Facing up to Thatcherism

Facing up to Thatcherism

The History of NALGO 1979–1993

MIKE IRONSIDE

AND

ROGER SEIFERT

OXFORD
UNIVERSITY PRESS

OXFORD
UNIVERSITY PRESS

Great Clarendon Street, Oxford OX2 6DP

Oxford University Press is a department of the University of Oxford.
It furthers the University's objective of excellence in research, scholarship,
and education by publishing worldwide in

Oxford New York

Athens Auckland Bangkok Bogotá Buenos Aires Calcutta
Cape Town Chennai Dar es Salaam Delhi Florence Hong Kong Istanbul
Karachi Kuala Lumpur Madrid Melbourne Mexico City Mumbai
Nairobi Paris São Paulo Shanghai Singapore Taipei Tokyo Toronto Warsaw

and associated companies in Berlin Ibadan

Oxford is a registered trade mark of Oxford University Press
in the UK and in certain other countries

Published in the United States
by Oxford University Press Inc., New York

© UNISON 2000

British Library Cataloguing in Publication Data

Data available

Library of Congress Cataloging in Publication Data
Ironside, Mike.
Facing up to Thatcherism: the history of NALGO, 1979–1993 / Mike Ironside and
Roger Seifert.
p. cm.
Includes bibliographical references.
1. National and Local Government Officers Association.   2. Government employee
unions—Great Britain.   3. Great Britain—Politics and government—1979–1997.
I. Seifert, Roger V.   II. Title.
HD8005.2.G7 I76   2001   331.88'1135141—dc21   00-064999
ISBN 0–19–924075–2

1 3 5 7 9 10 8 6 4 2

Typeset by Hope Services (Abingdon) Ltd.
Printed in Great Britain
on acid-free paper by
T.J. International Ltd.,
Padstow, Cornwall

From Mike to Rachel, Matthew, Calum, and Claire.

From Roger to Anne, and to the children: Sarah, Joseph, Rachel, Adam, Hannah, Judith, Miriam, and Benjamin.

Foreword

This is the third volume of the history of NALGO, a story that began in 1905 and ended in 1993, when the union merged with its partners, COHSE and NUPE, to become UNISON. NALGO's founding fathers would have been astonished by the manner in which their offspring developed, since the concept of trades unionism was anathema to them.

When I joined the union's staff in 1960, NALGO was described by many in the wider movement as a 'tea-and-bun club'. It was commonplace for branches to be presided over by the county or town clerk, and to be provided by their employers with operational and social facilities that were beyond the dreams of our blue-collar sisters and brothers. And yet, within the membership ranks, there was already a rapidly increasing number who recognized that they were not immune from the policies of governments who were their ultimate paymasters.

These more aware and politically motivated members would not have envisaged the bare knuckles fight with Thatcherism that is central to this volume, but they and their successors initiated the essential components of the survival kit and, simultaneously, changed the face and the nature of the union: the adoption of a strike clause, affiliation to the TUC, to Trades Councils, and to Public Services International, and the eventual adoption of a Political Fund.

Thus equipped, NALGO embarked upon the last chapter of its history, dominated by campaigning and, at times, frenetic activity. Ironside and Seifert, academic industrial-relations specialists, unlike their predecessor authors who were both former officers of the union, describe and analyse events. Generally speaking, I concur with their analyses. During the period covered, NALGO was bruised but, unlike some other unions, was not mortally wounded. I agree specifically with the authors that one of the factors saving it from that fate was the union's extraordinary bargaining and organizational adaptability.

Thatcherism became the global phenomenon of the era. Many NALGO members were angered by an ideology that undermined the post-war welfare settlement, that worshipped monetarism, the market, and the individual, that asserted that there was 'no such thing as society', and that sought to humiliate public servants and trade unions.

The practical implementation of this ideology seemed interminable—privatization, contracting-out, compulsory competitive tendering, the creation of internal markets, cash limits, unspoken public-sector pay policy, the decentralization of collective bargaining, the abolition of a tier of local government, and wave upon wave of anti-trade-union legislation.

In a state of shock, anger, and frustration, the initial trade union response was to reach for the scattergun. That gave way fairly rapidly to more focused campaigning on a wide range of issues. When the employers ditched fairness and dialogue, we were not afraid to use industrial action. We had some successes but, it has to be said, some failures. We played to our strengths. At national level, NALGO had built up teams of highly skilled and motivated staff in its research, publicity, education, and legal departments. With the aid of an outside agency we mounted much-admired, hard-hitting advertising campaigns.

NALGO's characteristic stamp was the resilience of its internal democracy at all levels through which policies were formulated. Through our uniquely well-resourced branches and steward system we could focus on local issues as required, including action to defend individual members. The authors rightly refer to nationally orchestrated but locally based campaigns. The union did, indeed, remain resilient. A peak membership of 783,000 never fell below three-quarters of a million.

Moreover, in what were often dark days, NALGO never ceased to throw its considerable weight behind human and civil-rights issues. It was always in the vanguard of the fight for equal opportunities and it campaigned against threatened deportations. Its international activities were highly regarded, and it was a source of great pride when Honorary NALGO Member Nelson Mandela became President of post-apartheid South Africa.

One of the lessons we learned during this period of our history was the need to work with others, whether other unions, employers, or the users of services provided by NALGO members. It was the deepening relationship between NALGO, NUPE, and COHSE, my perception of the erosion, in the emerging world, of the traditional distinctions and hostilities between white- and blue-collar workers, together with the need to put public-service worker unity on a permanent organizational base, that caused me and others to see NALGO's future in a merged union.

As I write, activism in the labour movement is somewhat unfashionable. I make no apology for declaring that the real heroes of this book were the NALGO activists. I salute them, and I am proud to have worked with them.

Alan Jinkinson

May 2000

Preface

Writing the history of an organization presents a series of problems not normally encountered in academic accounts of issues, events, and people. The constant temptation is to treat the organization as a sentient being, as if 'it' has prejudices and policies and as if 'it' is capable of both thoughtless and thoughtful actions. The fallacy of reification is easy to commit. For us, NALGO often appeared to be a living and evolving organism, and we had to keep reminding each other that trade unions are but institutions within which humans act.

Union histories are a mixed bunch. Many concentrate on describing the services provided, others recount the deeds of national leaders, and another group provides joined-up stories of the red-letter days—from triumph to victory to success. Our prime objective was to demonstrate how the varied and common experiences of union members determine the practices and policies of activists, leaders, and officials at all levels and within all sections of the union. In the last twenty years of the twentieth century the main experiences of NALGO members came from a substantial set of changes in British capitalism. They took three main forms: a dramatic shift in the financing, ownership, and management of the industries within which they worked; an uneven and qualitatively variable alteration in their labour processes; and an increasingly hostile political economy for both trade unions and public services. The overarching ideology that came to dominate the lives of NALGO members during this period was that of neo-liberalism—all power to the powerful interests of a US-dominated international capitalist system.

Our task, therefore, was to trace the impact of such developments upon NALGO the organization. This meant identifying key issues—discrimination, falling relative pay, anti-union laws, solidarity, privatization—and then witnessing how and why members, activists, leaders, and officials fought to establish policy, and then analysing how those policies were executed within a collective-bargaining agenda supported by industrial disputes and political campaigns. All this was contested inside the union, and the contests themselves as well as their outcomes created the dynamic for change in the union that eventually resulted in the formation of UNISON.

In the end this was no easy task. We had to sift through a mass of archives, to unpick the impact of external forces, and to follow internal debates and actions into a maze of interwoven special interests and common causes. We believe it was worthwhile, since the story reveals just how hard it was to fight in the circumstances faced by NALGO members in the years 1979–93, and that, while some battles were won and others lost, maintaining the struggle itself was a victory. It shows above all that history is made by men and women through struggle and not simply by leaders and opinion-formers. Our researches for this book have convinced us more than ever that the ideals and practices of trade unionism are fundamental to democratic struggle against the powerful interests in society.

A number of people helped us on our way. David Whitfield got us started with a van-load of documents. Throughout the book's long gestation, John Monks and Rod Robertson provided us with advice and guidance whenever we needed it, filled in gaps from their vast insider knowledge, gave us critical feedback, and sorted out problems with great courtesy and patience. Sheila McGinley and Matt Smith supplied us with documents from UNISON's West Midland and Scottish Regional offices respectively. David Musson of Oxford University Press gave us considerable support and encouragement. Dave Lyddon, a colleague at Keele, read our first draft and made exhaustive and useful comments. We record our thanks here.

Mike Ironside
Roger Seifert

Keele University
June 2000

Acknowledgements

The authors wish to thank the following photographers for their kind permission to include material in this volume:

John Harris (reportdigital.co.uk) for 'Muhammad Must Stay!', 1985.

Edward Winpenny for 'Make School Secs. Matter', 1987.

Andrew Wiard (reportphotos.com) for 'Stop Repression of Trade Unionists in South Africa and Namibia', 1988; 'Protect Equal Opportunities', 1991; and Low Pay? No Way!', 1992.

Melanie Friend for 'Real Pay Not Pocket Money', 1988.

Steve McTaggart for 'Fight for Scotland's Steel' 1990.

Anthony Fisher for 'Save Our Home', 1993.

Contents

List of Plates

List of Figures

List of Tables

Abbreviations

A&C	Administrative and Clerical
AAM	Anti-Apartheid Movement
ACAS	Advisory, Conciliation, and Arbitration Service
ACC	Association of County Councils
ACTS	Administrative, Clerical, Technical, and Supervisory Staff section of the TGWU
ADC	Association of District Councils
AEEU	Amalgamated Engineering and Electrical Union
AEI	average earnings index
AES	Alternative Economic Strategy
AEU	Amalgamated Engineering Union, later the Amalgamated Union of Engineering Workers (AUEW), and now the Amalgamated Engineering and Electrical Union (AEEU)
AGM	Annual General Meeting
AHA	Area Health Authority
AMA	Association of Metropolitan Authorities
ANC	African National Congress
APEX	Association of Professional, Executive, and Computer Staffs, later merged with the GMB
APT&C	administrative, professional, technical, and clerical
ARA	Anti-Racist Alliance
ASLEF	Amalgamated Society of Locomotive Engineers and Firemen
ASTMS	Association of Scientific, Technical, and Managerial Staff, later merged with TASS to form MSF
AUEW	Amalgamated Union of Engineering Workers
AUT	Association of University Teachers
BACM	British Association of Colliery Managers
BASW	British Association of Social Workers
BCCI	Bank of Credit and Commerce International
BIFU	Banking, Insurance, and Finance Union, now part of UNIFI
BMA	British Medical Association
BUSW	British Union of Social Workers
BWB	British Waterways Board

CAC	Central Arbitration Committee
CBI	Confederation of British Industry
CCT	compulsory competitive tendering
CEGB	Central Electricity Generating Board
CNALP	Campaign for NALGO Affiliation to the Labour Party
CND	Campaign for Nuclear Disarmament
COHSE	Confederation of Health Service Employees
COSATU	Confederation of South African Trade Unions
COSLA	Convention of Scottish Local Authorities
CPSA	Civil and Public Services Association, later merged with PTC to form PCS
CRE	Commission for Racial Equality
CSP	Chartered Society of Physiotherapy
CSU	Civil Service Union, later merged with SCPS to form NUCPS, now part of PCS
CVCP	Committee of Vice-Chancellors and Principals
CWU	Communication Workers' Union
DES	Department of Education and Science
DEOC	District Equal Opportunities Committee (NALGO)
DHA	District Health Authority
DHSS	Department of Health and Social Security
DLO	direct labour organization
DTI	Department of Trade and Industry
EAT	Employment Appeals Tribunal
EC	European Community
EC	Electricity Council
EETPU	Electrical, Electronic, Telecommunication, and Plumbing Union, later merged with AEU to form AEEU
EIS	Educational Institute of Scotland
ERM	Exchange Rate Mechanism
ESI	Electrical Supply Industry
ESOP	Employee Share Ownership Plan
ETU	Electrical Trades Union
EU	European Union
FDA	Association of First Division Civil Servants
FBU	Fire Brigades Union
FE	further education
FLAG	Fight for Labour Affiliation Group (NALGO)
FTE	Full-Time Equivalent
FUMPO	Federated Union of Managerial and Professional Officers
FUSE	The Federation of Unions Supplying Electricity
GCHQ	General Communications Head Quarters
GLC	Greater London Council

GMB	The GMB, formed by merger of APEX with the General Municipal Boilermakers, and Allied Trade Union (GMBATU), formerly the National Union of General and Municipal Workers (NUGMW), then the General and Municipal Workers' Union (GMWU)
GMBATU	General Municipal Boilermakers' and Allied Trade Union
GMWU	General and Municipal Workers' Union
GPMU	Graphical, Paper, and Media Union
GSSO	Gas Staffs and Senior Officers
GUARD	Gas Unions Against the Report to Dismantle British Gas
HAWU	Health and Allied Workers' Union
HCO	Higher Clerical Officer
HRM	human resource management
IDS	Incomes Data Services
IEA	Institute of Economic Affairs
ILEA	Inner London Education Authority
ILO	International Labour Organization
IMF	International Monetary Fund
IRA	Irish Republican Army
IRS	Industrial Relations Services
IRSF	Inland Revenue Staff Federation, now part of PCS
IT	industrial tribunal
JCC	Joint Consultative Committee
JNC	Joint Negotiating Committee
JTS	Job Training Scheme
LACSAB	Local Authorities' Conditions of Service Advisory Board
LCC	London County Council
LEA	Local Education Authority
LGIU	Local Government Information Unit
LGMB	Local Government Management Board
LMS	local management of schools
LRD	Labour Research Department
MATSA	Managerial, Administrative, Technical, and Supervisory section of the GMB
MEP	Member of the European Parliament
MMC	Monopolies and Mergers Commission
MOA	Municipal Officers' Association
MSF	Manufacture, Science, Finance union
MWUSA	Municipal Workers' Union of South Africa
NACODS	National Association of Colliery Overmen, Deputies, and Shotfirers
NAG	NALGO Action Group
NALGO	National and Local Government Officers' Association
NATFHE	National Association of Teachers in Further and Higher Education

NASUWT	National Association of Schoolmasters and Union of Women Teachers
NBC	National Bus Company
NBMCC	National Black Members' Coordinating Committee (NALGO)
NBPI	National Board for Prices and Incomes
NCB	National Coal Board
NCU	National Communication Union
NEC	National Executive Committee
NEHAWU	National Education Health and Allied Workers' Union
NEOC	National Equal Opportunities Committee (NALGO)
NGA	National Graphical Association, later merged with SOGAT to form GPMU
NHS	National Health Service
NIPSA	Northern Ireland Public Services Alliance
NJC	National Joint Council
NLGC	National Local Government Committee (NALGO)
NN	*NALGO News*
NRA	National Rivers Authority
NUCPS	National Union of Civil and Public Servants, later PTC, and now PCS
NUGMW	National Union of General and Municipal Workers
NUPE	National Union of Public Employees
NUM	National Union of Mineworkers
NUMAST	National Union of Marine, Aviation, and Shipping Transport Officers
NUR	National Union of Railwaymen, later merged with the NUS to form the Rail, Maritime and Transport Union (RMT)
NUS	National Union of Seamen, later merged with the NUR to form the Rail, Maritime and Transport Union (RMT)
NUS	National Union of Students
NUT	National Union of Teachers
NVQ	National Vocational Qualification
NWSA	National Westminster Staff Association, later part of UNIFI
PAM	profession allied to medicine
PAWP	Positive Action Working Party (NALGO)
PBR	payment by results
PCFC	Polytechnic Central Funding Council
PCS	Public and Commercial Services Union
PRP	performance-related pay
PS	*Public Service*
PSI	Public Services International
PSBR	public-sector borrowing requirement
PSPRU	Public Services Privatization Research Unit
PT	Professional and Technical, as in PT'A' and PT'B', being Whitley Committees in the NHS

PTC	Public Services, Tax, and Commerce Union, later merged with CPSA to form PCS
PTE	Passenger Transport Executive
PULSE	Public and Local Service Efficiency Campaign
RCN	Royal College of Nursing
REWP	Race Equality Working Party (NALGO)
RHA	Regional Health Authority
RIPA	Royal Institute of Public Administration
RJC	Regional Joint Council
RMT	National Union of Rail, Maritime, and Transport Workers
RPI	retail price index
RSG	rate support grant
SACTU	South African Congress of Trade Unions
SAT	Standard Assessment Test
SCAT	Services to Community Action and Trade Unions
SCPS	Society of Civil and Public Servants, later NUCPS, later PTC and now PCS
SDP	Social Democratic Party
SERTUC	South East Region of the Trades Union Congress
SGT	self-governing trust
SOG	self-organized group (NALGO)
SOGAT	Society of Graphical and Allied Trades, later merged with the NGA to form GPMU
STUC	Scottish Trades Union Congress
SWAPO	South West Africa People's Organization
SWP	Socialist Workers' Party
TASS	Technical, Administrative, and Supervisory Section of the AUEW, later merged with ASTMS to form MSF
TGWU	Transport and General Workers' Union
TQM	total quality management
TUC	Trades Union Congress
TUPE	Transfer of Undertakings (Protection of Employment) Regulations 1981
TURC	Trade Union Resource Centre
TWSA	Thames Water Staff Association
UCATT	Union of Construction, Allied Trades, and Technicians
UCCA	Universities Central Council on Admissions
UCW	Union of Communication Workers, later merged with NCU to form CWU
UDF	United Democratic Front
UNIFI	UNIFI, formed by merger of BIFU, NWSA, and UNiFi
VAT	Value Added Tax
YTS	Youth Training Scheme

I

NALGO—What Kind of Trade Union?

THIS volume of the history of the National and Local Government Officers' Association (NALGO) follows on from the works by Alec Spoor[1] and George Newman,[2] who covered the periods 1905–65 and 1965–80 respectively. We begin in 1979 and end in 1993 with the start of UNISON. Unlike our predecessor historians we are not and never have been NALGO full-time officers, and we therefore lack their daily intimacy with events and individuals inside the union. However, we have approached our task in the spirit of friendly, but critical, outsiders. We aimed to locate the union's story within the specific historical setting that moulded and challenged NALGO until cold logic, common circumstances, and the increasingly dangerous world of the 1990s moved the union towards its final merger with the National Union of Public Employees (NUPE) and the Confederation of Health Service Employees (COHSE) into UNISON.

Spoor criticized his own volume thus:

Perhaps the book's greatest fault . . . is its failure to bring out the collectivity of the movements, decisions, and actions it records. . . . The true history of NALGO does not lie in the sayings and doings of a few score 'leaders', officials, and speakers, but in the thoughts and deeds of the thousands of men and women who, through the years, have filled its national, branch and district offices, attending its meetings, and adding their voices and votes to the forming of its policies.[3]

We have tried to put those thousands of men and women at the centre of this book, through constant references to their trade-union activity in their

---

[1] A. Spoor, *White Collar Union: Sixty Years of NALGO* (London: Heinemann, 1967).
[2] G. Newman, *Path to Maturity: NALGO 1965–1980* (London: NALGO, 1982).
[3] Spoor, *White Collar Union*, p. vii.

workplaces and at branch, district, and national level. Collective bargaining is the motor of this activity: we describe the debates on policy, and we cover a large number of national and local strikes and campaigns to illustrate how the union's activists and members responded to events and grasped opportunities. We try to capture the dynamics of a union fighting hundreds of local battles and a fistful of national actions, through detailed accounts of the everyday, but far from ordinary, efforts made by members, activists, leaders, and officials. Our account is rooted in the wider issues and themes of trade unionism, seeing NALGO as an organization for collective bargaining, for action, for internal debates, and for solidarity with other workers through the Trades Union Congress (TUC), through individual unions, and through international links.

The union supported members and activists with educational, publicity, legal, and representational services. Structural changes were made, reflecting the forces levelled against both the members and the union itself. Here is a success story, in terms of organizational survival, democratic decision-making, victory in some actions, campaigns, and negotiations, and in raising issues both old and new to their proper place in national policy. But it is also a tale of the limits of union action when faced with a determined government utilizing the full force of state power with clear objectives to undo the gains of the working-class movement in the period 1945–73—Eric Hobsbawm's 'golden years'.[4]

This chapter sets the scene, laying out our analytical framework and our own position on industrial relations. It starts with a brief comment on the context of NALGO's activity in this period, stressing in particular the government's commitment to neo-liberal policies and the mobilization of state power to implement them. Essentially, our position is that all employed workers are exploited by their employer, and this leads to a discussion on the status of workers as employees and on the nature of waged work. Most people have no alternative but to work in order to secure a decent standard of life, and therefore they are in a weak position when they offer their services (their labour power) to employers. The contract of employment embraces legal notions of equality, fairness, and freedom between the buyer and the seller of labour power, but the real power imbalance between the two makes the contract the legal embodiment of inequality. It enables employers to exploit workers, by forcing down their wages to a level less than the value of their work. This exploitation requires the use of management practices that reduce the power of workers to control their own work, resulting in alienation.

---

[4] E. Hobsbawm, *Age of Extremes: The Short Twentieth Century 1914–1991* (London: Michael Joseph, 1994).

These twin aspects of capitalist employment relations—exploitation and alienation—result in resistance, varied and inconsistent, taking many forms, but most successful and sustained through trade-union organization. Trade-union activists pose a constant challenge to managerial authority, to unequal labour-market power, and to direct and indirect state involvement in exploitation.

This leads to a debate about the nature and purpose of trade unionism, and about what is a 'proper' trade union and who is a 'proper' trade unionist. We define trade unions as organizations simply by reference to their main function of engaging in collective bargaining. Their purpose in carrying out their function is more contentious, with two main versions of trade unionism reflecting the right and left wings of the labour movement. The first version assumes an identity of interest between the employer and the employees— the employees are better off if the employer does well, so the role of the union is to share in the running of the employer's business. The second version assumes a conflict of interest between employer and employees—the employees can be better off only at the expense of the employer, so the role of the union is to fight the employer at every opportunity. The right-wing version assumes that capitalism is beneficial and that workers' problems arise from business and/or management failures, while the left-wing version assumes that the workers' problems arise from capitalism itself.

It is this political disagreement about what trade unions are for that under-pins most policy debate. However, such debate also reflects the specific issues confronting the members at any given time. The actual nature of exploitation and alienation is constantly changing, sometimes slowly, sometimes rapidly. Shifting sands of economic circumstances, political conditions, technological change, and industrial reorganization all demand responses from trade unions. As the labour market changes in structure, old technologies and associated skills pass away, new industries emerge, and so the composition of the union membership changes as well as the jobs that they do. Change in the circumstances of the membership results in continuous discussion about the nature of change and in constant debate about how to respond to it. Such dialectic is always underpinned by the tension between left and right—over the form and substance of collective bargaining and industrial action.

Of course this tension is never resolved, and really existing union responses are based on both versions of trade unionism simultaneously. Union action reflects the balance of forces within the union, as the outcome of internal struggle within the framework of union democratic practice. Decisions about policy and action are made within a framework of formal structures of union government, but the processes through which policies are formulated, established, and translated into action extend beyond the formal institutions of

3

executives, regions, committees, branches, and industrial groups. Decisions made by those bodies are the outcomes of wider activity by members, activists, and officials, which itself reflects the type of union as defined by the structure and composition of its membership.

The final section of this chapter considers the nature of white-collar trade unionism and public-sector trade unionism. It explores the view that some organizations are not trade unions because their members are not exploited—because they are managers, or because they do not work for a capitalist, or because they are not directly involved in production.

Our main argument is that there are two dimensions to trade-union action. They respond to changes in the external circumstances confronting them, and they reshape themselves through internal debate over how to respond. The central theme of this book is that NALGO was a trade union that responded to fundamental and dramatic changes affecting the members' conditions of work. During the period covered by the book, NALGO policy developed in line with positions best known as 'broad left'. It rested on a consistent critique of government action to mobilize the state in support of big business and at the expense of both public services and public enterprises. It reflected the changes taking place in industry, management, and workforce, and it was driven by a uniquely open form of democratic practice.

Before the main narrative part of the book, Chapter 2 summarizes the union's development, drawing from both Spoor and Newman, from its foundation in 1905, through to its declaration of being a trade union in 1920, to affiliation to the TUC in 1965, to its first national strike in 1978. This sets the scene for a brief description of the union, its membership, and its main policies at the end of 1978, when this detailed history begins.

The next seven chapters cover the history of the period, followed by a concluding chapter on the merger into UNISON. Within each chapter four main themes are pursued: government practice and policy; NALGO's responses, and changes to its internal organization; campaigns; and collective bargaining and disputes. In addition, within most chapters there are more detailed case studies presented in boxed sections.

Chapters 3 and 4 cover the years from the 'winter of discontent' of 1978–9, followed by the Labour government's demise and Margaret Thatcher's first victory in June 1979, through to the general election of 1983. These years saw NALGO members drawn into three national disputes—the 1979 social workers' strike, the 1980 local-government comparability strike, and the 1982 NHS strike over pay and pay-bargaining machinery. The hallmark of this period was the government's determination to 'squeeze inflation' out of the system by cutting public expenditure, by deregulating services such as the buses, by applying cash limits for public-sector pay, and by reducing the legal rights of trade unions. NALGO fought not only to oppose these policies but also progressively to challenge them through the Alternative Economic Strategy (AES) and with campaigns such as 'Put People First'.

Chapters 5 and 6 cover the second Thatcher government, 1983–7, which with hindsight can be seen as the high point of what we now call Thatcherism. During this period the attack on organized labour was indeed severe, with the worst reserved for the National Union of Mineworkers (NUM), the print workers, and the staff at the Government Communications Head Quarters (GCHQ). Further anti-union legislation was linked with privatization, especially of British Gas, and with the use of compulsory competitive tendering (CCT) in local government and the National Health Service (NHS). The union organized against these policies as well as their consequences with increasing redundancies, the deregulation of labour management, and the restructuring of employment units. Industrial struggle fed into political action, with the defence of the Greater London Council (GLC), the fight against the rightward shift in the Labour Party and the TUC, and with another campaign, 'Make People Matter'.

In the final historical part of the book, Chapters 7, 8, and 9 deal with the period from 1987 to the summer of 1993. The government, having successfully privatized gas, applied the same formula to water and electricity. Crisis developed in the Conservative government as problems mounted up, symbolized by Mrs Thatcher's removal from the government over the issue of the poll tax in 1990. Under John Major, the health, education, and local-government reforms were implemented and the crisis deepened. These measures once again were fought tooth and nail by NALGO, alongside other public-sector unions and within the TUC. The union took strike action in 1989 over local-government pay and in the ambulance dispute, but increasingly concentrated its efforts in local fights to protect members against discrimination, bullying, low pay, the introduction of human resource management (HRM) practices such as performance-related pay, and training on the cheap. All this was set against a volatile international situation in which Nelson Mandela was released in South Africa while the collapse of the Soviet Union hastened the integration of the European Union (EU). By now merger seemed the best option for survival.

The book ends with the merger of NALGO with NUPE and COHSE to form UNISON in the summer of 1993. Chapter 10 discusses the two main sets of forces that operated to bring it about. First was the need to maximize the union's capacity to engage in collective bargaining. The movement for merger was rooted in the understanding of both activists and members that the structure of bargaining had become more fragmented and the issues for bargaining were increasingly located in the workplace rather than in national

Whitley Councils. Second was the need to speak with one voice on behalf of the increasingly homogeneous white-collar and manual employees. Some members were transferred into the private sector through privatization, and employment for those remaining in the public services became more like employment in the private sector. Under the impact of exploitative managerial techniques aimed at cheapening the workforce, NALGO, NUPE, and COHSE members found common cause over a wide range of employment issues, including low pay, deskilling, discrimination, and work intensification.

The main sources for the book were in the union's archives, which were made available to us. We made extensive use of official union documents such as annual reports, minutes, and conference papers. We also used the two union journals: *Public Service*, a monthly newspaper sent to all members, frequently with district supplements; and *NALGO News*, a weekly newspaper sent to all activists from 1981. *Public Service* often included activist-produced district supplements, such as *Mac* in Scotland, *Edlines* in the Eastern District, *News NoW* in the North West and North Wales, and *Met District News* in the Metropolitan District. In addition we searched through hundreds of pamphlets, leaflets, and other publicity materials. We interviewed several of the leading figures of the time, and spoke informally to many more. We supplemented these primary sources with annual reports of the TUC, accounts from national and local newspapers, Hansard, and material from union-friendly organizations such as Labour Research Department (LRD). In the field of industrial relations we used Incomes Data Service (IDS) and Industrial Relations Services (IRS) reports, as well as extra information from both the Fabian Society and the Institute of Employment Rights. We used secondary literature in the area of industrial relations and trade-union studies, and we drew from other first-hand accounts of the period, especially from members of the Conservative governments.

We work a large number of direct quotations from the primary sources into this text. Our intention is to give the union's own leaders and activists a strong voice in recounting the union's story, to set out policy positions from the union's own publications, and to explore discussion and argument through the protagonists' own words.

The Context—Global Neo-Liberalism

The reforms implemented by the Conservative governments of Margaret Thatcher (1979–90) and John Major (1990–7) dominate the period covered by this book. Their main policy initiatives were made in the name of free-market competition, rooted in neo-classical economic theory.[5] This in turn was part of a wider neo-liberal approach to the political economy of advanced capitalist nations. Noam Chomsky summarizes the neo-liberal position: 'The basic rules, in brief, are: liberalize trade and finance, let markets set prices ("get prices right"), end inflation ("macroeconomic stability"), privatize. The government should "get out of the way"—hence the population too, insofar as the government is democratic.'[6]

Another writer states the main features of neo-liberalism, and the global consequences of removing all fetters on monopoly capital's search for profits:

Neo-liberalism is the defining political economic paradigm of our time—it refers to the policies and processes whereby a relative handful of private interests are permitted to control as much as possible of social life in order to maximize their personal profit. Associated initially with Reagan and Thatcher, for the past two decades neoliberalism has been the dominant global political economic trend adopted by political parties of the center and much of the traditional left as well as the right. . . . The economic consequences of these policies have been the same just about everywhere, and exactly what one would expect: a massive increase in social and economic inequality, a marked increase in severe deprivation for the poorest nations and peoples of the world, a disastrous global environment, an unstable global economy and an unprecedented bonanza for the wealthy.[7]

The argument that the state should act to support the interests of large companies ('the business case'), often monopolies, at the expense of millions of citizens, further implies that the state must then promulgate the necessary myths to maintain social order: that there is no alternative; that profit-seeking activity is the sole source of wealth creation; that free competition (even though it does not exist most of the time) is the guarantor of efficient, effective, and economic use of resources; and that freedom to make money comes before equality and social justice.

Thus the last quarter of the twentieth century was characterized by an accelerating move away from Keynesian policies and by attacks on the welfare state, weak at first but ever more ferocious in the 1980s and 1990s. As Ralph Miliband persuasively argues in a book written in the early 1970s:

More than ever before men now live in the shadow of the state. What they want to achieve, individually or in groups, now mainly depends on the state's sanction and support. But since that sanction and support are not bestowed indiscriminately, they must, ever more directly, seek to influence and shape the state's power and purpose,

---

[5] J. Schumpeter, *History of Economic Analysis* (London: George Allen & Unwin, 1963).

[6] N. Chomsky, *Profit over People: Neoliberalism and the Global Order* (New York: Seven Stories Press, 1999), 20.

[7] R. McChesney, 'Introduction', in Chomsky, *Profit over People*, 7–8.

or try to appropriate it altogether. It is for the state's attention, or for its control, that men compete; and it is against the state that beat the waves of social conflict.[8]

NALGO members learned all about state power during the 1980s. They also learned that economic policies enacted in the name of competition actually fed the power of monopoly capitalism, and that 'the economy of large corporations is more, not less, dominated by the logic of profit-making than the economy of small entrepreneurs ever was'.[9] A small minority have control of the means of production and economic activity is dominated by the search for profits. Richard Hyman draws out the important labour-market consequences of this:

The worker surrenders control over his labour . . . the relationship between the employee and his employment is thus inherently unstable and conflictual. Moreover, wages and salaries represent only a portion of the value of what workers collectively produce; the remainder is appropriated as a natural element in the unequal economic relationship with the employer (they are thus, literally, 'exploited'; and this gives industrial conflict a *class* character).[10]

Harry Braverman,[11] in his analysis of the labour process, looks further at the consequences for workers employed in an economic system dominated by state-supported profit-maximizing private corporations. He argues that state monopoly capitalism speeded up certain modern developments: the internationalization of capital, the greater instability of the system, a widening of the rich–poor divide, and the need for government services to deal with greater urbanization. These have resulted in two significant developments since the 1960s: first, an expansion in certain types of occupation, particularly white-collar/professional and often within the state domain; and, secondly, the application of scientific management techniques to deskill the jobs done by these groups in the same way as jobs done by skilled manual workers were deskilled through the factory system. Both factors were crucial to NALGO's growth and development as a trade union in the 1980s. Conservative-government restructuring of health, local government, and education deliberately introduced pressures to cheapen the jobs of all categories of staff, resulting in widespread deskilling and degradation of job content.[12]

[8] R. Miliband, *The State in Capitalist Society* (London: Quartet Books, 1973), 3.

[9] P. Baran and P. Sweezy, *Monopoly Capital* (Harmondsworth: Pelican Books, 1966), 40.

[10] R. Hyman, *Industrial Relations: A Marxist Introduction* (London: Macmillan, 1975), 96.

[11] H. Braverman, *Labor and Monopoly Capital: The Degradation of Work in the Twentieth Century* (New York: Monthly Review Press, 1974).

[12] R. Seifert, *Industrial Relations in the NHS* (London: Chapman & Hall, 1992); M. Ironside and R. Seifert, *Industrial Relations in Schools* (London: Routledge, 1995); W. Gill, M. Ironside, and R. Seifert, 'The Reform of English Local Government Finance and Structure, and the Consequences for the Management of Labour', paper for the Critical Perspectives on Accounting Conference, New York (1999).

Practical neo-liberal initiatives in the UK included privatization, public sector cuts, public-sector restructuring, anti-trade-union legislation, and the reduction of civil rights, all as recommended by right-wing economic gurus such as Friedrich von Hayek[13] and Milton Friedman.[14] NALGO's responses to these policies were distinctive and radical, as the union fought, on the one hand, to defend jobs, pay, and services, and, on the other hand, to maintain the labour movement's commitment to public ownership.[15] As sections of both the Labour Party and the trade unions gradually shifted policy to embrace the logic of economy, efficiency, and effectiveness through private enterprise, the union became a major force on the centre left of the official movement. It broke new ground with its political campaigns, its international solidarity actions, its open democratic structures and practices, its coherent criticisms of the government's programmes, and its arguments for alternatives.

The Management of Labour: Markets, Processes, and Ideologies

Free workers under management control

Under the neo-classical free-market model, 'free' workers (not slaves) can choose to sell their labour power—their ability to do work—to employers. The formal legal relationship is contained in the contract of employment. The contract appears to embody a simple market exchange—the employee does work in exchange for a wage paid by the employer. In legal theory it is assumed that the contract is freely entered into by individual parties, the employer and the employee, who have equal status in the marketplace. However, in reality the position of the employee selling labour power is much weaker than that of the employer buying it—the notion of freely entering into work ignores the powerful economic and social forces that compel workers to seek employment.[16]

Furthermore, the extent to which the contract is fulfilled is largely indeterminate. In most employment situations the employee brings to the workplace the *capacity* to work—the actual *amount* of work and the actual *quality* of

---

[13] F. von Hayek, *The Road to Serfdom* (London: Routledge, 1944); F. von Hayek, *1980s Unemployment and the Unions* (London: IEA, 1984).

[14] M. Friedman, *Free to Choose* (Harmondsworth: Penguin, 1980).

[15] K. O'Donnell and M. Sawyer, *A Future for Public Ownership* (London: Lawrence & Wishart, 1999).

[16] O. Kahn-Freund, *Labour and the Law* (London: Stevens, 1977); Lord Wedderburn, *The Worker and the Law* (Harmondsworth: Penguin, 1986).

work are not specified in the contract. Consequently, employers need managers to act as their agents to ensure that, in return for being paid a wage, the employees provide the employer with as much work of the desired type as can possibly be extracted from them. There is a conflict built into the employment relationship, between employees seeking to maximize wages and to minimize effort, and employers seeking the opposite. The notion of a fair day's pay for a fair day's work obscures what is actually happening here— this underlying conflict cannot be resolved. As Owen, the hero of the *Ragged Trousered Philanthropists*, argued:

Yes; and those master painters are so eager to get the work that they cut the price down to what they think is the lowest possible point . . . and the lowest usually gets the job. The successful tenderer has usually cut the price so fine that to make it pay he has to scamp the work, pay low wages, and drive and sweat the men whom he employs. He wants them to do two days' work for one day's pay.[17]

The struggle between employer and employees is magnified by the employer's constant battle to survive, driven by an overriding need to maintain an acceptable rate of profit. Employers have to respond to a range of circumstances that can affect this, such as the extent of competition, the level of unemployment, technological change, the demands of the state and product/service users, and the behaviour of the workforce. This results in a never-ending quest to maximize output, to get work done more cheaply, and to ensure that both the volume and the nature of output are controlled in accordance with the needs of the business. Central to this is the control of labour. In this sense there is a frontier of control,[18] over which the respective collective organizations of capital and labour struggle to expand and defend their spheres of influence.

The employer strives to achieve unilateral decision-making over all aspects of the labour process: the pace of work, working time, the allocation of work between workers, the allocation of workers to jobs, and the work itself.[19] The most familiar and well-used methods are associated with F. W. Taylor's principles of scientific management, which are based on four classic aspects of labour management: finding the 'best' way for the job to be done; finding the 'best' worker to do the job; codifying the tasks involved in getting the job done; and ensuring these 'right' workers do their 'right' jobs in the 'right' ways by relating their pay to their output.[20]

[17] R. Tressell, *The Ragged Trousered Philanthropists* (London: Panther Books, 1965 edn.), 153.

[18] C. Goodrich, *The Frontier of Control* (London: G. Bell & Sons, 1920).

[19] Braverman, *Labor and Monopoly Capital*.

[20] F. Taylor, *Scientific Management* (New York: Harper & Bros., 1911); M. Rose, *Industrial Behaviour: Theoretical Development since Taylor* (Harmondsworth: Penguin Books, 1988).

Managerial logic is clear. Work is seen as a technical matter over which managers ought to have complete control without interference from workers. Work should be organized so that workers do not need to have a high degree of understanding of the processes and techniques involved, thus reducing management's dependence on skilled employees who may become scarce and powerful. As far as possible, work should be planned and controlled by managers, leaving workers 'free' to concentrate on completing their tasks.

This logic results in the familiar range of labour management techniques aimed at ensuring the workers carry out their legal duty under the employment contract. They include techniques to measure work, such as work study and job evaluation; to monitor work, such as appraisal; and to motivate workers to work, such as performance-related pay, fear of unemployment, and employee involvement schemes. Under generic terms such as human resource management (HRM) and total quality management (TQM) lie the familiar labour management activities of hiring and firing workers, watching workers, and inducing workers to work as hard and smartly as possible. Managerial control is enforced by the long hierarchical chains of supervisors, progress chasers, rate-fixers, and line managers, ensuring that the work done at the point of production/service delivery meets the needs of those who own the business.

The stark imperative of employers to control the labour process to the maximum possible detailed level could not be met if there was a general awareness of its exploitative and degrading nature, except by force and by the suppression of resistance. Managerial authority to control worker activity is cloaked in an ideology that presents the situation as both natural and desirable, often referred to as unitarism,[21] also known as managerialism. Its main elements can be summarized as follows. Managers are deemed to have the 'right' to manage, rooted in indisputable laws of property and economics, and, as the legal representatives of the owners, they have the legal right to enforce the contract of employment, to make decisions about the business, to see that the business makes a sufficient rate of profit, and to provide technical knowledge and expertise, applying 'scientific' management principles that are claimed to be entirely neutral and therefore not open to challenge. The assumed role of managers is to lead, motivate, and decide, while the employees' function is to follow, be loyal, work hard, and obey.

---

[21] A. Fox, *Industrial Sociology and Industrial Relations* (Research Paper 3, Donovan Commission, London: HMSO, 1966).

The wellspring of trade unionism

Employees throughout the capitalist world have invented a range of responses to strengthen their ability to control and protect their employment situation, the most important being the establishment of trade unions. When trade unions can provide a focus for worker resistance to managerial control, it may become less costly for managers to deal with them than to fight them.

This leads to recognition for collective bargaining, where trade unionists collectively representing employees deal with managers collectively representing employers, reaching collective agreements through negotiations, formal and informal, substantive and procedural. Job regulation, famously viewed as the making and implementing of rules at work, dealing with pay and conditions of service as well as with labour process issues, is seen in the mainstream industrial-relations literature as being the essential substance of collective bargaining.[22] Some aspects of job regulation may be decided unilaterally by management, others may be decided jointly, through negotiation, by management and trade union together.

Of course, once trade unions become involved in joint regulation, then the unitarist house of cards collapses, and an alternative management ideology—pluralism—is required. Pluralism differs from unitarism by recognizing that sometimes it is more efficient to accept worker representation into the managerial decision-making process than to leave it outside the tent. Its main proposition is that, while any organization is made up of a welter of conflicting interests, these can be reconciled through conflict resolution mechanisms such as collective bargaining and employee representation through formal joint procedures. However, pluralism shares with unitarism an acceptance of the view that everyone benefits from a harmonious partnership at work aimed at meeting the employer's goals. Prosperity and security for employees still stem from the success of the enterprise.

Marxism provides an alternative to the managerial perspectives. As managerialism has its variants, so does Marxism, but antagonism between employer and employee is one of the central notions. This antagonism springs from the very nature of the capitalist system. Capitalists own the means of production, and production has only one purpose: to enrich the owners. This is achieved by hiring workers to operate the means of production to produce goods and services. The value that is added during this process is equal to the value of the work done by the workers (including the value of the work done by the workers who made the means of production). The workers are

---

[22] A. Flanders, *Management and Unions* (London: Faber & Faber, 1968); H. Clegg, *The System of Industrial Relations in Great Britain* (Oxford: Blackwell, 1972).

exploited, because they are paid wages that are less than the value of the work that they do, enabling the employer to realize a profit in the market.[23]

Workers are impoverished by this process. Not only are they exploited; they are also alienated from crucial aspects of their human existence. They are alienated from the product of their work, because they do not own what they make, the employer does. They are alienated from each other, for they produce goods and services not for themselves, nor for their family, friends, neighbours, or fellow citizens, but for a capitalist who does not need them and immediately disposes of them on the market. They are alienated from the means of self-organization and self-sufficiency, as they do not own the tools of production and organization. They are alienated from what they do, for their actions have meaning only when performed for the employer. And they are alienated from their own futures, for they are forced into a contract of employment that gives the employers' agents the legal right to give them orders and to dispose of them when they are not required. In short, the worker's own labour power becomes a commodity that is under the control of the employer's agents during working hours.

In Karl Marx's own summary of the primacy of economic and work experience he argues for the importance of political and intellectual activity: 'The mode of production of material life conditions the social, political and intellectual life processes in general. It is not the consciousness of men that determines their being, but, on the contrary, their social being that determines their consciousness.'[24] So, while exploitation applies to all categories of workers and employers, part of the process requires that it is hidden from view. Gerry Cohen takes the argument further:

If the exploited were to see that they are exploited, they would resent their subjugation and threaten social stability. And if the exploiters were to see that they exploit, the composure they need to rule confidently would be disturbed. Being social animals, exploiters have to feel that their social behaviour is justifiable. When the feeling is difficult to reconcile with the truth, the truth must be hidden from them as well as from those they oppress. Illusion is therefore constitutive of class societies.[25]

Marx's theory of historical materialism provides us with the non-managerial framework for a worker-centred analysis of NALGO's history. He makes a general proposition that is helpful here: 'Men [*sic*] make their own history, but they do not make it just as they please; they do not make it under

---

[23] G. Cohen, *Karl Marx's Theory of History: A Defence* (Oxford: Clarendon Press, 1978), 40–5.
[24] K. Marx, 'Preface to a Contribution to the Critique of Political Economy', in K. Marx and F. Engels, *Selected Works Volume One* (Moscow: Progress Publishers, 1969), 502.
[25] Cohen, *Karl Marx's Theory of History*, 330.

circumstances chosen by themselves, but under circumstances directly encountered, given and transmitted from the past. The tradition of all the dead generations weighs like a nightmare on the brain of the living.'[26] Therefore, the history of a trade union can only be the history of the men and women who thought and acted; who fought, and either won or lost, in the extraordinary battles that shaped Britain at the end of the twentieth century.

In the core chapters of this book we try to link the activity of NALGO members to the events they experienced during the period, to their material experiences at work. Essentially these are rooted in 'marketization'. Privatization of utilities and parts of services, and structural reforms of the remainder of the public sector to introduce the cold logic of market-driven managerialism, resulted in changes to working conditions and working practices that had a profound impact on NALGO members' jobs. Working in the public services became ever more like working for a capitalist, as managers had no alternative but to impose a cost-cutting regime. Activists and leaders played a central role in organizing the fight to minimize the resulting increase of exploitation and alienation: by debating and deciding the policies and the practices to move the fight forwards, and by raising the members' understanding of both the nature and the form of their exploitation and their union's role in responding to it.

Ralph Miliband defines industrial relations as 'the consecrated euphemism for the permanent conflict, now acute, now subdued, between capital and labour'.[27] Trade-union organization and collective bargaining and action are part of the wider struggle against capitalist employment relations. While capitalism exists, compromise is necessary in order to win gains, to consolidate positions, and to avoid defeat. But such compromises are seen as just that, a limited and temporary solution to the deeper questions of exploitation and alienation.

Trade Unionism: Methods, Structures, and Organization

What is a trade union?

An organization that does not actually call itself a trade union may nevertheless still be one—examples include the Barclays Bank Staff Association (now part of UNIFI), the Association of University Teachers (AUT), the Royal

[26] K. Marx, 'The Eighteenth Brumaire of Louis Bonaparte', in K. Marx and F. Engels, *Selected Works Volume One* (Moscow: Progress Publishers, 1969), 398.
[27] Miliband, *The State in Capitalist Society*, 73.

College of Nursing (RCN), and NALGO itself. Along with the Webbs and other writers discussed later in this chapter, we would define a trade union by what it does, and our main point is that collective bargaining must be central to the definition. We argue that there are just three conditions to be met in order for an organization to qualify as a trade union: first, it must be organized independently of any employer; secondly, this must be for the purpose of engaging in collective bargaining with one or more employers; and, thirdly, it must be able to take action in order to secure collective-bargaining objectives. Trade unions engage in organized struggle to negotiate with the employer or their representatives at every twist and turn, on every issue, for any group of employees, and at every level—with management in the workplace, with the employer, or with the employers' organization. Their impact has been sufficient to make collective bargaining a matter of public policy, with public-sector industrial relations based on Whitleyism since 1919.

Just after the First World War, the Liberal–Conservative coalition government of the day tried to plan the reconstruction of the country and the empire. In the brief period between the war ending and British capital regrouping there was a need for greater state regulation to secure the rebuilding of the economy. This was especially important in the arena of industrial relations and labour management.[28] The unions were strong and, until the troops returned from overseas and the recession set in, labour remained scarce. Furthermore, there was also a demand for greater state regulation from the organized working class, drawing strength from the Russian Revolution in 1917 and spurred on by the rapid spread of socialist ideals. Under pressure from labour scarcity, popular protest, industrial action, and socialist agitation, the reactionary government of a victorious imperial state enacted three great democratic reforms: votes for women, the creation of what later came to be known as the welfare state, and Whitleyism. Only the first of these three reforms is untouched by the weakening of the preconditions that brought them about, all of which faded particularly rapidly during the period of this history: the 1980s saw high unemployment, the retreat of socialist ideals, and the fall of the Soviet Union.

Events in 1919 show that even a Conservative-dominated government will, under political and economic pressure, agree to extensive regulation of large areas of economic activity, including industrial relations (albeit on a voluntary basis). The Whitley Committee reports recommended that the best way to regulate industrial relations was through strong relationships between

[28] H. Clay, *The Problem of Industrial Relations* (London: Macmillan, 1929); W. McCarthy, *Making Whitley Work: A Review of the Operation of the NHS Whitley Council System* (London: HMSO, 1976); D. Farnham, 'Sixty Years of Whitleyism', *Personnel Management* (June 1978), 29–32.

well-organized employers and well-organized trade unions. Employers should recognize unions for collective-bargaining purposes, bargaining should take place on a regular basis, and disputes arising from the bargain (disputes of right) should be resolved through a formally agreed conciliation procedure.

In practice Whitley was never a starter in most of the private sector and, except in education[29] and the Civil Service,[30] it did not receive government support in the public sector until after the Second World War, when further concessions were made by a Labour government under similar pressures and NALGO won Whitleyism in local government. In 1979 Whitley was the dominant model of public-sector industrial relations and it seemed as if it had always been that way (see Chapter 2).

Within the Whitley system, codified national agreements are supplemented by bargaining at regional and employer levels, and even at sub-employer level. Both formal and informal bargaining occur over a wide range of both substantive and procedural issues, including bonuses, shift work, health and safety, working hours, holidays, new technology, redundancies, (re)grades, grievances, and disciplinary action. Trade-union negotiators—lay activists, workplace bargainers, full-time officials, and national officers—are all mobilized around collective bargaining, including individual representation.

There is a large body of literature on this.[31] Pluralist-minded British academics saw collective bargaining as 'a method of settling the terms and conditions of employment of employees',[32] refining the definition later as 'bilateral or joint regulation' of the 'rules governing employment together with the ways in which the rules are made and changed and their interpretation and administration'.[33] The pluralists focus on the system's capacity to prevent conflict between the parties by providing a method of resolving differences through some form of negotiation. This perspective understates the fact that bargaining also embodies conflict, because it usually results in a clear distrib-

---

[29] R. Seifert, *Teacher Militancy: A History of Teacher Strikes 1896–1987* (Sussex: Falmer Press, 1987).

[30] R. Blackwell and P. Lloyd, 'New Managerialism in the Civil Service: Industrial Relations under the Thatcher Administration 1979–1986', in R. Mailly, S. Dimmock, and A. Sethi (eds.), *Industrial Relations in the Public Services* (London: Routledge, 1989), 68–113.

[31] H. Clegg, *The System of Industrial Relations in Great Britain* (Oxford: Blackwell, 1972); H. Clegg, *The Changing System of Industrial Relations in Great Britain* (Oxford: Blackwell, 1979); G. Bain (ed.), *Industrial Relations in Britain* (Oxford: Blackwell, 1983); P. Edwards (ed.), *Industrial Relations* (Oxford: Blackwell, 1995).

[32] A. Flanders, 'Collective Bargaining', in A. Flanders and H. Clegg (eds.), *The System of Industrial Relations in Great Britain* (Oxford: Blackwell, 1954), 252.

[33] Clegg, *The System of Industrial Relations*, 1.

ution of spoils, where one party gains at the expense of the other. Thus there is plenty of room for argument about strategy and tactics both within and between the parties. The constant shifting of the main focus of bargaining, over the level at which bargaining should take place, over what is or is not negotiable, and over who is covered by any bargain and who is not, reflects the bargaining environment—the pressure of work processes themselves, the nature of the product, service, and labour markets, and the organizational power of the main parties to any bargaining that does or might take place.[34]

Unions exist for bargaining purposes, even if bargaining does not actually take place, as when the employer refuses to negotiate. Logically this leads to the third essential feature of trade unionism: trade unions fight to achieve their bargaining objectives. They fight to establish bargaining, they fight over the level, scope, and unit of bargaining, and they fight over bargaining outcomes. Without action, or at least the possibility of it, collective bargaining is an empty shell. So collective bargaining is both a means of resolving conflict and a method based on it. It implies the use of power within negotiations— namely, the potential or actual mobilization of union members to harm, disrupt, and distort the employer's business. This includes any form of industrial action, by any number of members, for any duration, whether or not sanctioned by law and/or union executives and/or ballots. Examples include overtime bans, strikes, downers, working to rule, boycotts, working without enthusiasm, and other restrictions of output.[35] The importance of taking and/or threatening to take action is paramount in the application of power by trade unions in their relationship with any employer.

In his discussion of these issues John Kelly[36] applies mobilization theory, in which 'interests' and their ascription have central importance. He investigates how grievances become articulated as injustices, and how such injustices become part of a collectively aware set of interests able to be channelled through the organization into collective action. Two points arise from this. First, trade-union activists and leaders play an important role in turning members' grievances into a widespread sense of injustice—they build union policy platforms that articulate the members' own experiences, and then feed these into the bargaining agenda and into trade-union action. Secondly, in most cases both the feelings of injustice and the remedies are contested,

---

[34] R. Walton and R. McKersie, *A Behavioral Theory of Labor Negotiations* (New York: McGraw Hill, 1967); K. Sisson, *The Management of Collective Bargaining* (Oxford: Blackwell, 1987).

[35] K. Knowles, *Strikes—a Study in Industrial Conflict* (Oxford: Blackwell, 1952); R. Hyman, *Strikes* (London: Macmillan, 1989); P. Edwards, 'Industrial Conflict', *British Journal of Industrial Relations*, 30/3 (1992), 361–404.

[36] J. Kelly, *Rethinking Industrial Relations* (London: Routledge, 1998).

between employers and employees and also within the trade unions. Indeed, each contested issue is located in a wider debate about where power resides in our society and how it can best be countered. Union decisions about why, when, and how to act—whether or not to affiliate to the TUC, or to strike, or to merge with others unions—are the outcomes of such debates.

Trade unions do engage in activities that are not collective bargaining. These may also apply pressure on employers, without directly disrupting their business, such as lobbying, campaigning, and linking up with political and single-issue groups. However, while together they constitute an important aspect of trade-union behaviour, organizations that are not trade unions might also use the same forms of activity to press their own case. Therefore it cannot be said to be either a necessary or a sufficient condition for trade unionism—trade unions that do not engage in this kind of action are still trade unions. But in the public sector, especially among white-collar staff, such campaigns do form an important part of union activity. They help stir members into action, they help win the understanding of sections of the public needed to support union action, they maintain morale among activists, and they nudge political decision-makers locally and nationally. NALGO became increasingly involved in a variety of important campaigns: backing an individual member facing deportation (see Box 7), raising awareness of equality issues (see Box 8), opposing the poll tax (see Box 13), and supporting the African National Congress (ANC) in South Africa (see Box 14). That any given trade union may or may not be involved in such campaigns takes us beyond the *function* of trade unions into the debate about their *goals*.[37]

What are trade unions for?

Having argued that trade unionism is a response of alienated and exploited workers, who create their independent organizations in order to engage in collective bargaining with employers, we now examine more closely the essential nature of these organizations, as seen through the debates about their purpose.

Beatrice and Sidney Webb famously define a trade union as 'a continuous association of wage earners for the purpose of maintaining or improving the conditions of their employment'.[38] They later refine this definition, changing 'employment' to the broader 'working lives'.[39] They went on to develop this position especially in their work *Industrial Democracy*.[40] The main thrust

[37] R. Martin, *Trade Unionism: Purposes and Forms* (Oxford: Clarendon Press, 1989).
[38] S. Webb and B. Webb, *The History of Trade Unionism* (London: Longman, 1894), 1.
[39] S. Webb and B. Webb, *The History of Trade Unionism* (London: Longman, 1920), 1.
[40] S. Webb and B. Webb, *Industrial Democracy* (London: Longman, 1897).

of their argument is that trade unions are known by their three methods of achieving the purpose set out in the definition: collective bargaining, mutual insurance, and legal enactment. The method of mutual insurance involves providing members with friendly society and out-of-work benefits, to prevent unemployed members from accepting employment on terms and conditions below the existing going rate. Collective bargaining is the establishment of conditions of employment through collective agreements between representatives of the employers and the trade unions. Legal enactment is the method of securing legal rights for workers to ensure a more permanent element to conditions of service beyond the reach of the vagaries of collective agreements that are themselves subject to market forces.

Taking their analysis of trade-union action further, the Webbs suggest that the three methods are underpinned by two devices: the restriction of numbers and the common rule. The latter simply states the benefits of common conditions of employment within occupational groups in order to prevent individuals and smaller groups from being picked off, typified by the national conditions established through national bargaining. The other device, the restriction of numbers, refers to efforts to control the price of labour by controlling its supply to the employers. Thus groups of workers establish a protected labour market, based on notions of skill and/or professionalism, and surrounded by a barrier of qualifications partly to control entry to their occupation. Cruder devices such as sexism, racism, and nepotism are also used by both professional and non-professional workers to prevent others from invading 'their' job territory.

The two devices in turn hinge on three doctrines (assumptions) of trade unionism: 'vested interests' refers to fighting to maintain customary conditions and pay rates; 'supply and demand' refers to the derived nature of labour so that the price of labour varies with the price of the goods or services provided by that labour; and the 'living wage' asserts that neither custom nor markets should be allowed to vary wages in ways that might ignore the importance of paying according to need. Debates about low pay, differentials, affordability, and comparability are rooted in these doctrines.[41]

Within the Webbs' model, the selection of method, device, and doctrine would vary according to trade, industry, and historical circumstance, resulting both in a wide variety in trade-union practice, and in constant arguments between trade unionists about which policies and practices to follow at any given moment. In the end any set of union policies and practices is seen as the outcome of endlessly shifting compromises within and between trade

---

[41] H. Phelps Brown, *The Inequality of Pay* (Oxford: Oxford University Press, 1977); G. Routh, *Occupation and Pay in Great Britain 1906–1979* (London: Macmillan, 1980).

unionists and the employers. The model gives considerable insight into the dynamics of trade unionism, but it is based on a narrowly limited conception of purpose.

Writers such as G. D. H. Cole[42] and Robert Hoxie[43] develop the ideas. Two of the categories outlined in Hoxie's analysis of American unions, business unionism and revolutionary unionism, represent types of possible trade-union behaviour based on either acceptance or rejection of the business enterprise as legitimate. Cole took this point further by locating such positions within a spectrum of consciousness. The limited version of 'here-and-now' trade unionism (the ultimate pragmatic position) was linked with a narrow interpretation of trade interests—trade consciousness. This contrasts with class consciousness, whereby the union is seen as an organization with which to fight against capitalism as both an entire system and as the main engine of the exploitation of employed workers. Tensions between the two positions account for debates within the trade-union movement, explaining differences in action and in methods. Actual union practice ends up most of the time somewhere between the two positions, reflecting the balance of forces within the union as well as the strength of the pressures on the union from outside.

Another American writer, Selig Perlman,[44] supports the business unionism position through the theory of limited engagement between unions and employers over the regulation of the job. Essentially his position, and that of others writing at the time,[45] is that exploitation and alienation may take place, and it may be felt by workers, but their natural inclination is to organize collectively to control their own employment situation and not to control their industry and/or their state. Perlman attacks left-wing views of trade unionism as originating among intellectuals, mostly Marxists, whose experiences are outside the scope of working peoples' knowledge. He argues, as do both Allan Flanders[46] and Tom Kochan[47] later, that the natural role of trade unions is the protection of job regulation and that this tends to maintain a proper job consciousness among workers. If and when unions and their members ever went beyond that limit then it was wrong, counterproductive, and largely due to the unwanted influence of outsiders with other political agendas.

[42] G. D. H. Cole, *British Trade Unionism Today* (London: Gollancz, 1939).

[43] R. Hoxie, 'Trade Unionism in the United States', in E. Bakke and C. Kerr (eds.), *Unions, Management and the Public* (New York: Harcourt, Brace & Co., 1948), 152–5.

[44] S. Perlman, *A Theory of the Labor Movement* (New York: Macmillan, 1928).

[45] J. Commons and Associates, *History of Labour in the United States* (New York: Macmillan, 1918).

[46] Flanders, *Management and Unions*.

[47] T. Kochan, H. Katz, and R. McKersie, *The Transformation of American Industrial Relations* (New York: Basic Books, 1986).

Ranged against this group of trade-union theories are the various Marxist positions.[48] Only when trade unionists sought common cause with others in struggle, based on a leftist critique of capitalism, could they successfully challenge both the management of the business and the social order that maintains the power inequality supporting business. Philip Foner, another American writer, comments on the limitations of Perlman's parochial argument:

The only labor organizations, according to this school, which could survive in America were those which . . . made their organizations revolve about the individual worker's job. Others which preached principles of labor solidarity and common action, the unity of skilled and unskilled in industrial unions, of the foreign born and native Americans, of Negro and white, of women and men, and dared to project issues other than the limited objective of wage and job control, went counter to the only acceptable 'consciousness' for American labor as a whole and were doomed to failure.[49]

Karl Marx and Friedrich Engels argue the general proposition that capitalism, by its very nature, creates the forces most likely to end its reign of economic domination. By organizing the workers into collective activity, educating them and drawing them into politics, the workers themselves become sufficiently powerful and organized to challenge the system through class struggle and to become its grave-diggers.[50] They argue that trade unions would play an important part in this process, but they are hampered by two factors: first by their tendency to narrow their practice to the limited possibilities of what could be achieved for their special case; and, secondly, by the ability of sections of capital with a temporary advantage in world markets to make concessions sufficient to dull the edge of the greater class challenge.

This ability to pay more than strictly market rates is used by employers to create a 'labour aristocracy' that might identify more closely with the employer than with other workers. Such an identification might also come from the nature of work, so that clerks are associated (only partly justifiably) with snobbishness and with anti-union traditions. Their extra pay and advantages might also lead them to believe that they are socially and culturally superior to other workers—not only to the less skilled and the less well educated, but also to women, to those from ethnic minorities, and to any other groups in an inferior labour-market situation. These deeply entrenched attitudes are not

[48] V. Allen, *Militant Trade Unionism* (London: Merlin Press, 1966); R. Hyman, *Industrial Relations: A Marxist Introduction* (London: Macmillan, 1975); J. Kelly, *Trade Unions and Socialist Politics* (London: Verso, 1988).

[49] P. Foner, *History of the Labor Movement in the USA* (New York: International Publishers, 1947), 10–11.

[50] K. Marx and F. Engels, 'The Manifesto of the Communist Party', in K. Marx and F. Engels, *Selected Works Volume One* (Moscow: Progress Publishers, 1969), 98–137.

only the preserve of white-collar and professional workers; they are equally pervasive throughout the hierarchy of administrative, professional, technical, clerical, craft, skilled, semi-skilled, and unskilled workers, and they are therefore prevalent in their trade unions. Breaking them down is part and parcel of leftist activity within the labour and trade-union movement.

Vladimir Lenin,[51] and later Antonio Gramsci,[52] argued that trade unions in and of themselves tend to have limited vision with regard to challenging and changing the system of capital itself. Political parties and agitations are needed, along with their industrial struggles, to feed into and to feed from that daily organized contest with the representatives of capital in the form of managers and employers. This position contrasts with the powerfully expressed views of syndicalists such as Tom Mann,[53] James Connolly,[54] and the Wobblies.[55] This amalgam of revolutionary trade unionism with more traditional guild socialism aimed to unite workers in an industry to take over the industry, and then, along with others, to take over the system. Its modern forms include the workers' democracy and control movements,[56] and sometimes it surfaces in union merger movements. It allows for managerial and professional grades to be incorporated into unions as part of the inclusive need to mobilize all employees for maximum impact under the banner of 'one big union'. Such an inclusive, vertically united, industrial union does not preclude links with political organizations, since, to be successful in trade unions, leftist groups need both to express the unifying principle of common cause with workers outside the union and to unite members of all occupations and ranks within the union.

For over a hundred years the left, in Britain, and in most other European countries, has been split between assorted communists and socialists espousing the end of capitalism, and an all-sorts of social democrats and progressive liberals arguing for the amelioration and control of capitalism. Alliances, based on desperate pragmatism as well as on high idealism, result in a bewildering variety of policy positions. 'Broad left' groupings—communists, socialists on the Labour Party left, and non-aligned socialist activists—usually exclude the ultra-left. The right is less coherent, including social democrats from inside and outside the Labour Party, liberals, and Tories, who embrace capitalism. This does not prevent them from being militant in defence of their

[51] V. Lenin, *What Is To Be Done?* (Oxford: Oxford University Press, 1963).

[52] A. Gramsci, *Selections from the Prison Notebooks* (London: Lawrence & Wishart, 1971).

[53] T. Mann, *Memoirs* (London: Labour Publishing Company, 1923).

[54] J. Connolly, 'Old Wine in New Bottles', in P. Ellis (ed.), *James Connolly: Selected Writings* (Harmondsworth: Penguin, 1973).

[55] Industrial Workers of the World—the Wobblies, 'Preamble', in S. Larson and B. Nissen (eds.), *Theories of the Labor Movement* (Detroit: Wayne State University Press, 1987), 66.

[56] K. Coates and T. Topham (eds.), *Workers' Control* (London: Panther Books, 1970).

rights from time to time, but it does prevent them engaging in struggles beyond the 'here and now' business unionism and trade consciousness outlined by Hoxie and Cole. In contrast, the left argues for wider and deeper opposition to employment conditions through a class position based on the unity of the sellers of labour power irrespective of the nature of the buyers.

Emile Burns, responding to the weaknesses and ultimate failures of the 1945–50 Labour government, provides a clear statement of what can be involved in the wider debate between the two main wings of the British labour movement:

There emerged 'New Thinkers' on the right, who sought to reformulate Labour's aims and programme and to build up a theoretical justification for change. . . . But the right-wing New Thinkers looked backward, not forward. . . . Nor were the thoughts which the New Thinkers embodied in their writings really new: they were based on the stock-in-trade of propagandists of the ruling class on the beauties of capitalism and the viles of socialism. If anything was new it was that these thoughts were set down and elaborated by spokesmen of the Labour movement . . . these apologetics could not seem convincing to the rank and file of the Labour movement—especially the active members whose outlook was socialist—unless the right-wing theoreticians could succeed in doing two things.[57]

These two things were to present post-war capitalism as something entirely different from older forms of capitalism, and to present socialism in the post-war world as something much worse than the socialism embraced by socialists before the war. This work was carried out by Dick Crossman, Tony Crossland, Hugh Gaitskell, and John Stratchey. Later in his book, Burns argues that, 'since it is in the industrial field that right wing theory and practice come most sharply into collision with the facts of life, the fight on wages and conditions gives the left movement its principal strength and momentum'.[58] Workers' experiences at work are linked by the broad left analysis to the fight beyond workplace issues, and this ability to deepen and widen the theory and practice of industrial struggle is what makes the left both successful and feared. Keeping the beast of militant trade unionism in its cage is still part and parcel of the limited right-wing vision of the trade-union role.[59]

Union democracy

Decisions about whether, how, and when to act are contested within the union's decision-making structures. Most unions appear similar, having branch, regional, and national structures, including bodies of delegates, executive committees, and conferences, through which policy decisions are

---

[57] E. Burns, *Rightwing Labour* (London: Lawrence & Wishart, 1961), 6–7.
[58] Ibid. 119.   [59] A. Blair, 'Consensual Feelings', *Unions Today* (Jan. 2000), 8–10.

made. Democratic safeguards include such issues as the rights of members—for example, on exclusion from office and expulsion from membership.[60] The constitution might also ensure that certain groups, such as women members, are represented within the structures.[61] However, union democracy does not begin and end with the formal constitutional structures.

The Webbs,[62] and later Turner,[63] describe and analyse different types of union government and relate these to both membership type and employer activity. Turner links union democratic practice to the boundary of union recruitment. Small unions of skilled workers, where the organizing principle is based more or less on establishing union control over the supply of labour to the employers in order to maximize both the price of labour and job security, have little interest in expanding their membership. There is a high degree of identity of interest between the skilled members, shared also by full-time officers who are likely to have practised the skill themselves. Union politics is thus characterized by a narrow concern for job-related issues.

The position of these 'closed' unions contrasts with that of the 'open' general unions, which have more inclusive and expansionary aims. Organizing workers who are not scarce in the labour markets, they rely more on the use of mass action to apply pressure on the employers, and also on securing wider political and legal rights for workers generally such as a minimum wage. There is less identity of interest based on the job, both among the membership and between members and full-time officers—the officials are likely to be more educated and better paid than the majority of the members. Membership participation in trade-union affairs is characteristically low.

Both government and employers take an interest in trade-union practice, finding some forms more unacceptable than others. In the anti-communist hysteria of the 1950s some academics friendly to government and to employers argued for a model of democracy based on the US Constitution, with formal and free opposition, in order to ensure that union behaviour matched the needs and demands of members, who were assumed to be in favour of high

---

[60] J. Gennard, M. Gregory, and S. Dunn, 'Throwing the Book', *Employment Gazette*, 88/6 (1980), 591–600; IRS, 'Union Procedures on the Admission and Expulsion of Members', *Industrial Relations Review and Report*, 272 (1982), 2–7; Wedderburn, *The Worker and the Law*.

[61] J. Hughes, *Trade Union Structure and Government* (Research Paper 5, Donovan Commission; London: HMSO, 1966); LRD, *Women in Trade Unions* (London: LRD, 1991); UNISON, *Getting the Balance Right: Guidelines on Proportionality* (London: UNISON, 1994); A. McBride, 'Reshaping Trade Union Democracy: Developing Effective Representation for Women', Ph.D. thesis (Warwick, 1997).

[62] Webb and Webb, *History of Trade Unionism*.

[63] H. Turner, *Trade Union Growth, Structure and Policy* (London: Allen & Unwin, 1962).

levels of cooperation with the employer.[64] This was taken up in the UK by writers such as Joseph Goldstein, Ben Roberts, and J. David Edelstein and Malcolm Warner, and then later Roger Undy.[65] The argument was that corrupt (as with Jimmy Hoffa of the teamsters[66]) and/or communist unions (such as the Electrical Trades Union (ETU)[67]) distorted the essential nature of trade unionism to such an extent that they ceased to be unions and became the instruments of gangster and/or political tendencies. Union democracy was judged by the norms of liberal–pluralist democracy.[68]

Writing from a left perspective, Richard Hyman[69] distinguishes between the optimistic views of the Webbs and Vic Allen,[70] and the more pessimistic ones of Robert Michels.[71] The latter's 'iron law of oligarchy' suggests that all mass organizations of the working class inevitably end up dominated by small cliques. This tension feeds into debates about the role of full-time officials in making and implementing union policy, and about their relationship to the rest of the union. Should they be accountable to the membership in the manner of elected representatives, or of appointed civil servants? In some unions, such as the NUM and the Amalgamated Engineering Union (AEU), they were elected, but in NALGO they were appointed by the National Executive Committee (NEC). Of course the formal lines of accountability do not actually describe real practice. How are elected leaders accountable to the electorate between elections, and what is their relationship to delegate conferences and councils? And is accountability of appointed officials through line management control any less democratic than this? Democratic accountability is something more organic and political than the formal lines established in the rules.

National leaders and full-time officers at all levels are frequently accused of betraying their own members. Of the few systematic studies that have been carried out, none has produced any evidence for that position. They recount

[64] S. Lipset, M. Trow, and J. Coleman, *Union Democracy: The Internal Politics of the International Typographical Union* (Glencoe, Ill.: Free Press, 1956).

[65] J. Goldstein, *The Government of British Trade Unions* (London: Allen & Unwin, 1952); B. Roberts, *Trade Union Government and Administration in Great Britain* (London: G. Bell & Sons, 1956); J. D. Edelstein and M. Warner, *Comparative Union Democracy* (London: Allen & Unwin, 1975); R. Undy, V. Ellis, W. McCarthy, and A. Halmos, *Change in Trade Unions: The Development of UK Unions since the 1960s* (London: Hutchinson, 1981).

[66] A. Sloane, *Hoffa* (London: MIT Press, 1991).

[67] C. Rolph, *All those in Favour: The ETU Trial* (London: André Deutsch, 1962).

[68] R. Martin, 'Union Democracy: An Explanatory Framework', in W. McCarthy (ed.), *Trade Unions* (Harmondsworth: Penguin, 1985), 224–42.

[69] R. Hyman, 'Trade Unions: Structure, Policies and Politics', in G. Bain (ed.), *Industrial Relations in Britain* (Oxford: Blackwell, 1983), 35–65.

[70] V. Allen, *Power in Trade Unions* (London: Longman, 1954).

[71] R. Michels, *Political Parties* (New York: Hearsts, 1915).

the obvious tasks of full-time officials—negotiations, representation, recruitment, helping branches and stewards.[72] More detailed and specific studies of NUPE,[73] the National Union of Railwaymen (NUR),[74] and the National Union of Teachers (NUT)[75] indicate the wide range of practices and relationships that develop. Wright Mills famously argues that, 'even as the labor leader rebels, he holds back rebellion. He organizes discontent and then he sits on it, exploiting it to maintain a continuous organization, the labour leader is a manager of discontent.'[76] But, if trade-union leadership is so benign, why did so many leaders take up such bitter struggles against the Conservative governments of the 1980s? Moreover, why did the Thatcher governments feel the need to legislate against their power?

Accepting neither the 'parliamentary model' of trade unionism, nor the 'sell-out' model of leadership, the broad left has traditionally taken a more dynamic approach, which puts leadership in the context of the past, present, and future struggles against the employer. Empty exercises in democracy, however defined, are not serious tests of trade unionism. The real test is the delivery of outcomes that benefit the members—the 'bringing-home-the-bacon' argument. In other words, 'I did not join a union so that I can participate in decision making, but to secure protection of and improvement in my collective conditions of employment.' That is not to say that union members do not participate in decision-making (although for most of the time only a small minority does participate in the governance of most unions); it is just not the reason why they joined. So being democratic, however defined, is not a necessary condition to qualify as a trade union.

Nevertheless, democratic practice and leadership are significant issues at all levels within any trade union, and they are subject to constantly changing pressures both from within the membership and from external political and economic circumstances.[77] Political processes within unions, and struggle over the manner in which they develop their policies and pursue their objectives, are part and parcel of everyday practice. They are indeed the union's

---

[72] H. Clegg, A. Killick, and R. Adams, *Trade Union Officers: A Study of Full-Time Officers, Branch Secretaries and Shop Stewards in British Trade Unions* (Oxford: Blackwell, 1961); W. Brown and M. Lawson, 'The Training of Trade Union Officers', *British Journal of Industrial Relations*, 11/3 (1973), 431–48; J. Kelly and E. Heery, *Working for the Unions* (Cambridge: Cambridge University Press, 1994); D. Watson, *Managers of Discontent* (London: Routledge, 1988).

[73] R. Fryer, A. Fairclough, and T. Mason, *Organisation and Change in the National Union of Public Employees* (London: NUPE, 1974).

[74] R. Hyman, R. Price, and M. Terry, *Reshaping the NUR* (London: NUR, 1988).

[75] R. Seifert, 'Some Aspects of Factional Opposition: Rank and File and the National Union of Teachers 1967–1982', *British Journal of Industrial Relations*, 22/3 (1984), 372–90.

[76] C. Wright Mills, *The New Men of Power* (New York: Harcourt Brace, 1948), 8–9.

[77] T. Lane, *The Union Makes Us Strong* (London: Arrow Books, 1974).

lifeblood, an integral part of being a trade-union official or activist. But they are not trade unionism itself; they are a *consequence* of it.

Trade-union practice reflects the prevailing views of members, activists, and leaders. A union of employees banded together in the belief that they are exploited would behave consciously in ways to tackle their exploiters. On the other hand, a union of employees who believe that they are being treated unfairly within a system that is either potentially or actually fair would also band together in trade unions, but their different understanding would result in different behaviour. Whichever view predominates is significant, to government, to employers, and to trade unionists themselves—unfairness can be remedied, but exploitation goes on for as long as the system goes on. The battle for ideas among trade-union members has political significance far beyond some of the sterile debates about union democracy—hence the scale of anti-unionism when it appears to challenge the employment system rather than just the employer.

NALGO is a Trade Union and All NALGO Members are Trade Unionists

Now NALGO can be located within the above framework, in an attempt to analyse the union and its distinctive characteristics, both as an organization and as a set of practices. We can use this framework to clarify two of the particular debates about trade unionism: first, that some workers cannot be trade unionists, because of the job that they do (such as white-collar professionals); and, secondly, that some organizations are not trade unions because their members are not employed by capitalists who exploit workers for profit. According to these arguments, NALGO was not a 'proper' trade union and NALGO members were not 'proper' trade unionists.

First, we disagree with writers who argue that there can be degrees of unionism, that some unions have more unionism in them than others.[78] When NALGO started to campaign around election issues and adopted a political fund in the 1980s, it did not become any more of a trade union, just as it was no less of a trade union before it affiliated to the TUC. TUC affiliates are not trade unions because they are affiliated—they can affiliate only if they are already trade unions. So membership of the TUC cannot be part of the definition or essential nature of a union, as this would be a circular argument. An organization is either a trade union or it is not—it is a state of being. We

[78] R. Blackburn, *Union Character and Social Class* (London: Batsford, 1967); K. Coates and T. Topham, *Trade Unions in Britain* (London: Fontana Press, 1988).

have argued that a trade union is defined by a relatively straightforward set of objective facts: an independent organization of employees that aims to engage in collective bargaining with one or more employers, and that takes action to support its bargaining objectives is a trade union. By this definition, NALGO was a trade union for most of its lifetime, and we review the union's development in Chapter 2. We conclude this chapter by locating NALGO within debates on the nature of trade unionism.

Attempts to categorize trade unions, in both everyday language and in academic analysis, often focus on the structure of recruitment. Typical classifications include general, industrial, craft, and occupational unions.[79] Other categories include public-sector unions and white-collar unions— indeed Spoor's first volume of NALGO's history bears the title *White Collar Union*.

George Bain provides the first major academic study of white-collar unions in the UK.[80] Following David Lockwood's[81] study of clerical workers and their unions, the work of Robert Blackburn and Kenneth Prandy,[82] and the earlier work on clerical workers by Francis Klingender,[83] Bain argues that an increasingly shared employment situation among white-collar workers created some of the conditions for union growth, and NALGO's growth came with the establishment of national standards of service,[84] an argument already made for schoolteachers.[85]

Pluralist academics have some difficulty fitting white-collar unions into their classifications.[86] For example, Allan Flanders argues: 'The development of union organisation among non-manual or white-collar workers needs to be considered separately . . . An organisation like the National and Local Government Officers' Association, however, might be said to resemble a general union in the white-collar field.' He continues: 'NALGO also illustrates another noticeable trend in non-manual unionism: the gradual transformation of professional associations into trade unions, with the growth of union consciousness among employees who originally believed they had little in

[79] Clegg, *The System of Industrial Relations*.

[80] G. Bain, *The Growth of White-Collar Unionism* (Oxford: Oxford University Press, 1970).

[81] D. Lockwood, *The Black Coated Worker* (London: Allen & Unwin, 1958).

[82] R. Blackburn and K. Prandy, 'White Collar Unionization: A Conceptual Framework', *British Journal of Sociology*, 16 (1965), 111–22.

[83] F. Klingender, *The Condition of Clerical Labour in Britain* (London: Martin Lawrence, 1935).

[84] Bain, *The Growth of White-Collar Unionism*, 75.

[85] A. Tropp, *The School Teachers* (London: Heinemann, 1957); R. Manzer, *Teachers and Politics* (Manchester: Manchester University Press, 1970).

[86] K. Prandy, A. Stewart, and R. Blackburn, *White-Collar Unionism* (London: Macmillan, 1983).

common with wage-earners and therefore did not share the same need for protective organisation.'[87]

Attaching some importance to the ways in which NALGO was unlike other unions, these writers turn to a sociological view of class, influenced by Max Weber[88] and Émile Durkheim,[89] and apply it *pari passu* to trade unions. Blackburn's influential account of white-collar unionism, albeit based on staff in the banking sector, argues: 'White collar unions are particularly interesting because the distinctive class positions of the workers have led to greater concern with the nature of their unionisms, and a resultant variety of forms.'[90] But the variety of forms was neither stranger nor more varied than those existing in other unions, and little account is taken of trade-union organization amongst, for example, health visitors and teachers. Others disagreed with Blackburn's overemphasis of status; for example, Roger Lumley argued that 'social status in fact has little direct effect on the membership density of unionism'.[91] But why the need to argue this at all? If NALGO consisted of wage-earners formed together into a union based on collective bargaining, then it was like other trade unions as well as being unlike them.

Accounts of trade unionism based on the differences in its forms, rather than in its substance, neglect the underlying dynamics of trade-union action. Turner's notion of 'open' and 'closed' unions gives a more dialectical approach than such static descriptive accounts. He explores the extent to which early local trade unions, based on occupational groups, were prepared to open their doors to other occupations and/or other localities, or whether they believed that their strength resided in their exclusiveness.[92] Clearly NALGO opened itself up, shifting its recruitment boundary from local-government administrative, professional, technical, and clerical (APT&C) staffs only, and rapidly becoming more 'open' in terms of both occupational and industrial recruitment. Indeed, its final act of amalgamation with NUPE and COHSE to form UNISON in the summer of 1993 was an acceptance that its growth and power rested in remaining open.

The argument that certain types of worker cannot be trade unionists is rooted in some rather static views about class, work, and unionization. It applies typically to managerial, professional, and other white-collar employees, along the following lines. First, as better-paid workers they are middle

[87] A. Flanders, *Trade Unions* (London: Hutchinson University Library, 1968), 34.

[88] M. Weber, *The Protestant Ethic and the Spirit of Capitalism* (London: Unwin University Books, 1970).

[89] É. Durkheim, *The Division of Labour in Society* (Toronto: Macmillan, 1964).

[90] Blackburn, *Union Character*, 7.

[91] R. Lumley, *White Collar Unionism in Britain* (London: Methuen & Co., 1973), 31–2.

[92] Turner, *Trade Union Growth*.

class and not working class, and they are thus socially, culturally, and politically unsuited to collective, solidaristic, and socialistic activity. Secondly, their position at work means that they may well be the instrument of exploitation, implementing sackings and disciplinaries, and exercising control over the labour process through speed-up and deskilling. Thirdly, they do not directly experience common exploitation, since they are far removed from the productive process: either because of the nature of their work, such as being a librarian, an architect, or a nurse; or because their position in the hierarchy makes them immune from the harsh realities of the employment relationship. The term 'staff' itself has both biblical and military connotations of authority over others.

In 1917 the Webbs argued that 'brain workers' might form together into associations owing to three 'impulses': the creative impulse to advance the knowledge and practice of the profession; the fellowship impulse of solidarity with the like-minded (and exclusion of others); and the possessive impulse to win status and pay based on community appreciation of their worth.[93] Certainly all three impulses were present in NALGO's development, with perhaps its real strength being to utilize all three to create a whole more powerful than its parts. However, the Webbs failed to follow the logic of their own model of trade unionism, agreeing that such groups did form organizations that adopted trade-union-like behaviour but still insisting that only organizations of manual workers were actually trade unions. If it looks like a duck and it quacks like a duck then why not accept that it is a duck!

David Lockwood's study of clerical work and clerical workers in the late 1950s provides some important insights into what happened to many NALGO members during the 1980s. He argues thus: 'To study the class consciousness of the clerk is to study the factors affecting his [*sic*] sense of identification with, or alienation from, the working class. More precisely, such a study should aim at an understanding of the relationship of the black-coated worker to the trade union movement, the main vehicle of working-class consciousness.'[94] He continues that, although clerks were clearly part of the working class, the real issue was their awareness of collective interests, since many seemed to suffer from 'false consciousness'. While clerks could form unions around an awareness of group consciousness, this was quite distinct from class consciousness. He suggests that:

In the case of blackcoated workers, class consciousness may be said to emerge when the members of a clerical association realize, first, that their common interests are

---

[93] S. Webb and B. Webb, 'Special Supplement on Professional Associations, Part Two', *New Statesman*, 9/212 (1917), 36.
[94] Lockwood, *The Black Coated Worker*, 13.

engendered by the conflict of interest between employer and employee, and secondly, that their common interests are not fundamentally dissimilar in type from those underlying the concerted actions of manual workers. The trade union movement is a working-class movement, and to the extent that clerical workers become involved in trade unionism they have to come to terms with its wider class character.[95]

We agree, except that we see no special case for white-collar workers here; for the same arguments can apply with equal force to a whole range of manual and craft workers who themselves have been referred to as the 'aristocracy of labour'. Lockwood accepts, as we do, that white-collar workers in general have to sell their labour power to make a living, but his answer to the puzzle of why they do not identify with the mass of manual workers and their organizations appears to be status. He avoids some tricky questions about status itself and about the importance to employers of both hiding the exploitative nature of the employment relationship and dividing the workforce in order to rule over it. Status is not only an issue for clerical workers; it applies to the workforce as a whole. Status was also an issue within NALGO, as it organized vertically up and down the job hierarchy. This brings us to the distribution of workers between and within unions. In particular, one option is the formation of occupation-specific unions, including unions for managers such as the National Association of Colliery Overmen, Deputies, and Shotfirers (NACODS) and the British Association of Collier Managers (BACM) in the mining industry, NUMAST in the merchant navy, the Association of First Division Civil Servants (FDA) in the Civil Service, and Federated Union of Managerial and Professional Officers (FUMPO) in local government.[96] The other main option is vertical unionism, where the union recruits up and down the job hierarchy, such as the NUT for schoolteachers and head teachers, most 'amalgamated' unions such as the Manufacture, Science, Finance (MSF) union and the Amalgamated Engineering and Electrical Union (AEEU), general unions such as the Transport and General Workers' Union (TGWU), the GMB, and NALGO itself. One study of NALGO argues that:

In the past the lack of differentiation between senior and lower grades of white-collar worker in the public sector, the consensus nature of union character and the

---

[95] Ibid. 137.

[96] A. Arthurs, 'Management and Managerial Unionism', in K. Thurley and S. Wood (eds.), *Industrial Relations and Management Strategy* (Cambridge: Cambridge University Press, 1983), 13–18; D. Simpson, 'Managers in Workers' Trade Unions: The Case of the NUJ', in Thurley and Wood (eds.), *Industrial Relations and Management Strategy*, 19–26; E. Snape and G. Bamber, 'Managerial and Professional Employees: Conceptualising Union Strategies and Structure', *British Journal of Industrial Relations*, 27/1 (1989), 93–110.

centralisation of collective bargaining have tended to militate against the identification of separate interests within white collar organisation, and against the potential for intra-union conflict which lies in the recruitment of both managerial and subordinate grades to one union body.[97]

The union encountered some difficulties in the 1980s and 1990s, when some of those conditions weakened, as did the Association of Scientific, Technical, and Managerial Staff (ASTMS)[98] and the Technical, Administrative, and Supervisory Section of the AUEW (TASS).[99]

Thus we are not convinced by any argument that NALGO was less of a trade union because it had managers, professionals, administrators, technicians, and clerks in membership. NALGO fought hard to hold onto managerial grades, and this was part of its development as a progressive and inclusive trade union. Furthermore, the government itself tried to remove managers from both collective bargaining and unions in the 1980s. It also prohibits union membership among the police and the armed forces. This was not always the case, but since 1919 the police have been members of the Police Federation,[100] which behaves as if it were a trade union, but is not one. This section of workers is non-union not because of their wishes, nor because others in the trade-union movement wish to exclude them, but because the state decrees it. This was famously extended to workers at GCHQ during the period of this history, and NALGO's strong defence of their trade-union rights owed something to the wider debate.

Finally, we turn to the line of argument that only those workers who are engaged by employers pursuing profits can have the relevant experience of exploitation to form organizations that qualify as proper trade unions—that workers employed by the state, by state agencies, and by non-profit private-sector organizations are not proper trade unionists. The main argument is that, when the principal owners of capital instruct their agent-managers to maximize their profits by whatever means, then the extraction of surplus value from the workforce requires *inter alia* the exploitation of that workforce. It is this act of exploitation, where the total remuneration package is less than the value created/added by the workers, that provides the basis for worker resistance, which is mobilized through working-class organizations

---

[97] P. Blyton and G. Ursell, 'Vertical Recruitment in White-Collar Trade Unions: Some Causes and Consequences', *British Journal of Industrial Relations*, 20/2 (1982), 189.

[98] R. Carter, *Capitalism, Class Conflict and the New Middle Class* (London: Routledge & Kegan Paul, 1985).

[99] C. Smith, *Technical Workers: Class, Labour and Trade Unionism* (London: Macmillan, 1987).

[100] R. Reiner, *The Blue-Coated Worker: A Sociological Study of Police Unionism* (Cambridge: Cambridge University Press, 1978).

such as trade unions. Profit-making for the employer is the mainspring of the entire process, and if this is absent then the workers are not exploited and they therefore cannot be organized to fight exploitation.

This line of argument leads to some curious conclusions. Employers in non-profit public or private sectors that behaved in the same ways as those in the profit sectors—paying low wages, hiring and firing arbitrarily, driving employees to work harder and cheaper—would not actually be exploiting the workers and would therefore not expect to be resisted. In order to bypass this apparent theoretical problem, leftist thinkers argued that under capitalism even state workers were exploited: first because state employment is funded out of taxation, which is part of the surplus created by workers and which therefore stands in the same relationship to profit; and, secondly, because state activity and agencies exist to provide additional means by which profit-makers could make profits. Teachers, for example, teach future workers in order that they can be exploited, so the teachers also are exploited. Local-government officers provide infrastructure to support profit-making, and thereby are themselves exploited as part of the state direction and collec-tivization of capital. There is a body of esoteric literature that attempts to the-orize a way through the contradictions of state employment.

In the end, state employment does carry with it the main trappings of exploitation—workers in the state sector do belong to trade unions that do engage in collective bargaining and do take industrial action to support it. Perhaps we can simply argue that, where the capitalist wage system dominates economic activity, then all employees must be subjected to the same exploit-ative employment relationship, and therefore no alternative relationship is actually possible. Thus debates about productive and unproductive labour and about ownership miss the point—the dominant employment relation-ship applies throughout all sectors of the economy, and is based on both exploitation and alienation of workers. All workers are exploited because they are forced to sell their labour power in a market, and it is this common experience that decides their class position. 'This is so despite differences in the level of income, authority, status and life-style of sellers of labour power.'[101] Trade unions are the original collective response to these experi-ences, and how they deal with their members' interests is determined through a specific historical set of circumstances, articulated and activated through political and structural forms of the unions themselves.

This summarizes our position: trade unions organize employees indepen-dently to pursue collective bargaining with their employer, using sanctions

[101] V. Allen, 'The Differentiation of the Working Class', in A. Hunt (ed.), *Class and Class Structure* (London: Lawrence & Wishart, 1977), 66.

against the employer to support their collective-bargaining objectives. Our definition includes all categories of employees, whatever their work, whatever their position in the employer's organization, and whatever the nature of their employer. Hence we can expect unions to take many a varied shape and form. In addition, the decisions taken that move a union towards both a bargaining organization and an action organization are the outcomes of industrial and political actions taken by the web of members, activists, and officials at all levels within the union, in response to whatever specific external and internal conditions apply at the time. This history seeks to demonstrate these points, through the case of NALGO.

2

NALGO: 1905–1978

T HIS chapter provides an overview of NALGO's history up to 1978, and briefly looks forward to the 1980s. It identifies the changing forms of trade unionism adopted, in line with our general model of trade unionism set out in Chapter 1. Our main argument is that all trade unions are necessarily rooted in collective bargaining as a response to exploitation and alienation at work—an underlying dynamic shared by all unions representing all types of worker.

Where unions differ is in their policies and their practices, which are themselves shaped by two sets of forces. First is the external pressures that bear down upon the union and its activists and members. In the case of NALGO these were mainly brought about by government actions. Second is struggle within the union, as members and activists try to come to terms with their ever-changing situation. There is a continual need to debate and to analyse the political, social, and economic environment surrounding the union, to understand external events, to respond to them, and even to shape them. So, while the essential organizing principle is simply that of collective bargaining, this is constantly overlaid by discussion and debate about what are the most appropriate forms of policy and practice at any given moment in order to secure maximum influence in the bargaining arena.

The first two sections of this chapter retrace the union's development, as covered by Spoor[1] and Newman[2] respectively, from its origins as an association with leaders who declared that it was not a trade union to its entry into the mainstream of the British labour movement. The third section summarizes NALGO as it was in 1978, describing its main structures and the types

[1] A. Spoor, *White Collar Union: Sixty Years of NALGO* (London: Heinemann, 1967).
[2] G. Newman, *Path to Maturity: NALGO 1965–1980* (London: NALGO, 1982). See also K. Bell, 'A History of NALGO in Scotland', Ph.D. thesis (Strathclyde, 1989).

of employees and industries covered, and identifying the main collective-bargaining arrangements and outcomes. The final section introduces the main issues with which the union dealt during the period of this volume, from 1979 to 1993. NALGO developed a distinctive approach to both policy and practice in this final period, rooted in a culture that was inclusive and partic-ipative and that enabled open debate at all levels of the union. Furthermore, the particular variety of trade unionism that came to flourish within the union was broad left and outward-looking, and NALGO took its policies and its practices into the wider trade-union and labour movement.

Sixty Years of Development, 1905–1965

The National Association of Local Government Officers (NALGO) was formed on 29 July 1905, by merger of the Municipal Officers' Association (MOA) and the Liverpool Municipal Officers Guild. The London-based MOA had been set up in 1894, with the main aim of establishing pension rights. The Liverpool Guild, formed in 1896 under the leadership of Herbert Blain, was more inclusive and was the model for local guilds in towns up and down the country, such as Hull, Derby, Oldham, Belfast, Poplar, Tunbridge Wells, and Macclesfield. There were other organizations of municipal employees alongside NALGO, such as the Institution of Municipal and County Engineers founded in 1873 and the Sanitary Inspectors Association of 1883.

None of these associations is mentioned in the Webbs' famous *History of Trade Unionism*, even in its 1920 version. The sole reference to NALGO comes thus: 'The employees of the Local Authorities—thirty years ago entirely without organisation—are still not so well combined as those of the National Government . . . the National Association of Local Government Officers and Clerks is a large and powerful body, composed mainly of the clerical and supervisory grades.'[3] They argue that trade unionism in the pub-lic services benefited greatly from a ministerial decision to recognize and deal with unions of government employees in 1906, followed by the 1912 inde-pendent arbitration tribunal for civil servants, and then by the 1917 Whitley reports.[4] Trade unions in local government grew and developed alongside those of other public-sector workers, especially those in education and the Civil Service, where Whitleyism was established early.

Government action is itself mainly driven by two sets of forces: first to meet the demands of sections of British industry and commerce to maintain con-

---

[3] S. Webb and B. Webb, *The History of Trade Unionism* (London: Longman, 1920), 508.
[4] Ibid. 647.

ditions for them to operate within a secure infrastructure to support profit-making; and, secondly, to meet the demands of citizens for health and security, for protection from crude and overt exploitation, and for a responsive and democratic system of government. At the start of the twentieth century Britain's imperial trade came under challenge from businesses in the USA, in other parts of Europe, and in the far east, while groups of reformers, including socialists, 'gas and water' Fabians, and active members of local communities also put pressure on the state. The very purpose of local government shifted, from the Victorian model of nuisance control towards the positive provision of health, education, welfare, culture, and well-being, which embraced a more progressive role for the local authority in economic and social conditions of the communities. Importantly, the impetus to achieve this modernization was rooted in wider social forces that included the local-government officers.

In 1900 the 2,000 local councils independently employed their staff. 'The tasks, pay, and working conditions of every officer, determined by his employer, varied greatly between one town and another.'[5] No women were employed and contact with the public was minimal. The vast majority of workers were low-paid clerks with secure jobs but subject to the tyranny of the town clerk. In turn, the handful of senior officers were gentlemen chiefs and professionals with good pay and high status locally. Nepotism and corruption were rife. In order to improve pay and conditions, as well as to increase control over their jobs, the clerks combined to try to reform both the employment situation and the local-government system together.

The new association's leadership explicitly opposed the notion that NALGO was a trade union—the first general secretary, Levi Hill, wrote in 1910 that 'anything savouring of trade unionism is nausea to the local government officer and his Association'.[6] But the organizational substance of trade unionism took shape over those early years. In 1906 the newly formed NEC announced six objectives, including the development of the organization through further mergers and the establishment of local associations (achieved in 1909), the pursuit of issues such as pensions, tenure, legal security, and generally to further the interests of local-government officers. A journal, *The Local Government Officer*, was established. By 1912 membership had reached 28,000 with affiliations from Scotland and Ireland, and the first full-time official was appointed.

The Tory leadership advanced the liberal argument, still prevalent today, that rational employers recognize that a well-paid and well-treated workforce would worker harder and be more loyal. But, as in other employment

---

[5] Spoor, *White Collar Union*, 3.   [6] Ibid. 47.

sectors, the weakness of this wishful dogma was exposed by the actions of actual employers: in 1908 the Borough of East Ham sacked twenty-two officers and cut the pay and increased the hours of the others. As members began leaching to the more militant National Union of Clerks, events like this forced the national leadership to rethink its position. However, the start of war had more impact than the particular acts of bad employers—most local-government officers under the age of 40 joined up, and by 1916 NALGO was on the verge of collapse.

The war changed everything. Members returning from the armed forces were part of a tidal wave of renewal, through social reform, socialist ideals, and active participation. The association became more open, admitting women into membership and holding an annual delegate conference, and the NEC became more representative and responsive. The 193 delegates attending NALGO's first annual conference in Blackpool in 1918 demanded a national salary scale, and called for a blacklist of councils that behaved unjustly to members. In 1919, with inflation threatening standards of living and members again joining more radical rival unions, the old-guard leadership finally gave way, and in June 1920, after a referendum of members, a special conference voted for NALGO to become a trade union.

The early 1920s saw membership rise to nearly 37,000. Of these about 16 per cent were women, of whom half were clerks and typists, about a third health visitors and nurses, and the rest library assistants, sanitary inspectors, and doctors. These groups forced the NEC to concede a special seat for women in 1925 (increased to two by 1935). Radicalism also appeared in the form of strike threats, in Pontypridd over payment of the war bonus, and in Oldham and Wolverhampton over the failure to implement agreed national scales. A national Whitley system was established in 1920, but by 1922 it was dead as employers broke away to seek advantage from recession. Cuts in public expenditure became a feature of the 1920s, as the *Daily Mail* launched a now familiar campaign against 'squandermania', and the flames of NALGO radicalism were damped down. Members had relatively secure jobs in a period of high unemployment, and the Superannuation Act 1922 provided a voluntary basis for local-government pensions. Conditions were unfavourable for collective bargaining, and the union turned towards strengthening services to members, establishing a convalescent home and a provident and building society. The 1921 conference rejected a move to affiliate to the TUC as too political.

Recession and unemployment dominated the 1930s, along with reactionary governments and an official trade-union movement committed to partnership through the famous Mond–Turner talks. However, as the decade unfolded, the international situation forced the UK government to expand public expenditure, and towards the end of the peace there was some restoration of pay levels. An emerging consensus in favour of national pay scales brought about moves to set up a Whitley system, although at the outbreak of war in 1939 each local authority was still setting its own rates of pay. NALGO campaigned on equal pay for women, a move brought about by activist pressure and by the attempts by some employers to undercut male wages through the substitution of female for male labour. Equal pay for equal work became official NALGO policy in 1936, but the union still opposed the employment of married women in local government.

During this period NALGO still had no industrial action tradition—Levi Hill, still General Secretary after twenty-six years, wrote: 'So far as administrative, professional, technical, and clerical staffs of local authorities are concerned, there is no record of the settlement of differences by what may be termed a "trial of strength" between employer and employee".'[7] However, the association campaigned, publicly and politically, to convince the wider community of the need for decent local-government service. Pay and conditions research activity was also put on a systematic footing, helped along by international comparisons through affiliation to the International Union of Local Authorities in 1932. Such campaigning and organizing bore fruit in 1939, when at last the union won one of its most fundamental first demands— pension rights for all local government officers.

Once again wartime pressures pushed the government to concede some long-standing demands of labour. NALGO used the provisions of the Conditions of Employment and National Arbitration Order 1940, through which collective bargaining over disputes could be mandatory, to secure a National Joint Council (NJC) in 1943. This mirrored the Scottish NJC, which had been reconvened in 1937. The coalition of forces in favour of Whitley—the unions, Labour Party, Civil Service, and War Cabinet—was stronger than the mainly Conservative opposition. But the main opposition arguments resurfaced in the 1980s: that when Labour councils were in a majority on the employers' side they would be overly sympathetic to NALGO, and that the national system would abolish the right of each local authority to be free 'to appoint, pay, treat, and dismiss their officers "at the pleasure of the council"'.[8]

As with 1919, so a post-war mood of radicalism took hold in 1945. Equal pay for women was formally agreed in the new NJC, and was first implemented in full by the London County Council (LCC) in 1952. The association's 1953 conference defeated the NEC's timid line on wage issues, after years of rank-and-file agitation from younger radical elements within the

---

[7] L. Hill, 'The Municipal Service', in H. Laski, W. Jennings, and W. Robson (eds.), *A Century of Municipal Service: The Last Hundred Years* (London: George Allen & Unwin, 1935), 130.

[8] Spoor, *White Collar Union*, 226–7.

union. The following year these branch-based activists initiated the union's first special conference called by branches, demanding serious action to secure better wage deals. But, despite both the size of NALGO and its increasing importance within a range of industries, it continued to receive scant attention from academic and trade-union commentators of the day.[9]

The period from 1950 to 1965 saw general expansion of the public services and of the newly nationalized gas and electricity industries, accompanied by a stop–go economic cycle. Although the Conservative government was keen to modernize, it was also reluctant to implement change, which left senior officials to establish a modern set of working practices in a somewhat patchy manner. So in electricity supply, for example, productivity pay was introduced in the 1950s along with private-sector comparability. The staff believed, quite rightly, that in a modern and expanding industry with scarce labour their main hope of better pay was through local deals with management. Indeed in 1965 they voted for an overtime ban, the first major industrial action by any NALGO group. This could have developed into a full strike, but the new Labour government defused the dispute by referring it to the National Board for Prices and Incomes (NBPI).

With nationalizations and the creation of the NHS, NALGO involvement in Whitley Councils increased to a total of thirty-five. This included eighteen in the NHS, where NALGO was represented on most of the new Whitley Councils and Committees but rarely had a majority, owing to the plethora of other staff side organizations. For example, the twenty-four staff side members of the Professional and Technical (PT) 'A' Whitley Council, representing sixteen different organizations, covered thirteen different staff groups all on different rates of pay! Most NALGO members were within the Administrative and Clerical (A&C) groups and their pay fell relatively during the 1950s, leading to calls for overtime bans. In other industries, NJCs were established for both gas and electricity supply by 1951, in the New Towns by 1955, and in water by 1965.

NALGO recruited and organized in all these industries, and formally recognized that it was no longer a local-government union by changing its name to the National and Local Government Officers' Association and by changing the journal's name from *Local Government Service* to *Public Service*. A trade-union identity was emerging, embracing administrative, professional, technical, and clerical staff in several parts of the public sector. Most employees in these industries faced similar problems of falling relative wages, as manual workers in more militant unions narrowed the pay gap.[10] At the same

9 N. Barou, *British Trade Unions* (London: Victor Gollancz, 1947).
10 H. Phelps Brown, *The Inequality of Pay* (Oxford: Oxford University Press, 1977); G. Routh, *Occupation and Pay in Great Britain 1906–1979* (London: Macmillan, 1980).

time, government intervened ever more openly in the pay, conditions of service, and management of labour of such staff, providing fertile territory for the growing number of left-wing and radical activists to advance their arguments within the union. Their influence was felt with the expansion of democracy within the union, as separate annual conferences (group meetings, to discuss pay and conditions issues) became the practice for all service/industry groups. There was a marked increase in NALGO's education activities, both for its own industrial-relations purposes and for the expansion of correspondence courses for members eager to become better qualified. Spoor summarized the twenty years after the war thus: 'NALGO's expansion from a single- to a multi-service union, the development of national collective bargaining, the near trebling of membership, and the fight to shelter members from the blast of inflation, absorbed most of the Association's energies.'[11]

By 1965 NALGO had members in twelve public services: local government, gas, electricity, water, the NHS, new towns, provincial buses, canals and waterways, ports and harbours, industrial estates, local valuation panels, and colleges of advanced technology. The union had won equal pay for women in the vast majority of areas it covered. It had put a strike clause into the rule book in 1961, it had started to threaten strikes, and members in the factor's department in Glasgow council went on unofficial strike for a day over gradings in 1964. A full-time officer for international work was appointed, also in 1964. Finally, in 1965, the union affiliated to the TUC after ballots held in 1955, 1958, and 1962 had all been lost by narrow margins. The 1964 ballot, with the NEC supporting affiliation, resulted in 138,120 in favour and 118,531 against—a turnout of 78 per cent!

Membership increased from 146,057 members in 1946 to 360,691 members in 1966, an increase of 147 per cent (see Fig. 2.1). Local-government officers turned to NALGO as employers and managers implemented changes in their working lives. More and more the union's orientation was towards collective bargaining, supported by research, education, and publicity. Full-time officials and lay activists were more broadly educated and knowledgeable, not only of their own worlds but also of the labour movement nationally and internationally. NALGO was set to play a fuller role within the wider trade-union and labour movement. Spoor comments on the union's rapid evolution during the ten years after 1955: 'Then, it was still held by the chains of its municipal and friendly-society origins, insular, proud, and reluctant to launch into the mainstream of trade union and national life. By 1965, it had cast off those chains and was in the centre of the current, moving strongly in the TUC convoy.'[12]

[11] Spoor, *White Collar Union*, 437.   [12] Ibid., p. v.

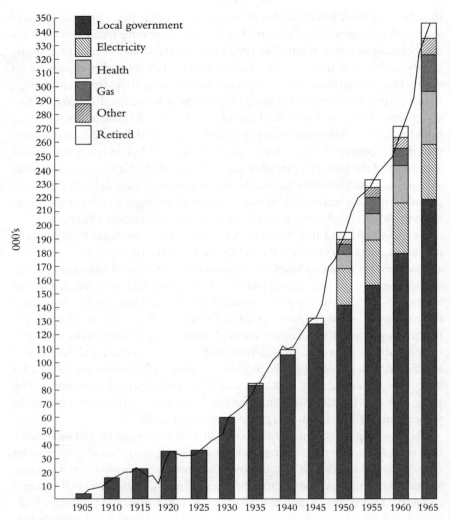

Fig. 2.1 NALGO membership 1905–65, by service
Source: A. Spoor, *White Collar Union: Sixty Years of NALGO* (London: Heinemann, 1967), 501.

Spoor, himself a union official, ends his book on a deserved note of triumph for NALGO the organization. However, he also reminds us of the central dilemmas for the union: how to represent white-collar staff who were not in a profession and who had no obvious product to market or profit to share; and how to react when the government took initiatives that damaged both the services and the members' conditions of service. The answer lay through col-

lective bargaining with employers and campaigning in the public and parliamentary arenas.

National Collective Bargaining and Industrial Action, 1965–1978

Newman,[13] himself a Deputy General Secretary, recounts the next fourteen
years of NALGO's long journey from local-government officers' guild to
multi-occupational, multi-industrial, TUC-affiliated trade union, involved
more than any other union in public-sector bargaining, action, and campaigning. As Geoffrey Drain, the General Secretary from 1973 to 1983, argues
in his preface to Newman's book, the main aspects of NALGO's development were in the use of industrial action, and in occupying a place in the
mainstream of the TUC and labour-movement politics.

During the Labour government of 1964–70 the union's leadership faced a
series of new challenges arising from government action. Government controls over pay affected workers in the public services disproportionately
harshly, and the reference of several pay claims to the NBPI resulted both in
higher levels of research to support claims and in the use of public awareness
campaigns to put the government under pressure. Prime Minister Harold
Wilson set up the Royal Commission on Trade Unions and Employers'
Associations, under Lord Donovan,[14] to investigate the causes of poor industrial relations and to recommend possible remedies. It recommended that
bargaining should take place at the level of the employer and/or the plant,
rather than nationally, and this caused some worries for NALGO negotiators.
Finally there were the shifting sands of public-sector finances and service priorities. The Labour government, while often progressive in comparison to its
Conservative predecessor, ran into trouble with the handling of macroeconomic issues, with a balance-of-payments crisis leading to devaluation in
1967, perceived low relative growth and productivity, and the niggling problem of inflation, outdated infrastructure, and a general failure to plan Britain's
industrial structure.

On top of this there was the revolution in both behaviour and expectations
of large sections of the population. Many aspects of this were channelled into
demands, from both service users and the government, for more responsive
local services at better value. More vigorous demands for representativeness
and for more dynamic policies came from within the union. With little scope

[13] Newman, *Path to Maturity*.
[14] Lord Donovan, *Royal Commission on Trade Unions and Employers' Associations*, Cmnd
3623 (London: HMSO, 1968).

for general pay rises under the government's incomes policies, the union searched for non-pay improvements such as better training, career opportunities, and jobs for married women, and for pay improvements through forms of productivity bargaining. NALGO expanded its training programmes and its campaigning work, and the legal department took on more personal cases, especially on pensions, accidents at work, and conditions of service.

These developments brought NALGO closer to the public-sector manual-worker unions whose members were also suffering disproportionately from the effects of incomes policies. Such closer workings were strengthened by affiliation to the TUC and the Scottish Trades Union Congress (STUC) in 1965,[15] and to the Wales Trades Union Conference when it was founded in 1974. The size of NALGO's membership guaranteed its General Secretary, Walter Anderson, a place on the TUC General Council from the outset. When NALGO joined it nearly doubled the entire membership of the public employees' group, which expanded far faster than any other TUC group—by the end of this period in 1978 it covered about two million employees, an increase of 54 per cent compared with a total TUC increase of 18 per cent. As George Newman noted, 'the entry into the comity of the TUC . . . was to bring influences to bear which would gradually have profound effect on the Union'.[16] These included a sharpening of internal political debates, which in turn fed into a further opening-up of the union's democratic structures. In addition, branches were free to affiliate to their local trades councils, although by 1978 only about a quarter had done so (311 out of 1,223 branches).

Most industrial-relations academics still put NALGO on the sidelines of trade unionism in the early 1970s. A standard textbook, almost the official textbook of British trade unions, rewritten by Henry Pelling,[17] mentions the union only as a coming force, and Allen Hutt's left-wing account of union history fails to mention it at all.[18] Even Allan Flanders can make only two points about NALGO, as mentioned earlier.[19] However, one book of the time, *White Collar Unionism in Britain*, has on its cover a picture of marchers at a large demonstration carrying banners with the words 'NALGO says NO'.[20] NALGO's first official strike, of eighteen members in the Cleansing Department of Leeds Corporation, was in February 1970.

---

[15] D. Volker, 'NALGO's Affiliation to the TUC', *British Journal of Industrial Relations*, 4/1 (1966), 59–66.

[16] Newman, *Path to Maturity*, 4.

[17] H. Pelling, *A History of British Trade Unionism* (Harmondsworth: Penguin, 1976), 273.

[18] A. Hutt, *British Trade Unionism: A Short History* (London: Lawrence & Wishart, 1975).

[19] A. Flanders, *Trade Unions* (London: Hutchinson University Library, 1968).

[20] R. Lumley, *White Collar Unionism in Britain* (London: Methuen & Co., 1973).

Edward Heath's Conservative government took office in 1970, committed to free-market ideals and promising the country a new deal with laws to restrict trade-union activity and a reduction in the scope and cost of public services. The infamous Industrial Relations Act 1971 resulted in a wave of strikes, including two in the public sector—post-office workers in 1971 and miners in 1972. In both cases NALGO voted to support fellow workers and to donate funds, a solidarity position that was further extended to the Shrewsbury building worker pickets jailed for conspiracy. When NUPE prepared to strike in local government in 1970, NALGO's leadership urged members to support their manual colleagues by not undermining their strike, under the classic trade union slogan: 'Their fight is our fight'.[21]

Thus the union resisted legal restraint, pay restraint, and public-expenditure cuts, all based on 'the Government's belief that strikes, pay increases and inflated public expenditure were the root causes of Britain's economic troubles'.[22] General Secretary Walter Anderson believed that the Industrial Relations Act 'would embitter, not alleviate, industrial difficulties; would impair, not strengthen, the authority of the trade unions and their representatives; and would sap, not reinforce, the procedures for avoiding and settling disputes'.[23] NALGO fought against the Act, supporting TUC policy by refusing to register under it.

These few turbulent years saw a world energy crisis, widespread industrial action during pay freezes, and, in 1974, a state of emergency declared during a miners' strike followed by the complete collapse of the government. But, before the Conservative government's brief and stormy hold on office came to an end, it enacted several major reforms. The water industry was reorganized into ten multi-purpose Regional Water Authorities under a National Water Council with a new NJC for water services staff. Local government was restructured and rationalized under exhortations to introduce corporate management structures. But the main changes were in the NHS, with the creation of fourteen Regional Health Authorities (RHAs) and seventy Area Health Authorities (AHAs), which was so badly botched that, for Newman, 'The story . . . is one of frustration, indecision, delay and absolute dismay for those in the service'.[24]

Driven by this combination of external shocks and internal pressure, the union altered its structures and practices. Branch structures were rationalized and merged as the employers themselves were reorganized, some changes were made to the method of election and operation of the NEC and annual conference, and policy positions hardened through a stronger commitment to fight to protect jobs and to tell the members what was going on. A culture

[21] Newman, *Path to Maturity*, 182.   [22] Ibid. 180.   [23] Ibid. 181.
[24] Ibid. 377.

of openness was promoted from the centre, with strong national support for the local publicity machinery.

A range of factors was making white-collar workers increasingly vulnerable to management reforms, to labour-market contingencies, and to government whim: falling relative pay caused by incomes policies; changes in working practices and technology caused by the modernization of industry and services; and government's lack of willingness to maintain and protect the post-war balance of power in terms of the relative gains of labour at the expense of capital. As a consequence, one possible and popular solution was to join a union, become active locally, and push for reform of union decision-making to take it away from the influence of national government and media and to place at least some of it in local hands, a solution famously exploited by ASTMS.[25]

In 1973, both the NALGO and the TUC old guard were replaced by new General Secretaries Geoffrey Drain and Len Murray respectively, and in 1974 a more friendly Labour government came into office. Initially the ill-fated Wilson–Callaghan administration enacted favourable trade-union and social legislation (including the Health and Safety at Work etc. Act 1974, the Trade Union and Labour Relations Act 1974, the Employment Protection Act 1975, and the Sex Discrimination Act 1975) in return for a notional tripartite agreement on wages and public expenditure.[26] This resulted in more and more pressure from public-service union members for pay increases. By April 1974 there were already over 35,000 local-government and 6,000 electricity staff on overtime bans or other action. The five Labour years were as eventful as the first half of the decade. Global capitalism ran into a dangerous morass of inflation without growth, unemployment without benefit reform, and low productivity without high profits. Labour faced the double squeeze of chronic underinvestment and the anarchy of the global markets. In such a position the choices were stark. For the left the way forward was to strengthen state ownership and to harness mass support for social reform, greater equality, and sharper economic planning, a set of policies that became known as the Alternative Economic Strategy (AES). But the government decided to take a loan from the International Monetary Fund (IMF), with now familiar monetarist conditions attached that shoved costs and risks down the social scale to the economically poorest and weakest.

This period saw large-scale protests against cuts in public spending. There were one-day strikes, national demonstrations, publicity campaigns, weeks of

[25] C. Jenkins and B. Sherman, *White Collar Unionism: The Rebellious Salariat* (London: Routledge & Kegan Paul, 1979).

[26] S. Kessler and F. Bayliss, *Contemporary British Industrial Relations* (London: Macmillan, 1998), ch. 2.

action, and mass rallies. These were frequently led by the emerging broad left coalition of communists, the Labour Party left, and other left groups. An increasing number of women, black, disabled, and gay and lesbian workers were brought into political and trade-union struggle through their bitter experiences of uneven and arbitrary rule in the employment relationship. They brought with them new dimensions of struggle, and they forced through progressive policies. In NALGO these included positive action for women in 1973, and action against discrimination on grounds of sexual orientation in 1976. Debates among women about the relevance of established union practices resulted in NALGO quitting the TUC women's conference, seen in 1976 as a sideshow. This upsurge in activists' interests brought with it a new impetus to set up the steward system—in 1978 the union had 30,000 workplace representatives.

In 1977–8 nearly 250 cases of industrial action went to the union's Emergency Committee. George Newman expresses anxiety: 'Yet again, Conference tried to sort out NALGO strike policy. It was evident that there was a strongly militant element in NALGO, including extreme political groups, who wanted to foster aggressive militant action frequently and for various causes.'[27] However, he also noted that industrial action had become commonplace: 'The experience of local or small-scale industrial action had been largely successful and the techniques involved were becoming increasingly familiar.'[28] The social workers' strike, NALGO's first national strike involving a major group of members, was characterized as 'the most expensive and extravagant industrial action in NALGO's history' (see Box 1).[29] Apart from that, the union's role in the industrial action in the 'winter of discontent' of 1978–9 was limited to supporting the TUC's general position against the 5 per cent pay policy.

The Labour government's shift to the monetarist right, with its damning of many Labour supporters and its turn away from social democracy, carried a high price. Deep divisions developed inside the labour movement as compromise gave way to confrontation with the winter of discontent, an outburst of outrage by public-sector workers, which created the conditions not just for the election of the Conservatives under Margaret Thatcher but also for the aggressive implementation of their neo-liberal agenda. As Ralph Miliband so rightly foretold, 'the failure of social democracy implicates not only those responsible for it, but all the forces of the Left. Because of it, the path is made smoother for would-be popular saviours whose extreme conservatism is carefully concealed beneath a demagogic rhetoric of national renewal and social redemption.'[30]

[27] Newman, *Path to Maturity*, 428.   [28] Ibid. 429.   [29] Ibid. 448.
[30] R. Miliband, *The State in Capitalist Society* (London: Quartet Books, 1973), 245.

NALGO's World *c.* 1978

Union action and structure

In 1978 NALGO was the fourth largest TUC affiliate, after the TGWU, the Amalgamated Union of Engineering Workers (AUEW), and the National Union of General and Municipal Workers (NUGMW). It employed more women organizers than any other union, although this was only one organizer in ten at a time when four members in ten were women. With a print run of 740,000 copies, *Public Service* had by far the largest circulation of any union journal. This supported an emerging steward system, which stimulated a more active membership.[31] NALGO had become an organizationally sound and democratic large union, organizing in growing sectors of the economy. For some commentators the union had become more 'unionate' and 'occupational sectoral'[32]—the changing composition of membership, along with changes in both government policies and labour-management practices, had made it a more 'normal' union in terms of taking action, supporting the TUC, and addressing fundamental employment protection objectives.

Characterizing it as a new public-sector giant, Robert Taylor argues that 'NALGO has come a long way since the early 1960s'. He quotes from an article in *Public Service* in May 1975, remembering life in the union as 'comfortable, uncomplaining and isolated from the trials and tribulations of the world outside. Once in a job you stayed in. NALGO itself had an air of destiny: if the Almighty was a card holder in a union then NALGO would hold his ticket. No strikes, no trouble and a quiet fusty-dusty daily round that meant wearing a dark suit from Monday until Friday.' This apparently clubby union was led by General Secretary 'Geoffrey Drain, the rotund, affable, cigar-smoking ex-Bevanite'.[33] By 1975, industrial action was part of NALGO's trade unionism, including sustained action over the London weighting issue. Taylor overstates NALGO's actual use of the strike weapon—'NALGO now appears to have few scruples about taking militant action, when it thinks fit. It has gradually become aware of the power it can wield to paralyse society'[34]—but he shows the degree of influence that the union had within a generally strong and left-leaning labour movement at the end of the decade. NALGO had become an open and active union that was well financed, well resourced, and playing a role proportionate with its size at last. It was a powerful instrument of persuasion on employers, government, and the public.

[31] N. Nicholson and G. Ursell, 'The NALGO Activists', *New Society*, 15 Dec. 1977, 581–2.
[32] K. Coates and T. Topham, *Trade Unions in Britain* (London: Fontana Press, 1988), 6, 36.
[33] R. Taylor, *The Fifth Estate* (London: Routledge & Kegan Paul, 1978), 240.
[34] Ibid. 245.

In October 1978 NALGO had 729,405 members, with 63 per cent in local government, with 11 per cent in health, 6 per cent in gas, 5 per cent in electricity, and 3 per cent in water. The rest were in transport, New Towns, port authorities, universities, and police authorities (see Table 2.1). This sectoral spread was uneven across NALGO's twelve districts, reflecting both local history and concentration of types of activity. There were over 100,000 in the two largest districts, North West and North Wales, and Metropolitan, and fewer than 35,000 in the smallest, South Wales. This meant that, for example, the three largest bits of the union were local government in the North West and North Wales (74,000), Metropolitan (70,000), and Scottish (58,000) districts, compared with the smallest groups such as twenty in the port authorities in the North West, 224 in New Towns in South Wales, and sixty-three in transport in Southern.

This history takes account of this preponderance of membership while not forgetting the importance of the smaller groups both for themselves and for their sometimes disproportionate impact on union affairs. As Neill tell us, 'it is widely known that Nalgo . . . organises "everyone from the town clerk to the tea boy" in British local government offices and that the union structure is without parallel in public administration or in private industry'.[35] Table 2.2 provides some idea of the ways in which NALGO's local-government membership was distributed between departments. Throughout the period 1979–92 the largest group of full-time and part-time staff was within social services. Others were spread in specialist areas such as housing, libraries, and environmental health, while the remainder were concentrated into the central bureaucracy of planning, finance, and corporate affairs.

NALGO's decision-making structure followed a textbook form of democratic accountability. Individual members belonged to one of over 1,200 branches, predominantly employer-based, which varied in size from the thirteen strong Rhondda Transport Branch to the Strathclyde Region Branch with nearly 20,000 members. Each branch was located within one of the twelve geographical districts and one of the eight service/industry groups (local government, health, water, electricity, gas, transport, New Towns, and universities). Branch members elected the NEC members for their district by secret ballot.[36] Branches could influence general policy by pushing motions through the system directly to annual conference and group meetings, and indirectly through the District Council to the NEC and through the District Service Conditions Committees to the National Committees (see Fig. 2.2).

---

[35] C. Neill, 'Nalgo and the Development of Occupational Associations in Local Government', *Industrial Relations Journal*, 10/2 (1970), 31.

[36] IRS, 'Union Rules: Election Procedures for Officials and Governing Bodies', *Industrial Relations Review and Report*, 282 (1982), 2–11.

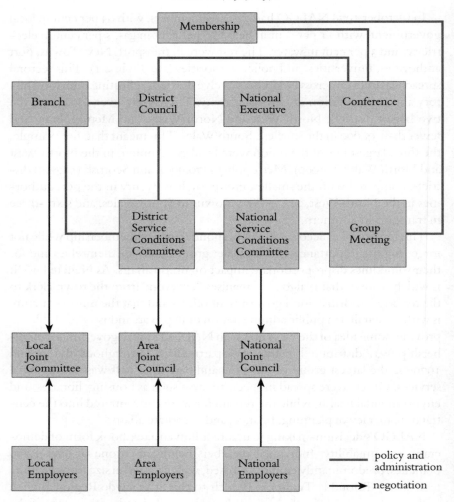

Fig. 2.2 NALGO organization

Collective bargaining and agreements

We argued in Chapter 1 that the main function of a union is to represent members individually and collectively in all forms of bargaining at all levels, and NALGO was heavily involved in carrying out this function. Pluralist political thinkers see collective bargaining as a system of conflict avoidance, and as part of the fabric of democratic capitalist society. At its best it makes a positive contribution to progress through an integrative approach to problem solving, where apparently everyone can be a winner. Productivity bargaining is an example of this. Within this ideological framework, trade-union involvement in collective bargaining is seen as a sign of both strength and political maturity, associated with moderation and modernization. Industrial action is seen as arising from an unfortunate but preventable breakdown of the system. Causes of breakdown included defective conflict resolution mechanisms; misjudgements by individual leaders; poor communications; and left-wing agitators. Such an analysis resulted in endless searches for 'solutions' to the strike 'problem', particularly through new conflict-avoidance mechanisms and institutions, such as industrial tribunals, ACAS, and health and safety committees, that favoured all parties equally.

Allan Flanders captures the tension in this in his contribution to the first textbook on British industrial relations in the post-1945 period:

Collective bargaining means different things to different people. Many look on it as the best way of keeping peace in industry. More than a few trade unionists would take the opposite view; for them it is the expression of class struggle with the overthrow of capitalism as its ultimate goal. Efficient employers may appreciate it because it prevents their less efficient competitors from undercutting them by paying lower wages.

He supports the American John Dunlop's view of industrial relations as a 'system' with three essential features: it fixes the price of labour services, it provides a system of industrial jurisprudence for the establishment and administration of other conditions of service, and it provides a voice for employees in decisions affecting their interests.[37]

Writing a decade later, Ben Roberts considers this view inadequate for a modern world needing greater control over wage settlements, when both labour shortages and the reluctance of British shareholders to invest provided workplace bargainers with levers to push up wages.[38] The decision to introduce incomes policies, whatever else it did, split the labour movement and helped to create the conditions for the fall of Labour in the spring of 1979.

Hugh Clegg[39] concisely argues that modern collective bargaining was the result of the partial coming together of two distinct trends: first a tradition of workplace bargaining through stewards and rooted in the establishment and defence of custom and practice, and, secondly, the widespread coverage of national agreements negotiated and supported through union officials outside the workplace. He makes a special point about the public sector:

---

[37] A. Flanders, 'Collective Bargaining', in A. Flanders and H. Clegg, *The System of Industrial Relations in Great Britain* (Oxford: Blackwell, 1954), 316.

[38] B. Roberts, *Industrial Relations: Contemporary Problems and Perspectives* (London: Methuen & Co., 1968), 23–8.

[39] H. Clegg, *The System of Industrial Relations in Great Britain* (Oxford: Blackwell, 1972); H. Clegg, *The Changing System of Industrial Relations in Great Britain* (Oxford: Blackwell, 1979).

Because of its highly centralized methods of management, its collective bargaining was also centralized. Nevertheless some public industries and services inherited trade union workplace representation with considerable control over work organization; and, with growing economic stringency, all of them experienced the same need for greater managerial control as had manufacturing industry, and made use of many of the same techniques in order to achieve it. In local government, education and the health service, the use of these techniques led to the conscious introduction by management and unions of shop steward organization where it did not exist before.[40]

Those insights are useful, but they are limited by the pluralist preoccupation with collective bargaining as an integrative solution to temporary disagreements between the potentially equal two sides of industry, now referred to as the social partners. Rather it brings about temporary outbreaks of peace between the parties to a fundamentally unequal employment relationship. But more than that, it provides a framework within which trade unionists can rebel against exploitation, advance and retreat, and take a break from the struggle without giving up. In the central chapters of this book we set out the range and the dynamics of NALGO's bargaining activities in this light.

Willie Brown's survey of British industrial relations in the late 1970s[41] shows that in the manufacturing sector there was a sharp move away from multi-employer bargaining to single-employer bargaining. Along with the increasing size of firms this created a greater division of managerial labour, resulting in an increasing number of personnel and industrial-relations specialists. There were more shop stewards, more full-time stewards, more closed shops (normally supported by management), and better trade-union support for both officials and stewards. NALGO was part of a large and successful trade-union movement that was influential in Downing Street, in company head offices, and in thousands of workplaces. Unions and their stewards were widely supported within a formalized system of collective bargaining underpinned by pluralist ideologies, legal support, and economic stability. TUC membership reached twelve million, the high point of post-war membership.

In the public services, especially the NHS, education, the Civil Service, and local government, the pattern of industrial relations was clear. There was a national system, usually of the Whitley type, for bargaining over most pay and conditions of service issues between multi-employer and multi-union sides.[42] At local level, union branch officials or stewards were mainly involved

---

[40] Clegg, *The Changing System of Industrial Relations*, 445.

[41] W. Brown, *The Changing Contours of British Industrial Relations* (Oxford: Blackwell, 1981).

[42] R. Mailly, S. Dimmock, and A. Sethi (eds.), *Industrial Relations in the Public Services* (London: Routledge, 1989).

with the implementation of national agreements and with grievance and disciplinary hearings. There was some limited scope for local bargaining, but generally local-level industrial relations were rather muted. National bargaining resulted in elaborately codified pay and conditions of service. For example, the largest single group, APT&C staff in local government, was covered by the 134-page 'Purple Book'. There was little scope for company and workplace bargaining, other than over issues not covered in the national agreement. This section outlines the main bargaining arrangements as they existed in 1979.

In 1979 the local-government service employed about 2.8 million people. The main employers belonged to the Association of County Councils (ACC), the Association of Metropolitan Authorities (AMA), the Association of District Councils (ADC), and the Convention of Scottish Local Authorities (COSLA). Except for COSLA, these are now merged into the Local Government Association. There was an industrial-relations advisory service for them, Local Authorities' Conditions of Service Advisory Board (LACSAB) (now the Employers' Organization for Local Government), which was also the employers' side secretariat for national negotiations. Union density was high (65 per cent), with sixty recognized trade unions and professional associations.

There were twenty-nine national bargaining units, with NALGO representation on seven (see Table 2.3). The main ones were the NJC for APT&C, covering over 500,000 staff, with five unions dominated by NALGO; and the NJC for APT&C in Scotland, covering about 65,000 staff. At regional level there were twenty-seven separately constituted Provincial Councils in England and Wales. Their main activities were around implementation of national agreements, and negotiating on local working practices, training, grades, and special rates. At local level there were Joint Consultative Committees (JCCs), which dealt with productivity and bonus schemes, job evaluation, demarcation, special leave, redundancy procedures, and health and safety. In London the GLC and the Inner London Education Authority (ILEA) operated an autonomous Whitley Council with pay and conditions negotiated outside the APT&C NJC.[43]

In the NHS most national negotiations were through eight Whitley Councils, each representing a functional category of staff.[44] Most of NALGO's 90,000 NHS members were among the 117,000 employees covered by negotiations in the A&C Whitley Council, where NALGO was the largest of eight unions. The union was also represented on the nurses' and midwives'

---

[43] ACAS, *Industrial Relations Handbook* (London: HMSO, 1980), 284–6.
[44] Ibid. 251.

council covering about 404,000 staff, although in this case NALGO membership was small compared with the large nursing unions. The other main interest for NALGO was in the PT'A' (where there is patient contact) and 'B' (minimal patient contact) Whitley Councils covering 65,000 staff. The PT'A' staff side was dominated by the single profession unions such as the Chartered Society of Physiotherapy (CSP), and PT'B' by ASTMS (see Table 2.4).

In the largest of the then public utilities, gas, electricity and water, NALGO's total membership was about 110,000. In 1979 the British Gas Corporation employed about 103,000 people. It was divided into twelve regions. NALGO's 46,000 members were among the 58,000 APT&C staff covered by the NJC for gas staffs and senior officers, and union density amongst this group was over 80 per cent. The white-collar sections of the GMWU (MATSA) and the TGWU (ACTS), ASTMS, and TASS were also recognized. The NJC established national grading and salary structures with Regional Joint Councils (RJCs) determining the grading of any given post. The Higher Management NJC covered 2,500 staff with NALGO as the sole union.[45]

The electricity industry employed 178,000 people. In England and Wales the main employers were the Electricity Council (EC) and the Central Electricity Generating Board (CEGB), while in Scotland there were two Scottish boards—the North of Scotland Hydro Electric Board and the South of Scotland Electricity Board. The NJC for Professional, Administrative, Clerical, and Sales staff covered 50,000 workers of which 38,000 were in NALGO, with others represented by the Association of Professional, Executive, and Computer Staffs (APEX), MATSA, and ACTS. The 1,700 staff in Managerial and Higher Executive Grades (NJMC) were mainly in EPEA, but some in NALGO and the Electrical and Engineering Staff Association (EESA), a white-collar section of the Electrical, Electronic, Telecommunication, and Plumbing Union (EETPU). National bargaining dealt with pay and conditions, while there were local and district bodies to oversee implementation, as well as to deal with issues over shift working and grievances.[46]

The water supply industry employed 74,000, with nine regional water authorities in England, a Welsh National Water Development Authority, and thirty other statutory water companies. The National Water Council was in charge of industrial relations. About 26,000 of the 37,000 white-collar workers were in NALGO, and were represented on the NJC for Water Service Staffs where NUPE, the General and Municipal Workers' Union (GMWU), and other smaller associations were also recognized. There was a JNC for

---

[45] ACAS, *Industrial Relations Handbook*, 192–3.
[46] Ibid. 194–7.

Water Service Senior Staffs, covering about 500, mainly represented by NALGO. Most activity was at national level with limited issues dealt with through RJCs. In Scotland industrial relations took place through local-government machinery.[47]

Other smaller groups were also represented by NALGO. These included junior administrative, clerical, and secretarial staffs, employed in a consortium of forty-one universities, with staff in other universities on either locally negotiated pay scales or on local-government scales. There was a Joint Committee for Computer Operating Staffs, with NALGO and ASTMS on the staff side.[48] The public transport employers included the London Transport Executive, the seven Passenger Transport Executives (PTEs) running bus services in the larger conurbations, fifty other local authorities running bus services, the National Bus Company, and the Scottish Bus Group Limited. NALGO's main interest was in the JNC for Non-Manual Staff, which covered four of the PTEs. Members in municipal bus services were covered by local-government negotiations.[49] NALGO represented the A&C grades in port and inland water transport. In municipal ports such as Bristol, local-government APT&C rates applied, and NALGO also represented salaried staff employed by the British Waterways Board.[50] Local authority rates applied to staff in municipal airports, of which Manchester was the largest.[51]

What NALGO did Next

NALGO went into the year 1979 financially and organizationally fit, part of a strong TUC. Its main policies were both clear and in line with the dominant centre left within the TUC: opposition to public-expenditure cuts, opposition to cash limits, opposition to moves to localize bargaining, and opposition to any watering-down of the commitment to public services in general. It supported the tenets of the AES, and it backed other workers in struggle throughout the world, especially in southern Africa. It was committed to improving the education of its members, to equality, to recruitment, and to union democracy rooted in both communication and representation. Writing about the period 1965–80 in George Newman's second volume of NALGO's history, Geoffrey Drain emphasizes the union's collective-bargaining role:

Always skilled in the art and science of joint negotiation and arbitration we strengthened our will and ability to stand up for the interest of our members by accepting fully the place of industrial action and by learning how to use it effectively in protecting

---

[47] Ibid. 197–8.   [48] Ibid. 243–4.   [49] Ibid. 204–6.   [50] Ibid. 214–15.
[51] Ibid. 218.

those interests. Through many reorganisations and structural changes in our services we fully met our obligation of protecting the individual member in situations of high risk. As the public sector came under growing pressure we met every challenge head on and, working with like-minded unions, shaped policies and created instruments (such as the TUC Public Services Committee) which armed us for the conflict we had to face.[52]

Significant changes were also taking place within the apparently stable Whitley system. The average size of employment unit was increasing; new technologies were altering traditional job classifications; personnel officers were playing a stronger role, creating more local activity around issues such as recruitment and discrimination; legal changes, especially in the areas of health and safety, allowed shop stewards to expand their role; changing expectations of service users generated new patterns of work; new financial regimes from central government meant a more severe application of cost-cutting measures; and private-sector notions of efficient and effective management were creeping into the political debates. For NALGO members there was little here for immediate concern, although the failure of national bargaining during these years had meant greater pressure on the leadership to use collective action to fight cuts in both pay and services. The general expectation was that the national system would continue in the 1980s in much the same way as it had in the 1970s.

Over the remaining fourteen years of NALGO's existence the members saw major changes in their industries: in structure, in management, and, in some cases, in ownership. An important minority was transferred from publicly owned corporations to private enterprises, most clearly in the gas, water, electricity supply, and bus industries, and also in parts of the health and local-government services. Whether privatized or not, the new situation created new pressures and problems for members and the union: senior managers were under pressure to quit NALGO altogether; there were redundancies amongst some grades of staff, although these were mainly dealt with through voluntary severance or early retirements; and for those who stayed on there were changes in both conditions of service and in the determination of those conditions. In some industries national collective bargaining was replaced by company-wide bargaining; and in all cases the scope of bargaining was squeezed. For all members the employment situation changed dramatically, affecting their attitudes both to employment itself and to the role of their union. This section outlines the outcomes of pay bargaining for a selection of NALGO groups.

For APT&C staff in local government, NALGO's largest bargaining unit,

---

[52] Geoffrey Drain's preface in Newman, *Path to Maturity*, p. vii.

pay outcomes were driven by government policy on cash limits, the union's strategy on industrial action, and the actual negotiations with employers. The details are discussed later in the book, but a brief glance at the figures provides us with some general notion of how the union and the system coped, with Table 2.5 providing an overview of pay agreements in local government.

Both male and female full-time APT&C grades experienced almost continuous relative decline in their pay after 1976, compared with the private sector, with temporary uplifts after the 1980 and 1989 strikes (see Fig. 2.3 and Table 2.6). In the period 1979–92, average earnings of full-time male APT&C staff increased by less than the national average increase for nine out of the fifteen years covered. Settlements were above inflation, but the overall picture is one of relative decline. Earnings of females also declined, but to a slightly lesser degree for full-timers, and to a distinctly lesser degree for part-timers.

Further details from the New Earnings Survey reinforce the picture of decline for full-time staff in England and Wales (see Tables 2.7 and 2.8). But these also tell us that earnings for most of the group were determined through the basic rate with little impact of either shift payments or payment-by-results schemes. The main addition to basic pay came from overtime, typically including about one in seven men and one in ten women. But the amount of overtime remained very limited, at less than one hour per week for most groups.

NHS staff fared similarly to those in local government—there were more staff generally covered by payment-by-results schemes, but there was limited use of overtime and shift payments. This again resulted in the importance of basic rates of pay and therefore their part in NHS disputes in 1982 and later in the ambulance dispute in 1989. Tables 2.9 and 2.10 indicate the relative decline of this group's pay compared with others, and the figures also show that the distribution of earnings worsened with low pay, especially amongst women staff, being skewed to the lower end.

The pay and conditions for white-collar staff in the utilities were determined by Whitley national bargaining with some local plant and company negotiation until the late 1980s, when privatization led to single-employer bargaining and in some cases single-table bargaining. Tables 2.11 through to 2.15 show that the make-up of pay was substantially different from local government and the NHS. Overtime working was much more widespread among men in the gas industry, although all other groups, especially women, started to be covered by more overtime in the early 1990s. Also in gas, PBR schemes covered about a quarter of staff, while after 1980 there was little evidence of such practices in either electricity supply or water. Shift work for all groups was also limited, covering between 5 and 10 per cent. In terms of pay, therefore, there was more scope for local bargaining over overtime and

Males, full-time

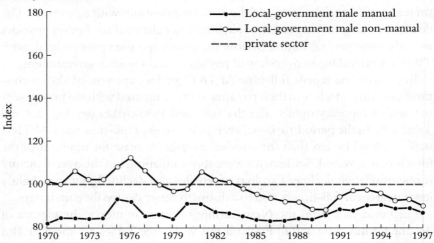

Females, full-time

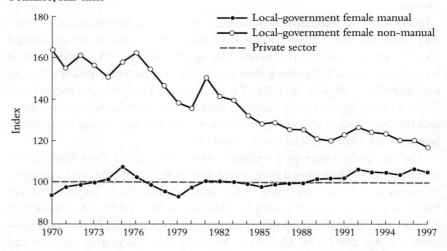

Fig. 2.3 Earnings of full-time local-government employees, measured against private-sector comparators, 1970–1997

Source: LACSAB, New Earnings Survey.

bonuses, and this is reflected in attitudes and behaviour of NALGO members in those industries.

Most members remained employed in the public sector, but the structure and practice of management shifted. In health and parts of higher and further education the employment unit changed to coincide with new business units—further education (FE) colleges became incorporated and hospitals became trusts. Local–government management was restructured, with more authority invested in senior management teams. There were redundancies, changes in skill mix, and new management techniques that introduced flexible conditions of service, with some local pay setting within national guidelines, and with changes in the labour process. This involved tighter management controls over staff performance, under the constraints of national performance indicators, financial controls, and coercive comparisons between local authorities. At the same time as conditions were squeezed for most employees, so union influence and power were restricted and reduced.

These pressures could have split the union apart, but its relatively complex system of government held together remarkably well. We discussed the workings of this system with the last General Secretary, with four senior officials from the gas, water, and electricity groups, and leading negotiators from the local–government, health, and universities groups. All agreed that a key part of NALGO's democracy was equality between full-time officers and lay representatives, rooted in the indirect election of negotiators. There was a strong working relationship between officials and activist leaders, with a high level of agreement on bargaining policies, strategies, and tactics.

Such cohesion also applied across the service-group boundaries. Although many still saw NALGO as predominantly a local-government union, there were no moves by the 'minority' groups to break away. The prevailing consensus was that, as Mike Blick said, 'all services got an equal crack of the whip'. Rita Donaghy suggested that the universities group was 'influential out of all proportion to our size'. In the utilities, Dave Stirzaker said that gas members 'never felt that their views were treated as second class views . . . There was never a difficulty.' Alex Thomson believed that the water group received its share from the national union—'I don't think they skimped on resources'— and Mike Jeram said 'we were left alone to do the electricity thing'.

In the 1980s the democratic system was supplemented by *ad hoc* national delegate meetings for occupational groups with particular service conditions issues under national negotiation, mainly in local government. These included meat inspectors, residential social workers, and registrars of births, marriages, and deaths. Mike Blick explained their role: '[Many] national campaigns . . . were all triggered off from the bottom up . . . There would be a request for a delegate meeting or it might be a series of them, and that would then help to brief us.' He argued that this was especially useful in local government because: 'It was a very very complex group. There was no way that a national committee can have any kind of expertise across the board. . . . It was a useful way of you telling us what the issues are, what problems there are. And via that route then it was felt claims ought to be made and sometimes these claims would work.' Alan Jinkinson said: 'As far as the leadership was concerned they were accepted as a good device because it couldn't make policy as it was always made clear, if you like, it was a sounding board.' Jim White thought that they 'were useful as a means of trying to identify concerns and offer suggestions'.

Another innovative development in this period was the establishment of 'self-organized' groups of women, disabled, gay and lesbian, and black members, which cut across service group boundaries and fed into the agendas of both annual conference and national committees. Initially established on an informal basis by activists themselves, they were recognized by the union and finally put on a formal basis with national and district structures in the late 1980s—and now form section D4 of the UNISON rule book. This was achieved in spite of some problems, as outlined by Rita Donaghy in an interview: 'To what extent do you allow structures that don't become unions within unions? To what extent do you allow autonomy and to what extent can you enforce policy on those autonomous groups? To what extent can those autonomous groups change policy and have bypass representation by means of automatic seats?'

Within these evolving democratic structures, political debate sharpened and intensified, driven by events outside the union but also stimulated by an increasingly influential left wing. The left's rise in the 1970s was helped along by the emergence of the NALGO Action Group (NAG). The main force behind NAG was the Socialist Workers' Party (SWP), which, along with other Trotskyist groups such as the Militant Tendency, remained small but at times influential. These ultra-leftists shared the view that trade-union leaders tend to betray the more revolutionary rank-and-file members by selling out to the representatives of capitalism. Their main impact in NALGO was through local actions in some branches and on a few national issues. General Secretary Alan Jinkinson told us his view: 'The ultra-left was nationally never very strong, I mean where the ultra-left deployed its strength was at the annual conference and in the local government group and in some branches'. He also said that 'they had an impact on the union's approach to industrial relations law . . . to national collective bargaining . . . on flat rate increases and . . . [in] constant calls for one-day strikes and demonstrations'.

The union's right wing was a mixture of a few active Tories, some Labour supporters who lined up with the SDP, and a less politically clear collection of local and national leaders characterized by national local-government negotiator Jean Geldart as 'apolitical, very naive, and inconsistent'. Mike Blick, chair of the National Local Government Committee (NLGC) for many years, and later national President, was a leading SDP trade unionist. He explained his version of NALGO's strength to us: 'I think a trade union is at its best when it's doing bread-and-butter things for its members', an echo of here-and-now pragmatism.

Throughout this period the dominant political grouping was the broad left, in NALGO's case very broad, including the Communist Party of Great Britain, left-wingers in the Labour Party, and a number of non-aligned socialists. There was a broad left presence in the NEC and in several districts, the Scottish, Metropolitan, and North West and North Wales in particular. Although never a numerical majority, the broad left nonetheless tended to put forward policies that found support among a majority of full-time officials and activists at local and national levels. Rita Donaghy, universities leader, national President, and TUC general councillor, told us that by the end of the 1970s 'a significant phalanx of say twenty on the left would meet beforehand and try to influence the agenda'. During the 1980s 'we became very effective and we became the majority during that period'. Alan Jinkinson and national local-government leader Jim White took the view that throughout the 1980s and early 1990s the union took a progressive left stance on most issues, mainly driven by the broad left, but under increasing pressure from both the right and the ultra-left.

Central to broad left policies was a recognition of the need to develop common cause against the government and, when necessary, against the employers. Such common cause had two ingredients. First, building unity with other trade unionists, peace campaigners, tenants' associations, anti-apartheid groups, and environmentalists, by linking the wholesale nature of capitalist exploitation of citizens and resources to local struggles over issues affecting people in their communities. Secondly, building unity inside the union, across established divisions of gender, race, disability, sexual orientation, industry, and occupation. The changing nature of the jobs done by NALGO members, through technology, restructuring, privatization, and managerialism, created the objective conditions for greater unity, but to put that into practice required constant arguing, campaigning, and action.

As the 1970s came to an end it was clear that NALGO was set to play a key role in the labour movement. Geoffrey Drain concluded his preface to Newman's volume thus: 'when the third history comes to be written there will be many further honourable and exciting achievements to relate in the life of one of the greatest trade unions Britain has known.'[53] However, neither he nor anyone else could have foreseen the extent to which NALGO was to be embroiled in root-and-branch restructuring of both the public sector and the labour movement as the new Conservative government set about dismantling the welfare state.

---

[53] Geoffrey Drain's preface in Newman, *Path to Maturity*, p. viii.

Appendix

TABLE 2.1. *NALGO membership, 31 October 1978*

District	Number of branches	Paid-up membership		Members in arrear and membership of branches excluded from voting		Total membership			
		Voting	Retired	Ordinary	Retired	Ordinary	Retired	Honorary	Total
Eastern	130	48,909	3,776	66	—	48,975	3,776	—	52,751
East Midland	104	43,043	2,978	47	—	43,090	2,978	—	46,068
Metropolitan	128	93,200	8,896	797	39	93,997	8,935	—	102,932
North Eastern	75	39,028	1,859	309	13	139,337	1,872	—	41,209
North Western	135	100,664	5,688	168	—	100,832	5,688	—	106,520
Scottish	121	65,571	1,359	179	2	65,750	1,361	—	67,111
South Eastern	98	45,030	5,279	140	—	45,170	5,279	—	50,449
Southern	77	38,630	3,054	67	—	38,697	3,054	—	41,751
South Wales	91	32,633	1,391	207	—	32,840	1,391	—	34,231
South Western	97	45,733	3,190	139	2	45,872	3,192	—	49,064
West Midland	94	67,651	4,373	180	13	67,811	4,386	—	72,197
Yorkshire and Humberside	78	61,697	3,371	44	—	61,741	3,371	—	65,112
Honorary members	—	—	—	—	—	—	—	10	10
TOTALS	11,228	681,769	45,214	2,343	69	684,112	45,283	10	729,405

TABLE 2.2. *Non-manual employment in selected local-authority departments in England and Wales, 1979–1992*

Department	1979		1983		1987		1992	
	FT	PT	FT	PT	FT	PT	FT	PT
Construction	16,000	100	16,700	100	19,547	300	16,900	600
Social services	87,600	13,800	92,300	16,800	102,700	25,100	116,300	39,800
Libraries	22,200	10,900	21,300	12,000	22,000	14,000	21,400	17,100
Recreation	15,500	3,100	17,500	4,200	21,100	6,200	27,300	10,400
Environmental health	14,100	200	13,800	300	14,400	400	16,400	1,000
Refuse	3,900	0	3,700	0	3,700	100	4,000	100
Housing	33,000	2,900	37,200	3,600	43,300	4,300	52,400	6,700
Planning	21,700	500	20,800	500	21,700	800	23,700	1,800
Engineering	69,800	2,100	66,500	2,200	63,500	4,400	60,700	3,900
Finance	50,500	2,700	51,400	2,800	53,500	3,500	70,900	6,900
Other corporate	61,300	4,900	59,000	5,100	61,000	6,200	63,600	9,500

Note: figures are to nearest 100.
Source: LACSAB, New Earnings Survey.

TABLE 2.3. *NALGO representation on negotiating bodies in local government*

Negotiating body	Employee representation
National Joint Council for Local Authorities' Administrative, Professional, Technical, and Clerical Staff (NJC–APT&C) (covering over 500,000 employees)	Provincial Council Staff Sides, Scottish Council Staff Sides, National and Local Government Officers' Association (NALGO), National Union of Public Employees (NUPE), Confederation of Health Service Employees (COHSE), GMWU's Managerial, Administrative, Technical and Supervisory Section (MATSA), TGWU
Residential Establishments Officer Committee and Standing Joint Advisory Committee for Staffs of Children's Homes	COHSE, NALGO, NUPE, MATSA, Association of Community Home Schools, Association of Hospital and Residential Care Officers, Association of Heads and Matrons of Assessment Centres, TGWU's Association of Clerical, Technical, and Supervisory Staffs (ACTS)
NJC–APT&C (Scottish Council) (covering 65,000 employees)	NALGO, NUPE, MATSA, TGWU
JNC for Chief Officers of Local Authorities	NALGO, Society of Education Officers, Association of Public Service Professional Engineers (APSPE), Association of Public Service Finance Officers (APSFO), Association of Passenger Transport Executives and Managers, Association of Planning Officers, Association of Local Authority Chief Architects, Union of County and District Surveyors, Guild of Directors of Social Services
JNC for Chief Officials of Local Authorities (Scotland)	NALGO, APSFO, APSPE, Association of Local Authorities' Chief Executives, Association of Directors of Administration, Association of Directors of Education in Scotland, Scottish Assessors' Association, Association of Directors of Social Work, Association of Directors of Water and Sewerage Services, Scottish Society of Directors of Planning, Association of Scottish Passenger Transport Executives and Transport Managers, Association of Local Government Engineers and Surveyors, Association of Chief Architects of Scottish Local Authorities

TABLE 2.3 *cont.*

Negotiating body	Employee representation
Whitley Council for New Town Staff	NALGO, New Towns' Chief Officers' Association
Whitley Council for the Staffs of the Industrial Estates Corporations and Development Agencies	NALGO

Source: ACAS, *Industrial Relations Handbook* (London: HMSO, 1980), 284–6.

TABLE 2.4. *NALGO representation on negotiating bodies in the National Health Service*

Negotiating body	Management side	Staff side
General Council	Chairmen of management sides of each functional council	Staff side representatives from each functional council
	Representatives from: RHAs; AHAs; Scottish Health Authorities (SHAS); Welsh Health Authorities (WHAS); DHSS; Scottish Home and Health Department (SHHD); Welsh Office (WO)	
Administrative and Clerical Council	RHAs, AHAs, SHAs, WHAs, DHSS, SHHD, WO, Dental Estimates Board, Prescription Pricing Authority	NALGO, NUPE, TGWU, and Association of Hospital and Residential Care Officers (AHRCO), Association of NHS Officers, Confederation of Health Service Employees (COHSE), GMWU's Managerial, Administrative, Technical and Supervisory Section (MATSA), Society of Administrators of Family Practitioner Committees
Nurses' and Midwives' Council	RHAs, AHAs, SHAs, WHAs, DHSS, SHHD	AHRCO, COHSE, MATSA, NALGO, NUPE, Association of Nurse Administrators
Professional and Technical Council 'A'	RHAs, AHAs, SHAs, WHAs, DHSS, SHHD, WO	ASTMS, COHSE, NALGO, NUPE, Association of Clinical Biochemists, British Association of Occupational Therapists, British

TABLE 2.4 *cont.*

Negotiating body	Management side	Staff side
		Dietetic Association, British Orthoptic Society, Chartered Society of Physiotherapy, Hospital Physicists' Association, Society of Chiropodists, Society of Radiographers, Society of Remedial Gymnasts
Professional and Technical Council 'B'	RHAs, BGs, SHAs, WHAs, DHSS, SHHD, WO	ASTMS, COHSE, NALGO, NUPE, Supervisory, Technical, Administrative, Managerial and Professional Section of UCATT (STAMP), National Union of Gold, Silver and Allied Trades, Union of Shop, Distributive and Allied Workers (USDAW)

Source: ACAS, *Industrial Relations Handbook* (London: HMSO, 1980), 250–7.

TABLE 2.5. *Local-government pay settlements, 1979/80–1996/7 (%)*

Year	Private sector[a]	Manuals	APT&C	Teachers	Firefighters	Police
1979/80	16.7	11.9	15.0	14.6	20.5	13.5
1980/1	9.6	7.5	7.5	7.5	18.8	21.3
1981/2	7.0	6.9	5.7	6.0	10.1	13.2
1982/3	5.8	4.9	4.9	5.0	7.5	10.5
1983/4	6.0	4.5	4.8	5.1	7.8	8.4
1984/5	6.4	5.1	5.6	8.5	6.9	5.1
1985/6	6.3	8.1	5.9	5.7	7.2	7.5
1986/7	5.1	18.0	7.5	16.4	7.3	7.5
1987/8	5.9		5.6	5.4	7.3	7.75
1988/9	7.6	5.6	8.8	7.0	8.6	8.5
1989/90	8.7	8.8	9.38	9.5	8.6	9.25
1990/1	8.0	9.38	6.4	9.3	9.5	9.75
1991/2	4.4	6.4	4.1	7.5	5.6	8.5
1992/3	2.7	4.1	1.5	1.5	4.9	6.5
1993/4	2.5	1.5	2.4	2.9	1.4	1.5
1994/5	3.0	2.4+2.2	2.2	2.7	2.2	3.0
1995/6	3.2	2.91	2.9	3.75	3.5	3.0
1996/7	3.0	2.82	2.82	3.3	4.4	3.5

[a] Until 1989/90 all private-sector settlements are manufacturing settlements; later settlements include all private-sector employers.

Source: Local Government Management Board.

TABLE 2.6. *Average earnings indices for selected local-government groups in relation to their whole economy comparators, 1970–1997*

Category	1970	1975	1980	1985	1990	1995	1997
FULL-TIME MALES							
Whole economy							
non-manual	100.0	100.0	100.0	100.0	100.0	100.0	100.0
APT&C	89.9	96.9	92.0	85.7	82.0	86.3	83.4
Teachers	100.3	106.0	88.5	92.6	93.6	103.7	100.1
Police	86.6	104.1	109.5	115.6	99.8	103.0	101.4
Whole economy							
manual	100.0	100.0	100.0	100.0	100.0	100.0	100.0
Local-government							
manuals	79.1	85.3	86.4	79.1	80.9	84.4	82.3
Firefighters	114.2	117.2	105.1	113.3	115.1	118.9	123.3
FULL-TIME FEMALES							
Whole economy							
non-manual	100.0	100.0	100.0	100.0	100.0	100.0	100.0
APT&C	104.5	104.5	103.9	100.4	95.6	96.5	93.1
Teachers	163.5	151.5	131.7	134.5	134.5	138.1	135.1
Whole economy							
manual	100.0	100.0	100.0	100.0	100.0	100.0	100.0
Local-government							
manual	89.6	102.2	95.3	94.5	97.6	97.5	97.2
PART-TIME FEMALES							
Whole economy							
non-manual		100.0	100.0	100.0	100.0	100.0	100.0
APT&C		111.1	104.6	101.6	100.6	98.3	100.0
Whole economy							
manual		100.0	100.0	100.0	100.0	100.0	100.0
Local-government							
manual		106.8	100.8	100.0	103.8	108.6	105.5

Source: LACSAB, New Earnings Survey.

TABLE 2.7. *Distribution of pay for male local authorities' administrative, professional, technical, and clerical NJC, England and Wales, 1978–1993*

Year	Average gross weekly pay				Distribution of weekly pay		Average weekly hours		Percentage of the employees who received		
	Total (£)	of which			10% of employees earned		Total including overtime	Overtime	Overtime pay (%)	PBR (%)	Shift (%)
		Overtime pay (£)	PBR etc. (£)	Shift etc. premium pay (£)	less than (£)	more than (£)					
1978	92.0	1.6	0.0	0.3	58.5	129.5	37.4	0.7	12.9	0.4	4.8
1979	101.6	1.8	0.1	0.3	63.7	142.4	37.5	0.6	12.2	0.8	4.3
1980	130.0	2.1	0.1	0.6	80.1	188.8	37.3	0.6	11.1	0.7	4.9
1981	154.5	2.7	0.1	0.7	95.2	222.3	37.4	0.6	11.9	0.9	5.4
1982	166.6	3.2	0.2	0.8	101.2	239.0	37.4	0.6	11.8	1.3	5.0
1983	176.6	4.1	0.3	0.9	107.3	253.8	37.5	0.7	14.5	2.4	6.3
1984	183.5	4.0	0.2	0.9	110.5	264.6	37.4	0.7	13.9	0.9	6.2
1985	193.0	4.2	0.1	1.1	116.2	281.6	37.5	0.7	14.0	0.9	6.1
1986	207.2	4.6	0.2	1.5	125.4	301.4	37.4	0.7	16.2	1.1	7.3
1987	221.7	5.6	0.3	1.5	130.7	322.1	37.5	0.8	15.2	1.0	6.3
1988	241.1	5.9	0.3	1.6	143.9	352.7	37.5	0.8	15.1	1.4	6.7
1989	259.7	7.0	0.3	2.3	155.1	380.5	37.6	0.9	17.4	1.1	7.8
1990	291.0	9.9	1.3	2.1	168.3	430.0	37.9	1.2	19.9	3.3	6.9
1991	324.7	8.5	1.6	2.5	187.8	476.5	37.6	0.9	17.5	3.1	7.5
1992	351.8	7.7	1.6	2.1	198.1	519.8	37.5	0.8	15.5	3.1	5.8
1993	372.4	7.0	2.0	1.9	213.1	539.0	37.3	0.6	13.2	4.3	5.6

Source: New Earnings Survey.

Note: Figures are for full-time males on adult rates, whose pay for the survey period was not affected by absence.

TABLE 2.8. *Distribution of pay for female local authorities' administrative, professional, technical, and clerical NJC, England and Wales, 1978–1993*

Year	Average gross weekly pay				Distribution of weekly pay		Average weekly hours		Percentage of the employees who received		
	Total (£)	of which			10% of employees earned						
		Overtime pay (£)	PBR etc. (£)	Shift etc. premium pay (£)	less than (£)	more than (£)	Total including overtime	Overtime	Overtime pay (%)	PBR (%)	Shift (%)
1978	60.3	0.6	0.0	0.2	45.0	82.2	37.1	0.3	8.6	0.3	5.3
1979	67.0	0.9	0.0	0.4	49.6	91.9	37.4	0.4	8.5	0.4	7.4
1980	85.9	0.9	0.0	0.6	60.2	121.7	37.1	0.3	7.0	0.7	6.6
1981	101.1	1.0	0.1	0.7	70.7	145.2	37.1	0.3	6.8	0.6	7.5
1982	109.9	1.0	0.1	0.8	76.0	156.2	37.0	0.2	6.4	0.5	7.3
1983	119.3	1.4	0.2	1.0	82.3	170.2	37.1	0.3	9.1	0.7	8.7
1984	126.5	1.2	0.1	0.9	86.1	181.9	36.9	0.3	8.4	0.5	8.4
1985	134.4	1.2	0.1	1.3	90.7	193.0	37.0	0.3	8.6	0.7	8.7
1986	144.5	1.7	0.1	1.4	100.3	207.4	37.0	0.3	10.5	0.3	9.6
1987	153.9	1.9	0.1	1.4	105.0	217.1	37.0	0.3	9.8	0.7	8.7
1988	170.3	2.5	0.1	1.5	115.8	246.2	37.0	0.4	12.0	1.0	8.9
1989	184.0	2.8	0.1	1.6	125.2	265.6	37.0	0.4	12.8	0.5	8.7
1990	206.1	4.2	0.4	1.5	137.1	298.4	37.3	0.6	13.4	1.0	7.3
1991	228.1	3.2	0.2	1.8	158.4	331.9	36.9	0.4	11.1	1.0	7.5
1992	248.6	3.3	0.4	1.5	171.1	363.4	36.9	0.4	10.0	1.3	6.8
1993	263.2	3.5	0.7	1.8	179.8	377.9	36.8	0.4	10.4	2.6	6.5

Note: Figures are for full-time females on adult rates, whose pay for the survey period was not affected by absence.

Source: New Earnings Survey.

TABLE 2.9. *Distribution of pay for male NHS administrative and clerical staffs, Whitley Council, 1979–1993*

| Year | Average gross weekly pay | | | | Distribution of weekly pay 10% of employees earned | | Average weekly hours | | Percentage of the employees who received | | |
| | Total (£) | of which | | | less than (£) | more than (£) | Total including overtime | Overtime | Overtime pay (%) | PBR (%) | Shift (%) |
		Overtime pay (£)	PBR etc. (£)	Shift etc. premium pay (£)							
1979	109.3	2.4	0.6	0.1	64.9	172.8	38.9	1.8	13.3	3.0	1.5
1980	135.6	4.1	0.2	0.3	79.1	195.0	38.3	1.2	15.6	2.0	3.4
1981	155.3	2.7	0.5	1.2	84.5	241.5	37.6	0.6	12.4	3.8	6.4
1982	167.4	2.7	1.1	1.1	94.7	246.5	37.7	0.6	10.7	7.1	4.5
1983	184.3	2.9	1.3	2.3	101.6	268.3	37.7	0.6	10.2	8.3	10.7
1984	179.8	2.8	0.9	1.2	98.7	263.0	37.6	0.5	12.1	7.9	4.7
1985	188.5	2.1	0.7	1.7	98.5	288.8	37.4	0.4	14.6	5.4	7.8
1986	209.3	3.7	1.0	1.4	109.6	313.3	37.6	0.7	14.7	6.1	7.1
1987	225.2	3.5	1.1	2.0	109.6	380.2	37.6	0.6	12.4	6.2	6.2
1988	253.1	1.8	1.9	0.6	126.2	451.2	37.3	0.3	7.8	8.2	3.7
1989	262.4	4.6	1.0	1.6	138.5	429.5	37.7	0.7	11.9	5.3	8.8
1990	294.2	4.1	0.7	1.8	143.7	488.7	37.5	0.6	9.6	4.8	4.8
1991	308.5	6.3	1.0	1.7	143.9	540.5	37.7	0.9	12.3	4.4	5.2
1992	332.6	5.9	1.3	0.8	165.9	542.7	37.6	0.7	12.8	6.2	3.5
1993	338.5	4.1	3.2	1.5	162.3	546.8	37.3	0.5	11.0	11.4	4.2

Note: Figures are for full-time males on adult rates, whose pay for the survey period was not affected by absence.

Source: New Earnings Survey.

TABLE 2.10. Distribution of pay for female NHS administrative and clerical staffs, Whitley Council, 1978–1993

Year	Average gross weekly pay				Distribution of weekly pay		Average weekly hours		Percentage of the employees who received		
	Total (£)	of which			10% of employees earned		Total including overtime	Overtime	Overtime pay (%)	PBR (%)	Shift (%)
		Overtime pay (£)	PBR etc. (£)	Shift etc. premium pay (£)	less than (£)	more than (£)					
1978	56.4	0.4	0.1	0.1	40.5	74.5	37.0	0.2	6.2	2.8	2.8
1979	63.0	0.6	0.1	0.2	44.7	83.7	37.1	0.3	5.8	3.2	2.6
1980	76.8	1.1	0.2	0.2	52.5	106.3	37.1	0.3	7.4	3.6	3.4
1981	88.5	0.6	0.3	0.2	62.5	120.3	36.9	0.2	6.7	4.7	2.6
1982	94.6	0.7	0.2	0.2	65.0	127.6	36.9	0.2	6.4	3.4	3.5
1983	104.8	1.0	0.3	1.0	73.1	142.2	37.0	0.3	9.2	3.1	6.7
1984	105.8	0.7	1.1	0.4	73.9	141.1	36.9	0.2	6.9	5.1	3.8
1985	112.1	1.3	0.4	0.5	80.2	155.6	37.0	0.3	10.8	4.7	3.6
1986	120.4	1.1	0.3	0.6	84.8	165.3	37.0	0.2	10.1	3.3	5.1
1987	128.3	1.2	0.4	0.6	90.2	183.9	37.0	0.2	9.7	2.9	4.3
1988	137.6	2.0	0.5	0.5	94.9	197.0	37.1	0.4	12.0	3.1	4.1
1989	146.5	2.3	0.4	1.0	101.2	208.1	37.1	0.4	12.5	2.9	6.9
1990	169.5	2.3	0.3	0.8	118.8	239.9	37.1	0.4	10.2	1.7	4.5
1991	190.0	2.5	0.5	0.9	130.8	269.0	37.1	0.4	9.5	2.7	4.9
1992	211.4	2.7	0.6	0.7	148.4	292.0	37.1	0.4	10.7	3.5	3.5
1993	225.4	3.0	0.4	1.0	157.2	317.1	37.1	0.4	11.3	2.3	4.3

Note: Figures are for full-time females on adult rates, whose pay for the survey period was not affected by absence.

Source: New Earnings Survey.

TABLE 2.11. Distribution of pay for male British Gas staffs and senior officers, NJC, 1978–1993

| Year | Average gross weekly pay | | | | Distribution of weekly pay 10% of employees earned | | Average weekly hours | | Percentage of the employees who received | | |
| | Total (£) | of which | | | less than (£) | more than (£) | Total including overtime | Overtime | Overtime pay (%) | PBR (%) | Shift (%) |
		Overtime pay (£)	PBR etc. (£)	Shift etc. premium pay (£)							
1978	91.1	5.0	5.2	0.4	62.8	125.0	39.0	1.9	40.4	27.9	5.0
1979	112.0	8.2	9.3	0.9	74.8	152.9	39.4	2.3	40.7	64.4	8.3
1980	134.4	6.7	6.4	1.6	91.0	178.5	39.5	2.5	32.0	30.3	12.7
1981	159.3	7.7	7.3	1.4	104.8	214.1	38.6	1.4	35.4	33.1	7.4
1982	180.9	7.8	7.1	1.1	116.8	246.5	38.4	1.4	43.4	34.9	6.8
1983	195.4	7.9	8.4	1.2	131.3	262.5	38.2	1.2	35.1	23.4	9.1
1984	206.6	9.2	8.4	1.7	130.4	281.3	38.2	1.2	31.8	22.5	11.2
1985	214.3	12.8	9.8	1.7	134.4	287.9	38.6	1.6	40.0	22.0	8.2
1986	231.4	13.9	8.5	2.8	146.9	312.3	38.8	1.8	40.3	21.7	10.6
1987	243.8	13.9	11.0	2.2	149.1	348.1	38.7	1.6	37.3	26.7	10.7
1988	257.2	12.2	11.3	2.7	156.4	353.5	38.3	1.2	40.9	27.0	10.0
1989	287.1	15.2	9.8	1.8	174.4	403.7	38.6	1.6	40.2	22.9	6.4
1990	323.2	23.2	9.6	2.1	196.2	463.7	39.2	2.1	48.6	26.1	6.8
1991	361.4	25.1	10.3	2.5	228.7	496.2	39.4	2.4	50.6	19.3	5.6
1992	375.7	21.7	12.5	3.1	245.5	502.4	38.9	1.9	45.1	21.1	6.5
1993	399.3	22.9	20.9	2.2	256.7	520.2	38.7	1.8	43.5	26.9	5.7

Note: Figures are for full-time males on adult rates, whose pay for the survey period was not affected by absence.

Source: New Earnings Survey.

TABLE 2.12. *Distribution of pay for female British Gas staffs and senior officers, NJC, 1978–1993*

Year	Average gross weekly pay				Distribution of weekly pay 10% of employees earned		Average weekly hours		Percentage of the employees who received		
	Total (£)	of which			less than (£)	more than (£)	Total including overtime	Overtime	Overtime pay (%)	PBR (%)	Shift (%)
		Overtime pay (£)	PBR etc. (£)	Shift etc. premium pay (£)							
1978	60.2	0.7	2.1	0.0	47.3	77.2	37.3	0.4	14.0	30.9	2.2
1979	70.9	0.7	4.4	0.1	55.2	88.7	37.3	0.3	16.5	52.8	6.8
1980	87.4	1.5	2.3	0.4	67.6	111.0	37.4	0.4	14.9	40.5	6.0
1981	103.3	1.3	2.0	0.1	81.4	127.3	37.3	0.3	14.3	50.5	2.2
1982	116.2	1.5	2.6	0.1	93.7	140.5	37.5	0.5	28.4	51.0	1.5
1983	126.7	0.9	2.0	0.1	102.4	156.5	37.2	0.2	11.6	42.4	3.0
1984	132.8	1.6	1.0	0.3	107.9	165.1	37.3	0.3	14.9	35.6	3.7
1985	145.4	3.8	1.6	0.3	116.8	181.1	37.6	0.6	25.1	28.7	2.3
1986	156.2	7.0	1.9	0.3	122.0	195.7	38.1	1.1	26.6	29.4	3.4
1987	162.8	4.1	2.0	0.4	128.9	199.5	37.6	0.6	25.3	35.6	4.0
1988	177.0	7.2	1.8	0.4	140.5	218.4	38.0	1.0	29.2	34.8	2.5
1989	187.9	6.5	2.8	0.3	139.9	243.2	37.9	0.9	22.2	34.7	1.7
1990	212.0	9.2	2.4	0.7	158.7	276.9	38.1	1.1	27.3	38.3	3.2
1991	254.5	11.8	2.5	0.9	182.6	345.6	38.2	1.2	35.3	22.4	5.9
1992	263.5	9.5	2.6	1.2	191.3	352.6	37.9	0.9	26.1	15.8	6.1
1993	279.1	9.9	3.9	1.0	202.5	376.5	37.8	0.9	31.0	12.0	7.0

Note: Figures are for full-time females on adult rates, whose pay for the survey period was not affected by absence.

Source: New Earnings Survey.

TABLE 2.13. *Distribution of pay for male electricity supply, administrative, and clerical grades, NJC, 1979–1992*

Year	Average gross weekly pay				Distribution of weekly pay		Average weekly hours		Percentage of the employees who received		
	Total (£)	of which			10% of employees earned		Total including overtime	Overtime	Overtime pay (%)	PBR (%)	Shift (%)
		Overtime pay (£)	PBR etc. (£)	Shift etc. premium pay (£)	less than (£)	more than (£)					
1979	103.5	1.6	1.4	0.9	66.4	154.3	38.5	0.5	19.5	27.9	11.0
1980	118.5	1.2	0.0	1.3	81.0	170.5	38.3	0.3	10.9	0.0	10.9
1981	142.5	3.5	0.0	1.8	97.5	210.0	38.6	0.6	15.7	0.0	10.7
1982	153.5	2.1	0.4	1.4	110.0	213.2	37.3	0.3	12.2	4.6	6.9
1983	173.2	3.7	0.3	2.5	117.6	242.0	37.6	0.6	18.9	3.0	11.4
1984	181.4	4.8	0.3	2.2	115.5	257.0	37.6	0.6	21.6	3.0	9.7
1985	188.7	1.5	0.1	2.6	120.9	267.5	37.2	0.2	8.1	1.5	11.1
1986	221.1	7.4	0.2	2.9	133.7	342.9	37.8	0.8	25.4	2.2	11.9
1987	221.7	5.9	0.5	2.1	142.7	317.2	37.7	0.7	22.1	3.8	8.4
1988	237.6	8.9	0.3	1.7	149.7	357.7	37.9	0.9	21.1	3.3	8.1
1989	Not available										
1990	Not available										
1991	324.7	15.7	0.0	2.8	195.5	514.5	38.2	1.2	26.1	1.3	7.8
1992	380.0	12.9	2.8	2.3	220.7	592.1	37.9	0.9	23.6	4.3	3.6

Note: Figures are for full-time males on adult rates, whose pay for the survey period was not affected by absence.

Source: New Earnings Survey.

TABLE 2.14. *Distribution of pay for female electricity supply, administrative, and clerical grades, NJC, 1978–1992*

| Year | Average gross weekly pay | | | | Distribution of weekly pay | | Average weekly hours | | Percentage of the employees who received | | |
| | Total (£) | of which | | | 10% of employees earned | | Total including overtime | Overtime | Overtime pay (%) | PBR (%) | Shift (%) |
		Overtime pay (£)	PBR etc. (£)	Shift etc. premium pay (£)	less than (£)	more than (£)					
1978	57.0	0.3	1.2	0.2	46.0	70.1	38.2	0.2	7.4	24.9	5.3
1979	67.7	0.5	1.4	0.2	51.6	85.1	38.2	0.2	8.5	31.7	4.2
1980	82.9	0.6	0.1	0.3	64.4	106.5	38.1	0.1	7.8	1.0	5.2
1981	101.1	0.3	0.0	0.2	77.8	132.7	38.1	0.1	4.4	1.0	3.4
1982	114.3	0.8	0.1	0.2	88.2	147.6	37.1	0.2	7.0	1.5	2.5
1983	126.1	1.0	0.2	0.4	97.6	162.3	37.2	0.2	9.8	3.6	5.7
1984	134.3	1.5	0.2	0.9	101.3	176.3	37.3	0.3	12.1	2.1	7.9
1985	141.2	0.7	0.1	0.4	108.0	184.7	37.1	0.1	5.7	2.1	6.3
1986	152.9	2.3	0.2	0.4	110.8	202.5	37.3	0.3	15.6	2.2	4.4
1987	164.5	3.8	0.4	0.4	114.1	223.2	37.5	0.5	24.2	3.6	3.6
1988	173.6	2.9	0.2	0.2	123.1	236.7	37.4	0.4	18.1	3.0	2.5
1989	192.0	5.6	0.1	0.5	134.5	265.2	37.6	0.6	25.6	1.4	3.8
1990	209.8	8.2	0.0	0.8	144.8	280.1	37.9	0.9	27.8	0.4	4.5
1991	229.9	10.0	0.0	0.7	158.4	298.5	37.8	0.9	0.7	0.9	4.1
1992	252.4	9.4	0.4	0.9	176.4	338.2	37.8	0.8	22.8	2.3	4.2

Note: Figures are for full-time females on adult rates, whose pay for the survey period was not affected by absence.

Source: New Earnings Survey.

TABLE 2.15. *Distribution of pay for male water-service non-manual staffs, NJC, 1979–1989*

Year	Average gross weekly pay				Distribution of weekly pay 10% of employees earned		Average weekly hours		Percentage of the employees who received		
	Total (£)	of which			less than (£)	more than (£)	Total including overtime	Overtime	Overtime pay (%)	PBR (%)	Shift (%)
		Overtime pay (£)	PBR etc. (£)	Shift etc. premium pay (£)							
1979	114.9	3.9	0.4	0.5	77.6	162.4	39.5	3.0	26.1	5.6	6.3
1980	137.0	4.4	0.4	0.6	87.0	190.4	37.5	1.0	20.9	3.4	6.1
1981	167.6	4.1	0.9	0.6	106.7	233.3	37.5	0.8	20.0	4.7	5.3
1982	182.8	8.1	0.2	0.4	115.5	251.3	38.2	1.4	28.9	2.0	4.6
1983	195.4	6.4	0.8	0.6	133.0	258.7	37.8	0.9	27.8	4.4	5.7
1984	213.1	7.6	0.9	1.0	123.8	287.5	37.7	1.1	29.7	4.1	4.1
1985	213.5	7.7	0.8	0.3	128.0	287.8	37.8	1.1	27.1	3.0	2.3
1986	245.2	10.0	0.6	0.9	144.3	326.5	37.8	1.3	26.8	1.4	6.3
1987	257.4	12.2	1.6	0.6	163.0	356.0	38.0	1.5	28.8	5.5	3.4
1988	258.4	8.8	0.8	0.7	152.1	365.7	37.9	0.9	25.4	2.5	2.5
1989	287.8	15.0	1.5	1.4	168.7	398.7	38.5	1.6	28.4	1.8	2.8

Note: Figures are for full-time males on adult rates, whose pay for the survey period was not affected by absence.
Source: New Earnings Survey.

3

The Advent of Thatcherism

THIS chapter starts in early 1979 with the last few months of the Labour government. It includes an account of the strike by social workers (see Box 1), during the 'winter of discontent', and of the crisis over public-sector pay and incomes policies. It then covers the election of the Conservative Party under Mrs Thatcher in May 1979, followed by the main developments during the early years of the Conservative government. First we outline the government's drive to 'squeeze inflation out of the system' through a combination of cutting public expenditure, weakening union power, and increasing unemployment. Secondly, we discuss NALGO's responses to these policy initiatives by maintaining a 'business-as-usual' approach to industrial relations and collective bargaining in all sectors, illustrated by the 1980 local-government comparability pay dispute (see Box 2). Thirdly, we explore the linkage between government policy and monetarist dogma. Finally, we discuss the impact of these and other forces on the union itself. We identify the emerging tensions: over representativeness; coping with an increasingly fragmented and diverse membership; and facing up to the nature of political opposition to government. Our aim is to trace the sequence of events as they unfolded over time, while also discussing the complex interplay between political and economic forces, trade-union action in the arena of collective bargaining, trade-union policy development and campaigning, and internal democratic practice.

The Advent of Thatcherism

The Fall of the Labour Government and the
Winter of Discontent

At the start of 1979 the Labour government's main policies were in tatters as its accord with the trade unions broke down over one incomes policy too many.[1] The monetarists at the IMF, with their economic and consequent social and welfare policies, had tightened their grip on Chancellor Dennis Healey. The Western capitalist economies faced unrelenting pressures from the falling growth rate, from the challenges from Japan and other Asian exporters, and from the shock waves caused by huge increases in the price of oil. Implementing international monetarist belt-tightening criteria, the burden of which fell on its own supporters, the Callaghan Cabinet stumbled through the winter of discontent towards the spring of defeat.

Incomes policy was central to the government's attempt to resolve their economic problems in line with the IMF's requirements. The year 1979 began with a tide of opposition to the latest phase, a 5 per cent ceiling on pay settlements. The pay limit reflected the government's quandary at the end of the previous incomes policy phase, as James Callaghan remembered:

Denis Healey and I had previously discussed what steps would be needed after August 1978 when the current incomes policy would expire, and although we recognized the strength of the unions' demand for a return to so-called free collective bargaining, both of us were in agreement that we could not simply throw the reins on the horse's back and allow it to gallop away.[2]

Settlements were running at about 8 per cent, and Callaghan reckoned that wage drift would mean actual increases would be greater than the 5 per cent limit. But, while wage drift might occur in the private manufacturing sector, it would not happen in the public sector. The result was the winter of discontent, with manual workers in the NHS and in local government out on strike in February 1979.[3]

Callaghan does not hide his anger with public-sector workers and their union leaders: 'I find it painful to write about some of the excesses that took place',[4] and he puts the blame for the strikes and subsequent loss of electoral support firmly with the TUC, its constituent unions, and their members. This view is shared by Callaghan's biographer: 'His dismay, indeed anger, at the

---

[1] UK Government, *Winning the Battle against Inflation*, Cmnd 7293 (London: HMSO, 1978).

[2] J. Callaghan, *Time and Chance* (London: Collins, 1987), 519.

[3] S. Kessler and F. Bayliss, *Contemporary British Industrial Relations* (London: Macmillan, 1998), 28.

[4] Callaghan, *Time and Chance*, 537.

course of events was transparent . . . but he offered no alternative strategy and no lead.'[5]

Having botched its dealings with the unions, and underestimated the pent-up frustration of organized workers after years of pay restraint, the government sought a way out through the Standing Commission on Pay Comparability, chaired by Professor Hugh Clegg. Established in March as a pay deal in waiting until after the coming general election, the Clegg Commission was seen as a rational and fair way out of years of public-sector pay dilemmas. However, under the Conservative policies of the 1980s it became the tomb marker on the grave of pay comparability.

Both the abortive 5 per cent norm and Clegg served to harden attitudes over pay—national water chairman Ken Onslow spoke for many in NALGO when he said that the limit 'militates unfairly against the public sector'.[6] Moreover, the government exploited the Whitley bargaining machinery to postpone reaching settlements for as long as possible, and members in the New Towns among others sided with their employers to attack the government's deliberate delays. British Waterways staff took industrial action after government ministers intervened to reject their claim that they had a special case for a pay increase greater than the government's limit.

NALGO members in the NHS had already been involved in eleven disputes since 1976, and A&C members were preparing to take action again over a claim for a minimum of twenty days annual leave. Ada Maddocks, national officer for health, urged members to 'think about the sort of industrial action you would be willing to take in support of the annual leave claim . . . it now seems inevitable that tough action will have to be taken'.[7]

The right-wing press portrayed health-service trade unionists as uncaring militants who believed that the health service was run for their benefit rather than for patients. Such arguments later impressed the Royal Commission into the NHS[8] and convinced the TUC to issue guidance placing limits on industrial action.[9] This reflected a desire within some unions to retreat from confrontations with the government, and increasingly they became helpless spectators as the NHS was impoverished. In contrast, NALGO Deputy General Secretary Bill Rankin defended the right of public-sector workers, especially health workers, to strike. He argued that 'management and government in turn must not be so cynical as to allow great frustrations to build up because they calculate that there is no effective muscle behind workers' demands no

[5] K. Morgan, *Callaghan: A Life* (Oxford: Oxford University Press, 1997), 664.
[6] *Public Service* (*PS*) (Jan. 1979), 3.   [7] Ibid. (Apr. 1979), 5.
[8] A. Merrison, *Royal Commission into the NHS*, Cmnd 7615 (London: HMSO, 1979).
[9] TUC, *Improving Industrial Relations in the NHS* (London: TUC, 1981).

matter how justified a claim might be'.[10] Later the *Daily Telegraph* reported from the annual conference that 'the largest white-collar union yesterday voted heavily against a proposal to condemn industrial action which placed life in jeopardy'.[11]

As manual workers piled on the pressure, under the looming prospect of the tottering Labour government being replaced by a Tory one, NALGO leaders got their various claims in quickly. Local-government activists wanted an end to the long-running negotiations over the 1978 13 per cent London weighting offer; a condition of service claim for water staff was put to their NJC; and there was industrial action over the length of the working week by NHS staff on PT'B' conditions. NALGO put its weight behind a claim for more pay for nurses on account, pending agreement on a comparability study, and opposed a Department of Health deskilling exercise involving foot-care assistants. Other claims included gas staff on pay, electricity members on salary structure, and staff in New Towns on productivity deals. Members threatened action in the universities over a 5 per cent offer that Rita Donaghy, national committee chair, condemned.

Activists were divided over the use of incomes policies. Some argued for them on the basis that a properly constituted policy might be fairer during periods of rising inflation, while those opposed noted their unequal operation and their doubtful efficacy in dealing with inflation. However, official union policy remained ambiguously in favour. Geoffrey Drain took the arguments to the Wales TUC in Tenby in May, calling for

a pay and prices policy to include tripartite annual talks between unions, employers and the government, a revived central advisory role for the TUC, a new independent Agency on the lines of the former Prices and Incomes Board to apply the policy to pay, prices, profits and dividends, tougher government powers to freeze or cut prices and an investigation of the role of profits and of continental style capital-sharing schemes.[12]

Bill Gill continued the theme at the TUC Annual Congress in Blackpool: NALGO 'was not seeking support for the rigid arbitrary pay policies of the past but that a permanent, jointly agreed system of wage determination as an integral part of economic and social policy would ensure a more just and equitable distribution of wage increases than has been done by free collective bargaining'.[13] The argument was rejected.

One of NALGO's main concerns during the run-up to the election was the progress of its first national strike action of any major significance, that of social workers (see Box 1). The group of workers involved, and the attitudes

---

[10] *PS* (Jan. 1979), 4.   [11] *Daily Telegraph*, 14 June 1979, 2.
[12] *NALGO Annual Report 1979* (London: NALGO, 1980), 10.   [13] Ibid. 7.

of both the employers and other members towards them, symbolized especially clearly the contradictions facing workers who are both public-service employees and trade unionists.

Box 1: NALGO and the Social Workers' Strike of 1978–9

In 1975 there were nearly 19,000 social workers, senior social workers, team leaders, community workers, trainees, and social-work assistants in England, Wales, and Scotland. Their pay was restricted to within a narrow range of grades (the 'grading prescriptions') set down in the Purple Book (the national agreement covering APT&C staffs in local authorities). Emergency services during nights, bank holidays, and weekends were based on the 'standby' system, where social workers were available on call on a rota basis. In return for this they received a small payment, which was the same whether or not they were called out. The demands made of a social worker in one part of the country might be quite different from those in another, and this fuelled the dispute.

NALGO tried to negotiate both nationally and locally. The 1975 local-government group meeting called for new provisions on social-worker grades, and in 1976 it told the national committee to call industrial action if negotiations failed to bring social workers within the Purple Book's overtime provisions. Members in a number of branches were prepared to take industrial action to secure negotiations on standby, but, pending national agreement on the issue, they were forbidden to do so by the national leadership. A national survey showed that most branches were dissatisfied with the standby scheme, and that most favoured the establishment of special night duty teams.

In January 1977 a special conference launched membership-wide industrial action against cuts, instructing all members in all services not to work overtime and not to cover the duties of posts held vacant. In June the local-government group meeting called for the abolition of the national scale for social workers and instructed branches to commence negotiations with their employers. It also called for local negotiations to be allowed on standby if national negotiations were not successful by the end of 1977.

Within the next twelve months over twenty branches asked NALGO's Emergency Committee to support them in withdrawing their members from standby rotas. The 1978 group meeting threw out a series of motions calling for national negotiations on a career grade. The British Association of Social Workers (BASW), which was then affiliated to NALGO, wanted the national prescribed scale extended, with progression at the top of the scale based on the capability of the individual social worker. They argued that this would enable social workers to develop their careers without leaving social work. This ran against NALGO's 'rate-for-the-job' policy based on a link between duties/responsibilities and grades. BASW went on to set up the British Union of Social Workers (BUSW), and NALGO ended its relationship.

On 8 August 1978 it became clear that abolition of the national scale was not negotiable, and all 128 social service authorities refused to negotiate over grades, arguing that the Purple Book provisions should apply. Within a month the social workers in Southwark, Tower Hamlets, and Newcastle upon Tyne were on strike. Liverpool and Lewisham joined them in October, followed by Greenwich, Gateshead, Sheffield, Knowsley, and Leeds. By the end of the year Cheshire, Islington, Rochdale, Havering, and Gloucestershire had joined the strike, bringing the number of branches to fifteen and involving 2,600 strikers with another 1,700 taking action short of strike in five other branches. The action went on until April.

One of the first lessons learned was how to run a strike. At this time NALGO was one of the few large unions without any sort of strike tradition. Social workers set up picket lines and hardship funds, and worked out how to keep strikers fed, warm, and informed. Branch officers and stewards had to deal with overreacting managers, strike-breakers, and other members hostile to the strike. They made difficult decisions about how emergency services would be organized and who would provide them. They worked it out as they went along, but they also drew strength from the local labour-movement networks. Experienced trade unionists handed their knowledge on and helped to establish the routine and rhythm of strike activity—a combination of tight administration to coordinate picket rotas and to establish effective communications, along with measures to build confidence, sustain morale, democratize the strike, and generate wider support.

As with any strike the tricky question of unity kept surfacing in variable forms. In Tower Hamlets some senior managers were sent home for refusing to cross picket lines, and 573 of their staff walked out in protest. In Newcastle some members attempted to requisition a branch meeting to discuss repudiation of the strike, and the emergency committee agreed that a district officer should be based full-time with the branch during the strike. Strike pay was conditional on participation in picket duty. Newham and Coventry branches sought official support for a strike ballot of both field and residential social workers, but this was refused. Activist networks such as those set up by the strikers in London and in the north-west were very important in keeping the dispute alive, with national organizations such as NAG maintaining continuous pressure on the national leadership. Strikers demonstrated outside union headquarters as well as against their employers.

National leaders also learned how to operate during a strike. The NEC established a Strike Action Bulletin, which kept all branches informed about the social workers' case and about their action for the duration of the strike. It also set up a Strike Operations' Committee, which held its first meeting on 22 September. The leadership stuck to the principle that the strike was about a national dispute to secure local negotiations. By the end of October a joint national working party was set up to negotiate a national framework to be applied by local joint agreement. The working party's recommendations were sent to branches for consultation in November, containing proposals that were the basis for the eventual settlement. They were recommended to a special group meeting on 26 January.

Group meetings consisted of delegates from local-government branches, including delegates from over 400 branches that had no social workers in membership, putting the delegates from the fifteen branches with striking social workers into a small minority. Many strikers turned up to urge their fellow members to step up their support, having arranged for a string of motions to be tabled. These included criticisms of the NEC and the Strike Operations' Committee, calls for escalation of the strike to include all social workers and other groups of members, and a levy on working members. The delegates refused to discuss any of these, and at one point considered going into private session because of the barracking by angry strikers in the visitors' gallery. They agreed with the national committee's recommendation to accept the working party deal, and supported strikes where local negotiations based on the national framework broke down. The national committee agreed that no branch would be required to return social workers to work if meaningful negotiations were not under way.

The national agreement was signed on 9 February 1979, and, by the end of the month, after considerable debate about whether or not local talks amounted to 'meaningful discussions', the emergency committee sent all strikers back to work except in Gateshead, Tower Hamlets, and Knowsley. This was after some delay while the provincial employers tried to agree among themselves a common line for the local negotiations, resisting local bargaining to the last. The last strikers went back to work in Knowsley on 23 April.

The strike raises some major questions about the national union's position on sectional struggles. What is the limit to the amount of national resources to be devoted to a small proportion of the membership? How can members be involved in decisions about strikes? How can public-service professionals put pressure on employers without putting people at risk? What response should be made to ultra-left demands, often superficially attractive to enthusiastic young activists, to turn every local or sectional dispute into a struggle to the death, regardless of the cost? Aspects of this came to the fore in the question of strike pay. The January group meeting occurred against a background of NEC concern about the £500,000 paid out to strikers monthly. National committee chair Mike Blick said that NALGO's traditional policy of paying net pay to those on strike was in jeopardy and that members in all services had an interest in what was happening. January's *Public Service* reported that, 'Despite the effort put into the action, backed by some £1.75 million, it had not as yet forced local area bargaining in any area in which strike action was taking place. Yet some members had been out since mid-August.' Jim White, national committee vice-chair at the time, told us: 'It lasted too long. It was a destructive dispute within the union. . . . It separated social workers from a lot of their colleagues in the rest of local government.'

The social workers' strike was part of a rapid increase in the use of industrial action during the late 1970s. In 1979 the union's Emergency Committee received 126 calls from branches for official support for industrial action—101 of these were in local government, and seventy-two were directly supported.[14] The rise in militancy was matched by warning signs of the coming anti-union offensive that would confront all unions in the movement. The media continued their endless stream of attacks on trade unions and their influence over the Labour government, and the Conservatives promised that their government would legislate away what they called trade-union privileges. This line of argument was firmly rebutted in Lord Wedderburn's article in *Public Service*, where he argued that the rights to strike and to picket are civil rights that had already been eroded by the judges and were under further threat from Conservative proposals.[15]

The Conservatives are Coming

With the election of Mrs Thatcher's government on 3 May 1979 came a profound and lasting change to the fortunes of NALGO and its members. Two issues rang out loud and clear from the Tories' election platform: the enactment of legislation to limit trade unions as both organizations and as organizers of collective action; and cuts in public services through both reduced funding and transfer into the private sector. Both were the direct consequences of a government determined to 'squeeze inflation out of the system' at any cost, a policy rooted in monetarist supply-side economics, which sees the public services as consumers rather than as generators of wealth. Every pound spent on public services is regarded as a pound that could otherwise have been spent in the wealth-creating private sector—wealth creation is 'crowded out'.[16] Trade unions are seen as preventing the markets for labour from operating freely and therefore preventing the labour flexibility necessary for the efficient generation of profits. There is no evidence that this economic model has any validity and NALGO, along with other TUC unions, began to develop both a criticism of the model and a powerful alternative vision—the Alternative Economic Strategy (AES).

'Thatcherism' entered the language, sloganizing a mixture of policy initiatives, a style of government in which central state power was used apparently to reduce that same central state power, and a populist approach to many deep-seated and deeply felt problems facing large numbers of citizens. Left-wing writers at the time highlighted the key features that made Thatcherism something distinctive in modern British history: anti-collectivism, including

---

[14] *NALGO Annual Report 1979*, 45–7.

[15] *PS* (Mar. 1979), 8–9.

[16] R. Bacon and W. Eltis, *Britain's Economic Problem: Too Few Producers* (London: Macmillan, 1976).

attacks on the so-called dependency culture;[17] arguments that 'the public sector is an unproductive burden on the wealth-creating sector in general and on taxpayers in particular';[18] that 'the chief aim of government economic policy should be maintaining price stability by firm control of the money supply';[19] and that trade unions should be hampered whenever possible from doing their job effectively.[20]

A few years later, after Margaret Thatcher's third and final election victory in 1987, there remained strong support for the view that 'the Conservative victory of 1979 represented an important break from the historic compromise of post-war Britain, a break organised and managed by the Right'.[21] This view was shared, more or less, by the left in the trade union movement. Thatcherism was seen as a virulent right-wing version of post-1945 Conservatism, dedicated to achieving both popular and capitalist aims of improving productivity and profitability, reducing the direct tax burden, keeping prices under control, and pursuing hard policies on law, order, defence, welfare, and international relations.

Inflation was one central issue: 'Over the course of her government she kept to the priority of reducing inflation above all else.'[22] Privatization was another: 'If control of inflation was the key economic objective during Thatcher's first government, privatization became the central goal during the second.'[23] The Tories had already announced, at their 1978 conference, a policy of hiving off NHS support services, based on a recommendation from the Conservative Medical Society under the influence of the head of a private American medical company. Within a few weeks of the election there were some early signs of government plans: 'Sir Keith Joseph's thoughts on denationalisation are reported to take in the hiving off/merger of electricity and gas showrooms where NALGO members work. The extensive sale of council houses and proposed curbs on local authority direct works departments are both contrary to NALGO policy.'[24] Industry Secretary Joseph's credentials as an anti-union and anti-nationalized industry crusader were confirmed

---

[17] S. Hall, 'The Great Moving Right Show', in S. Hall and M. Jacques (eds.), *The Politics of Thatcherism* (London: Lawrence & Wishart, 1983), 27–34.

[18] A. Gamble, 'Thatcherism and Conservative Politics', in Hall and Jacques (eds.), *The Politics of Thatcherism*, 114.

[19] Ibid. 115.

[20] T. Lane, 'The Tories and the Trade Unions: Rhetoric and Reality', in Hall and Jacques (eds.), *The Politics of Thatcherism*, 169–87.

[21] B. Schwarz, 'The Thatcher Years', in *Socialist Register 1987* (London: Merlin Press, 1987), 118.

[22] M. Holmes, *The First Thatcher Government 1979–1983* (Boulder, Colo.: Westview Press, 1985), 50.

[23] E. Evans, *Thatcher and Thatcherism* (London: Routledge, 1997), 34.

[24] *PS* (June 1979), 8.

early in 1980 with his intransigent handling of the steel dispute.[25] NALGO leaders were right to fear this latter-day class avenger: 'The Joseph period at the DoI did in fact see the first steps towards what became known as privatisation.'[26]

The new government argued that state finances had to be balanced in order to reduce inflation: 'the Conservative government came into office with a clear policy to cut public expenditure and to reduce state intervention.'[27] Ronald Reagan won his 1980 US presidential election on a similar platform. Both Thatcher and Reagan argued for a reduced state role in economic policy, with the result that 'income inequality increased sharply in both countries in the 1980s'.[28] Mrs Thatcher was quite clear about the public policy implications: 'Because our analysis of what was wrong with Britain's industrial performance centred on low productivity and its causes—rather than on levels of pay—incomes policy had no place in our economic strategy.'[29] For her, trade unionism itself was a cause of low productivity: 'We also had to deal with the problem of trade union power, made worse by successive Labour governments and exploited by communists and militants who had risen to key positions within the trade union movement.'[30]

The government's main targets for reducing its expenditure were heralded in Geoffrey Howe's budget, which cut public spending by £1.6 billion and prepared to sell state assets worth £1 billion. These cuts paved the way for the other part of the strategy, tax cuts: 'At the heart of this first Budget, we had one overriding question to resolve: how and how far should we implement our central, well-trailed promise of significant improvements in incentives at all levels—by means, of course, of substantial cuts in the income taxes?'[31] In another repressive policy move, Michael Heseltine, Secretary of State for the Environment, announced cash limits and a post freeze in local government. There were to be real cuts in expenditure in health and education too. The utilities—gas, water, electricity, and some parts of transport—would be allowed to continue their day-to-day industrial relations but under the increasingly vocal threat of privatization.

Michael Heseltine argues that 'by 1979 local government had become a barely controllable free-wheeling employment machine which for year after

---

[25] M. Halcrow, *Keith Joseph: A Single Mind* (London: Macmillan, 1989), 138–9.

[26] Ibid. 142.

[27] K. Andrews and J. Jacobs, *Punishing the Poor: Poverty under Thatcher* (London: Macmillan, 1990), 3.

[28] P. Pierson, *Dismantling the Welfare State? Reagan, Thatcher and the Politics of Retrenchment* (Cambridge: Cambridge University Press, 1994), 5.

[29] M. Thatcher, *The Downing Street Years* (London: Harper Collins, 1993), 93.

[30] Ibid. 97.   [31] G. Howe, *Conflict of Loyalty* (London: Macmillan, 1994), 128.

year had been run largely for the benefit of the machine-minders'.[32] Cuts were about much more than simply cutting expenditure: 'By cutting state spending the government help to make room for tax cuts, allow interest rates to fall, help to curb inflation and, more philosophically, to reduce the role of the state in society as a whole.'[33]

The Monetarists Bare their Teeth

NALGO started 1980, its seventy-fifth year of existence, with its financial accounts in a shaky condition as campaigning and industrial action took their toll on resources. While trying to rein in some areas of expenditure, the union was also faced with the daunting prospect of pressing forward with the members' claims and with sustaining its opposition to government on many fronts in many industries. This was a giant task, but the consequences of not acting would be even more damaging to both the union and its members. Geoffrey Drain's New Year message called for 'strong actions' against the cuts: '1980 must be the year in which we all become protagonists for and activists in defence of our welfare state and our trade unions.'[34]

Using the full panoply of state organs, and supportive news media, the government started to articulate its legislative programme to restructure British economic and social life, while also invoking the notion of a return to some mythical glorious Victorian past. This was never rooted in any actually existing traditional past; it was rather a shadow of a less than wonderland American dream. Right-wing economic theories, as represented by the arguments of Friedrich von Hayek[35] and Milton Friedman,[36] provided ideological support for the government's attacks on the public services and on the unions.

Put simply, the monetarist position is that there is a fixed amount of money available for wages at any given time. This means that higher wages can only be distributed among fewer employees, as there is a direct trade-off between jobs and pay. In other words, if you wanted to keep jobs then you had to keep pay awards low. Monetarist dogma was promoted through simplistic notions of maintaining balanced books, staying out of debt, and not paying ourselves more than we can afford.

---

[32] M. Heseltine, *Where There's a Will* (London: Hutchinson, 1987), 43.

[33] P. Riddell, *The Thatcher Government* (Oxford: Blackwell, 1985), 105.

[34] NALGO, *Stop the Cuts Action Bulletin*, no. 11, 3 Jan. 1980 (London: NALGO).

[35] F. von Hayek, *The Road to Serfdom* (London: Routledge, 1944); F. Hayek, *1980s Unemployment and the Unions* (London: IEA, 1984).

[36] M. Friedman, *Free to Choose* (Harmondsworth: Penguin, 1980).

Following the logic through to its conclusion, trade unions can only be seen as a negative force—they bully employers into paying their members wages that are artificially inflated above their 'natural' level, thus causing inflation in the wider economy, reduced wages for non-union employees, and unemployment among the wider workforce. Lord Blake summarizes these main elements of Margaret Thatcher's policies: 'She intended to reverse the long-term decline of the economy by a policy of "monetarism", reduction in expenditure and taxation, curbing of union power, no subsidisation of "lame ducks", and "privatisation" of publicly owned industry. She was sceptical about the blanket provisions of the "welfare state". She was against "corporatism", "collectivism" and "Keynesianism".'[37] As she put it herself: 'Firm control of the money supply was necessary to bring down inflation. Cuts in public expenditure and borrowing were needed to lift the burden on the wealth-creating private sector.'[38]

There were some famous Tory dissidents who dismissed 'the distilled monetarist "frenzy" that swept through much of the Conservative party', and rejected two of its central assumptions—that inflation could be controlled through a reduction in the money supply, and that 'a market economy is fundamentally self-regulating'.[39] However, what they contemptuously despised as dogma had practical implications when it came to policy implementation[40]—for example, when Chancellor Geoffrey Howe's 1980 budget cut public expenditure by a further 4 per cent.

NALGO policy-makers were aware of the dangers, and constantly rebutted the monetarist arguments:

Our analysis of the March budget made even clearer the judgment of your Council that the Government's economic strategy was (and remains) fundamentally mistaken. The disincentive effects of taxation, the crowding-out of private sector output, the impact of the PSBR [public-sector borrowing requirement] on the money supply and the money supply on the rate of inflation are all shown to be of dubious validity, having neither firm theoretical nor empirical foundations. However, the Government seemed determined to follow their economic strategy even if it involved, in the words of the Chief Secretary to the Treasury: 'Three years of unparalleled austerity.' Your Council concluded that the short to medium-term prospects were bleak.[41]

Another monetarist anti-inflation measure came with the Employment Bill 1980, which set out to weaken the closed shop, and to restrict the ability

---

[37] R. Blake, *The Conservative Party from Peel to Thatcher* (London: Methuen, 1985), 337.

[38] Thatcher, *The Downing Street Years*, 41–2.

[39] I. Gilmour, *Dancing with Dogma: Britain under Thatcherism* (London: Pocket Books, 1992), 15.

[40] H. Young, *One of Us: A Biography of Margaret Thatcher* (London: Macmillan, 1991).

[41] *NALGO Annual Report 1980* (London: NALGO, 1981), 27.

of unions to mount lawful pickets and take lawful industrial action in solidarity with workers in dispute. NALGO's leaders attacked this Bill as a clear attempt to 'weaken trade unions and the protection they offer their members',[42] developing a position of opposing legal restrictions on trade-union organization and on trade-union action throughout the subsequent succession of new laws (see Box 5). The Tories had no doubts about the importance of restricting union activity. Norman Tebbit wrote proudly of his 1982 legislation: 'I have no doubt that Act was my greatest achievement in Government and I believe it has been one of the principal pillars on which the Thatcher economic reforms have been built.'[43] His view was shared by wet and dry Tories alike. For Francis Pym, 'the Government's approach to trades union legislation has been an outstanding success . . . the policy of gradual action to prevent abuses of union power has won consent from the country at large'.[44] And for Nicholas Ridley, 'the combined effect of these four statutes was to push the trade unions firmly back within a very tightly restricted framework of law'.[45]

At the 1980 NALGO conference, outgoing President John Meek told delegates: 'We have seen a massive and sustained campaign to denigrate and malign the public sector. Only recently, Environment Secretary Michael Heseltine vented his spleen in an attack on NALGO when he called us Luddites.'[46] Attacks on local government, transport, and the NHS were continued.

It was in these early days of the first Thatcher administration that the significance of the public sector to the Tory anti-inflation project began to emerge. The ultimate objective was to reduce public spending by changing the fundamental structures of the public sector, although the eventual scale of this was not immediately apparent. 'The Treasury and the Department of the Environment had two main priorities: first, to ensure that local government expenditure was contained within the overall targets for public spending; second to hold down increases in local rates in accordance with the Government's counter-inflation policy.'[47] The Local Government, Planning, and Land Bill started the process with its proposals to introduce business-like criteria for the management of council activities such as house repairs through directly employed labour. As Michael Heseltine later remembered, it was the introduction of MINIS (Management Information System for Ministers) that showed 'how slack the disciplines of the public sector had grown in compar-

---

[42] *PS* (Jan. 1980), 1.

[43] N. Tebbit, *Upwardly Mobile* (London: Weidenfeld & Nicolson, 1988), 184.

[44] F. Pym, *The Politics of Consent* (London: Hamish Hamilton, 1984), 12.

[45] N. Ridley, *My Style of Government* (London: Hutchinson, 1991), 15.

[46] *PS* (July 1980), 11.   [47] Riddell, *The Thatcher Government*, 127.

ison with those in the private sector'.[48] Under the Local Government Finance Act 1982 the Audit Commission was created to enforce central government's financial strictures. The unions were acutely aware of the dangers from the start: 'Government policies are designed to produce substantial job losses in local government.'[49]

In transport, the return of the bus and coach industry to the private sector started 'when the 1980 Transport Act abolished price control . . . [and] deregulated long-distance coach services'.[50] Norman Fowler's Transport Bill proposed opening up to private operators the entire system of municipal services that had been pioneered by the local authorities. As the Secretary of State remembered:

The 1980 Transport Act took all the action necessary to transfer the National Freight Corporation to the private sector and reform the Traffic Commissioner system so that new inter-city and commuter coach services could develop. . . . With the momentum of privatization established, I was able to argue successfully for further legislation. The 1981 Transport Act enabled private investment to be introduced.[51]

In the NHS the White Paper *Patients First*[52] proposed to replace the AHAs with the apparently more coherent District Health Authorities (DHAs). These proposals went hand in hand with efforts to use job evaluation to assess the work of nurses, an early warning of the wave of deskilling to come in later years. The White Paper proposed giving greater powers to managers at hospital level, believing a more efficient and effective service, releasing scarce resources for more patient care, would be the result.

The DHSS still referred to the importance of 'good personnel policies and practices . . . [and] proper consultation with staff interests',[53] but its attitude to industrial relations actually toughened, spelled out in the reactionary anti-union document *If Industrial Relations Break Down* (Health Circular HC (79) 20). This called for the use of strike-breakers: 'Authorities should, if they feel it necessary during a dispute, make use of volunteers as they think fit' (para. 9).

As part of its general belief in the need to incorporate private-sector business practices into public services, government planners started down three

[48] Heseltine, *Where There's A Will*, 21.

[49] D. Heald, 'Tory Policies towards the Public Sector', *Scottish Trade Union Review*, 7 (1979), 7.

[50] J. Hibbs, 'Privatization and Competition in Road Passenger Transport', in C. Veljanovski (ed.), *Privatization and Competition* (London: IEA, 1989), 161.

[51] N. Fowler, *Ministers Decide* (London: Chapmans, 1991), 133.

[52] DHSS, *Patients First: Consultation Paper on the Structure and Management of the NHS in England and Wales* (London: DHSS, 1979).

[53] Ibid. 16.

related routes: measuring public-service performance; forcing public-service managers to subcontract work to the private sector even if they believed it was against the public interest; and increasing involvement of management consultants. So, as well as interfering in the pay-determination process, the government was developing other new methods of centralizing control over public services. One of the most significant was the use of performance indicators to establish league tables in local government, later used in the NHS and education. The government also supported the involvement of private companies in public services, encouraging employers to use the courts to force through changes associated with contracting-out of services. For example, a computer company involved in the NHS took action against NALGO in the High Court over an instruction to members not to cooperate with the firm's activities. As *The Times* law report noted, 'Health Computing Ltd, a newly formed company wishing to develop and market computer services in the health care area, failed in their application for an interim injunction to restrain NALGO from instructing branches not to cooperate with them.'[54]

Pay Bargaining—Business as Usual

Union negotiators submitted traditional pay claims through Whitley in 1979 and 1980 despite the existence of the Clegg Commission and the arrival of the Conservatives. They drew on the five sets of traditional trade-union arguments.[55] Cost-of-living arguments are based on the idea that pay should at least keep up with the rate of inflation, usually defined by the rate of increase of the retail price index (RPI). Comparability arguments, known in the USA as 'me-too' claims, are based on the idea that pay should at least keep up with increases in earnings as measured by the average earnings index (AEI), and/or with specific named comparators. Of course, comparability was attacked by the Conservatives, who argued that public-sector workers should not expect a pay increase just because private-sector workers earn more, perhaps because of profit and/or productivity gains. Increasing public-sector pay without proportionate increases in performance was seen as economically dangerous and morally repugnant. Both types of argument, comparability and cost of living, are based on notions of fairness, on the extent to which pay is felt to be fair having regard to general increases in prices and wages. The main purpose of the argument is to articulate the justice of the members' case, to win their sup-

[54] *The Times*, 5 Mar. 1980, 14.
[55] B. Wootton, *The Social Foundations of Wage Policy* (London: Unwin University Books, 1962).

port for the claim, and to present a strongly supported claim to managers during negotiations.

The third set of arguments is based on increases in performance and/or productivity and/or workload. Here there are always problems of definition and measurement, but the general proposition is that, everything else being equal, workers should be rewarded for an increase in effort, especially if it also results in an increase in output.

The fourth line of argument is that of profitability and/or affordability. You can pay more because you can afford it, in the private sector because of increased profits and in the public sector because of increased budgets. However, linking pay to such variables as these can be double edged. Will union negotiators also accept pay cuts if performance falls and profits or budgets decline? In addition there are endless problems both with the measurement of these terms and, ultimately, even if we all agree that profits have risen, in establishing that there is a link between that and the workers' contribution. Why should the employer increase the pay of those who did not directly contribute to rising profits and productivity?

The fifth and final set of arguments is concerned with the state of the labour markets and the ability of the organization to recruit and retain the best mix of workers. In the short term it may be difficult for the organization to replace workers, substitute them with lower-skilled workers, or exchange them for machinery. Therefore, if there are staff shortages managers are under pressure to pay more and improve conditions to attract staff and retain them.

As the bargaining climate shifts, so does the balance of argument. Public-service union negotiators' reliance on comparability and cost-of-living arguments was tested. The process by which the union arrives at its position and pursues it can reflect the political tensions inside the union as well as the strategies of employers. Indeed, the entire bargaining round needs to be seen as a process of intense debate and deliberation inside the union. In NALGO's case the usual pattern was for negotiations, involving activists and full-time officials within the service group, to arrive at a common position within national policy guidelines. This was frequently tested out by consulting active members in the workplaces. Once agreed it would be presented to the employers through the relevant joint negotiating committee. Sometimes, as in the NHS, NALGO representatives had to negotiate further with other unions.

Once the claim was with the employers, there would be the ritual of counter-offer, breaks for consultation, and further negotiations. If the fall-back position of the two sides overlapped, then the expectation was for a settlement. If not, then the union national committee would sound out members over some form of industrial action. Three processes were therefore involved: an intensive period of intra-organizational bargaining within NALGO and the union sides, actual negotiations with the employers, and the threat and/or use of industrial action.[56]

The traditional line of argument over pay for public-sector workers was that there was no easy or obvious way in which to judge and measure their performance and their worth. Notions of value added seemed inappropriate and yet the public-sector wage bill was a large part of total public expenditure and was believed to have an impact on other macroeconomic variables such as the rate of inflation. In early 1979 the determination of public-sector pay became an acute economic and political issue, which still remains unresolved. At the time a majority of government decision makers were persuaded by a combination of some trade-union leaders and friendly experts that a scientific type of comparability study was both possible and credible. The attraction for a beleaguered Labour government was clear—here was a mechanism that at least appeared fair and free of government interference.

The Standing Commission on Pay Comparability was established in 1979, headed by Professor Hugh Clegg, a respected social-democratic pluralist from the academic world. Once the commission was operating, several key questions began to emerge: would the actual recommendations resolve long-standing pay demands and improve the lot of the workers; what impact might such settlements have on wider economic issues; and what was the basis for the alleged science behind comparing the work of a nurse, a teacher, a firefighter, an administrator, and a manager with jobs in the private sector?[57]

Many had grave doubts, including the TUC Public Services Committee: 'Four key problems were identified in relation to establishing comparability systems: identifying appropriate external comparisons; establishing arrangements to maintain them; avoiding the disruption of internal relativities; and clarifying the relationship of comparability studies to cash limits.'[58] The LRD found that Clegg awards were lower than those given by other review bodies; Clegg's methods were unsatisfactory and inconsistent; Clegg's awards worsened the plight of the low paid; and those receiving non-Clegg awards did better in both money and percentage terms.[59] An extensive survey by IDS showed that the pay position of public-sector employees improved relative to national averages until 1975, but worsened after 1979, whether they were referred to Clegg or not.[60]

[56] R. Walton and R. McKersie, *A Behavioral Theory of Labor Negotiations* (New York: McGraw Hill, 1967).

[57] IRS, 'Pay Comparability: The Standing Commission Reports', *Industrial Relations Review and Report*, 206 (1979), 2–5.

[58] *TUC Annual Report 1979* (London: TUC, 1980), 277.

[59] LRD, 'Goodbye, Mr Clegg', *Labour Research*, 69/9 (1980), 196–8.

[60] IDS, *Pay in the Public Sector*, study 263 (London: IDS, 1982), 4.

The relationship between the Clegg studies and the debate on incomes policies was, of course, close. Hugh Clegg had himself been intimately involved with both. The general argument was that wage rises pursued by organized labour to catch up with price rises fed a vicious circle—one person's pay rise was another's price rise. Incomes control was a temporary method of breaking the wage–price price–wage spiral to restore normality to wage demands and lower inflation. The economics behind this position were far from clear, but that did not deter government ministers and leading experts from proclaiming its truth. This matters, because, when incomes policies were implemented, under both Conservative and Labour governments, most public-sector workers did less well than others, even though all should have fared equally well/badly. Many post-mortems were held after the failure of each policy,[61] and in 1979 the Conservatives pledged to abandon such government interference in wage setting.

Many public-sector pay settlements for 1979–80 reflected the pressures of an election year, as well as the failures of incomes policies, and the adjustments of Clegg. The main claim was in local government, for 15 per cent from July. Mike Blick, chair of the national committee, said: 'There are many problems facing the negotiators this year, not least the attitude of the new government to public sector pay in general and further references to Professor Clegg's comparability commission in particular.'[62] The group accepted a rise of 9.4 per cent and the offer of a comparability study. A&C grades in the NHS accepted a settlement linked to Civil Service pay, and New Town staff accepted 9 per cent and £10 for comparability. BWB staff accepted 18 per cent and water staff 17 per cent. In the NHS PT'B' staff took 9 per cent now and 5 per cent later, and electricity agreed 12 per cent now and 8 per cent later (see Tables 2.5–2.15).

Disputes loomed in the gas and university sectors. Gas staff rejected a 16 per cent pay offer linked to job losses. As Dave Stirzaker noted, 'British Gas made record profits last year of £361m and the national gas committee felt there was no reason why the industry should not match the best pay settlements in the country.'[63] After threats of industrial action, a settlement was reached around the 16.5 per cent mark plus consolidation of productivity payments, and restructuring of clerical grades. A&C members in the universities rejected an 8.9 per cent offer and threatened action after the employers refused to go to arbitration. As Rita Donaghy said, 'the other groups in the university service have settled for much more than we have been offered',[64] and the NEC approved the group's first national strike. There was a one-day token strike

---

[61] H. Clegg, *How to Run an Incomes Policy, and Why We Made a Mess of the Last One* (London: Heinemann, 1971).

[62] *PS* (May 1979), 1.   [63] Ibid. (Sept. 1979), 7.   [64] Ibid. (Oct. 1979), 5.

with a rally in London, and other forms of selective action such as a ban on overtime and no cover for unfilled vacancies. Some employers, following both their instincts and government advice, took a hard line and suspended staff, including thirty-four at Warwick, ten at Swansea, and eight at Kent. This dispute ended with a 9.4 per cent rise and an agreed reference to the Clegg Commission.

NHS groups like the nurses and the members covered by the PT'A' and PT'B' Whitley Councils were furious with the low levels recommended by the Clegg Commission, and at the possibility of the recommendations being implemented in phases. They managed to persuade the government fully to fund the Clegg pay rises and to move towards a 37.5 hour week. Opposition to the government came from an unexpected quarter when professional staff mainly in single-profession unions not affiliated to the TUC took industrial action over pay awards. The professions allied to medicine (PAMs) were unhappy with Clegg's award of 15.4 per cent, and days of action followed on 27 March, 10 and 18 April. These early grumblings grew into a major dispute affecting the whole NHS two years later. One spin-off from the Clegg awards was the development of JCCs in hospitals and DHAs. Some discretion over employment issues was pushed down to DHA level, and this helped to develop local bargaining over the introduction of bonus schemes for A&C staff and over local changes to stand-by and on-call payments.[65]

When the Tories came to office there was a strong call to disband Clegg, but the leadership felt bound by its pledges: 'The government's early policy was made more difficult by the refusal to disavow the 1979 election pledge to respect the Clegg comparability awards, which continued into 1980 dispensing wage rises with regard to matters totally irrelevant to such crucial criteria as labour supply and demand.'[66] Lord Blake agrees: 'Matters were made worse by the Conservative promise during the election campaign to abide by the recommendations of Professor Clegg's Commission on pay comparability. This was an error bitterly and soon regretted.'[67]

Nevertheless, the new government had a clear view about the issue. When she disbanded Clegg, Prime Minister Margaret Thatcher said that '[public-sector] pay needs to be negotiated with full regard to the country's economic circumstances, to the need to improve the efficiency of the public services and to what the taxpayer and ratepayer can be expected to afford'.[68] For negotiators in the utilities she had this message:

---

[65] R. Seifert, *Industrial Relations in the NHS* (London: Chapman & Hall, 1992).
[66] Holmes, *The First Thatcher Government*, 69.   [67] Blake, *The Conservative Party*, 340.
[68] IRS, 'Doomed Comparability Commission Forecasts its Rebirth', *Industrial Relations Review and Report*, 231 (1980), 10.

As regards pay bargaining in the nationalized industries, we decided that the responsible ministers should stand back from the process as far as possible. Our strategy would be to apply the necessary financial discipline and then let the management and unions directly involved make their own decisions. But that would require progress in complementary areas—competition, privatization and trade union reform—before it would show results.[69]

This apparently non-interventionist view was short-lived:

The Thatcher administration started off with the view that, having set cash limits for the increase in money available for a particular programme, employers and trade unions should bargain within this constraint. . . . This turned out to be a hopelessly naive approach, which ignored the strength of centralized bargaining and of public-sector unions . . . Consequently two years were wasted in a series of bloody and fruitless battles . . . the initial problem was that the cash limits were implausible because of the Government's commitment to honour the awards made by the Clegg Commission on Pay Comparability.[70]

As a result by late 1980 the government recognized that it had to interfere more directly by putting pressures on senior managers to keep within cash limits by holding pay down and further to weaken the unions and the bargaining structures. The government rejected formal incomes policies, both because they had failed and because they were too Keynesian, and instead 'devoted a great deal of effort to convincing trade unionists that it would not finance pay increases by printing money'.[71]

The logic therefore remains inescapable—that unions, and especially those operating in the public sector, had to be controlled: 'Under Mrs Thatcher, Conservatives were more outspoken in blaming the unions for low productivity, overmanning, restrictive practices, and strikes, particularly in the public sector where the unions were often able to exploit their monopoly position.'[72] The Prime Minister had no doubt as to the enemy: 'Battle was to be joined over the next two years [1980–1] on three related issues: monetary policy, public spending and trade union reform.'[73] As Margaret Thatcher mobilized state power, she 'demonstrated how effectively the state could intervene by legislation which deprived workers of rights'.[74]

Under these difficult circumstances, NALGO and the other unions continued to engage with the employers in collective bargaining.

[69] Thatcher, *The Downing Street Years*, 32–3.

[70] Riddell, *The Thatcher Government*, 125.

[71] S. Dunn and M. Gregory, 'Chronicle: Industrial Relations in the United Kingdom, April–July 1980', *British Journal of Industrial Relations*, 18/3 (1980), 380.

[72] D. Kavanagh, *Thatcherism and British Politics* (Oxford: Oxford University Press, 1987), 237.

[73] Thatcher, *The Downing Street Years*, 123.   [74] Evans, *Thatcher and Thatcherism*, 370.

Local-government members took on their employers for reneging on the agreement on comparability to settle the 1979 pay claim, in their first ever experience of industrial action involving the entire membership (see Box 2). The establishment press took the opportunity to advertise the adverse consequences of union action on the public. *The Times* reported:

Industrial action by nearly 500,000 local authority white collar workers, aimed at halting the collection of rates, could lead to local councils facing severe financial difficulties. The first programme of national industrial action by town hall staff is to start immediately. Included in a wide-ranging series of sanctions by NALGO is the threat of disruption of Easter holiday flights from provincial airports.[75]

Box 2: NALGO and the Local-Government Comparability Dispute, 1980

The National Local Government Committee (NLGC) recommended a 1979 claim including a 15 per cent increase, additional increases based on comparability as promised to other public-sector groups, a thirty-five-hour week for all, one extra day's leave, and more long-service leave. Responding to calls for wider discussion of the claim they decided to call a special group meeting of delegates. This resulted in an agenda containing fifty-five amendments sent in by branches, including calls for a flat-rate increase rather than a percentage; for a mixture of a flat rate plus a percentage; for a percentage higher than fifteen; for additional fringe improvements; and for industrial action and/or further group meetings should the claim not be met.

At the group meeting in May, Dennis Reed, from Middlesex Polytechnic Branch, called for a flat-rate claim in order to win the support of the broad membership, arguing that the lower paid would take action only if they were to gain equal rewards for an equal sacrifice. The delegates voted heavily against the flat rate and the debate moved on to the straight percentage, with similar arguments about justice for the lower paid being made by opponents. This was rejected by a narrow majority on a card vote. Now the delegates discussed the options for mixed claims, with NLGC vice-chair Jim White arguing that they should be rejected because 'if you carry this amendment you wipe away any possibility of a comparability exercise'. In his view a straight percentage and the comparability argument were indivisible. A card vote saw a mixed claim voted down by a solid majority. The delegates finally agreed on the claim supported by the NLGC—15 per cent and a £60 minimum.

The debate highlighted the difficulty of building unity on pay within a membership encompassing wide pay differentials. Of the 472 branches represented at the meeting, 167 cast their card votes to reject the straight percentage and 246 against rejecting it (the remainder either divided their vote, spoilt it, or did not cast it). Clearly the opposition to the straight percentage was concentrated within the larger branches, where activist concerns about low pay were stronger.

---

[75] *The Times*, 12 Mar. 1980, 1.

On 6 July the NJC met and the employers made an offer of 9 per cent on the pay bill, including the costs of consolidating a £312 supplement and settling the social workers' strike (see Box 1), and a comparability study. This was improved to 9.4 per cent on all salary points, and the NLGC recommended acceptance to a group meeting on 27 July. The meeting accepted only one of thirty-five amendments for debate, from Knowsley, calling for rejection of the offer and an escalating campaign of industrial action. This would include one-day all-out strikes, selective strikes of key workers, lobbies and demonstrations, financed by a levy of the local government membership.

Mike Blick argued that the lessons of the social workers' strike and the London weighting dispute showed that only an all-out indefinite strike would be effective, and the membership would not want that, but few delegates were convinced by this line of argument. Jim White warned of the dangers of rejecting the offer, and losing a ballot on industrial action. The employers would return to the negotiations with more confidence. Furthermore, selective action among 450 different employers could leave groups of members isolated and vulnerable to being laid off or locked out. The delegates voted three to two to accept the offer.

The NJC set up a joint steering group to carry out the comparability study, which was based on comparisons of pay movements among comparable groups of workers over an agreed period of time. After several months' work the inevitable problems over interpretation of the data came to a head at the NJC on 18 February 1980. Arguing breach of faith by the employers, or, as Alan Jinkinson told us, 'the employers ratted on us twice', the unions rejected their offer and the NLGC asked the NEC to support a programme of industrial action. Immediate instructions were given to all local-government members to cease cooperation with outside consultants, contractors, and agency staff, and to black all work relating to the issue of rate demands. Eight days later another group meeting gave its support to a programme of action recommended by the NLGC, including a national one-day strike in April, rallies in districts and branches during working hours, withdrawal of cooperation with councillors, and an overtime ban. Branches were asked to set a voluntary levy of £1 per week on all members, and to identify groups of members willing to take strike or other disruptive industrial action. Mike Blick dismissed the employers' offer as 'a con-trick'. It amounted to 8 per cent of the pay bill, while the comparability data suggested it should be 14 per cent. The delegates gave resounding support for the NLGC's action.

This was the first ever national industrial action covering the entire local-government group. Jim White pointed out to us that 'it was the first time that most of the local government membership had actually taken any industrial action of any kind whatsoever'. Groups of members volunteered to strike, and there was determined resistance to management reprisals such as suspensions of those who refused to work normally. Air traffic controllers at municipal airports voted to strike over Easter. Ten days after the delegate meeting, with the action escalating and members demonstrating real anger at their betrayal, the employers returned to the negotiating table and conceded increases ranging from 9.5 per cent at the bottom of the scale to 18 per cent at the top, equivalent to 13 per cent on the pay bill, backdated to 1 January 1980.

The Thatcher era started with a resounding defeat for the local-government employers—when we interviewed Mike Blick he said 'I look upon the comparability action as one of the most successful pieces of industrial action the union had ever taken'.

The success of this campaign owed much to its origins. A long period of incomes policy had resulted in a general compression of wage differentials. Secondly, the exceptions built into some of the incomes policy mechanisms had discriminated against employees in the public services. For the APT&C staff, much of this discontent focused on differentials, as foretold with the 1977 group meeting vote calling for them to be restored. On the other hand, the cash limits imposed on local authorities by the Callaghan government and continued by Thatcher's were beginning to bite. The employers anticipated further budget cuts, and were already arguing that excessive pay rises would mean staffing cuts. However, there were deep divisions between the employers—at least thirty-eight of them were prepared to enter into local agreements that were better than the national offer.

Throughout the UK, many local authorities were giving tacit support to NALGO's case over comparability, particularly because the findings of the exercise had been so blatantly ignored by the Employers' Side. This was becoming more and more obvious . . . when several Scottish local authorities approached their individual NALGO branches with a view to reaching a locally negotiated settlement.[76]

As this was NALGO's first large-scale national action, it carried a number of lessons. In particular it emphasized the importance of a central strike operations room, staffed by national officers and publicity specialists. More dedicated telephone lines were needed, and finance staff should be present. There had been only a very few isolated cases of strike-breaking activity by members, but these showed that the union's disciplinary procedures needed speeding up.

Despite the show of strength in the NHS and the resounding success of the local-government comparability dispute, there were few other reasons to be cheerful. By the spring of 1980 the economic climate was bleak for NALGO's members and their negotiators. The rate of unemployment was nearly 7 per cent, and was soon to reach 10 per cent. The AEI remained much higher than government experts had predicted at nearly 19 per cent, and inflation was running at 20 per cent. This made the union's task of representing its 753,226 members so much harder (see Tables 3.1 and 3.2). Everywhere it turned the government was cutting, restructuring, and holding out. As TUC General Secretary Len Murray put it, 'the cuts have put the economy into a nosedive'.[77]

By the autumn of 1980 Mrs Thatcher's deflationary policies were working their way through the economic and social system, with 'the attention of pol-

[76] *NALGO Scottish District Council Annual Report 1980* (Glasgow: NALGO, 1981), 37.
[77] *PS* (Mar. 1980), 1.

icy makers increasingly turned towards further limitations on the public sector'.[78] So the more aggressive union claims of the early part of the year were yielding to the new economics and workers were revising their expectations of keeping their standard of living on the up. As the sands of bargaining power shifted, more cases went to arbitration, as neither side was sure about the strength of its position.

Arbitration was an integral part of the Whitley system, functioning as a means of resolving conflicts and avoiding large-scale disruption of essential public services.[79] National strikes are always possible under national multi-employer bargaining. For the monetarists, arbitration awards are inherently inflationary, as the arbitrators tend to split the difference between the employers and the unions. This represents an interference with the free operation of the labour market, as rates of pay are prevented from adjusting to the new market conditions of high unemployment. The government exhorted employers to resist arbitration and to make pay offers based on affordability and on labour-market conditions rather than on cost-of-living increases and comparability. Employers acting to avoid disputes by agreeing to arbitration passed these positions on to arbitrators, arguing their case on affordability. The government wanted to restrict access to arbitration by removing the right of either party to initiate it unilaterally, achieving this for schoolteachers in 1981, and indicating that it would act further in British Gas, the National Water Council, British Rail, and British Steel.[80]

NALGO wanted the local government employers' 1980–1 offer of 13 per cent in response to the 20 per cent claim to go to arbitration, but recognized that another round of industrial action might be an option to fulfil the aim of hanging onto the gains achieved from the comparability settlement. As Mike Blick argued, 'a 12 per cent offer in the face of a 21 per cent rise in the cost of living is an attempt by the employers to claw back our comparability increases'.[81] In November the CAC awarded 15 per cent on all spinal column points (13 per cent from July and 2 per cent from the next April) and improved holiday entitlements.[82] The panel's report expressed both its recognition of the employers' case and the need to make an award that would be acceptable to the unions: 'The committee has kept the question of the ability to pay very

[78] S. Dunn and M. Gregory, 'Chronicle: Industrial Relations in the United Kingdom, August–November 1981', *British Journal of Industrial Relations*, 19/1 (1981), 96.

[79] IRS, 'Arbitration as a Means of Settling Disputes, Part 1: The Public Sector', *Industrial Relations Review and Report*, 259 (1981), 2–7.

[80] *TUC Annual Report 1982* (London: TUC, 1983), 283.   [81] *PS* (Oct. 1980), 2.

[82] IRS, 'Local Government Staff Win 15% Arbitration Award', *Industrial Relations Review and Report*, 239 (1981), 10.

firmly in mind throughout its deliberations. We have also borne in mind the levels at which other local government groups have been settling.'[83]

Nurses and water staff put in claims for 30 per cent, and gas staff for 25 per cent, while university staff accepted 13.5 per cent and Clegg recommendations. New Towns talks broke down over a 12 per cent interim offer, and electricity managers were also in pay deadlock. Other electricity staff rejected an offer of 17 per cent.

NHS district works staff rejected a 13 per cent pay offer as too far below the rate of inflation, and *Public Service* reported that 'a programme of industrial action by health service administrative and clerical staffs was approved last month by NALGO's emergency committee. It had been drawn up by the national health committee in an attempt to stop the Government and NHS employers from breaking a 20-years-old agreement on pay links between A&C staffs and white collar civil servants'.[84] The national committee sought authorization for a one-day national strike, further one-day strikes, strikes of key workers, work to rule, ban on non-contractual overtime, no cover for unfilled vacancies, complete non-cooperation with commercial agency staff, and non-cooperation on reorganization with central government departments, on the introduction of new technology, and with employing authority meetings. All this was 'in view of the refusal of the management Side of the A&C Whitley Council to honour the traditional links which NHS A&C staffs have with the Civil Service'.[85] The newspapers were quick to comment:

Members of NALGO are proposing industrial action in the health service if the government sticks to the 14 per cent limit on pay increases . . . There was also strong criticism of the Government's refusal to continue the unofficial link with civil servants' pay which administrative and clerical staff have enjoyed over the last 20 years. This year Civil Service pay increases averaged 16.85 per cent.[86]

Fight the Cuts! Defend the Union!

The main thrust of the government's attack remained in local government, and the union firmed up its resistance, as *The Times* reported:

Mr Michael Heseltine, Secretary of State for the Environment, yesterday bitterly criticised NALGO for its decision to refuse to cooperate in providing staffing figures in local government. He said that the union's attitude saddened and depressed him. 'It

---

[83] *PS* (Dec. 1980), 2.   [84] Ibid. (Sept. 1980), 4.
[85] *NALGO Emergency Committee Meeting Minutes*, 9b (London: NALGO, 1980), 158.
[86] *The Times*, 9 June 1980, 3.

lies at the heart of this country's relative decline. It is typical of the negative and hostile, almost Luddite, attitude that so many people criticise local government for.'[87]

Already, the union had a well-established national policy to support local action against cuts:

An emergency motion was carried declaring NALGO's total opposition to the Government's plans to cut public expenditure and its determination to resist any proposals to undermine the public services. It went on to call for: support to branches taking industrial action to stop redundancies; monitoring of government proposals and wide dissemination of the positive case for public expenditure; vigorous collective action through the TUC; continuation of instructions to branches not to cover posts held vacant and to oppose the use of agency staff; non-cooperation with government legislation or instructions where additional financial provision was not made.[88]

The *Daily Telegraph* was happy to provide prominent coverage of the union's 'fight-the-cuts' message and its opposition to the elected government's policies: 'confrontation is likely over two issues . . . the first is a pay claim . . . The second is opposition to the government's proposed cuts in public spending.'[89] Two important documents reaffirmed union policy: *Public Expenditure—into the Eighties*, and, on the public accountability of spending plans, *Behind Closed Doors*.

But there seemed to be a rising tide of job losses. A thousand local-government members in Liverpool went on strike for two hours to lobby a meeting of the city council over job cuts. Somerset County Council announced the dismissal of all its 256 classroom assistants after warnings in the local press: 'Redundancies among education staff in Somerset are inevitable if the county council goes ahead with a seven and a half per cent cut in next year's budget.'[90] There was fierce opposition from the NUT and parent–teacher associations, and the NALGO branch wanted to support the seventy members involved by banning the processing of redundancies. Alan Jinkinson, national officer for local government, launched a charter for non-teaching staff, which aimed 'to compel local education authorities, NALGO branches, and non-teaching staff themselves, to recognise that all the paid staff in schools and colleges are as much employees of a local authority as any other officer and, as such, enjoy the rights conferred on them as union members by national and local agreements'.[91]

Disputes continued throughout 1980. Day-care workers in Camden walked out over low pay, winning the regrading of some posts after four weeks of action. London disputes were reported in *Met District News*. Andy

[87] Ibid., 10 May 1980, 2.   [88] *NALGO Annual Report 1979*, 37.
[89] *Daily Telegraph*, 12 June 1979, 2.   [90] *Western Morning News*, 12 Sept. 1979, 7.
[91] *PS* (Dec. 1979), 2.

Batkin of Wandsworth Branch wrote in the June issue about Wandsworth council: 'After a short but bitter confrontation, Wandsworth NALGO celebrated May Day having forced a complete management backdown over the decision to lock out thirty-nine housing management assistants for refusing to cover for axed posts.' The July edition reported on the strike by Islington Council's building works department staff over the sacking of a foreman painter, and on the successful four-week strike in Merton Council's housing department over suspension of NALGO members for placing an embargo on some activities in support of their claim for improved conditions of service. As the *Morden News* reported, 'nobody ever wins on a strike action . . . but it was a victory in as much as the employers were shown that local government workers are not as easy meat as they thought'.[92]

September's *Met District News* reported on yet more industrial action, by 115 Ealing Council day-care workers. They banned admissions, blacked all work with agency staff, adhered to strict staff–client ratios, and stopped all administrative returns in their aim for regrading, non-use of agency staff, and improved staffing levels.[93] One consequence was a rapid deterioration in previously good relations with management: 'Social workers are warning of a mass walkout if disciplinary action is taken against anyone involved in sanctions over pay. Officials of the National and Local Government Officers Association involved in the industrial action claim Social Services Director Mr Ken Anderson threatened to discipline ten senior day care centre managers who refused to attend a meeting.'[94] Another factor in this dispute was the widespread local support, which was significant because of the limited industrial power of the strikers and also because it was local people who would be worst affected. Securing support from the local community became a hallmark of NALGO action.

Examples of other local opposition to restructuring and underfunding in local government include blacklisting jobs at Trafford Metropolitan Borough over redundancies, a dispute at Kent social services over the closure of residential homes, and industrial action in Newcastle over use of disciplinary procedures against a NALGO member for refusing to cover unfilled posts in line with union policy. In this case the Emergency Committee agreed 'retrospective approval be given to the action of certain members in the Recreation Department in stopping work for one hour to attend a meeting'.[95] This was a typical example of the union's flexible and practical approach to the realities of local industrial relations in circumstances when ballots were inappropriate.

[92] *Morden News*, 6 June 1980, 5.
[93] *NALGO Emergency Committee Meeting Minutes*, 9b (1980), 228–9.
[94] *Ealing Gazette*, 1 Apr. 1980, 1.
[95] *NALGO Emergency Committee Meeting Minutes*, 9a (1980), 91.

Wandsworth Elderly People's Homes
are no place for private firms

Published by Wandsworth NALGO, Municipal Buildings, Wandsworth SW18 2PU on behalf of Elderly People's Homes Defence Campaign and printed by Centurion Print Ltd.

NALGO says:
if Blackpool's bins go private

you'll throw away
more than rubbish

Published by NALGO, 1 Mabledon Place, London WC1H 9AJ.
Printed by the Co-operative Press Ltd, 158 Buckingham Palace Road, London SW1 (PD/82/304/10,000)

Is this how you saw your career in the health service?

The way things are going it will not be long before the NHS is run like a supermarket. Already, private firms are being invited to make money out of running parts of the NHS. And the Government is undermining the service still further by:

■ keeping the NHS short of cash;
■ cutting the number of staff.

NALGO is campaigning in all ways to protect your job and to stop the erosion of the NHS by fighting cuts, private medicine and 'privatisation'.

DEFEND THE NHS WITH NALGO

Published by NALGO, 1 Mabledon Place, London WC1H 9AJ
Printed by Centurion Press Ltd. PD/84/88/10,000

DON'T LET WHITEHALL TAKE OVER YOUR TOWN HALL

KEEP
LOCAL GOVERNMENT
LOCAL

PUT PEOPLE FIRST.

nalgo

Published by NALGO
1 Mabledon Place, London WC1H 9AJ
and printed by Centurion Print Ltd.
PO/84/227/20,000

PROFITEERS KEEP OUT!

No private profit from public need

PUT PEOPLE FIRST.

nalgo

Published by NALGO, 1 Mabledon Place, London WC1H 9AJ
Printed by Centurion Print Ltd. (Hertford)
PD/84/299/30,000

British Gas
and your Future
Under the Hammer

Stop the Gas sell-off
Vote `Yes´ in the ballot

nalgo

BREAK FREE OF LOW PAY

NALGO
-FIGHTING FOR FAIR PAY IN THE NHS

Published by NALGO, 1 Mabledon Place, London WC1H 9AJ Printed by The JASON PRESS Ltd. PD/86/20/38

CAUTION
ELECTRICITY
PRIVATISATION

The government is going to privatise electricity. Overnight, your industry will become a high risk business, with job security and service conditions in the firing line.

NALGO

In other cases, such as Kent Branch's non-cooperation with social services cuts, the Emergency Committee insisted on a ballot and then authorized action after there was a two-to-one majority in favour.[96]

As 1980 came to a close, NALGO branches in London were fighting cuts in Hillingdon, Tower Hamlets, and Lewisham, and in the Eastern District *Edlines* reported attacks on job cuts in Cambridgeshire and action by non-teaching staff in Bedfordshire schools. All 1,700 members of Knowsley Branch walked out after disciplinary action was taken against a member for refusing to cooperate with management consultants looking at the work of housing staff. Over 700 staff walked out of the housing department in Manchester, as explained in a letter from the NALGO branch to the local press:

Our members are on strike not because they oppose redeployment but that 10 of their colleagues have been summarily dismissed for refusing to do two persons work by not covering vacant posts. This is national policy for MATSA, NUPE and NALGO, the principal unions involved in the dispute. Although sufficient funds are available to recruit replacement staff, management have deliberately provoked an unnecessary confrontation.[97]

This wave of traditional trade-union activity, the classic response to exploitation in the workplace, was relatively new to members and activists alike, and it represented an important stage in the union's development. White-collar public-service workers were applying sanctions against their workplace managers just as generations of other workers had done before them—when employees come under attack then their trade unions fight back, over the bargaining table when they can, and through industrial action where necessary and possible. While learning how to do this, they were also evolving new forms of workplace struggle to suit their particular situation as public-service workers, and this was reflected in the development of the union's action as well as its broader policies. NAG produced a pamphlet *Fighting the Cuts*, which set out the various forms of action, such as non-cooperation, no cover, overtime bans, occupations, boycotting new technology, and going on strike. As they pointed out, 'more and more NALGO members are being forced to go on strike to defend services, living standards and jobs. During the last couple of years, there have been strikes by social workers, typists, telephonists, residential workers and admin workers amongst others.'[98]

Policy moved forward at the 1980 conference, encouraging branches to take a tougher line on local action against local cuts. Jim White, chair of the NLGC, argued that 'it was logical that if NALGO was running a campaign to

[96] Ibid. 88.
[97] Letter from S. Kukalowicz to *Manchester Evening News*, 12 Nov. 1980, 14.
[98] Nalgo Action Group, *Fighting the Cuts* (London, NAG, 1980), 10.

convince the public that it was their services and their standard of living that was at risk, then it should show itself prepared to take industrial action in defence of those services'.[99] *The Times* noticed this policy development: 'Britain's fourth largest union yesterday launched a campaign of opposition to the Government's public expenditure cuts and made a commitment to take industrial action in defence of services. The traditionally moderate NALGO came out against the cuts in principle and not only in cases where union members' jobs were affected.'[100]

NALGO Gets Political

The 1980 conference debated the causes and consequences of public-sector cuts, and how to develop both industrial and political methods to oppose them. NEC member Ivan Beavis supported a successful call for reductions in arms spending, noting that, 'at this time of deep economic decline, the Government has embarked on a policy of aggression towards the Soviet Union and a massive increase in the amount of money spent on arms'.[101] One issue remained unresolved: 'An attempt to put an end to NALGO's continuing adherence to a form of incomes policy was easily defeated after NEC speakers had made it clear that the policy was in abeyance for the time being because it was impossible to pursue with the present government.'[102]

The union was in tune with the rest of the trade-union movement on the main issues of 1980. On 9 March 3,000 members lined up behind NALGO's banner to join up to 100,000 others, including striking steel workers, in the TUC's march from Hyde Park to a rally in Trafalgar Square in London, demonstrating against cuts and the anti-union Employment Bill. Members supported another TUC day of action on 14 May at 130 separate rallies. Geoffrey Drain called for 'a day of all-out action' against government policies: 'An alternative strategy must be adopted based on economic growth stimulated by expansion of the public sector and the regeneration of manufacturing industry through increased public and state participation.'[103] The Labour Party also piled in, holding a demonstration on 29 November in Liverpool against unemployment and cuts attended by over 100,000, including nearly 2,500 NALGO members.[104]

These actions, driven by the sheer scale of government reforms, reactivated debate within the union over affiliation to the Labour Party and, more real-

---

[99] *PS* (July 1980), 3.   [100] *The Times*, 12 June 1980, 2.
[101] *PS* (July 1980), 5.   [102] Ibid. 4.
[103] NALGO, *Stop the Cuts Action Bulletin*, no. 17, 23 Apr. 1980.
[104] Ibid., no. 27, 3 Dec. 1980.

istically, over a political fund. National leaders began to put the case: 'The arguments for establishing a political fund are that NALGO by its very nature is a political organisation and may be hampered in the pursuit of members' interests.' The NALGO in the Eighties Committee argued simply that 'the general approach of the Labour Party towards the public services, social welfare, industrial regeneration and trade union rights is far closer to NALGO's position than that of any other political party' (see Box 9).[105]

NALGO was having to come to terms with one of the central tensions within trade unions. On the one hand, they have the unique function as organizations that negotiate with employers over pay and conditions of service, dealing with issues both collectively and as individual cases. On the other hand, particularly for those in the public sector, the environment in which such bargaining takes place is itself determined by the political economy of the industry, the country, and the government. Therefore unions also engage in some form of activity to influence the political decision-makers, to gain access to the opinion-formers, and to confront the controllers of funds. Both negotiating with employers to secure rights through collective bargaining *and* dealing with government and other parts of the state to secure wider economic, political, and social rights is part of union business. Thus political action and collective bargaining can become closely intertwined, as in the 'social-contract' period of 1974–8. More traditionally, wider political action either is left alone or is dealt with at arm's length through political parties that act mainly, but not only, in the interests of unions and their members—usually, in Britain, the Labour Party.[106] As we argued in Chapter 1, any activity that contributes, one way or another, to the success of the core bargaining method is of paramount importance to the union's success and survival, and therefore is subjected to intense internal debate and discussion.

NALGO was often characterized as 'non-political', but in fact it had long practised the art of political lobbying. By the summer of 1979 union relationships with the government were broken, and political activity shifted towards raising membership awareness of social and economic objectives. By this time Geoffrey Drain had been made chairman of the Public Services Committee at its first meeting on 30 January 1979. The TUC had set this up to look at issues of public-service expenditure, funding, and pay.[107] After Geoffrey Howe's emergency budget in September 1979, NALGO launched the 'Stop the Cuts' campaign to attack the government's economic policy. A regular bulletin provided information for branches on cuts proposed or made by employers, on union responses, and on union anti-cuts action and

[105] *PS* (May 1980), 8–9.
[106] D. Sassoon, *One Hundred Years of Socialism* (London: Fontana Press, 1996).
[107] *TUC Annual Report 1979*, 276.

propaganda materials. The first bulletin reported on industrial action in eight branches, including Sheffield, where 350 members stopped work to join a 1,000-strong protest when Environment Secretary Michael Heseltine toured their city.[108] Liverpool City Council's personnel subcommittee voted to give employees the day off with pay to attend the anti-cuts march and lobby of Parliament on 28 November,[109] where 50,000 people took part, including 2,500 NALGO members behind the national banner.[110]

At the 1979 Annual Congress in Blackpool TUC General Secretary Len Murray attacked privatization and anti-union laws. The TUC's Campaign for Economic and Social Advance, based on an analysis linked to the AES, argued the case for five key points: first, ensure growth in both employment and output, supported by import controls and building on the benefits of North Sea oil and gas; secondly, modernize through technological change, with reduced working time and improved industrial democracy; thirdly, introduce progressive taxation rather than a high rate of VAT, to secure price stability and a national consensus on the distribution of income and wealth; fourthly, use the public services to generate economic activity and reduce inequality; and, fifthly, promote public enterprise, public investment, and public ownership.[111] Supporting a composite moved by Geoffrey Drain, the Congress was concerned that government policy would 'result in a society with private affluence for the fortunate and public squalor for the majority'.[112]

Geoffrey Drain moved the main TUC motion on public expenditure at the 1980 Annual Congress, rejecting the government's economic strategy and continuing the Campaign for Economic and Social Advance. He lambasted the 'extremist Government of the far right', identifying the divisions that resulted from its policies—rich against poor, employed against unemployed, private industry against public, region against region.[113] *Public Service* included a supplement published by the TUC:

The squeeze on local authority spending is now beginning to have a devastating effect on services and jobs up and down the country. . . . At the same time as the Government has stoked up inflation to more than 20% it has only allowed local authorities a 13% increase in spending. As a result of these backdoor cuts of hundreds of millions of pounds the quality of local services is deteriorating rapidly.[114]

The campaign statement continues: 'In the midst of all this gloom, there is one important sign for hope. Broad-based Anti-Cuts Committees are now

---

[108] NALGO, *Stop the Cuts Action Bulletin*, no. 1, 29 Oct. 1979.
[109] Ibid., no. 3, 2 Nov. 1979.   [110] Ibid., no. 9, 29 Nov. 1979.
[111] *TUC Annual Report 1979*, 513.   [112] *PS* (Oct. 1979), 13.
[113] *TUC Annual Report 1980* (London: TUC, 1981), 467–8.
[114] *PS* (Sept. 1980), TUC extract, 1.

receiving considerable support, in hundreds of different localities.'[115] Even the establishment press picked up this important development, with an uncanny forecast of its eventual outcome:

Tentative steps are being taken towards forging a link between three public sector unions in an attempt to oppose together the Government's public expenditure cuts. The latest development in a continuing series of talks involving NALGO, NUPE and COHSE has been encouragement by COHSE to approaches made by NUPE officials. The long-term aim among officials of the unions is an alliance, possibly in the form of a federation, between the three unions, which would produce a formidable public sector union of nearly 1.7 million members.[116]

This was in 1980!

Building Unity and Common Cause

The sheer scale of activity within the union had several consequences for internal organization, raising questions of resource allocation, democratic practice, and the protection of the more vulnerable sections of the membership. More and more members were drawn into sporadic battles affecting their industry, their employer, their department, or their workplace, like an endless guerrilla warfare fought in some murky terrain. These struggles sent shafts of light into the darkness, revealing the underlying conflict in the employment relationship and demonstrating the importance of trade-union organization. Fighting on so many fronts, the union needed to maintain both national coherence and local support.

Public-sector union cooperation took in both national and local issues. NALGO members were instructed not to cross a NUT picket line in Nottingham during a dispute over class sizes, and there was support for the Isle of Grain action against redundancies in the CEGB. The North West and North Wales District paper, *News NoW*, reported on spending cuts in the power industry, and on financial support for the steel workers under threat from government policy towards the British Steel Corporation. This combination of local action against government cuts and local backing by NALGO for other groups involved in similar disputes with the government was a major aspect of the political battles within the union. It is certainly arguable that these types of actions were essential, but nevertheless they began to open old divisions within the union and to hint at new ones. Tory members wrote to *Public Service* to complain about attacks on government policy, and other sectional and factional interests started to concern themselves with the direction of policy

---

[115] Ibid. 4.   [116] *The Times*, 2 June 1980, 2.

and action. The political and ideological content of internal debate was greatly sharpened under these conditions, and the potential for division was graphically demonstrated later, by the special conference in 1984, over donations to the striking mineworkers' hardship fund (see Box 6).

Tensions emerged over the conduct of disputes, and this prompted activists to re-examine the union's industrial action procedures.[117] Although there had been disagreements over the social workers' strike in 1979, the NEC report 'contains no recommendations for radical changes in NALGO rules and regulations governing such procedures'.[118] The NEC did not agree that the rules themselves hindered industrial action, arguing that the procedures neither prevented members from becoming militant nor did they prevent action from being effective. The line presented was a balance between too much central restriction preventing effective action and too loose arrangements allowing doomed action to weaken both sections of the membership and the integrity of the national union.

Such was the union's operational structure that these differences could create delays and divisions more readily than in some highly centralized and less democratic unions. Internal tensions were fought out in several places, and they did constrain policy developments. Furthermore, the ways in which NALGO's stretched resources should be deployed and used were neither clear nor simple. Previously it had been assumed that the union would continue to grow and would remain a unitary organization, but that was now under scrutiny by the NALGO in the Eighties Committee: 'We have a common interest as public service employees with roughly comparable jobs. However, in pay and conditions, each service increasingly sets its own pace in its own way. NALGO faces inevitable transformation into a federal union in which the differences are recognised but the common strength in dealing with major economic matters will count for more.'[119] Recognition by national leaders of the importance of subgroups triggered a debate on the role of district committees in negotiations and disputes, and each district committee was urged to review its own representativeness and its dissemination of decisions. Mike Blick's position was this: 'I personally am dedicated to the principle of open government in NALGO.'[120] However, the need for discipline and control that is necessary to win strikes can cut across such openness, and as the amount of industrial action escalated the issue became more urgent. The NEC's position on procedures for calling action was opposed by many,

---

[117] IRS, 'Survey of Union Strike Rules, Part 1: Authorisation and Procedure for Calling Industrial Action', *Industrial Relations Review and Report*, 276 (1982), 2–12; IRS, 'Union Strike Rules, Part 2: Strike Pay, Strike Committees and Disciplinary Rules', *Industrial Relations Review and Report*, 279 (1982), 2–9.

[118] *PS* (Apr. 1980), 10.　　　　[119] Ibid. (Jan. 1980), 2.　　　　[120] Ibid. 5.

including Birmingham local-government branch representative Max Bowen, who argued at conference that 'we are more concerned with the dozens of local disputes for which basic guidelines are still needed'.[121]

These debates highlighted some of the dynamics of trade unionism. Whatever the circumstances, union activists fight to assert the rights of members through collective bargaining over whatever issues are practically presented by the everyday life of employment. As new concerns emerge, so this raises questions about how the union should respond and about the development of new policies. This is achieved by the establishment of campaigning movements *within* the union, as policy development is pushed forward in the teeth of opposition and delay. One of the most important movements was that encompassing the general notion of fighting discrimination against certain categories of members and workers. In general this meant the development of policies, organizational structures, actions, and awareness around the needs, fears, and demands of women, ethnic minorities, disabled workers, lesbians, and gay men.

Women activists were fighting their way into the union mainstream, although a motion from the Metropolitan District Council for NALGO to end its boycott of the women's TUC was rejected: 'Your council feels that the TUC women's conference no longer serves any useful purpose and by its divisiveness acts against the best interests of the trade union movement as a whole' (see Box 11).[122] Women activists on the National Equal Opportunities Committee (NEOC) concentrated on defining and agitating for policy and procedures on concrete issues such as childcare and sexual harassment.[123] Some of this was based on the report on the 400 branch responses to a survey, which concluded that women were still proportionately under-represented in union activity and that 'their lack of involvement at the general level may mean that issues pertinent to the working conditions of women in particular, are not being brought to the attention of the branch executive'.[124] One consequence was the issuing by NEOC of advisory pamphlets for negotiators—for example, the one on *Workplace Nurseries*.

NALGO supported the formation of Nalgay, almost alone in the trade-union movement in declaring support for the rights of gay members. More broadly, low pay and the cuts were having a disproportionate impact on women, part-timers, disabled, and black members, and their struggles both drew support from the union and fed into its development: 'The TUC model equality clause has now been incorporated into national agreements in all

---

[121] *PS* (July 1980), 4.   [122] *NALGO Annual Report 1980*, 160.

[123] NALGO, *Sexual Harassment is a Trade Union Issue* (London: NALGO, 1980).

[124] NALGO, *Equal Rights Survey: Preliminary Results of the NALGO 1979 Branch Survey Prepared for the 1980 Annual Conference* (London: NALGO, 1980), 16.

services. The main task of the Committee during 1979 was, therefore, the development and negotiation of equal opportunities policies to put flesh on the bones of national statements of intent.'[125] However, these mild improvements also revealed both the limitations of the law, a lesson with very wide implications, and the difficulty of pushing up the agenda the issues that mattered most in these struggles.

Self-organized pressure groups within NALGO shared the objective of reducing inequality, but they were not always united either between or within themselves as to how best to pursue this. What was becoming clear was that fighting inequality was immediately relevant to a very substantial proportion of the membership. Furthermore, it raised a set of very difficult practical issues, including the attitudes of many members, the establishment of bargaining objectives, the suitability of existing union structures, and, not least, the establishment of some consensus as to the *causes* of inequality.

At the level of the workplace the union took up issues affecting both small groups and individual members. It acted after the smallpox incident at Birmingham University in which Professor Shooter's official report commented on 'bad laboratory practices and ineffective controls'.[126] It fought an important unfair dismissal case over a librarian who had been sacked when her employer, the ILEA, discovered that she had epilepsy. This was just one of over 2,300 personal cases taken up by NALGO's legal department that year. Another was in Dorset to win an improved pay deal for six medical receptionists under a 'schedule 11' claim for pay parity, resulting in many more joining the union. Such cases, while always intensely individual in nature, illustrate how individual workers' needs and aspirations are realized through the strength of collective action and union support. They also provide evidence of the common experience of work throughout all the industries and occupational groups represented by NALGO. Fighting one case within a trade-union context with any given employer is always fighting the collective case, learning lessons, putting down markers, and creating the collective awareness of the variety and subtlety of struggle itself. These classic cases of traditional trade-union virtues illustrate well the power of persuasion through deeds.

The union also took up the fight internationally. Economic depression in the UK in 1979–80 reflected a wider international crisis built on the financial dominance of American banks and the imperialist ambitions of the US government. Here was the source of a worldwide dogma of strict monetarist economics enforced by political repression. Extremely dangerous developments in Iran followed the ousting of the dictatorial Shah, and the world order was

---

[125] *NALGO Annual Report 1979*, 40.   [126] *PS* (Feb. 1979), 5.

plunged into further crisis as the USA under Ronald Reagan reacted aggressively to Sandinista rule in Nicaragua and to the Soviet Union's intervention in Afghanistan. The mood for more arms and more support for dictatorships was encouraged in the USA when hostages were taken in Iran, and the climate deteriorated in the UK with the IRA killings of Airey Neave and later Earl Mountbatten. The UK government was happy to increase public expenditure on defence, apparently ignoring its own economic warnings about public expenditure when it was related to foreign policy. Alliance with the USA meant a UK government supporting counter-revolution in the world, and promoting a more reactionary set of policies at home.[127] In South Africa, for example, apartheid took comfort from its friends in the UK and US governments determined to hold this economically and militarily strategic land for their interests against the claims of the majority. Margaret Thatcher openly admired Chile's military dictator General Pinochet, leader of the CIA-supported *coup* that ousted the democratically elected government of the left in September 1973, killing president Salvatore Allende. Thousands of Chilean citizens, including trade unionists, disappeared during the ensuing fierce suppression of resistance. Closer to home, state employers in West Germany were dismissing communists and other left activists under the policy of *Berufsverbot*.

NALGO's expanding international activity reflected this intensification of oppression, lending real practical support and commitment to freedom in these distant and not so distant countries—their struggle was NALGO's struggle. In this the activists and most of the leadership agreed, although large sections of the members were either uninterested or unconvinced. Nonetheless, this activity, which was both highly visible in some respects and politically sensitive and sophisticated in others, gave the union a unique internationalist dimension of activity beyond the usual formal participation in international networks of like-minded union officers in world and European confederations.

Concluding Remarks

The year 1980 ended with the economic crisis reaching new depths: unemployment was at 10 per cent and rising. The government announced a 6 per cent limit on all public-sector pay, despite some opposition from civil-service unions to the suspension of the Pay Research Unit, and another £1 billion

---

[127] R. Miliband, 'Freedom, Democracy and the American Alliance', in *Socialist Register 1987* (London: Merlin Press, 1987), 480–501; E. Hobsbawm, *Age of Extremes: The Short Twentieth Century 1914–1991* (London: Michael Joseph, 1994).

was lopped off public expenditure. The union's worst fears were beginning to be realized, encapsulated by the appearance of a new verb—'to privatize'. The unions' ability to fight this and the consequential job losses was further eroded when Parliament approved the codes of practice on picketing and the closed shop on 13 December.

During eighteen months of a Conservative government some clear policies emerged, mainly associated with cuts in public expenditure, attacks on trade-union organization, and the abandonment of incomes policies. NALGO had been drawn into conflict, both with the Callaghan government over its own policies of controls over public expenditure and pay, and consequentially with the employers as in the social workers' strike. Once the Tories were elected, the scale and coherence of opposition grew rapidly, with the union joining alongside other labour-movement organizations in a broadly progressive set of campaigns against public belt tightening, against anti-union legislation, against early examples of deregulation and privatization, against some disgraceful foreign policies, and for the maintenance of national pay bargaining based on comparability. As the year ended NALGO's leaders, activists, and members braced themselves for a further dose of deflation.

Other worrying features were beginning to emerge: first, although there was general support for the union's policies, many members were not actively involved in union rallies, actions, and policy stances; secondly, the government's commitment to cutting public services, especially in local government, was more focused; and, thirdly, there were extensive and widely supported moves for increased legal containment of trade unionism. Perhaps a fourth should be added, although its emergence at this time was less obvious, and that was the disarray of the Labour Party.

Appendix

TABLE 3.1. *NALGO Membership, 31 October 1979*

District	Number of branches	Paid-up membership		Members in arrear and membership of branches excluded from voting		Total membership			
		Voting	Retired (student)	Ordinary	Retired	Ordinary	Retired (student)	Honorary	Total
Eastern	130	48,241	4,050(1)	1,693	53	49,934	4,103(1)	—	54,038
East Midland	105	44,182	3,231	46	—	44,228	3,231	—	47,459
Metropolitan	129	95,044	9,414(2)	317	3	95,361	9,417(2)	—	104,780
North Eastern	75	40,560	1,989(1)	159	4	40,719	1,993(1)	—	42,713
North Western and North Wales	136	104,673	6,385(2)	95	—	104,678	6,385(2)	—	111,155
Scottish	120	69,386	1,399(4)	164	2	69,550	1,401(4)	—	70,955
South Eastern	97	45,555	5,461(1)	9	—	45,564	5,461(1)	—	51,026
Southern	76	38,236	3,246	1,373	65	39,609	3,311	—	42,920
South Wales	91	33,606	1,605(3)	56	—	33,662	1,605(3)	—	35,270
South Western	97	46,982	3,527	649	22	47,631	3,549	—	51,180
West Midland	92	69,392	4,736	883	102	70,275	4,838	—	75,113
Yorkshire and Humberside	78	60,175	3,340(2)	3,090	—	63,265	3,340(2)	—	66,607
Honorary members	—	—	—	—	—	—	—	10	10
TOTALS	1,226	696,032	48,383(16)	8,534	251	704,566	48,634(16)	—	753,226

TABLE 3.2. *NALGO membership, 31 October 1980*

District	Number of branches	Paid-up membership: Voting	Paid-up membership: Retired (student)	Members in arrear and membership of branches excluded from voting: Ordinary	Members in arrear ...: Retired	Total membership: Ordinary	Total membership: Retired	Total membership: Honorary (student)	Total membership: Total	Total membership	Increase over 1979	Percentage increase
Eastern	129	50,936	4,491(1)	242	2	51,178	4,493(1)	—	55,672	54,038	1,634	3.03
East Midland	104	45,740	3,448(2)	—	—	45,740	3,448(2)	—	49,190	47,459	1,731	3.65
Metropolitan	130	97,869	10,348(5)	1,469	78	99,338	10,426(5)	—	109,769	104,780	4,989	4.76
North Eastern	75	41,554	2,214	7	—	41,561	2,214	—	43,775	42,713	1,062	2.49
North Western and North Wales	135	108,981	6,939(2)	21	—	109,002	6,939(2)	—	115,943	111,155	4,788	4.31
Scottish	120	74,080	1,438(9)	129	2	74,209	1,440(9)	—	75,658	70,955	4,703	6.63
South Eastern	97	46,136	5,821(2)	25	—	46,161	5,821(2)	—	51,984	51,026	958	1.88
Southern	76	40,747	3,525	3	—	40,750	3,525	—	44,275	42,920	1,355	3.16
South Wales	92	34,466	1,683(4)	241	1	34,707	1,684(4)	—	36,395	35,270	1,125	3.19
South Western	97	48,246	3,805(3)	116	4	48,362	3,809(3)	—	52,174	51,180	994	1.94
West Midland	92	73,299	5,229	131	15	73,430	5,244	—	78,674	75,113	3,561	4.74
Yorkshire and Humberside	78	67,007	3,793(5)	19	—	65,026	3,793(5)	—	68,824	66,607	2,217	3.33
Honorary members	—	—	—	—	—	—	—	10	10	10	—	—
TOTALS	1,225	727,061	52,734(33)	2,403	102	729,464	52,836(33)	10	782,343	753,226	29,117	3.87

4

The Squeeze Tightens

T HIS chapter covers the remainder of the Thatcher government's first term of office, from 1981 until the June 1983 election. As the Conservative right tightened its grip on the government, so NALGO strengthened both its policies and its structures. It became more involved in supporting, one way or another, the struggles of others as they were drawn into the net of anti-inflationary monetarism. The union backed other workers' campaigns on pay, jobs, and unemployment, locally and nationally. Local branches and stewards played an important part in this, within a policy framework that generated awareness of economic and social alternatives. NALGO's John Edwards outlined the importance of the trade-union response, as the privatization agenda became clearer: 'The only power now left to defend these public assets is the organised power of the trade unions. In the gas authority we are prepared to use that power.'[1]

As the NUM took successful strike action over pit closures and as workers in the NHS and Civil Service took industrial action against government pay policies, so it seemed to many in the labour movement that, while the world might be worse than it was before, it was not significantly different—despite the economic recession and an aggressive government, the trade unions could still defend their members in some circumstances in some industries, given the proper leadership. This general mood of defiance was reflected in the TUC's commitment to alternative economic strategies, published in its *Plan for Growth* and *Unemployment: The Fight for TUC Alternatives*, and summarized in NALGO's own pamphlet *Give Britain a Boost*. NALGO, along with other TUC unions and the increasingly divided Labour Party, consistently argued a set of realistic alternatives around this plan, giving coherence to the range of national and local struggles over job losses, cuts, efficiency drives, and

[1] *NALGO Annual Report 1981* (London: NALGO, 1982), 10.

privatization. TUC General Secretary Len Murray attacked the government over its economic policies, which had generated the worst slump since the early 1930s, with nearly 12 per cent unemployed, almost 7,000 bankruptcies, and industrial production down by over 10 per cent.

The Political Economy of Thatcherism—Defiance and Despair

Chancellor Geoffrey Howe writes bluntly about his 1981 budget: 'The final structure of the entire budgetary package was as harsh as it was comparatively straightforward.'[2] In his efforts to keep down the PSBR as a proxy for holding back inflationary pressures he increased taxes substantially, and in order to tighten the Treasury's grip on public spending there was a vital technical change from volume to cash controls. One famous consequence of the budget was a letter to *The Times* signed by 364 economists decrying the government's economic theories and policies. It was a massively deflationary budget that eventually brought inflation down by driving unemployment up.

Later in 1981 the appointment of Norman Tebbit as Secretary of State for Employment signalled a renewed determination to restrict trade-union opposition. Here was the genuine article, the class warrior explicitly attacking workers and their organizations without clinging to any of the outdated notions of patrician one-nation Toryism. As he said about his own appointment, 'to some it was a calculated insult to the unemployed, to others a welcome challenge at last to the abuses of trades union power and the closed shop in particular'.[3]

Over the summer months the government underlined its commitment to driving inflation down through a mixture of high interest rates and low public expenditure. For NALGO, 'this year was characterised by the government's adherence to its monetarist economic strategy in the face of mounting evidence that it was bound to fail'.[4] The consequences were a huge leap in unemployment and an almost equal loss in total trade-union membership. While the situation was desperate, many in the TUC, the unions, and the Labour Party still assumed that there had been no fundamental shift in the political allegiances of the voting population. The depth of the economic crisis was known, but the severity of the political crisis for socialists and social democrats was hardly realized, partly disguised by Labour gains in local elections.

[2] G. Howe, *Conflict of Loyalty* (London: Macmillan, 1994), 204.
[3] N. Tebbit, *Upwardly Mobile* (London: Weidenfeld & Nicolson, 1988), 181.
[4] *NALGO Annual Report 1981*, 39.

One unexpected response to the consequences of Tory policy was rioting in Brixton and later in Toxteth. In other more structured ripostes Arthur Scargill was elected as President of the NUM with a landslide victory, and Ken Livingstone became the leader of the GLC to pursue a radical left-of-centre agenda. These events illustrated the depth of political opposition to the government in some sections of the population, and they illustrated the importance of leadership in rallying the struggle around the pivotal issues of public control and jobs, which were made more urgent as unemployment moved towards three million. There was popular support for the People's March for Jobs, with NALGO playing a large part in its success.

The year ended with the government attacking the collective-bargaining power of public-sector unions at national level, withstanding 'lengthy and costly industrial action in 1981, which the civil service unions took in response to a low pay offer and to the abolition of "fair comparability"'.[5] One commentator summed it all up at the time:

The problems were brought to a head in the lengthy and bitter civil service pay dispute of 1981. Nine separate unions formed a united front and took selective strike action that focused on the national computer centre. The strikes were eventually called off with a settlement of a little over the Government's previous offer and the establishment of an independent inquiry under Sir John Megaw, a retired judge. Its report, in July 1982, suggested a shift from the former comparability approach whereby pay levels were fixed in relation to equivalent jobs in the private sector. Instead the Megaw inquiry preferred a system of job evaluation, with a more detailed analysis of relative accountability and responsibility. This gave greater weight to prevailing market forces.[6]

Thus the government established that it owed no special duty to public-sector workers and that comparability was no longer the proper basis for pay increases. This was the key moment when the government decided that cash limits should drive pay determination. The 4 per cent cash limit set in 1981–2 was intended as a flexible solution—separate groups could settle above or below that amount. It was an apparent rejection of corporate tripartism implicit in incomes policies, and a move, along with merit pay schemes, towards the profit-centred private sector. The impact on NALGO members was felt first in the NHS among A&C grades, but eventually in local government and universities as well.

By the start of 1982 two and a half years of cuts, job losses, and falling relative pay were eroding the confidence of the labour movement. The annual report captured this mood within NALGO:

[5] S. Kessler and F. Bayliss, *Contemporary British Industrial Relations* (London: Macmillan, 1998), 135.

[6] P. Riddell, *The Thatcher Government* (Oxford: Blackwell, 1985), 126.

Your Council find it hard to describe the events of the last year without sounding a note of despair. It is an understatement to say that the British economy is now in crisis . . . unemployment is high and rising . . . output is falling . . . chronically low levels of investment in both the public and private sectors are leading to deindustrialization and a decaying infrastructure . . . living standards are now clearly declining.[7]

Despair among the trade-union movement was accompanied by an increasing triumphalism within the government. This was the year that the right wing of the labour movement deserted to join the fledgling Social Democratic Party (SDP), while the government used the crisis in the Falklands to register a huge boost in its popularity ratings. The war in the Falklands was a strange political throwback to a bygone age of nineteenth-century British Imperialism, characterized by ruthless exploitation and aggression overseas and economic self-interest at home. At the STUC Annual Congress in April, for example, delegates 'were in the grimmest mood seen for years . . . news came hourly of new and dangerous moves in the Falkland crisis . . . the other factor which dominated congress was the Glasgow Hillhead by-election result'[8] (where a traditional Labour seat was taken by Roy Jenkins, one of the 'gang-of-four' leadership of the SDP). The NEC called on the UK and Argentine governments 'to end aggressive activity and to seek a peaceful solution under the auspices of the United Nations'.[9]

Specific government action against the unions took a more definite shape, with Norman Tebbit's Employment Bill wending its way through the procedures of the House of Commons, supported by the Liberals and the SDP. The TUC coordinated several mobilizations during 1982, including a day of opposition to Tebbit's proposals on 10 June. NALGO publicized Len Murray's warning that 'this Bill, when it becomes law, will in effect hand to employers a loaded gun and invite them to point it at trade unions'. The TUC's special Wembley Conference believed that government ministers 'are making it clear that they are out to break the power of trade unions by reducing their ability to take effective action on behalf of members'.[10] As jobs became less secure, so fear and hostility spread among employed workers—fear of unemployment for themselves, making them more compliant at work, and hostility towards the unemployed, who might take their jobs. Government's claim to be modernizing and restructuring the public sector was attractive to many workers, both among those who had found that services were inadequate and among those who worked in the public services for little

---

[7] *NALGO Annual Report 1982* (London: NALGO, 1983), 4.

[8] *Public Service (PS)* (May 1982), 20.   [9] *NALGO News (NN)*, 14 May 1982, 4.

[10] TUC, *Industrial Relations Legislation: The Employment Act 1980 and Employment Bill 1982. Report by the TUC General Council Adopted by the Conference of Executives of Affiliated Unions at the Wembley Conference Centre on April 5, 1982* (London: TUC, 1982), para. 2.

reward. Ideas based on economic, social, and political liberalism, rooted in the pronouncements of right-wing think-tanks, wormed their way into mainstream debate and were given credence by being discussed seriously in the established press (including *The Times*, recently purchased by Rupert Murdoch) and broadcasting organizations. Popular debate was invaded by the dubious economic logic of sound money and of wealth creation only through profit-making private enterprise.

As 1982 drew to a close the government's political dominance was strengthened not only by their military adventure in the Falklands but also by the increasing internecine strife within the Labour Party. Unemployment, recession, and legislation were ranged against workers and their unions. A further revival from an earlier age also emerged: spies and strike-breakers.[11] An NEC report to conference was concerned with 'the regular use of troops for strike-breaking, possibly illegally and certainly without proper Parliamentary control', and 'routine spying by police and security services on trade unionists and legitimate trade union activity, and the collection of information which is sometimes secretly supplied to employers'.[12]

Against such forces the labour movement stood firm for its main demands: fair pay based on bargaining, expansion of the economy through investment and public services, and justice for those pushed to the margins of economic and social life. It employed tried and tested methods to fight for these aims— strikes, other forms of industrial action, protests, propaganda, demonstrations, rallies, and expert opinion publicized to whomever cared to listen and learn. The intensity of the struggle and the commitment of those involved in action in 1982 were dispassionately summarized in one academic journal: 'Despite the impact of increasing levels of unemployment upon the bargaining power and the militancy of many groups of workers . . . the numbers of workers involved in disputes and the numbers of working days lost remained well above the low figures for the same period last year.'[13]

The early months of 1983 witnessed both a growing confidence in government as the anti-Conservative vote split, and a growing fear within the unions that, despite record levels of unemployment, the government would succeed in cutting public services and driving down wages while winning enough of the electorate to its side to ensure another victory. Both the 1982 and 1983 budgets gave away tax concessions to businesses and income-tax payers at the expense of indirect taxation, part of the Medium Term

[11] A. Pinkerton, *Strikers, Communists, Tramps and Detectives* (New York: G. W. Carleton & Co.,1878); R. Geary, *Policing Industrial Disputes: 1893 to 1985* (Cambridge: Cambridge University Press,1985).

[12] *PS* (Feb. 1983), 10.

[13] D. Marsden, 'Chronicle: Industrial Relations in the United Kingdom, August 1982– November 1982', *British Journal of Industrial Relations*, 21/1 (1983), 117.

Financial Strategy, which stated more enthusiastically than ever the need for supply-side solutions to unemployment. In particular, having increased unemployment through their own policies, the Conservatives shifted the blame onto the unemployed themselves. So in 1982 Geoffrey Howe introduced the Community Programme, 'carefully avoiding the more emotional notion of "workfare"'.[14] Union fortunes took a further turn for the worse on 9 June, when the Tories won the general election with an increased majority. As the union's annual report baldly stated, '1983 was another bad year'.[15]

Attacks on Local Government

Local democracy

The government's main attack on public services fell onto local government, with reductions in local accountability, finances, and relative pay. Michael Heseltine, the man who would be king, struck a great blow at local-authority finances. Noting that 'some of us felt that councils had more in reserve than they were willing to reveal when asked for cuts',[16] he reduced the 1981–2 rate support grant. The resultant job losses were a price which the government was prepared for others to pay. On top of this, the right of local authorities to levy rates also came under attack as part of the campaign to subordinate local authorities to central government. NALGO saw that 'the new system represented a formidable attack on local autonomy'.[17] As Nicholas Ridley remembers, when Mrs Thatcher asked Michael Heseltine to reform the local rate system, he came forward with three alternatives: 'a local income tax, a local sales tax and a poll tax. Margaret Thatcher could find no way forward. The reform was shelved.'[18] But not for long.

A year later, reeling under the impact of a £2 billion cut in spending, the AMA pointed out that 'without money your council is without power. It can't make decisions. It can't go against Whitehall.'[19] NALGO elaborated: 'The 1982–3 RSG settlement represents a continuation of the government's assault on local authority spending, services and jobs. As in the past years, cuts are being forced on councils by a combination of reduced spending targets and inadequate cash limits . . . NALGO calculates that overall cuts of around 6% in current spending would be required to meet government targets.'[20]

---

[14] Howe, *Conflict of Loyalty*, 243.
[15] *NALGO Annual Report 1983* (London: NALGO: 1984), 59.
[16] M. Heseltine, *Where There's a Will* (London: Hutchinson,1987), 38.
[17] *NALGO Annual Report 1981*, 39.
[18] N. Ridley, *My Style of Government* (London: Hutchinson,1991), 122.
[19] *PS* (Nov. 1981), 1.   [20] *NN*, 12 Feb. 1982, 1.

But the threat to local government was further intensified by the Local Government Finance Act 1982, which set up the Audit Commission and also enhanced central government's powers to impose selective penalties on 'overspending' councils and to prevent councils from setting supplementary rates.[21] This was underlined by the Green Paper on the *Alternative to Domestic Rates* (Cmnd 8449), which paved the way for the hated poll tax, introduced first in Scotland in 1989. NALGO argued that the system needed reform but that rates should stay since 'rates are cheap to collect, easy to administer, hard to evade, predictable in their yield, highly perceptible'.[22] The union adopted the campaign slogan 'For democracy's sake—stop Heseltine and Younger now'.[23]

Pay bargaining

After the local-government pay fight of 1980 and the modest 7.3 per cent settlement plus some scale restructuring in 1981, NALGO started to consider joint pay strategies with the other unions. As Alan Jinkinson, national officer, argued: 'The view appears to be that a common strategy does not necessarily require common claims . . . The most important objective is to create and maintain a united front in opposition to policies which would result in members' standards of living declining.'[24] This idea grew in attractiveness:

Public-service unions, including NALGO, are now taking the first steps to prevent the Government from picking them off one by one in the battle to impose its new four per cent pay limitation. There was a unanimous vote at last month's TUC for a motion that 'every effort should be made to organise co-ordinated action by public service unions during the next pay round.'[25]

As a result the 1982 claim was drawn up with a common core of 12 per cent on salaries and a thirty-five-hour week. An academic article summarizes the arguments:

The TUC Public Services Committee has recently discussed the problems posed by different settlement dates in its attempts to encourage more effective co-ordination of collective bargaining by affiliated unions. There would be a number of potential advantages if local government unions shared a common April settlement date: a more co-ordinated bargaining strategy would emerge from rationalization of union resources in preparing pay claims, the prospect of simultaneous industrial action, and the removal of the pressure from the manual workers' negotiations.[26]

---

[21] LRD, 'Attacks on Local Councils', *Labour Research*, 71/10 (1982), 218.
[22] *NALGO Annual Report 1982*, 56–7.   [23] *NN*, 6 Nov. 1981, 1.
[24] *PS* (Sept. 1981), 2.   [25] Ibid. (Oct. 1981), 1.
[26] I. Kessler and D. Winchester, 'Pay Negotiations in Local Government—the 1981–82 Wage Round'. *Local Government Studies* (Nov./Dec. 1982), 21.

In 1983 the local-government group meeting passed a resolution that 'supports the common pay strategy for the current pay year, and instructs the National Committee to work closely with appropriate unions, through the TUC'.[27]

Action against cuts

But the main action focused on the consequences of the cuts, and the union moved its policy and procedures into line with members' experiences. Joint statements with NUPE, *Local Government under Attack* and *Scottish Local Government under Attack*, called on 'branches to form joint action committees with other local government unions, to oppose all redundancies, refuse to cover for unfilled vacancies, and carry out a campaign on the effects of the cuts'.[28]

In the public construction sector, cuts were damaging the infrastructure and direct labour organizations (DLOs) were under attack as capital programmes were cut back. NALGO 'condemns attacks on DLOs as being unjustified and ideologically motivated . . . and it is recommended that a future government should promote a massive renewal of local authority direct labour'.[29] This neatly combined the union's commitment to protect the jobs of members in construction and maintenance as well as restating a Keynesian commitment to planned economic expansion through public works.

The 1981 annual conference agreed a NEC motion 'which deplored the government's hostility to the concept of public service exemplified by the gradual undermining of independent local democracy and rejecting the image of a profligate local government service and the constant denigration of local government workers'.[30] The conference went further: 'NALGO upholds its right to take action to defend services and jobs while recognising that such action may fall outwith the Government's or courts' definition of a trades dispute. This was the important paragraph in a Scottish district motion which delegates carried and the NEC opposed with no great conviction.'[31] By the spring of 1982, policy was clear: 'Endorsement by the NEC on 6 March of the strike clauses in the national cuts strategy means that a branch's use of indefinite and total strike action in defence of jobs and services is now official NALGO policy.'[32] The union saw 'mounting evidence that the major cause of our difficulties is the government's own policies'.[33] The Scottish Dis-

---

[27] *NALGO Annual Report 1982*, 68.

[28] *PS* (Feb. 1981), 20; *Stop the Cuts Action Bulletin*, no. 29, 2 Feb. 1981.

[29] NALGO, *Crisis in Construction* (London: NALGO, 1981), 15.

[30] *NALGO Annual Report 1981*, 40.   [31] *PS* (July 1981), 4.

[32] Ibid. (Apr. 1982), 2.   [33] *NALGO Annual Report 1982*, 41.

trict Council 'resolved to welcome and encourage full involvement with branches in the event of strike action over public expenditure cuts'.[34]

In parts of Scotland, under Secretary of State George Younger, the impact of cuts was severe. At a mass demonstration in Dundee at the end of 1980 Jim White had served notice on the government 'that NALGO members will not go to the dole queues willingly, every cut and every redundancy will be fought with all the strength we can muster'.[35] The Scottish District Council provided a strong focus for the challenge to the government's policies. Michael Foot, leader of the Labour Party, and Bruce Millan, Labour Party Scottish spokesman, made speeches at a rally in Glasgow which the *Scotsman* reported under the headline 'Awesome Show of Anti-Tory Solidarity', stating that 'the trade unions were the backbone . . . but there were others. The Church of Scotland was there. So were the Communists. And the Nationalists: at least three factions.'[36]

The fight was particularly intense in Lothian Region, where the joint union committee attacked Younger's cuts as 'an intolerable piece of criminal lunacy'.[37] There was a series of industrial actions, including 'blacking of all statistical returns to Central Government, blacking of all work connected with redundancies, blacking of all contractors and consultants'.[38] Speaking at a rally in Edinburgh, Geoffrey Drain said: 'This meeting is about three issues which are all part of one great issue and the three separate ones are services, jobs and liberty. The larger issue of which they are all part is the issue of people and what happens to them.'[39] Phyllis Herriot, leader of the Lothian Region labour group, said: 'We make no apologies for offering better services, schools, community centres, home helps, buses and everything else, than any other local authority in Scotland—we were elected to do just that and we have not dodged the task in any way.'[40]

In spite of this fierce resistance, the government managed to force through cuts of £30 million, but as with other defeats positive lessons could be learnt. Archie Fairlie argued that 'the joint trade union committee which led the campaign and organised the massive strike on 30th June brought together the giants of public service trade unionism—NALGO, NUPE (manual workers), the TGWU (busmen), the FBU (firemen) and the EIS (teachers). This in itself was a major step forward.'[41] Some councillors claimed a partial victory in Lothian since the final cuts were less than government demands, and were achieved through freezing posts but not by redundancies. The Lothian

---

[34] *NALGO Scottish District Council Annual Report 1982* (Glasgow: NALGO, 1983), 31.
[35] *Mac* (Feb. 1981), 1. [36] *Scotsman*, 23 Feb. 1981, 1.
[37] *PS* (Sept. 1981), 1.
[38] *NALGO Emergency Committee Meeting Minutes*, 10b (London: NALGO, 1981), 149.
[39] *NN*, 25 Sept. 1981, 6. [40] *Mac* (Oct. 1981), 1. [41] Ibid. (Nov. 1981), 3.

struggle linked into wider debate about the AES, explaining the impact of government cuts on local economies in publications such as *Unemployment or Prosperity: The Battle for Lothian.*

The meat inspectors and the births, marriages, and deaths registrars

Two national disputes in 1981 illustrated how members could be galvanized into taking industrial action by their sense of frustration and injustice when employers refuse to deal with pay problems. The members involved, meat inspectors and registrars, showed that trade-union militancy is not the preserve of stereotypical proletarian workers. They also showed the range of non-strike sanctions that public-service workers might impose against their employers. The registration officers banned weekend working, refused to answer their telephones, and worked to rule to press their pay and grading demands.

Meat inspectors also took industrial action over their grades, as 'the duties of meat inspectors had changed considerably since 1972 when the grade was last altered. They also undertook duties in excess of the basic meat inspection regulations and were involved in such matters as meat hygiene, animal welfare, animal disease and animal by-products.'[42] A special delegate meeting passed a motion to support 'the proposed work-to-rule in accordance with the 1963 meat inspection regulations, which should continue until the employers have met the claim in full'.[43] Support for the action was solid and the impact on abattoirs slowed down the rate of slaughter. Fears that employers were getting round the work to rule led to an escalation: 'The message from meat inspectors is that they now want positive and effective action to be taken as quickly as possible to force the employers to reopen negotiations.'[44] In November the General Secretary urged an all-out strike vote in response to members' frustrations, but failed to get a majority in the ballot.

Both the meat inspectors and the registration officers returned to normal working having won some concessions short of their claims. One of the most important features of these national disputes was that they involved a very large number of local-government branches in sectional industrial action for the first time, building on the experience gained by the larger branches during the social workers' strike and by the increasing number of local actions over cuts and jobs. Branch activists and district officers learned many lessons about the role of district offices and district committees in planning and coordinating such difficult national sectional campaigns.

---

[42] *NALGO Emergency Committee Meeting Minutes*, 10b (1981), 137.
[43] *PS* (Sept. 1981), 2.   [44] *NN*, 16 Oct. 1981, 1.

Local industrial action, from Penzance to Edinburgh

The amount of local industrial action escalated, as employers implemented the government's cuts. One lesson of industrial action was about solidarity in the face of victimization. For example, in rural Penwith, 140 members found themselves pitched into an indefinite strike in defence of the chair of their sub-branch (see Box 3).

Box 3. NALGO and the Penwith Strike—the Dismissal of Alec Maund

Penwith District Council is a small local authority in Cornwall. In 1979 Brigadier John C. Moore became the Council's Chief Executive, shortly after leaving the army. In 1980 Alec Maund, the Council's Principal Architect, became chair and lead negotiator of the 140-strong Penwith Sub-Branch of the West Cornwall NALGO Branch. Their first major dispute occurred when the Brigadier engaged management consultants to 'streamline' the administration, without agreeing any safeguards for the staff. NALGO intervention, led by Alec Maund, resulted in agreed safeguards being put in place. The consultant's report was implemented without any compulsory redundancies, although Alec Maund's status was reduced to senior architect.

In January 1981 the council set up a new Architects Section, with Alec Maund as senior. Only five months later it hired an independent architect to report on the section, following which it put a housing scheme out to a private contractor, leaving the section with very little work. In August it decided to disband the section altogether and hive off all its work to private contractors.

NALGO responded rapidly. Penwith members saw this as a direct attack on their officers, and on Alec Maund in particular, in an attempt to break their developing opposition to dictatorial management. A sub-branch meeting decided to boycott all work connected with the contracted-out housing scheme and to oppose compulsory redundancies. The council redeployed all the staff in the section except for Alec Maund, who was dismissed on grounds of redundancy on 21 October. The next day over 100 members came out on strike in an impressive display of anger over the privatization of a council service and of solidarity with their victimized union leader. The NEC resolved 'That this National Executive Council congratulates and expresses its full support for the members in the Penwith sub-branch undertaking industrial action in defence of jobs and fundamental trade union principles and trusts that this action will lead to a speedy and successful conclusion.'

The strike was headline news in the local press:

Penwith's first-ever strike by 120 of its District Council NALGO staff enters its second week today. There was no sign yesterday of any early meeting between the two sides which could resolve the deadlock. On the one side stood the Council, with its decision to disband the architects services department, and make the Council architect, Mr Alec Maund, also a central figure in the dispute as local NALGO branch chairman, redundant. On the other stood the staff, with their pickets on duty outside the offices at St Clare, Penzance, determined to fight for no redundancy and a restoration of the architect's section.[45]

A week later the paper reported 'No Break in NALGO Strike', and that an ACAS official had spoken with the strikers but had not met the chairman of the council.[46]

What followed was a graphic demonstration of the weakness of the law in protecting workplace union activists from vindictive employers. Ignoring the obvious concerns of its entire workforce, the council refused to consider Alec's reinstatement and redeployment. The strike continued while NALGO took his claim for unfair dismissal to an industrial tribunal (IT) in November. The case was lost, and the Penwith members returned to work in January, after twelve weeks on strike.

In May 1982 the Employment Appeals Tribunal (EAT) referred the case back to the IT on a point of law. Nothing happened for another seventeen months while the council appealed unsuccessfully to the Court of Appeal. The IT reconsidered the case early in 1984, deciding again that the dismissal was not unfair. After taking detailed legal advice NALGO decided not to appeal and finally ended its financial support for Alec Maund two and a half years after his dismissal, on 14 March 1984.

Most activists did not face such blatant victimization, and many branches sought assurances from sympathetic employers over job losses and erosion of conditions of service. Even some Tory councils were inclined to be sympathetic, reflecting local election results and worries over the impact of successive cuts. General dismay over job losses was turning into more persistent dogged resistance at local and sectional levels. Glasgow Council agreed to a thirty-five-hour week and a new technology agreement for its APT&C staff, but in Middlesex Polytechnic, Hillingdon Council, and Dorset County Council members took action over redundancies. Wandsworth Council withdrew its threat to 400 staff jobs after two weeks of selective strikes by key personnel. The Wandsworth Branch was supported by the Emergency Committee, worried by the claim that 'recent statements by the leader of the Council have indicated that previous informal undertakings that no-one would be made compulsorily redundant, are no longer operative'.[47] Job cuts were withdrawn in Milton Keynes after threats of action. There was a large rally in Peterborough during a visit by Michael Heseltine to protest against cuts. There were demonstrations against cuts in Hertford and in Thurrock, and jobs were blacklisted over regrading issues at Weymouth and Portland Borough Council. Lambeth Council put 300 jobs at risk over land sales and the branch balloted for a union boycott, social workers in Lothian Region held a three-week strike after threats of disciplinary action for not covering a vacant post, and staff in Roxburgh went on strike to fight redundancies.

[45] *Cornishman*, 29 Oct. 1981, 1.   [46] Ibid. 5 Nov. 1981, 1.

[47] *NALGO Emergency Committee Meeting Minutes*, 10a (1981), 29–30.

NALGO's first major strike around the issue of new technology started in October 1982 over South Tyneside Council's refusal to abide by a new technology agreement, which said that the benefits of new technology would be greater if 'the technology is introduced in a controlled and mutually acceptable way and operated within the terms of this Agreement'.[48] This was not, however, how the local paper saw things:

400 NALGO members employed by South Tyneside Council have been on strike for a week because of a trivial argument about the introduction of new technology . . . Council services are threatened with weekly paralysis—the effect of which will have an effect beyond the Mondays off—and South Tyneside has already been waiting a week for £1/2 million in rents and rates . . . Where, outside the public sector, could an argument about whether or not there was anything to argue about, spark off a strike today? . . . 800 companies went bust in the North East between New Year and the end of September, 260 of them going under in the third quarter . . . All of these firms and their employees had no choice but to bear the burden of rates. We hope the South Tyneside clerks may take the hint, accept the council offer and get back to their jobs that are the envy of millions.[49]

This industrial action, as with so many others cases, was rooted in disputes over job security, grading, and status quo provisions. The employers' repudiation of the recently negotiated agreement led to further escalation: 'By early November hundreds of members of South Tyneside Local Government Branch had been on strike for five weeks.'[50]

Privatization and Efficiency: The Terrible Twins

Many commentators emphasize privatization as a hallmark of the government's break with past policies:

The impact of the government's new thinking has most obviously been felt in the privatization programme for the state-owned industries and state-provided services. The programme covers both denationalization (or the sale of assets and shares owned by the state) and liberalization (or the relaxation or abolition of a service's statutory monopoly). Perhaps in no other area of policy has the discontinuity between the present and previous governments been so marked.[51]

One of the main neo-classical arguments for privatization was that, in an idealized perfectly competitive market, producers can compete against each

---

[48] Ibid. 11 (1982), 484.   [49] *Evening Chronicle* (Newcastle), 14 Oct. 1982, 12.
[50] *North East News* (Dec. 1982), 4.
[51] D. Kavanagh, *Thatcherism and British Politics* (Oxford: Oxford University Press, 1987), 217–18.

other only on price. In this case the most profitable and successful firms are those that produce their products at the lowest unit cost, so they are forced to find every way to improve their production techniques, lower their unit costs, and hence be more efficient. Thus efficiency is equated with lower unit costs and this in turn means higher profits.

Two points follow from this. First, everyone appears to benefit from efficient production, since the best firms come to dominate the market and if the others do not copy then they will go under—market discipline favours best practice. Secondly, systems without a profit motive, such as public services, have no incentive to achieve efficient performance and therefore they waste resources, impoverish the rest of the country, and fail to deliver the best service to users. To remedy this market forces must be introduced, either directly through transfer to private ownership or indirectly through the importation of private-sector management.

The problem is that most of the time firms do not behave like that at all: their managers do *not* seek out most efficient solutions in the technical sense. They can achieve lower unit costs through market power by driving down the costs of wages, of their suppliers (and hence their suppliers' profit margins), and other costs. This is not more efficient, it is simply cheaper for the firm that dominates the market. In fact by any sensible measure, from the point of view of those suppliers and workers who are in a position of weakness in the market, it is inefficient. They are under ceaseless pressure to produce more output for less income. The idea that public services and utilities can simply become more efficient by copying an idealized 'best' private-sector management practice is false. Privatization was central to the government's project to restructure the British economy, but its purpose was to increase profit-making rather than efficiency.

Margaret Thatcher was totally clear: 'Privatization, no less than the tax structure, was fundamental to improving Britain's economic performance. But for me it was also far more than that: it was one of the central means of reversing the corrosive and corrupting influence of socialism.'[52] By 1983 many of her Cabinet agreed that privatization was a workable and popular policy. Their belief in its efficacy stemmed from a simplistic grasp of economics: 'Private sector management is always likely to be more efficient than public sector management, not because the people are different but because of the twin stimuli of the profit-and-loss account and the workings of competition.'[53] Further, it spreads share ownership generally as well as 'among the employees of the company concerned', and it 'transferred the allegiance of

[52] M. Thatcher, *The Downing Street Years* (London: Harper Collins, 1993), 676.
[53] Heseltine, *Where There's a Will*, 71.

the workforce and management to working for their customers rather than for themselves. It cut out the obtrusive power of the trade unions, and enabled management to remove all restrictive practices.'[54] No wonder the unions feared it and no wonder they fought against its consequences.

When the government announced the sale of its holding in the Wytch Farm oilfield, one of the first cases of denationalization, Ron Walsh, chair of the National Gas Committee, responded: 'It is an absolute disgrace that after public money has been used to carry out exploration and the benefits are just about to accrue to the nation, that this government should see fit to hand it over to private profit pirates.'[55] For Geoffrey Drain, 'it shows the desire to sell off the public sector to private profit at public expense. They are handing out the spoils to their backers.'[56] NALGO issued a leaflet, *In Defence of New Towns*, as part of its opposition to the 'irresponsible sale of invaluable public assets in the new towns'.[57]

The Competition Act 1980 gave the Monopoly and Mergers Commission (MMC) additional powers to investigate the public sector, which fuelled the wider economic debate on efficiency and on the assumed benefits of profit-seeking competition. This device promoted the illusion that sound economic theory lay behind the principle of competition. The MMC's report on the gas industry recommended that it shed its domestic appliance business and, when the programme to sell off the 900 gas showrooms was announced, Labour's Shadow Trade Secretary John Smith called it one of the 'most appalling and spiteful decisions' ever announced in Parliament, promising that the next Labour government would reverse it. Geoffrey Drain said: 'We will not have this cynical manipulation of public assets for the benefit of private profit under the pretence of an ethical approach to the country's economic problems.'[58] In his presidential speech to the annual conference, Peter Morgan attacked the government's plan: 'The more attractive parts are to be hacked away and surrendered to freebooting privateers.'[59]

A ballot over the threat to jobs in the gas appliance market was won by three to one, and Gas Unions Against the Report for Dismantling the British Gas Corporation (GUARD) organized a one-day strike against the 'great gas robbery'.[60] Dave Stirzaker, national gas organizer, reported that 'GUARD is . . . drawing up plans for industrial action this winter',[61] and Bob Strother, chair of Edinburgh and District gas branch, said: 'Members must be prepared for all out action.'[62] The union refuted the government's case, arguing that

---

54 Ridley, *My Style of Government*, 60.
55 *Gas Action News*, no. 3, 29 June 1981.
56 *PS* (Sept. 1981), 12.
57 *NALGO Annual Report 1981*, 133.
58 *Gas Action News*, no. 4, 14 July 1981.
59 *PS* (July 1981), 11.
60 *NALGO Annual Report 1981*, 94; *PS* (Sept. 1981), 9–12.
61 *PS* (Oct. 1981), 6.
62 *Mac* (Oct. 1981), 2.

customers would be worse off, safety standards undermined, services reduced, job losses escalated, and all in order to make excessive profits for private companies.

A combination of factors, including union opposition, forced Energy Secretary Nigel Lawson to postpone the sell-offs until after the next election:

Few of us realized what a storm would be unleashed over what could hardly be called one of the commanding heights of the economy. The Labour Party and the gas trade unions, encouraged by Dennis Rooke who was incensed by the idea of losing any part of his empire, were up in arms. The government's opponents were remarkably successful in portraying the privatization of this state-owned chain of shops . . . as an ideologically inspired attack on the British way of life.[63]

However, the notion that services and utilities could be provided to the public more efficiently and at lower cost to the tax payer was a powerful one, and job losses and restructuring developments were presented by employers as the outcomes of efficiency studies. Water authorities used these to justify further staffing reductions, the National Bus Company (NBC) agreed new guidelines on redundancies before its announcement of 4,000 job losses, and over 1,200 jobs were lost when the electricity boards were reorganized.

The electricity group deplored government policy and restated the link between jobs and services: 'This group meeting is concerned at the disastrous impact that the government's policies are having on the electricity supply industry's ability to provide an efficient service to the people of this country.'[64] Water industry national organizer E. J. Roberts argued that 'the assumption by Mrs Thatcher that customers' bills for water services this year would be excessive because of the inefficiency of regional water authorities prompted her to order a lightning investigation by three accountancy firms into the authorities' 1981–2 budgets'.[65]

The water industry was simply allowed to deteriorate through deliberate underfunding, and the cuts affected public health: 'Since NALGO's statement to the press last month about the consequences of neglect of services the public takes for granted, the union's district offices have been inundated with calls from local journalists about the dangers of river and drinking water pollution, flood risks, mains bursts, sewer collapse and the safety of impounding reservoirs.'[66] In the south-west, for example, even the senior managers at Wessex Water and South West Water warned of cuts creating real public health problems.

---

[63] N. Lawson, *The View from No. 11* (London: Corgi Books, 1992), 213.
[64] *NALGO Annual Report 1981*, 82.   [65] *PS* (Mar. 1981), 5.
[66] Ibid. (Feb. 1982), 4.

Restructuring and new technology in the electricity industry, with limited funds, meant a grim future for jobs. In a deal with APEX over destructive competitive recruitment, both general secretaries agreed 'to work in the spirit and not only the letter of the TUC Bridlington principles'.[67] In the gas industry the union opposed the Oil and Gas Bill, which threatened three in every five jobs and, according to Dave Stirzaker, would mean compulsory redundancies.[68] The crisis in the energy sector was discussed in the NEC report *Energy for the Future*, in which an integrated and planned energy policy was put forward as a key aspect of national resources and environmental safety, stressing the central role of NALGO members in a public-sector fuel and power industry. It concluded that 'the core of NALGO's policy for the energy sector is the need for public ownership, public control and a planned approach to the future of energy supply and consumption'.[69]

Battles over the role of the GLC and the operation of London Transport reveal the politics beneath the efficiency rhetoric. Tory alarm bells rang out before the 1981 local elections, when one MP claimed that 'London is in real danger of becoming an increasingly lawless city if the Labour Party win control of the GLC'.[70] Labour, with Ken Livingstone as leader, took the GLC from the Tories and went on to challenge Margaret Thatcher's popularity and her claims that services could be properly managed only in the private sector. The GLC introduced the 'Fares Fair' scheme, subsidizing public transport and thereby increasing usage, reducing accidents, traffic congestion, and pollution, and running the system more efficiently. A group of Conservative-run London boroughs challenged the legality of cheap fares, on the basis that the GLC had broken central government requirements not to use the rates to alter the basic economics of fares.

Early in January 1982 *The Times* reported on the response: 'Union leaders representing more than 60,000 London Transport employees met yesterday to coordinate a campaign in support of the 'Fares Fair' scheme, which has been declared illegal.'[71] A few days later the same paper covered the growing trade-union resistance to imposed fare increases: 'London bus and tube workers could be urged by the NUR not to collect fares when they are increased in March as a protest at the Law Lords ruling on the GLC's cheap transport policy.'[72] The next day it reported: 'London Underground stations will be shut, peak-hour trains will be fewer and more crowded, and bus services will be cut as a result of the Law Lords' judgment on the "Fares Fair" policy, London Transport said yesterday.'[73] It continued running the story as the GLC

---

[67] Ibid. (Feb. 1982), 7.   [68] Ibid. 6.
[69] NALGO, *Energy for the Future* (London: NALGO, 1982), 96.
[70] *The Times*, 30 Apr. 1981, 4.   [71] Ibid., 5 Jan. 1982, 3.
[72] Ibid., 22 Jan. 1982, 2.   [73] Ibid., 23 Jan. 1982, 2.

responded: 'Parliament alone can now tell how much Londoners ought to pay for travel by bus and tube, Mr Ken Livingstone, leader of the GLC, said yesterday as he launched a campaign costing £200,000 of lobbying and advertising in favour of cheap fares.'[74] Towards the end of February: 'Mr Ken Livingstone, Labour leader of the GLC, yesterday described as imaginative a proposal that London Transport staff might allow passengers to travel free or not collect the extra fares to be charged next month. Unions have called a one-day strike in protest at the decision to double fares on London Transport.'[75] The new fares were implemented on 21 March.

At the same time as this the MMC was examining four bus undertakings in the run-up to deregulation. Norman Fowler, Secretary of State for Transport, commented that 'this investigation is part of the government's drive for increased efficiency and value for money in the bus industry'. In NALGO's view, 'the government has sought to undermine the public undertakings to the point where subsidies are withdrawn from public operators and then paid to "commercial" concerns to operate the very same unprofitable services'.[76] Local authorities were worried that the planned legislation 'will administer a devastating blow to network bus operations', and the AMA organized a campaign of opposition supported by NALGO.[77] The union's policy statement *Public Transport Now* concluded: 'The country's bus services are currently facing an acute crisis which threatens the continued existence of a comprehensive network of passenger transport and seriously jeopardises the achievement of a fully integrated national transport system.'[78]

In local government, contracting out was the main, relatively new, form of privatization. The union argued that it resulted in bogus savings, reduced public accountability, job losses, weaker unions, and worse conditions of service. *Edlines*, the Eastern District's supplement to *Public Service*, summarized the situation in a spoof definition: 'privatise: vb. Orig. USA circa late 1970s. To contract out, run public services at a profit, undermine trade unions.'[79] The combination of cuts and privatization cost 173 job losses in Suffolk County Council, and Essex and Hertfordshire County Councils were planning more privatization.

In Birmingham Social Services Department over 1,500 members went on strike when three members were dismissed for refusing to take part in an efficiency study. This was part of a wider campaign triggered by the new Conservative council to consider privatizing several services. As *The Times* noticed, 'the use by councils of private consultants to help cut costs was con-

---

[74] *The Times*, 5 Feb. 1982, 3.   [75] Ibid., 22 Feb. 1982, 2.
[76] *NN*, 22 Jan. 1982, 4.   [77] *PS* (Nov. 1982), 3.
[78] NALGO, *Public Transport Now* (London: NALGO, 1982), 2.
[79] *Edlines* (Mar. 1982), 4.

demned by the council staff section of NALGO'.[80] District Organization Officer Sid Platt reported that 'the branch is seeking to black all investigative work etc. in preparation for possible privatisation'.[81] Over 9,000 Birmingham members were 'refusing to co-operate in any measures invoked by the council to advance the planning or realisation of the contracting-out of existing council services', and after threats from the Conservative leader of the council the NALGO branch agreed to take strike action should any member be disciplined.[82] The local paper reported this under the headline 'Town Hall Men in Tough Line on Jobs Threat':

Nearly 10,000 white collar council workers in Birmingham have been given the all clear by their union to take industrial action if compulsory redundancies are proposed. The action will include refusing to cover vacant jobs during sickness and holidays, non co-operation with contractors, blacking the collection of money, and councillors being 'sent to Coventry'. . . . The Birmingham branch of Nalgo has also voted in a ballot to black the introduction of any more new technology.[83]

At the 1982 conference the leadership pledged a million pounds to help fight privatization and 'to boost morale among NALGO members and all trade unionists in the face of government sabotage and denigration of the public services and of their own work'.[84] This became the 'Put People First' campaign in 1983, a key development of the union's political campaigning (see Box 9). The TUC Public Services Committee issued a pamphlet *Keep Public Services Public—the TUC Case against Contracting out*, and NALGO put its case in *Fighting Privatisation*:

Privatisation is politically motivated. It is doing enormous damage to the social fabric and creating mounting problems for the future. The government and its friends in private industry argue that the private sector is efficient and public services are inefficient and wasteful. They use false arguments and empty slogans to support their case. We must show them up for what they are—profiteers, whose sole object is to make money out of people's needs. Contractors make their profits by cutting jobs, pay, standards of service and working conditions. Their employees have worse sick pay schemes, less holidays, reduced pensions, longer hours, no career structure and increasing workloads.[85]

Consequences of contracting out were clear to manual local-government workers in June 1983, when Birmingham City Council awarded its refuse collection service to an in-house bid, which resulted in 262 redundancies.

---

[80] *The Times*, 15 June 1982, 3.

[81] *NALGO Emergency Committee Meeting Minutes*, 11 (London: NALGO, 1982), 341.

[82] *PS* (Sept. 1982), 2.   [83] *Birmingham Evening Mail*, 1 June 1982, 5.

[84] *PS* (Oct. 1982), 1.

[85] NALGO, *Fighting Privatisation: A NALGO Campaign Guide for Districts and Branches* (NALGO, 1982), 3.

Even without actual privatization, the contracting process achieved the shake-out of jobs demanded by government policy. There were disputes in councils such as Kensington and, more famously, in Wandsworth, where council leader Christopher Chope, later Minister for Housing, initiated a programme that was vigorously opposed by the council unions.[86] Bury Metropolitan Council was forced to drop its privatization plans after a joint trade-union campaign.[87] However, the union view was that 'the success reported here in the battle against privatisation should not be taken as a sign that the tide is turning in NALGO's favour. It simply means that more councils are planning such measures and that some, not all, are being frustrated.'[88] In the main it was manual worker jobs that disappeared. Although the writing was on the wall for white-collar staff, they could not in general be convinced of the need to take supportive action. Nevertheless, the NEC proposed rule changes to admit into membership workers employed in the private sector.

NALGO Policy and Practice

NALGO takes the left alternative

Throughout 1981 the union developed its policies in opposition to the government's programme, including commercialization of some parts of the transport system; sales of council houses; a de facto public-sector pay norm; and a Green Paper that threatened to remove trade-union immunities when members took industrial action (see Box 5). This national opposition generally failed to block these changes, but it kept alive the distinctive trade-union approach to workers' rights. Local resistance was enabled by relaxing some central union controls over industrial action, granting more powers to branches on decisions over picketing and strike funds, and speeding up the whole process of approving action. *The Times's* version was that 'leaders of the largest white collar union representing local government workers want to introduce rule changes that would have the effect of making it easier for members to take industrial action'.[89] Almost a year later *The Times* reported further: 'NALGO yesterday urged local authority white collar workers who are affected by councils' attempts to cut expenditure to go on "indefinite and total" strike.'[90]

---

[86] Wandsworth Joint Trade Union Committee, *Public Jobs for Private Profit: Fighting Contractors in Wandsworth* (London: Wandsworth Trade Union Publications, 1983).

[87] Bury Joint Trade Union Committee, *Hands Off Bury's Bins: How We Stopped Privatisation* (Bury: Bury Joint Trade Union Committee, 1984).

[88] *PS* (Feb. 1983), 2.   [89] *The Times*, 18 May 1981, 2.   [90] Ibid., 6 Mar. 1982, 3.

NALGO reported on the TUC's 1982 Annual Congress in Brighton: 'Beleaguered was the feeling generated by this year's TUC. Motion after motion and delegate after delegate made it clear that working people and the trade unions were under attack from every side.'[91] NUPE General Secretary Rodney Bickerstaffe successfully moved a motion that 'rejects as divisive and inequitable the use of cash limits as a Public Sector Incomes Policy and the use of public sector workers as pawns in a campaign to bring about a substantial real reduction in wage levels'. Here the TUC finally voted in favour of NUPE's long campaign for a national minimum wage, supported only cautiously by the General Council.[92]

Geoffrey Drain won wide support for a composite motion attacking the government's monetarist policies. In his speech he identified five frontal attacks by the government on the public services: first, the attack on resources through cuts, cash limits, and restraints on external sources of funds; secondly, the attack on the base of the public sector through privatization; thirdly, the attack on local democracy through centralization of state power and through new legislation; fourthly, the attack on public-service employees through a campaign of 'sneers and denigration'; and, fifthly, the 'deliberate use of unemployment as an instrument of policy'.[93]

Opposition to the government's policies was strengthened by a clear alternative—NALGO endorsed the AES, put forward by the TUC and the TUC Labour Party Liaison Committee, with its well-argued alternative to market-based neo-liberalism. The 1982 annual conference supported selective import controls; opposed any privatization, and backed renationalization; supported incomes policy but only as 'part of a comprehensive strategy including all forms of income and price controls within the framework of a planned economy'; and called for expansion of public-sector expenditure. Delegates voted for a composite motion:

Conference reiterates its complete opposition to the divisive economic strategy of the present Government which is based on cuts in public expenditure . . . Conference believes that a continuation of present policies would bring about the irreversible impoverishment of our communities with inadequate benefits and services . . . Conference reaffirms its support for the TUC's alternative economic strategy . . . Conference further calls on the NEC, through the TUC, to strengthen the public sector pay strategy and prepare a campaign of publicity and concerted industrial action to rally the membership in opposition to all anti-union Government policies as a whole.[94]

One summary of the aims of the AES includes the following: to stop the waste of human and material resources in mass unemployment and underused

---

[91] *PS* (Oct. 1982), 8. [92] *TUC Annual Report 1982*, 574–7.
[93] Ibid. 578. [94] *PS* (July 1982), 3.

capacity; to attack poverty, class inequalities, and discrimination; to expand the economy through large-scale public investment and spending; to increase democratic control and economic planning; and to reshape the welfare system.[95] 'Central to the AES is the demand that unemployment is reduced decisively by expansionary policies' and in particular by 'an expansion of public sector employment'.[96] NALGO played a major part in both developing the AES within the TUC and promoting it among union activists through a sixty-page conference paper.

The TUC's 1983 economic review urged 'increased public spending . . . a £10 billion expansionary package'.[97] The review explained 'the positive part played by the public sector in the TUC's alternative economic strategy. It shows that we need public spending: to protect the needy; to invest in industries and services which supply the whole community; and to implement strategies for growth, industry, employment and equality.'[98] This linked with the Labour Party's 1983 election manifesto: 'The present hideous level of unemployment is not an accident. It is the direct result of the policies of this government. The Tories have cut public investment and services . . . our approach is different. We will expand the economy, by providing a strong and measured increase in spending.'[99]

A new awareness among sections of the labour movement grew out of the battles against the government, about the nature of state power and about the ruthless nature of state action based on monetarist economic principles. The countervailing labour-movement principle of struggle through common cause emerged more strongly both in the immediate fight and in shifting the political balance of the wider movement. This was amply demonstrated by the 1983 People's March for Jobs, which the TUC reluctantly agreed to support only under pressure from NALGO and other unions. As *The Times* gleefully reported, 'the TUC is facing revolt over its decision not to support a planned Glasgow to London demonstration on unemployment . . . the executive of NALGO Britain's fourth largest union has unexpectedly decided to brush aside an official TUC call not to take part in the protest and instead give it "full financial and moral" support'.[100] Deputy General Secretary Alan Jinkinson was secretary of the national organizing

[95] S. Aaronovitch, *The Road from Thatcherism: The Alternative Economic Strategy* (London: Lawrence & Wishart, 1981), 2–3.

[96] D. Currie, 'World Capitalism in Recession', in S. Hall and M. Jacques (eds.), *The Politics of Thatcherism* (London: Lawrence & Wishart, 1983), 102–3.

[97] TUC, *The Battle for Jobs: TUC Economic Review 1983* (London: TUC, 1983), 17.

[98] Ibid. 28.

[99] Labour Party, *The New Hope for Britain—Labour's Manifesto 1983* (London: Labour Party, 1983), 8.

[100] *The Times*, 29 Nov. 1982, 2.

committee for the march. NALGO Research Officer Rod Robertson was the assistant secretary, and he told us that he and Alan Jinkinson 'had their eyes opened to TUC politics' through this.

As wage settlements fell in response to higher unemployment and lower inflation, so the mobilizing efforts of unions became further strained. The need to fight on so many fronts caused tensions within both NALGO and the wider movement. A split deepened in Labour's ranks, between what became known as the 'hard' left, at that time associated with Tony Benn's 1981 challenge to be deputy leader of the party, and the 'soft' left, later under Neil Kinnock, moving to the right.[101] The former stuck to the main elements of the AES, while the latter drifted into a no-man's-land of economic policy that certainly contributed to the election defeats of 1987 and 1992. Defeat in 1983 dealt a crushing electoral blow to the left.

NALGO's publicity department summarized the pre-election situation in the 1982 annual report: 'It has been another grim year for ordinary people all over the world, for the trade union movement, for the increasing numbers unable to find work, particularly young people and school leavers and for older people struggling to bring up a family on the dole. All this and more has been reflected in the pages of *Public Service*, which has hardly made cheerful reading.'[102] Most activists supported national opposition to the government's expenditure cuts in health, education, local-government services, and energy and transport, and to their increases in nuclear and military expenditure. This large group, the very broad left, also argued and fought for greater local autonomy, at the place of work through stewards, and at branch and group level to pursue objectives through collective bargaining. But as far as the wider membership was concerned, whatever had to be done could be done without either affiliating to the Labour Party or having a political fund. On 22 March 1982 the result of the ballot on these issues was announced—with a 58 per cent turnout, 89 per cent had voted against a political fund and 88 per cent against Labour Party affiliation (see Box 9).

Wear and tear

There was no doubting the urgency of union action to face the future, but one area of difficulty was well illustrated in a report in *Met District News* on membership participation in official union meetings. Ron Tennant, chair of the Metropolitan District Council, sadly noted that low turnout at meetings meant 'the rest of us huddled together opposing the 6 per cent pay policy—which isn't a pay policy; supporting the firemen, opposing Urban

---

[101] D. Sassoon, *One Hundred Years of Socialism* (London: Fontana Press, 1996), 698–9.
[102] *NALGO Annual Report 1982*, 196.

Development Corporations and the sale of council houses, and taking collections for the NALGO members on strike in Manchester . . . And we all shuffled off into the night.'[103] Rita Donaghy reported that the last two meetings had been inquorate, preventing the District Council from playing its role in maintaining NALGO policies and actions between conferences, which could lead to the union failing to respond to the acute problems of members.

Activists faced a conundrum—as the need for union responses became more acute, so the level of union activity declined. As *Met District News* put it: 'Cuts in services. Lengthening dole queues. Falling living standards. It's obvious that there is very little to cheer about these days given the economic crisis inspired by the government's policies. There has, as a result, been a general fall in morale within the trade union movement reflected by falling attendances at meetings at almost every level.'[104] Concerned about the implications of this for union democracy, Metropolitan District Secretary Ivan Beavis noted that

London has over 100,000 NALGO members in over 150 branches and the district is the forum through which members channel their views to the NEC and to the national negotiators and should be a dynamic body. The lack of interest enabled the national executive members to express their own views and this lack of accountability further weakened the relevance of the district.[105]

Branch AGMs in Worthing and Durham were so poorly attended that reluctant members were press-ganged into taking office. *Public Service* journalist Jeff Spooner reported that 'a buoyant convivial atmosphere gave way to an eerie silence when an appeal was made for somebody to become secretary of the Worthing health branch', and 'heavy verbals were expected at the first AGM of the Durham health branch. The branch executive committee had been pilloried for eight months for the way it handled industrial action locally . . . so the scene was set for a showdown . . . but the members who ventured out on a wet evening were either content with recent decisions or unwilling to make their criticisms public.'[106]

Even when 1,200 members of Camden local-government branch turned up to a branch meeting on 18 February 1981, they did so to vote overwhelmingly against any action to fight the cuts. Mike Blick moved the victorious motion, passed by 764 to 404: 'This branch condemns the government's policies which are having such a disastrous effect on Camden's finances. It considers that NALGO's members best interests will not be served by a policy of confrontation with the Council while it attempts to deal with these problems.'[107] Thirty members of the branch executive resigned. It

---

[103] *Met News* (Jan. 1981), 2. [104] Ibid. 3. [105] Ibid. (Dec. 1982), 3.
[106] *PS* (Dec. 1982), 2. [107] *Met News* (Apr. 1981), 1.

indicated that membership turnout at meetings was dependent on the issues: routine business and even plans to fight back were ignored, while efforts to take action were rebuffed by large numbers.

This shows several important points about trade unionism in local government, where the employers are elected and can claim some legitimacy in carrying through their policies as endorsed by the electorate. More importantly, Labour councils may be genuinely sympathetic to union positions (as argued by opponents of the national scale in the 1920s (see Chapter 2)). National policies that suggest fighting every cut might well be appropriate for most other sections of NALGO, but in local government they might need to be refined. During a broad labour-movement struggle against the government, including Labour councillors and trade unionists sharing broad objectives, the range of tactical options and the numerous shades of political differences provide fertile territory for muddles and splits.

As we suggest in Chapter 1, during the 1980s the issues faced in everyday work by an increasing number of members became more and more similar to those traditionally faced by manual workers. As a result many widely held objections to industrial action and political campaigning began to wither away, and the broad left leadership in regions such as Scotland, the North West, and London established a clear line of policy and practical opposition to government. Inevitably during such a period there were deviations and blind alleys that activists followed, creating additional tensions between rival factions, and over the next few years both the ultra-left and the SDP right sought to undermine the dominant progressive alliance at the heart of the union.

Despite all of this NALGO held together: in 1981 only the North East region lost members. In Scotland, West Midland, Metropolitan, and Eastern districts membership increased by over 2 per cent. More specifically, the Eastern region lost members only in electricity while making real gains in local government, and in Scotland, for example, there were gains in membership in the NHS and university sectors. As a result, national membership increased by 20,000 to over 796,000 in 1981, strengthening the union's financial position in combination with increased subscriptions and with no large-scale national industrial action (see Tables 4.1 and 4.2). This position was in stark contrast with some of the larger manual unions and the TUC in general (see Table 4.3).

NALGO in the 1980s

Market forces and cost-cutting tested the unity of the national union, as particular groups experienced different pressures and argued for different solutions to their problems. Holding together the national union was going to be one of the major challenges for the leadership, and, since NALGO was one of the largest and most influential of the TUC's affiliates, the integrity of the union had implications for the labour movement as a whole.

Many activists believed that, despite the high-profile campaigns and the sometimes successful challenges to cuts, nonetheless the union and the membership in general were not responding robustly enough. The need for a stronger union response was a crucial part of the discussions in the NALGO in the Eighties Committee, set up 'to test NALGO's structure against the challenge of the decade'.[108] This committee provided important ideas as to how the union might cope with what was to come.

Its first report mainly endorsed the status quo, but the specific issues that it discussed give a flavour of the debates going on inside the union at the time. It covered four areas of concern, the main one being the tensions that arise in a vertical trade union, between members who are managers and those who are managed.[109] As the report notes, 'managers tend to regard themselves as agents for their employers and may find themselves in a dilemma when this position comes into conflict with their membership of a union. Also they may be regarded with suspicion by other members of the branch who see their loyalty as divided.'[110] The committee favoured retaining managers within the union, noting in particular that some high-graded staff might have no managerial role while some low-graded staff might be in charge of others. Some senior staff were leaving NALGO for the supposed benefits of separate representation, particularly in the NHS. No structural changes were recommended to accommodate managers, but the possibility of branches establishing steward constituencies for senior managers was suggested. This debate resurfaced with the UNISON merger talks.

The next main point was on the scope of membership, with a particular emphasis on industrial unionism. Options included the establishment of single unions for each of the services containing NALGO members, merger with other unions, and the adoption of a federal structure. The committee was in favour of industrial unionism as a long-term objective, but rejected expansion into areas of manual employment. On mergers they concluded that none was likely at the time. They also rejected notions of a federal union with greater autonomy for sections, and believed that the best hope of expansion was by recruiting non-members such as the 130,000 non-manual employees in local government. In addition the committee rejected both

---

[108] *NALGO in the Eighties*, First Report (London: NALGO, 1981), 2.

[109] P. Blyton and G. Ursell, 'Vertical Recruitment in White-Collar Trade Unions: Some Causes and Consequences', *British Journal of Industrial Relations*, 20/2 (1982), 186–94.

[110] *NALGO in the Eighties*, First Report (1981), 4.

affiliation to the Labour Party and the creation of a political fund (see Box 9).

But the decentralization of power was the main issue. In local government there were more national delegate meetings for particular occupational groups, and the NHS members wanted more frequent group meetings. There were moves to make NEC members more accountable to District Councils. A decision to continue appointing, rather than electing, the General Secretary was picked upon by *The Times* as a sign of the need for trade union reform. It reported that the NALGO NEC saw direct election of officials as 'fundamentally undemocratic'.[111] Nevertheless, moves aimed at making the union more responsive on traditional negotiating issues of pay, conditions of service, jobs, and equality were supported by most activists, officials, and elected leaders. They aimed to enable the union as a whole and the union as the sum of its parts to fight the cuts and to defend public services. Opposition to a Conservative government on these issues was not lost on the press: 'The biggest union representing town hall staff set course yesterday for a confrontation with the Government over cuts being demanded in local council spending' and 'the conference also called on the union leadership to coordinate the campaign with the TUC, Labour Party and local Labour groups to oppose cuts'.[112]

Campaigns—nationally orchestrated and locally based

NALGO policy remained expansionist and Keynesian, fighting for jobs and services. This stimulated a stronger role for local activists and widened union action into common cause with others fighting on a range of broad political, economic, and social issues. Internal developments, spurred on by growing local activist power, focused on holding leaders and officials more tightly to account for policy-making and implementation, with the debates on this being sharpened, reflected, and refracted through the campaigns for and against the political fund and Labour Party affiliation. The important role of local activists and stewards was both recognized and strengthened with the launch in 1981 of *NALGO News*, a weekly four page (and sometimes eight-page) newspaper: '*NALGO News* is sent to some 25,000 branch and district officials and stewards and is intended to keep them up to date on all main developments at national level in all areas of the union's work.'[113]

The union forged closer links with others in the public sector and played a more important role within the TUC, but its own democratic practices and structures were coming under fire. Initially a local-government trade union

---

[111] *The Times*, 26 Jan. 1981, 2.   [112] Ibid., 11 June 1981, 2.
[113] *NALGO Annual Report 1981*, 157.

for white-collar and professional staff, NALGO had become a broader-based organization. There was a clear logic to this when the utilities and other services were run in ways similar, although never identical, to local government. But when the government pushed market competition, private enterprise, and different financial and managerial arrangements into these industries, then the similarities began to disappear and the resultant diverging interests of sections of the union were not so easily reconciled. The union's federal unity became more fragile as, for example, members facing a future in the private sector and those facing continuing employment in the cash-strapped public services considered their respective positions.

Vertical recruitment also came under pressure, as employers started to split senior managers from trade unionism in order to achieve their managerial reforms through the introduction of HRM techniques in the later 1980s and 1990s. Some higher managers set up a breakaway union in the gas industry. Publicizing the case against this, *Public Service* reported that it 'has not been granted certification as a trade union, claims 1300 members from the ranks of higher managers . . . and is not recognised by British Gas for negotiating'.[114] Breakaway unions are rare in British history and are usually caused by a mixture of small-group disaffection and employer encouragement. They normally do not survive long.[115]

Leaders and activists gained confidence in their ability to make alliances with a variety of causes and organizations without compromising the union's integrity or its identity. On issues such as the new employment legislation to restrict trade-union action, NALGO had no trouble in siding with the TUC. On matters of discrimination, it was happy to join with other groups to fight the employment consequences of unfair treatment against gay workers. On racism, it encouraged both raising awareness and taking action, as with the Lambeth Branch publication, *Race and Racism*. Shoulder to shoulder with others, members joined a march on 1 December 1981, organized by teacher unions and the South East Region of the TUC (SERTUC), to protest against education cuts in London. In Scotland John Pollock, STUC chair, argued that the battle against cuts in Lothian had shown the benefits of common campaigns: 'the union battle was fought not by individual unions, but on the basis of fighting to preserve the jobs of all. They were fighting not only for their own jobs, but for the maintenance and improvement of the services also.'[116]

But broadly based national action was increasingly overshadowed by local activity, ranging from small-scale skirmishes to all-out strike action through-

[114] *PS* (Feb. 1982), 6.
[115] S. Lerner, *Breakaway Unions and the Small Trade Union* (London: Allen & Unwin, 1961); J. Hemmingway, *Conflict and Democracy* (Oxford: Oxford University Press, 1978).
[116] *Mac* (Jan. 1982), 4.

out the country. As a result workplace shop stewards began to play a much more prominent role (see Box 4).

Box 4. The NALGO Steward System

From NALGO's early days as a local–government officers' union, branch organization was based on officers elected at the annual general meeting and holding functional positions, such as president, secretary, and treasurer. The main point of contact between branch and employer was through the branch officers. Branch business was overseen by an executive committee, consisting of the officers and 'departmental representatives' elected from among the members in each local-authority department. Departmental representatives were the link between the branch and the members—they had no formal role in negotiating with management. Branch officers met with employer representatives and senior managers on a regular basis in local JCCs, and they dealt with most grievances and disciplinary cases, perhaps assisted by full-time officers.

This system began to show signs of strain during the 1970s. The 1974 local-government reorganization created some very large local authorities, and, along with the electricity, gas, and water employers, they adopted new management structures with stronger personnel functions, taking tighter approaches to workforce planning including the use of work study, job evaluation, and 'organization and methods' techniques. Departmental representatives took on some of the work previously done by branch secretaries and full-time officers. Departmental JCCs were established in many larger employers, where departmental representatives had regular formal meetings with their top managers. As membership doubled from under 350,000 in 1965 to over 700,000 in 1978, members needed better contact with the union, better representation, more information, and more involvement in union decisions.

New employment laws, such as the Industrial Relations Act 1971 and the Trade Union and Labour Relations Act 1974, gave the 'officials' of recognized trade unions the right to paid time off and office facilities appropriate to their activities on pay and conditions issues.

The NEC Working Party on Communications recommended the immediate implementation of a steward system,[117] and the 1977 conference agreed. Branches were to seek 'facilities agreements' with employers, providing for recognition of stewards, office accommodation, furniture, equipment, clerical support, access to employer documents, check-off and paid time off for union duties. Steward training was to be provided at branch, district, and national levels, and a weekly information publication was to be sent to activists.

The 1977 conference resolution defined two aspects of the steward. First, the steward was to be 'responsible to and for a particular group of members'. Secondly, the steward 'shall negotiate on behalf of his [sic] group and individuals within his group'. Many large branches had already moved towards this model, and departmental

---

[117] G. Newman, *Path to Maturity: NALGO 1965–1980* (London: NALGO, 1982), 522.

representatives negotiated with managers and handled grievance and disciplinary cases. Constituency-based representation had already been adopted in some branches. The Sheffield Branch, for example, already had a form of steward system, including stewards who were members of departmental steward committees but not of the branch executive committee.

Adoption of the steward system was patchy, and, in spite of a survey of branches suggesting that there were 30,000 NALGO stewards in 1978, progress was sufficiently slow for the issue to be raised again in the 1980s. The activists' bulletin finally appeared in the form of *NALGO News* in 1981. A survey of stewards carried out by Glasgow University, reported in *Public Service* in April 1982, identified that, of the average two and three quarter hours per week on union business, 46 per cent was spent with members and 54 per cent with other stewards and branch officers. No mention is made of negotiations with management. To some extent the use and growth of stewards owed something to their more general existence among the manual workers in NUPE and the General and Municipal Workers' Union (GMWU).[118]

The 1983 conference resolution suggested a more urgent approach and clarified two main principles. First, the basic unit of branch organization should be the constituency or shop, consisting of a relatively small number of members grouped in a workplace and, if appropriate, by job function. Shop boundaries should reflect patterns of negotiations between stewards and managers. Secondly, shop stewards should be grouped together into steward committees. Branch executive committees should consist of stewards elected by and from the steward committees, along with the branch officers. But 'limits on the ability of most stewards to play a full role in turn suggests difficulties in stewards associating effectively at levels above the immediate place of work'.[119]

The importance of this model was that it allowed for many more members to be brought into union activity and for a much broader base of both representation and participation. An increase in the number of representatives through the new steward system meant better union campaigning among the members and greater union responsiveness to member demands.

The change to the steward system, however patchy and gradual, became an essential part of NALGO's democratic and organizing fabric. It reached the parts of the membership that had been untouched by the outdated departmental representative system, providing both a voice for the members in the union and a platform for the union in the workplace.[120] Stewards played a vital role in national union campaigns,

---

[118] M. Terry, 'Organising a Fragmented Workforce: Shop Stewards in Local Government', *British Journal of Industrial Relations*, 20/1 (1982), 1–19; I. Kessler, 'Shop Stewards in Local Government Revisited', *British Journal of Industrial Relations*, 24/3 (1986), 419–41; R. Fryer, 'Public Service Trade Unionism in the Twentieth Century', in R. Mailly, S. Dimmock, and A. Sethi (eds.), *Industrial Relations in the Public Services* (London: Routledge, 1989).

[119] I. Kessler, 'Bargaining Strategies in Local Government', in R. Mailly, S. Dimmock, and A. Sethi (eds.), *Industrial Relations in the Public Services* (London: Routledge, 1989), 183.

[120] N. Nicholson, G. Ursell, and P. Blyton, 'Social Background Attitudes and Behaviour of White-Collar Shop Stewards', *British Journal of Industrial Relations*, 18/2 (1980), 231–9.

such as the 1987 political fund campaign (see Box 9), the 1989 recruitment campaign, and the 1989 strike in local government (see Box 12), taking the union arguments to the members and countering government and employer propaganda. Steward structures, such as steward committees and their links with branch committees, provide the basis for the kind of permanent and stable organization that is necessary to sustain a continuing union presence at work, to provide support to members with problems, and to raise the awareness of new activists entering the world of trade unionism and negotiations with managers.

As the steward system developed, reports from branches provided evidence of its success. Suffolk County Council Branch found that there had been 'a marked increase in the level of participation. Stewards are now beginning to deal with service conditions problems, there is more interest in branch training, there has been new life breathed into Departmental Committees (now Stewards' Committees) and there is a greater interest in other activities ancillary to NALGO such as Trades Councils.'[121] The union stepped up its programme of courses for activists and branch officers, to improve both their skills and their knowledge, which also operated as an informal setting for discussion and debate and for building activist networks within and between branches.[122]

Discussion and action were stimulated by the campaign to 'Put People First', 'the slogan for NALGO's national campaign against cuts and privatisation'[123] aimed at generating support for public services in an election year (see Box 9). The politically sensitive title was well chosen: people—citizens, users of services, trade-union members, and workers—were seen as more important than profit and the three 'E's of economy, efficiency, and effectiveness. The campaign was launched in April 1983 with a £1 million budget for events to take union arguments all over the country: in Scotland the 7:84 theatre company used street performances of a play called *On the Pigs' Back*; in Yorkshire and Humberside John Daly, the incoming General Secretary, spoke at the press launch; in Hull the campaign bus appeared in the local carnival; in the West Midlands there was a rally in Stafford; a NALGO balloon took President Peter Holt up in the air in South Wales; and in Liverpool the North Western and North Wales District adopted a zoo animal threatened with extinction in the wild. The letters page of *Public Service* shows that a section of the membership opposed the campaign, on the grounds that it

---

[121] *Edlines* (Mar. 1983), 4.
[122] IRS, 'Training Union Representatives: NALGO's Policy', *Industrial Relations Review and Report*, 225 (1980), 9–10.
[123] *NN*, 25 Feb. 1983, 1.

was outside the proper scope of trade union activity and anti-government to boot!

The list of campaign issues taken up by the union grew ever longer: the People's March for Jobs, which left Glasgow on 23 April 1983, with a £20,000 NALGO donation; the Police and Criminal Evidence Bill, which aimed to criminalize some forms of protest; and early hints about abolishing the GLC. In the NHS NALGO opposed the Griffiths Report[124] on new management structures; launched the 'Say No to Private Medicine' campaign; and also supplied information on the changes brought about by the 1983 Mental Health Act. The new Transport Act was attacked as giving too much power to the Secretary of State; the government's Green Paper on trade-union democracy was strongly criticized; and the privatization of Wytch Farm onshore oilfield was condemned.

International work expanded through affiliation to the Public Services International (PSI) and through strengthened support for South African trade unionists in their struggle for freedom (see Box 14). NALGO was among the unions from nineteen European countries that organized a demonstration in Brussels against unemployment. Recognizing the international dimension to the problems of spending for war but not spending for people, activists backed anti-war activity at the 'Women All Out for Peace' day of action at the women's peace camp at the Greenham Common US bomber base. Those women opposing military might gave hope to others fighting to protect the services that enabled a peaceful and dignified existence. They underpinned action against the closure of the South London Hospital for Women in Wandsworth.

These campaigns brought to the fore the importance of women's identity with other women, linking to other struggles, including that within NALGO, for higher levels of representation for women. In yet another investigation, 'NALGO's equality survey had demonstrated that women were still clustered in the low paid jobs, had breaks in service to care for children and were under-represented in the union hierarchy'.[125] The NEOC, ably supported by Tess Woodcraft, broke new ground by issuing union guidelines for campaigning on sexual harassment and positive action at work, and a pamphlet on *Rights of Working Parents*. Another pamphlet, *Gay Rights: NALGO Fighting against Prejudice*, emphasized the importance of union action to defend gay and lesbian members from victimization at work. For example, Ian Davies was sacked by Tower Hamlets social services department after he voluntarily told his director that he had been fined £25 for a minor offence

---

[124] R. Griffiths, *NHS Management Inquiry* (Letter to Secretary of State; London: DHSS, 1983).
[125] *PS* (Feb. 1983), 20.

relating to his homosexuality. Union support, including an IT hearing and a strike by the NALGO branch, secured his reinstatement. NALGO worked with the National Council for Civil Liberties to support the rights of gay workers.

There were other important developments on discrimination issues. The Central Arbitration Committee (CAC) reported on a national local-government maternity agreement, ruling that 'maternity leave beginning on or after 1 April 1982 should count for the accrual of annual and sick leave— in the case of unpaid leave for 22 weeks, or such lesser period where the scheme provides discretion'.[126] Lambeth Council agreed a positive action policy for black people, but recognized that it would work only if there was 'clear political commitment', backing by senior management, and independent monitoring, and that 'trade unions must join with management in establishing goals'.[127] Furthermore, an increasing number of activists, nationally and locally, understood that their trade-union aims were linked to the aims of anti-apartheid, anti-nuclear, and anti-discrimination protestors, both morally and politically. Such a catalogue of disparate but related causes shows how NALGO was politicized as activists responded to the forces of reaction both at home and abroad.

Collective Bargaining and Local Disputes

The bargaining climate in 1981

In some industries the bargaining machinery itself came under attack. The National Water Council was abolished, ending the related bargaining system and its agreements, and later in 1982 the government created pay review bodies for some NHS staff. Norman Tebbit announced, in a written parliamentary answer on 28 July, that the government was to scrap the 1946 Fair Wages resolution, breaching the International Labour Organization's Convention C94. An academic survey of the manufacturing sector found several important general developments in industrial relations, including the move to single-employer bargaining, a more professional approach to negotiations by managers, pay-fixing at the level of the employer and/or the business unit, and a more widespread use of job evaluation.[128]

Some of this rubbed off on parts of the public sector as employers aimed to alter the scope and level of collective bargaining. In local government, for

---

[126] Ibid. (May 1982), 3.   [127] Ibid. (Apr. 1982), 15.
[128] W. Brown, *The Changing Contours of British Industrial Relations* (Oxford: Blackwell, 1981).

example, there was a mood among some employers that just maybe the time was coming when national negotiations were less important. The real push to change the entire bargaining framework came from the cash limits introduced in 1976, because 'the question of local authority pay, and therefore pay bargaining, now led directly into that of local authority expenditure as a whole'.[129] Early signs of the importance of local pay determination showed in the growing number of local regrading disputes, even when they were nationally supported as with the social workers in 1978–9 (see Box 1). Also, during the 1980 comparability dispute (see Box 2) some local authorities made their own deals. In 1982 a survey of 235 local authorities showed that there was 'a significant amount of supplementary bargaining in local government. This is, of course, important in that it implies that central government could not hope to control local spending via the mechanism of influencing national negotiations.'[130]

By 1981 the recession started to bring down the rates of increase of both prices and average wages to around 11 per cent. British Waterways Board workers settled for 8 per cent and a job security pledge, while staff in water supply won 11 per cent. In the health services NALGO, NUPE, and COHSE voted against accepting a 6 per cent pay rise for nurses and PT'B' staff, but they were outvoted by the non-TUC organizations, and had to face the government's determination to break the link between NHS A&C grades and those in the civil service. 'The last two years has [*sic*] seen a rigid application of government cash limits in the NHS. As a consequence the links which most NALGO members had either formally or informally with related civil service staff have been severed.'[131] The same 6 per cent offer was rejected by A&C staff where NALGO had a majority, but soon after the negotiators accepted it. PTE staff settled for pay increases of 7.5–7.9 per cent. In the universities, the Clegg Commission awarded 5 per cent to clerical staff, and then the computer staff received the final Clegg award, of 15.3 per cent.

But collective-bargaining activity became increasingly concerned with jobs. There were threats of job loss by electricity employers to frighten the union into a low wage claim. Fierce cuts throughout the university system made job losses inevitable, and NALGO, along with the other main campus unions, NUPE, ASTMS, and AUT, launched a campaign to reverse the damage: 'Unanimous support for a national rally and mass lobby of MPs on 18 November was given by delegates to the reconvened universities group

[129] K. Walsh, 'Centralisation and Decentralisation in Local Government Bargaining', *Industrial Relations Journal*, 12/5 (1981), 47.

[130] M. Ingham, 'Industrial Relations in British Local Government', *Industrial Relations Journal*, 16/1 (1985), 15.

[131] *NALGO Annual Report 1981*, 102.

meeting.'[132] NALGO argued for an expanded further and higher education sector and pointed out that cuts mean redundancies, affect local economies, and reduce the system to a home for a dwindling elite.[133] As Alex Thompson, national organizer, argued: 'The attack on university finance has nothing to do with economics but is part of the government's philosophy . . . to make university education elitist'. This view was powerfully supported by Geoffrey Drain speaking to the rally in London: 'It is an attack on liberties and freedom of opportunity because cuts in universities mean a reduction of at least one in seven of those qualified by Robbins criteria to be there. It also blights the hopes of mature and part-time students and creates more youth unemployment.'[134]

When members lobbied the Aston University Senate meeting to protest about redundancies, supported by members from other unions and other universities, their district organization officer, Sid Platt, told them: 'Either they could give up or they could fight for their jobs.'[135] The Aston members did fight, and the redundancies were withdrawn. The local press reported 'furious workers are to ask unions in Birmingham to call for the scrapping of the body that recommended sweeping cuts in Universities'.[136]

Bedfordshire and Cambridge County Councils slashed services despite large demonstrations and union protests. The *Cambridge Evening News* reported that 'about 200 demonstrators stood outside Shire Hall in Cambridge today to protest against Cambridge County Council cut-backs', and later that 'trade unionists from all over East Anglia were told in Cambridge yesterday to expect 400 redundancies among local government employees'.[137] In the NHS, South Glamorgan AHA announced sixty-seven redundancies as branch chair Bill Williams argued: 'We have asked the authority to look at other ways of saving the money but they just do not want to know. Now we are going to fight these redundancies all along the line.'[138]

In Scotland *Mac* reported a 'war against the cuts' with 'a series of brief skirmishes and much posturing, consultation and negotiation'.[139] *Met District News* covered Hillingdon Council's decision to axe 238 jobs and the NALGO branch's industrial action, including ceasing cooperation with councillors, withdrawing cooperation from the council's expenditure review, and banning all work on the council's second review of land sales. Staff in Enfield Council's architect's department fought against redundancies, declared

---

[132] *PS* (Oct. 1981), 5.
[133] NALGO, *Post-School Education* (London: NALGO, 1981).
[134] *NN*, 20 Nov. 1981, 1.   [135] *PS* (Nov. 1981), 5.
[136] *Birmingham Evening Mail*, 1 Oct. 1981, 18.
[137] *Cambridge Evening News*, 24 Feb. 1981, 1; and 5 Mar. 1981, 8.
[138] *PS* (Apr. 1981), 6.   [139] *Mac* (Mar. 1981), 4.

without union consultation, and in Hackney social services there was successful no-cover action over unfilled posts. There were strikes in Wandsworth over privatization proposals and NALGO members in Westminster went on strike for a day over job cuts recommended by the management consultancy firm McKinsey. In the North West and North Wales District *News NoW* reported on the scandal of unemployment and job losses in towns with higher than average unemployment, reaching over 15 per cent in Liverpool, Wrexham, and Ormskirk.

But the biggest local action was a six-month strike of 400 Liverpool City Council typists over grades. Branch chair Graham Burgess said: 'The typists are low paid and often the only wage earner in the family. The city council is refusing to budge—they seem intent on starving the typists back to work. But our members are determined to win.'[140] The action became more bitter as managers suspended some members who refused to do the strikers' work, and the branch escalated the action with the support of the NEC—it was agreed 'that members employed as typists, secretaries, etc. previously balloted be instructed to take indefinite strike action with effect from 6 July 1981 with strike pay of £20 per week from National funds.'[141] In December, after twenty-four weeks on strike, the typists returned to work based on an agreement to settle through a committee of inquiry chaired by an Advisory, Conciliation, and Arbitration Service (ACAS) nominee. One problem in agreeing the terms of the return to work was in NALGO's treatment of strike-breaking members, an issue that dogged the union throughout the decade.

The 1982 NHS dispute

The most important national action of 1982 was organized through the TUC around pay claims for health-service workers. Deteriorating industrial relations were highlighted in the TUC's report, *Improving Industrial Relations in the NHS*,[142] requested by the Royal Commission into the NHS concerned with the damage done by national disputes. The TUC argued that 'pay should be freely negotiated before central cash is allotted annually to health authorities', and that there should be an NHS arbitration tribunal with the power to make binding awards. Responding to the government's pay limit, the joint staff side of Whitley A&C 'stated that if pay in 1982 increased by 4% only, staff in the NHS would be taking a reduction in pay and a cut in living standards'.[143] In formulating the claim, 'delegates to NALGO's special health

---

[140] *PS* (Sept. 1981), 2.

[141] *NALGO Emergency Committee Meeting Minutes*, 10b (1981), 70.

[142] TUC, *Improving Industrial Relations in the NHS* (London: TUC, 1981).

[143] *NN*, 25 Sept. 1981, 1.

group meeting on pay will be urged to support a plan to break through the Government's four per cent limit on public sector salary deals because that is the only way of ensuring fair awards for the membership'.[144]

The TUC-affiliated unions agreed a common claim of 12 per cent, setting course for a major clash: 'An alliance of 14 TUC health service unions, including NALGO, has asked the public to back their bid to break through the government's four per cent public sector pay norm . . . For the first time, unions and professional associations on all 17 NHS Whitley negotiating councils and committees have lodged claims with this common core.'[145] John Monks, assistant publicity field officer, urged NALGO branches to use the local media on a regular basis to counter 'the massive propaganda from the employers'.[146]

After a rally on 15 March, there was a series of strikes and days of action that attracted widespread support from the labour and trade-union movement, and from the wider public. NALGO, representing mainly A&C staff, played a full part, as reported in *Public Service*:

Our cause is just—now pay up. That was the message driven home last month to the government by the three quarters of NALGO's health service members who took action on 19 May in support of 12 per cent pay claims. It was the first ever one day strike by all groups of health service staff in TUC health service unions. The desperation of NALGO members was summed up in the leaflet *Striking for a Living Wage*, where it was argued that 'none of us wants to go on strike. It was always an act of last resort. But sometimes it cannot be avoided—when it becomes the only effective way to register our protest. Whole NALGO branches walked out on strike as NALGO members joined demonstrations, workplace meetings and picket lines. Miners at four Yorkshire pits joined the campaign . . . Hospitals, offices and clinics from the Highlands and Islands of Scotland to Sussex coast resorts were hit as NALGO's traditionally moderate members protested at a blatant injustice.[147]

The conduct of the dispute was very important given the union need for public support and the employers' aim to divide the workforce. NALGO's view was that 'it soon became clear . . . that the government had instructed management sides to hold the line of four per cent',[148] and that there was no intention to allow the parties to settle amongst themselves. Action ranged from local activities such as in Harrow when 200 health workers walked out of Northwick Park Hospital to one-day strikes on 19 May and again on 4 and 8 June. ACAS involvement helped Norman Fowler, Secretary of State, to improve the government's offer to 7.5 per cent for professional staff and 6 per cent for others, but this only sparked further protests with a day of action in

---

[144] *PS* (Dec. 1981), 9.   [145] Ibid. (Mar. 1982), 8.   [146] Ibid. (Apr. 1982), 5.
[147] Ibid. (June 1982), 1.   [148] *NALGO Annual Report 1982*, 104.

London and Glasgow on 23 June. There was a three-day national stoppage on 19–21 July, followed by more days of action in August and September, with the TUC calling for maximum support, including stoppages, from all affiliates. There were selective strikes, which were supported by action from other groups such as the Yorkshire NUM.

The government was shaken by the breadth of support and unity of purpose. Norman Fowler recalled: 'August was even worse than July. As the dispute hardened, demonstrations became everyday affairs. Whenever I drove to a hospital my question would not be whether there was a demonstration but how big.'[149] On 9–13 August there was a five-day stoppage that received support from groups such as Fleet Street electricians and the Clydesdale Mill of British Steel. There were more and more large rallies throughout the country, and other sections of the membership joined with solidarity action. On 17 October there were regional days of protest over health staff pay following a vote for an all-out NHS strike.

Public support put the government in danger of destroying its Falkland-based popularity. Talks started at the end of October, and the dispute was settled after ACAS intervention with a two-year pay deal (6 per cent from April 1982 with another 4.5 per cent from April 1983) and the offer of a pay review body for nurses and PAMs.[150] On 14 December the health group meeting was asked to decide between more strikes or acceptance of the offer. The pressure was to accept, as industrial action was fading and unity between the unions was weakening. In addition some benefits were seen from the proposed streamlined Whitley. NALGO decided to oppose the pay review body, noting that 'the proposal will result in a greater fragmentation of manpower and pay arrangements' and that the review body itself would not be politically independent of government.[151]

This dispute broke the government's pay limit and also showed the strength of support for the NHS. The unions' action was partly responsible for persuading the government to downplay its NHS reforms in terms of privatization and pay-setting. However, by setting up the pay review bodies for professional staff, and by partially reforming the Whitley system, the government had succeeded in hanging onto most of its main objectives in the areas of pay and employer rights, sounding a clear warning to other public-sector workers ready to defend their pay and jobs.[152] The government was convinced it had won an important victory. Norman Fowler believed 'the 1982

[149] N. Fowler, *Ministers Decide* (London: Chapmans, 1991), 172.
[150] G. Thomason, 'The Pay Review Bodies', *Health Services Manpower Review*, 11/3 (1985), 3–6.
[151] *PS* (May 1983), 8.
[152] R. Seifert, *Industrial Relations in the NHS* (London: Chapman & Hall, 1992).

health dispute served notice that the Government would not easily give way in a strike. That message was later underlined in the 1984–5 miners' strike.'[153]

The bargaining climate in 1982–3

The government's strategy to cheapen public-sector labour and to reduce public services gained strength, and NALGO activists and leaders saw it would have drastic results for both members and service users. As they voted in the general election, members in all parts of the union knew that their pay was being squeezed, conditions threatened, and job security weakened. Under such circumstances workers might respond in a variety of ways. Some take a resigned view and plough on. Some react in personal ways such as quitting, reducing effort, or sabotage. Others try to organize collective resistance and struggle through their union branches.

It is sometimes the most apparently unlikely groups that react in the most positive ways. One important aspect of NALGO's resistance at this time was the major protest movement that began to well up from among nursery nurses, drawing confidence from other women's struggles. Groups of workers traditionally in a weak position in the labour market can react more directly to the combined effects of low pay, bad treatment, and worsening service conditions to take up the vanguard role within a large organization. Such a note of optimism may appear at odds with such a ferocious four years of government attacks against working people, their organizations, and their services. But it is just that, the unexpected level of resistance among objectively weak groups, that enabled the union to maintain its organizational shape, to reform its internal decision-making to be more representative, and to mount campaigns against government policies.

With inflation and the average earnings index both increasing at about 9 per cent, public-sector pay settlements continued to fall in 1982. Water staff settled for 7.5 per cent, electricity for 7.2–7.6 per cent, gas for 6.8–7.5 per cent, New Towns for 5.9 per cent, National Bus for 6.6 per cent, and British Waterways for 6.5–7 per cent. Other groups were forced to accept lower settlements after arbitration, with an award of 5.4–7.3 per cent to university staff, and one of 5.7 per cent in local government. For most groups there was a loss of pay, both in real terms and in comparison with other employees.

In 1983, settlements were around the 5 per cent mark in local government (4.64–5.47 per cent), electricity (3.5–5.8 per cent), gas (5.5 per cent), waterways (5 per cent), PTE (4 per cent in April with another 1.5 per cent in October), buses (5.5 per cent), New Towns (4.8 per cent), water (5.6 per cent), industrial estates (4.85 per cent in England and Wales and 4.57 per cent in

---

[153] Fowler, *Ministers Decide*, 178.

Scotland), and universities (4.6–5.47 per cent). Again these were below both the rate of inflation and settlements elsewhere in the economy, emphasizing the government clampdown on public-sector pay irrespective of the consequences. The consistent pattern shows that, whatever the industry's own situation, and whatever the supposed independence of arbitration systems, the going rate is the going rate, and it is largely determined by crude pay limits decided by the Treasury (Tables 2.5–2.15).

Cutbacks were widespread. Lothian Regional Council shed 4,400 jobs after control went from Labour to a Conservative–SDP–Liberal coalition. In London's fifty-two hospitals 4,000 jobs were lost. Job losses spread to the voluntary sector, set to expand rapidly in the 1990s, causing its first major outbreak of industrial conflict. All social-worker posts were blacklisted at the famous charity Barnados after redundancy threats. The case of Barnardos was especially important:

Up till now Barnardos, National Children's Homes, and the Children's Society have refused recognition of NALGO mainly from a position of strength. Membership has been steadily increasing in these organisations and residential staff are awaiting the outcome of this dispute before judging the effectiveness of trade unionism against anti-union employers. The past has shown lack of fight by residential staff over closures because of lack of members or lack of time to organise. This closure has arrived in an established NALGO home, with good organisation in the Division plus willingness to fight the employer from all the Spennells staff.[154]

In 1983 the union responded as water employers began their moves to end national bargaining: 'This group meeting recognises that current proposals for breaking up the negotiating machinery at national and regional level are based on the Government's desire to reduce the effectiveness of the trade unions within the industry, and reduce the level of salary and conditions of service settlements.'[155] Similar motions were passed by the gas and electricity groups. The position was publicized in a NALGO leaflet that said the Water Bill means 'death of all existing national and local agreements; end to national pay talks; attack on training and other services; threat to more jobs; and halts the industry's voice'.

The crisis in the water industry worsened with the first national strike by manual workers. John Pitt, national water officer, said: 'Branches throughout the country are rallying to the call given nationally not to undermine the action in any way.'[156] NALGO's 30,000 members in the industry were persuaded that the manual workers' fight over pay was also their fight, and the union instructed them to work normally and not to cross picket lines. The

[154] *NALGO Emergency Committee Meeting Minutes*, 11 (1982), 243.
[155] *NALGO Annual Report 1983*, 159.   [156] *NN*, 28 Jan. 1983, 1.

strike lasted from 23 January to 23 February 1983.[157] It highlighted the more aggressive and divisive labour-management policies being introduced against staff and their unions.

In the NHS some services were being privatized, which threatened 'hard won terms and conditions of employment'.[158] Under similar pressures, members at the London Institute of Education walked out over the appointment of a clerical worker on a fixed-term contract, a labour-management practice that was to become more and more widespread. In local government 30,000 residential workers called for industrial action to settle their long-running demands for improved conditions, especially in working time and payments for unsocial hours. Union action to protect jobs, to defend conditions, and to fight the cuts had an impact in the workplaces, putting managers under pressure. They responded by attacking trade-union organization, and two important victories at ITs show how NALGO responded. British Gas stopped two branch secretaries having time off to attend meetings opposing the Oil and Gas Bill, and Haringey Council stopped safety representatives having paid time off. In both cases employers aimed to restrict workplace representatives' activity in order to reduce union effectiveness, and in both cases the union successfully used the courts to enforce their rights.

Concluding Remarks

So the first period of Conservative government ended with their second general-election victory in 1983. NALGO members faced up to the consequences of government policy: cuts and redundancies, restructuring and privatization, efficiency drives and managerial controls, and a reduction in democratic accountability. All of this was against a background of an increasingly unstable international political world and the re-emergence of right-wing ideals in government. Unions used all the methods available to them to fight back, and NALGO extended its own internal democratic practices of consultation, bringing in new groups, developing stewards at the workplace, and maintaining its position on the left of centre of the British trade-union movement.

Pessimism was mixed with muted defiance as activists and leaders carried on protecting members' interests at the place of work, and forging the wider unity and political understanding necessary to redirect government practices

---

[157] S. Ogden, 'Water', in A. Pendleton and J. Winterton (eds.), *Public Enterprise in Transition: Industrial Relations in State and Privatized Corporations* (London: Routledge, 1993), 140–2.
[158] *PS* (Apr. 1983), 7.

and Labour Party policies towards union goals of full employment, higher investment, and better public services. The 1983 annual report expresses the pessimism:

Your Council published its white paper on *The Alternative Economic Strategy*, which marked the culmination of several years' work in developing a carefully thought out programme for a new government. But before it had even been adopted by Conference the general election campaign had ended with the return of a government committed to the continued pursuit of a relentless, monetarist-inspired strategy of deflation and major cuts in public expenditure and public employment. In earlier years your Council has stressed the doomed folly of such a course. There are still no signs of sustainable economic growth or any improvement in employment prospects. Yet still the government persists and with an increased parliamentary majority NALGO must brace itself for continuing attacks on virtually all the services in which members are employed.[159]

Geoffrey Drain expressed the defiance at the conference after the election: 'We must say in the aftermath of that disastrous Thursday, NALGO stands firm; NALGO knows where it is going; NALGO deserves, wishes and demands that these policies be followed at the earliest opportunity; and, in the meantime, in every possible action it can take it will seek to implement them in any area where there is a possibility of making progress.'[160] The annual report summarized the year as 'very difficult . . . which reflected NALGO's transition into a campaigning union at the forefront of the trade union battle against cuts and the Government's economic policies'.[161]

Monetarism and privatization were the hallmarks of the first Thatcher government, but it was general policies in favour of a social market economy and against a dependency culture that mattered more. In its simplest form monetarism appeared attractive, since it seemed to provide politicians with a cure for the inflation that had dogged them throughout the 1970s. The answer to inflation was first to assume the cause to be excessive growth in the money supply and then to provide a solution through government reduction of its own borrowing by cutting spending. NALGO and other unions argued sophisticated alternatives to that simplistic (and wrong) analysis, pointing out the repeated policy failures and arguing that the real cause of falling inflation was the recessionary contraction in economic activity, partly unleashed by the government itself.

Nevertheless, 'the privatization of public enterprises was one of the most important and distinctive features of the record of the 1979–1983 Conserva-

---

[159] *NALGO Annual Report 1983*, 59.   [160] *PS* (July 1983), 2.
[161] *NALGO Annual Report 1983*, 215.

tive Government',[162] based on four main assumptions. These were, first, that private companies are more efficient because of the discipline of the markets; secondly, that 'public ownership impinges upon economic freedom';[163] thirdly, that 'whereas trade unions in the private sector know that an excessive pay award may lead to bankruptcy no equivalent constraint exists in the public sector';[164] and, fourthly, that it reduces the public-sector borrowing requirement.

These assertions remain potent reminders of the early 1980s and their legacy continues to haunt and divide the trade-union movement, including UNISON itself. Thatcherism had a moral dimension that played an equally crucial part in the experiment. The ideal of the social market economy was partially copied from the German Christian Democrats and their *Soziale Marktwirtschaft*. It came in through leading ideologue Keith Joseph, and was taken to mean 'a market economy with social obligations'.[165] Such obligations included the provision of free health, education, and social security, but targeted only for those who could not afford to pay. As Nicholas Ridley explains about the Prime Minister, 'she disliked what she called "the dependency culture". By this she meant a society where people became dependent on the State for their education, or health care, or pensions, or housing, and in some cases their income.'[166] It was against these aspects of government policy that NALGO found it harder to campaign: many members approved of the government's initiatives. The national leadership was sometimes clearly opposed, and sometimes clearly confused. The union had much to fear from another term of Conservative office. And so it proved.

---

[162] D. Steel and D. Heald, 'The Privatization of Public Enterprises 1979–1983', in P. Jackson (ed.), *Implementing Government Policy Initiatives: the Thatcher Administration 1979–1983* (London: Royal Institute of Public Administration, 1985), 69.

[163] Ibid. 72.   [164] Ibid.[165] Ridley, *My Style of Government*, 78.

[166] Ibid. 79.

Appendix

TABLE 4.1. *NALGO membership, 31 October 1981*

District	Number of branches	Paid-up membership Voting (student)	Paid-up membership Retired	Members in arrear and membership of branches excluded from voting Ordinary	Members in arrear and membership of branches excluded from voting Retired	Total membership Ordinary (student)	Total membership Retired	Total membership Honorary	Total membership Total	Total membership	Increase over 1980	Percentage increase
Eastern	129	51,605	4,990(3)	471	37	52,076	5,027(3)	—	57,106	55,672	1,434	2.58
East Midland	105	45,797	3,692(3)	267	10(1)	46,064	3,702(4)	—	49,770	49,190	580	1.18
Metropolitan	132	98,440	11,045(8)	3,035	207	101,475	11,252(8)	—	112,735	109,769	2,996	2.71
North Eastern	75	41,266	2,192(2)	193	—	41,459	2,192(2)	—	43,653	43,775	(122)	(0.28)
North Western and North Wales	136	107,482	7,342(5)	2,509	53	109,990	7,395(5)	—	117,390	115,943	1,447	1.25
Scottish	120	74,324	1,548(1)	2,590	13	76,914	1,561(1)	—	78,476	75,658	2,818	3.73
South Eastern	98	45,645	6,305(10)	109	—	45,754	6,305(10)	—	52,069	51,984	85	0.17
Southern	76	40,726	3,729(1)	59	8	40,785	3,789(1)	—	44,575	44,275	300	0.68
South Wales	92	34,458	1,775(2)	445	11	34,903	1,783(2)	—	36,688	36,395	293	0.81
South Western	97	47,495	4,241(11)	472	26	47,967	4,252(11)	—	52,230	52,174	96	0.11
West Midland	92	74,334	5,753(3)	304	7	75,638	5,779(3)	—	81,420	73,674	2,746	3.49
Yorkshire and Humberside	79	65,833	4,026(3)	155		65,988	4,033(3)	—	70,024	68,824	1,200	1.75
Honorary members	—	—	—	—	—	—	—	9	9	10	(1)	—
TOTALS	1,230	728,405	156,698(52)	10,608	372(1)	739,013	57,070(53)	9	796,145	782,343	13,802	1.77

TABLE 4.2. *NALGO membership, 30 September 1982*

District	Number of branches	Paid-up membership				Members in arrear and membership of branches excluded from voting		Total membership					Total membership
		Voting	Retired	Student	Unemployed	Ordinary	Retired	Ordinary	Retired	Student	Unemployed	Honorary	
Eastern	125	50,886	5,046	2	3	69	—	50,955	5,046	2	3	—	56,006
East Midland	104	45,653	3,836	1	3	84	—	45,737	3,836	1	3	—	49,577
Metropolitan	152	95,775	11,011	13	12	2,843	139	98,618	11,150	13	12	—	109,793
North Eastern	81	40,772	2,296	3	1	58	—	40,830	2,296	3	1	—	43,130
North Western and North Wales	135	108,358	7,068	5	1	16	—	108,374	7,068	5	1	—	115,448
Scottish	119	76,638	1,566	8	1	222	1	76,860	1,567	8	1	—	78,436
South Eastern	97	43,978	6,322	13	5	131	—	44,109	6,322	13	5	—	50,449
Southern	89	39,574	4,155	2	6	74	—	39,648	4,155	2	6	—	43,811
South Wales	93	33,977	1,830	2	1	52	6	34,029	1,836	2	1	—	35,868
South Western	97	46,424	4,108	1	—	296	16	46,720	4,124	1	—	—	50,845
West Midland	92	74,862	6,070	14	4	48	—	74,910	6,070	14	4	—	80,998
Yorkshire and Humberside	77	65,562	4,271	3	2	89	—	65,651	4,271	3	2	—	69,927
Honorary members	—	—	—	—	—	—	—	—	—	—	—	9	9
TOTALS	1,261	722,459	57,579	67	39	3,982	162	726,441	57,741	67	39	9	784,297

161

TABLE 4.3. *Membership of the largest British trade unions, including NALGO, NUPE, and COHSE, 1981, 1986, and 1991*

1981		1986		1991	
Union	Membership	Union	Membership	Union	Membership
TGWU	1,696,000	TGWU	1,378,000	TGWU	1,127,000
AUEW	1,266,000	AEU	858,000	GMB	863,000
NUGMW	866,000	GMBATU	814,000	NALGO	760,000
NALGO	739,000	NALGO	750,000	AEU	623,000
NUPE	704,000	NUPE	658,000	MSF	604,000
COHSE	230,709	COHSE	212,312	NUPE	551,165
				COHSE	201,993
ALL	12,311,000	ALL	10,598,000	ALL	9,489,000

Note: Figures are to the nearest thousand.
Source: Annual Reports of the Certification Officer.

5

Thatcherites versus the
Trade-Union Movement

WINNING 42 per cent of the votes cast, and a majority of 144 seats, the Conservatives gained a resounding victory in the general election on 9 June 1983. Opposition was divided between Labour with only 28 per cent of the vote and the SDP–Liberal Alliance with 26 per cent. Margaret Thatcher saw the result as

the single most devastating defeat ever inflicted upon democratic socialism in Britain. After being defeated on a manifesto that was the most candid statement of socialist aims ever made in this country, the Left could never again credibly claim popular appeal for their programme of massive nationalization, hugely increased public expenditure, greater trade union power and unilateral nuclear disarmament.[1]

Greatly encouraged, the government immediately got down to business. Margaret Thatcher strengthened her position in the Cabinet by promoting Nicholas Ridley and Cecil Parkinson (before his abrupt departure), who joined Norman Tebbit, Nigel Lawson (now Chancellor), Norman Fowler, and Geoffrey Howe (now Foreign Secretary).

This team set about cutting, privatizing, attacking trade unions, and reducing the power of local authorities with renewed enthusiasm. Within a month Chancellor Nigel Lawson announced another £500 million cut in public expenditure and a further £500 million sale of government assets. The next day Patrick Jenkin presented the case for abolishing the GLC and for imposing penalties on local councils if they overspent government limits. Within the next week Norman Fowler announced cuts in the NHS and Peter Walker accelerated the closure of coal mines.

[1] M. Thatcher, *The Downing Street Years* (London: Harper Collins, 1993), 339.

The events of 1984 resonated uncannily with George Orwell's nightmare portrayal of rampant authoritarian and anti-democratic forces, although these real attacks on the rights of citizens and their democratic organizations came from a right-wing elected autocracy and not from the socialism that Orwell feared so much. NALGO's annual report for the year showed how the government's objectives of weakening the public services were related to their wider objectives to support the accumulation of profit in private hands:

The hostility of the Government to public provision has been given added impetus by the economic recession and the lack of profit in private industry. Urged on by their city and business friends, and supported by right wing pressure groups such as the Adam Smith Institute and the Institute for Economic Affairs, a wide range of measures have been taken to undermine the public sector and curtail public provision of essential services . . . Your Council has watched developments with growing despair.[2]

NALGO supported striking miners, print workers, and GCHQ trade unionists; argued against more anti-union laws; opposed CCT in health and local government; and continued to campaign, bargain, and take action in all services at national and local levels.

The Politics of Defeat

The winter months of 1983–84 saw the chilled hand of government tightening its grip over both trade unionism and local democracy, suppressing anything that might challenge its dominance of civil society. On 25 January 1984 Geoffrey Howe announced that trade union membership was no longer compatible with employment at the government's surveillance centre, the GCHQ. He later recalled that 'the substance of the matter was, in fact, relatively easy . . . MI5 and MI6 already were [non-union]; for reasons of historical accident, GCHQ was not, and had been put at risk and damaged by the kind of industrial conflict from which it was meant to be immune. Our vital intelligence partners, the Americans, had been as worried about this as we were.'[3] A day of protest in Cheltenham on 28 February became an annual event until trade unionism was restored there thirteen years later by the new Labour government.

The Trade Union Act 1984 placed further restrictions on union organization, union funding for the Labour Party, union political campaigns, and industrial action. At the June annual conference 'delegates resolved that, if necessary, NALGO should be prepared to break the law when faced with the

---

[2] *NALGO Annual Report 1984* (London: NALGO, 1985), 51.
[3] G. Howe, *Conflict of Loyalty* (London: Macmillan, 1994), 341.

Government's anti-trade union legislation'.[4] In its own inimitable style, *The Times* picked up on this decision: 'The moderate union which represents town hall staff adopted a policy of militant opposition yesterday to the Government's employment legislation which commits the leadership to supporting acts of law-breaking.'[5]

Box 5. NALGO and the Anti-Union Laws

Conservative government attacks on the legal rights of unions and their members became one of its distinguishing features. Union responses to the new laws were varied. Some eventually embraced many of the government's changes, and the TUC was often ambivalent towards them, but NALGO maintained a consistently strong line of opposition.

Trade unions can be held legally liable to compensate employers who are damaged as a result of industrial action being organized by them, except for industrial action that is taken in connection with a 'trade dispute' as specified in legislation. This 'immunity' was weakened by successive laws in the 1980s that reduced its scope by narrowing the definition of a trade dispute, and by imposing complicated requirements for ballots and other administrative actions. Effective forms of picketing became unlawful.

This disruption of union organization was intensified by giving new rights to union dissidents. Members could take legal action against their union not only when it took unlawful industrial action but also when their union disciplined them for refusing to take part in action that was lawful. A government commissioner was appointed to help these anti-union actions by disaffected members.

NALGO campaigned alongside the TUC against the first two Acts in 1980 and 1982. The TUC General Council called a special conference of trade-union executives on 5 April 1982 (the 'Wembley Conference'), which agreed an eight-point campaign plan against the 1982 Bill ('Tebbit's Law'). TUC General Secretary Len Murray described the Bill as 'a manifesto for a union-free society' from a government 'which regards unions as a form of environmental pollution'. NALGO's Geoffrey Drain added that: 'Public service employees will be in peril when they fight against public expenditure cuts, against the wrecking of services, and against privatisation. The narrowing of immunities means that they will not be able to fight for jobs and pay, for welfare provisions and for services.'[6]

Anticipating future debates he added 'We are not embarking on a campaign of civil disobedience and law-breaking but, if the sword is forced into our hands, then we will use it.' The TUC campaign included refusal to hold ballots on closed shop and union membership agreements; refusal to accept government funds for union ballots; and coordinated industrial action and financial support for unions in dispute with

---

[4] *Public Service (PS)* (July 1984), 1.   [5] *The Times*, 14 June 1984, 2.
[6] *PS* (Apr. 1982), 1.

employers. NALGO endorsed the campaign and contributed £78,000 to the TUC's £1 million fighting fund.

The union's 1984 conference was concerned about the general issue of state activity in industrial relations, including legal powers to invoke states of emergency, and to mobilize armed forces personnel and equipment to break strikes. These powers had been used against workers in the railways, ambulance, firefighting, refuse collection, docks, power stations, lorry transport, air traffic control, and the Buckingham Palace boiler room. NALGO was concerned that members might be forced to take part in contingency measures during disputes, and reaffirmed its policy of not carrying out the work of members of striking unions. There was concern about the mobilization of spies against trade unionists by the Special Branch sections of police forces, and about police requests of NALGO members to provide information on their subordinate staff or on their clients.[7] The conference specifically condemned the use of police in industrial disputes and supported calls for public inquiries into the role of the police at Warrington and in the miners' dispute.

The delegates also narrowly passed, by a card vote against the recommendation of the NEC, a strongly worded motion endorsing the Wembley Conference principles, accepting 'that support for these principles may involve unlawful activity by NALGO . . . supporting any activities necessary to defeat any anti-trade union legislation', and agreeing that 'the trade union movement must be prepared to make positive breaches of the law and to defy court orders'.

The Trade Union Act 1984 contained provisions on ballots for industrial action with significant implications for NALGO. While the union usually held ballots before instructing members to take industrial action, this was not done where members had already walked out, or when members were authorized rather than instructed to take part in days of action and other demonstrations. Changing the union's rules or procedures to accommodate the legislation 'would lend credibility to what we regard as unjust laws which not only tip the balance of power even more towards employers but sour good industrial relations and bring the rule of law itself into disrepute'.[8] The union took a 'business-as-usual' approach, which included no response to the Act's requirements on political funds, although it was recognized that 'were the court to rule that a perfectly legitimate campaign was unlawful it would no doubt be possible to secure a majority for the establishment of a political fund'.

In 1985 the TUC began to back off from the Wembley Conference decisions, initiating a series of reviews of the industrial-relations legislation. NALGO's NEC criticized the TUC for taking a short-term view based on the expediency of securing the election of a Labour government:

It is important that the opportunity is taken to draw up proposals which the trade union movement genuinely believes are necessary for the protection and advancement of working people and their organisations and are not just designed to improve the prospects of a Labour Party

[7] *Government Activities against Trade Unions* (London: NALGO, 1984). See also *NALGO Annual Conference 1984 Minutes* (London: NALGO, 1985), Minute no. 103.
[8] *NALGO News (NN)*, 7 Dec. 1986.

victory . . . the TUC should not be afraid of putting forward industrial relations policies just because they are perceived as unpopular.[9]

Pointing to the resolution of the TUC's 1985 Annual Congress, NALGO policy was for a return to the 1979 position, for the restoration of immunity rather than the introduction of positive rights, and against statutory recognition procedures that would give strike-breaking splinter groups the right to a place at the bargaining table. Speaking at the Scottish TUC Alan Jinkinson argued that rights and immunities were two sides of the same coin, and both were needed.

That same year Alan Paul, a member of NALGO and chair of the Conservative Trade Unionists' national committee, made fourteen complaints to the Certification Officer. Only three were upheld, and these covered technical points of administration. But in August 1987 the Certification Officer upheld a complaint by another member, Tracy Shears. The main problems were the election of the Junior Vice-President and of the six chairs of the national service conditions committees onto the NEC indirectly by the national committees rather than by ballot of the membership. Also in 1987 Alan Paul and Simon Fraser obtained a High Court injunction to stop NALGO's 'Make People Matter' campaign (see Box 9).

These two decisions led to the first breaks with the 'business-as-usual' approach. The 1987 conference called for a ballot to create a political fund, and the NEC reluctantly proposed rule changes to protect the right of service groups to be represented on the NEC, but removing their right to vote. The 1988 conference agreed these changes and, noting the Employment Act 1988, called for a full report the following year. The 1989 conference invented a system of 'confirmatory ballots', where the district service conditions committees and branches would become entitled to make nominations for the service conditions representatives' seats on the NEC. The hope was that there would be no nominations from these quarters, leaving the national committee nominees to be elected unopposed. A more significant change was the decision to hold a membership ballot every five years for the election of General Secretary.

The next test came after the 1989 strike in local government (see Box 12), when branches started disciplinary action against strike-breakers. The Employment Act 1988 gave union members the right to seek compensation of between £2,520 and £14,085 if their union disciplined them for refusing to join industrial action, even where a majority had voted for it in a ballot. After their successful strike the local-government group meeting asked the NEC to give full legal and financial support to any branch facing claims for compensation from disciplined members. President Rita Donaghy said: 'We are between the devil and the deep blue sea, we could be outside the law but we must keep faith with those who took action. If we are going to be vulnerable, let's be vulnerable on the side of our members.' Arguing in favour of a special conference, local-government committee vice-chair Jean Geldart said: 'If we are to take on defying the law, then that should be a matter for the whole union. It is such an important decision in financial terms the decision has to be taken at the highest

[9] Ibid., 21 Mar. 1986, 5.

point of the union.' The NEC voted against a special conference, advised branches of the legal implications, suggested that they could ask strike-breakers to resign from the union, and decided to complain to the International Labour Organization (ILO) and/or the European Court of Human Rights.

By the end of January 686 members had been expelled by twenty-six branches, and fifty-eight of the dissidents had referred the issue to ITs. Balking at the massive financial consequences, the NEC changed its mind. Branches were told to stop all disciplinary actions, or face having their powers suspended by the NEC and having any tribunal awards recovered from branch funds. The NEC decided to support eleven expulsions already implemented in South Tyneside, by defending its case at an EAT. Eventually, in February 1991, the EAT found in favour of the strike-breakers but awarded them the minimum possible under the Act.

The NEC placed a rule change to prevent branches from taking disciplinary action defined in law as 'unjustifiable' on the 1990 conference agenda, and then withdrew it. The conference recognized 'that continued principled opposition (to the law) would financially destroy NALGO and put more money in the pockets of scabs than any pay settlement could do'. It agreed 'to continue to operate our rules, but recognised the need for constraint when it ceases to be in the interest of the Association to do otherwise'.[10] It decided against any rule changes to restrict the rights of branches to discipline members.

By now the Labour Party's employment spokesman Tony Blair had announced support for some of the Tory initiatives, setting the scene for a row at the TUC when NALGO's call for a future Labour government to repeal all the anti-union legislation and to restore immunities was narrowly defeated (see Box 11).

NALGO's 1991 conference rejected the national officers' repudiation of industrial action by members in Liverpool City Council. It also adopted a charter of positive rights of workers to join unions, to strike including solidarity action, and to picket effectively. It restated the position that unions should have the right to enter workplaces to organize, to determine their own constitutions and procedures, to be consulted and informed by employers, and to take political action. This was followed by the 1992 conference's uncompromising statement in the 'Unshackle the Unions' campaign.

The 1984 conference also discussed the role of NALGO's representatives in the TUC General Council's vote not to support action in solidarity with an affiliated union's strike. The National Graphical Association (NGA) was in dispute with the Stockport Messenger Group, and pickets had been involved in violent clashes with police protecting production at the printing plant.[11] The courts acted against the NGA, which called for support from the

[10] *NALGO Annual Conference 1990 Minutes* (London: NALGO, 1991), Composite H, 32.

[11] M. Dickinson, *To Break a Union: The Messenger, the State and the NGA* (Manchester: Booklist Ltd., 1984).

labour movement. When the General Council discussed this, NALGO's four representatives were divided. Lay representatives Bill Gill and Norrie Steele voted to support the NGA in line with union policy, but new General Secretary John Daly and National Officer Ada Maddocks voted with the majority against, and the NGA conceded defeat on 18 January 1984. This was discussed at the Metropolitan District Council's AGM:

A major debate developed from a motion by the Islington branch expressing concern at the lack of support from the TUC General Council for the National Graphical Association in its fight against Government anti-trade union legislation. The motion criticized the two NALGO representatives on the TUC General Council who voted against support for the NGA. In particular it condemned the National Executive Council for deciding to limit NALGO's support for the NGA which is seen to be in clear breach of the trade union's policy.[12]

Ada Maddocks and John Daly were formally censured by conference, which 'carried a composite resolution criticising your Council's endorsement of the TUC General Council decision not to support the national stoppage called by the NGA . . . a further composite resolution was carried criticising severely the two NALGO members of the TUC General Council'.[13]

In March 1984 the unions fighting national disputes at GCHQ and in the car industry were joined by the coal miners in their strike against pit closures and for better pay and conditions. This historic struggle dominated British politics and the labour movement for the next twelve months. Class and political divisions widened and NALGO was caught up in the controversies.

Initially NALGO mobilized its national and branch resources to support the striking miners, and over the summer, with support from steelworkers, railway staff, seamen, and later dockers, it looked as if they would win.[14] NALGO promoted the miners' case, giving their leader, Arthur Scargill, space in *Public Service*. He argued that, 'throughout Britain, miners are fighting not only for their pits and jobs, but for the very survival of the coal industry. Passionate concern for the future of people and their communities is matched by sound economic common sense, and determination to protect a vital national asset—coal.'[15] This line of argument, so well articulated by the miners, went to the heart of the transformation of British economic and social life in the 1980s. It was so sharply expressed in both words and deeds that it flung open a window on the dynamics of class struggle. The NEC voted to give £10,000 to the solidarity fund, an expression of both support and

---

[12] *Met District News* (Mar. 1984), 2.   [13] *NALGO Annual Report 1984*, 70.
[14] R. Samuel, B. Bloomfield, and G. Boanas (eds.), *The Enemy Within: Pit Villages and the Miners' Strike of 1984–5* (Routledge & Kegan Paul, 1986).
[15] *PS* (May 1984), 14.

recognition that the miners' fight for the coal industry was part of NALGO members' fights for their own industries and services. But this action also revealed substantial differences in the depth of political understanding among members, activists, and leaders (see Box 6).

March 1984 may well be one of the turning points in modern history, as the government mobilized state resources against the organizations of the working class. Taking on and defeating the NUM was the dominant industrial act of these years—Nicholas Ridley, the alleged architect of the government's plans for coal and Transport Secretary at the time, had no doubts about that: 'It was a strike against the government. The government couldn't leave it to the Chairman of the Coal Board—Ian MacGregor—not only because he was quite incapable of winning the propaganda battle, but also because far more forces had to be organized than the Coal Board alone could command: police, transport, electricity generators, docks, even the law courts.'[16]

A small group of Cabinet ministers ran the fight against the strike, and their own comments about it make interesting reading. For Ridley

[The strike] really was closer to a revolution than to a strike. The bitterness, the vindictiveness and the violence with which some behaved were ugly indeed—they were the acts of people with a deep political cause, not usually found in industrial disputes. It was very much in the nature of a Peasant's Revolt, or a Luddite assault upon new textile machinery, as well as a political attempt to humiliate and perhaps destroy the Government.[17]

For Cecil Parkinson the enemy was not only the trade union; it was the nationalized industry itself: 'He [Scargill] proved in 1985 that no government could allow itself to be at the mercy of an industry and a trade union which would use its economic power for political purposes . . . I never understood the argument that Britain somehow owes a great debt to the mining industry. The industry was given a privileged position and it abused the privilege.'[18]

The importance of winning was not lost on Norman Tebbit: 'had the Thatcher government been broken and the craven Mr Kinnock installed in office by Scargill's thugs Britain would have been a grim place indeed.'[19] Not so clearly stated at the time but boasted of later was the fact that the defeat of the miners was the precondition for the privatization of gas and later electricity supply.[20] Not only would it chasten the unions in general, but it would remove the main opposition to the destruction of any planned energy policy and to the handing-over of valuable state assets to the private sector.

[16] N. Ridley, *My Style of Government* (London: Hutchinson, 1991), 69.   [17] Ibid. 70.

[18] C. Parkinson, *Right at the Centre* (London: Weidenfeld & Nicolson, 1992), 281.

[19] N. Tebbit, *Upwardly Mobile* (London: Weidenfeld & Nicolson, 1988), 239.

[20] P. Walker, *Staying Power* (London: Bloomsbury,1991); N. Lawson, *The View from No. 11* (London: Corgi Books,1992).

Box 6. NALGO and the 1984–5 Miners' Strike

The year-long miners' strike reverberated far beyond the British coalfields. It tested both the endurance of miners and their families and the resolve of activists and leaders throughout the labour and trade-union movement. To understand the strike, and NALGO's reaction to it, we need to trace its beginnings in the early 1970s.

The 1970 general election put the Conservatives back into office, under the leadership of Edward Heath. Their incomes policies caused public-sector pay to fall relative to other private sector groups, and the miners started a national strike at the start of 1972. The NUM did not issue strike pay, using its funds to organize mass pickets at pits, power stations, and docks to prevent the movement of coal around the country. NALGO's NEC donated £1,000 to support the union's picketing and publicity activity, in spite of some limited opposition.[21] After six weeks the National Coal Board (NCB) and the NUM reached an agreement that had the support of the government, and the miners went back to work.

They voted to strike again two years later, in January 1974, when a combination of economic crisis and fuel shortage put the miners in a strong position and the NCB and the government in a weak one. Under emergency powers the government imposed power cuts on the population on a rota basis, and a maximum three-day working week on most manufacturing industry. The dispute was rapidly resolved with the return of a Labour government. NALGO, along with the other TUC unions, had supported the miners' case and had agreed not to use any pay increase granted to the miners as ammunition in their own pay claims.

These two defeats left deep scars in the Tory Party, and a policy group led by Nicolas Ridley set out a strategy for the next Tory government: build up coal stocks, particularly at power stations; make plans for importing coal; equip power stations to operate on alternative fuels; encourage the movement of coal by less unionized road hauliers instead of rail; and establish a large mobile police force to deal with pickets.

The strategy was implemented, and the epic strike started, on 5 March 1984, when the NCB unilaterally announced the closure of Cortonwood colliery in Yorkshire, breaking the pit closure procedure agreement with the NUM. The Yorkshire men received union support on 8 March, and the national strike began four days later with over 90,000 out. It lasted for almost exactly a year, ending on 5 March 1985 when miners marched back to work behind their union banners defiant but defeated.

With unemployment rising rapidly there was widespread agreement with the miners' 'Coal-not-Dole' slogan. Support groups sprang up everywhere. Miners' wives organized themselves to raise money, mind children, provide food, sustain morale, join demonstrations, and speak at meetings. This grew into the national 'Women-Against-Pit-Closures' organization, which provided a campaigning focus that drew thousands of women into contact with each other and into organized activism.

In April NALGO's NEC responded to the TUC's call for financial support[22] by donating £10,000 to the NUM's hardship fund and by calling on districts and

[21] G. Newman, *Path to Maturity: NALGO 1965–1980* (London: NALGO, 1982), 176, 426.
[22] *TUC Annual Report 1984* (London: TUC, 1985), 398–403.

branches to make donations and to organize weekly workplace collections. *NALGO News* and *Public Service* carried articles about the NUM's case, and the Scottish District published a four-page broadsheet that was circulated throughout the union. Many NALGO branches set up support groups and joined other groups set up by trades councils, Labour Party branches, and other local organizations. Countless activists were involved in collecting money, food, and household essentials, helping with holidays and Christmas parties for children, taking NUM fundraisers from the coalfields into their homes in the cities, and generally doing anything and everything possible to help win the strike. The activists at the annual conference supported the NEC's position and made a further collection and donation, bringing the national total to £36,342, less than five pence per member.

But not all trade unionists shared this view. While never publicly denying the justice of the NUM's arguments, some sections condemned the NUM for not holding a ballot and would not support mass picketing. Five NALGO branches told the union that they intended to withhold subscription income because they disagreed with the donation. Other branches passed resolutions criticizing the NEC and a few hundred members, particularly police civilian staff, resigned in protest. In August 200 branches challenged the NEC and annual conference decisions to support the miners with donations to the hardship fund—the decisions 'proved controversial and a special conference was requisitioned by the East Northamptonshire Branch on 10 October to debate a motion instructing the NEC to make no further donations to the NUM until a secret ballot of the membership is held'.[23] *The Times* understood the importance of this: 'A special conference is to be held in October as part of a campaign to prevent Britain's fourth largest union from making any further donations to the miners' strike.'[24] Its fellow political paper, the *Daily Telegraph*, reported with glee that 'about 20 members of the Nalgo branch in Northamptonshire have resigned in protest over the union making a £35,000 donation to a fund for the families of striking miners'.[25] Mike Jeram, national officer for electricity at the time, told us that 'a lot of electricity branches were numbered amongst the people that called for the special conference', which was held in October.

The *Morning Star* over-optimistically reported that 'executive members of . . . NALGO are confident that today's one-day conference in London will reinforce their union's support for the miners'.[26] Jim White stressed the importance of the vote when he told us, 'had the NEC lost that particular debate, then not just the NEC but virtually every district council structure in the country with I think the exception of East Midlands would have been almost terminally undermined . . . the NEC's credibility would have been shot, as would have been the leadership in all of the districts'. Graham Wise from East Northamptonshire Branch, the mover of the motion and the only speaker from the fifty requisitioning branches, said that the majority of members were disaffected with many NALGO policies, especially on donations to the NUM, which appeared to be more political than fraternal. Other speakers condemned the NUM leadership for failing to hold a national ballot, to condemn violence by their

[23] *NALGO Annual Report 1984*, 72.　　[24] *The Times*, 16 Aug. 1984, 2.
[25] *Daily Telegraph*, 23 Oct. 1984, 6.　　[26] *Morning Star*, 10 Oct. 1984, 2.

members, or to observe TUC guidelines on picketing. They argued that individual NALGO members could still support the miners if they wished. The dissidents did not achieve the two-thirds majority required to bring about a national ballot, but the vote was large enough to stop any further national donations.

Another motion to reaffirm the policy agreed at the June conference was heavily defeated, leaving NALGO without a national policy for the remainder of one of the toughest industrial conflicts of the century. The NEC met on 24 November, endorsed the conference motion, agreed that union money could not be sent to the strikers, and urged members to send moneys to the TUC's miners' hardship fund. Branches remained free to organize their own fund-raising and campaigning activity, but without the support of materials, coordination, and argument under the umbrella of a national policy. The ending of national financial support for the strike meant that some branches had to scale down their official support, fearful of a similar membership revolt closer to home. However, activists everywhere continued their local support group activities until the bitter end in March 1985.

The miners' strike dragged on against an increasingly bleak economic and political background. Chancellor Nigel Lawson's first budget contained the same mix of monetarism and privatization as before, with a public-sector pay target of 3 per cent, public-sector spending cuts, and severe controls over local-government expenditure. The Green Paper, *The Next Ten Years: Public Expenditure and Taxation into the 1990s* (Cmnd 9989), made it all too clear. As the Chancellor concluded in his budget speech, 'the purpose of the reforms is to rehabilitate the role of profits in the British economy'.[27] The TUC General Council expressed strong opposition to these measures, especially to 'cutting back public expenditure in order to finance tax cuts', and it argued that the results of not expanding public spending for a further ten years would be 'greater poverty, greater inequality and collapse of the economic infrastructure'.[28] Further government efforts to deregulate the labour market were signalled by their threats to reform Wages Councils (abolished in 1993), seen by the Chancellor as bodies 'which destroy jobs by making it illegal for employers to offer work at wages they can afford and the unemployed are prepared to accept'.[29]

The strike dominated the autumn conference season, and divisions around its meaning for the unions deepened as Norman Willis took office as the new TUC General Secretary. The year 1984 ended with the miners still out and beginning to flag, with over three million unemployed, and with the government revealing its preparedness to govern by secret force and by

---

[27] Lawson, *The View from No. 11*, 354.   [28] *TUC Annual Report 1984*, 245.
[29] Lawson, *The View from No. 11*, 362.

propaganda war. The labour movement stared defeat in the face. When it finally came in March 1985 it was a moment of high tragedy for miners and their families who had sacrificed everything in a year of hardship, and it was a crushing blow for organized labour. The government had taken on and destroyed one of the most disciplined fighting forces in the movement. By the end of the year the newspaper employers took on the powerful printing unions, the government took on the teacher unions in preparation for their attacks on the state school system, and local government was in disarray over rate capping. The government brought down the hammer, raining blow after blow on the foundations of free trade unionism. NALGO's annual report summarized this: 'For yet another year your Council must record the continuation of a government economic strategy malevolent in its intent towards the public services and the public sector generally and malicious in its effects on the British economy,'[30] and 'recent months have seen an intensification of the government's privatisation drive fuelled not only by dogma but also by the need to generate the resources for tax cuts'.[31]

The Thatcher government was reaching its zenith, buoyed up by Ronald Reagan's re-election in the USA, its resolve strengthened by the IRA bombing of the Tory Party Conference, as it pursued a wide range of economic and industrial policies aimed ostensibly at modernizing British capitalism. Its main objective was to reverse the declining rate of profit, and a major consequence of this was greater exploitation of the weakest and poorest citizens, both at home and abroad. With the defeat of the miners it was in a position to push on with its other activities: 'Along with privatization, supply-side finance, and "union-bashing", the government expressed its radicalism with a series of assaults on major segments and institutions within British society. In effect, the security and strength of major professions were undermined for ever. This meant in particular a direct attack on public-sector institutions and their custodians.'[32] Chancellor Lawson's budget again underlined the government's determination to control the economic agenda to meet these purposes, restating its aims to cut public spending and services, to privatize, and to deregulate.

With unemployment reaching an all-time high of 3,341,000, the government produced a White Paper, *Employment: The Challenge for the Nation*. This the TUC dismissed as a 'Blue Paper', as nothing more than party political propaganda paid from public funds, because it contained no new government policies or proposals for action. The TUC's analysis showed that government saw no role for itself in either causing or reducing unemployment—the trade

[30] *NALGO Annual Report 1985* (London: NALGO, 1986), 61.   [31] Ibid. 64.

[32] K. Morgan, *The People's Peace: British History 1945–1989* (Oxford: Oxford University Press, 1990), 475–6.

unions and the unemployed themselves were to blame. Arguing that, 'even on the most optimistic reading of the Government's analysis, the sum total of their measures would be to leave unemployment virtually unchanged', the TUC concluded that 'the government had absolutely no answer to unemployment'.[33] The government could have gone further—a high level of unemployment was actually essential to the completion of its project to restructure both British capitalism and the state. Encouraged by high unemployment and low inflation, the government's ideologues restated with greater vigour their intellectual rationalization for privatization: the corrosive mixture of efficiency through market forces and lower labour costs through a deregulated labour market. Confronted with a confident and revanchist government firing at all of the industrial sectors organized by NALGO and at union organization itself, it was no surprise to find the union in a certain amount of tense confusion during these years.

The Right, the Wrong, and the Left in NALGO

Both the TUC and NALGO reflected on the Labour Party's second election defeat. The TUC General Council decided that as the TUC's case had apparently been rejected as not valid there should be a 'careful strategic analysis of the direction and presentation of policy'. Furthermore, it was no longer true 'that there was a clear consensus on the need for economic management and redistribution, or that a Government of any persuasion would want to do a deal with the TUC'.[34] This signalled the start of a shift in TUC support, towards a greater acceptance of the 'business case' and away from radical alternatives.

NALGO was less conciliatory, recognizing that the new government was 'committed to the continued pursuit of a relentless, monetarist-inspired strategy of deflation and major cuts in public expenditure and public employment . . . NALGO must brace itself for continuing attacks on virtually all the services in which members are employed'.[35] Peter Holt, the incoming President, marked out the issues at the start of Thatcher's second term: 'Our trade union rights and freedoms, our civil liberties and our traditions of public enterprise and welfare have come under ruthless attack . . . privatisation is an ugly word for an ugly policy'. On unemployment he was scathing: 'No speeches can ever convey its true misery, degradation and despair,' and on Chile and South Africa he argued for 'continuous support from NALGO'.

---

[33] *TUC Annual Report 1985* (London: TUC, 1986), 284.
[34] *TUC Annual Report 1983* (London: TUC, 1984), 241.
[35] *NALGO Annual Report 1983*, 59.

His position was rooted in a firm political grasp of the main trade-union tasks—to oppose government policy, to support fellow trade unionists elsewhere, to condemn unemployment, and to oppose privatization. All this was necessary to fight effectively for members. In his farewell address to conference, Geoffrey Drain argued for a continuation of the union's distinctive approach: 'NALGO cannot grow, cannot even survive, cannot serve its members unless it is fully part of the society in which it exists, operating at every level and in every way, and being political in doing so.'[36]

When a new public-sector pay freeze was announced, the NEC carried the following motion: 'NALGO completely rejects the Government's three per cent pay target. Announced as it was unilaterally after a short Cabinet meeting, it shows the Government's complete disregard for the real world of industrial relations and collective bargaining.'[37] A mood of pessimism was obvious in the annual report for 1983:

The government's clear intention now is to cut public expenditure; to reduce the scope of public sector industry and the public services; to reduce the number of public employees; to bring down relative pay levels; and to weaken public sector trade unions. It represents a frontal assault on NALGO members' jobs, on the services in which they are employed and, if the policies are successful, on the existence of the union itself.[38]

For the NALGO delegation at the TUC Annual Congress in Blackpool in September it

was a sombre occasion in the light of the Conservative Government's return to office with an increased majority on 9 June. The continuation of the Government's economic policies combined with its intense hostility to the trade union movement presents a major challenge to the membership, powers and political influence of trade unions and the mood was described by *The Economist* as one of 'reluctant realism'.[39]

At this Congress NALGO and many other unions voted decisively in favour of a statutory national minimum wage. This important debate turned on the belief expressed by Tony Clark of the West Midlands PTE: such a wage would 'for the first time . . . give every worker the most fundamental employment right of all—a fair day's pay for a fair day's work'.[40] Opponents took the view that it would be ineffective and might hinder workers fighting in traditionally militant ways for higher wages.

The activists at NALGO's post-election 1983 conference struggled to hold the line and to build activity around the three trade-union themes of this history. First, at the place of work the union adopted the only practical course of

---

[36] *PS* (Oct. 1983), 11. [37] Ibid. 16. [38] *NALGO Annual Report 1983*, 77.
[39] Ibid. 2–3. [40] *PS* (Oct. 1983), 3.

action available—namely, to respond to employer initiatives by negotiating and taking action, in consultation with members and within the national policy framework. Secondly, the union developed its own organization, structures, and democracy in order to reflect and support its 'business-as-usual' approach to collective bargaining in all its forms. Thirdly, it beefed up its role in a range of broad political areas in order to present a NALGO position to decision-makers and policy formulators through public campaigns. However, the increasing sense of powerlessness in the face of the government driven recession also deepened internal strife within the union over each of those spheres of union action. There were internal disputes about the conduct of negotiations and industrial action, there was dithering over NALGO's own internal regulations, and there were arguments about political alignments. When John Daly took over as General Secretary, *The Times* commented that he was seen by other trade unionists 'as an administrator rather than a class warrior' and that 'he is described as someone who resides firmly on the right of the Labour Party'.[41]

The residential workers' dispute in local government reveals the tensions in the union's approach to collective bargaining. Stemming from years of frustration at being unable to reach agreements in the NJC for premium payments for shifts, irregular hours, and public holidays, and for a shorter working week, these members voted to ban overtime and admissions from 12 September 1983. The union was aware of the difficulties of taking such action—it could easily lose the support of both the wider NALGO membership and the general public, and the government always used disputes like these to raise the issue of preventing industrial action in so-called essential services—an old demand in the guise of protecting the innocent, but always aimed at preventing workers exercising their democratic rights.[42] Union posters and leaflets carried the message 'Be Fair to Those Who Care', and branches were given guidelines to help sustain the action.

The employers refused to negotiate, despite the severe impact of the industrial action. In Scotland the dispute escalated when the employers issued false statements about the impact of the action on homes. Nearly 600 members in seventy homes went on indefinite strike, and members occupied Strathclyde Region's Roberton Assessment Centre:

The NALGO office was besieged by demands for action—and act we did! When negotiations finally broke down on Thursday night, we took the decisive decision to pull four children's homes out on strike in support of Roberton. The support for this

---

[41] *The Times*, 25 Nov. 1983, 2.

[42] L. Neal, L. Bloch, and C. Grunfeld, *Essential Services—Whose Rights?* (London: Centre for Policy Studies, 1984).

action was solid. In addition, from Thursday night Roberton staff went on all out strike, and occupied the building.[43]

The threat of national strike action hinged on improved offers from the employers. As the action grew throughout October the union won backing from other unions, such as NUPE and the NUT, and published a range of publicity materials. By December the action was set to escalate again with national demands for working the office hours of other local-authority employees.

During all drawn-out periods of action there is bound to be discussion and debate about the best way to make progress—this is both a political reality and a central aspect of democratic trade-union accountability. Under these circumstances negotiations *within* the union, intra-organizational bargaining between different groups inside the union, can overshadow the negotiations that take place between the union and the employer, inter-organizational bargaining. With the employers refusing to negotiate, the residential social workers became more angry and frustrated and a number of branches put forward resolutions to the national delegate advisory meeting on 17 November. Some of these were strident in their criticism of the national leadership. For example, one from Southwark Branch: 'we call on the national local government committee/strike operations committee to organise the action more effectively' and 'this national advisory delegate conference condemns the decision of a meeting between NALGO and Association of London Authorities' representatives'.[44] Eventually this frustration led to direct action by some strikers against their own union: '200 striking residential workers invaded NALGO Headquarters where they voiced their dissatisfaction in two hours of angry exchanges with officials and NEC members.'[45]

On 9 January 1984 they returned to work with the promise of an independent inquiry, which reported in October 1984 and failed to resolve the issues. The bitterness of the dispute was one telling example of how NALGO's own policies and leadership were to come under close and sometimes hostile scrutiny from those members taking action or supporting the action of others. The residential and allied staff group felt that the action itself was hamstrung by the union's central decision-makers, who failed 'to recognise at an early stage the strategic importance of the dispute for all NALGO members' and failed 'to campaign in a positive and professional manner with the full resources of the union'.[46]

Debates about the organization and structure of the union were also difficult. The union was unable to make a decision about whether or not to

---

[43] *Mac* (Nov. 1983), 1. [44] *NN*, 25 Nov. 1983, 3.
[45] *PS* (Dec. 1983), 5. [46] *NALGO Annual Report 1984*, 94.

recruit in the private sector, following members who happened to be employed in privatized services (see Tables 5.1–5.4). There seemed to be some concern that by agreeing to recruit in privatized industries the union would have given up the fight to stop privatization, a rather perverse argument that was opposed by NEC members such as John Allan, who saw it as simply preventing the union from representing members forced to change employers. In another aspect of this, groups of women and black members, many of them in jobs vulnerable to cuts, contracting-out, casualization, and speed-up, pressed their demands on union representation with increasing vigour. They wanted stronger representation by the union, and they wanted better representation in the union's structures. They questioned the union's commitment to action and made demands that raised complex questions about the integrity of the structures. At this point the NEC's race equality working party was embroiled in controversy as its report on fighting racism was delayed (see Box 8), prefiguring the difficult debates to come about self-organization.

In the wider political arena, the union was drawn into a dangerous, potentially divisive flirtation with the SDP following the Labour Party's electoral collapse. Even before the election, several prominent and not so prominent labour-movement figures had defected to the SDP, including some in NALGO. Most notable of these was chair of the NLGC and NEC member Mike Blick, who was a member of the SDP's trade-union affairs committee. The NEC narrowly agreed a proposal by Bill Gill and Pat Kelly: 'A top level NALGO delegation is to meet the Social Democratic Party at the invitation of its leader Dr David Owen to discuss the SDP's attitude to proposed Government legislation on trade unions.'[47] The TUC had declined David Owen's invitation on the grounds that the SDP largely supported government policy in this area, and only one other TUC affiliate broke ranks, the NASUWT. This was the first time that NALGO had sent a formal delegation to meet any political party.

However, it would be wrong to draw too many conclusions about the extent of disunity. First, although the residential workers' action collapsed, it was only one phase in a longer campaign to protect residential establishments and those who worked in them. The seriousness of the government's position only fully emerged nearly ten years later with the 'care-in-the-community' restructuring. Secondly, while the internal struggles over equal representation had some dangerous undertones, they were nevertheless rooted in real injustices both at work and in the wider society. Demands from women, black members, and other sections of the membership facing

[47] *PS* (Oct. 1983), 1.

179

prejudice and discrimination had to be given a voice, and their pressure-group activity within the union eventually provided a strong impetus for greater openness and inclusiveness throughout the union as a whole. Thirdly, the NEC's flirtation with the SDP did not grow into anything lasting and NALGO continued to develop its role as a major player on the progressive wing of the labour movement.

Other important and positive developments in 1983 included greater support for the development of the steward system (see Box 4), and further impetus for a separate NALGO health and safety department to support the work of workplace safety representatives (see Box 10). The union held its first ever women-only conference in Manchester, attended by over 200 delegates, who put forward a series of proposals including reaffiliation to the Women's TUC (see Box 11), racism-awareness training for members, recognition of sexual harassment as a disciplinary offence, negotiation with employers to provide access to breast and cervical cancer screening, and research and education courses on new technology. This activity built on the increasing efforts by other unions and the TUC to strengthen women's roles within the trade-union movement. The TUC put on a display covering the history of women in trade unions on the fiftieth anniversary of the women's TUC.

NALGO published pamphlets to support womens organization in NALGO, such as *51 per cent* and *How Equal are your Opportunities?* Work continued in the race equality working party and on the equal pay for work of equal value campaign. The union's 1984 conference voted to return to the TUC women's conference, and NALGO's delegation was welcomed back to a defiant meeting of the STUC women's conference chaired by Ada Maddocks in Kirkaldy (see Box 11). Action on gay and lesbian rights was becoming more widespread, and Norfolk Branch appointed two gay rights officers. But one of the most important initiatives was to support the campaign to prevent the deportation of NALGO member Muhammad Idrish (see Box 7).

Box 7. NALGO'S Defence of Muhammad Idrish

The Muhammad Idrish Defence Campaign was formed to establish his right to stay in Britain and to challenge the arbitrary nature of immigration law. This was a broad-based campaign led by community activists, and NALGO's support was a major factor in its success.

Muhammad came to Britain from Bangladesh to study at Bristol University in 1976. He married a Scottish woman in 1979 and then applied for permanent residence. There was a long delay of fourteen months when the application could have been approved. However, fourteen months after his application Muhammad and his wife separated, and he was almost immediately served with a deportation order. His appeal to an adjudicator was turned down.

By this time Muhammad was working as a social worker at a Barnardo's home in West Bromwich and was a founder member of the Barnardo's NALGO branch. The Muhammad Idrish Defence Campaign was established to support High Court action to have the adjudicator's decision set aside. The campaign was supported by many organizations in the West Midlands, including NALGO and other union branches, trades councils, and ethnic minority organizations. An emergency resolution at the 1983 conference committed the union to supporting the campaign by organizing a demonstration in Birmingham in September and calling on unions with members involved in deportations to boycott the handling of his deportation. NALGO produced campaign leaflets and posters in many languages, organized the first march and rally in Birmingham in October, and hosted a fringe meeting at the TUC Congress in September.

Two days after the Birmingham rally Muhammad was called to his court hearing with only a day's notice—his application for a judicial review was dismissed. During the run-up to his appeal to the High Court he and his supporters spoke at hundreds of meetings up and down the country, a petition was circulated, a campaign video was produced, and BBC2 broadcast a programme on the case on 22 February 1984. Over 1,000 supporters gathered to demonstrate on 9 May, the day scheduled for the appeal, only for the hearing to be postponed. Deputy General Secretary Alan Jinkinson said:

Neither we nor Muhammad will be put off by recent official suggestions that those who campaign publicly against their own deportation would be better advised not to do so. We read such suggestions as nothing more than crude threats designed to intimidate trades unionists into not exercising their civil rights. We are determined to ensure that Muhammad is not deported and to continue the campaign against the racist laws which threaten him.

NALGO's 1984 conference reaffirmed its support, and demonstrations took place on 4 and 5 July outside the Court of Appeal, which rejected the appeal and refused leave to appeal to the House of Lords. The union produced a leaflet, *Muhammad Idrish—the Case against Deportation*, and sent it to MPs to gain support for a petition for leave to appeal. His oral appeal to the House of Lords was turned down in November, and the Home Office issued a deportation order on the same day. Another demonstration of over 2,000 took place in Birmingham on 30 January 1985.

A vigil was held after another unsuccessful appeal to the Immigration Appeals Adjudicator on 11 March 1985, and the broader campaign gathered momentum with a national demonstration on 23 March in Manchester organized by the growing number of defence campaigns and the city council. The Campaign against Racist Laws was established to secure the repeal of the immigration legislation. Speaking to the TUC Annual Congress on the eve of the final appeal to the Immigration Appeal Tribunal, Alan Jinkinson said, 'If he loses he will be liable to immediate arrest and detention . . . Congress, I ask for your unanimous support for a fellow trade unionist who is possibly but a few days from jail and deportation.' In what General Secretary

John Daly described as 'a blow against the racist bias in the immigration laws', the tribunal upheld the appeal.

In another move to protect the basic rights of workers, electricity staff boycotted the Youth Training Scheme (YTS) because

whatever the potential merits of a scheme such as the YTS, it is the lack of funds available to improve the scheme, the refusal of employers such as the Electricity Council to top up trainee allowances, and the proposal to introduce sanctions on social security benefits which would have the effect of making schemes compulsory which have influenced the national electricity committee's thinking on this matter.[48]

The 1984 conference extended this action, resolving that 'workplace based youth training schemes should not be approved by branches unless the trainees' £25 allowance is topped up "to a significant degree"'.[49] *The Times* took notice: 'Britain's biggest white collar union is to urge the labour movement to withdraw support from the Youth Training Scheme (YTS) unless there are immediate signs of improvement.'[50] Selwyn Gummer, Minister of State for Employment, answering a friendly question planted in the House of Commons, said, 'I should much prefer Opposition Members to speak in a non-party political way about the youth training scheme. It is for that reason that I have gone in for a self-denying ordinance of not pointing out the outrageous activities of those who seek to oppose the scheme.'[51]

It is arguable that by the end of 1983 the centre of the class struggle was shifting. Between 1979 and 1983 the labour movement fought a right-wing Tory government. Then the emphasis changed, as elements within the ranks of the movement itself drifted to the right, most visibly in defections to the SDP, but finding expression elsewhere in a wide range of policy debates under the banner of 'new realism'. An NEC member's damaging criticisms of the union were broadcast in a *Diverse Reports* programme on Channel 4 during the 1984 annual conference.[52] Such enemies within were hard to take when the real foe was not far away.

Collective Bargaining—the Beat Goes On

National bargaining

With great dramas unfolding in the coalfields, in Fleet Street, and in the surveillance centres, national negotiations took place against an inauspicious

[48] *NN*, 27 Apr. 1984, 1.
[49] *PS* (July 1984), 4.
[50] *The Times*, 13 Aug. 1984, 2.
[51] *Hansard*, 3 July 1984, oral answers, 77.
[52] *PS* (July 1984), 7; (Sept. 1984), 16.

backdrop in 1984–5. Efforts to secure collective agreements on the usual range of issues fell on stony ground. Many employers simply rejected pay claims, while others delayed giving any response. NALGO service group leaders consulted with their members on ways to bring greater pressure on the employers as pay negotiations became bogged down. With the going rate around 4.5 per cent, most negotiators settled without action. PTE staff did threaten to strike over their 3 per cent offer. Individual employers made local approaches on both topping up the national pay deal and threatening job losses, putting pressure on the national JNC's credibility. The union leadership wanted a national response to the national offer, and the union committee agreed on industrial action: no cooperation with outside consultants; no cooperation with changes from new technology and new job techniques; and no cover for vacant posts or for absences. Eventually a 4.5 per cent deal was struck: 'the agreement was reached following a succession of inconclusive negotiating meetings and industrial action throughout the PTEs.'[53]

Other settlements in the summer of 1984 included the NBC at 4.9 per cent, and gas staff agreed 4.8 per cent with an extra day's holiday. Electricity staff received 5.2 per cent, which was the least of the negotiators' worries given the MMC reports on Yorkshire and South Wales Electricity Boards and the CEGB reorganization—electricity staff were struggling to maintain both jobs and their negotiating machinery. On the waterways the settlement was 4.6 per cent, water 5 per cent, industrial estates 4.5 per cent, and University staff 3.5–5.75 per cent.

In the NHS the A&C grades, most of PT'B', and the ambulance officers all accepted 4.5 per cent in contrast with the pay review body award of 7.8 per cent to PT'A' staff. The health group was unhappy: 'the group meeting acknowledges that an improved pay offer will only be achieved if a programme of industrial action is undertaken.'[54] Meanwhile the TUC had launched the 'Save Your Health Service' campaign at the start of the year (see Tables 2.5–2.15).

In local government the claim for 7 per cent and better grading for nursery nurses was rejected by the employers, who responded with an offer of 4.5 per cent. The NLGC recommended arbitration since the employers refused further negotiations and there was some indication that industrial action would not receive the level of support from members required for victory. This position was endorsed at a meeting of 1,200 local-government delegates, and later, after further wrangling, terms of reference were agreed with the employers to be sent to the arbitration panel.

---

[53] *NALGO Annual Report 1984*, 148.   [54] Ibid. 130–2.

Even NALGO was not immune from industrial strife, finding itself in dispute with its own employees. In the spring of 1984, disrupted production of *NALGO News* was modestly reported by the journal: 'We apologize for the lateness and reduced size of this issue of *NALGO News*. Production difficulties have arisen as a result of industrial action being taken by NALGO staff's unions over a pay dispute.'[55] Almost a year later the union suffered more action, reported in the national press: 'The public service union Nalgo was paralysed yesterday when its entire staff of 850 began strike action in support of its press officer, Mr Jim Roberts, who was dismissed for allegedly leaking documents to Mr Derek Hatton, the deputy leader of Liverpool City Council. The strike has shut down Nalgo's London headquarters.'[56]

Local bargaining

Local bargaining became increasingly significant during these years, as managers searched for reductions in labour costs so that they could operate within their declining levels of funding. Four related issues came to dominate employer-level industrial relations, with managers trying to force through changes in the organization of work and trade unionists resisting attacks on pay, job security, and working conditions. First was the issue of unilaterally declared compulsory redundancies and/or redeployment to achieve lower staffing levels. Secondly, managers introduced new technology without agreement. Thirdly, grading structures were manipulated in order to reduce wage costs, and low-paid groups putting in regrading claims faced management indifference and inaction. Finally, managers took vigorous action to assert their 'right to manage', victimizing individual workers and union representatives. Under the conditions imposed by the government, individual employers trying to maintain services with less cash had no option but to intensify the exploitation of staff, extracting more work from a smaller and cheaper workforce. This meant launching strong attacks on well-organized NALGO branches. Some examples of management action and union responses are given below.

Compulsory redundancies caused Brighton Polytechnic staff to walk out when the County Council cut the budget. Croydon Branch won reinstatement of a Senior Training Officer post after a nine-month boycott of training by 500 members in the social services department. Northern General Transport members established a formal agreed procedure on redeployment. *Met District News* told how members took action to protect one of their colleagues: 'Attempts by Middlesex Polytechnic management to enforce a compulsory redeployment have been defeated after a wave of strikes by NALGO members throughout the Polytechnic.'[57]

When Lochaber District Council in the Highland Region of Scotland made three officers redundant in June 1983, this sparked off a longer strike by fifty-two NALGO members, reported in *Public Service*: 'As it entered its fifth week, Lochaber sub-branch officials accused the 12-member local council of mismanagement, financial incompetence, and vindictive refusal to discuss alternatives to compulsory redundancy.' Senior District Officer Matt Smith commented, 'the union has set its face against compulsion whether applied to one member or one hundred. The council must learn how to put people first.'[58] The Highland Region Branch called on mass support for the strikers, and the Emergency Committee approved national blacklisting of Lochaber jobs. A key to the success of this dispute was support from the national Emergency Committee following a ballot of sixty-two members of whom forty-three voted in favour of action.[59]

The story of the strike was told in the press:

A strike by 52 members of the National and Local Government Officers' Association employed by Lochaber District Council entered its seventh week yesterday to the strain of bagpipes but with both sides very much out of tune. Even two council meetings within 20 hours and the appearance of Mr Arthur Steer, the president of NALGO, at Fort William failed to produce a formula for an early return to work and left a possibility of support action from the union's 800,000 members. The stoppage is over a council decision to make three NALGO members redundant to effect savings. They are the only council in Scotland so far to introduce compulsory redundancies. By six votes to four, with one councillor abstaining, the council agreed yesterday to refer the dispute to the national joint consultative machinery for councils. . . . About 15 employees are keeping the council's services going but the strikers claim that there must be a huge backlog of work. About half of those working resigned from NALGO in the past few weeks and the others are non-union. More than 100 union members, made up of strikers and delegates from other branches in Scotland, marched along Fort William High Street led by four pipers. Mr Steer told the marchers: 'I can promise you all the support you need at national level and from fellow members throughout the country. I have never seen such a reactionary council as the one you suffer here in this town.'[60]

The strikers and the members who supported them played the vital role: 'Their determination to win this dispute is impressive and morale is high. There is little doubt that their action is causing serious disturbance to the

---

[57] *Met District News* (Feb. 1984), 1.   [58] *PS* (July–Aug. 1983), 1.

[59] *NALGO Emergency Committee Meeting Minutes*, 12 (London: NALGO, 1983), 180.

[60] *Scotsman*, 27 July 1983, 6.

orderly running of the District Council's business.'[61] By early August the council withdrew the redundancy notices and the strike ended in victory.

NALGO News reported another strike against redundancies:

Two hundred NALGO members at North West Water Authority headquarters walked out on Tuesday over the first compulsory redundancy in the water industry. NALGO member Dave King was given two hours' notice to quit without any prior consultation last Friday, despite an agreement between the authority and NALGO that there would be no compulsory redundancies under reorganisation plans.[62]

This action received retrospective approval from the Emergency Committee and the branch went on to win the dispute. In St Helens a strike by 1,400 NALGO members over suspensions following a refusal to relocate to another workplace lasted seven weeks.

Difficult collective-bargaining issues ensued when Sheffield City Council terminated the new technology agreement and offered another without a status quo clause. Council leader David Blunkett commented that, 'under the previous agreement, NALGO held on to status quo, no matter how long. We found that managers could not make progress. We felt we were handing over our power to the unions and giving them a veto over our political decisions.'[63] Sheffield Branch members went on strike over this refusal to negotiate in good faith, and again the local press tells the story with these three extracts from consecutive days, starting on 2 October 1984:

Town Hall Revolt Looms: Several Sheffield Town Hall workers are expected at a meeting tonight to discuss ways of escalating the current dispute with the city council. The move follows the walkout of 19 cashiers in the city's rates hall this morning which has brought an end to over-the-counter payments of rent and rates. The city council could now face open revolt from key workers in various town hall sections in the dispute with Nalgo union members over new working practices.[64]

Town Hall on Brink of Chaos: Sheffield City Council is on the brink of total chaos this afternoon as white collar staff prepare to escalate their strike action. Council bosses fear that Nalgo members will close down the City Treasurer's Department bringing a total halt to all financial transactions. The news comes on a day of turmoil that was an embarrassment at the Blackpool Labour Conference for City Council leader David Blunkett. Mr Blunkett—due to speak in a local government debate— faced pickets from Nalgo workers at the conference who leafleted Labour delegates on the 'high handed' style of the City council towards its workers.[65]

400 Walk Out in City Treasury: Sheffield City Council was rocked by further industrial action today when more than 400 staff in the City Treasurer's Department walked out. The strike has brought the department to a virtual standstill with only

[61] Ibid. 194. [62] *NN*, 11 May 1984, 1. [63] *PS* (Nov. 1984), 2.
[64] *Star*, 2 Oct. 1984, 1. [65] Ibid., 3 Oct. 1984, 1.

senior officers working and will affect a wide range of financial transactions. White collar union Nalgo say staff will return tomorrow after protest over colleagues being asked to do work that should have been done by people on strike. The City Council could face further chaos in the education department, where Nalgo claims members are being asked to operate new technology . . . the dispute over new working practices now looks set to turn into a head-on confrontation between the white collar staff and the council bosses. Nalgo has made it clear that it will escalate its action across the whole range of Town Hall services unless the council backs down from insisting on having a final say over new working practices.[66]

Local regrading claims began to attract national attention as low-paid groups took action. Sandwell Branch took up a regrading claim for 250 school secretaries, who refused to handle telephone calls and to collect cash. Their employer threatened to stop their pay, and national support was given for a strike when 'as a result of the action the authority has suspended the school secretaries'.[67] The action ended after twelve weeks with an agreement to examine their grading issues through a joint working party with an independent chair.

Islington's Labour council rejected efforts to end a three-month strike by 170 nursery workers at day centres. The NALGO branch decided to ballot all 2,000 members to force the council to negotiate in good faith. A national campaign over nursery workers' gradings was developing, which spilled into local action elsewhere: 'Bolton's 200 nursery nurses in educational establishments are still out on indefinite strike over the Bolton council's refusal to implement a regrading recommended in a joint council/NALGO report.'[68] The *Bolton Evening News* reported one of the more dramatic actions under the headline: 'Women Strikers Hit Town Hall: a group of striking women nursery nurses brought chaos to Bolton Town Hall today when they barricaded themselves inside the switchboard room . . . the 16 nurses say their action was to mark the 20th week of their strike which is over the authority's refusal to sign a local agreement giving them better pay and conditions.'[69]

Inevitably, some staff were attacked by their employers for following union policy to protect jobs, and time after time their work colleagues mobilized to defend them. In Merseyside, 2,000 went on strike when the council suspended a member refusing to cover a vacant post. There was a strike in Westminster for the reinstatement of a dismissed branch secretary among library staff, and another strike by 1,600 members in Southwark over the sacking of a peripatetic residential social worker.

---

[66] Ibid., 4 Oct. 1984, 1.
[67] *NALGO Emergency Committee Meeting Minutes*, 12 (1983), 422.
[68] *News Now* (Oct. 1984), 1.   [69] *Bolton Evening News*, 18 Sept. 1984, 1.

Employers were more ready to victimize individual members. *Public Service* reports on one serious case in September 1983: 'Haringey NALGO won the reinstatement of a dismissed colleague last month by taking massive strike action for eight days. More than 2,200 staff voted with their feet when Les Butler, a works foreman on probationary service, was sacked without regard to procedures.'[70] The local newspaper reported: 'The NALGO storm began on September 8 when foreman Les Butler was told he was the subject of disciplinary action after a meeting to discuss his performance. . . . The council "tore up" its employment agreements over the sacking of building worker Les Butler, claims NALGO.' The report also reveals the extent of membership involvement in the strike.

Services Paralysed: Council services were paralysed this week after two thousand Haringey NALGO members backed the call for continued strike action at a mass meeting at Alexandra Palace on Monday. All NALGO departments were represented in the mass which assembled on the BBC car park, including staff from libraries, housing, social services, education, planning, architects, economic development and borough valuers. . . . They were called to vote on this resolution: 'this branch meeting totally rejects the employer's cynical and derisory offer and confirms and resolves to continue the industrial action'. The show of hands was acknowledged by convenor Reg Hart's words: 'thank you very much, the motion is overwhelmingly carried.'[71]

Although the council admitted that it had broken its own code of practice, it was reluctant to reverse the decision. This dispute was a good example of how quick action could stop employers arbitrarily breaching procedures. A report on the dispute to the union's national Emergency Committee also showed how the union was capable of rapid responses at all levels, to give support to members who needed to take swift action: 'The branch executive resolved to support the member . . . Before the branch executive's resolution could be implemented, some 70 members . . . took strike action . . . The chairperson of the NEC retrospectively approved this action with strike pay.'[72]

While Haringey members were supporting their victimized work colleague, social workers in Kent came out for three months to defend their shop steward: 'At noon on Wednesday 3 August, John Kirkpatrick, a leading steward in the social services department, was summarily dismissed for refusing to carry out a management instruction which would have undermined official NALGO industrial action.'[73] Over 300 members walked out immediately, and NUPE's divisional office gave full support. Within two weeks 500 mem-

[70] *PS* (Oct. 1983), 7.   [71] *Journal*, 23 Sept. 1983, 3.
[72] *NALGO Emergency Committee Meeting Minutes*, 12 (1983), 279.
[73] *NN*, 12 Aug. 1983, 3.

bers were out and demanding John Kirkpatrick's full reinstatement while the dispute went to ACAS. Activists from COHSE, NUT, NUM, ASLEF, NGA, SCPS, and the AUEW joined a protest march in September. Kent County Council went to the courts to stop the union picketing, but the judge ruled against them. Geoffrey Drain said: 'We are delighted with this victory. We hope now that Kent County Council will accept that courts are not the place to settle industrial disputes, any more than victimising individual trade unionists is the way to do so . . . Kent County's cavalier approach to its employees is what led to this dispute and its escalation.'[74] The dispute dragged on to the end of the year with the employers refusing in advance to abide by any decision of an IT. The *Kentish Gazette* could not resist reporting on the resignation from NALGO of Nicholas Stacey, Director of Social Services, because 'he believed a large number of "vulnerable and innocent" clients were suffering as a result of the strike'.[75]

A more unusual case was that of Pat Coxon, a social worker and NALGO activist sacked by Gateshead Council after being arrested and imprisoned for her activities at the Greenham Common women's peace camp. The camp was a continuous protest at the government's decision to allow the US air force to keep nuclear bombs and cruise missiles there in readiness for an attack on the Soviet Union. NALGO supported her, and the council later reinstated her, treating her three-week prison term as unpaid leave of absence.

Another important victory came after strike action in Hartlepool over a racially motivated sacking. The council simply told a NALGO member there was no future for him, took him off the mailing list, and took all his work from him. Again, the local press took up the story:

Strike Threat At Civic Centre: NALGO to Act Over Job Loss: Hartlepool Civic Centre staff are being urged to stage a one-day strike on Friday in support of a colleague whose job disappeared in a council reshuffle. And the council's planning department could go on all out indefinite strike if union leaders' recommendations are taken up by civic centre staff. The 400 members of the council's NALGO branch will meet on Thursday to reaffirm their support for former Deputy Borough Planning Officer Arun Sathe, who for the past six months has been without any work to do. NALGO says he has been the subject of discrimination.[76]

Nearly 400 members went on strike for a day and twenty-one from the planning department were out for three weeks. The branch won support from the CRE and from Labour MP Jack Straw, and won the case with an agreement 'that Arun Sathe's job is safeguarded on full protected salary . . . that he will be given suitable work to do pending the result of negotiations . . .

---

[74] Ibid., 30 Sept. 1983, 1.   [75] *Kentish Gazette*, 19 Aug. 1983.
[76] *Hartlepool Mail*, 3 July 1984, 1.

and that the Tribunal case under the Race Relations Act stands adjourned'.[77] The *Hartlepool Mail* headlines summarize the victory: 'Acas Talks End Job Loss Strike: Relieved Planner Given New Post'.[78]

These actions to defend individual union members also defended the union locally, so that action could be taken over key issues of regrading, redundancies, and changing work practices.

Facing up to the Conservative Counter-Revolution

Other sections of this chapter have discussed NALGO's failure to support some key struggles of other union members—the miners and the print workers—when they came under attack. Right-wing theories, about inefficient industries, restrictive labour practices, and domineering unions, held sway over the alternative analysis—that state power was being both centralized and strengthened to support profit-making. Powerful forces were being mobilized to secure a transfer of risk away from the shareholders and onto the workers, and a flow of wealth in the opposite direction. These were the same forces that were being turned against union members. But, at all levels of the union, the implications of defeat for the miners and printers were not fully appreciated by sufficient numbers. However, when the government acted to restructure industries and services employing NALGO members, most leaders and activists had a sharper understanding of the issues and their responses were much more clearly thought out. This section covers the union's mobilization to try to stem the counter-revolution and to modify its impact on members' job security, pay, conditions of service, and labour process.

Counter-revolution in local government—the case for a dented shield

Soon after the 1983 election, on 27 October, the government published the White Paper *Streamlining the Cities*, setting out its intention to abolish the GLC and the six metropolitan county councils. This was followed on 20 December by the Rate-Capping Bill. NALGO was clear about the government's intentions: 'Since 1980 the system of local government finance in England has gone through seven distinct phases as the Government has sought greater control of local government spending. Rate capping must be seen as the culmination of those processes.'[79] Worried about the implications,

---

[77] *NALGO Emergency Committee Meeting Minutes*, 13b (London: NALGO, 1984), 103.
[78] *Hartlepool Mail*, 31 July 1984, 9.   [79] *NALGO Annual Report 1983*, 61.

NALGO News reported that 'the government's attack on the independence of local government is becoming even more ferocious'.[80]

In the following year the local-government group condemned the government's announcement on the 1984/5 rate support grant, on the grounds that 'it was clearly designed to force many local authorities either to make massive cuts in spending or to increase rates significantly and thereby appear to justify the proposed rate-capping legislation'.[81] Councils faced a serious and difficult dilemma. The government was reducing its share of spending on local government, but half of local-authority income was still received from national government. Every 1 per cent cut in spending imposed by the government could only be cancelled out through a proportionately larger increase in the rates levied on local households. *NALGO News* argued the case:

Local government, the jobs of its workers, and the services they provide to the community have been under sustained attack for several years. The government has imposed increasingly severe constraints on local government spending and has engineered a highly complex system of central funding to confuse public understanding of local services and their funding. Massive reductions in rate support grant (from 58.2 per cent in 1979/80 to an estimated 49.9 per cent in 1983/4, as a percentage of relevant expenditures in England) have forced local authorities to choose between cuts in services or increases in rates. Manipulation of grant-related expenditure figures to produce artificially low levels of acceptable expenditure have aggravated this effect by reducing the 'relevant expenditure' on which Rate Support grant is calculated. Low spending targets, arbitrarily fixed on a crude basis to force spending down even more, have resulted in severe financial penalties being exacted from the very many local authorities which spend above government targets. Despite the huge reductions brought about by these policies (local authority spending has fallen as a percentage of Gross Domestic Product from 15.9 per cent in 1974/5 to 12.8 per cent in 1983/4), and the consequent loss of over 100,000 local government jobs since 1979, the government has not yet secured the full control it wants in order to cut local services to the minimum and it is now extending its powers through the imposition of rate control and severe penalties, the establishment of unaccountable quangos to run major public enterprises, the abolition of the GLC and the metropolitan counties to whose policies it is opposed and the abolition of the 1985 elections in those areas. At the very time when funding and local investment are required to respond to serious problems of economic decline, social deprivation and urban decay, the government is determined to cut services to the public, and to do so by crude centralist devices which take no account of the needs of each local community.[82]

These moves to curtail local-government powers became another Thatcherite totem, although not without some infighting:

[80] *NN*, 18 Nov. 1983, 3.   [81] *NALGO Annual Report 1984*, 53.
[82] *NN*, 30 Mar. 1984, 1.

Local government reform divided the Conservative Party between those—Pym was one—who adhered to the traditional view of local democracy rooted in the shires and the boroughs, sustained by local squires and burgesses (Alderman Roberts of Grantham, for example), while others were of the opinion that reversing Britain's decline was too serious a business to be left to the sort of people who these days got themselves elected to town and county halls.[83]

However, the reformers' three main arguments won through: levels of spending were too high; the leaders of the GLC and other large councils were too left wing; and the Tories had already promised to abolish/reform the rates.

During the period 1979–83 left-wing councillors had put up rates rather than slash spending.[84] 'The government's answer to this in its second term was rate-capping. It was made illegal to set rates above a certain level. The Rates Act 1984 was due to come into effect in the spring of 1985.'[85] This sparked an important battle inside both the Labour Party and NALGO. The left generally argued that there should be non-compliance with government through not setting a rate at all, but Neil Kinnock famously argued, at a meeting in Birmingham in February 1985, 'better a dented shield than no shield at all . . . better a Labour council doing its best to help than Government placemen extending the full force of Government policy'.[86]

NALGO produced clear evidence that scrapping the GLC and the metropolitan county authorities would be more expensive than keeping them. The union's submission concluded that, 'for all its commitment to cutting public spending, the government seems to be prepared to pay any price, however huge, to eliminate its political opponents'.[87] GLC branch officers also produced a report, linking abolition with attacks on democracy, cuts in services, and redundancies. They concluded that abolition was undemocratic, impractical, would destroy jobs, increase centralization, and be inefficient and wasteful,[88] and that 'the results will be an unworkable proliferation of mostly unelected organisations'.[89]

The union launched industrial action to boycott all work connected with abolition, and organized massive demonstrations around the country with tens of thousands of members attending. On 24 January 1984 over 30,000 demonstrators supported a day of action in London. John Daly told the rally

---

[83] P. Jenkins, *Mrs Thatcher's Revolution* (London: Jonathan Cape, 1987), 179.

[84] 'Local Government: Attacks and Responses', *Labour Research* (June 1984), 156–8.

[85] Jenkins, *Mrs Thatcher's Revolution*, 238.   [86] Ibid. 239.

[87] *NN*, 27 Jan. 1984, 1.

[88] NALGO, *Why NALGO Opposes the Abolition of the Metropolitan Counties and the GLC* (London: NALGO, 1984), 3.

[89] LRD, *Rate Capping and Abolition: Councils in Danger* (London: LRD, 1984), 20.

that 'the future of democracy, the future of jobs and the future of public services are all at stake in the campaign'.[90]

The TUC set up a Campaign Co-ordinating Committee 'to develop the Movement's activities in opposition to the Rate Bill and also to the proposed abolition of the Metropolitan County Councils and the GLC',[91] which led a week of nationwide activities by the local-government unions and TUC Regional Councils. As part of this, 29 March was designated 'Democracy Day', and there were demonstrations in London, Liverpool, Leeds, Birmingham, and the north-east.

NALGO supported the establishment of the more broadly based Local Government Information Unit:

A national campaign unit, staffed by professionals and funded by local authorities and trade unions, is to be set up to co-ordinate the defence of local government against central government's legislative attacks. The unit's main task will be to fight the Government's proposals on rate-capping, abolition of the Greater London Council and metropolitan county councils, and the future organisation of London Transport.[92]

The union 'joined with rate-capped and heavily penalised authorities and other trade unions in the Local Government Capping Unit . . . and participated in the development of the joint campaign against the controls'.[93] The TUC maintained communications with the eighteen councils first in line to be rate-capped, and held a conference on 4 December 1984, attended by over 100 trade-union delegates and forty Labour councillors. The fight against abolition lasted until 31 March 1986 and is covered in more detail in Chapter 6.

Counter-revolution in the NHS

Embattled NHS staff faced yet more privatization and reorganization, summarized by one expert at the time:

The report of the Central Policy Review Staff in September 1982 argued that one way by which the projected gap between government revenue and expenditure could be bridged was the denationalization or privatization of the National Health Service. Public reaction was hostile and the Conservative government responded by apparently rejecting this option. Most people believe this rejection was a temporary measure, as the government continued to advocate 'partnership' between the public and private sectors, and various pressure groups continued to demand 'competition' in health care markets, the 'reduction of bureaucracy' and 'greater choice' for consumers.[94]

---

[90] *PS* (Feb. 1984), 1.　　　　　　　　　　　　[91] *TUC Annual Report 1984*, 322.
[92] *PS* (Nov. 1983), 1.
[93] *NALGO Annual Report 1985* (London: NALGO, 1986), 109.
[94] A. Maynard, 'Privatizing the National Health Service', in C. Johnson (ed.), *Privatization and Ownership* (London: Pinter, 1988), 47.

In the autumn the crisis became more acute with Secretary of State Norman Fowler announcing a mere 0.5 per cent growth target. He supported the government's general position that the NHS should remain largely public: 'My view (the view of a confirmed industrial privatizer) was that the National Health Service should remain at the centre of our health care system and that politically we would reap the whirlwind if we could be portrayed as moving away from it.'[95] Hence the famous slogan of the Prime Minister that the NHS is safe in our hands! As *Public Service* reported: 'Spending cuts have hit the NHS in the past month as never before. Cuts of £140m were announced by Health Secretary Mr Norman Fowler, along with staff cuts of between 6,000 and 7,000 jobs. But health unions have said that, in reality, up to 20,000 jobs are at risk.' Ada Maddocks said: 'It is impossible to cut staff without also cutting the standard of patient care. Our members are not prepared to sit back and watch the destruction of their jobs and the services they help to provide, and will vigorously oppose this new attack on both.'[96] Mike Thorpe, chair of the East Midlands District Health Committee, spelled out the implications:

It is difficult to contemplate, let alone believe that any further reductions in administrative costs are possible in a service which is acknowledged as having the lowest administrative costs of any health service in the world . . . inevitably every member in the service will be affected by the threat . . . And it is vital that each member recognises the role that needs to be played.[97]

NALGO's health group reported on 1983: 'The year was dominated by government measures to reduce NHS manpower and expenditure levels and to increase private provision of services.'[98] The health group annual meeting urged opposition to the contracting-out of domestic, catering, and laundry services. The meeting was 'alarmed at the recent dramatic growth of privatisation . . . [and] records its total opposition to privatisation in the NHS',[99] prompting *The Times* to report that 'militant action against the private health sector is being planned by NALGO'.[100] In its 1984 report the health group recognized 'that the government's determination to encourage the growth of private health care facilities and privatisation of the NHS support services will cause serious damage to the fabric of the nation's health care services'.[101]

NHS unions were coming to terms with two significant developments that followed from their successful industrial action in 1982. First was the pay review bodies established by the government for nurses, midwives, health visitors, and the professions allied to medicine. A rare academic comment on

95 N. Fowler, *Ministers Decide* (London: Chapmans, 1991), 185.

96 *PS* (Sept. 1983), 1.   97 *Empress* (Sept. 1983), 3.

98 *NALGO Annual Report 1983*, 133.   99 *NN*, 2 Sept. 1983, 2.

100 *The Times*, 8 Aug. 1983, 2.   101 *NALGO Annual Report 1984*, 130.

pay review bodies, made by a member of two of them, suggested that there were four reasons why free collective bargaining was inappropriate for such groups: there is no trading activity; the state is a monopsonistic buyer of labour; the state has the final say over pay anyhow; and the Whitley Councils themselves are regulated by the state.[102] For NHS staff outside the review body system, including most NALGO members who were in the A&C grades, changes to the management side of Whitley were criticized by National Officer for Health Ada Maddocks: 'This marks yet another step away from accountability within the NHS. The Government appears intent on rushing through the establishment of a small, tightly knit group of negotiators who would owe their positions entirely to patronage from the Secretary of State.'[103]

The second outcome of the 1982 strikes was a review of management structures. A NALGO leaflet sums this up: 'Mr Roy Griffiths, Sainsbury's supermarket chief, was called in by the government to apply the principles of the market place to a caring service.' NALGO's early concerns that he would initiate changes in pay determination systems, in local management practices, and in management control systems, later proved correct. An article in *NALGO News* examined several aspects of the Griffiths agenda: more centralized political control; higher density of management without necessary funds; substitution of budgets for need as the priority issue; and attacks on existing industrial-relations machinery and traditions.[104]

These concerns were shared by the TUC[105] and by other commentators: 'The Griffiths Report's adoption and implementation signifies [sic] a new style of management in the Health Service, which could clash with more traditional industrial relations practice . . . Some existing managers felt that strong management was synonymous with a tough approach to unions.'[106] By 1985 the health group was very anxious: 'This group meeting recognises the grave danger posed to NHS jobs and services by the deepening of the economic crisis. The immediate prospect of further massive attacks on public expenditure, in addition to privatisation, the implementation of the Griffiths report and the growing list of hospital closures requires a decisive and unequivocal strategy to defend jobs and services.'[107]

---

[102] G. Thomason, 'The Pay Review Bodies', *Health Services Manpower Review*, 11/3 (1985), 3–6.

[103] *PS* (Oct. 1983), 3.   [104] *NN*, 4 Nov. 1983, 4.

[105] *TUC Annual Report 1984*, 316.

[106] A. Swabe, P. Collins, and R. Walden, 'The Resolution of Disputes in the NHS', *Health Services Manpower Review*, 12/1 (1986), 5.

[107] *NALGO Annual Report 1985*, 137.

Getting on with privatization

The biggest direct threat to members came from privatization, which had become so popular that the government had decided to include gas, water, and electricity supply alongside subcontracting to the private sector in health and local government. NALGO issued leaflets opposing privatization in all industries in which it organized staff. The general theme was that 'nationalised industries and services should not be sold to powerful City institutions whose first aim is to make money, not to serve the nation. NALGO wants to halt this mad march back to the nineteenth century. Support your union's campaign to stop "privatisation".'[108] For the time being the action focused on two services, buses and gas.

The White Paper *Buses* (Cmnd 9300) contained three core elements: to break up and sell off the NBC to the private sector; to reorganize municipal operators into companies to be owned by the councils prior to privatization; and to break up and sell off the services operated by the PTEs. The costs of the transitional plans would be subsidized through direct government moneys and through job losses and management restructuring. The Transport Act 1985 'extended deregulation to all types of bus service . . . Local authorities were also given various rules to prevent them inhibiting competition . . . but its biggest new development was provision for the privatisation of the two-thirds of British buses and coaches that were currently in the ownership of either local authorities or the state.'[109]

A pro-privatization report concluded that 'the optimal solution is competition for the market rather than in it. This would suggest that a system of competitive contracting or franchising of services should result.'[110] This view, derived from neo-classical economic assumptions, and rooted in the dogmatic assertion of inherent efficiency in the private sector, failed to predict any of the actual outcomes of bus deregulation. In contrast, NALGO activists predicted the outcomes with great accuracy: reduced services; worse conditions of employment; unsafe vehicles; closure of unprofitable routes; higher fares; and lower usage. Its 1984 pamphlet *Our Buses Our Fight* sets out the consequences: 'The most significant of the government's plans is to abolish Road Service Licensing throughout Britain (except London) resulting in free-for-all competition between any operator who can manage to put a bus on the road. This, if allowed to be implemented, will destroy services and

---

[108] NALGO, *They Sell We Pay* (London: NALGO, 1984).

[109] J. Hibbs, 'Privatization and Competition in Road Passenger Transport', in C. Veljanovski (ed.), *Privatization and Competition* (London: IEA, 1989), 161–2.

[110] I. Savage, *Deregulation of Bus Services* (London: Gower and Institute for Transport Studies, 1985), 255.

thereby effectively immobilise countless numbers of people, hitting hardest the most disadvantaged groups.' Another study found that there was 'little dissension amongst commentators regarding the traumatic impact of the Transport Act on the employees within the industry and secondly, on the industrial relations institutions and practices'.[111] With 70 per cent labour costs it meant job losses, wage cuts, and increased hours.

The National Gas Committee took a hard line opposing management proposals on redundancies, on the abolition of the national bargaining machinery, and on showroom closures in readiness for privatization. They threatened non-cooperation with new technology as part of their campaign for better conditions such as a thirty-five-hour week and more annual leave. EMGAS technicians went on strike for eight weeks when two technicians were suspended for refusing to work to a new job description, and eventually the company conceded an agreement 'much better than a status quo'.[112] An overtime ban at North West Gas resulted in the appointment of two new staff. Compulsory redundancies became more likely after a report by management consultants Deloitte, Haskins, & Sells recommended that greater profits could be achieved through efficiency measures. As Roy Jones, National Gas Committee chair, pointed out: 'the report is a major threat to staff in the industry and its recommendations would lead to a reduction in the quality of service to the public.'[113]

On 7 May 1985 the government announced its plans for the British Gas sell-off. As the gas group reported, 'the campaign against gas privatisation was one of NALGO's main priorities for the remainder of the year . . . Much of the campaign has been co-ordinated with other gas unions.'[114] The union donated £9,000 to the anti-privatization campaign. *The Times* reported that 'strikes over privatization can be expected before Christmas in the gas industry, a union leader said yesterday. Mr David Stirzaker, national gas officer of NALGO, said the action would start with a 24-hour stoppage.'[115]

Similar alarms were ringing in other sectors: motions from the water and electricity groups expressed their concern that they would be next to be privatized. At Thames Water there was talk of the employer pulling out of the national agreement, and, without consultation with the staff side, management consultants drew up plans to cut up to 1,000 jobs, a fifth of the total, and to prepare the way for privatization. Similar moves at the South West Water Authority threatened 250 jobs, and 'Severn Trent Water moved nearer to a

---

[111] K. Forrester, 'Buses', in A. Pendleton and J. Winterton (eds.), *Public Enterprise in Transition: Industrial Relations in State and Privatized Corporations* (London: Routledge, 1993), 223.

[112] *NALGO Emergency Committee Meeting Minutes*, 12 (1983), 264.

[113] *PS* (Oct. 1983), 6.   [114] *NALGO Annual Report 1985*, 126.

[115] *The Times*, 11 June 1985, 2.

major industrial dispute . . . when the authority's instruction to divisional managers to put 25% of their regular design work out to private consultants began to take effect . . . Engineers in the projects section were told that one in four must go.'[116] The Wales TUC meeting in Tenby on 2–4 May 1985 opposed the privatization of the Welsh Water Authority.

These issues were at the forefront of NALGO's campaigning activity: 'By the middle of the year privatisation had clearly become the biggest challenge and was given top priority.'[117] The main annual conference debate on privatization was about how to fight against the downgrading of public services. It was understood that the fight must include 'linking with other unions; supporting employers sympathetic to the union's position; and, in the long term, electing a Labour Government'.[118] *Public Service* reported on how this was to be implemented:

The case for keeping the water industry in public ownership is being brought to the attention of the main political party conferences this autumn. They are being lobbied and leafleted and, where possible, NALGO speakers are being provided for fringe meetings. A leaflet entitled *Hands Off!* has been prepared by the water industry unions' committee comprising NALGO, GMBATU [General Municipal Boilermakers' and Allied Trade Union], NUPE, TGWU, TWSA [Thames Water Staff Association] and UCATT [Union of Construction, Allied Trades, and Technicians].[119]

At the 1985 TUC Annual Congress in Blackpool John Daly started his speech by attacking the government's record: 'In the past six years Thatcher's Government has robbed the working people of this country of £8,000 million-worth of public assets. It is the biggest case of grand theft in the recorded history of crime.'[120] The TUC's report *Stripping our Assets—the City's Privatisation Killing* identified how financial institutions and consultants, many having made donations to the Conservative Party, benefited from the sell-offs of profitable and successful public enterprises.

Concluding Remarks

The year 1985 ended as it began, with a major national dispute over the future of an entire industry. Rupert Murdoch, a key supporter of the government, took on the print unions NGA and Society of Graphical and Allied Trades (SOGAT) '82 at his Wapping plant as he imposed a new order on the work-

---

[116] *PS* (Aug. 1984), 3. [117] *NALGO Annual Report 1985*, 215.
[118] *PS* (July 1985), 2. [119] Ibid. (Oct. 1985), 3.
[120] *TUC Annual Report 1985*, 547.

force in his News International empire. As with the miners, the determination of the trade unionists was met with employer intransigence supported by police protection. Violent clashes in the coalfields and at Wapping strengthened the resolve of some and weakened that of others. By the end of 1985 NALGO had gone through some very hard battles, both internally and against its immediate opponents, and had emerged in relatively good shape. However, the biggest battles were yet to come, in the programmes to privatize the utilities and to restructure local government, the NHS, and education.

With a large majority in Parliament after the 1983 election, the Conservatives had cleared the road to continue with their main programmes. But first they had to achieve two key tasks: to defeat the NUM and to abolish the GLC. Here were the apparent strongholds of the left, democratic alternatives to government with their own mandates. In tackling the miners the government sought to triumph over organized labour and to send shock waves through the movement. The defeat, and it was a terrible defeat, strengthened right-wing labourism and created confusion, defeatism, and new realism within the trade-union movement. This was not new—in previous defeats parts of the labour movement had veered right and become more conciliatory in words and deeds than the objective situation demanded. NALGO was deeply involved in the policy debates, and sometimes policy commitments wavered, nerves were lost, and direction drifted. But, despite that, the union maintained its support for national and local activities around collective bargaining, and continued its support for others in even worse circumstances. There was a broad degree of unity on issues such as union rights at GCHQ, non-cooperation with trade-union laws, and for the AES.

Appendix

TABLE 5.1. *NALGO membership, 30 September 1983*

District	Number of branches	Voting members	Members in arrear	Membership of branches excluded from voting	Ordinary (cols. 2–4)	Total membership					Total membership (cols. 5–10)
						Retired	Student	Unemployed	Trainee	Honorary	
	(1)	(2)	(3)	(4)	(5)	(6)	(7)	(8)	(9)	(10)	(11)
Eastern	119	49,308	52	461	49,821	5,883	1	6	15	—	55,726
East Midland	104	45,419	50	—	45,469	4,100	3	4	25	—	49,601
Metropolitan	151	96,594	308	1,443	98,345	11,901	13	23	17	—	110,299
North Eastern	80	40,192	91	—	40,283	2,159	2	1	83	—	42,528
North Western and North Wales	141	107,774	141	—	107,915	7,968	7	1	52	—	115,943
Scottish	117	74,915	48	1,843	76,806	1,768	14	2	57	—	78,647
South Eastern	96	41,798	120	196	42,114	7,154	8	10	14	—	49,300
Southern	80	37,988	67	301	38,356	4,483	4	5	—	—	42,848
South Wales	89	33,845	51	—	33,896	2,004	3	1	24	—	35,928
South Western	97	45,624	91	109	45,824	4,138	1	3	29	—	49,995
West Midland	91	73,144	45	—	73,189	6,262	6	2	27	—	79,486
Yorkshire and Humberside	79	65,758	45	—	65,803	3,912	1	4	11	—	69,731
Honorary members	—	—	—	—	—	—	—	—	—	5	5
TOTAL	1,224	712,359	1,109	4,353	717,821	61,732	63	62	354	5	780,037

TABLE 5.2. *Allocation of NALGO membership, by service, 30 September 1983*

District	Local government	Gas	Electricity	Health	Transport (inc. PTEs)	Water	New Towns	Port authorities	Universities	Police authorities	Retired
Eastern	33,603	3,227	2,672	4,676	543	2,979	676	23	492	930	5,883
East Midland	31,419	3,859	2,603	5,462	433	—	114	—	470	1,109	4,100
Metropolitan	70,138	7,414	4,482	10,810	453	3,111	250	—	1,687	—	11,901
North Eastern	27,446	2,406	1,974	4,445	784	1,348	505	99	336	940	2,159
North Western and North Wales	73,790	6,016	5,781	12,217	2,949	3,462	1,108	20	1,163	1,409	7,968
Scottish	57,852	2,906	4,061	8,493	404	15	1,259	41	1,570	205	1,768
South Eastern	25,956	3,809	2,755	5,763	281	2,104	—	—	520	926	7,154
Southern	23,946	2,625	2,730	6,397	63	—	710	—	1,069	816	4,483
South Wales	21,526	2,356	1,176	4,004	175	2,370	224	—	1,010	1,055	2,004
South Western	32,522	2,083	2,551	4,355	181	2,348	—	103	599	1,082	4,138
West Midland	47,985	5,171	2,875	8,651	1,571	4,571	662	—	919	1,082	6,262
Yorkshire and Humberside	49,978	2,280	3,078	5,260	1,508	2,339	—	—	1,360	784	3,912
Honorary members	—	—	—	—	—	—	—	—	—	—	—
1983 Totals	496,161	44,152	36,738	80,533	9,345	24,647	5,508	286	11,195	9,256	61,732
Percentages	63.61	5.66	4.71	10.32	1.20	3.16	0.71	0.04	1.44	1.19	7.19
1982 Totals	493,504	45,920	38,305	86,364	8,772	26,407	6,047	296	11,729	9,097	57,741
Percentages	62.92	5.86	4.88	11.01	1.12	3.37	0.77	0.04	1.50	1.16	7.36

TABLE 5.3. *NALGO membership, 30 September 1984*

District	Number of branches	Voting members	Members in arrears	Membership of branches excluded from voting	Total membership						Total membership (cols. 5–10)
					Ordinary (cols. 2–4)	Retired	Student	Unemployed	Trainee	Honorary	
	(1)	(2)	(3)	(4)	(5)	(6)	(7)	(8)	(9)	(10)	(11)
Eastern	117	47,501	46	208	47,755	5,864	6	8	52	—	53,685
East Midland	104	43,692	57	571	44,320	4,070	4	7	6	—	48,407
Metropolitan	151	95,996	247	1,436	97,679	12,022	19	20	24	—	109,764
North Eastern	80	39,317	87	114	39,518	2,647	7	3	108	—	42,283
North Western and North Wales	134	107,846	148	—	107,994	7,293	32	19	137	—	115,475
Scottish	117	75,912	40	767	76,719	1,774	5	9	135	—	78,642
South Eastern	97	38,296	144	304	38,744	7,299	7	8	36	—	46,094
Southern	81	35,692	64	663	36,419	4,722	5	7	34	—	41,187
South Wales	88	3,022	89	67	33,178	2,268	14	5	34	—	35,499
South Western	96	44,333	88	—	44,421	4,362	222	6	80	—	49,091
West Midland	92	68,136	1,058	25	69,219	6,556	1	3	47	—	75,826
Yorkshire and Humberside	80	65,739	75	—	65,814	4,569	8	6	35	—	70,432
Honorary members	—	—	—	—	—	—	—	—	—	5	5
TOTAL	1,237	695,482	2,143	4,155	701,780	63,446	330	101	728	5	766,390

202

TABLE 5.4. *Allocation of NALGO membership, by service, 30 September 1984*

District	Local government	Gas	Electricity	Health	Transport (inc. PTEs)	Water	New Towns	Port authorities	Universities	Police authorities	Retired	Student unemployed, trainee	Honorary	Total membership
Eastern	32,519	3,052	2,694	4,283	507	2,846	620	20	466	748	5,864	66	—	53,685
East Midland	30,792	3,849	2,582	5,201	401	—	93	—	434	968	4,070	17	—	48,407
Metropolitan	71,160	6,839	4,363	10,002	459	2,885	256	—	1,715	—	12,022	63	—	109,764
North Eastern	27,209	2,343	1,807	4,266	780	1,266	458	97	330	872	2,647	118	—	42,283
North Western and North Wales	74,672	5,770	5,612	11,935	2,967	3,354	1,087	20	1,189	1,388	7,293	188	—	115,475
Scottish	58,167	2,862	3,988	8,213	415	17	1,246	35	1,577	199	1,774	149	—	78,642
South Eastern	23,980	3,697	2,699	5,148	277	1,987	—	—	494	462	7,299	51	—	46,094
Southern	22,882	2,527	2,616	5,924	63	—	663	—	1,019	725	4,722	46	—	41,187
South Wales	21,542	160	1,178	3,808	176	2,197	206	—	914	997	2,268	53	—	35,499
South Western	31,836	4,059	2,450	4,149	188	2,144	—	2	572	1,021	4,362	308	—	49,091
West Midland	44,776	5,167	2,814	8,237	1,495	4,406	637	—	882	805	6,556	51	—	75,826
Yorkshire and Humberside	50,508	2,177	3,094	4,806	1,492	2,456	—	—	1,281	—	4,569	49	—	70,432
Honorary members	—	—	—	—	—	—	—	—	—	—	—	—	5	5
1984 Totals	490,043	42,502	35,987	75,972	9,220	23,558	5,266	174	10,873	8,185	63,446	1,159	5	766,390
Percentages	63.95	5.55	4.70	9.92	1.20	3.08	0.68	0.02	1.41	1.06	8.28	0.15	5	100.0
1983 Totals	496,161	44,152	36,738	80,533	9,345	34,647	5,508	286	11,195	9,256	61,732	479	5	780,037
Percentages	63.61	5.66	4.71	10.32	1.20	3.16	0.71	0.04	1.44	1.19	7.91	0.05	—	100.0

203

6

Privatization and the Retreat from National Bargaining

ALFWAY through their second term, the Conservatives so dominated political life that it seemed nothing and nobody could deflect the Prime Minister from her objectives—even the Westland crisis in the summer of 1985 left her unscathed. One historian dubbed this period 'high noon for the new right'.[1] For the next two years until the 1987 general election the government proceeded with its plans to abolish the GLC, to privatize gas and water, to restructure local-government finance, and to establish contracted-out services in local government and the NHS. NALGO responded by shifting the bargaining agenda to issues such as equality, health and safety, and low pay, and by setting up a political fund to prevent the right from paralysing its campaigns.

With over three million unemployed, workers were afraid of unemployment. Most employed workers' pay was still rising faster than prices, although most NALGO members saw their pay fall behind other workers as their pay settlements were below the national norm (see Tables 2.5 and 2.6). There were many reasons for employed workers to keep their heads down.

NALGO continued arguing for pay determination based on comparability and on the duty of government to look after those employees unable or unwilling to take industrial action because of the potential harm to the public. A delegate to the STUC women's conference in Perth on 20–21 November expressed this well: 'The government claims that health service workers have a moral obligation to the patient, well we say that the government has a moral obligation to the health service workers.'[2] Sir Terence Beckett, Direc-

---

[1] K. Morgan, *The People's Peace: British History 1945–1989* (Oxford: Oxford University Press, 1990).

[2] *NALGO Annual Report 1985*, 23.

tor General of the Confederation of British Industry (CBI), put the government's contrasting view when he called for 'the complete elimination of pay increases not related to an increase in the output of goods and services'.[3] Ministers such as Ken Clarke and Nicholas Ridley banged the drum against national pay deals based on inflation and comparability, favouring local deals based on affordability and on labour-market conditions.

The March of the Marketeers

Meanwhile, Chancellor Nigel Lawson cut the basic rate of income tax by a penny in his 1986 budget. Such tax-cutting was not only about winning votes: as Michael Heseltine saw it, 'tax rates had to be made competitive, an incentive society recreated, the ill-disciplined subsidies to the nationalised industries removed, a forest of forms, restrictions and government impertinences removed'.[4] Inflation reached its lowest level during the Tory years, allowing the Chancellor to cut two pence off income tax in the 1987 budget and pave the way, as he believed, for an election victory based on the success of the economy.[5]

In the summer the government used its parliamentary majority to enact legislation on the privatization of gas and municipal airports, on social security measures, and sex discrimination, and, through a Wages Act, the removal of 500,000 workers under 21 years old from wages council protection. Britain's gas industry was sold off with a cynical publicity campaign extolling the virtues of the 'shareholder democracy' and 'popular capitalism', which sadly captured the mood of large sections of the population—there was massive demand for shares. British Gas employees were offered some free shares and discounts on others, but NALGO emphasized that, even if all employees took up the offer in full, the total employee share ownership would amount only to 4 per cent, not enough to wield any influence over company policy.[6] NALGO campaigned vigorously for strike action against gas privatization and in local government over pay, but the members rejected the union's call in both cases.

The bad news mounted up, especially in local government: 'The Government has reiterated, in a Green Paper "Paying for Local Government", its intention of replacing domestic rates with an archaic poll tax or "community

[3] D. Marsden, 'Chronicle: Industrial Relations in the United Kingdom, August–November 1985', *British Journal of Industrial Relations*, 24/1 (1985), 123.
[4] M. Heseltine, *Where There's a Will* (London: Hutchinson, 1987), 103.
[5] N. Lawson, *The View from No. 11* (London: Corgi Books, 1992), ch. 56.
[6] GUARD, *Before You Decide, Read the Facts* (London: GUARD, 1986).

charge".'[7] This was soon implemented in Scotland—the Abolition of Domestic Rates (Scotland) Bill became law—but the government postponed its introduction into England and Wales until after the next general election (see Chapter 7).

NALGO's annual report for 1986 summed up the fate of both the economy and the unions under the Conservatives:

The consequences of the Government's policies since 1979 include high and increasingly long-term unemployment; the collapse of manufacturing industry; an unprecedented balance of payments deficit; the neglect of investment, research and development, and industrial training; decaying infrastructure and inadequate public services; a growing housing crisis with mounting homelessness in the wake of savage cuts in expenditure on public housing. . . . Your Council can only look forward to continuing hard times for NALGO members.[8]

In the wider world outside collective bargaining and economic statistics, but not disconnected from it, the international political scene was dominated by the intensified new cold war under US President Reagan. Harking back to the old days of British gunboat diplomacy, the newer imperial power of America launched bombing raids with terrifying force against Libya. At enormous cost to the American and world economy, Ronald Reagan pursued the so-called Star Wars weapons development initiatives. Margaret Thatcher strengthened Britain's 'special relationship' with America, through the Trident programme and the stationing of American Cruise missiles on British territory. NALGO was one of a handful of unions supporting unilateral nuclear disarmament, because of concerns about 'the increase in the number of nuclear weapons in the world; the introduction of a new generation of weapons . . . the growing threat, by accident or design, of a nuclear holocaust . . . the waste of money on means of destroying life at the expense of ways of enhancing life'.[9]

The labour movement was demoralized and weakened, in part by the strength of the forces it faced and in part by its own inability to maintain clear positions. Trade-union policy became more muddled and confused, under pressure from the electoral needs of the Labour Party and from the sectional conservatism of some trade unionists. Defeat at the ballot box, accompanied by populist attacks on the trade-union and labour movement's traditional social democratic views of society, gave strength to those who supported the other main British trade-union tradition of 'business unionism', resurrected under the slogan of 'new realism'. The TUC and Labour Party retreated

---

[7] *NALGO Annual Report 1986* (london: NALGO, 1987), 57.   [8] Ibid.
[9] NALGO, *Sanity in our Time: Why NALGO is Affiliated to the CND* (London: NALGO, 1985).

from their centre-left positions on broad issues of economic and industrial policy.

The dominance of Conservatism, supported by most of the media, helped to ensure that more left-wingers and left-wing views were rooted out not only from local councils but also from both the trade-union movement and the Labour Party. Neil Kinnock, as part of his modernization of Labour policy, but also to consolidate his own position as leader, launched a bitter and sustained attack on a tiny number of Militant Tendency members, especially in Liverpool. This famously publicized action was a thin disguise for attacks on the entire broad left, and was applauded both in the Tory press and in the boardrooms. As one commentator suggested:

This battle had become the paramount preoccupation of the new leadership. The story of the party from 1983 until 1987 and beyond was essentially the story of the successful campaign against the hard Left conducted by Neil Kinnock. It was symptomatic of the profound crisis of the Labour Party that so much time and effort had to be expended by a major party of the European Left to get rid of a rather unsophisticated Trotskyist sect, able to count on no more than a few thousand members.[10]

NALGO's leadership kept to a line that was clear enough. President Sheila Smith kicked off the election year with a New Year message in *NALGO News*: 'The quality of life in Britain is being progressively corroded by policies which put profits before people.'[11] Deputy General Secretary Alan Jinkinson followed this up with a call that 'the present government's blitzkrieg against the public sector is against the public interest and must be stopped'.[12] This was underlined in the union's annual report: 'Every one of the services in which the Association has members, but especially local government, the water and electricity industries, and the NHS, have faced new measures or threats of privatisation on an unprecedented scale.'[13]

The pace of political life quickens before a general election. More citizens and union members take notice of the big issues of the day, and this provides a rare opportunity for the labour movement to have some of its ideas debated in a public arena. Faced with the daunting prospect of a third Tory government, NALGO put huge resources into the 'Make People Matter' campaign (see Box 9), linked to the TUC's 'Public Services Year' campaign initiated by a NALGO resolution at Congress. The union pressed for improvements to the economic conditions of members and for stronger political and social rights for workers. During election campaigns union action gains

---

[10] D. Sassoon, *One Hundred Years of Socialism* (London: Fontana Press, 1996), 701.
[11] *NALGO News* (NN), 9 Jan. 1987, 1.   [12] Ibid., 16 Jan. 1987, 5.
[13] *NALGO Annual Report 1987* (London: NALGO, 1988), 30.

significance, adding a wider propaganda dimension to the usual mixture of street demonstrations and lobbying in the corridors of power.

As the Webbs persuasively argued (see Chapter 1), union action swings between this method of winning government protection for workers and the method of winning improved pay and conditions through collective bargaining. Unions use both methods, but at times they perceive that there is more advantage to be gained by focusing more on one method than the other. Needless to say, they cannot withdraw from collective bargaining, and on this front NALGO aimed to persuade employers in the public sector of the need to tread carefully in the run-up to the election. There is a sense of both a dash to settle disputes and pay rounds in case of unforeseen political advantage/disadvantage going to the other side, and a postponement of major decisions until the political power in Westminster is settled for another four or five years.

The Webbs also pointed out that when trade unionists find themselves unable to win improvements through formal collective agreements at national level then they shift the focus of their collective strength to different issues at different levels. The breadth of NALGO campaigns expanded to cover a wider and wider range of membership concerns, as the union established a political fund and developed important new policies on workplace issues such as discrimination and violence at work.

Pragmatism in the Face of the Enemy

Dismay and confusion among trade unionists, and divisions over the best way to respond, deepened as the government pressed forward on so many fronts at once. NALGO's internal democracy showed signs of strain. Ten NEC members lost their seats in 1985. Subscriptions went up by 10 per cent to cover the costs of campaigns and actions. More worrying was the West Midlands County Council branch decision to break ranks by talking with the government over the abolition of the council, against explicit NALGO policy to the contrary. The General Secretary wrote to the branch's 2,300 members, pointing out the potential wrecking effect of their decisions on the national campaign against abolition. The members were not convinced, and the union dissolved the branch.

NALGO's 1985 conference was low key and inward looking. It acknowledged that government policy had forced the union into a more political stance, a point picked up by *The Times*: 'The 752,000 members of Nalgo were advised yesterday to vote the Conservatives out of office in defence of jobs and public services. At its annual conference in Bournemouth, Mr Norrie

Steele, the public employees' union leader, condemned cuts in public spending and privatization and said career prospects and job security were being threatened.'[14]

Under such difficult conditions some turned their attention inward to seek out the enemies within the movement. Fingers pointed in several directions: at defeatists amongst the members; at freemasons; at the Militant Tendency; and at dissidents among the union's staff. In the case of freemasons a report to conference found, not surprisingly, little hard evidence of influence. National union policy was similar to the position taken up by the Metropolitan Police; in the light of the 'exclusivity, strange rites, social conservatism and secrecy of the craft' it advised its members not to join![15]

The leadership came under challenge from both the right-of-centre guardians of the 'ordinary' members and the further-left guardians of trade-union purity. There were some determined challenges to the broad left's dominance of union policy, not for the first or last time, from small Trotskyite groups encouraged by events in Liverpool (see later in this chapter). Even the General Secretary felt the need to go public on this. In a speech at the 1985 District Publicity Officers' annual weekend meeting he argued persuasively that:

This year Congress approved the TUC/Labour Party statement *A New Partnership— A New Britain*. Within the next three years there will be a general election, and the Labour Movement must be able when that call comes to present a united approach with constructive policies designed to revitalise the economy. To seriously tackle the major evil of mass unemployment and provide a programme whereby the Public Sector is in the forefront of developing measures to improve social provisions and provide a stimulus to the economy.[16]

But he went on to argue that this could be done only through Parliament, and not by some revolutionary left groups. Seeking to convince members, Labour politicians, and the watching press of NALGO's mainstream credentials, he attacked both the Trotskyite left for its part in the Liverpool strike and the broad left for its challenge to his position over a range of issues including the Stockport Messenger dispute.

By 1986 membership fell to 680,000 working members, down from 739,000 in 1981—a loss of almost 8 per cent in five years. Losses were high in New Towns (39 per cent), transport (27 per cent), health (23 per cent), gas (21 per cent), water (18 per cent), electricity (15 per cent), universities (11 per cent), and ports (10 per cent). But in the union's local-government heartland the loss was much lower at only 2 per cent (see Tables 6.1–6.4). Part of the loss

---

[14] *The Times*, 18 June 1986, 2.   [15] *NALGO Annual Report 1985*, 81.
[16] *NN*, 25 Oct. 1985, 1.

is accounted for by job losses and unemployment, part by changes in employment status, and part by staff turnover—perhaps in the 1980s it was harder to recruit new staff to keep up with losses. This is partly a matter of image in terms of how individuals might perceive union membership to be beneficial to them, but it is also strongly influenced by wider political views about the extent to which unions make a difference to the economy and to society at large.

Such questions can be tackled through propaganda and campaigns, but the most useful way is through action, so that individual employees have direct experience of the union, alive and relevant at their immediate place of work—to most members the steward is the union. The *Steward's Guide to Recruitment*, issued in 1986, emphasized this point: 'The best possible recruitment advertisement is an active and concerned steward. It is therefore important that recruiting is not considered in isolation from your other roles as a steward. Non-members will want to join when they see others benefiting from membership of an active NALGO branch that takes up issues on behalf of its members.'[17]

This is why campaigns aimed at including minority groups of members in union activity are vital for the health of trade unionism. One key development in NALGO was the way that the demands of black members were taken up. Activists recognized that these members needed to identify with the union as *the* organization that represents not only their general employment interests but also their specific needs. Such needs included a legitimate space within the union for black members to take forward particular fights on issues such as racism and to formulate collective positions treating discrimination at work as a subset of wider and deeper racist practices.

Box 8. NALGO and the Fight for Equal Rights

'Equal rights' is a key slogan of progressive trade unionism. The struggle for equality at work has two relatively uncontroversial main aspects: first, to establish rights of employees to equal treatment by managers through collective agreements and through action to prevent managers from violating those rights; and secondly, to secure legal rights to equal treatment for all workers through political action. However, the struggle for equal rights is located within profound economic and social inequality, and this adds a third dimension that is not at all uncontroversial—changing union policy and practice itself.

In the workplace, managers have power over those whom they manage. This may become apparent through recruitment and selection decisions, promotion, supervision, work allocation, dismissal, and even in the ability to intimidate, to harass, and

---

[17] NALGO, *Steward's Guide to Recruitment* (London: NALGO, 1986), 2.

to demand favours without fear of interference. The fight for equality is one example of the endless need to assert the rights of workers. The potential for abuse of authority is immense, and the authority structure itself is underpinned by the management's claim to the 'right to manage'. There is systematic discrimination against sections of the workforce on the basis of personal characteristics—sex, race, disability, and sexual orientation.

NALGO adopted a series of conference resolutions in the 1970s, establishing a set of policies to tackle disadvantage faced by women workers, including: equal job and promotion opportunities; action against low pay generally; child-care provision; equal pension rights; stronger rights for employees to take part in union activity; equal rights for part-time employees; stronger rights to take maternity or paternity leave and return to work; equal pay for work of equal value; and action against sexual harassment. Surveys of NALGO branches carried out in 1974 and 1979 showed that women were under-represented on branch committees and among branch officer positions, and a survey of 5,000 members, carried out by researchers at University College, Cardiff, added further information on the extent of the disadvantage facing women members.[18]

In the 1980s the debate broadened to encompass other sections of the membership facing discrimination. Drawing from a bewildering array of ideas, including many strands of feminism and black consciousness, activists forged strong networks and alliances to confront discrimination within the union and to get their concerns accepted as legitimate. They formed *ad hoc* groups, operating at branch level and in some cases at district level, and started to challenge the union establishment. Some of the debates of the 1980s left the participants bloody and battered; those around the reports of the union's Race Equality Working Party (REWP) and the Positive Action Working Party (PAWP) give a flavour of the issues involved.

REWP was set up by the NEC early in 1982, with a brief 'to study the position of ethnic minority workers in NALGO services and elsewhere in the labour force and amongst the unemployed, to attempt to quantify the degree and nature of racism and discrimination that exists both at work and in the union and to make recommendations on an organisation and structure within the union that might adequately address these problems'.

At the annual conference that summer there were two motions on the issues. One from Liverpool called on the NEC to establish a race equality committee and on branches to take up some specific issues with employers: special recruitment and training initiatives for workers from ethnic minorities; training for managers dealing with employment issues and with service provision; monitoring of recruitment and selection; and appointment of race advisers in key departments, with branch agreement to waive internal advertisement requirements prior to these posts being filled externally.

The second motion, from Ealing Branch, called for national campaigns to encourage participation by ethnic minority members; anti-racism courses for negotiators;

---

[18] NALGO, *Equality? Report of a Survey of NALGO Members* (London: NALGO, 1981).

investigation of racist practices within services employing NALGO members; improvements in employers' recruitment and employment practices; union rules to secure the expulsion of members found to be perpetuating racism; and a new national committee on racism. The Liverpool motion was carried, and, after much confusion, the Ealing motion was referred to the NEC. Thus REWP got off to a difficult start.

REWP's report, issued in January 1984, summarized the prevalence of racism, citing research evidence on the persistent employment discrimination faced by black workers. The following extracts give an outline of the thinking behind REWP's recommendations on union structures:

NALGO's blend of representative democracy (one member one vote) and participative democracy (in which participation is open to all, and those who participate shoulder the responsibility of decision-making) has important advantages but, as it stands, may not be capable of reflecting adequately and representing the aspirations of the union's ethnic minority members, since they lack the numerical strength necessary to compel action within this structure.... One of [REWP's] primary aims had to be to stimulate the creation of a proper representative structure for ethnic minority members from branches through district to national level, *as well as* their proportionate involvement in the mainstream of union activity.

Furthermore, '[REWP] has assumed in its deliberations that those most closely affected by oppression and disadvantage should take the lead in determining the strategy for fighting it. But, because there is strength in unity and most NALGO members are white, it believes that any structure devised by the union must involve all members in the struggle.'

Thus REWP aimed to protect the structural integrity of the union's traditional representative structures while maximizing the possibilities for participation specifically by black members. It proposed the establishment of race equality officers, black members' groups, and race equality committees at both branch and district levels to fulfil these twin objectives. At national level REWP proposed a permanent national race equality committee, equal in status to the NEOC.

REWP's report was carried at the 1984 conference with some amendments, notably one from the Scottish District Council that established the principle of national support for district and national delegate conferences of black members. Some 500 activists attended the first national conference of black members in May 1986, followed by a further conference in Liverpool in January 1987, which agreed a new structure for the National Black Members Coordinating Committee (NBMCC).

The issue of representation was tackled more generally in a resolution at the 1985 annual conference. It instructed the NEC to make recommendations on how the interests of women, black, lesbian and gay, and disabled members 'can be better promoted and represented at all levels within the union'. In another resolution the conference supported facilities to establish and develop groups and committees at all levels of the union. The NEC set up the PAWP to devise a strategy to implement these aims. At their first meeting in November 1985 the nine NEC members initially appointed to PAWP co-opted two representatives from each of the NBMCC, the Disability Consultative Committee, and the Lesbian and Gay Steering Committee (the organized 'groups of members facing particular forms of discrimination' became known as self-organized groups (SOGs) during PAWP's deliberations).

PAWP launched a programme of research and consultation throughout the union, and it reported to the NEC in November 1986. It recommended that union funding should be made available to establish and support SOGs, and a re-drafted report went to the NEC in March 1987, recommending the establishment at district level of four committees under the umbrella of the existing District Equal Opportunities Committees (DEOCs), with reserved seats for SOG representatives on both DEOCs and district councils. At national level they recommended establishing a National Lesbian and Gay Committee made up of two representatives from the SOG in each district, with two reserved seats on the NEC; continuing the NBMCC, with the right to refer issues direct to the NEC; a Disability Committee with two reserved seats on the NEC; and a National Women's Rights Committee with one reserved seat on the NEC.

The NEC agreed to circulate this report, though 'members felt that these proposals [for reserved seats on the NEC] raised very serious questions, both of principle and practicality. In principle, the grafting onto the NEC of a quite different form of representation to that which already exists was found by some to be quite disturbing.'[19] The 1987 conference passed a motion expressing 'extreme concern' that the NEC had not adopted the report.

The NEC's own 'Report on Positive Action' went to the 1988 conference, recommending union support for SOGs to organize at branch and district levels, and recommending the establishment of four new national committees with the right to make recommendations to the NEC. There would be consultations between the SOGs and the national committees, but there would be no reserved seats. The conference debated a motion supporting the NEC's report and an amendment supporting PAWP's. Both were voted down. A similar debate in 1989 also saw no proposal gaining conference support.

By then the national committees existed, and national conferences based on the SOGs were taking place, with NEC support. Policy and practice developed on the basis of pragmatism and accommodations with the SOGs. In tune with many other areas of union practice, the real developments occurred in the wide political spaces that exist between the formal meetings of annual conferences, national executives, and district councils. In spite of the muddle and the hurt that was attached to the issues, union practice did develop, new structures for participation were established, and NALGO was recognized as being at the forefront of campaigns to tackle discrimination and disadvantage.

As well as reforming its own structures, the union took up individual cases—for example, in Doncaster, where an IT ruled that 'a council who refused to short list a woman for an interview for a more senior post was guilty

---

[19] NALGO, General Secretary's circular to branches, 27 Apr. 1987.

of sex discrimination'.[20] It advised branch negotiators with *NALGO Negotiating Guidelines* on part-time work and on job-sharing, and with the pamphlet *More than Ramps* aimed at securing better union facilities for disabled members. It supported the week of action for women in trade unions: 'On Saturday 18 October, trade unionists all over the country will be taking part in meetings, fairs, demonstrations and other events to mark TUC Women's Action Day.' The date coincided with the centenary of the death of a leading figure in early trade unionism, Emma Paterson.[21]

Present-day concerns were linked to past struggles, especially those where workers fought against the odds. The union gave financial support and publicity to a march from Jarrow that harked back to the spirit of the 1930s protests against unemployment: 'Carrying the original Jarrow crusade banner the Jarrow '86 marchers left Jarrow last Sunday on the first leg of their march to London . . . at the front of the march, carrying the original petition box, is unemployed NALGO member John Badger whose father designed the original Jarrow crusade banner and whose uncle Alf was one of the 1936 marchers.'[22]

Increasingly the union campaigned overtly against government policies and politics, unemployment, anti-union laws, and privatization, which eventually led to the creation of a political fund. While some unions were backsliding, NALGO's 1986 annual conference stood by the TUC's Wembley Conference decision not to apply for money from the government for union ballots. The issue surfaced again in 1987, and again 'the NEC considers that the advantages of a public subsidy are outweighed by the real and potential loss of union independence which would result'.[23] On the proposed new curbs on trade unions, NALGO pointed out that 'it is extraordinary that the independence of trade unions, the principle of freedom of association and the right of trade union members to determine their own affairs are apparently no longer seen as part of the British democratic tradition'.[24]

NALGO was among the minority of delegations at the 1986 TUC Annual Congress in Brighton that opposed the joint TUC/Labour Party statement on labour law, *People at Work: New Rights New Responsibilities*. John Daly told Congress that 'NALGO was currently involved in the largest strike ballot in history because our members expected it. We needed no lectures on secret ballots from this government or Labour Party leadership.'[25] For TUC President Ken Gill, 'despite the desolate economic and social landscape, there is reason for optimism; the political tide has turned since last Congress' owing to the 'heroic year long miners struggle. Their fight for jobs and communi-

---

[20] *Public Service (PS)* (Sept. 1986), 12.   [21] *NN*, 3 Oct. 1986, 7–8.

[22] Ibid., 10 Oct. 1986, 1.   [23] Ibid., 27 Mar. 1987, 5.

[24] Ibid., 8 May 1987, 5.   [25] *NALGO Annual Report 1986*, 4.

ties, and the ten billion pound cost destabilised the Tories.'[26] But the majority did not see it like that. Despite adopting supportive policies towards the GCHQ trade unions, the print workers at Wapping, and the strikers at Silentnight beds, overall there was a shift towards Labour Party leader Neil Kinnock's position.[27] During his address to Congress Kinnock attacked the ultra-left in Liverpool, providing a basis for reformulating the Labour Party's agenda and reorienting the labour and trade-union movement towards a role more supportive to business interests.

As seen with the miners' strike, the Conservative government had opened up new avenues for discontented members to attack their union, forcing unions to waste precious resources in defending the democratically decided rules. NALGO had to defend itself against a complaint brought by a member to the Certification Officer about the union's election procedures. Then two members took High Court action against the 'Make People Matter' campaign in the run-up to the 1987 election, happily reported in *The Times*: 'Two Conservative trade unionists yesterday launched an action in the High Court in an attempt to halt a union's £1 million campaign for more money for public services,'[28] and 'NALGO, the local government union, spent £250,000 on posters targeted at Conservative marginal constituencies as part of its campaign against Tory policies, the High Court in London was told.'[29]

Box 9. NALGO and the Politics of Campaigns—Getting the Union Message Across

There are two main ways for trade unions to establish and defend the rights of their members—by entering into collective agreements with employers, over terms and conditions of employment for employees, and by securing legal and political rights for workers and their organizations. Effectiveness in the second of these requires involvement in the political system.

By the 1980s NALGO policy had evolved into a strong blend of progressive left positions, reflecting broad social campaigns such as the women's, anti-racist, and peace movements. Here we examine some of the initiatives to win support for the union's policies, both among the membership and among policy-makers in government and elsewhere.

As the nature and composition of the membership changed with expanding public services, so the economic concerns of successive governments to place limits on public spending generated pressures that the union could not ignore. The response of the union to the dramatic political and economic events of the 1980s illustrates the

---

[26] Ibid. 3.

[27] N. Kinnock, *The Future of Socialism*, Fabian Society Tract no. 509 (London: Fabian Society, 1986).

[28] *The Times*, 28 May 1987, 2. [29] Ibid., 30 May 1987, 20.

significance of political campaigning. The NALGO in the Eighties committee report to the 1981 conference considered the legality of two campaigns—to support Welsh devolution and to sponsor the Anti-Nazi League—but legal opinion was that neither had breached the provisions of the Trade Union Act 1913. The committee believed that NALGO could widen the coverage of its rules to allow political campaigns, funded from the general fund, on anything not expressly mentioned in the Act.

The conference disagreed, ordering a ballot on both affiliation to the Labour Party and the establishment of a political fund, with publicity covering the cases for and against to be sent to the members. Twenty-two NEC members formed the Fight for Labour Affiliation Group (FLAG), while the Militant Tendency established the Campaign for NALGO Affiliation to the Labour Party (CNALP). Early signs that the move towards affiliation were misjudged came at a meeting at Luton College where NLGC chair and defector from Labour to the SDP Mike Blick publicly debated the issues with NLGC vice-chair and Labour member Jim White. Only twenty people turned up. In the absence of a focused campaign the result was inevitable—the members rejected both the political fund and affiliation by eight to one, in a surprisingly high turnout of nearly 60 per cent, giving a sharp warning to activists that members would vote for such a move only if the benefits were clearly apparent.

The Conservative government's assault on the public sector resulted in NALGO policy becoming more explicitly opposed to the government. The 'Stop the Cuts' campaign, running since the mid-1970s, had lost momentum and the union launched the 'Put People First' campaign in 1983. Costing £1 million, it was the biggest ever trade union campaign. Planned to run from March to July, it coincided with the general election held on 9 June. It was designed to alert the public to the damaging effects of cuts and privatization, and to persuade people to fight back.

Leaflets, posters, rallies, and demonstrations carried the union message, and local activists organized a broad range of events aimed at bringing people together—festivals, carnivals, exhibitions, sponsored events, events for schools and children generally, media programmes, film, theatre, and so on. Twelve extra specialist staff were taken on, and half of the campaign budget was spent on advertising. Hard-hitting pictures with captions highlighting concerns about cuts causing unemployment among both young people and professionals, about collapsing welfare services, and about the high priority given to spending on weapons, appeared on nearly 300 poster sites in prime urban locations and as full-page adverts in forty-five editions of national daily newspapers, in eighteen editions of the ethnic press, and in twenty-four editions of specialist journals.

'Put People First' was coordinated by a strong campaigning centre supporting district and branch activities, and resulted in stronger communications links and in stronger propaganda techniques. The 1986 conference called for a similar campaign to be run in 1987, to persuade NALGO members to vote to defend services in the local elections. The resulting 'Make People Matter' campaign had another £1 million budget.

National and district staff were seconded to the campaign, the hot-air balloon was brought back into action, along with three bouncy inflatables for outdoor events, and posters went up on 500 billboards in prominent positions in marginal constituencies. Mothers of babies born in NHS hospitals on May Day were presented with 'silver' spoons and a union message, attracting substantial favourable media coverage.

Two members, both Conservative Party activists, halted the campaign by securing a court injunction on the day that the 1987 general election was called. The union's conference responded immediately by voting to campaign among the members for the establishment of a political fund, as required by the Trade Union Act 1984. This Act was intended to cut off union funds to the Labour Party, by requiring all unions with political funds, as well as those creating new ones, to hold ballots to establish or retain them. The TUC had set up a campaign coordinating group to oversee the first ballots, and one after another the Labour Party affiliates renewed their political funds with resounding ballot majorities involving high turnouts. NALGO was the first large union to vote on setting up a fund for the first time.

The staff resources that had been dedicated to 'Make People Matter' were switched to the political fund campaign. NALGO activists were brought into action through a cascading series of briefings using the TUC education service. Monitoring systems were set up to check that campaign activities were implemented and targets were met. The West Midland District set itself the objective of having every member spoken to about the ballot. Staff and activists visited nearly 48,000 members before the ballot papers were distributed in February 1988. In larger workplaces the ballot papers were issued at meetings, checked against a register, and members were encouraged to vote having listened to the union's arguments.

The arguments for the political fund were clear and specific: it would enable NALGO to continue its normal campaigning activities; it was necessary because the law had changed (by narrowing the definition of 'political objects'), not NALGO; and NALGO's political independence would not change as a result. Strong campaign messages were combined with well-organized campaign activities. Activists were engaged in a unity of purpose over a relatively short period of time with specific and limited objectives. These were the conditions for a massive vote of over 390,000 in favour of the fund—over three-quarters of those voting, on a turnout of two-thirds of the entire membership. Members understood; as Alan Jinkinson said to us, 'it was going to be political action that changed government minds'.

NALGO switched its resources to secure a yes vote by members in a ballot to establish a political fund. Sheila Smith commented on the importance of union campaigns: 'If we are to stop the wholesale destruction of our public services, and in our turn roll back the frontiers of private greed, we must increase public understanding of the issues.'[30] The shift in NALGO towards campaigning ever more explicitly around a broad set of political, economic, and social issues, generally arguing a broad left position, reflected the

[30] *NN*, 12 June 1987, 8.

substantial changes during the 1980s in NALGO's whole approach to government and to extra-parliamentary activity.

Against Deregulation and Privatization, for Making People Matter

This second half of the second Tory term saw the further development and implementation of the government's deregulation and privatization agenda. The 1985 Green Paper, *Competition in the Provision of Local Authority Services*, started the process to introduce CCT for refuse collection, street cleaning, office cleaning, ground maintenance, and vehicle and catering services, and later this was applied to the NHS. As well as opposing these developments, NALGO also argued against privatization of gas, water, and electricity supply, and warned members of the related dangers to collective bargaining and working practices.

Royal Assent was given to the Transport Act on 30 October 1985, and abolition of the GLC and the six metropolitan county councils was finalized early in 1986. Abolition resulted in 8,100 job losses, and it removed at a stroke some successful counter-examples to the Conservatives' support for market forces as the best providers of services. Indeed, just as it was necessary to defeat the NUM in order to pave the way for the privatization of the energy industries, so it was essential to defeat Ken Livingstone at the GLC before the full policy of CCT for local government could be enacted in 1988.

At the 'Keep it Public' conference in Sheffield, organized by the Local Government Information Unit (LGIU), all speakers opposed privatization, but several were aware of the problems facing employees and the unions. The main themes were the improvement of services, and the strengthening of links between employers, service users, and staff. Jim White, chair of NALGO's NLGC, said: 'We have not yet won the argument against privatisation. It is sometimes difficult to convince an employee of a local authority that his, and particularly her, working life would be any worse outside.' Vice-chair Jean Geldart extended the analysis: 'The problem is one of radically altering trade union members' attitudes to the services they provide, and of how far the unions are obliged to remain separate from councils in order to defend their members' interests.'[31]

NALGO leaders urged local-government branches to coordinate their actions against CCT with NUPE, because they saw the consequences: 'These proposals are aimed at producing job losses in local government, deteriora-

---

[31] *PS* (Jan. 1986), 10–11.

tion of pay and conditions, a further restriction on local democracy and a weakening of trade union organisation.'[32] The TUC responded to the Green Paper with *Privatisation by Order—the Government Plan for Local Services*, which highlighted the same dangers. A report from Sheffield City Council argued that 'those Conservative councils which have voluntarily handed over such work to contractors has [sic] already shown the fall in standards of service, the loss of jobs, and the worsening of pay and conditions that results from such moves'.[33]

Nicholas Ridley, the Secretary of State responsible for both local government and water, was a most effective exponent of privatization, supported by research from academics in institutions such as the London Business School and the Institute for Fiscal Studies, and by government supporters in the national newspapers. *The Times* printed one mischievous story in 1987, allegedly based on a leaked NALGO report, purporting to show that

the government's policy of privatizing local services is supported by members of the public sector unions and Labour councils . . . Senior NALGO officials are dismayed at the increasing popularity of privatization within the union movement . . . Inter-union rivalry poses a further problem: the National Union of Public Employees suspects NALGO of being soft on the privatization issue because it is a 'professional and managerial' union whose members are not threatened by privatization.[34]

Events in Buckinghamshire had revealed the truth in 1986, when the County Council decided to stop most school meals provision, leading to a worsening service to the children and their parents and to threatened redundancies of staff including thirty NALGO members. NALGO joined with NUPE to form a trade-union action committee, which linked up with local parents and the Child Poverty Action Group. Despite this campaign and overwhelming local opinion, the service was slashed by the council and 1,600 staff were sacked. *NALGO News* reported that the gap in provision was soon filled by private companies: 'Private firms have been quick to cash in on parents' demands for more substantial lunchtime meals. In 18 schools, Sutcliffe catering has taken over the kitchens.'[35]

Earlier in 1986 the TUC organized a week of action, with demonstrations to protect local democracy and services on 5 March in Coventry, 6 March in Manchester and London, and 7 March in Liverpool. *Public Service* reported:

All members have been authorised by NALGO's emergency committee to take part in the TUC national day of action on 6 March against rate-capping and against the

---

[32] *PS* (Aug. 1985), 2.

[33] LRD, SCAT, and Birmingham Trade Union Resource Centre, *Putting the Rates to Work* (London: LRD, 1985), 3.

[34] *The Times*, 18 May 1987, 2.   [35] *NN*, 7 Nov. 1986, 1.

take-over bid mounted by the Government against local authorities. Members are urged and encouraged to turn out in their thousands to show that they are behind the local authorities who, on 7 March, will be refusing to budget for more cuts in services and jobs.[36]

Activists faced a similar situation in the health service, with the creeping privatization of laundry, catering, and domestic services. Although the awful consequences were clear, most workers were not in the mood to oppose: 'Evidence has been building up that the government's "contracting-out" strategy has had the effect not of bringing in private companies to every hospital but of forcing health workers to accept poorer pay and conditions in order to avoid redundancy.'[37] In the TUC Health Service Committee the same conclusion was drawn: 'Current evidence suggested that the main source of savings was the reduced cost of in-house services. Health authorities had found that the cheapest tender did not always yield the promised savings and that the quality and continuity of services had been affected by privatisation.'[38] So the link between worse services, privatization, and worse conditions of service was firmly established.

In the gas industry NALGO embarked on its biggest anti-privatization campaign yet. National Officer Dave Stirzaker told us that the union gave full support to the gas group: 'NALGO provided all the money they needed, all the resources, I mean they never skimped on anything.' There were regional rallies, and Dave Stirzaker travelled the country to speak at public meetings with Shadow Minister Ted Rowlands and other MPs. But at many meetings they addressed empty chairs, finding a distinct lack of public interest. In April 1986 the union campaigned amongst the membership for a vote to take industrial action against the sell-off, but they voted 8,120 in favour and 11,477 against. There was a bitter argument over the handling of the campaign, the ballot, and the announcement of the ballot results: 'This gas group meeting regrets the National Gas Committee has refused to support the publication of the result of the privatisation ballot in a bulletin to the branches. It believes that the failure to publish the results discredits NALGO's industrial action procedure in the eyes of the gas membership.'[39] Dave Stirzaker told us that 'the membership were divided because a lot of members had seen what had happened in other privatizations and thought well there's a few bob in this for us'.

Margaret Thatcher claimed that the privatization of British Gas was 'a resounding success . . . four and a half million people invested in the shares,

---

[36] *PS* (Mar. 1985), 1.   [37] *NALGO Annual Report 1986*, 140.

[38] *TUC Annual Report 1986* (London: TUC, 1987), 345.

[39] *NALGO Annual Report 1986*, 131.

including almost all of the company's 130,000 employees'.[40] Peter Walker,[41] then Energy Secretary, and Nigel Lawson,[42] then Chancellor of the Exchequer, disagreed on how to privatize the industry. Lawson and others in the Cabinet wanted to break the company up to induce competition. Walker argued, along with British Gas senior management, for the industry to be sold off in one job lot, keeping the monopoly, and this view prevailed. Here was a highly successful and profitable nationalized industry being sold off not to reap the much trumpeted benefits of free competition, and not to save taxpayers' money from propping up another lame duck, but to raise money for tax cuts and to hand over national assets to private shareholders.

It is not surprising that centralized control of the industry was maintained, given its history. By 1912 about one-third of the industry was controlled by local authorities, and by then it had become both unionized and rife with industrial struggles. There had been collective-bargaining machinery since 1919, and in 1943 NALGO represented all A&C grades.[43] Along with coal, electricity supply, and transport, the gas industry was nationalized just after the 1945 peace settlement. In 1972 the Conservatives set up the British Gas Corporation in time to take advantage of the benefits of North Sea gas. As NALGO's Margaret Webb argued at the STUC Annual Congress in Aberdeen: 'Gas, she told the Congress, was taken into public ownership when no-one else wanted it. Workers had built it up to a multi-million pound company with profits which helped fund the health service, education and welfare. This flow of revenue to government would stop with privatisation because future profit would fall into the hands of the private speculators.'[44]

One argument for keeping the industry under state control, and one used worldwide, is that it is a natural monopoly. As one expert indicated, 'such an industry is clearly not self-regulating and some degree of state regulation or control may be necessary to prevent monopoly abuse'.[45] This line of argument may not apply with equal force to the production, distribution, and transmission parts of the industry, but it was clear in 1986, and it is even clearer fourteen years later, that market instability is deemed by all governments as too dangerous. As a result, they either maintain the industry in the public sector or provide a heavily regulated and interventionist role for the state. Thus none of the benefits claimed for post-privatization free markets has accrued

[40] M. Thatcher, *The Downing Street Years* (London: Harper Collins, 1993), 682.

[41] P. Walker, *Staying Power* (London: Bloomsbury, 1991).

[42] Lawson, *The View from No. 11.*

[43] T. Williams, *A History of the British Gas Industry* (Oxford: Oxford University Press, 1981).

[44] *NN*, 2 May 1986, 3.

[45] J. Davis, *Blue Gold: The Political Economy of Natural Gas* (London: George Allen & Unwin, 1984).

to customers, workers, and government, only to shareholders and senior managers.

Union opposition to water privatization, announced in the 1986 White Paper *Privatisation of the Water Authorities* (Cmnd 9734), was equally fierce but more popular. The joint union anti-privatization booklet, *A Water-Tight Case*, argued against the government plans. As with the gas industry, the leadership looked for support from the members: 'This group meeting reaffirms its total opposition to the Government's plans to privatise the nation's water services and urges all NALGO members employed by Water Authorities and Statutory Water Companies to actively support the campaign to resist the Government's proposals.'[46] At the Wales TUC annual conference John Daly argued that 'the next Labour government should have a planned programme to restore to public ownership all privatised public assets, starting with the public utilities'.[47] In this case the campaign had some impact, when in July Secretary of State Nicholas Ridley told the House of Commons that he had decided to postpone the measures (see Chapter 7).

However, it had become clear that the unions had real difficulty in mounting effective opposition to privatization, in spite of the strength of their case, and the TUC began to make some concessions to those hostile to public ownership—the 1985 Congress 'called for the General Council to continue the preparation of a revised approach to public ownership that would acknowledge the limitations of nationalisation'. Nevertheless, the TUC continued to highlight those who really benefit from privatization with its reports on *The £16 Billion Gas Bill*, and on *Privatisation and Top Pay*. The latter revealed that the top executives of privatized companies awarded themselves pay rises averaging £19,000 within one year and over £45,000 within two years of privatization.[48]

As the 1987 general election approached, the electricity industry entered the privatization programme. The electricity group meeting, 'noting that the Conservative Party's manifesto includes the privatisation of the Electricity Supply Industry, agrees that the Industry's trade unions oppose by every means available to them the privatisation of, in whole or part, the ESI and fully endorses the current FUSE campaign'.[49] In the same vein, the water group meeting 'condemns the latest plans for privatising the water industry put forward by the Secretary of State, Nicholas Ridley, in a letter to Gordon Jones, chairman of the Water Authorities' Association'. The gas group meeting 'calls upon the next Labour Government to renationalise the British Gas Industry.

---

[46] *NALGO Annual Report 1986*, 165.   [47] *NN*, 9 May 1986, 3.
[48] *TUC Annual Report 1986*, 288–9.   [49] *NALGO Annual Report 1987*, 58.

The Industry should be wholly owned by the British public via the British government.'[50]

During this period the links between privatization and management reorganization became more explicit. It was clear enough that labour management practices would change once a public utility or a public service was transferred to private ownership, as the needs of private owners are different from those of the previous public body employers. But increasingly public-sector employees were finding that labour management practices were changing even before the transfer to public ownership. Once the government had announced that it intended to bring about privatization, either by selling off or by contracting out, so senior managers within individual public-sector employers started to introduce a range of employment practices designed to weaken the collective and individual strength of employees.

The government played its part by weakening national bargaining, as Paymaster General Kenneth Clarke argued for the disappearance of annual pay increases and comparability. The TUC's Economic Committee 'concluded that the attack on national pay bargaining was primarily directed at public service unions and presaged a new onslaught to establish regional pay and a fragmentation of bargaining in the public sector'.[51]

Managerial aims of building a flexible workforce required a redefinition of the employment relationship. Safeguards were removed from contracts of employment, weakening employees' contractual rights on job security, working time, rate for the job, and a host of other protections that restricted managerial freedoms to hire, pay, deploy, and fire at will. Flexibility also meant weakening the main opponents of managerial freedom, the trade unions. Public-service managers claimed the right to manage, in particular the right to decide how work and employment conditions should be organized, without interference either from individual employees claiming their individual rights or from trade unions acting on behalf of the collective workforce.

This trend is illustrated by a growing number of examples: efforts to break away from national bargaining at Thames Water and Westminster City Council; proposals in British Gas to shed 10,500 jobs within three years; management consultants recommending increases in the use of temporary and agency staff in British Waterways Board; new 'flexible' working practices in universities. The privatized municipal airports unsuccessfully tried to remove staff from the national local-government conditions of service, although employers at Blackpool and Leeds/Bradford agreed only reluctantly.

---

[50] Ibid. 62.   [51] *TUC Annual Report 1987* (London: TUC, 1988), 255.

Settling for the Going Rate Nationally, Fighting Back Locally

National bargaining

While it was still business as usual for the national negotiators and for the group meeting delegates, the negotiations and their outcomes were not living up to the claims. With members not inclined to take industrial action, settlements during this period were clustered tightly around a public-sector going rate that was lower than that in the private sector. For all members the pay position worsened, but the lower paid were particularly badly affected. The union began to address the low-pay issue more systematically, supporting regrading campaigns for specific groups and producing well-researched campaign material on behalf of low-paid members generally, and putting in flat-rate as well as percentage claims.

The staff side evidence to the CAC arbitration on the 1984 local-government claim was based on its objectives 'to halt the decline of APT&C salaries relative to inflation and the level of pay in the economy as a whole; and to overcome the problem of low pay'.[52] The CAC awarded 4.6–5.6 per cent, and some regradings for nursery nurses. National organizer for local government, Keith Sonnet, said: 'The award falls far short of our claim but is an improvement on the employers' "final offer".'[53] Branch delegates accepted it but did not like it: 'This group meeting regards the 1984 arbitration award as derisory, particularly in respect of the claim for regrading on behalf of nursery nurses in education.'[54] So the 1985 claim demanded a £15 per week increase and further salary scale restructuring, proclaimed on the front page of *Public Service*: 'NALGO's local government membership is for the first time seeking a flat rate cash addition to salary in their 1985 pay claim submitted to the national employers.'[55]

The other main campaign was against low pay in the NHS: 'This group meeting is totally committed to eradicating the chronic low pay of NALGO members within the NHS which it finds morally and ethically indefensible.'[56] The 1985 claim was for £8 per week plus 8 per cent, in order to shift two-thirds of A&C staff out of low pay. It included a call for a thirty-five-hour working week and thirty days' minimum annual holiday. After a delegation had met Health Minister Kenneth Clarke, John Daly commented that: 'The minister did not want to hear what we were saying. He does not accept that if morale suffers, as is happening now, patient care suffers too. . . . We were

---

[52] *NN*, 1 Feb. 1985, 4.
[53] Ibid., 25 Jan. 1985, 1.
[54] *NALGO Annual Report 1985*, 93.
[55] *PS*, Apr. 1985, 1.
[56] *NALGO Annual Report 1985*, 134.

very disappointed with his attitude. It is not the way to further good industrial relations in the service.'[57]

Other claims went in: university clerical and administrative staff claimed £14 per week on all points; employees in the threatened NBC claimed £10 per week; and the gas group had privatization in mind and sought significant changes in the way the claims were decided, proposed, and agreed by the National Gas Committee. Electricity's 39,000 members voted for an overtime ban, non-cooperation with the introduction of new technology and a no cover policy as part of their action for a thirty-five-hour week, part of their strategy to keep jobs in the face of rationalization and restructuring. Alan Jinkinson, Deputy General Secretary, argued at a thirty-five-hour week campaign rally in Glasgow that jobs were threatened through economic policies, reorganizations, and new technology: 'The Government's pathetic prescription for the four million on the dole is to reduce the wages of the lower paid, to reduce the income tax of the higher paid, to reduce the value of social security benefits, to sell off the nation's assets and to seek to undermine the effectiveness of free trade unions.'[58]

There was no mood among the membership for the type of titanic struggle they were witnessing with miners and print workers. In the 1960s white-collar public-sector staff copied their then successful manual colleagues and started to take industrial action, but in the 1980s they saw that industrial action was ill advised. NALGO groups settled without going into dispute, but without any enthusiasm either. Most settlements fell within a narrow range around a 5 per cent norm, behind the national increase of 7 or 8 per cent in the average earnings index. Public-sector pay just kept up with inflation, running at 5–6 per cent, despite the still high unemployment figures of nearly 14 per cent. Waterways staff settled for 5.2 per cent, PTE staff for 3–5 per cent; National Bus for 4.9–5.2 per cent, gas for 5.5–6.2 per cent, New Towns for 4.9 per cent, electricity for 4–6.7 per cent, water for 5.4 per cent, and local government for 5.25 per cent with another 0.35 per cent for scale restructuring. In the NHS the unions were forced to accept a divisive deal, with A&C staff and most of PT'B' taking 4.7 per cent in contrast with the nurses and PT'A' who received 4.7–16.6 per cent from the pay review body. The health group's bitter response 'recognises this government's inflexible attitude and callous exploitation of the concern of health workers not to affect patient care by taking industrial action, this Group Meeting reluctantly instructs its negotiators to achieve the best possible settlements' (see Tables 2.5–2.15).[59]

The TUC Public Services Committee, now chaired by NUPE's Rodney Bickerstaffe, stepped up its efforts to strengthen negotiations by playing a

---

[57] *PS*, Mar. 1985, 8.   [58] Ibid., Apr. 1985, 6.
[59] *NALGO Annual Report 1985*, 136.

coordinating role on pay. It set out seven general principles to underpin collective bargaining policies: public-service workers should be treated fairly in relation to others; public-service pay cannot be decided purely by market principles; lower pay does not mean more jobs; low-paid workers must be given a fair deal; public-sector workers' living standards should rise in line with living standards in the rest of the economy; priority must be given to shorter working time; and public spending must allow for fair pay. A TUC conference in March discussed this, attended by 136 executive members and negotiating officers from twenty-six public-service unions.[60]

As the 1986 round got under way a *Public Service Pay Special* set out the case for just awards: 'For the past five years, public sector pay—the salaries of NALGO members—has fallen behind pay in the private sector . . . low pay leads to low morale, high turnover and staff shortages. It results in poor services and customer dissatisfaction'. Claims for this year included: 12 per cent in local government with a minimum rise of £900; £20 for health; £7 and 7 per cent in water; 10 per cent in gas; 10 per cent or £520 in universities; and substantial increases in electricity and transport (NBC). There was some expectation that the government might allow employers to settle more generously, since this was the year before an election.

As in 1985, claims were weighted so that the lowest paid would receive proportionally larger pay rises, recognizing both the historical failure to tackle low pay and the worsening plight of the low paid themselves. Delegates from health-service branches set the scene for the NHS claim: 'This group meeting reaffirms its total commitment to end the low pay of NALGO members in the NHS and deplores the continual wage erosion of successive pay settlements.'[61] *NALGO News* carried the arguments: 'The health service is one big team. We could not manage without professional, technical and clerical staff. It is time they had a fair pay rise.'[62] On 12 May the union took the case to Parliament, when 'hundreds of NALGO's 70,000 technical, administrative and clerical health members lobbied their MPs'.[63] The union's pamphlet *Underpaid and Undervalued: Secretarial and Clerical Workers in the NHS* supported the claim: 'The work of NHS secretarial and clerical staff is as essential to the quality of patient care as that of doctors and nurses. They are skilled workers who do demanding and responsible work under often intolerable pressure—yet they are *grossly* underpaid for the vital contribution they make to the health service.'[64] But collective bargaining was still hampered by cash limits, as summarized by the TUC:

[60] *TUC Annual Report 1985*, 317–19.

[61] *NALGO Annual Report 1986*, 138.

[62] *NN*, 28 Feb. 1986, 4.

[63] Ibid., 16 May 1986, 1.

[64] NALGO, *Underpaid and Undervalued: Secretarial and Clerical Workers in the NHS* (London: NALGO, 1986), 3.

The failure to match NHS needs and resources had particularly affected the cash limited hospital and community health service. NHS beds had been lost, services
restricted and entire wards and hospitals closed to meet the imposed targets which
took little account of rising costs and increased needs. Another consequence had been
the fall of 13,000 in the number of full-time directly employed staff in the service since
1982 when hospital staff were dealing with more in-patient cases per hospital bed than
ever before.[65]

In general the settlements for NALGO members were similar to most
other public-sector groups, with two exceptions: the teachers, who had been
involved in a bitter national strike, and the groups covered by pay review
bodies. Universities settled after a one-day strike on 15 January 1986 alongside AUT members. Rita Donaghy, chair of NALGO's National Universities
Committee, said 'this was an unprecedented day in the history of universities,
because it was the first time that unions have taken strike action on a joint basis
to save their service and defend their standard of living'.[66] The agreement, at
£4.50–£6.50 for grades one to three and 5.2 per cent for grades four and five,
did not satisfy the union's low-pay concerns. Most groups settled for around
6 per cent, including A&C grades and most PT'B' grades in the NHS at 5.9
per cent; universities' clerical staff at 5 per cent or £5 per week, and computer
staff at 5.5 per cent; electricity supply at 6.5 per cent; and New Towns at 5.9
per cent. In water, against the background of threats to privatize, there was a
low settlement of 5 per cent for the period 15 April 1986 to 30 June 1987.

Local-government negotiators rejected a 5 per cent offer on their 12 per
cent/£900 claim. Andy Sweeney, vice-chair of the Scottish district local-
government committee, told a rally in Glasgow on 17 May: 'We should be
preparing the membership for the prospect of industrial action . . . We deserve
the claim we have asked for and it's up to every branch officer to make sure
that the members understand that.'[67] Delegates at the annual group meeting
agreed, and called a ballot on industrial action. NALGO asked the Low Pay
Unit to investigate low pay in local government, and Nasreen Rahman's pamphlet, *Council Non-Manual Workers and Low Pay*, set out the case for the claim.
It concluded that 'the cuts in the real level of wages for low paid local government staff mean that more and more are having to rely on means-tested
benefits to top up inadequate incomes. Since 1980 the number of public servants dependent on Family Income Supplement has more than doubled.
Dependence on housing benefit is widespread.'[68]

However, despite the autumn ballot campaign, NALGO members voted
by around 55 per cent against industrial action in the Eastern, East Midlands,

---

[65] *TUC Annual Report 1986*, 343.   [66] *PS* (Feb. 1986), 5.
[67] *MAC* (May 1986), 2.   [68] *NN*, 15 Aug. 1986, 5.

North East, Metropolitan, North West and North Wales, Scotland, Southern, South West, and West Midland districts. The exceptions were in the South East, where only 36 per cent voted for action, and in South Wales, which recorded the only district majority for action at 58 per cent. Jim White, lead negotiator and chair of the NLGC, subsequently reported: 'The 1986 pay claim has been settled at 5.96%. But the problems remain. We still have to end low pay and restore the value of comparability with the earnings of other workers. . . . The ballot result was a warning to the employers.'[69]

Gas staff went into dispute over their 1986 claim, but as in local government it ended when members voted 52 per cent against industrial action and accepted a 5.5 per cent deal. Gas higher managers took an arbitration award of 5.5 per cent.

In 1987 most groups wanted early settlements before electoral politics clouded the issue. PTE bus staff put in a common claim for 8 per cent or £700, university clerical and related staff for 8 per cent or £600, NHS A&C and PT'B' for £20 a week, water staff for 7.5 per cent or £740, local government for 12 per cent or £900, and New Towns for 10 per cent or £800. As the election approached, university staff accepted 5.8 per cent, local-government staff agreed 7 per cent, and PTEs in Greater Manchester, Merseyside, and Yorkshire got around 5 per cent. NHS members in A&C and PT'B' grades received a 5 per cent agreement, and in December the group meeting again stated that 'the fight against low pay remains the central task facing the health membership'.[70] Health branch delegates resolved: 'This group meeting is determined to continue its campaign to end the scandal of low pay in the NHS.'[71]

Six years after the successful industrial action based on pay comparability in local government, the collective-bargaining climate had changed. Government policies had reduced staffing levels, injected efficiency notions into management, and constrained finances. The consequences included challenges to national collective bargaining, and shifts in bargaining tactics. 'The exact formulation of claims reflected the ebb and flow of internal NALGO debates on flat rate or percentage increases.'[72] The union's key arguments based on comparability were opposed by employers' affordability arguments, and NALGO responded by focusing on low pay.

NALGO's commitment to tackle low pay was shared by both the TUC and the Labour Party, through the TUC–Labour Party Liaison Committee, of which John Daly was a member. Their joint statement *Low Pay: Policies and Priorities* started by setting out low pay as a fundamental issue for a civilized

---

[69] *PS* (Oct. 1986), 1.   [70] *NALGO Annual Report 1987*, 66.   [71] Ibid. 64.

[72] I. Kessler, 'Bargaining Strategies in Local Government', in R. Mailly, S. Dimmock, and A. Sethi (eds.), *Industrial Relations in the Public Services* (London: Routledge, 1989), 172.

society: it reinforced social divisions; it militated against democracy; it worsened under the impact of government policy, which caused unemployment; and it was a measure of the extent to which people and their work were valued. The statement offered a strategy for tackling low pay: 'A central feature of this will be the introduction of a national minimum wage with statutory backing.'[73] It also argued for strong trade-union organization around collective bargaining: 'An effective programme to end low pay will require more than the introduction of a statutory minimum wage. In particular it will need concerted action through collective bargaining. It will also mean the strengthening of legislative support for collective bargaining—and supporting economic, industrial and social policies.'[74]

Local bargaining

Bargaining at local level became more important as it became more difficult to secure gains through national negotiations. Furthermore, local bargaining activity increased as government policies worked their way through structural change to local reorganization and to workplace management action. There were four main aspects of union action: first, to tackle the immediate effects of government policies such as rate-capping and privatization; secondly, to negotiate over managerial initiatives to change the labour process, through new technology and new working practices; thirdly, to push up pay through regrading and local pay supplements; and, fourthly, to defend members under pressures at work such as violence and racism. NALGO activists developed new patterns of trade-union action, establishing a tradition of local militancy that had a direct bearing on the everyday lives of members.

In the autumn of 1985 the rate-capping crisis fermenting within the local-government system finally broke in Liverpool, sweeping over the labour movement, local government, and NALGO. As the City Council was dominated by the Militant Tendency, led by Derek Hatton and Tony Mulhearn, it was not unexpected that it 'became the centre for disputes about rate-capping for excessive expenditure and then for surcharging when it tried to defy the government over expenditure cuts'.[75] The drama of the time was captured by local press reports: 'YOU'RE ALL SACKED!' ran the headline of the *Liverpool Echo* on the 5 September. The council decided to make the entire workforce redundant rather than make cuts.

Such simple-minded plans to direct the entire movement against the government could not succeed. Union stewards lined up with the council and called for total support from members and from transport and power

---

[73] *TUC Annual Report 1986*, app. 2, 411.   [74] Ibid. 413.
[75] Morgan, *The People's Peace*, 477.

workers. However, some unions pursued more partial industrial objectives, as the *Liverpool Echo* reported: 'NALGO members have already been instructed not to co-operate in drawing up [redundancy] notices',[76] and it was on the redundancy issue alone that industrial action would take place.

John Daly reported that he, along with general secretaries David Basnett (GMBATU), Ron Todd (TGWU), and Rodney Bickerstaff (NUPE), met Labour councillors, but the City Council pressed ahead with its decision to declare 31,000 employees redundant. In the end, with members increasingly uneasy, it was no surprise when they voted against strike action: 'On September 24, shop stewards' plans for an indefinite strike in support of the city council in demanding government money to ease the city's financial crisis were scrapped following a vote by NALGO members against action.'[77] This effectively ended the Labour council's challenge to the government's legislation. The Conservatives used the Liverpool crisis to scorn 'loony-left' ideas and practices, and Neil Kinnock used it to attack the left within the labour movement and thereby consolidate the rightward shift in policy. Overall it was a disaster for the left and for the council employees.

Opposition to management was a constant feature of this period. In 1985 the Generation Branch at Tilbury "B" Power Station won authorization from the union's Emergency Committee to 'picket Tilbury "B" Power Station on Saturday, 9 February 1985 and successive Saturdays as it was believed some staff intended to work overtime despite the national instruction'.[78] There were disputes in Gloucestershire County Council over not crossing a NUPE picket line of school meals staff; social workers in Bury refused to cooperate with the introduction of new technology; Islington health branch lobbied its DHA over privatization of catering; electricity members picketed the CEGB headquarters for a thirty-five-hour week; Severn Trent Water Authority branch members refused cooperation over new billing arrangements; and Beverly District Council branch members refused to help with new computers.

Action continued in 1987: 'The social services in Liverpool came to a standstill this week when 1250 NALGO members walked out after five workers were removed from the payroll . . . The city's NALGO branch backed them with a half day strike last week, and when the five were threatened with dismissal NALGO members twice prevented a disciplinary hearing going ahead.'[79] In Bristol a member was sacked after he queried a management decision on terms of service. The employer claimed it was gross misconduct because his memo represented 'an open challenge and lack of

---

[76] *Liverpool Echo*, 13 Sept., 1.   [77] Marsden, 'Chronicle', 127.
[78] *NALGO Emergency Committee Meeting Minutes*, 14 (1985), 19.
[79] *NN*, 13 Feb. 1987, 1.

support for a management decision'.[80] There was a one-day strike in Manchester's town clerk's department over intimidation. Social workers went on strike in Waltham Forest over staffing shortages. So the list goes on.

Three groups in particular took localized action over their gradings and rates of pay—medical secretaries, nursery nurses, and school secretaries. These groups received national support: 'This group meeting instructs the National Local Government Committee to pursue actively a national claim for the rationalisation of service conditions and leave entitlement for APT&C staff in educational establishments. This section of staff is predominantly women and are amongst the lowest paid.'[81] Action spread across the country, as members followed the lead of others.

In Luton the health branch took up the medical secretaries' cause. The branch won 'approval for members previously balloted to take indefinite strike action, following the Health Authority's refusal to regrade the post of medical secretary'.[82] *The Luton News* covered the story: 'The bitter pay feud that has brought chaos to Luton and Dunstable Hospital finally ended yesterday when the striking secretaries went back to work. The 34 medical secretaries have agreed to suspend their three-week old strike while talks aimed at solving their regrading dispute continue.'[83] Jean Taylor, the branch secretary, made it clear that 'if management don't come up with the goods we will be out on strike again'.[84] She went on to argue at the Eastern District Council meeting that 'the timid girls became the strongest. The reticent girls became the most vocal, and the weakest became the most determined . . . not only is our togetherness apparent to ourselves, it is apparent to management.'[85] This dispute was one of many equally determined actions by medical secretaries up and down the country (see Box 15).

A strike by 270 school librarians and support staff in Strathclyde won official support 'when approval was given to members in the above branch to take strike action in support of their claim for regrading . . . The action has been suspended . . . while negotiations are proceeding.'[86] This was another example of employers dragging their feet over grading grievances until staff took more decisive action, which then forced the 'good-faith' negotiations sought by the union in the first place.

Nursery nurses imposed a work to rule in Cheshire, where their work was being expanded and extended by the employer to cover staffing shortages. Such action by employers often results in staff demands for better grading in

[80] Ibid., 8 May 1987, 1.   [81] *NALGO Annual Report 1987*, 53.
[82] *NALGO Emergency Committee Meeting Minutes*, 15 (London: NALGO, 1986), 46.
[83] *Luton News*, 3 Apr. 1986, 12.   [84] *PS* (May 1986), 10.
[85] *Edlines* (July 1986), 1.
[86] *NALGO Emergency Committee Meeting Minutes*, 16 (London: NALGO, 1987), 58.

recognition of the extra work, and in employer refusals to negotiate. Employer delaying tactics over long periods, sometimes up to two years, finally bring the NALGO membership to take direct industrial action. This depressingly familiar pattern is based on cynical exploitation of those least able to fight back, and on dividing the workforce through stirring up rivalries over skill and status.

One of the largest local disputes of this type involved all APT&C staff in Ealing Council over a claim for a local allowance, to reflect the extra costs of living and working in Ealing. Again the employer refused to negotiate, which, after two years, led to limited action by staff, which in turn provoked the council into sending home some staff, and this then escalated into full-blown strike action. Local paper the *Gazette* reported:

A one-day strike next Thursday by members of local government workers union Nalgo will hit the rate-making meeting where the new rate was due to be announced. . . . More one-day strikes and an overtime ban are planned. The action is being taken because town hall white collar workers are angry that their London weighting is not being increased. . . . More than 80 per cent of Nalgo's 2650 members voted for the industrial action.[87]

Indefinite strike action started after a secret ballot resulted in a three-to-one majority. It was reported at length to the union's emergency committee:

For many years, NALGO at Ealing has been dissatisfied at its classification as an outer London Borough for the purposes of London Weighting. It has regularly been raised as a matter for negotiation . . . On 4 September 1986 . . . the leader (of the council) said he was sympathetic and accepted the arguments in favour . . . A joint report . . . recommended that the cost of living be ameliorated by a substantial increase in London Weighting, by negotiation, with effect from 1 April 1987, of an Ealing supplement . . . The council indicated that they were considering the possibility of moving to that position . . . A ballot paper was prepared and dispatched with a dead-line for return of 13 February 1987.

The ballot covered a range of sanctions against the council, and the results were: on the instruction not to collect moneys due to the council, 1,583 yes and 194 no; overtime ban, 1,621 yes and 171 no; non-cooperation with councillors, 1,587 yes and 206 no; and one-day strikes, 1,481 yes and 375 no. The first one-day strike was on 6 March, and from 7 March 'the whole of the membership were on strike'. On 11 March a further ballot voted to continue the strike action. The dispute ended on 2 April after conciliation by the joint secretaries from the Greater London Whitley Council.[88]

---

[87] *Gazette*, 27 Feb. 1987, 3.
[88] *NALGO Emergency Committee Meeting Minutes*, 16 (1987), 101–3.

BANG GOES ANOTHER KIDNEY UNIT.

A kidney unit costs about £15,000. They won't say what an air-to-air missile costs. But a simple anti-tank missile is about £7,000.

And it's not just kidney units that are going up in smoke.

The Government spends nearly eight times as much on defence research as medical research.

And that's the least of your worries.

Newly built hospitals are keeping wards shut because the Government won't give them enough money to run properly.

Since 1979 Government policies have forced 90 hospitals to close down.

Over 13,000 beds have gone out of the window since 1979. Common sense will tell you there aren't 13,000 fewer sick people.

If everyone who's waiting for an operation were to stand in one long queue, it would stretch for close on 200 miles.

But none of this really has to happen.

This Government claims we haven't got any more money to increase spending on the health service.

Want to know the real truth?

It just isn't high enough on their list to warrant the extra cash that's needed.

Defence is. And that is why from 1981 to 1984

spending on defence will have risen by 30%.

For a country that isn't supposed to have any money, don't you think it's amazing what we're spending it on?

PUT PEOPLE FIRST.

IF THIS GETS YOUR VOTE MAKE SURE YOU USE IT.

THIS ADVERTISEMENT IS SPONSORED BY NALGO, THE PUBLIC SERVICE UNION.

Building friendship -
WORKING
FOR FREEDOM

FORWARD WITH THE
WORKERS' STRUGGLE

AN INJURY TO ONE
IS AN INJURY TO ALL

Report of a NALGO delegation to South Africa June/July 1987

THEY'VE GOT WELFARE
THE WRONG WAY ROUND.

The latest cuts mean only one child in three will be lucky enough to get a nursery place.

The Government grant for new buses will be cut from £71 million in 1979/80 to nil in 1984/85.

A 13% increase in the number of people over the age of 75 has been matched by only a 3% rise in money spent on them.

Over 500,000 council homes have been sold off and the building of new ones has fallen by 62,000 a year since 1979.

The Government says that we can't afford to spend more money on the Welfare State.

Then how come they've constantly increased spending on defence since they came to power?

They seem to think warfare is more important than welfare.

Finally, this period saw local negotiators taking up some workplace issues much more vigorously. The basic issue of safety at work has particular characteristics in the public services, as 'the public' itself is a potential hazard. Tackling violence against public-service employees became a priority issue, especially after the tragic murders of three social workers killed in different incidents while at work. As *Public Service* noted, 'these are extreme examples of the risks faced by public sector employees in their work. But daily they face verbal abuse, intimidation, threats or physical injury from people who are driven to desperate acts by the pressures under which they live.'[89] This was seen as a mainstream industrial-relations issue in which members informed their union negotiators, who in turn fought to get the employer to introduce measures to reduce risks of attacks. For example, 1,200 Glasgow members in the housing department went on strike for five days in a dispute 'over a unilateral decision by some Councillors to remove protective screens in Housing Offices'.[90] The strike was supported by the emergency committee, and was successful. Twelve members who crossed the picket line were expelled by the branch, but their appeal to the NEC was upheld, to the 'anger and disgust' of the majority of the branch.

Box 10. NALGO and Violence at Work—a Health and Safety Issue

Public-service employees may come into conflict with their managers, their co-workers, and the public. Managers are in a position of authority, and are authorized by the employer to give orders to their subordinates. This fundamentally unequal power relationship can become unbearably oppressive in two main sets of circumstances. First, power holders may abuse their power—for example, by giving instructions that they are not entitled to give; by showing favouritism; by using their subordinates' vulnerability to force them to do favours; or by using their position as an outlet for their own prejudices. Secondly, managers may themselves be placed by their own superiors under such intense pressure to achieve results that they resort to bullying their subordinate staff to improve their performance.

Violent tempers, bigotry, frustration, alcoholism, and mental illness are present in the workplace, just as they are in the world outside. Most of the time most workers find ways of getting along with each other, as they do in their neighbourhoods, but when one worker starts to abuse another in the workplace then there is little scope for the victim to escape.

Finally, many NALGO members work with the public, either in the public-service workplace or out in the wider community. The nature of the public services can generate tensions between public servants and the public, especially where cash is involved, or the public servant has some authority over the public, or the member of the public is dependent on the service. The nature of employment, and the nature

---

[89] *PS* (Oct. 1986), 1.   [90] *MAC* (Jan. 1986), 1.

of public-service work, mean that public-service employees are constantly placed in situations that have the potential for violence, abuse, and harassment.[91]

NALGO ensured that the employers' obligation to protect employees from abuse was kept on the agenda, maintaining a strong record on the issues of racial and sexual harassment. In 1985 the Islington Branch organized strike action over racial harassment by a supervisor. In 1989 a medical records officer was sacked by a health authority in south Cumbria after NALGO gathered complaints from twenty-six women who had been victimized or sexually harassed by him. Cases like these reveal the importance of visible action. Many cases of workplace harassment come to light only when those being harassed are confident that they will receive support from their union or from management.

Some extreme cases serve to demonstrate the importance of secure protection. In 1989 a Blackburn housing benefits officer was killed in an arson attack on his office. The council responded to the tragedy with support and sympathy for his colleagues, but also continued with its policy of making council services more open and accessible to users. This resulted in all twenty-five housing management staff going on strike over the council's refusal to provide protective screens on public counters.

Out in the community, Tower Hamlets Branch succeeded in persuading the council to produce a policy on preventing violence at work after a social worker was threatened with petrol bombing and an estate officer was injured when he had three Staffordshire bull terriers set on him in 1990. In 1991 a Derwentside planning officer was shot dead while serving an enforcement notice, and a Gloucester City Council clerk was raped and strangled on her way from work to the council car park. The Gloucester incident occurred after the council offices had relocated to a dockside area beside the River Severn. Managers were given car-parking spaces beside the offices, but everyone else had to use a car park over 500 yards away in the middle of the river's flood plain. After the murder the 270-strong Gloucester City Branch demanded that women be allowed to use the managers' car park. The council initially agreed, but changed its mind a year later. The branch placed pickets on the management car park, organized a petition, and gave interviews to local radio and newspapers, campaigning until the council changed its mind again and agreed to let women park there. They also agreed to set up working parties to look at safety inside and outside council buildings.

In 1992 another NALGO member was murdered while carrying out her rent collection round in Rotherham. In this case the Health and Safety Executive actually took some action by serving an improvement notice on Rotherham Borough Council requiring it to carry out an assessment of the risks faced by employees while they were at work.

Alongside these extreme cases are all the unreported incidents of minor assaults, bullying, intimidation, verbal abuse, and an anti-public-service climate that makes public servants appear fair game. Often disregarded as 'trivial' by managers, these incidents taken together ratchet up the stress level. NALGO has challenged management

---

[91] T. Rothwell, 'Violence to Staff—the National and Local Responses', *Local Government Employment*, 31/5 (1987), 9.

on these issues, arguing that no abuse should be tolerated, and that workplace violence is a trade-union issue. Union training, supported by a range of publications, provided safety representatives with the resources to take up workplace safety issues through negotiation.

Tackling local issues such as workplace safety strengthened the relevance of trade unionism: here was a matter that nobody could gainsay, it had some appeal in the popular press, and for many members it was a more or less constant issue in the workplace. Many public-service workers faced danger of violence by members of the public as well as by colleagues at work, and women and black members faced the threat of sexual and/or racial harassment. This issue was taken up, along with more general matters of health, at the TUC women's conference at Blackpool in March 1987. Despite NALGO's view that there was a 'subdued inevitability about the proceedings' of this conference,[92] in terms of the low morale of the wider movement and lack of sharp disagreement among delegates, yet again its real importance lay in its being a place for activists to share experiences, for newcomers to become assimilated, and for women to have a focus for their discontent uniquely expressed and discussed by and with other women workers.

There was a long strike in Islington over racial harassment, reported in *Public Service*:

An official one-day strike was due to be staged by NALGO's Islington local government branch in support of 435 colleagues who walked out on 5 August in a dispute over alleged racial harassment. The 435 members in housing, neighbourhood and area social service offices are on strike because the council is refusing to redeploy a housing supervisor found guilty by the council of a breach of its equal opportunities employment policy.[93]

The local press picked up the story:

Hundreds of Islington Council staff went on strike this week in a bid to stop a council worker starting a new job. The staff, members of NALGO, walked out of neighbourhood offices, the housing advisory service, and the social services department, after the council refused to take further action against housing official Ms Vi Howell over an alleged breach of the racial harassment code.[94]

Islington Branch took this action after the council found that three employees had been involved in harassing black workers for eighteen months. The council redeployed two, but left one in post. A branch meeting resolved:

[92] *NALGO Annual Report 1987*, 13.   [93] *PS* (Sept. 1985), 16.
[94] *Islington Gazette*, 9 Aug. 1985, 1.

In view of the serious nature of the harassment suffered by our members in the Housing department and in light of continued intimidation of members involved in the case this branch:— agrees that in those specific cases the members of staff found guilty by the council of racial harassment should not work with the public, agrees that NALGO members should refuse to cooperate with these staff if they are allowed to continue working with the public.[95]

This important dispute raised many serious questions about the obligations of managers to protect employees from racist abuse, about the existence of racism among NALGO members, and about the role of the union in protecting members from racism and in dealing with racist members. It was part of a broad range of union initiatives for equality at branch, district and national levels, helped by publications such as the organizing pack *Fighting against Prejudice* on gay and lesbian rights, and the *Disability is No Handicap: Negotiators Guide* pamphlet. It was also yet another example of the large number of local battles taken up by activists and members.

Concluding Remarks

So ended Margaret Thatcher's second term, in which she took on and defeated two of her greatest foes, the feared NUM and the GLC, and their hated figureheads Arthur Scargill and Ken Livingstone. Neither of these 'enemies within' went quietly, and in both cases the campaigns and struggles to defend them left indelible marks on British society. But those victories paved the way for privatization of the utilities and parts of the public services.

Most of the switch from public to private so far affected NALGO members only indirectly (except of course in gas and the buses), but they were about to become much more involved; through subcontracting in local government and health; through the sell-off of water and electricity supply; and, crucially, for NALGO's biggest membership base, though the reform of local-government rates. It was in these industries that NALGO's members would feel the full blast of state restructuring, and so the union came under pressure to reform itself and to shift its main policy base away from the AES towards the new realism that formed the basis for new Labour and the new TUC. The Labour Party election manifesto included a £12 billion emergency programme to tackle unemployment, poverty, and crime, but made 'no commitment to repeal all Conservative labour legislation'.[96]

Election for a third term set the seal on Margaret Thatcher's victory, as the government's popularity held up with those who actually voted, boosted by

---

[95] *NALGO Emergency Committee Meeting Minutes*, 14 (London: NALGO, 1985), 190.
[96] *The Times*, 20 May 1987, 5.

Nigel Lawson's pre-election budget cut of 2p off income-tax basic rate. The result was widely predicted and NALGO had to admit that 'the ditching of monetarism, a modest reflation and a considerable depreciation of sterling—all of which had been anathema to Mrs Thatcher's Government in earlier years—had had predictable and beneficial effects on the economy'.[97] This and the continued disarray of the Labour Party and wider movement helped secure the third success for Mrs Thatcher, and the NEC's dismal view was widely shared: 'the re-election of the Government in June realised your Council's worst fears'.[98]

[97] *NALGO Annual Report 1987*, 29.   [98] Ibid.

Appendix

TABLE 6.1. *NALGO membership, 30 September 1985*

District	Number of branches	Voting members	Members in arrears	Membership of branches excluded from voting	Ordinary (cols. 2–4)	Total membership					Total membership (cols. 5–10)
						Retired	Student	Unemployed	Trainee	Honorary	
	(1)	(2)	(3)	(4)	(5)	(6)	(7)	(8)	(9)	(10)	(11)
Eastern	117	45,810	36	—	45,846	5,896	8	14	50	—	51,814
East Midland	102	43,373	67	125	43,565	223	11	11	9	—	47,819
Metropolitan	149	95,043	150	448	95,641	11,799	25	61	50	—	107,576
North Eastern	81	39,007	92	—	39,099	214	11	35	85	—	41,444
North Western and North Wales	133	107,453	128	70	107,651	8,177	33	35	57	—	115,953
Scottish	118	75,953	60	466	76,479	1,921	14	8	170	—	78,592
South Eastern	100	37,301	149	—	37,450	7,612	8	14	28	—	45,112
Southern	82	34,727	72	—	34,799	4,409	3	14	29	—	39,254
South Wales	89	32,064	70	—	32,134	2,386	2	3	4	—	34,529
South Western	95	43,127	115	—	43,242	4,694	8	10	138	—	48,092
West Midland	92	67,216	60	9	67,285	6,999	2	6	84	—	74,376
Yorkshire and Humberside	80	63,404	51	—	63,458	4,004	11	9	81	—	67,563
Honorary members	—	—	—	—	—	—	—	—	—	7	7
TOTAL	1,238	684,478	1,053	1,118	686,649	64,334	136	220	785	7	752,131

Table 6.2. Allocation of NALGO membership, by service, 30 September 1985

District	Local government	Gas	Electricity	Health	Transport (inc. PTEs)	Water	New Towns	Port authorities	Universities	Police authorities	Retired	Student, unemployed, trainee	Honorary	Total membership
Eastern	31,570	2,863	2,660	3,091	468	2,706	532	17	470	659	5,896	72	—	51,814
East Midland	30,551	3,684	2,469	4,951	419	—	—	—	450	1,041	4,223	31	—	47,819
Metropolitan	71,624	6,219	4,070	8,771	420	2,498	352	—	1,687	—	11,799	136	—	107,576
North Eastern	27,220	2,242	1,833	4,105	807	1,213	400	83	328	868	2,214	131	—	41,444
North Western and North Wales	75,755	5,503	5,407	11,367	2,892	3,365	776	20	1,217	1,349	8,177	125	—	115,953
Scottish	58,178	2,768	3,942	8,143	381	17	1,246	27	1,566	211	1,921	192	—	78,592
South Eastern	23,336	3,456	2,609	4,916	246	1,924	—	14	472	477	7,612	50	—	45,112
Southern	22,083	2,382	2,473	5,508	64	—	613	—	1,024	652	4,409	46	—	39,254
South Wales	21,154	1,976	1,132	3,581	165	2,061	178	—	906	981	2,386	9	—	34,529
South Western	31,220	1,996	2,329	3,935	195	2,064	—	—	535	968	4,694	156	—	48,092
West Midland	44,334	4,985	2,714	7,611	1,350	4,249	447	—	876	719	6,999	92	—	74,376
Yorkshire and Humberside	48,949	1,900	3,031	4,510	1,465	2,310	—	—	1,233	—	4,004	101	—	67,563
Honorary members	—	—	—	—	—	—	—	—	—	—	—	—	7	7
1985 totals	485,974	40,034	34,669	71,299	8,872	22,407	4,544	161	10,764	7,925	64,334	1,141	7	752,131
Percentages	64.62	5.33	4.61	9.48	1.17	2.98	0.60	0.02	1.43	1.05	8.56	—	7	100.00
1984 totals	490,043	42,502	35,987	75,972	9,220	23,558	5,266	174	10,873	8,185	63,446	1,159	5	766,390
Percentages	63.95	5.55	4.70	9.92	1.20	3.08	0.68	0.02	1.41	1.06	8.28	0.15	5	100.00

TABLE 6.3. *NALGO membership, 30 September 1986*

District	Number of branches (1)	Voting members (2)	Members in arrears (3)	Membership of branches excluded from voting (4)	Total ordinary membership (cols. 2–4) (5)	Retired (6)	Student (7)	Unemployed (8)	Honorary (9)	Total membership (cols. 5–9)	Total membership 30 Sept. 1985	Increase/decrease	Increase/decrease (%)
Eastern	117	44,262	—	537	44,799	6,504	6	32	—	51,341	51,814	−473	−0.91
East Midland	100	43,717	4	236	43,957	4,471	10	21	—	48,459	47,819	+640	+1.34
Metropolitan	145	90,709	71	4,069	94,849	13,296	32	77	—	108,254	107,576	+678	+0.63
North Eastern	78	38,924	37	—	38,961	2,384	5	4	—	41,354	41,444	−90	−0.22
North Western and North Wales	134	106,184	13	613	106,810	8,953	15	207	—	115,985	115,953	+32	+0.03
Scottish	119	76,004	41	728	76,773	1,970	11	9	—	78,763	78,592	+171	+0.22
South Eastern	100	35,796	32	900	36,728	7,752	6	29	—	44,515	45,112	−597	−1.32
Southern	82	34,166	3	445	34,614	4,602	9	11	—	39,236	39,254	−18	−0.05
South Wales	87	31,567	11	399	31,977	2,221	9	4	—	34,211	34,529	−318	−0.92
South Western	97	43,488	13	318	43,819	4,655	5	21	—	48,500	48,092	+408	+0.85
West Midland	94	66,857	20	110	66,987	7,173	19	11	—	74,190	74,376	−186	−0.25
Yorkshire and Humberside	77	61,383	4	157	61,544	4,057	2	12	—	65,615	67,563	−1,948	−2.88
Honorary members	—	—	—	—	—	—	—	—	7	7	7	—	—
TOTAL	1,230	673,057	249	8,512	681,818	68,038	129	438	7	750,430	752,131	−1,701	−0.23

TABLE 6.4. *Allocation of NALGO membership, by service, 30 September 1986*

District	Local government	Gas	Electricity	Health	Transport	Water	New Towns	Port authorities	Universities	Police authorities	Retired	Student, unemployed	Honorary	Total membership
Eastern	31,277	2,699	2,644	3,612	273	2,561	534	15	459	725	6,504	38	—	51,341
East Midland	31,291	3,597	2,422	4,885	276	—	—	—	448	1,038	4,471	31	—	48,459
Metropolitan	72,336	5,665	3,962	8,193	301	2,510	280	—	1,602	—	13,296	109	—	108,254
North Eastern	27,573	2,193	1,783	4,109	672	1,121	226	82	330	872	2,384	9	—	41,354
North Western and North Wales	75,570	5,217	5,365	11,008	2,312	3,355	704	24	1,186	2,069	8,953	222	—	115,985
Scottish	58,392	2,674	3,885	8,351	396	15	1,247	28	1,588	197	1,970	20	—	78,763
South Eastern	23,128	3,283	2,508	4,808	87	1,934	—	15	459	506	7,752	35	—	44,515
Southern	22,522	2,284	2,359	5,192	—	—	576	—	1,000	681	4,602	20	—	39,236
South Wales	21,222	1,891	1,127	3,490	95	2,226	88	—	889	949	2,221	13	—	34,211
South Western	32,054	1,925	2,296	3,857	109	2,047	—	2	537	992	4,655	26	—	48,500
West Midland	44,639	4,873	2,621	7,314	1,220	4,071	436	—	847	966	7,173	30	—	74,190
Yorkshire and Humberside	47,187	1,848	2,771	4,436	1,216	2,237	—	—	1,245	604	4,057	14	—	65,615
Honorary members	—	—	—	—	—	—	—	—	—	—	—	—	7	7
1986 totals	487,191	38,149	33,743	69,255	6,957	22,077	4,091	166	10,590	9,599	68,038	567	7	750,430
Percentages	64.92	5.08	4.50	9.23	0.93	2.94	0.54	0.02	1.41	1.28	9.07	0.08	7	100.00
1985 totals	485,974	40,034	34,669	71,299	8,872	22,407	544	161	10,764	7,925	64,334	1,141	7	752,131
Percentages	64.62	5.33	4.61	9.48	1.17	2.98	0.60	0.20	1.43	1.05	8.56	0.15	7	100.00

7

Storms—Financial, Climatic, and Industrial

THE results of the 1987 general election showed steady voter support for the Conservatives and some improvement in the position of Labour. Peter Jenkins summarized: 'On polling day the result was Conservative 43 per cent, Labour 32, Alliance 23. Labour had made some marginal progress at the expense of the Alliance. That was all that happened. The government was re-elected because of a prosperous economy and a divided opposition. To that extent 1987 was a re-run of 1983.'[1]

Debates in the trade-union movement about the lessons to be learned from this were complex, but they could be grouped into two main schools of thought. One group would position the unions behind the middle–England-oriented revolution in the Labour Party led by Neil Kinnock, formulating the business-friendly new Labour proto-type. The other supported traditional left-of-centre policies to confront the government by tapping into resentment towards the resulting insecure world of work. Activists and leaders searched for policy direction and for practical solutions, coming up with an array of contradictory policies and activities, some reflecting one line of thought and some reflecting the other, as the battle raged over the direction of policy renewal.

Central to this debate within NALGO were difficult questions about public ownership and about how state employees are managed, questions that are fundamental to both public-service and economic performance. Indeed, as discussed in Chapter 1, debate on the role of the state and its agencies was either neglected or muddled. Thorny questions about how economic policy and political power are linked were avoided by many trade unionists. How-

[1] P. Jenkins, *Mrs Thatcher's Revolution* (London: Jonathan Cape, 1987), 369.

ever, NALGO continued to oppose the government's main policies: privatization of water and electricity supply; CCT and the internal market for education and health; and the poll tax. The union also maintained its pay battles, with a major strike in local government. It strengthened its position in the TUC, and it started merger talks with NUPE and COHSE.

Still Losing Ground

The long autumn after the election was tempestuous in more ways than one. In October most parts of the country, especially the southern half, were affected by some of the worst storms of the century and NALGO members were heavily involved in restoring services. On Black Monday, 19 October, just two weeks after the triumphant Tory Party conference, the stock-market crash blew through the world's financial institutions. The government spent millions to 'protect' the pound, ignoring the consequences for British workers in both the public and private sectors, and relying on privatization to pay for it all.

More was wiped off the value of shares, nearly a quarter, than in any previous crash. Conservative forces in the press and business called for state intervention to restore confidence and to reduce the fearful possibility that the fall in share prices would trigger a recession. The then Chancellor recalled his actions: 'While I myself did not share the general crash hysteria, for the first and only time during my period as Chancellor I judged the risk of serious recession as greater than the risk of inflation.'[2] Interest rates were cut, and the seeds were sown for a series of economic policy blunders that split the Cabinet and helped to end Margaret Thatcher's term in office. But that was still three years away. The crash was followed by the 1988 budget giveaways that fuelled the recession of the early 1990s. John Major, then in the Cabinet and to become Chancellor two years later, took the view that, while mistakes were made, they could not have been foreseen.[3] Of course they were foreseen by some, but the government ignored their critics, including many in the trade-union movement, who did predict the awful consequences of their policies.

Over the next three years the local-government, education, and health services, along with the public utilities, would be changed dramatically. NALGO, with most other unions and the TUC, fought against the reforms as each was proposed and enacted: 'Your Council has continued to guide, co-ordinate and organise resources for campaigns against privatisation,

[2] N. Lawson, *The View from No. 11* (London: Corgi Books, 1992), 747.
[3] J. Major, *The Autobiography* (London: Harper Collins, 1999), 660.

contracting out and competitive tendering.'[4] The NEC was crystal clear about the importance of public ownership:

A motion by the Tottenham Gas Branch submitted by the Eastern District Council instructs your Council to make representations to the Labour Party during its policy review to ensure that the Labour Party continues its policy to renationalise British Gas plc in the first term of the next Labour Government. Your Council supports the motion as it is in line with NALGO policy to return British Gas to full public ownership.[5]

Union President John Saunders's 1988 New Year message was upbeat:

The last year has not been all gloom. We ran a successful Make People Matter campaign . . . Branches are improving their own organisation and this is paying off in better recruitment and ability to respond to members' needs . . . We also have cause for optimism on the service conditions front. We have seen members prepared to stand up for themselves, with NALGO's support, to improve their pay and working conditions.[6]

This last point is particularly important. As unions faltered in their political ability to stop detrimental legislation, so they concentrated on their national and local strengths in collective bargaining. Such struggles both fed into and fed off the popular movement against the poll tax; this genuine labour-movement coalition, which swept Mrs Thatcher from office in 1990, might also have removed her party from government. While much of the Tories' programme to restructure both public ownership and public service was actually implemented during their third term, NALGO never stopped campaigning against the reforms and for the members' pay and conditions.

With widespread opposition to the poll tax, and a growing realization that this third term of market remedies was threatening too many jobs and too many services to be quietly accepted, there was still a general mood of defiance. An academic review of the industrial relations of the year shows how this was perceived.

On the surface, 1987–88 marked a continuation of many trends of the 1980s. Output, earnings, profit rates and employment continued to grow, whilst unemployment fell for the second year in succession. Strikes remained at the level of the previous year, unions continued to lose members (albeit at a slow rate) despite the fall in unemployment, there was some decline in the numbers of workers covered by multi-employer agreements, and a further round of labour legislation reached the statute books . . . The public sector has continued to display a remarkable succession of traditional, protracted and bitter disputes over pay and effort levels. If there is any change

---

[4] *NALGO Annual Report 1988* (London: NALGO, 1989), 27.
[5] Ibid. 21.   [6] *NALGO News (NN)*, 15 Jan. 1988, 1.

in the public sector it has been in the direction of an 'old' adversarial industrial relations built on low trust, tough management and union militancy.[7]

Accounts like this suggest some puzzlement among commentators on industrial relations. They did not accept notions that workplace reforms to apply HRM techniques could eliminate adversarial industrial relations, notions promoted by managers and supported by many business school academics and popular pundits. However, they still seem surprised to find that, when they believe union power to be vanishing as a result of falling membership and rising unemployment, workers still took collective action. NALGO's history shows that trade-union resistance to unacceptable change, through a broad sweep of defence actions, continues even under the severest of pressures.

The Chancellor's economic strategy of creating a boom fuelled by tax cuts proved to be a disaster in the years to follow. As the Chancellor himself recalled, the 1988 budget's main element 'was the establishment of a single higher rate of income tax of 40 per cent'.[8] The balance-of-payments situation worsened, along with rising inflation, and government policy was in tatters. John Major reflects on the problems: 'The 1988 budget would cast a long shadow . . . When the economy fell off the cliff and boom turned to recession, made worse by an adverse world economy, the housing market stagnated, prices tumbled, and millions found themselves burdened with negative equity, owing more on their homes than they were worth. This problem was to paralyse the economy in the early nineties.'[9] The 1989 budget, Nigel Lawson's last, did little more than fiddle around the issues as efforts to link up with the Exchange Rate Mechanism (ERM) ran aground. So, from the election victory of 1987 until the end of 1989, government mistakes in the handling of the economy created boom and then bust, which alongside other reforms meant a sharp fall in its popularity.

Yet the Labour opposition and the TUC failed to capitalize on the government's crisis. They responded to woefully inadequate economic theory and practical clangers with depressing restraint. These two central institutions of the British labour movement did oppose water and electricity supply privatization, and they did have doubts over the reforms of the remaining public services, but they failed to develop a root-and-branch critique of government policy. So, despite the government being in a complete shambles by 1992, Labour still managed to lose that general election as well.

A Labour Party policy document, published in 1988, illustrates the loss of direction and the acceptance of the discredited government's position. Under

---

[7] J. Kelly and R. Richardson, 'Annual Review Article 1988', *British Journal of Industrial Relations*, 27/1 (1989), 152–3.

[8] Lawson, *The View from No. 11*, 815. [9] Major, *The Autobiography*, 106.

the heading 'A Productive and Competitive Economy' it is argued that a market economy is the key to prosperity, and that the key to a workable market economy is to reform the supply side—training, working practices, investment, tax reform, and monetary control over inflation.[10] This document reveals the dominance of the right wing within the party, and the retreat from policies associated with Keynesian demand-side management and with public ownership.

In contrast, NALGO's national leadership was in no doubt about the backsliding on policy:

Your Council expressed measured criticisms of the TUC submission in the relatively low profile given to the needs of the public services, the overall caution and modesty of its spending proposals and the absence of a comprehensively argued statement of opposition to the government's economic strategy. The TUC's restrained tone and apparent lack of confidence was perhaps understandable in the wake of Mrs Thatcher's third comprehensive general election victory.[11]

Among activists there was an awareness of a turning tide for the labour movement, with delegates at the 1988 TUC women's conference in Blackpool 'in more determined mood than recent years have seen, buoyed up by the surge of action in unions over the winter. Low pay, poor working conditions and discrimination were . . . high on the agenda.'[12] However, this groundswell of resistance was not apparent among the craven and crestfallen leaders of the TUC and the Labour Party.

Without doubt NALGO reached a great turning point in this period. Founded as a narrow professional body of local-government officers determined to establish a decent and uniform officialdom to advise and support the locally elected councillors, it had become the largest white-collar trade union in the land, representing most grades of non-manual staff in local government, education, health, transport, and the utilities, and it was in the vanguard of progressive labour-movement thought and deeds. Two union decisions showed how far NALGO had travelled. The vote to set up a political fund, in order to channel money, effort, and time into fighting trade-union causes, made explicit the fact that NALGO was now pursuing its dominant purposes of collective bargaining and representation in the wider world of politics. NALGO's collective-bargaining objectives were now supported by high-profile activity outside both the workplace and the national collective bargaining structures. The second decision, to merge with NUPE, completed the union's transition during a decade of attacks into an active formulator of policy and decisions at the heart of the British labour movement.

---

[10] Labour Party, *Social Justice and Economic Efficiency* (London: Labour Party, 1988), 3.
[11] *NALGO Annual Report 1988*, 27.   [12] *NN*, 18 Mar. 1988, 3.

After nearly a decade as Prime Minister, Margaret Thatcher still appeared to hold an unassailable position in her party, supported by the main mass communications media, further strengthened by the launch of Sky TV in February 1989. As *Public Service* reported:

Mrs Thatcher celebrates ten years as Prime Minister this month. But for public service and trades unionism the Prime Minister's party will be a wake. The Conservative Prime Minister summed up how she feels about the welfare state: 'no one would have remembered the good Samaritan if he'd only had good intentions. He had money as well.' Since then Mrs Thatcher has passed on the other side as more and more people have fallen by the wayside.[13]

But just as her grip on power and her place in history seemed assured, she began to lose both. Her defence of the poll tax sounded increasingly hollow, as opposition to it gathered in strength until it formed the silver bullet that fatally wounded her. More generally, there was a growing unease amongst a clear majority of the voting population, reflected both in opinion polls and in the unease of many leading Tories, about her persona and about those policies with which she was most closely associated.

Most of this was yet to crystallize, for the juggernaut of neo-liberal market reforms was moving steadily forward. NALGO made a dismal assessment of the country's plight:

The Council watched economic developments during 1989 with increasing concern, as the union's worst fears were confirmed . . . As 1989 ended, the Council's unhappy predictions were seen to have been close to the reality of events . . . and the prospects for 1990 looked grim. The analysis of Britain's economic ills, the long term weakness on which every spurt of growth seemed to founder, was identified by the Council as early as 1975, with broadly similar subsequent analyses. Such remedies as the union has proposed have not been found wanting, merely untried.[14]

This was followed by a more optimistic assessment of the government's standing:

Mr Lawson's mismanagement of the economy was so monumental that the edifice of Thatcherism itself began to crack as winter arrived. Low inflation, home ownership, free market economics and tax cuts—all allegedly pillars of the Tory temple— were visibly collapsing or under threat . . . The final demolition of Thatcherism came closer as higher taxes emerged as a possible last resort for new Chancellor Major as he picked his way through the fallen masonry of the Lawson era.[15]

By holding to a progressive line on public service and public ownership, NALGO helped to turn around the image of trade unions, in spite of

---

[13] *Public Service (PS)* (May 1989), 10.
[14] *NALGO Annual Report 1989* (London: NALGO, 1990), 21.   [15] Ibid.

tightening legal restrictions and widespread membership losses. All this, and the subsequent creation of UNISON, was part of the process that ensured the election of a Labour government a decade later. Solid foundations were laid for campaigns against the tide of Tory reforms, leading up to the storming anti-poll tax protests and driving the Conservatives' popularity to a humiliatingly low level, which culminated with Margaret Thatcher's overthrow by her own adoring party in 1990.

At the TUC Annual Congress, not long after NALGO's successful 1989 national strike in local government (see Box 12), even General Secretary Norman Willis shared the view that the crisis at the heart of government provided a breathing space for the labour movement.

In recent months, he argued, we had seen a number of unions undertake successful industrial action, without losing public support. Recent opinion polls were showing that the vast majority of the public believed unions to be essential to protect workers' interests, and while that support had not yet been transformed into increased membership it provided a firm foundation for recruitment work.[16]

Solidarity: The Friends Within

NALGO's internal democracy came under attack during 1987, as members of the Conservative Trade Unionists' organization made a series of complaints to the Certification Officer under the 1984 Trade Union Act. The report to the NEC meeting on 19 September emphasized NALGO's standing as a law-abiding organization while also worrying about the implications:

While NALGO has adopted 'a business as usual' approach to the Trade Union Act its main concern has been not to defy the law but to protect and preserve longstanding constitutional arrangements which have served the union well and have hitherto never been questioned. It was presumably never the government's intention that Part I of the Act should cause difficulties for unions like NALGO with long traditions of secret individual balloting; however the sweeping and unsophisticated nature of the legislation has meant that as a side effect the delicate and elaborate constitution developed over the years to bind the various sections of the union together is put at risk.[17]

Resulting rule changes were relatively minor, but they did effectively reduce democratic controls on the senior officials. Most significantly, they ended the NALGO tradition of having service committee representatives indirectly elected to the NEC. This weakened the NEC's representativeness at a time when many crucial decisions about the future practices of the union within service groups were being determined. The changes that emerged

---

[16] *NALGO Annual Report 1989*, 2.   [17] *NN*, 2 Oct. 1987, 4.

reflected not only legal wrangles but also a perhaps over-cautious concern among the leadership to limit the likelihood of internal conflict. The decision to have the General Secretary elected by ballot of the membership rather than by the NEC was followed by John Daly's announcement of his retirement at the 1989 conference, and the union prepared for its first and only election for this position.

The union took heart from the substantial yes vote to set up a political fund, following another legal challenge that stopped the 'Make People Matter' election campaign. Over 70 per cent voted in favour on a 67 per cent turnout, and NALGO became the fiftieth union to win a ballot under the 1984 Act, providing it with a separate 'war chest' to fund campaigns during elections. The strength of the vote also legitimated the union's campaigns to save public welfare provision through public services. It continued resourcing the fights against privatization of electricity and water, against contracting-out in local government and the NHS, and against local management of schools (LMS). In these campaigns the union mobilized the broadest range of arguments, including: price rises for customers; environmental concerns; job losses; health and safety hazards for staff and for local communities; lack of accountability; poor quality of service provision; reduced rights for staff and for service users; resources shifted away from socially defined need towards efficiency-defined demand; new managerialism; and sections of the population forced into a choice between either taking up private provision or having no services at all.

Reaching out to the wider world, the union's international activity increased in volume and intensity. Members joined pickets at South Africa House and at supermarkets selling South African produce. The union published detailed accounts of the realities of life and politics in South Africa in *Building Friendship—Working for Freedom*, and in Israel, the West Bank, and the Gaza Strip in *NALGO Visit to Israel and the Occupied Territories*, as seen by union delegations during their visits in the previous year. The union's work in southern Africa now included official links with trade unions in Namibia, and support for the South West Africa People's Organization (SWAPO) liberation movement.[18] Returning from the turmoil of Central America in 1988, the NALGO delegation reported how visits by official union delegations were important to trade unionists fighting for peace and freedom in their own country: 'It was brought home to us time and again during our visit the extent to which these unions valued international solidarity and the tremendous encouragement this gives them to continue to operate in the face of overwhelming adversity.'[19]

[18] NALGO, *Namibia: The Forgotten Colony* (London: NALGO, 1988).
[19] NALGO, *Central America: The Right to Live in Peace* (London: NALGO, 1989).

NALGO sponsored the launch of the Trade Union Network on Ireland, as the union began its important and significant support to those working through the trade union and labour movement towards a political settlement.[20] This started to put into practical effect the policy adopted by the 1987 conference: 'that the only just and lasting solution to the problems in Ireland lies in a united and independent Ireland established by peaceful means'. A delegation from the Metropolitan, North Western and North Wales, and Scottish District Councils met trade-union and labour-movement representatives in both Northern Ireland and the Republic. Their aims were: to raise their own understanding of the problems faced by trade unionists; to seek views about NALGO's policy; and to seek views about how issues should be raised in the British trade-union and labour movement.[21]

At the traditional CND Easter march NALGO was there, endorsing the slogan, 'No nostalgia, No Trident, No Nukes'.[22] All this activity around the big issues of world peace and freedom in South Africa, and around attacks on public services through privatization and cuts in the UK, reflected the union's broad left position, which linked rights at work to human rights more generally. NALGO's Scottish District Organization Officer, Charles Drury, summed it all up in his presidential address to the STUC 1988 Annual Congress in Ayr, when he argued for a change in political power to 'provide the people we represent with the jobs, with the quality of life, and with the public services they deserve'.[23]

However, splits in the labour movement were clearly evident at the TUC's 1988 Annual Congress in Bournemouth. Congress gave its support to the P&O strikers, the GCHQ trade unionists, and the print union members involved in the Wapping dispute with Rupert Murdoch. But the expulsion of the Electrical, Electronic, Telecommunication, and Plumbing Union (EETPU), over its activities at Wapping and elsewhere, revealed the depth of the problem reported soberly in NALGO's annual report: 'A major split, a long time coming but increasingly inevitable, was achieved with some dignity.' Also at this Congress, 'the Leader of the Opposition, intervening unwisely in one of the major controversies of the week was soundly rebuffed'.[24] This referred to the debate on the government's Employment Training Scheme—the majority ignored Neil Kinnock and followed NALGO's position on a boycott in this case.

[20] NALGO, *Ireland: A Trade Union Concern* (London: NALGO, n.d., *c*.1988).
[21] NALGO, *Report of a Delegation to Ireland 21–25 October 1990*, Metropolitan, North Western and North Wales, and Scottish District Councils (London: NALGO, n.d., *c*.1990).
[22] *NN*, 8 Apr. 1988, 1.   [23] *NALGO Annual Report 1988*, 7.
[24] Ibid. 1.

Box 11. NALGO in the TUC

The TUC is Britain's only national trade-union centre, surviving intact and without any major split since its foundation by a meeting of trade unions and trades councils at the Mechanics Institute in Manchester in June 1868. It set up the Labour Representation Committee in 1900, which soon after became a federation of trade unions and socialist organizations known as the Labour Party.[25]

NALGO affiliated in 1964, and by 1979 was established in decision-making both within the General Council and at Congress. General Secretary Geoffrey Drain and National Officer for Health Ada Maddocks were on the General Council, and NEC member Glynn Phillips was on the General Purposes Committee. The Scottish District Organization Officer, Charles Drury, was president of the STUC's 1979 Annual Congress. Between 1979 and 1992 the number of affiliated unions fell from 109 to 72, reflecting the intense merger activity of the period. Membership among affiliated unions fell from over twelve million to less than eight million, as the industrial landscape changed. The Thatcher government withdrew from all meaningful contact, provoking a crisis for the TUC: if it could no longer carry out its historic role of influencing the government, then what role should it perform?

NALGO played a considerable part in the ensuing controversies, especially around the central issues of incomes policy, anti-trade-union legislation, Europe, and training. In 1991 the union was heavily involved in pre-Congress negotiations that resulted in a compromise backed by all the big unions, rejecting incomes policies while backing a tripartite national economic assessment by the TUC, the government, and the employers, and supporting a statutory minimum wage.

As the Tories' legislative assault on the unions gathered pace, and, later, as the opposition Labour Party started to concede many important aspects of the Tory legislation, the ideological debate within the TUC sharpened considerably. Initial unanimity behind the 'business-as-usual' response to the earlier rounds of legislation began to break up in the mid-1980s. The 1986 Congress began to back off, accepting the rightward-drifting Labour Party's decision to retain legal restrictions on strike ballot rules in return for a commitment to repeal the three Acts passed in 1980, 1982 and 1984. NALGO voted against this policy change, and maintained its oppositional stance by taking motions to the 1990 and 1991 Congresses calling for complete repeal of all of the anti-union laws of the 1980s.

Policy on European integration provided another example of changing and diverging differences between NALGO and the orthodox TUC mainstream. In 1981 the TUC was in favour of withdrawal from the European Community (EC), with NALGO among a small opposing minority. Only seven years later the President of the European Commission, Jacques Delors, was welcomed onto the Congress platform, where, to general acclaim, he outlined his vision of a 'social Europe' with the right to collective bargaining, the right to participate in European company councils, and the right to life-long education. This would provide the counterbalance to the

[25] R. M. Martin, *The TUC: The Growth of a Pressure Group, 1868–1976* (Oxford: Clarendon Press, 1980).

single European market due to be established at the end of 1992. With only limited opposition, Congress bowed to further integration of the European economies.

By 1992 the General Council was arguing that the benefits contained in the social chapter of the Maastricht Treaty offered hope to employees. NALGO spoke virtually alone against the monetarist principles embedded in the Treaty, as delegate Richard Maybin put the union's case that it would result in more unemployment, cuts in wages, and cuts in public services.

NALGO fought hard to protect the integrity of training provision, rejecting the idea that workers should train themselves out of unemployment and into jobs, and opposing the government's aim of linking training to its drive to cut welfare benefits. Government training schemes contained increasing elements of compulsion, in an attempt to reduce the unemployment figures, as workers were threatened with loss of benefits if they refused to participate. By 1984 NALGO's policy was both clear and out of step with the General Council when it argued that the TUC should withdraw support from the YTS, unless trainees received the rate for the job and young workers were not forced into schemes. YTS was succeeded by the even worse Job Training Scheme (JTS). Government proposals, including pay of benefits plus £10 per week, withdrawal of benefits from those who refuse to participate, and abolition of the trade-union veto, were subsequently incorporated into the Employment Training Scheme. NALGO won support for a union movement boycott from both the STUC and the Wales TUC, but had to wait until 1988 finally to secure Congress backing for non-cooperation with the Employment Training Scheme. Subsequent TUC guidance fell short of NALGO's interpretation of what had been agreed.

This pointed towards issues of decision-making and accountability within the TUC, which surfaces from time to time in a variety of forms. One aspect relates to the structure of the TUC itself, and the 1980s saw several debates about the composition of the General Council. NALGO was particularly concerned that on some important issues—such as Employment Training, the conduct of the Wapping dispute, and nuclear power—the General Council did not take full regard of decisions made by Congress. By the 1989 Congress NALGO was calling for substantial change to the industrial and sectoral grouping arrangements, so that the General Council would be more representative of the numerical and political strength of the affiliated unions. However, Congress voted for a compromise that preserved the political status quo while also allocating more reserved seats for women.

Both the TUC and the STUC hold annual women's conferences (since 1930 and 1927 respectively). In the 1970s NALGO called for them to be abolished, on the grounds that they were divisive and that the problems of working women should be considered by the full Congress rather than being sidelined to a separate body with no power to decide Congress policy. The union stopped participating in 1976.

In 1983 NEOC decided to support the resumption of attendance, disagreeing with the union's powerful economic committee. One of the stumbling blocks was that the women's conference did not have the right to send resolutions to the TUC Congress. Liverpool's Vicky Rosin said that it was wrong for NALGO to sit on the sidelines while women trade unionists fought within the TUC for proper recognition of the

conference. NALGO's first women-only conference also called for resumed attendance, setting the scene for the union's 1984 conference to reverse the 1976 decision.

The social policies of the movement are given shape through debates before and
at the annual congresses. NALGO took its own distinctive policies into the debates,
playing a part in winning support for unilateral nuclear disarmament; opposition to
nuclear power generation; support for the armed struggle in, and for sanctions
against, South Africa (see Box 14); support for anti-poll-tax campaigns; support for
Scottish and Welsh devolution; and opposition to the Prevention of Terrorism Act.
Contrast this with NALGO's position in the late 1960s, just after it first affiliated,
when the delegation abstained from votes on peace and disarmament, nationalization
of the drug industry, the Vietnam War, the sale of arms to South Africa, and the military *coup* in Greece, in order 'to preserve NALGO's independent position on party
political matters'.[26]

John Daly's Congress speech illustrates the extent to which it was necessary to spell out to the faint of heart the need for militant resistance to the
worst of the government's reforms. In a debate on the poll tax he argued
against the General Council's restraint: 'NALGO considers it premature at
this time to commit itself to confining our opposition to activities which are
within the law. NALGO has no wish to engage in unlawful activities but
should the need arise these unjust laws must be opposed by every means available, even if we have to go outside the law.'[27] NALGO's position was clearly
expressed in the leaflet *Poll-Taxed or Pole-Axed?* 'Through the poll tax Mrs
Thatcher will thus achieve more easily two of her primary aims: to reduce the
overall level of public service provision and to centralise, or increase central
government control over, local authority services.' In a nutshell: 'It will rob
from the poor to give to the rich.'[28]

At the STUC Annual Congress in Aberdeen, President Ronnie Webster
'went on to castigate the poll tax and unemployment before ending with an
appeal for peace and nuclear disarmament'.[29] NALGO successfully argued
that local-government staff should not be used as 'the shock troops who will
bring down the poll tax', against the arguments of ultra-left factions in many
unions.[30] A few weeks later in Swansea, Elwyn Morgan, chair of the Wales
TUC, argued that 'even the most hardened supporters of the present
Government were now turning against the Thatcher regime as they became
sickened with what the Government were doing to the health service, social
welfare and education. Compulsory competitive tendering in the public

[26] G. Newman, *Path to Maturity: NALGO 1965–1980* (London: NALGO, 1982), 108.
[27] *TUC Annual Report 1988* (London: TUC, 1989), 533.
[28] NALGO, *Poll-Taxed or Pole-Axed?* (London: NALGO, 1988).
[29] *NALGO Annual Report 1989*, 7.   [30] *PS* (June 1989), 4 .

services was a ploy to drive down wages. Putting public services into private hands was done for profit.'[31]

In 1988 the piecemeal bricks of government reforms started to come together as solid new structures. Strategic responses were needed to combat the increasing isolation of the unions within a political world of exclusion and denigration. One response was to change the shape of British trade unionism irrevocably—at the annual conference 'NALGO took an historic step towards merger with NUPE when Conference agreed that the idea was an urgent priority'.[32] The momentous decision was reported factually in the annual report:

Conference 1988 carried a resolution welcoming the principle of a merger with NUPE and instructing your Council to approach NUPE in a positive way and, following discussions, to produce a white paper for Conference 1990 outlining the obstacles to a merger and how these could be overcome. At its own conference in May NUPE carried a motion re-affirming its commitment to an enlarged public service union including NUPE, COHSE and NALGO and calling for a feasibility study for its 1989 Conference.[33]

The merger proposals were part of a wider merger movement among British trade unions, with the NGA and SOGAT forming the Graphical, Paper, and Media Union (GPMU), the Union of Communication Workers (UCW) and National Communication Union (NCU) forming the Communication Workers' Union (CWU), and TASS and ASTMS forming MSF. All were examples of efforts to consolidate shared strengths in the face of changing employer structures, new technology, and government policy (see Chapter 10).

At a joint NALGO/NUPE conference Tom Sawyer, NUPE's Deputy General Secretary, understood that the unions were 'walking on ground we have never walked before' and Alan Jinkinson saw this as a 'unique opportunity'.[34] NALGO and NUPE executive committees met jointly for the first time in March 1989. The NEC gave the merger top priority, and joint activity with NUPE expanded, especially in the NHS. A joint database on CCT was set up. The very nature of CCT brought workers of all occupational groups together and this gave a grass-roots feel to merger plans. Inter-union cooperation on CCT extended further with the publication by NALGO, NUPE, TGWU, and GMB of *Who Cares Wins: A Trade Union Guide to Compulsory Competitive Tendering for Local Services*, with a series of *Tender Care* supplements on the tendering processes covering catering, refuse collection and street cleaning, building cleaning, and ground maintenance.

---

[31] *NALGO Annual Report 1989*, 10.   [32] *NN*, 17 June 1988, 1.
[33] *NALGO Annual Report 1988*, 35.   [34] *NN*, 28 Oct. 1988, 3.

The sudden urgency of the merger idea within NALGO was in part a reaction to a decade of stresses and strains: a stream of successive government reforms; a torrent of local action; the pressure cooker of free-market mechanisms; and wearying internal divisions in the search for policy responses. Taken together, everyone was anxious about the future. For example, between 1981 and 1987 NALGO lost about a quarter of its members in British Gas and this rate of decline was accelerating. As a result the union looked to merge branches, to streamline their operation with national help, and to improve steward facilities at work to encourage more of these key union recruiters to take on the task. All of this created a stronger feeling among activists and among the leadership that the big idea of a merger offered a solution.

Another part of the motivation for merger talks was a realization of the common core of problems faced by the three unions. Privatization, CCT, job losses, flexible working practices, partial derecognition, and low pay were the specific sticks used to beat the workforce, with government policy on employment regulation, union laws, and public ownership forming a general bludgeon of powerful forces to break away from the post-war consensus of economic and social progress for the majority of citizens. As John Daly put it: 'The government wants health care on the cheap for profit.'[35] Bill Seawright, speaking in his presidential address to the 1989 conference, suggested a clear political direction: 'People are learning again the truth that collectivism and public provision are positive, humane and also efficient principles.'[36] Looking forward to the merger, he put the case: 'I believe that merger is the way forward. The new union that would be formed from the merger would have collectively greater strength than we each have separately today.'[37] By then *The Times* could report another development: 'Delegates at COHSE's annual conference at Bridlington, Humberside, voted overwhelmingly for a motion calling for a new public sector union incorporating NUPE, NALGO and COHSE.'[38]

Merger activity reveals yet again how unions function. It demonstrates the dialectics of trade unionism, manifested in endless discussion between members, activists, and leaders about the right course of action to take under the circumstances of the moment. Policy and action are pushed and pulled by constantly shifting tensions: between immediate prosaic daily fights against injustice to the individual and the group, on the one hand, and the national battles of principle and practice, on the other; between the sections of the union, divided by occupation, industry, sex, race, disability, sexuality, and politics; and within the union as an independent organization and as a part of

[35] *PS* (Mar. 1989), 6.
[36] *NN*, 16 June 1989, 1.
[37] *PS* (July 1989), 13.
[38] *The Times*, 21 June 1989, 3.

the union movement, the labour movement and the international working-class movement. Static models of unions as pressure groups, and those that simplistically pit the 'ordinary' members against the 'union bureaucrats', miss both the point of union existence and the point of struggle. It is only by examining the whole and the parts together in action that NALGO's progress into the 1990s and into its final years of existence can be understood.

Deregulation and Management Reforms

Managerialism comes out of the closet

During this term of office the government made great strides in its privatization programme, with CCT in local government, with the Education Reform Act 1988 for schools and colleges, with self-governing trusts in the NHS, and with outright sell-off in water and electricity supply. All were accompanied by moves to change employment practices towards so-called flexible working in the name of new public management.[39] The programme was justified by economic assertions, misrepresenting Adam Smith as some once and future privatizer. For example, one prominent writer claims that, 'according to Smith, private ownership improves productivity and efficiency . . . put simply, because private ownership concentrates the costs and benefits of decisions on the owners of capital, they have strong incentives to use resources efficiently'.[40] This ideal was developed by academic economists using simplistic cost-benefit analysis, as argued by the future electricity supply regulator Stephen Littlechild: 'In principle, one might examine the effects of each alternative privatization proposal on different interest groups such as existing and potential customers, tax-payers, suppliers of labour and capital etc. Trade-offs between these interest groups could be established and decisions made accordingly.'[41]

John Daly put the alternative trade-union view at the 1987 TUC Annual Congress: 'The present Government, in pursuing its policy of establishing a free market economy, has created and deliberately maintained mass unemployment while at the same time it has sold off at give-away or knock-down prices valuable public assets.'[42] Despite the case of gas illustrating the sham

---

[39] C. Pollitt, *Managerialism and the Public Services: Cuts or Cultural Change in the 1990s?* (Oxford: Blackwell, 1993).

[40] C. Veljanovski, 'Privatization: Monopoly Money or Competition?', in C. Veljanovski (ed.), *Privatization and Competition* (London: IEA, 1989), 35–6.

[41] M. Beesley and S. Littlechild, 'Privatization: Principles, Problems and Priorities', *Lloyds Bank Annual Review*, 149 (1983), 11; M. Beesley and S. Littlechild, 'The Regulation of Privatized Monopolies in the United Kingdom', *RAND Journal of Economics*, 20/3 (1989), 454–72.

[42] *TUC Annual Report 1987*, 533.

economics of marketization, merely swapping a public monopoly for a private one, the government remained undeterred in the case of water and electricity supply. However, the unions could and did mount much more effective opposition, and privatization lost much of its populist appeal during this period. One commentary notes that:

Whilst water privatisation in December 1989 was (again) substantially oversubscribed by the public as investors, public opinion was no longer nearly so much in favour of these privatizations, fearing the consequences of the creation of powerful private monopolies. The record of OFTEL and OFGAS, whilst not itself poor, had seemingly failed to convince the public as consumers that regulation would prevent prices rising and services declining.[43]

Alongside the sell-offs of the utilities, the government pressed on with its plans to introduce so-called internal markets for health, education, and local government. Here a split is made between the providers of the service—for example, hospitals—and the purchasers of the service, not patients but Health Authorities. The theoretical justification, to some extent based on the work of American academics,[44] is that the bureaucrats in charge of supplying the service will respond to market-like pressures with budget-maximizing behaviour.[45]

The result is that labour management practice takes on more of the characteristics of the private sector, as managers adopt the twin notions of flexibility and downsizing, combining job losses with intensification of work for those staff remaining. With high and prolonged unemployment, weakened trade unions, right-wing leadership of the Labour Party, a dominant market ideology, and a comfortable government majority in the Commons, conditions were right for managers to take unilateral control over the workplace and to extract more work from fewer employees. Managers grabbed opportunities to maximize their budgets by reducing labour costs through attacks on staffing levels, staffing and grading structures, conditions of service, working practices, and trade-union organization. Management consultants, hired to advise on how to run services, often recommended increased labour flexibility in contracts, hours, skills, and payment systems.

Familiar management practices, repackaged with friendly sounding language of quality, empowerment, teamwork, and involvement, were adapted

---

[43] M. Dunn and S. Smith, 'Economic Policy and Privatisation', in S. Savage and L. Robins (eds.), *Public Policy under Thatcher* (London: Macmillan, 1990), 38.

[44] W. Niskanen, *Bureaucracy and Representative Government* (Chicago: Aldine Atherton, 1971); W. Niskanen, 'Bureaucrats and Politicians', *Journal of Law and Economics*, 18/3 (1975), 617–43.

[45] P. Dunleavy, *Democracy, Bureaucracy and Public Choice: Economic Explanations in Political Science* (New York: Harvester Wheatsheaf, 1991).

from the private sector for use in the public sector. 'New Public Management', as it later became known, was an important part of the attack on the public sector. The enemies of the public services and utilities argued that they were less efficiently managed than organizations under private control. Hence outright privatization or, alternatively, forcing public-sector services to operate *as if* they were in the private sector, would benefit everyone. One important aspect of the argument was that the public sector was systematically overstaffed and generally had higher labour costs than necessary. Furthermore, a logical extension of the analysis is that trade unions are to blame for high costs by pushing up wages and by blocking management attempts to increase efficiency.

Examples of job losses and closures came thick and fast: fifteen staff at Milton Keynes Development Corporation faced the sack after refusing to join a new private company created to do the work of the corporation's building directorate; Nicholas Ridley ordered the closure of most of Lambeth Council's DLO after losses were blamed on poor management by an independent inquiry; private bus company Yorkshire Rider shed seventy-five jobs, amid 'fears that Yorkshire Rider's management is trying to line its own pockets by cutting jobs'.[46] Another privatized bus company, Greater Manchester Buses, announced plans to shed 670 jobs in order to raise the money to buy new buses.

Plans to privatize parts of the NHS, such as pharmacy, pathology, and radiology, were announced at the Conservative Party conference by John Moore, the Social Services Secretary. Nicholas Ridley put forward his programme to privatize housing with the help of the Public and Local Service Efficiency Campaign (PULSE), a privatization lobby group supported by private contractors, right-wing Conservative MPs, and organizations such as the Freedom Association.

NALGO opposed techniques aimed at tightening management control over both pay and performance, warning NHS activists of the dangers in appraisal and performance-related pay for health professionals, and of the need to reach agreements that protected members. Pay flexibility was being introduced into British Gas, through supplements to basic pay.

One academic view, based on a wide range of privatization experiences, was that, 'despite the gloom of trade union opponents of privatization, and the expectations of its champions, the effects on industrial relations have been ambiguous'.[47] Nevertheless, there were plenty of examples of collective bargaining being undermined by the new employers in the privatized sector and

[46] *NN*, 31 Mar. 1989, 1.

[47] A. Ferner and T. Colling, 'Privatization, Regulation and Industrial Relations', *British Journal of Industrial Relations*, 29/3 (1991), 405.

liberated managers in the public-service sector. Bargaining machinery was dismantled as industries changed structure and employers made good their escape from some of the national bargaining institutions, backed by government attacks on rigid national settlements that were immune from local labour-market forces.

In National Power, 'personnel director, Robert Jackson has warned that 3,000 staff could be made redundant in an attempt to cut costs. National Power management would also want to end national pay bargaining.'[48] New collective-bargaining machinery was agreed for staffs in colleges and polytechnics, a forerunner of changes to come in the water industry, and later the NHS, and much later in local government with the Single Status Agreement of 1997. Already, LACSAB's view was that, 'while it may not be realistic to abolish the national system, there are arguments for devolving more power to local authority level'.[49]

By the end of 1989, privatization, and its link to labour management practice, was a dominant issue for NALGO's NEC:

The Council has continued to guide, co-ordinate and organise resources for campaigns to defend public ownership and control of public utilities and services; to maintain and restore direct labour; to maintain and improve the quality, scope, accessibility, responsiveness and democratic accountability of local and other public services; and to protect the jobs, pay, conditions, health and safety, equal opportunities, negotiating machinery and trade union rights of members affected by privatisation and compulsory competitive tendering. The main focal points of these efforts during the year, determined by the emphasis of the Government's privatisation measures, were in local government, water, electricity and the National Health Service.[50]

CCT in local government

In June 1987 the Local Government (No. 2) Bill was given its first reading, with proposals for CCT for street and building cleaning, vehicle and ground maintenance, catering, and refuse collection. Masquerading as a measure to introduce local flexibility over the running of council services, the CCT proposals were part of a substantial tightening of central state power. At the 1987 TUC Annual Congress Rodney Bickerstaffe slammed 'the blitz on local services that is at the heart of this Government's programme: the poll tax, the Education Bill, the Housing Bill, privatisation and the moves to end contract compliance. The sub-title of the Queen's Speech this year might well have been "How we plan to destroy local government".'[51] A decade later the impact could be summarized thus: 'Having been broken by the first and

---

[48] *NN*, 20 Jan. 1989, 1. [49] LACSAB press release, 25 Nov. 1987.
[50] *NALGO Annual Report 1989*, 21. [51] *TUC Annual Report 1987*, 532.

second Thatcher governments, local government was converted into a competitive "service enabler" by the third. . . . The Local Government Act 1988 required local authorities to put most of their existing services out to competitive tender and ensured that only commercial criteria should determine which organizations provided services.'[52] Based on bidding procedures that were structured in favour of private contractors' bids rather than in-house tenders, it meant a loss of jobs and worse services.

NALGO produced a handbook *Fighting Privatisation in Local Government* and stepped up production of the *Stop your Council Contracting* bulletin.[53] It sent out a series of detailed guidelines 'to aid branches in negotiations with local authorities in the preparation of contract specifications which are required to be prepared under the provisions of the 1988 Local Government Act No. 2. . . . it is the policy of the national local government committee to endeavour to ensure that local authority services are retained in-house and that contractors do not take over local authority services'.[54] The guidelines included clear statements on standards of service, identifying the diversity of existing provision. For example, 'local authority refuse collection is a comprehensive service, dealing with the collection of household, trade, bulky, special, recyclable, and clinical and other types of waste',[55] and in vehicle maintenance 'local authorities currently operate on preventive maintenance rather than reactive maintenance, e.g. the elimination of specific *ad hoc* repairs'.[56] The aim was to prevent private contractors from cherry-picking the most profitable elements of provision and running contracts for short-term maximum profit.

Confident of government support, the CBI unsurprisingly campaigned in the opposite direction, pushing for faster and fuller CCT. In its report *The Competitive Advantage*, 'the private business lobby called for competition to become the rule rather than the exception'.[57] The attack on local government entered a new phase, with government acting to 'depoliticize' decision-making. CCT was part of a wider move to weaken local democracy, turning local authorities into functional arms of central government run by technical management cadres rather than by elected politicians. The Education Reform Act and the Housing Act were particular examples of several pieces of legislation that replaced local discretion with centrally determined decrees and with funding formulae. Another example was the government White Paper proposals arising from the Widdecombe Committee of Inquiry into the Con-

---

[52] E. Evans, *Thatcher and Thatcherism* (London: Routledge, 1997), 61–2.

[53] D. Foster, 'Privatization Policy in Local Government: The Response of Public Sector Trade Unions', Ph.D. thesis (Bath, 1991).

[54] *NN*, 22 July 1988, 4.   [55] Ibid., 29 July 1988, 4.

[56] Ibid., 5 Aug. 1988, 4.   [57] Ibid., 21 Oct. 1988, 1.

duct of Local Authority Business. Jim White called on the TUC to oppose Widdecombe's proposal to remove the right of senior and other council staff in 'politically sensitive posts' to be involved in political activity.

Strengthening the senior management cadres meant that they had to be separated from their junior and professional colleagues. National collective bargaining and vertical trade unionism helped to maintain an identity of interest between manager and managed. To break this allegedly cosy relationship, an increasing number of senior managers were paid on personal contracts based on so-called market rates fixed by management consultants such as Inbucon. 'Advanced' councils such as Kent County introduced local performance pay structures despite local and national union opposition. As national officer Keith Sonnet argued: 'NALGO is opposed to performance related pay because it is divisive, counter-productive to teamwork and undermines the national pay bargaining system which is based on the rate for the job . . . [It] is about cutting costs. If local authorities are concerned about performance they should put more money into staff training and development.'[58]

Local-government workers responded to all this by joining NALGO, against the general trend of decline in other sectors of employment. In 1987–8 NALGO's local-government membership rose by nearly 7,000 to 494,000, accounting for about 80 per cent of total membership growth in NALGO over that period (see Tables 7.1–7.6). As Alan Jinkinson said: 'This increase shows that despite government attacks on trade unions, workers value them highly.'[59]

The Education Reform Act 1988

Government attacks on local democracy were particularly intense in the local-authority part of the education sector. When the government decided to abolish ILEA, NALGO joined others in lobbying the House of Lords to reverse the decision. As education officer Regina Kibel said: 'The government wants more choice in education, but ILEA parents are overwhelmingly in favour of ILEA—they are being denied their choice.'[60] ILEA members were balloted for strike action over the sacking of a union activist, and they joined NUPE, the NUT, the National Association of Teachers in Further and Higher Education (NATFHE), and the TGWU in a one-day strike.

The Education Reform Act gave most secondary schools the right to opt for grant maintained status; gave control of Local Education Authority (LEA) budgets to schools; set up the national curriculum and associated Standard Assessment Tests (SATs); allowed selection of pupils; and removed further

[58] Ibid., 22 Jan. 1988, 1.   [59] Ibid., 29 Jan. 1988, 1.   [60] Ibid., 20 May 1988, 1.

261

and higher education colleges from LEA control.[61] The Prime Minister was a fervent advocate of parental choice especially in the case of Grant Maintained Schools, an invention whereby schools could opt out altogether of LEA control and opt instead for Department of Education and Science (DES) direct rule.

NALGO's response, echoing the opposition of most other unions and educational organizations, highlighted the loss of planning and coordination by LEAs; growing unaccountability in the use of resources; adverse employment consequences for tens of thousands of APT&C staff; and, of course, the fear that all of this would result in cuts in government cash and ultimately of standards. A major threat was the suggestion that polytechnics and larger further and higher education colleges would benefit from managerial and financial independence from the LEAs. Under the guise of releasing the colleges from bureaucracy, local politics, and outmoded management, the government sought to create educational institutions with lower public funding, more than ever directing their activities towards the labour-market commands of the private sector. NALGO campaigned against the Education Bill alongside the teacher unions, the NUS, and the TUC. The union also protected its school-level activists, winning a claim at an IT on behalf of a member who had been refused promotion at Liverpool De La Salle Catholic secondary school because of her trade-union activity.

The NHS and the Community Care Act 1990

The government launched its proposals for the NHS in the White Paper *Working for Patients* (Cm 555). The reforms were based on the claim, which was not rooted in any empirical study, that 'what is peculiar to the NHS is its almost total lack of any incentives to greater efficiency'.[62] The solution was the introduction of competition. John Major, Prime Minister when the reforms were implemented in 1991, believed it was a success, but 'introducing the internal market, however, was a noisy business. The British Medical Association—the doctors' trade union—defended the way things had always been done . . . We were harried by the suggestion that the creation of the internal market was a covert step on a path to full privatisation of the NHS. It was not.'[63]

This position was accepted by hardly anyone else, especially those who joined the nationwide demonstrations on 3 February 1988, as *NALGO News* reported:

---

[61] M. Ironside and R. Seifert, *Industrial Relations in Schools* (London: Routledge, 1995).

[62] J. Peet, *Healthy Competition: How to Improve the NHS* (London: Centre for Policy Studies, 1987), 6.

[63] Major, *The Autobiography*, 391.

Thousands of health workers throughout Britain joined picket lines, lobbies and marches on Wednesday in an unprecedented protest against NHS under-funding. The action focused on London where staff at 40 hospitals staged pickets . . . Their anger was increased by news, denied by the government, that ministers want to offer nurses a pay rise of just 3%, while health secretary John Moore has refused to guarantee that pay awards would be fully funded.[64]

Hector MacKenzie, COHSE's General Secretary, said that the White Paper ought to be titled *Working for Profits*, as he moved a resolution at TUC Annual Congress stating that the proposals would 'have disastrous consequences for the effective and efficient delivery of health care'.[65] Lynne Robson, chair of NALGO's National Health Committee, told the union's conference that self-governing hospitals sounded more like private companies: 'Opted-out hospitals would not have to provide a full range of services, they would raise revenue from the services they did offer, and employ staff on any rates of pay.'[66] In the end there would be job losses, bed closures, and a worse service to patients.

The NEC's policy was 'that NALGO should focus on the effects of the white paper on all NALGO members and the general public as *users* of the NHS as well as the implications for NALGO members in the NHS as *employees*', and to support the TUC's Health Service Committee in lobbying political parties and liaising with the British Medical Association (BMA).[67] A joint NALGO and NUPE critique of *Working for Patients* was sent to all branches.

Already there were massive cuts accumulating throughout the NHS, well in advance of the structural reforms outlined in the White Paper, and yet more were in the pipeline. In the London ambulance service, for example, 'NALGO fears the plans will leave the service ticking over from day to day but seriously exposed to incidents such as the King's Cross tube fire'.[68] The union highlighted the role of the ambulance and other emergency services after that fire and after the Clapham train crash, both at the end of 1987. Some ambulance service managers took on the most anti-union positions, and in 1989 all this culminated in a bitter pay dispute that resulted in a defeat for the unions. NALGO accused the new wave of NHS managers of secrecy: 'there is evidence that health authorities are simply referring contentious matters of public concern to committees and subcommittees to avoid the presence of the public.'[69] This increased lack of accountability added to the already existing democratic deficit within the NHS, and foreshadowed the severe crisis of public control in the 1990s.

---

[64] *NN*, 5 Feb. 1988, 1.   [65] *TUC Annual Report 1989* (London: TUC, 1990), 360–1.
[66] *PS* (July 1989), 4.   [67] *NN*, 21 Apr. 1989, 7.
[68] Ibid., 22 Jan. 1988, 1.   [69] Ibid., 26 Aug. 1988, 3.

Mounting evidence of the crisis of underfunding fuelled both the right-wing government reformers seeking market changes and those on the left trying to protect the basis upon which health care is delivered: the Black Report[70] provided hard information on the growing inequality of health provision in the UK; and the government refused to fund the pay rises recommended by the pay review body for nurses and PAMs, thus putting increased pressure on health-authority budgets. Mrs Thatcher justified the cuts when she said 'you have a duty to look at the whole burden on the taxpayer'.[71] Lynne Robson took a different view: 'The consequences of consistent underfunding affect every corner of the NHS. All health workers are part of a health care team. At the moment their work is based on goodwill rather than good pay.'[72] As John Pestle, chair of the Health Service Committee, said: 'There is a point at which members will no longer put up with cuts and low pay. That point has been reached.'[73] NHS industrial relations took a new twist when 1,200 senior health managers, mostly NALGO members, were unilaterally taken out of Whitley bargaining machinery under Department of Health and Social Security (DHSS) circular HC(87)22.

Trade unionists rallied to defend the service. In London health members voted to join a twenty-four-hour strike with COHSE and NUPE. Lothian health board's decision to axe 500 jobs sparked a mass demonstration in Scotland on 24 February 1988, with over 50,000 joining STUC rallies in Glasgow, Edinburgh, Dundee, and Aberdeen. Health workers lobbied their health boards in Glasgow and Edinburgh, and striking hospital staff invaded a meeting of Central Manchester health authority over job cuts. The protests intensified, with over 100,000 at a massive TUC march against cuts in London, and with local demonstrations in South Wales, South Derbyshire, Leeds, Birmingham, and Stirling. Actions like these brought together trade unions, community groups, and political organizations fighting against government refusals properly to fund the NHS and to keep its election promises.

This protest movement was part of a broader-based set of campaigns on the issues of privatization, cuts, job security, and conditions of service. Those concerns were linked to notions of safeguarding quality in public services, rooted in deeper arguments about the moral and practical limitations of market forces and deregulation. Union arguments often understated the potential for social reform through extending social ownership and deepening democratic accountability. Nevertheless, NALGO consistently argued the

---

[70] Sir Douglas Black, *Inequalities in Health—the Black Report* (Harmondsworth: Penguin, 1982).

[71] *NN*, 29 Jan. 1988, 3.   [72] Ibid., 26 Feb. 1988, Health Action Special.

[73] Ibid., 29 Jan. 1988, 1.

case against unfettered market forces and for an alternative to the government's economic strategies.

Privatization of Water and Electricity Supply

Opposition to the privatization of water and electricity was widespread and popular. Although ultimately unsuccessful, the union campaigns mobilized analysis and argument that attracted much attention and support. They also linked with campaign groups from a wide spectrum of causes, as well as conducting well-organized lobbying around Parliament. NALGO President John Saunders expressed the general feelings within the union at the 1988 conference: 'The message to the privateers is simple. Leave the public services to those who have built them, to those who believe in them, to those who devote their lives to them.'[74] The union took a high campaigning profile in the water industry, where one of the resources basic to all forms of life was to be turned into a saleable commodity.

From Roman times a supply of safe communal drinking water had been considered fundamental to life. In the middle of the nineteenth century, when demand outgrew natural supply and cholera epidemics had swept through many large cities, the links between public health and water were well established and accepted. A publicly owned and controlled supply of water to the larger communities became the norm. The post-1945 government concentrated on rationalizing the industry to reduce the number of suppliers.[75] By the time of the 1974 reorganization the relationship between water supply and clean rivers was well known. As another expert later summarized the situation in 1974, 'integrated river basin management represented the full recognition of the interdependence of the three water functions. It was unique to Britain and admired by water professionals all over the world. The system was seen as improving efficiency and effectiveness by facilitating optimum use of resources, especially in emergencies such as drought, floods or major pollution incidents.'[76]

NALGO published *Water Down the Drain?*, which gave a potted history of the development of the water supply and sewage systems and argued the case against private ownership. The union provided twenty-eight reasons why investors should steer clear of water stocks, and the union's response to the draft regulations was that there was a 'profit before purity threat to water'.[77]

[74] Ibid., 17 June 1988, 2.
[75] K. Smith, *Water in Britain* (London: Macmillan, 1972).
[76] J. Davidson, *Privatization and Employment Relations: The Case of the Water Industry* (London: Mansell, 1993), 23.
[77] *NN*, 27 May 1988, 3.

One expert was scathing of the privatization plans: 'The government and water authorities stumbled into it without any clear or coherent view of its implications,'[78] and 'the DoE published a most unconvincing White paper, with one chapter of gross privatisation rhetoric and several others of more detailed defiance of reality'.[79]

Another observer reports on the success of the Water Joint Trade Union Industry Committee's role, with NALGO's Alan Jackson as secretary, in coordinating national and regional political opposition. They repudiated the government's line on efficiency and competition, and promoted the positive benefits of 'a unified approach to the management of the whole water cycle',[80] pollution controls, and repair of infrastructure, achievable through public ownership. The case was cogently argued in *Public Ownership: A Water Tight Case* issued by the joint trade-union committee, alongside propaganda materials including badges, adverts, and video. The union even used the courts: 'NALGO did successfully bring a court case against Thames Water for spending money on furthering the cause of privatisation before formal Parliamentary authority had been given.'[81]

National officer Alex Thomson told us: 'Our best tactic was to actually build up as many opposition groups as possible'. As the Water Bill reached the committee stage in March, the government came under intense pressure on questions such as rate rises, immunity from prosecution over pollution issues, and limited promises on capital investment by the water companies. Alan Jackson told us that the union funded a worker in opposition spokesman Jack Cunningham's office, and NALGO researchers prepared briefings for Labour MPs. *Public Service* reported on a rally on 12 April 1989:

The depth of public opposition to water privatisation was made clear last month when thousands lobbied parliament and a 250,000 name petition was handed into Downing Street . . . NALGO General Secretary John Daly expressed the anger of many. He told the rally 'this measure is utterly cynical and immoral. It shows that Margaret Thatcher and her colleagues are prepared to subordinate the interests of the whole community to those of the financial institutions.'[82]

Even Margaret Thatcher was sensible to problems with water: 'The privatization of the water industry was a more politically sensitive issue. Much emotive nonsense was talked along the lines of, "look, she's even privatizing the rain which falls from the heavens". I used to retort that the rain may come

---

[78] D. Kinnersley, *Troubled Water: Rivers, Politics and Pollution* (London: Shipman, 1988), 127.

[79] Ibid. 132.

[80] S. Ogden, 'The Trade Union Campaign against Water Privatization', *Industrial Relations Journal*, 22/1 (1991), 27.

[81] Ibid. 29.   [82] *PS* (May 1989), 3.

from the Almighty but he did not send the pipes, plumbing and engineering to go with it.'[83] Other members of the Cabinet took the view that, although water privatization was both sound and successful, there had been presentational problems that forced them to strengthen safety regulation and environmental protection.[84] However, the real fears of large sections of the population, the opposition of experts and the unions, and the historical lessons of the industry all seemed to wash over the government decision-makers.

Privatization plans for the electricity supply industry were announced by Cecil Parkinson in two White Papers (Cm 322 and Cm 327) early in 1988. NALGO responded that 'the proposals in the White Paper do not in any way change NALGO's long held view that the privatisation of the electricity industry is fundamentally wrong in principle, and contrary to the national interest'.[85] The union opposed the break-up of the CEGB into two bits before selling it off, and so did Lord Marshall, the chair of the CEGB. Electricity branch delegates at the 1988 conference reiterated the union's line: 'this group meeting remains fundamentally opposed to the privatisation of the ESI [Electrical Supply Industry].'[86] The industry's unions formed a joint campaign organization, the Federation of Unions Supplying Electricity (FUSE), which was supported by the TUC.

The fight against ESI privatization was less public than the water campaign, and did not catch popular imagination in the same way. Again Margaret Thatcher acknowledged the problems with selling off this industry, 'the most technically and politically difficult privatization'.[87] The minister in charge, Cecil Parkinson, was sufficiently in the Thatcher mould to be relied upon to sell at any price with no real safeguards. His views were clear: 'The nationalized industries were trade-union dominated and chronically overmanned; the customer was at the bottom of their list of priorities. All too often it appeared that industries were being run for the benefit of the workforce and that the customer was merely a necessary evil.'[88] The actual difficulties in the case of the ESI were great indeed, supplemented by Lord Marshall's fierce opposition. Harking back to the government's investment in defeating the miners in 1984, Parkinson later revealed: 'Although privatization of electricity dominated my time at the Department of Energy, it was my announcement of another privatization which most pleased the 1988 Conservative Party Conference . . . the coal industry.'[89]

---

[83] M. Thatcher, *The Downing Street Years* (London: Harper Collins, 1993), 682.
[84] Lawson, *The View from No. 11*, 230–4.   [85] *NN*, 18 Mar. 1988, 7.
[86] *NALGO Annual Report 1988*, 52.   [87] Thatcher, *The Downing Street Years*, 682.
[88] C. Parkinson, *Right at the Centre* (London: Weidenfeld & Nicolson, 1992), 259.
[89] Ibid. 280.

Once again economic theory and political practice did not match. Various academics tried to argue that electricity supply was not a natural monopoly, despite the evident lack of competition when it was in private hands, as in the USA.[90] Various reports of the MMC prepared the ground.[91] Again, private ownership ran against the tide of history of the industry in Britain. By the 1870s the large town municipalities took on the essential task of ensuring supplies of gas, water, and electricity to local industry and citizens. Electricity supply created the lighting in homes, streets, and workplaces essential for modern life; and only through the capital investment of local authorities was it possible to provide the developments needed to create a modern public transport system of railways and trams. One historian of the industry concluded that 'electricity supply and tramways were both run cheaply and well by the corporations'.[92] After the Second World War its fate was similar to other utilities, with reorganizations aimed at streamlining the structure under the CEGB and supporting investment. This underpinned the union's case, as explained to us by electricity national officer Mike Jeram: 'We argued it's like an integrated supply system and that if you break that up you will bring about dis-economies of scale, unnecessary duplication . . . and additional costs.' By the time of its sell-off there were virtually no commentators, experts, employees, or customers in favour. But this was no deterrent to the government, despite fears surrounding nuclear power generation, especially after Chernobyl.

From the union position, the best that could be done in practice, besides attacking the dominant thinking of market-force ideology, was to secure redundancy agreements and to protect the integrity of the collective bargaining system. Mike Jeram told a conference of branch activists: 'NALGO's fundamental job in the private sector will be to negotiate on behalf of its members,' especially as National Power was threatening to break away from the national negotiating machinery after the twelve-month guaranteed period.[93] NALGO's National Electricity Committee campaigned against privatization with the hope of stopping it, while also setting itself a realistic five-point strategy to protect bargaining:

Take whatever steps are necessary to maintain NALGO's position as the major union for NJC staffs. Equip ourselves for negotiating in the private sector. Recruit and retain

[90] W. Primeaux, 'Electricity Supply: An End to Natural Monopoly', in C. Veljanovski (ed.), *Privatization and Competition* (London: IEA, 1989), 129–34.

[91] MMC, *The Revenue Collection Systems of Four Area Electricity Boards*, Cmnd 9427 (London: HMSO, 1985); MMC, *North of Scotland Hydro-Electric Board*, Cmnd 9628 (London: HMSO, 1985).

[92] I. Byatt, *The British Electricity Industry 1875–1944* (Oxford: Clarendon Press, 1979), 204.

[93] *PS* (Mar. 1989), 12.

our members in the private sector and including new areas into which the company may diversify. Encourage members to participate in the union and stand as representatives and branch officers. Review branch organisation to ensure that we are giving members the service they want.[94]

A working party put its proposals for a new branch structure before electricity branch secretaries at a meeting in December. Similarly pragmatic approaches were adopted at the TUC, which organized a conference on the issue and then drew up a report 'highlighting the effects [of privatization] on power manufacturing and industry in general, the damaging effects on the coal industry, and the impact on the nuclear industry'. The TUC's position was supported by Labour's Shadow Energy Spokesperson Tony Blair.[95]

The Last Throw of the National Pay Bargaining Dice?

National bargaining after the election

The history of this union, like all others, is dominated by the cycle of collective bargaining. The annual round of drafting and submitting claims, and then getting down to bargaining, which may include strikes, lock-outs, and arbitration, remain at the heart of unionism. Collective bargaining is the main motor of union activity, and when it changes then so do union activity and union organization. Structural changes in bargaining have great significance for union leaders and activists. However, the essential nature of the bargaining round lives on. An impressive combination of knowledge and skills, both technical and political, is required to frame and pursue a claim. The need for open debate, whether about profits or productivity, recruitment and retention, comparability or cost of living, indicates the real democracy in unions.

A wave of pay settlements followed the general election. Both gas and electricity staff settled for 5.6 per cent, a couple of percentage points off the going rate in the country. Other groups settled for less as the pressure built up to secure something. So water staff accepted 5 per cent, against their national committee's recommendation, A&C grades in the NHS reluctantly settled for 5 per cent despite its failure to address the problems of low pay, and British Waterways staff accepted 5 per cent after talks at ACAS failed to shift management's position. In local government there was serious talk of reforming the negotiating machinery and introducing flexibility, in line with both the logic of subcontracting and the squeeze on council budgets through rate-capping: 'At the end of July Labour-led local authority employers and union leaders reached outline agreement on a radical pay, flexibility and regrading

---

[94] *NN*, 28 Apr. 1989, 4–5.   [95] *TUC Annual Report 1989*, 243.

deal for one million council manual workers.'[96] This foreshadowed the same approach for white-collar staff, held back by the strike in 1989 (see Box 12) but completed in the 1997 Single Status Agreement.

The 1988 round began around Easter time. Water staff wanted 'a substantial percentage increase on all salary points reflecting the staffs' contribution to the success of the water industry', along with two days' extra basic leave and progress on hours of work and shifts.[97] Gas staff asked for 'a substantial common percentage increase on all salary points' along with a reduction in the working week and longer holidays.[98] Claims in transport and the university sector addressed the issue of low pay. Electricity staff were asked by their national committee to accept the employers' offer on the long-standing claim for schedule B staff in shops: 'On the plus side the proposals improve the salary position of a substantial number of members, free the supervisors grading structure . . . introduces an improved holiday formula . . . On the negative side, local negotiations over the introduction of new technology will be more difficult.'[99] Local government APT&C staff called for a 10 per cent rise, while colleagues working in the New Towns put in a demand 'for a substantial increase for all staff'.[100] Claims for £24 per week for PT'B' NHS staff on Committees B (dental technicians), C (pharmacy technicians), E (other technicians), H (dental therapists), and W (works staff) went in.

These pay claims, coordinated but separate, were submitted against the backdrop of Chancellor Nigel Lawson's budget, which John Daly summarized as 'the greedy have shoved the needy aside'.[101] With falling unemployment and early signs of the Lawson boom, some groups did better than others. Electricity staff rejected a 7 per cent with strings offer, although later it was accepted, and water staff accepted 6.5 per cent. University staff lobbied in London over their pay and rejected a 3 per cent offer, later accepting 5.13 per cent. In early May nurses and PT'A' staff settled for the recommendations of the pay review body of 8.8 per cent, while PT'B' staff rejected a 4.8 per cent offer. Their A&C colleagues rejected 5.5 per cent but settled for that a few weeks later, albeit unhappily: 'this group meeting recognises that the management side's offer to A&C staff fails to tackle the problem of low pay; fails to restore the ground lost relative to other groups of workers in the economy as a whole and within the NHS itself; and contains no improvements in respect of working hours or annual leave' (see Tables 2.5–2.15).[102]

In local government the national committee took a hard line on APT&C pay:

[96] E. Heerey, 'Chronicle: Industrial Relations in the United Kingdom April–July 1987', *British Journal of Industrial Relations*, 25/3 (1987), 443.

[97] *NN*, 4 Mar. 1988, 5. [98] Ibid., 11 Mar. 1988, 5. [99] Ibid., 4 Mar. 1988, 5.

[100] Ibid., 18 Mar. 1988, 4. [101] Ibid. 1. [102] *NALGO Annual Report 1988*, 57.

Delegates to NALGO's local government group meeting on 26 July will be asked to reject an offer of 5.4% pay rises for council white collar staff. But in a report to the meeting, the local government committee warns that rejection has to be backed by 'serious' industrial action. Token gestures and calls for further negotiations will be 'pointless' it says. Arbitration is spurned as unlikely to result in 'significant increases' and as setting the pattern for future claims. The committee calls for a ballot on a pro-gramme of industrial action including a national one-day strike at the end of September and further two-day strikes by NALGO districts in October.[103]

Facing strong counter-propaganda from the employers, the union took the view that 'this blatant attempt to interfere in the internal democratic processes of NALGO will prove counter-productive'.[104] Sure enough the delegates voted by 327,235 to 123,636 on a card vote to reject the employers' offer and the union began campaigning for a strike vote. The General Secretary sent an open letter to all local-government members: 'I urge you during the coming ballot to read our publicity material carefully and to attend branch meetings called to discuss the matter—and to vote YES in the ballot.'[105] However, the vote went against strike action by 56 per cent to 44 per cent, on a 60 per cent turnout. South Wales District achieved a majority in support of the strike, and the closeness of the vote in other districts was recognized by the delegates at the reconvened meeting:

This group meeting notes the narrow defeat in the ballot for industrial action on the 1988 APT&C pay claim. The group meeting recognises, however, that the strength of feeling shown by the membership in the ballot provides a platform for a vigorous campaign in 1989 to achieve the twin objectives of eradicating low pay and restoring APT&C pay levels in comparison to other groups of workers.[106]

Delegates accepted the 5.6 per cent offer, but the scene was set for the major mobilization to come in 1989 (see Box 12).

A national union fighting local issues

The focus of union resistance shifted inexorably to the local level after the election, as local employers implemented the cuts imposed by central gov-ernment. Cuts in local government were laid at the door of central govern-ment: 'local government continued its unequal struggle to provide adequate services for their local communities within the restrictive financial arrange-ments.'[107] Local collective bargaining continued to grow in importance, requiring action to defend members on four types of issue in particular: cuts and subsequent job losses; attacks on conditions of service; efforts to win

[103] *NN*, 15 July 1988, 1.   [104] Ibid., 22 July 1988, 2.   [105] Ibid., 12 Aug. 1988, 2.
[106] Ibid., 7 Oct. 1988, 2.   [107] *NALGO Annual Report 1988*, 27.

regrading for low-paid groups; and protection of activists and agreements from management. NALGO members, often along with members of other public-service unions and their supporters from the wider labour movement and local communities, took up the fight.

Some disputes were mainly concerned with the impact of financial cuts on staff and the services they were able to provide to the public. Management locked out home-care organizers in Islington when they refused to move offices because of fears that it would result in a worse service to the public, especially the sick and elderly. There was a one-day stoppage over staffing levels by forty staff at the chief executive's office in Lambeth.

Anti-cuts demonstrations and strikes became a constant feature of reports in *NALGO News*: 'Some 2000 people demonstrated outside Haringey London borough civic offices last Thursday in protest over £15 million cuts and the prospect of more to come next April. The NALGO demonstrators who had been on strike for the day, were joined by women's groups and child care campaigners.'[108] Like many other actions, this was officially endorsed by the union: 'The Chairperson of the NEC, after consultation with the General Secretary, authorised . . . the branch to participate in a day of action on 22 October 1987 in protest at the authority implementing cuts without prior consultation.'[109] There was a one-day strike by 2,000 staff in Brent over cuts, 1,500 demonstrated at Waltham Forest, and another 1,000 demonstrated against cuts in Camden.

Staff in Camden and Lewisham held one-day strikes supported by local community and client groups, and in Birmingham there was joint action with NUPE and the West Midlands Pensioners' Convention to save four old people's homes. NUPE, GMB, and NALGO members took a one-day stoppage to lobby Gateshead Council over cuts and privatization plans for the parks department. There was a lobby of Westminster Council to oppose its massive privatization programme, followed by a one-day strike by 2,000 NALGO members in protest over the selling-off of 11,000 council homes. The action was supported by local tenants, and Sheila Brass, NALGO branch secretary, told the strikers that 'the success of today is that it is the first time we have stood together with tenants on an issue of joint concern to us'.[110] In Malvern, a joint NALGO–NUPE picket stood alongside residents protesting against the sell-off of local-authority homes. These were just some examples of widespread action by members in a desperate bid to persuade councils to minimize the impact of the central government's rundown of local services.

---

[108] *NN*, 30 Oct. 1987, 3.
[109] *NALGO Emergency Committee Meeting Minutes*, 16 (1987), 156.
[110] *NN*, 25 Sept. 1987, 1.

Fights against threatened redundancies took on a higher profile, as councils used threats of mass sackings to escape from the constraints of collective agreements. In Camden members voted against an all-out strike over compulsory redeployment (42 per cent yes to 58 per cent no), but in Lewisham there was a one-day strike by 2,500 NALGO members in support of thirty-seven members out on indefinite strike over compulsory redundancies. *NALGO News* reported on the fight in Brent:

NALGO members could face compulsory redundancy in the wake of the latest wave of cost cutting by Brent council in north London. Hundreds of jobs are to be axed as the council seeks to chop its budget by £16.2 million by 1 September. The authority's ruling Labour group is to meet on Sunday and will discuss whether or not to go for mass sackings. Administrative, clerical, and teaching staff are likely to bear the brunt of redundancies, whether forced or voluntary.[111]

With a three-to-one majority in favour of one-day strikes, 'the chairperson of the NEC, after consultation with the General Secretary, authorised the action without reimbursement for any loss of income incurred from National funds'.[112] Over 1,000 white-collar jobs were to be axed, and that decision of the council sparked a call for a ballot on indefinite strike action. This was rescinded after the council removed the threat of compulsory redundancies.

In Bradford, Councillor Pickles made proposals for swingeing cuts backed up with a direct attack on national conditions of service, reported in *NALGO News*. 'The Pickles proposals include replacing council bargaining structures with local negotiations between unions and managers; performance-related pay for directors; the loss of at least 2,500 jobs; and savings of more than £5 million a year.'[113] As a result, 'union members went on strike for the afternoon and a crowded rally in the city's St George's Hall was addressed by NALGO assistant general secretary Dave Prentis and three local Labour MPs. More than 3,000 people lobbied councillors before the council meeting.'[114] Later, 'A national one day strike in support of Bradford NALGO and other branches fighting cuts was demanded by delegates to the union's reconvened local government group meeting . . . national committee leader Jim White pledged that every penny in NALGO's £16.25 million strike fund would be used to beat Bradford if necessary.'[115] Bradford Branch engaged Services to Community Action and Trade Unions (SCAT) to write up its experiences, publishing *The Bradford Experiment: Counting the Cost* in 1990.

Meanwhile, branch activists continued the routine of defending members' workplace rights. In Brent housing department a strike over safe working

---

[111] Ibid., 5 Aug. 1988, 1.
[112] *NALGO Emergency Committee Meeting Minutes*, 17 (London: NALGO, 1988), 195.
[113] *NN*, 14 Oct. 1988, 1.   [114] Ibid., 28 Oct. 1988, 1.   [115] Ibid., 4 Nov. 1988, 1.

conditions in the housing department lasted four months until the council offered a deal. This was over the problem of safety screens, demanded by staff dealing with desperate homeless people angry at inadequate help and likely to take it out on the only people in authority they saw, NALGO members. In Southampton City Council a two-day strike by housing benefit staff over violence at work resulted in improved safety. In a dispute with larger implications, NALGO won an equal pay victory for sixty-six social services staff in Avon.

The emergency committee approved action after 'a request was received from the [Tyne and Wear PTE] branch . . . for members previously balloted and employed by Busways Travel Service to undertake a programme of industrial action'.[116] *NALGO News* reported: 'United action by Nalgo bus staff has won recognition for overtime, holiday and shift work. Overworked staff were putting in up to 73 hours a week as competition gripped following deregulation.'[117] After the threat of a total overtime ban, the employer made an offer in recognition of the long and unsocial hours worked by the staff. The local press reported the anarchy that had resulted from deregulation as told to them by a rival operator: 'They have just flooded the place with buses . . . This has just killed our trade point blank.'[118]

Local flexibility within a nationally negotiated framework provided further opportunities for local union action, as with the nationally agreed 'groundbreaking equal opportunities guidelines for local authorities'[119] in local government in 1987. The NHS clinical regrading exercise for nurses and midwives also provided a basis for local decisions, resulting in some 100,000 appeals against grading decisions made by managers by January 1989. There were 500 appeals lodged at one health authority alone, and the resulting backlog clogged up NHS management time and stimulated union action—for example, there was a protest march in Winchester, organized by the TUC, against the new grading structure implemented by Wessex RHA. NALGO and the other NHS unions issued detailed advice to officers and stewards dealing with cases on the principles and practices involved. Regrading became part of efforts by health managers, acting under orders from the government, to alter skill and grade mix in an attempt to reduce wage bills without cutting pay rates.

For the union the regrading claim provided a focus for action over low pay. Management attacks on grading structures further entrenched the traditional structure of the internal labour market, trapping thousands of low-paid women clerical workers in low-grade ghettos, a blunt instrument for under-

---

[116] *NALGO Emergency Committee Meeting Minutes*, 16 (1987), 94.
[117] *NN*, 4 Sept. 1987, 1.   [118] *Evening Chronicle*, 8 July 1987, 3.
[119] *NN*, 11 Dec. 1987, 1.

mining national pay awards and payment systems. NALGO responded by taking up the cause of the low paid, winning popular support, recruiting new members, and persuading more members to be active. Nursery nurses waged a national campaign based on local action for promotion opportunities and upgradings. In Haringey, for example, they took action in July 1987 along with welfare assistants, and Sheffield nursery nurses voted to strike over their grades later in the year. Nursery nurses in dispute with Bradford Metropolitan Borough voted to take industrial action and hold rallies during Bradford's showcase Education Week. As a result, the council backed down and made an offer on improved conditions and grades. Even when there was a new national agreement in 1989, incorporating a new grade definition and assimilation onto a new main grade, NALGO warned nursery nurses that some employers might seek to alter their duties in order to classify them as outside the new grades and pay scales.

Over 300 housing staff in Birmingham took indefinite strike action over pay and regrading issues. This escalated into a one-day strike by 7,000 Birmingham Branch members in support of their low-paid clerical colleagues. Later, in 1989, 150 staff in Birmingham's housing benefit office came out on strike over their regrading demands. Branch secretary Nick Hay said: 'Members' patience has run out. Management have neither negotiated seriously nor taken the threat of industrial action seriously . . . this situation indicates that industrial relations in Birmingham city council are in complete shambles.'[120] The council used the local press to hit back at NALGO: 'Birmingham council leader, councillor Dick Knowles, today accused "a giant union" behind the two strikes of hitting the poorest people in the city.'[121] This did not prevent the action from winning the support of the national union, which approved 'a request . . . for members employed in the Housing Benefit Section and previously balloted to take indefinite strike action with strike pay at the rate of £50 per week from National funds in support of their regrading claim'.[122]

Back in the NHS, other groups fought over their grades. At North Manchester General Hospital 200 clerical and secretarial staff went on strike for half a day, angered by both the low pay offer nationally and the employers' proposals on flexible pay and regrading. This was followed by a picket in London at the DHSS over the NHS pay offer to A&C grades. As one picket put it, 'we are considered the lowest of the low but we are part of the health care team too'.[123] The long-running battle over regrading for medical secretaries and medical records staff continued. In Shotley Bridge, Durham, thirty-five

---

[120] Ibid., 7 Apr. 1989, 3.   [121] *Birmingham Evening Mail*, 3 Apr. 1989, 4.
[122] *NALGO Emergency Committee Meeting Minutes*, 18 (London: NALGO, 1989), 18.
[123] *NN*, 18 Sept. 1987, 1.

staff went on strike over regrading and the refusal of management to go to independent arbitration, ending after nine weeks when North West Durham Health Authority agreed to an ACAS nominee to chair the appeals panel. In Coventry seventy-seven medical secretaries won a major victory after six weeks on strike, and others in Tameside Health Authority reached an important agreement after a year of action when the employer agreed to both regrading and progression through the scales to management jobs. Thirty-seven medical secretaries took strike action after their long-running dispute over grades had come to nothing at the Raigmore Hospital in Inverness. Eighty medical records staff were locked out by management at University Hospital Cardiff, following limited industrial action taken against low pay, poor conditions, and severe understaffing problems. These and other disputes, even though some were lost, provided some hope for NALGO NHS members engaged in a long-term struggle for better pay and the recognition of the relative importance of their work in the total health-care service (see Box 15 for more detail on the medical secretaries).

Local struggles over regradings and cutbacks often turned into defences of union rights. In Leicester City Council's housing department 350 members went on strike in October 1987, winning the reinstatement of a colleague after he had taken limited industrial action in line with NALGO policy. The original dispute arose because the 'procedure by which the vacant posts in the Housing Directorate have been created was contrary to all agreements', and this resulted in a ballot of members of the housing department to boycott certain tasks and 'to take strike action if necessary in support of any member who may be disciplined as a consequence of this action'.[124] The situation was made worse by a report critical of staff and NALGO members deliberately leaked to the *Leicester Mercury*.[125]

In a strikingly similar dispute in 1989 housing staff in Dundee went into dispute over 'management's proposals to breach an existing agreement on the application of salary scales'. As a result, they 'undertook a rolling programme of strike action of 3 days per week in protest at management's decision to grade 22 temporary posts GS1/2'. In the run-up to the strike local councillors and NALGO activists used the local press to put their respective cases. Under the headline 'Three Day Strike Set to Hit Services' the *Dundee Courier and Advertiser* reported: 'It was announced by Nalgo officials yesterday that all Dundee District Housing officers and housing services will be disrupted by strike action next week following a ballot by Nalgo housing members over the council's proposals to create 22 new jobs to collect the new community

---

[124] *NALGO Emergency Committee Meeting Minutes*, 17 (1988), 37–8.
[125] *Leicester Mercury*, 23 Oct. 1987, 27.

charge.'[126] The council suspended a manager who refused to cross a picket line, and the Emergency Committee gave support: 'as a consequence of the first three days of strike action on 26/28 April 1989 a member was disciplined by the authority and the members in the Department took indefinite strike action which the Chairperson of the Council, after consultation with the General Secretary, made official with strike pay at £50 per week from National funds.'[127] ACAS became involved for conciliation, but not before the dispute 'became more entrenched and bitter after the council suspended 250 NALGO members'.[128] There was an eventual return to work on 17 May.

There were many similar examples: staff at three homes for the mentally handicapped in Camden walked out after a supervisor was suspended for taking industrial action; 450 Glasgow library staff walked out over the suspension of a colleague for following NALGO policy on vacant posts, shutting every library in the city; forty library staff at Swiss Cottage in London stopped work after three colleagues were suspended without pay for refusing to 'help out' in areas where posts had not been filled. Some employers provoked rows by breaking long-standing agreements, such as when Leicester City Council refused 'to deal with a complaint of race and sex discrimination through its grievance procedure'.[129]

One danger of patchy local responses was the potential isolation of those in dispute. For example, the sacking of ILEA activist Tony Marriott was a particularly serious attack, which threatened to undermine the union's strategy of opposing the abolition of ILEA while also fighting for the best deals for staff affected by it.

The last national disputes of the decade—some you win, some you lose

The 1989 pay round got under way as normal, with claims reflecting union policy and with action to support claims reflecting union power. Wider economic and political factors, and the special issues for industrial sectors and occupational groups, also played their usual part. These varying forces can result in widely differing outcomes—this was the year of the local government APT&C strike and the ambulance staffs dispute.

As usual, several pay claims were presented to the employers in the weeks before Easter. University A&C staff claimed 15 per cent, a thirty-five-hour working week, and twenty-five days annual leave as a minimum, under the slogan 'time to fight for a living wage'.[130] The claim for a 'substantial percentage increase' for gas staffs and senior officers reflected 'worrying evidence

---

[126] *Dundee Courier and Advertiser*, 15 Apr. 1989, 4.
[127] *NALGO Emergency Committee Meeting Minutes*, 18 (1989), 10.
[128] *PS* (June 1989), 15.   [129] *NN*, 6 Nov. 1987, 8.   [130] Ibid., 20 Jan. 1989, 4.

that gas staff and senior officers' earnings have fallen behind the increase in earnings and . . . there is also a sharp rise in the cost of living'.[131] Staff in the soon to be privatized water industry claimed a substantial pay increase to combat the special problems of low pay, recruitment, and retention, and to account for the radical change and reorganization of the sector. New Towns staff put in for 14 per cent, NHS A&C staff asked for 10 per cent or £15 to counter low morale and high turnover,[132] and this was the basis of the ambulance staff claim for a substantial increase to maintain differentials. British Waterways Board (BWB) staff claimed 10 per cent to reflect the success of the organization as well as to be above both inflation and average earnings, and electricity staff demanded 'a substantial pay increase, no less favourable than awards in other parts of the electricity industry and other areas of the economy'.[133] The range and specificity of the claims reflect the negotiators' best guess of what would encourage members to act and what might persuade employers to negotiate in good faith.

Most negotiations dragged on to early summer, when gas staff were the first to settle for 7.75 per cent, followed by water staff for 8.75 per cent. NHS A&C grades accepted a complex restructuring offer with pay costed at 9.5 per cent but which divided activists over the fear that the higher grades would benefit at the expense of entrenching a low-pay ghetto at the bottom of the scales. Later in the year BWB staff accepted 8 per cent as the best deal available without industrial action, and most NHS PT'B' staff reluctantly agreed one of the lowest deals on offer at 6.5 per cent. PT'B' technicians did rather better, at 8.5–9 per cent with improvements to grading structures. The employers' 'final' offer of 8.3 per cent for APT&C staff in colleges and polytechnics was readily accepted, especially as there was extra benefit for those on low pay. A&C staff in universities settled for the going rate at 7.7–8.2 per cent. The range of settlements, whether won easily or with greater difficulty, reflected wider economic variables such as inflation and average earnings.

Events in local government caught the imagination and dominated 1989, when APT&C staff rejected successive offers and moved towards a national strike, as reported in *The Times*:

Industrial action by over 500,00 local government workers is likely to plunge Britain's town halls into chaos next month in the next major challenge to government pay policies in the 'summer of discontent' . . . Mr Jim White, NALGO's chief negotiator, said last night that if no negotiations were likely after the three-day walkout, a ballot for indefinite action would probably follow.[134]

[131] Ibid., 3 Feb. 1989, 4.
[132] NALGO, *I Can't Afford to Work Here Any More: The Recruitment and Retention of Administrative and Clerical Staff in the NHS* (London: NALGO, 1989).
[133] *NN*, 5 May 1989, 6.   [134] *The Times*, 28 June 1989, 2.

Six days of strikes, on 4, 11, 12, 18, 19 and 20 July, were supported in the historic yes vote, with 186,365 (59 per cent) in favour and 128,132 (41 per cent) against on a 62 per cent turnout. On 4 July half a million members went on strike and over 10,000 lobbied the employers, convinced that their leader, Keith Sonnet, was right when he said 'Once again the employers have treated the negotiations with contempt'.[135] As the strike took hold, Mrs Thatcher attacked the union in the House of Commons and members responded with a mass show of unity. After the six days the employers called for new talks but could not reach a settlement. Indefinite strikes started, after local ballots of staff in computers, rates offices, treasurers' departments, and others. Local strikes kept the pressure on employers, and soon the employers gave in. NALGO won a famous victory, with an 8.8 per cent increase without strings and more for the lower paid. Details of the issues behind the strike, and of the strike itself, are given in Box 12.

Box 12. NALGO and the Local Government Strike 1989

NALGO's biggest mobilization took place in the summer of 1989, involving all 500,000 members in local government in short strikes, with tens of thousands taking indefinite strike action. As with the comparability dispute of 1980, this was the culmination of pay problems that had been building up over several years. It was also a response to employer moves to weaken national conditions of employment by introducing a degree of 'flexibility' to the pay scales. The conduct of the strike reflected careful planning, campaigning, and leadership at both national and branch levels to lay the groundwork for a resounding victory. The sheer scale of the action is confirmed by the government's statistics—it accounted for over half of all the 'days lost' through strikes in Britain that year.

The NLGC had adopted the practice of consulting on the claim through delegate meetings at district level, aiming to draw up a claim that balanced the views of different sections of the membership. Their 1989 consultation paper argued that a 17 per cent increase on the pay bill was needed to bring the 1984 arbitration average pay level into line with movements in average earnings. Forty per cent of APT&C staff (about 250,000 FTEs) earned less than the Council of Europe's 'decency-threshold' measure of low pay. The NLGC re-rehearsed the arguments about straight percentage, flat rate, or mixed claims, trying to satisfy two priorities: eradicating low pay and restoring pay levels in comparison to other groups of workers.

The agreed claim, for £1,200 or 12 per cent, whichever was highest, was submitted earlier than usual, in January, reflecting the NLGC's aim to build a campaigning momentum. The employers' initial offer of 6 per cent was conditional on the abolition of all national grades, abolition of provincial and national grading appeals, relaxation of the national standards on working time and unsocial hours payments, and

---

[135] *NN*, 7 July 1989, 1.

performance-related incremental progression. This was guaranteed to provoke a hostile reaction; deputy national officer Dennis Reed condemned it as 'an insult'. When the employers increased the offer by only 1 per cent, retaining all the other conditions except for performance increments, the NLGC began campaigning anew. In fact the 1989 campaign was really a continuation of the previous year's work.

The employers' conditions, quickly dubbed the 'strings', gave massive impetus to the campaign. NLGC chair Jim White told the group meeting delegates that the 'strings represent the most dangerous and insidious attack on conditions of service of APT&C staff since the national agreement was first constituted in 1947'.[136] He said that, if the employers got away with this round of changes, they would be back the next year to attack other national provisions: 'We must take them on, beat them, and demonstrate that we are not a soft touch.' The mood of the members had changed, with 60 per cent voting in favour of a one-day all-out strike on 4 July, two consecutive days in the following week, and three consecutive days the week after that—the first ever vote for a national strike of council white-collar staff. This was backed up with a national demonstration on 6 June, when the scheduled NJC meeting lasted for only ten minutes before breaking up without agreement. Ten thousand members had marched past the employers' London headquarters in Belgrave Square, accompanied by three bands. However as national officer Keith Sonnet said: 'the employers refused to budge.'[137]

Branches aimed to mount pickets at all of the thousands of workplaces with striking members, from the smallest library and primary school to the largest town hall and civic centre. Branch picket officers drew up rotas that involved every single member, and acquired mobile phones to organize and deploy flying pickets. The strike unleashed a torrent of creativity, as members entered into the spirit of struggle. Picket lines carried out their serious task of isolating the few strike-breakers (mainly managers) who vainly pretended that services were operating. But there was also plenty of humour, through picket-line stunts, entertainments, and various activities that boosted the morale of the pickets and brought the dispute to the public's attention.

As the employers stood by their refusal to talk for the duration of the all-out strike programme, the members' anger intensified. A wave of indefinite stoppages started as groups of members queued up to be balloted and called out, and the NLGC prepared to run a national ballot for further all-out stoppages. Branches selected key staff, especially those involved in collecting money for the employer, to take local strike action on full pay. These actions cost Leeds and Manchester City Councils £1 million or more each week. The closure of the Tyne tunnel to all but emergency vehicles cost the strikers' employer £100,000 per week. Some 15,000 members in 325 branches joined in the indefinite stoppages of work.

It soon dawned on strikebound local authorities that they had bitten off more than they could chew. The employers returned to the bargaining table, letting go of the strings and increasing their offer to 8.8 per cent, weighted slightly towards the lower paid.

---

[136] *NN*, 2 June 1989, 1.   [137] Ibid., 7 July 1989, 1.

There was some fuss over return to work deals, and there was a nasty dispute in Tower Hamlets where the branch secretary, Derek Relph, was charged with gross misconduct following incidents on a picket line. More than 2,500 members went out on indefinite strike after a vote in favour of 1,276 against 435, successfully defending him against the charges after four weeks on strike. Some employers backed down over harsh deductions of strikers' pay after local action in Liverpool, Port Talbot, and Sefton.

But more serious issues were raised over the fate of strike-breakers. The delegate meeting that ratified the pay agreement also sought to discipline members who crossed picket lines. As *The Times* noted, 'The National and Local Government Officers' Association intends to become the first union to challenge the Employment Act, 1988, by taking action against its own strike breakers.'[138] The outcome was bad for the union; as *The Times* smugly noted, 'Britain's biggest town hall union may have to pay compensation of more than £300,000 to members who were disciplined after defying an instruction not to cross picket lines during a pay dispute last summer. An industrial tribunal has ruled that the National and Local Government Officers' Association acted unlawfully against 11 members in South Tyneside.'[139]

The victory in local government, involving two-thirds of the union's members, took an enormous effort of will and resources. The leadership, supported by activists and members, kept its nerve and won the pay dispute, but it did not neglect other members and other struggles. The autumn saw another major public-sector dispute, in the ambulance service.[140] But this time, despite a courageous and popular fight, the action was lost. The consequences of this defeat for the future of the service were more severe than even the most fearful government critics could forecast.

Ambulance officers and control staff, mostly NALGO members, voted to join the overtime ban already started by ambulance drivers, mostly NUPE members, after rejecting a 6.5 per cent pay offer. Underlining the threat to the integrity of the public-sector emergency service, the Northumbria ambulance service was set to become the first NHS Trust. The ambulance dispute became more vicious as the government stood firm, rejecting both union calls for arbitration and the growing popular support for the union case shown at demonstrations in London. Many saw the links with privatization, and deeply held passions and fears ran under the surface of this difficult dispute. The role of the ambulance staff in great public disasters, such as at Hillsborough football stadium earlier in the year, added to the large-scale public support, but the government's overriding concern was to drive down costs before setting up

---

[138] *The Times*, 23 Aug. 1989, 4.   [139] Ibid., 12 Dec. 1989, 4.
[140] A. Kerr and S. Sachdev, 'Third among Equals: An Analysis of the 1989 Ambulance Dispute', *British Journal of Industrial Relations*, 30/1 (1992), 127–43.

self-governing Trusts. The government decided to tough it out. Some health authorities responded to union action to handle only emergency work by locking out the staff and refusing to pay their wages. The TUC organized a rally in Trafalgar Square on 13 January 1990, attended by 40,000, and there were regional events on 30 January. Eventually the ambulance crews, controllers, and officers were driven back to normal working in February 1990, with an agreement that fell far short of the union's objectives. However, the hardline approach taken by the Prime Minister and her Cabinet made them even more unpopular and certainly played a part in Mrs Thatcher's personal downfall.

Concluding Remarks

These thirty months after the 1987 election saw momentous changes and political turmoil. Privatization took over, irrespective of its competitive virtues. In water and electricity supply, as earlier with gas, the substantial case against privatization was ignored, resulting in grossly inefficient outcomes, a generally worse service to customers, and a sharp deterioration in employee rights. Structural and managerial reforms also were put in place in the public services. In health, education, and local government the false goals of market competition were promulgated together with the linked objectives of efficiency and management power, as identified in several studies: in health, 'cash-limited, manager-led efficiency';[141] in education, 'another theme present during this period was the strengthening of management and the accompanying weakening of the power of the professionals and their trade unions';[142] and 'local government is being transformed from a provider of public services to an enabling agency facilitating, regulating and supporting a wide range of public and private institutions in meeting local needs'.[143]

This generated a continual stream of local disputes around large and small issues, arising from the everyday reality of work and from workers' experience of work. Constant efforts to humanize the workplace, and to counter the management techniques lifted from the pages of management texts, provide a wellspring of creativity as workers try to gain and regain control over the conditions of their working lives, through their trade unions. The endless lists of actions throughout all the industrial sectors, regions, and occupations

---

[141] I. Kendall and G. Moon, 'Health Policy', in S. Savage and L. Robins (eds.), *Public Policy under Thatcher* (London: Macmillan, 1990), 115.

[142] M. McVicar, 'Education Policy', in Savage and Robins (eds.), *Public Policy under Thatcher*, 136.

[143] S. Horton, 'Local Government, 1979–1989', in Savage and Robins (eds.), *Public Policy under Thatcher*, 172.

covered by NALGO tells us more surely about the pressures on managers to slash and cut, and about the nature and purpose of trade unionism, than either the dry academic portrayals of rational economic actors or the snide media commentators' attacks on union barons and restrictive practices.

A list of just a few NALGO actions being taken as the 1980s drew to a close gives an idea of the range of methods and devices that are practised by all unions responding to the needs of workers in trouble: solidarity with the GCHQ unions at their march and rallies; forcing Bradford Council to back away from redundancies; a strike by Brent social workers; protests by nurses over regradings in Manchester and Croydon; negotiations over redeployment schemes in the National Rivers Authority and over a pay deal for airport workers; union representation for individual members like Marion Gaima, successfully protected from deportation; improving union self-government, with new committee structures for women, disabled, black, and lesbian and gay members, and the new structure for members in colleges and polytechnics. Finally, the union maintained its activity in the wider political arena, arguing the union cases against the privatization of the water and electricity supply industries; against the Widdicombe proposals and the subsequent government White Paper on the conduct of business and the democratic process in local government; and, at the STUC women's conference in Perth, supporting a Scottish assembly and opposing the poll tax.

The first two and a half years of the Thatcher government's third term saw more important changes to industries in which NALGO members worked than in the whole of the previous decade. In local government a combination of cash limits supported by rate-capping and CCT weakened the basis of local democracy, undermined the national elements of the system including pay bargaining, and sent services into a spiral of decline. The best efforts of the union stopped the most extreme Tory plans in some councils, and maintained the form of national bargaining. In the NHS the push to decentralization and liberalization continued, with NALGO members in A&C grades more vulnerable than professional staff, who were partially protected by review bodies and by greater public support. With privatization of the utilities went the collapse of national bargaining and the rise of company-level negotiations. All of this was set against the failure of the government to control the new inflationary surge driven by its own policies. Storms had exposed the frailty of market economics, and the scene was now set for the first major crisis for the Conservatives in the Thatcher years, a crisis so deep that it split the party and resulted in its crushing defeat in 1997. Certainly NALGO played a part in the downfall of the Prime Minister and the subsequent loss of faith in her brand of Conservatism. But yet more damage was still to be done to the public sector, to working people's lives, and to their trade unions.

Appendix

TABLE 7.1. NALGO membership, 30 September 1987

District	Number of branches (1)	Voting members (2)	Members in arrears (3)	Membership of branches excluded from voting (4)	Total ordinary membership (cols. 2–4) (5)	Retired (6)	Student (7)	Unemployed (8)	Honorary (9)	Total membership (cols. 5–9) (10)	Total membership 30 Sept. 1986 (11)	Increase-decrease (12)	Increase/decrease (%) (13)
Eastern	116	43,524	15	884	44,423	6,624	7	34	—	51,088	51,341	−253	−0.49
East Midland	99	43,946	27	179	44,152	5,017	6	35	—	49,210	48,459	+751	+1.55
Metropolitan	142	88,413	118	7,591	96,122	14,320	54	68	—	110,564	108,254	+2,310	+2.13
North Eastern	77	39,831	37	—	39,868	2,583	4	9	—	42,464	41,354	+1,110	+2.68
North Western and North Wales	132	107,766	10	122	107,898	9,986	29	132	—	118,045	115,985	+2,060	+1.78
Scottish	115	77,192	60	237	77,489	2,185	4	11	—	79,689	78,763	+926	+1.18
South Eastern	98	35,476	127	404	36,007	7,534	14	35	—	43,590	44,515	−925	−2.08
Southern	82	30,195	2	3,578	33,775	5,077	9	9	—	38,870	39,236	−366	−0.93
South Wales	85	31,185	8	819	32,012	2,476	4	1	—	34,493	34,211	+282	+0.82
South Western	97	42,214	5	1,649	43,868	5,045	8	25	—	48,946	48,500	+446	+0.92
West Midland	95	59,439	2	7,169	66,610	7,828	7	23	—	74,468	74,190	+278	+0.37
Yorkshire and Humberside	77	62,347	0	287	62,634	4,679	15	18	—	67,346	65,615	+1,731	+2.64
Honorary members									7	7	7		—
TOTAL	1,215	661,528	411	22,919	684,858	73,354	161	400	7	758,780	750,430	+8,350	+1.11

TABLE 7.2. *Allocation of NALGO membership, by service, 30 September 1987*

District	Local government	Gas	Electricity	Health	Transport	Water	New Towns	Port authorities	Universities	Police authorities	Retired	Student, unemployed	Honorary	Total membership
Eastern	31,184	2,545	2,623	3,550	236	2,421	493	15	454	902	6,624	41	—	51,088
East Midland	31,400	3,471	2,431	4,995	310	—	16	—	440	1,089	5,017	41	—	49,210
Metropolitan	73,902	4,863	3,815	7,573	325	3,832	276	—	1,536	—	14,320	122	—	110,564
North Eastern	28,453	2,159	1,792	4,413	603	1,042	179	82	296	849	2,583	13	—	42,464
North Western and North Wales	77,075	5,062	5,427	11,169	1,801	3,369	641	23	1,230	2,101	9,986	161	—	118,045
Scottish	58,289	2,471	3,842	8,222	492	14	1,229	35	1,664	231	2,185	15	—	79,689
South Eastern	23,015	2,978	2,294	4,746	91	1,898	—	15	436	534	7,534	49	—	43,590
Southern	22,184	2,197	2,130	5,077	—	—	456	—	1,005	726	5,077	18	—	38,870
South Wales	20,794	1,740	1,127	3,029	76	2,181	82	—	872	900	2,476	5	—	34,493
South Western	32,475	1,823	2,276	3,712	106	1,994	—	2	526	954	5,045	33	—	48,946
West Midland	45,114	4,689	2,633	7,262	972	3,767	318	—	826	1,029	7,828	30	—	74,468
Yorkshire and Humberside	48,506	1,711	2,768	4,561	1,007	2,194	—	—	1,241	646	4,679	33	—	67,346
Honorary members	—	—	—	—	—	—	—	—	—	—	—	—	7	7
1987 totals	494,023	35,709	33,166	68,877	6,022	22,712	3,690	172	10,526	9,961	73,354	561	7	758,780
Percentages	65.11	4.71	4.37	9.08	0.79	2.99	0.49	0.02	1.39	1.31	9.67	0.07	—	100.00
1986 totals	487,191	38,149	33,743	69,255	6,957	22,077	4,091	166	10,590	9,599	68,038	567	7	750,430
Percentages	64.92	5.08	4.50	9.23	0.93	2.94	0.54	0.02	1.41	1.28	9.07	0.08	—	100.00

TABLE 7.3. *NALGO membership, 30 September 1988*

District	Number of branches	Voting members	Members in arrears	Membership of branches excluded from voting	Total ordinary membership (cols. 2–4)	Retired	Student	Unemployed	Honorary	Total membership (cols. 5–9)	Total membership 30 Sept. 1987	Increase/decrease	Increase/decrease (%)
	(1)	(2)	(3)	(4)	(5)	(6)	(7)	(8)	(9)	(10)	(11)	(12)	(13)
Eastern	118	44,112	12	0	44,124	6,880	6	48	—	51,058	51,088	−30	−0.06
East Midland	100	43,625	30	963	44,618	5,034	10	26	—	49,688	49,210	+478	+0.97
Metropolitan	142	90,730	59	1,745	92,534	14,362	43	133	—	107,072	110,564	−3,492	−3.16
North Eastern	77	39,781	39	36	39,886	2,911	4	15	—	42,786	42,464	+322	+0.76
North Western and North Wales	137	107,600	8	168	107,776	9,740	33	126	—	117,675	118,045	−370	−0.31
Scottish	115	77,981	39	38	78,058	2,228	5	8	—	80,299	79,689	+610	+0.77
South Eastern	99	34,192	30	452	34,674	7,803	16	21	—	42,514	43,590	−1,076	−2.47
Southern	78	32,655	2	384	33,041	4,889	10	14	—	37,954	38,870	−916	−2.36
South Wales	83	31,734	30	373	32,137	2,597	2	3	—	34,739	34,493	+246	+0.71
South Western	96	43,892	6	275	44,173	4,857	10	27	—	49,067	48,946	+121	+0.25
West Midland	91	66,031	6	862	66,899	7,701	7	26	—	74,633	74,468	+165	+0.22
Yorkshire and Humberside	78	62,559	3	111	62,673	41,443	46	13	—	67,175	67,346	−171	−0.25
Honorary members	—	—	—	—	—	—	—	—	41	41	7	+34	—
TOTAL	1,214	674,892	264	5,407	680,563	73,445	192	460	41	754,701	758,780	−4,079	−0.54

TABLE 7.4. *Allocation of NALGO membership, by service, 30 September 1988*

District	Local government	Gas	Electricity	Health	Transport	Water	New Towns	Port authorities	Universities	Police authorities	Retired	Student, unemployed	Honorary	Total membership
Eastern	31,152	2,393	2,502	3,299	336	2,647	331	17	434	1,013	6,880	54	—	51,058
East Midland	31,879	3,295	2,382	5,064	356	0	0	0	423	1,219	5,034	36	—	49,688
Metropolitan	71,769	4,595	3,216	7,239	251	3,923	148	0	1,393	0	14,362	176	—	107,072
North Eastern	28,974	2,129	1,618	4,216	613	980	75	78	279	894	2,911	19	—	42,786
North Western and North Wales	77,614	4,552	5,388	11,097	1,845	3,388	455	29	1,197	2,211	9,740	159	—	117,675
Scottish	60,201	2,387	3,783	8,140	455	16	1,191	33	1,584	268	2,228	13	—	80,299
South Eastern	22,532	2,663	2,129	4,384	84	1,366	536	15	416	549	7,803	37	—	42,514
Southern	22,009	2,071	2,057	4,821	0	95	326	0	917	745	4,889	24	—	37,954
South Wales	2,809	1,685	1,097	3,480	166	2,069	59	0	866	906	2,597	5	—	34,739
South Western	32,716	1,668	2,267	3,591	139	1,957	0	2	536	1,297	4,857	37	—	49,067
West Midland	46,222	4,597	2,579	6,871	915	3,622	234	0	769	1,090	7,701	33	—	74,633
Yorkshire and Humberside	49,102	1,588	2,708	4,281	922	2,181	0	0	1,134	757	4,443	59	—	67,175
Honorary members	—	—	—	—	—	—	—	—	—	—	—	—	41	41
1988 totals	495,979	33,623	31,726	66,483	6,082	22,244	3,355	174	9,948	10,949	73,445	652	41	754,701
Percentages	65.72	4.45	4.20	8.81	0.85	2.94	0.44	0.02	1.31	1.45	9.73	0.08	—	100.00
1987 totals	494,023	35,709	33,166	68,877	6,022	22,712	3,690	172	10,526	9,961	73,354	561	7	758,780
Percentages	65.11	4.71	4.37	9.08	0.79	2.99	0.49	0.02	1.39	1.31	9.67	0.07	—	100.00

TABLE 7.5. *NALGO membership, 30 September 1989*

District	Number of branches (1)	Voting members (2)	Members in arrears (3)	Membership of branches excluded from voting (4)	Total ordinary membership (cols. 2–4) (5)	Retired (6)	Student (7)	Unemployed (8)	Honorary (9)	Total membership (cols. 5–9) (10)	Total membership 30 Sept. 1986 (11)	Increase/decrease (12)	Increase/decrease (%) (13)
Eastern	117	40,715	13	704	41,432	6,250	12	39	—	47,733	51,058	–3,325	–6.51
East Midland	100	44,124	7	499	44,630	5,266	27	17	—	49,940	49,688	+252	+0.51
Metropolitan	142	85,495	317	4,062	89,874	14,810	49	121	—	104,854	107,072	–2,218	–2.07
North Eastern	79	41,599	37	36	41,672	3,069	4	17	—	44,762	42,786	+1,976	+4.62
North Western and North Wales	142	108,357	30	259	108,646	10,381	24	83	—	119,134	117,675	+1,459	+1.24
Scottish	109	79,676	1	102	79,779	2,618	11	20	—	82,428	80,299	+2,129	+2.65
South Eastern	92	32,700	2	302	33,004	7,376	47	29	—	40,456	42,514	–2,058	–4.84
Southern	79	31,275	10	845	32,130	4,827	21	23	—	37,001	37,954	–953	–2.51
South Wales	81	32,089	17	472	32,578	2,633	5	0	—	35,216	34,739	+477	+1.37
South Western	96	42,658	6	655	43,319	4,142	17	224	—	47,702	49,067	–1,365	–2.78
West Midland	89	67,108	19	49	67,176	7,793	9	22	—	75,000	74,633	+367	+0.49
Yorkshire and Humberside	73	61,209	11	0	61,220	4,991	4	21	—	66,236	67,175	–939	–1.40
Honorary members	—	—	—	—	—	—	—	—	40	40	41	–1	–2.43
TOTAL	1,199	667,005	470	7,985	675,460	74,156	230	616	40	750,502	754,701	–4,199	–0.56

288

TABLE 7.6. *Allocation of NALGO membership, by service, 30 September 1989*

District	Local government	Gas	Electricity	Health	Transport	Water	New Towns	Port authorities	Universities	Police authorities	Polytechnic colleges	Retired	Student, unemployed	Total membership
Eastern	29,497	2,260	2,258	3,112	308	2,017	191	14	423	955	397	6,250	51	47,733
East Midland	31,347	3,213	2,286	5,024	308	0	0	0	417	1,254	781	5,266	44	49,940
Metropolitan	68,320	4,434	3,608	6,625	219	3,469	293	0	1,277	0	1,629	14,810	170	104,854
North Eastern	29,887	2,093	1,676	4,149	657	892	43	77	265	886	1,047	3069	21	44,762
North Western and North Wales	77,593	4,379	5,224	10,950	1,690	3,315	315	2.8	1,182	2,128	1,842	10,381	107	119,134
Scottish	62,222	2,316	3,798	7,986	410	19	1,196	3	1,528	271	0	2,618	31	82,428
South Eastern	21,382	2,518	1,924	4,119	82	1,684	0	1.2	415	483	385	7,376	76	40,456
Southern	20,505	2,027	2,010	4,754	0	0	263	0	845	698	1,028	4,827	44	37,001
South Wales	22,556	1,683	1,100	3,387	152	1,850	86	0	803	961	0	2,633	5	35,216
South Western	31,461	1,619	2,276	3,489	124	1,908	0	2	527	1,347	566	4,142	241	47,702
West Midland	45,626	4,409	2,550	6,966	918	3,357	0	0	802	1,078	1,470	7,793	31	75,000
Yorkshire and Humberside	46,793	1,410	2,707	4,081	826	2,367	0	0	1,098	671	1,267	4,991	25	66,236
1989 totals	487,189	32,361	31,417	64,642	5,694	20,878	2,387	166	9,582	10,732	10,412	74,156	846	750,462
Percentages	64.92	4.31	4.19	8.61	0.76	2.78	0.32	0.02	1.28	1.43	1.39	9.88	0.11	100.00
1988 totals	495,979	33,623	31,726	66,483	6,082	22,244	3,355	174	9,948	10,949	—	73,445	652	754,660
Percentages	65.72	4.45	4.20	8.81	0.85	2.94	0.44	0.02	1.31	1.45	—	9.73	0.08	100.00

8

Markets, Managers, and the Merger

T HE new decade started against a backdrop of shattering world events as socialism was dismantled in Central and Eastern Europe, symbolized by the fall of the Berlin Wall in November 1989 and the collapse of the Soviet Union in 1991. Two deep-seated shifts had occurred in the political economy of the UK. First, economic reforms spearheaded by Mrs Thatcher were now well established, and mainstream labour-movement opposition to the principles of market efficiency and private profit reduced in each year that passed. Water was privately owned by the end of 1989, and electricity supply companies were set up by the end of 1990 with National Power and Power-Gen arriving soon after. Education and health reforms were enacted in 1988 and 1990 respectively, coming into operation alongside CCT. NALGO's annual report draws attention to the shrinkage of the public sector: 'By 1989–1990 public expenditure, as a percentage of gross domestic product, had fallen to 38.25% from its 1979 figure of 43.25%. Fifty major businesses and 65% of the nationalised industries have passed to the private sector.'[1] The union's 1990 economic update, published in *NALGO News*, took the gloomy view that 'the scene is set for a hard year which will demonstrate the complete failure of Mrs Thatcher's governments to correct Britain's underlying economic weaknesses'.[2]

The second shift was in response to the social consequences of those attacks on the public sector, stimulating an uncertain alliance between the worst off, the labour aristocracy, and sections of the middle class. An urge to pull back from the abyss was apparent in the debates within NALGO, the TUC, and

---

[1] *NALGO Annual Report 1990* (London: NALGO, 1991), 12.
[2] *NALGO News (NN)*, 16 Feb. 1990, 5.

the Labour Party, over new approaches to public services, to direct government ownership and control, and to economic policy itself. As anti–poll–tax campaigns gathered strength, and entry to the ERM was followed by economic crisis, Mrs Thatcher's popularity continued to wane.

Rita Donaghy's presidential New Year message reflected this, sounding an optimistic note:

It is a remarkable tribute to NALGO's resilience and perseverance that we have not only survived the past decade intact, but also seen it out with a major pay victory in local government and a magnificent campaign by our ambulance members. We have won the debate against water and electricity privatisation and have exposed the attacks on our education and transport services . . . The NALGO/NUPE/COHSE merger, if successful, will form an exciting new union which will be able to offer a massive improvement in strength, service and protection . . . There is a new air of confidence that we can outlast our would-be destroyers and carry our case for more public investment and less private greed.[3]

Aside from this optimism, whether well founded or misplaced, NALGO had established a remarkable unity of purpose—the next few years were characterized by a firm left-of-centre national leadership reflecting, by and large, the views and wishes of the majority of activists. Set within a context of largely stable membership and considerable financial resources, this broad consensus saw the formulation and pursuit of progressive policies across a range of industries and issues; policies that were supported through organizational and constitutional changes and that underpinned the confident moves towards merger.

There was also a perception that the beginning of the end was nigh for the government. The dominant view in the labour movement was that Labour under Neil Kinnock could win the next election, only eighteen months away, and that the main way to combat the uncertainties and weaknesses among union members was to unite around certain common principles; hence the increasing momentum behind the merger.

A New Prime Minister, the Same Old Song

As Mrs Thatcher's hold on office began to falter, she removed two key figures: Nigel Lawson and Geoffrey Howe. John Major's 1990 budget was fiscally neutral, since government policy-makers realized that the boom had ended and recession loomed. No return to Keynesian demand management, just more of the same failure to address substantial structural and equity issues. By

---

[3] *Public Service (PS)*, Jan. 1990, 1.

the end of 1990 Mrs Thatcher was gone, ditched by her party fearful of elec-toral defeat, and replaced by the apparently moderate John Major. The fall of this particularly dominant Prime Minister should have wrecked the govern-ment and allowed Labour to win the 1992 election. Many unions, including NALGO, assumed that this would happen and decided to go along with the Labour leadership's ultra-cautious line.

The year 1990 ended with mixed messages. In deep political trouble, the Tories had thrown out their great leader. Both their economic policies and the social consequences were ever more unpopular. As the NEC's economic report stated: '1990 saw the end of Mrs Thatcher's long premiership and con-clusive proof that the various economic strategies pursued by her govern-ments had all failed . . . As the year ended, inflation was in double figures, unemployment was rising at an accelerating rate and output was falling rapidly.'[4]

On the other hand, there was a new Prime Minister and a new war in the Gulf, and there seemed to be a rush to push through reforms in health, edu-cation, and local government so as to make them very difficult to reverse. Moreover, Labour and the unions themselves were in poor shape—the unions had lost members, money, and status, while the Labour Party was finding it increasingly difficult to present itself as an alternative. It had neither a strong critique of government nor a positive programme for improvement.

For NALGO members in the workplaces the messages were mixed too. For the majority their jobs were still reasonably secure, their pay kept up with inflation if not with private-sector earnings, and restructuring often merely replaced one set of anonymous employers and managers with another set. New technology threatened some but helped others. The union and some employers were much more open and serious about equality issues, but real change was still varied and patchy. Union organization remained intact, although activists were often overstretched. Merger talks were a good idea but they were not inspiring. The 1990s therefore might have held fears and demons, but they were familiar ones, and there was no obvious slayer of drag-ons to transform their working lives.

NALGO maintained both its attacks on government economic policy and its pressure on Labour to adopt more expansionary demand-led policies. Under the title of *Lawson, Major, Lamont and the Slide into Recession*, the union published its quarterly economic assessment: 'Britain is moving fast into its most serious recession in ten years. The transformation from Mr Lawson's claimed economic miracle—via forecasts of a soft landing and Mr Major's short and shallow recession—to Mr Lamont's predictions of bleakness ahead, has been dramatic.'[5] Another publication, *The Economy—a NALGO Review*, was summarized in the Annual Report:

Government stop–go economic policies had led to faltering growth and brought unemployment and poverty. Most serious of all had been the decline of British manufacturing . . . caused primarily by chronically low levels of investment, driven down by the repeated use of deflationary economic strategies by successive governments in panic response to inflation and balance of payments crises.[6]

The Major government's first budget, under Chancellor Norman Lamont, came a few days after an IRA bomb attack on Downing Street. The budget bore a striking similarity to those ten years earlier, as the Chancellor himself recalled: 'I emphasized that the most important objective was the reduction in inflation from its unacceptably high level.'[7] Since the remedies would be the same and since the wider economic setting was worse, such a policy was a reminder to all trade unionists of the price they would have to pay for government mistakes.

The TUC and NALGO urged the government to provide a fairer budget, not in the hope of winning one but as a marker for Labour. The 1991 *TUC Budget Submission* argued for higher child benefit, pensions, abolition of poll tax, and the reduction in the numbers of low-paid workers. *NALGO News* editor David Whitfield commented on the budget: 'With continuing high interest rates to maintain sterling in the Exchange Rate Mechanism, the prospect is bankruptcies and rising unemployment as the industrial base continues to collapse.'[8] By Easter unemployment had reached 3,201,600 and had not yet peaked. Government blamed the unemployed and union pay negotiators for this rise, while the unions blamed the government. NALGO's economist Kelvin Hopkins noted how bad things were: 'Output is falling, unemployment rising fast, investment is collapsing, the balance of trade is in substantial deficit and inflation is proving resistant even to severe and prolonged deflationary measures.'[9] Remedies that were suggested included devaluation, cutting interest rates, and higher public-sector spending especially on investment. In 1991 the government ditched the poll tax and cut interest rates. John Major suddenly became very popular, far more so than his party.

On public-sector pay in general NALGO fell in line with the TUC and Labour Party as part of a pre-election concordat. Willie Brown and Bob Rowthorn's Fabian Tract contributed to the development of this position: 'It is only by assuring the public service trade unions that their pay will not again

---

[5] *NN*, 18 Jan. 1991, 4–5.   [6] Quoted in *NALGO Annual Report* 1991, 11.
[7] N. Lamont, *In Office* (London: Little, Brown & Company, 1999), 55.
[8] *NN*, 22 Mar. 1991, 1.   [9] Ibid., 26 July 1991, 4–5.

be left behind that they can be expected to negotiate reciprocal assurances on industrial peace and on cooperation with change.'[10] NALGO's Rita Donaghy spoke firmly in 'rejection of any form of pay restraint and any form of statutory pay review machinery encompassing the whole of the public sector. So-called incomes policies have always in practice been pay restraint, discriminating against public service workers, unfairly applied, not touching the boss's pay rises, price rises or interest rates.' Worried that a national economic assessment should reflect the concerns of women and part-time workers, she argued that real progress on pay would be achieved 'through collective bargaining, membership-led from pay claim to settlement'.[11] A compromise position was cobbled together, between free collective bargaining based on pay comparability, on the one hand, and pay constraints in line with macroeconomic factors, on the other, through a proposed national assessment of all economic indicators before pay could be decided. This was in part prompted by the creation in 1991 of another pay review body, for schoolteachers,[12] but it also reflected increasing confusion at the heart of the labour movement's economic policy positions, which contributed to the disastrous 1992 election defeat.

By the end of the year there seemed to be some improvement, as the government sought to talk up the economy in time for the election. But, despite this, the recession remained a crisis, symbolized by the crash of the Bank of Credit and Commerce International (BCCI) in July and by the farcical tragedy of Robert Maxwell's drowning in November. The TUC and Labour Party's bland position on the implementation of the Single European Market at the end of 1992, and later on the drafting of the Maastricht Treaty and on the implementation of Economic and Monetary Union, amounted to little more than wishful thinking that these might help us out of a recession and that there might be something in it for trade-union members through the Social Charter. In a telling example of NALGO's policy development being spurred by discussion and debate, the 1989 conference agreed a position of opposition to the Single European Market and criticism of the TUC's position. This resolution recognized that 'attempts to positively influence developments in the European Community should not be dismissed', and the union put forward its arguments for adjustments to the EC's policies and practices.[13] Debate was

---

[10] W. Brown and R. Rowthorn, *A Public Services Pay Policy*, Fabian Society Tract no. 542 (London: Fabian Society, 1990), 18.

[11] *TUC Annual Report 1991* (London: TUC, 1992), 388–9.

[12] M. Ironside and R. Seifert, *Industrial Relations in Schools* (London: Routledge, 1995).

[13] NALGO, *The European Community and 1992: The Report of the National Executive Council's Single European Act Working Party* (London: NALGO, 1990); NALGO, *The Economy: A NALGO Review* (London: NALGO, 1991).

taken further when the 1992 conference voted to oppose the Maastricht Treaty, and in 1993 the North Western and North Wales District Council published, with the support of the Metropolitan, Scottish, and West Midland districts, *Maastricht: Implications for Public Services* written by economist Jonathan Michie.

NALGO policy-makers had grasped the implications of European integration, recognizing that there were vital political links between the drive to cut levels of public sector expenditure and the broader economic policies of monetarism, to meet the commercial needs of businesses in Europe. It matched the government's clarity in recognizing the political and economic significance of both public ownership and public services under local democratic control—both regarded by the government as undesirable. This strong ideological position was driving through the drastic programmes of privatization and marketization, in the face of a weak and muddled counterideology from the trade-union and labour movement. NALGO was one of the few unions that recognized the consequences for members—a loss of union and worker influence over pay, over traditional conditions of service issues, and over the newer issues related to managerial control over the labour processes in the workplaces.

Thus, in the run-up to the 1992 general election, NALGO was dominated by three main concerns. The first was the election itself, with the government's unpopularity as it presided over a tattered economy appearing to give Labour its best chance of regaining power since 1979. Second was the continuing restructuring of the public sector, through both the transfer of activities to the private sector and the marketization of the rest. Third was the proposed merger with NUPE and COHSE to form the largest public-sector union in Europe.

Movements—for Merger, Mandela, and Equality; against Poll Tax and Anti-Union Laws

NALGO's first and only elected General Secretary

NALGO's first ballot to elect the General Secretary got under way early in 1990. Debates about the formation of both the new union and a new type of union were reflected in the candidates' election statements.[14] Knowsley local-government branch secretary Roger Bannister, confusingly standing as a 'Broad Left Candidate', set out the classic ultra-left line in his manifesto: 'I want to help turn NALGO into a fighting, campaigning Union', which

---

[14] *PS* (Mar. 1990), 10–11.

would come about through a 'decisive change at the top of the Union'. He would forgo the General Secretary's salary, taking only his social worker's salary, and he would fight for flat-rate pay claims to eradicate low pay; for action to defend the NHS, jobs, and services; for the thirty-five-hour week; and for women. The key to this would be mass industrial action at national level against cuts and privatization and to stop the poll tax. On the merger he argued that 'we must not allow the domination of the merged Union by a powerful full-time bureaucracy. There must be adequately financed, autonomous Branches.' There should be elected full-time officers on salaries similar to their members, an end to junketing, more power for self-organized groups, affiliation to the Labour Party, and international action to support the anti-apartheid struggles and to support struggles against 'East Europe's Stalinist, police regimes'.

Islington health branch secretary and Workers' Revolutionary Party member Chris Goody stood on a similar platform, arguing for 'a leadership which will stand against the anti-trade union laws and give a clear lead in mobilising members to defend the NHS, by fighting in the TUC for an indefinite General Strike to get rid of this government'. She called on NALGO 'to fight for a real socialist government, a Workers' Revolutionary Government'.

In opposition to these two ultra-left rank-and-file candidates were two broad left full-time officials. West Midland District Organization Officer Sid Platt argued for a more efficient union organization to represent members and to pursue current policies over anti-government campaigns, for the merger, for a wider role in the TUC, and for a strong recruitment drive. He stood on his own considerable talents: 'My election pledge to you is that I will be the most effective advocate of our policies, on behalf of all the members.' The fourth candidate, and the clear favourite, Deputy General Secretary Alan Jinkinson, argued for a more efficient and decisive leadership of the union along roughly the lines it was heading: 'A vote for me will be a vote for strong leadership in the direction you the members want to go—not in a direction one individual or a political caucus wants to take you. It will be leadership which gives powerful support to every group of members in NALGO—in negotiation, at times of dispute and in public debate, especially in the media.'

In the end Alan Jinkinson won by a large margin, with 77,791 out of 156,369 valid votes cast. This compared with 37,474 for Sid Platt, 35,480 for Roger Bannister, and 5,624 for Chris Goody. The regional turnout varied from a low of 18 per cent in the Metropolitan District to a high of 30 per cent in the Scottish and Southern districts. Jinkinson's largest votes came from the three best-organized broad-left strongholds, the Scottish, the North Western and North Wales, and Metropolitan Districts. Sid Platt and Roger Bannister did best in their home districts. The result, announced in May, was greeted in the government's media voice, *The Times*, as 'a victory for the soft left'.[15] The *Morning Star* reported the winner's pledge 'to ensure that NALGO exercises its full weight on the radical and progressive wing of the trade union movement'.[16]

NALGO and the poll tax

The community charge, a reinvented and regressive poll tax, was the ultimate expression of neo-liberal economics. It revealed both a devastating ignorance of the conditions of life for the majority of citizens and a complete lack of social awareness when confronted with strong opposition. Unrepentant Tory leaders still maintained that 'instead of realizing that the wrong tax base—the property base—was being used to pay for social policies in relation to people—not property—successive governments decided to abate the impact of the high level of rates by paying ever-increasing grants to local councils in order to enable them to keep rates down'.[17] In other words, right-wing Conservatives had wanted out of rates since at least the mid-1970s, and by 1985 they were sufficiently strong in the Cabinet to bring in the poll tax. This was proposed strongly by Kenneth Baker and Nicholas Ridley, supported by the Prime Minister herself, and opposed by Nigel Lawson.

Box 13. NALGO and Opposition to the Poll Tax

The poll tax, introduced in Scotland in 1989 and in England and Wales in 1990 (it was never tried in Northern Ireland), was a central component of the government's attack on local democracy. It had flagship status, as it brought about massive restructuring of local government. Opposition to it was one of the main factors in the downfall of Margaret Thatcher.

For most of the twentieth century local authorities were funded through the collection of 'rates', a tax based on the value of the property occupied by citizens and businesses. The government contributed to local-authority revenue through the rate support grant (RSG), which was a fixed proportion of local authority spending (about 60 per cent). This meant that the expansion of local-authority services in the 1960s and 1970s resulted automatically in large increases in central government expenditure. The Labour government of the late 1970s, under pressure from the bankers controlling the IMF, began the process of placing cash limits on local-authority spending.

Cash limits were continued by the Tories, followed by rate-capping and, in 1987, proposals to reform the basis of local taxation. The property-based tax was to be replaced by a tax on each individual resident. As it was a tax based on a headcount of the local population, it became known as the poll tax rather than by its official title of

---

[15] *The Times*, 10 May 1990, 5.   [16] *Morning Star*, 10 May 1990, 3.
[17] N. Ridley, *My Style of Government* (London: Hutchinson, 1991), 120.

the community charge. The property-based tax on local businesses was replaced by a unified business rate set by central government. Any increase in local taxes in order to maintain or improve services could now be raised only through an increase in the local poll tax, without the increase being shared by either local businesses or the government.

All residents were required to register for the tax, with failure to register being punishable by fine. Unregistered residents could be traced through the electoral register, with the implication that anyone trying to avoid paying the tax would have to give up his or her right to vote. Some 11,000 people disappeared from the electoral registers in Glasgow before the tax was implemented, suggesting that a large number of people intended not to pay. The resulting shortfall could only be met either by cuts in services or by further large increases in the poll tax. Enforcement of the law, and especially the rights of the tax collectors to track the movements of individuals as they changed address, raised some complex civil liberties issues.

The net effect was an increase in the amount of local tax paid by the poorest families and a decrease in the amount paid by the better off, representing a dramatic shift of the burden of taxation from the rich to the poor and from prosperous regions to the poorest. This was so blatantly unfair that it resulted in a long-running wave of protest. Anti-poll-tax groups sprang up all over Scotland, and then spread to England and Wales.

NALGO members were at the centre of the storm. They were responsible for implementing a new system that was grossly unfair, that was hated by the majority of the local residents, that was very costly to run, and that struck a blow at the funding of local-authority services delivered by their fellow branch members. The union's NLGC issued posters and campaign packs, including material produced jointly with NUPE, and urged branches to throw their weight behind local anti-poll-tax campaigns.

The annual conference in 1988 voted to 'organise and encourage opposition in parliament'; to 'urge the TUC to take a leading role in stimulating mass opposition' as part of a coordinated national broad-based campaign involving all groups opposed to the tax; and to 'encourage branches and districts to campaign with the rest of the labour and trade union movement'. It did not give open-ended support for non-payment campaigns, recognizing that in Scotland most local authorities were opposed to the tax and that 'any campaign involving defiance of the law must be a part of the mass movement involving the overwhelming support of the Scottish people themselves'. The STUC organized a week of action with demonstrations held in many Scottish cities.

The issue of mass opposition was tested at the end of 1988, when Knowsley and Islington branches applied for official backing for branch ballots on non-cooperation with the creation of poll-tax collection jobs. The Emergency Committee turned this down as such action would involve only a small number of members at the front line, who would then become very vulnerable. It could also give employers an incentive to privatize poll-tax collection. Mass opposition was to be organized with the labour and trade-union movement generally, in conjunction with community and other groups.

As the tax came into operation in Scotland the 1989 conference strengthened its support for mass action, through non-payment and other forms of civil disobedience. The conference rejected adventurist calls for a campaign among NALGO members to urge them not to pay and to hold a ballot on non-collection of the tax. The STUC Annual Congress voted to support a broad campaign for repeal, for delay and disruption in tax collection, and for action to defend those unable to pay. The TUC held a demonstration in Manchester, and the Congress strengthened its commitment to lead the mass campaign.

As implementation in England and Wales approached in 1990, many branches launched protests, including strikes, against the impact of the tax on NALGO members' jobs. In Liverpool, where the council refused to implement the tax, members faced the prospect of their wages not being paid. Over 400 Sheffield members went on strike over a range of issues, including staffing levels, flexibility, office organization, and accommodation. The union committed £250,000 to a campaign focused on the council elections, under the slogan 'Poll tax means less for local services. Vote against it on May 3rd.' Many members were involved in a massive demonstration in the centre of London on 31 March.

Margaret Thatcher and her supporters continued to argue that the tax was both fair and workable, while the level of protest escalated. Local communities mounted demonstrations at both Labour and Conservative council meetings to set the level of the tax. Particularly hard hit were the first twenty-one local authorities to have their poll tax capped by the government, resulting in several strikes against cuts in jobs and services. Mrs Thatcher's misreading of the mood of the country proved fatal to her political career. She was replaced as Prime Minister by her protégé John Major, who quickly announced another review of local-government finance.

The protests continued into 1991, as councils trimmed their budgets to avoid capping. Branches reacted to the prospect of thousands of job losses, organizing protest meetings and token strikes. On 21 March 1991 Michael Heseltine announced the replacement of the poll tax by the council tax, with effect from 1993. This made concessions to popular resentment by reintroducing the property-based element, but on the basis of government-defined bands. The capping provisions were retained. Thus the government ended its ill-judged experiment with a wholly regressive tax, while keeping the basis for government-imposed cuts in local spending.

In 1989–90 many local councils revealed that the charge might be more than double the original estimates, causing panic in the government. Secretary of State for the Environment Chris Patten squeezed more money out of the Treasury for extra grants to keep the poll tax down. The government was split, the labour movement was able to mount a broadly based opposition, and challenges to Margaret Thatcher's leadership position could now find concrete form through Michael Heseltine, followed by Douglas Hurd, and finally, successfully, by John Major. The leaders of the party were in no doubt of its importance: 'By now Conservative backbenchers were becoming extremely restive . . . I received regular and depressing reports from the whips . . . the political atmosphere was becoming grim.'[18]

Another senior Cabinet member looks back on the shambles with horror: 'Never before in my political career had I found myself wholly unequipped with any intellectually credible explanation for what we were trying to do.'[19] For Chancellor Lawson 'one expedient followed another, most of which had the effect of reducing the distinctive characteristics of the Poll Tax and moving it towards a clumsy, arbitrary and ill-drafted caricature of an income tax'.[20] Even the new Prime Minister understood what had happened: 'the tax had proved a disaster: unfair, unworkable and unacceptable.'[21] The poll tax was a fiasco, which should have brought down the deeply unpopular government as well as Margaret Thatcher.

NALGO's part in the opposition was threefold: first it joined the general policy position that such a tax was perverse in its practice and unjust in its conception; secondly, the union protested against its actual impact on many of the low-paid workers it represented; and, thirdly, it was NALGO members who were faced with collecting and implementing the tax. Poll-tax issues began to dominate the industrial-relations scene:

Poll tax collection in Liverpool is at a virtual standstill and the city is in chaos as NALGO's strike action bites deep. 'There is no pursuance of non-payers, the vast majority of people who have not already made arrangements to pay the tax are not paying at all and the city is also unable to collect £34 million of outstanding rates as it had planned', said branch secretary Judy Cotter. Food is rotting at the docks as the strike of environmental health officers means that food export licences are not being processed, and infestation of all kinds are on the increase in kitchens and restaurants around the city. Eighty-four key staff walked out last week in protest at the council's decision to impose the deduction of fifths rather than sevenths from the pay of members on strike. The main group out on strike are poll tax management staff.[22]

The 1990 STUC meeting in Glasgow used the anti-poll-tax fight as a launching pad to revitalize other campaigns for a Scottish government, for a return to full trade-union rights, and for public support for strikes in the rail and ambulance services. Ada Maddocks argued that the tide was turning in favour of the labour movement with 'a message heralding hope, optimism and great changes'.[23] The TUC women's conference in Cardiff re-energized its campaigns on issues such as sexual harassment at work, equal pay, and the

---

[18] M. Thatcher, *The Downing Street Years* (London: Harper Collins, 1993), 656–8.
[19] G. Howe, *Conflict of Loyalty* (London: Macmillan, 1994), 604.
[20] N. Lawson, *The View from No. 11* (London: Corgi Books, 1992), 581.
[21] J. Major, *The Autobiography* (London: Harper Collins, 1999), 215.
[22] *NN*, 24 Aug. 1990, 1.   [23] *PS* (May 1990), 9.

right to abortion. This interconnecting mix of collective-bargaining issues, workplace exploitation, national campaigns, and unity behind key causes thrust the unions back onto the centre stage of British politics, as employers and policy-makers alike looked to the end of the Thatcher era. As was noted at the time, 'most national unions have adopted policies opposing the poll tax, the majority supporting the policy of the TUC and the Labour Party . . . the TUC's campaign aims to build broad-based opposition to the poll tax'.[24]

Freedom, equality, and unity

One single event captured and stimulated the growing optimism of the time: the release of Nelson Mandela on 11 February 1990. His faith in progress and his unshaken socialist beliefs inspired struggling workers everywhere. His homecoming symbolized the revolutionary ideals of liberty, equality, and solidarity. Here was a right to end many wrongs, a struggle to inspire others in struggle, and a triumph of individual will and collective power over cruel and unjust governments and political systems. The British anti-apartheid movement, for so long reviled in the press, infiltrated by the security forces with the knowledge of both Labour and Conservative leaders, and damned by faint support from too many in the labour movement, took great and deserved pride in the beginning of the end of that brutal social and cultural instance of modern inhumanity. And within the British and international anti-apartheid movement was the contribution of NALGO's members and leaders, fulfilling the slogan that an injustice to one is an injustice to all.

Box 14. NALGO and the Anti-Apartheid Movement

It is no exaggeration to say that NALGO played a real part in the overthrow of the appalling racist system of apartheid. Of course the South African liberation movement was the main force that toppled the ruling regime, finally bringing about its collapse in the early 1990s after long and bitter struggle. Their courage and sacrifice reveals the power that can be mobilized by a democratic mass movement under a strong political and fighting leadership. NALGO's contribution was to generate moral, political, and financial support for the liberation movement in Britain. This had great symbolic importance, because of the history of British involvement in the country.

During the state of emergency after the 1960 massacre of sixty-five black South African men, women, and children at a peaceful demonstration in Sharpeville, some 20,000 people were arrested in the ensuing wave of strikes and demonstrations, and the ANC was declared illegal. Further legislation was passed to suppress political opposition in 1962, and the ANC, deciding that it was no longer possible to secure

---

[24] LRD, *The Poll Tax* (London: LRD, 1990), 30.

change through non-violent means, formed a military wing called Umkhonto we Sizwe (Spear of the Nation) to launch the armed liberation struggle. Two years later Nelson Mandela was tried, along with others at the Rivonia trial, and was convicted and sentenced to life imprisonment for sabotage and treason.

South African industrial relations were complex, with laws on union registration that made it difficult for unions of black workers to gain legal status without becoming ineffective. Between 1973 and 1981, of 1,400 officially recorded strikes by African workers only three were declared legal. The multiracial South African Congress of Trade Unions (SACTU), founded in 1955, was explicitly committed to struggle on both economic and political fronts against all forms of oppression and exploitation. Its aims of organizing the unorganized, building unity between diverse social forces, and generally guiding, influencing, and persuading the trade-union movement along a revolutionary course meant that it was continually harassed. In the 1960s hundreds of activists were banned from union work, banished to remote parts of the country, imprisoned, and murdered. During the 1970s the political struggle took new forms as the ANC went underground. Resistance through community-based organizations resulted in the establishment of the United Democratic Front (UDF) in 1983.

Non-racial trade unions were an important part of the liberation movement, also providing the basis for solidarity links with trade unions in Britain. As they grew in strength by asserting the rights of employees and organizing strikes against employers, they developed permanent organizational stability in spite of their semi-legal status. The crowning achievement of these labour-movement activists came in 1986 with the establishment of the Confederation of South African Trade Unions (COSATU), supported by SACTU. COSATU organized a wave of union mergers to rationalize the structure on an industrial basis, and quickly became the third force in the liberation movement along with the ANC and the UDF. This linked together the main struggles against apartheid—military and political through the ANC, civic and community through the UDF, and industrial through COSATU.

NALGO's first formal national involvement in the British campaigns against apartheid came in the 1974 conference decision to support SACTU and to ask the TUC to do the same. In 1975 the union affiliated to the Anti-Apartheid Movement (AAM), which had been formed in 1959. NALGO activity on South Africa was focused through SACTU and the AAM, including sponsoring a conference in 1979 on building support for the United Nations call for economic sanctions. Demands for sanctions made by the trade union and political organizations of the black South African people fell on deaf ears in the British government, but NALGO's International Relations Section played a significant role in building activity. Officials provided local activists with information for the high-profile public campaigns, while also operating underground as a conduit for contacts with the South African trade unions at the highest level.

The union's 1983 conference made Nelson and Winnie Mandela honorary members, and the significance of this gesture was recognized when the ANC's Adelaide Tambo and Solly Smith visited the 1984 conference to receive membership certificates on their behalf. COSATU General Secretary Themba Nxumalo addressed the 1986 annual conference and toured Britain, along with National Secretary Kisa Dlamini, visiting many NALGO branches. These links grew out of the union's decision to focus its contacts through the recognized leaders of the organized struggle, which meant recognizing the legitimacy of organizations banned by the regime and branded by others as 'terrorist' or 'subversive'. NALGO took this to the 1985 TUC Annual Congress, proposing support for the ANC, SACTU, and the UDF. The TUC's International Department put intense pressure on the delegates to withdraw the proposition, which they resisted and won Congress agreement.

In 1987 the Municipal Workers' Union of South Africa (MWUSA) and the Health and Allied Workers' Union (HAWU), both COSATU affiliates, invited NALGO to send a delegation. NALGO consulted with SACTU and decided to accept, welcoming the opportunity to strengthen links with its sister unions, to witness the conditions faced by workers under the government-declared state of emergency, to be present at the launch of the establishment, through merger, of the National Education Health and Allied Workers' Union (NEHAWU), and to attend the second COSATU National Congress. NALGO was committed to a disciplined approach, and was highly critical of organizations that had visited South Africa with their own agendas and had stirred up publicity that made South African activists vulnerable to the security forces.

NEC members Rita Donaghy, John McFadden, and Ralph Gayton, and International Relations Officer Jan Stockwell travelled separately as tourists, linking up with their hosts under conditions of secrecy to maintain the safety of both themselves and those they were visiting. In their final report they described the difficulties that they had found, including the bombing of COSATU offices, detention of activists (Themba Nxumalo was in police custody during the visit), anti-union vigilante groups, and intimidation and dismissal of union activists and members. They also found a vibrant and progressive trade-union movement that was fighting back by campaigning on employment issues and by organizing practical support such as self-defence training. The delegation was impressed by the activists' clarity of purpose, typified by their attitude towards sympathetic non-South Africans, as expressed in the report:

The answer to our question 'What can we do to help?' was invariably to tell us that their future freedom lies in the strength of their organisation in trade unions and community-based groups. If we want to support their struggle, we should help them strengthen their organisations. And we should take all opportunities we have to undermine the position of the enemy, the apartheid regime.

This meant providing a regular source of financial, material, and political support as well as responding to emergency situations, channelled through proper organizations and procedures. NALGO conference had explicitly rejected suggestions that, as the South African labour movement became more confident and operated more openly, then direct links could be established between activists. The delegation's experience affirmed that this was a correct decision—the intensity of the liberation struggle, and the dangers faced by leaders and activists, made such links too risky. It was made clear to them that they would have been made less welcome if they had not taken advice from the ANC and SACTU before their visit. NALGO speakers argued this case throughout the British labour movement.

The final collapse of the rotten apartheid system was sudden. The ANC and the UDF were unbanned, and shortly after that Nelson Mandela was released, after twenty-seven years in jail, on 11 February 1990. During the intense negotiations that followed, NALGO played its part by supporting the retention of sanctions and by keeping the membership abreast of developments with accurate information to counter misleading reports that inflated the impact of minor reforms. NALGO member Nelson Mandela visited his union's head office during his first visit to the UK after his release, before going on to be elected President of South Africa under the country's new constitution in May 1994.

Mandela's release, and his subsequent role in the accord that ended apartheid rule, certainly helped the upbeat mood within the British labour movement. Its role in securing his release was rewarded by his attendance at the Wembley concert in April 1990 in his honour. Over 75,000 people went to see and hear him speak as the leader of the ANC.

NALGO continued to campaign on equality issues. It supported a conference of Asian social workers in Norwich, which heard participant Don Naik outline how 'myth, prejudice and racist assumptions stand between most Asian people in Britain and decent social services'. He argued: 'Many Asians contact social services departments only in the most desperate of circumstances because of their negative experience of white institutions.'[25] The union publicized MEP Glyn Ford's report on racism and xenophobia in Europe, which highlighted 'a steep rise in racist attacks and crimes'. The report called for more funds to fight right-wing groups through education, and for improved status for immigrant workers through collective-bargaining agendas at the workplace.[26]

This was linked to the economic climate within the EU and the possible creation of second-class citizenship through the 1992 single market system. NALGO's own report made a long list of demands, including: detailed monitoring of the free movement of workers; substantially increased structural funds to raise employment; legislation on working time and contracts of employment; strengthening and expansion of the Social Charter to ensure protection of jobs and opportunities for women and outlawing racial discrimination; a legal duty on employers to provide training with paid time off; requirements on information and consultation of the workforce; monitoring of how the UK implements the Directives on health and safety at work; two

---

[25] *PS* (Nov. 1990), 6–7.   [26] *NN*, 10 Aug. 1990, 4–5.

years' vocational training for all young people; the designation of 1993 as the year of the elderly; urgent effective legislation to promote equal employment and social opportunities for people with disabilities; and equal rights for lesbians and gay men.[27]

NALGO News reported union successes in collective bargaining over equality, for example in the NHS: 'The comprehensive claim on equal opportunities was submitted to the management side of the general Whitley council on 23 October 1989. As part of that claim detailed negotiations have taken place on the issue of retainer schemes.'[28] This type of agreement indicated a shift in trade-union activity into some broader-based issues, which included strong NALGO support for new National Vocational Qualifications (NVQs).

Action was also taken through the courts: 'A far-reaching victory for NALGO in the European Court of Justice has given the go-ahead for compensation claims on behalf of women who were forced to retire at age 60 by British Gas while men could retire at 65. NALGO's success opens the way for similar potential claims throughout the public services including local authorities.'[29] In the newly privatized electricity sector low-paid women clerical staff went to ITs arguing for equal pay and prospects with comparable men. NALGO made it clear that these were test cases, and David Whitfield argued that 'men as well as women working in clerical jobs and in electricity showrooms will benefit'.[30] Bill Morris, Deputy General Secretary of the TGWU and leading black trade unionist, argued the case in an interview for *NALGO News*: 'If the movement does not address itself to the question of equal opportunities and give people room to articulate their views, then before long it could gradually find itself isolated from those people.' He saw equal opportunities as 'an extension to the range of activities that a dynamic and progressive union that's about to safeguard its future must take on board if it is to survive, and to tap into the talent of all the skills and enthusiasm of the membership overall'.[31]

Measures aimed especially at women workers and low-paid workers struck a chord at the union's women's conference in Great Yarmouth in 1990. The message was clear: 'women want decent child care, women want an end to low pay, women want equal representation—and they want it now.'[32] At the NALGO black members' conference in Manchester in April the main priority was for legal representation for members involved in discrimination and harassment cases, and this flowed from a broader initiative taken by ten TUC unions to hold a conference earlier in the year on black workers' rights in the

[27] Ibid., 8 June 1990, 4. [28] Ibid., 3 Aug. 1990, 2. [29] Ibid., 20 July 1990, 1.
[30] *PS* (electricity) (June 1991), 1. [31] *NN*, 8 Feb. 1991, 7.
[32] Ibid., 19 Oct. 1990, 3.

1990s. Such activities meant that the next conference in Glasgow in December was stronger and better than ever, and its priorities included the wider issues of jobs, low pay, and the Asylum Bill.

Similar but distinct concerns troubled the delegates at the second NALGO conference for members with disabilities held in Coventry in April. There was particular concern over mental health, the quota system, and the move to treat disability as a narrow medical issue rather than as an equal-rights one. And there were tensions at the national gay and lesbian conference in Glasgow in November, with a decision to support 'outing'.

At the STUC women's conference at the start of 1991 the main issues were fighting the evils of pornography and sexual harassment, themes picked up at the TUC women's conference in Blackpool as well as the issues of part-time work, care choices, opposition to pay restraint, and improved public transport. NALGO delegates supported motions on carers, sickle-cell, disabilities, family policy, and racism. The next STUC women's conference was in Perth as the year ended, debating low pay, democracy in South Africa, AIDS, abortion, and racism. This was set within a general debate on the economy and on the problems for women as workers and citizens affected by cuts in public services. This broad-based approach did not rule out internal controversies, sometimes bitterly expressed. Patsy Boulton, co-chair of the women's committee, speaking at the NALGO women's conference, condemned the union's failure to establish district women's officers. She said, 'This is war and the only place the battle will be won is in the National Executive Council.'[33]

All of those initiatives helped to broaden the basis of unity in the union, which traditionally rested on the unifying activity of national collective bargaining, coupled with the aspects of working life that the members had in common: the type of work, their aspirations, the public-service ethos, and their sense of identification with the service, with service users, and with their union. However, government reforms were breaking up public industries and services, weakening national collective bargaining, destabilizing labour markets, and eroding long-cherished conditions of service.

The potential for division is always most acute around pay, as Alan Jinkinson recognized: 'Ending the scandal of low pay remains NALGO's top priority.'[34] The union shifted its historic position on pay and began the move towards a set of policies that had widespread populist appeal in principle. However, in practice workers who themselves were outside the union definition of low pay had overriding concerns about their own position within the labour market. A narrow union focus around the single issue of low pay had the potential to be more limited, less unifying, and more fragile than the previous more inclusive policies.

[33] *PS* (local government) (Dec. 1991), 3.   [34] Ibid. (Sept. 1991), 6.

Official recognition of self-organized groups, to combat the historical and continuing disadvantages experienced by women, black, disabled, and gay and lesbian members, also posed some difficult questions. How separate are the special interests of some members, and how can these tangled strands be woven into a coherent whole to embrace the interests of *all* the members? Such fundamental issues of union democracy remain permanently unresolved, reflecting structural inequalities in the wider society within which unions operate. Unity rests crucially on action, and both officials and activists recognized this. They swung behind measures to strengthen democratic structures and practices, and there was a much more systematic commitment to taking up individual cases of discrimination.

Against the anti-union laws

Belief that the Conservative shambles would soon give way to a new Labour government underpinned President Rita Donaghy's address to the 1990 annual conference: 'NALGO has a major role to play in building a stronger, fairer society and dismantling the legacy of the Thatcher era.'[35] NALGO was part of the leadership of the entire trade-union movement, symbolized when national officer for health Ada Maddocks took her place as President of the TUC at the Blackpool Congress.

One example of this role was in the union's public stand against the anti-union laws. Negotiators recognized that the laws hampered the union in bargaining over members' conditions of service. This basic union fear was well stated when the annual conference in Bournemouth opposed the package of employment law proposals put forward by Labour spokesman Tony Blair: 'Conference voted to oppose official Labour party policy on trade union law and campaign instead for a "reassertion of the principles of free trade unionism".'[36]

NALGO and the broad left in the wider union movement pushed hard to persuade other unions and the Labour leadership of their case. The union's resolution to the TUC stated that 'Congress notes that in 1989 the British government was condemned by the International Labour Organisation because of its repressive legislation against trade unions, in contravention of international conventions'.[37] John Hendy QC wrote in *NALGO News*: 'Mr Blair does not say so but any employment lawyer will tell him that whatever principles he wishes to retain from existing legislation, the TUC resolution is right that all the Conservative laws will need to be repealed.'[38] Labour law

[35] *NN*, 15 June 1990, 1.   [36] Ibid.
[37] TUC, *Annual Report for 1990* (London: TUC, 1991), 292.   [38] *NN*, 20 July 1990, 4–5.

academic Keith Ewing's pamphlet for the Institute of Employment Rights also backed up NALGO's position:

The Employment Act 1990 is the fifth major statute since 1980 concerned principally to restrict the freedoms of trade unions and their members. It is in some respects every bit as far reaching and 'radical' as several of the earlier initiatives; and is a clear indication that the steam has not run out of the Thatcher-inspired crusade against the unions.[39]

Alan Jinkinson made his famous Congress speech, regretting that the TUC's opposition to the Employment Bill was muted: 'Sadly, the response of many of the leaders of our movement to these continual assaults is to hide behind the parapet and throw out the odd concession in the hope the enemy will go away. Inevitably and invariably they come back for more.' He ended his speech by reminding the delegates of the slogans on their union banners:

'An Injury to One is an Injury to All' or 'Unity is Strength' or 'Workers of the World Unite'—If you haven't deposited them in the Museum of Labour History do so now before they run out of space. And if you ever again find yourself singing the anthem 'Solidarity for Ever' remember to incorporate these words into the chorus: only where there is a direct interest of an occupational or professional nature.[40]

Despite this contribution the motion was lost by a slender margin. Nevertheless, NALGO made its mark, with the *Independent* reporting the union's 'dogged promotion of a proposition on employment law . . . in the teeth of considerable Labour Party pressure to withdraw it', under the headline 'Nalgo Finds a New Role as Leader of the Left'.[41]

Concerns about the direction of legal changes were hardened by the Green Paper, *Industrial Relations in the 1990s*, which suggested that customers of public services could sue unions if the service was affected by unlawful industrial action. NALGO accumulated a number of bad experiences in the courts, as employers took legal action against branches. In Liverpool City Council a strike spread from its original and immediate causes to include resistance to the anti-union laws, but this brought the branch into conflict with the NEC. A highly charged debate at the 1991 conference in Glasgow was reported in *Public Service*:

Judy Cotter, Liverpool's branch secretary, who faced imprisonment for challenging the anti-union laws during a dispute last year was vindicated by a convincing vote of support in the final debate of conference. Standing Orders were suspended in the dying minutes of conference to give the speakers on motion 116 (anti-union laws)

---

[39] K. Ewing, *The Employment Act 1990: A European Perspective* (London: Institute of Employment Rights, 1991), 5.

[40] *NALGO Annual Report 1990*, 72.

[41] *Independent*, 4 Sept. 1990.

time to outline their reasons for defying the laws and carrying out the 'business as usual' policy in regard to the anti-union laws. Ms Cotter criticised the national executive council for repudiating the half day strike called by the branch for September 19, with a 'ragbag of excuses' in a letter which arrived before the strike rally. She said to applause: 'Six thousand of our members defied the law and came out on strike. This outstanding action clearly showed that they understood the issues were relevant to their own situation.'[42]

The Liverpool case revealed the limits of NALGO policy—opposition to the law did not entail breaking the law itself. Another case presented NALGO with problems, when members in South Tyneside went to court over their right to remain in membership even after crossing picket lines during the 1989 local-government strike. The scene was set early in 1991: 'Nine strikebreakers who were expelled by South Tyneside NALGO for refusing to support their colleagues in the 1989 local government strike took the union to court recently. The case, still being heard by the Employment Appeals Tribunal in London . . . makes legal history as the nine claim compensation for alleged distress as a result of their expulsion.'[43] The outcome was gleefully reported in *The Times*:

Britain's biggest white collar trade union was ordered to pay a total of £22,680 compensation to nine former members expelled for crossing picket lines during a strike in 1989. In the first case of its kind under the 1988 Employment Act, which introduced a right not to be unjustifiably disciplined by a trade union, the Employment Appeal Tribunal awarded the nine £2,520 each to compensate for injury to feelings caused by expulsion from the 750,000 strong National and Local Government Officers' Association. Mr Justice Wood, the tribunal president, said that the nine were 'witnesses of conscience, courage and integrity'. After the judgment, Alan Jinkinson , the union's general secretary, condemned the award as 'dirt money'.[44]

Economics—pay, training, and pensions

Delegates at the 1991 annual conference took a strong position on incomes policy: 'NALGO is totally opposed to any agreement between the TUC and a future Labour government which involves pay restraint. In an overwhelming vote yesterday, Conference committed the union to rejecting incomes policy no matter how it is dressed up as pay norms, accommodations or review bodies.'[45] This position was later endorsed by the TUC, along with calls for a national minimum wage.

Once again the union opposed government schemes to alleviate unemployment based on the supply-side economic argument that unemployment

---

[42] *PS* (local government) (July 1991), 4. [43] Ibid. (Jan. 1991), 3.
[44] *The Times*, 15 Feb. 1991, 7. [45] *PS* (local government) (July 1991), 4.

is essentially a problem caused by the workforce itself: 'Employment Action must be one of the most cynically misnamed government projects in 12 years of exploiting the fear of unemployment as a weapon against ordinary people . . . At last month's TUC NALGO successfully argued that the trade unions should boycott Employment Action. We said that it was no more than "workfare" taking us back towards '30s style workcamps.'[46] Instead the union backed demands from the STUC in Dundee for quality training schemes that are more accountable and with more trade-union involvement, a sentiment echoed at the Wales TUC in Llandudno.

NALGO's motion to the TUC began with one simple trade-union principle: 'Congress restates its commitment to full employment as the central objective of economic policy.' Alan Jinkinson reminded the delegates about the consequences of mass unemployment—'broken homes, repossessions, suicides, crime, young people begging in the streets, the sheer utter waste of human talent'—and he called on the trade-union movement to protect long-term unemployed workers 'from further harassment and exploitation from Government Workfare schemes'.[47]

As the general election approached, the union launched 'the biggest national advertising and leafleting campaign ever undertaken by a British trade union', with a £1.5 million budget.[48] It included full-page advertisements in national newspapers, highlighting the dire state of the NHS, education, community care, and the plight of the elderly. It rattled the government, provoking an outcry in newspapers such as the *Sun*, the *Mail*, and the *Express*. A report in *The Times* gives a flavour:

> The prime minister yesterday accused the local government union NALGO of using 'phoney pictures and fake statistics' in a £1.5 million advertising campaign attacking the government's record on the health service . . . Michael Jopling, Conservative MP for Westmorland and Lonsdale, called on the prime minister at question time to take action to ensure that all advertisements were decent and truthful, 'especially and including advertisements put in the press by trade unions on behalf of the Labour Party'. Mr Major replied: 'I join you in condemning the advertisements to which you refer, with phoney pictures and fake statistics.'[49]

As if attacks from the government and the anti-union press were not enough, NALGO also faced hostility from within the labour movement when GMB/APEX national officer Mick Graham, speaking at his union's conference, portrayed NALGO as a union of 'Tories led by Trots'. This slogan, which was picked up by the popular press, contained several separate sets of accusations: first, that most NALGO members voted Tory, assumed to be

---

[46] *PS* (local government) (July 1991), 6. [47] *TUC Annual Report 1991*, 274.
[48] *NN*, 28 Mar. 1991, 1. [49] *The Times*, 3 May 1991, 8.

rooted in their white-collar status and in the conservatism of traditional local-government employees; secondly, that an important section of activists and leaders were Trotskyists, a reference to the left-wing nature of their actions and campaigns but a ludicrous view of the vast majority of those involved; and, thirdly, that NALGO was less than democratic and representative because the majority was being (mis)led by a tiny minority.

This sideshow did not dent the continued optimism of the broadly left leadership. At the end of 1991 the union was in reasonable shape in terms of membership, organization, and finance. Membership declined only slightly in 1990 with a loss of about 6,000 members out of a total of just over 744,400 (see Tables 8.1–8.4). Endless fighting on several fronts had taken its toll, stretching resources, and exacerbating inner tensions, but the union had survived with most policies intact and in an optimistic mood for a Labour victory and for a merged union within the year. The hallmark of NALGO, and one of its legacies to the trade-union movement, was the extent of its internal democracy, recognized in at least one academic study of workplace democracy.[50]

David Stockford expressed these sentiments in his presidential speech to the conference: 'All over the world working people and their unions have learnt it—that union rights, workers' rights and human rights are one and the same thing . . . We are the breath of life to society, without which justice and truth in employment cannot exist.'[51]

Moving towards merger

The merger process was negotiated through a joint committee, with Deputy General Secretary Dave Prentis as one of the joint secretaries. NALGO Executive Officer Rod Robertson told us that the partnership approach to a three-way merger helped to ensure that the rule book and the new union structures were all agreed before the merger, which minimized post-merger problems.

Campaigning kicked off in 1990 with a weekend seminar for members of all three unions' executive committees. John Daly argued that 'we must involve the many thousands who are going to finally determine if this venture is going to be a success', while Rodney Bickerstaffe of NUPE concluded that 'we have to sink our identities to save our identity . . . without a new union all three unions would face troublesome times ahead'. Hector MacKenzie of COHSE added that 'as we move towards the new century we can no longer assume the loyalty of the members—we need to be better able to relate to our

[50] P. Fosh and E. Heery (eds.), *Trade Unions and their Members: Studies in Union Democracy and Organization* (Basingstoke: Macmillan, 1990).

[51] *PS* (local government) (July 1991), 6.

members'. By February all three executives had agreed on the joint report *The Challenge of the New Union*, to be presented to each annual conference later in the year. The union took the campaign to the members, with the benefits of merger outlined in a special supplement to *Public Service* in May 1990.

The first benefit was in responding to government action: 'Pressures to combine cuts in welfare provision with increased state controls and restrictions on union rights have necessarily fostered growing co-operation between the three unions in recent years.' A merged union would 'exert a major influence over future public service policy—in Britain and Europe'.

Secondly, it would strengthen the members' position with management:

Employers' strategies also pose a common threat to all three unions. These include threats to jobs, to the ability to negotiate effectively on behalf of members and to national collective bargaining, to trade union action, and to the maintenance of public services. The employers are clearly in a belligerent and vindictive mood, bolstered by government hostility to trade unionism and antagonism towards the public services. It would be far better for the three unions to join forces and combine their collective strength.

Thirdly, it would 'provide a better service for members', 'ensure members in larger and smaller services enjoy improved support and facilities', and 'it would also provide exciting opportunities to advance a new kind of trade unionism which would better represent the interests of the members'.

Fourthly, it would result in a more efficient union administration. Economies of scale would 'combine the three unions' resources, full-time officers, expertise, communications, publicity and democratic services', and 'end wasteful competition, conflict and duplication of resources'.

Fifthly, the merged union would have influence in outside bodies and campaigns. It would 'organise over 1.6 million workers . . . be the largest union in the TUC [and] . . . influence other trade unions, employers, governments, public debate and the climate of opinion and policy formulation within the European Community and wider international relations'.[52]

Alan Jinkinson argued that the merger 'will stand or fall by what members think it is going to be capable of doing in terms of increasing unity and solidarity in the workplace, to defend the interests of the members in the workplace and further their collective bargaining strength'.[53] Linking the merger with the fight for public services, he argued: 'NALGO members are at the sharp end behind the headlines. That puts NALGO at the sharp end in their defence. Devolution to put resources closer to members is a key point of the thinking behind the proposals to create a new union.'[54] He urged delegates

[52] *PS (Special Supplement)* (May 1990), 1.   [53] *PS* (June 1990), 8.
[54] *NN*, 31 Aug. 1990, 2–3.

at the 1990 conference to 'seize this greatest opportunity in our history', and academic adviser Bob Fryer, from Northern College, sloganized the historical importance of the merger thus: 'Secession is easy. Unity is hard.'[55] The conference voted to move forward, but not without controversy: 'Talks with NUPE and COHSE are to continue, it was decided, during a passionate and often bitter debate on merger.'[56]

Detailed merger proposals, *A Framework for a New Union*, were ready to send to the three unions' annual conferences in 1991. Bob Fryer restated the arguments: 'It must be that we are going to get a stronger trade union. Stronger in terms of collective bargaining, stronger in terms of individual representation, stronger in terms of providing services and resources to members and also stronger in influencing public policy both in Britain and Europe.'[57] NUPE and COHSE conferences voted to support the proposals, but NALGO's hesitated. Incoming President Mike Blick made his plea to the delegates: 'I sincerely hope that conference will vote in favour of moving forward and coming to an agreement with the other unions which will then be acceptable not only to the three conferences but to the members of the three unions.'[58] His hopes were eventually fulfilled, although the conference insisted on amending the report and as a result there was a period of tension in the summer when there was little progress on the Instruments of Amalgamation. Hector MacKenzie of COHSE argued that 'it is absolutely crucial that the three unions are united. Whatever the difficulties we have the most effect when we are working together. There is more that unites us than divides us. We either work together or hang separately.'[59]

As the year ended NALGO finally sorted out its misgivings on some of the important details, and the NEC gave the final go-ahead. The timetable was for NALGO to hold a special conference in March 1992, for all three union conferences in the summer of 1992 to decide on the final countdown to merger, subject to ratification by a membership ballot, and then for vesting day on 1 July 1993.

Labour Management and the Markets

A dirty business

Privatization created a mishmash of private-sector companies all seeking to maximize short-term profits by cheapening labour costs through weakening collective-bargaining arrangements and diluting collective agreements.

[55] *PS* (July 1990), 1, 9.   [56] *NN*, 15 June 1990, 1.   [57] *PS* (Feb. 1991), 8.
[58] *NN*, 7 June 1991, 8.   [59] *PS* (local government) (Oct. 1991), 7.

Judith Cook, author of *Dirty Water*, outlined the context in the water industry: 'Today water is back in private hands after being starved of investment for ten years.' Cook suggested that 'what's dirty about water is that it's full of nitrates and pesticides, rivers are full of industrial waste and raw sewage washes up on mile after mile of our beaches'. She went on to claim that 'if a private company has to choose between safety and profit, profit wins every time'.[60] Meanwhile NALGO altered its organization for water staff in line with the new industry structure. As Alex Thomson, national officer for water, said, 'it's vitally important that people are properly represented for talks on the new pay system, contracts and conditions . . . There is the threat of large scale redundancies posed by the takeovers of companies and the drive for profitability.'[61] Stuart Ogden argues that the main industrial–relations changes came after 1991 with company bargaining,[62] and that the employers' need for flexibility and skill mix changes made the move to single status and single table bargaining inevitable.[63]

Electricity privatization, on 1 April 1990, created a new industry structure based on the four main functions of generation, transmission, distribution, and supply. Since 1957 there had been two sections of the industry: the CEGB generated electricity and transmitted it through the National Grid; and the twelve area electricity boards were responsible for distribution and supply to customers. Under the new system the twelve area boards became public electricity supply companies. The CEGB was broken up into four main companies: PowerGen, with twenty fossil fuel and one hydropower stations; National Power, with thirty-four fossil-fuel and four hydropower stations; Nuclear Electric, with thirteen nuclear stations, hydropower, and gas turbine plant; and the National Grid Company. Price, performance, competitive practices, and safety were to be regulated by the Director General of Electricity Supply, the MMC, and the Director General of Fair Trading.

The actual privatization was shambolic, with what came to be known as 'spatchcock' legislation necessary to resolve endless difficulties and contradictions. 'Increasing competition in generation and supply was a primary objective of the ESI privatization, but this was hampered at the outset by the duopoly structure chosen for the generating side . . . paradoxically, the generating duopoly necessitated regulation to restrict competition even further'.[64]

---

[60] *PS* (Feb. 1990), 8.   [61] Ibid. 8–9.

[62] S. Ogden, 'Decline and Fall: National Bargaining in British Water', *Industrial Relations Journal*, 24/1 (1993), 52.

[63] S. Ogden, 'The Reconstruction of Industrial Relations in the Privatized Water Industry', *British Journal of Industrial Relations*, 32/1 (1994), 74.

[64] J. Roberts, D. Elliott, and T. Houghton, *Privatising Electricity: The Politics of Power* (London: Belhaven Press, 1991), 85–6.

Needless to say, the government said nothing about the prospects for either the environment or the employment of those who worked in the industry.

Once again it was a combination of the unions, environmentalists, and some concerned consumer groups that mounted opposition and predicted the future more accurately than either government or business experts. Alan Jinkinson wrote:

Electricity supply privatisation has been a shambles right from the start . . . Rather than float the national electricity generating company PowerGen on the stock market next February, the government wants a trade sale in the autumn. . . . Whichever company wins out, the service to the public, the standard and price of supply and jobs, conditions and pensions of electricity supply staff as well as the environment will all be under threat.[65]

Soon after privatization the industry's previously stable industrial relations were threatened by the end of national bargaining,[66] which was accompanied by redundancies, flexible working, and individual performance pay for managers.[67]

In 1991, as bus services worsened across the nation, NALGO published its own transport policy, *Moving Forward*, which won support from the Labour Party with its views on protecting the environment, planning integrated services, and linking up the community with the service providers. This contrasted with the potential chaos on London buses, as Joan Ruddock, Labour's Shadow Transport Minister, argued: 'Not only is the government turning its back on creating real priority for buses, it now proposes to introduce a system which has been an abject failure in every other part of Britain.'[68] In Scotland, for example, the sale of Fife Scottish Bus group to Stagecoach raised fears 'that private sector bus conglomerate Stagecoach will soon have established an overwhelming monopoly of Scottish bus services for itself'.[69] In another example of private management putting services at risk, West Midlands Passenger Transport Authority cut back on buses after the collapse of its bankers, BCCI.

Markets in health and social care

The government published its plans to reorganize health and social care services in *Care in the Community* at the end of 1989. NALGO's NLGC argued:

[65] *PS* (Sept. 1990), 6.

[66] T. Colling, 'Privatization and the Management of Industrial Relations in Electricity Distribution', *Industrial Relations Journal*, 22/2 (1991), 122.

[67] A. Ferner and T. Colling, 'Electricity Supply', in A. Pendleton and J. Winterton (eds.), *Public Enterprise in Transition: Industrial Relations in State and Privatized Corporations* (London: Routledge, 1993), 121.

[68] *NN*, 4 Oct. 1991, 4.   [69] *PS* (transport) (Nov. 1991), 2.

'The white paper has enormous implications for staff in social services and social work departments . . . These staff are low paid, often untrained and overworked . . . branches will need to ensure that no changes are implemented without their agreement and that particular attention is paid to: work load; pay levels; conditions of service; training.'[70]

NALGO News reported cautiously: 'Although there will remain considerable health service provision in the care of the elderly, disabled, mentally handicapped and mentally ill, the government's intention to increase care in the community, which will lead to the closure of some NHS facilities, will continue to pose threats to the health service employment of many of our members.'[71] In general 'NALGO is opposed to the fragmentation and privatisation of services threatened by the government's "care in the community" proposals'.[72] As the Bill went before Parliament, the main issues for the union were the threat to jobs and the introduction of a range of private, private-not-for-profit, and public employers, some of which might not recognize unions and might force pay and conditions down. As *NALGO News* explained: 'The White Paper Caring for People, and the provisions of the NHS and Community Care Bill lay considerable emphasis on developing a mixed economy of care . . . Authorities may decide either to put homes and services up for tender or simply contract to buy places/services from the private or voluntary sector.' This article listed sell-offs, transfers, and private- and voluntary-sector developments, which already represented a massive transfer of public funds into private hands, covering nine councils and ten health authorities. With no promise of extra funding from government, provision to patients and clients would suffer.[73] NEC member Barbara Hudson argued at the 1990 conference that 'care in the community is a bland, user friendly term but it is a contrick for all those who work for the health service and all those who use the health service'.[74]

The impact of competitive tendering was clear. Research by the Joint NHS Privatization Unit, set up in 1986 by COHSE, GMB, NUPE, and TGWU and subsequently joined by NALGO, found that virtually all catering contracts and nearly three quarters of domestic and laundry contracts were won by in-house organizations. However, the impact on ancillary staff was dramatic: 'A stable, committed and established workforce has been replaced by a casualised, almost entirely part-time staff, paid even less than regular NHS employees and expected to work even harder for their smaller wage packets.'[75] Putting it bluntly, 'Competitive tendering is, quite simply, a means of

[70] *NN*, 5 Jan. 1990, 4–5.   [71] Ibid., 19 Jan. 1990, 6.
[72] Ibid., 16 Mar. 1990, 4–5.   [73] Ibid., 29 June 1990, 4–5.   [74] *PS* (July 1990), 2.
[75] Joint NHS Privatisation Unit, *The NHS Privatisation Experience* (London: Joint NHS Privatisation Unit, 1990), 13.

forcing NHS staff to do the same work or to work harder for less money.'[76] The LRD reported that by the summer of 1990 nearly 2,000 NHS contracts had been put out to tender, 92,000 ancillary workers had lost their jobs as a result, and the service had deteriorated, with nearly one-quarter of contracts failing.[77]

During 1990 the first wave of hospitals prepared bids to 'opt out' of health authority control and gain self-governing trust (SGT) status. *News Now* listed the arguments against: 'They will be leaving an integrated, planned NHS which aims to help those most in need . . . this system sets each hospital in competition with another. . . . The trusts will have complete freedom to set aside long established conditions of employment; ignore pay review bodies and refuse to recognise trade unions and staff associations.'[78] Paul Marks, national officer for health, commented on the SGT bids: 'If you delete all the wishy, washy platitudes, you discover that they really are saying very little . . . With 75 to 80 per cent of NHS expense on staff, it really is scandalous how little applications say on the way they will be treated.'[79]

The union organized ballots and campaigned for votes against management plans, for example:

Health chiefs at the 400-bed Alexandra Hospital in Redditch decided they would not be putting the unit forward in the first wave for opting-out . . . NALGO, along with other health unions at the hospital, had good reason to celebrate. They believe their hard efforts which resulted in massive 'No' votes in ballots against opting out helped prompt the authority into a rethink.[80]

The campaign swept the country, with battles in Leeds, Sheffield, Oxford, Manchester, London, Newcastle, and Merseyside reported in *Public Service*: 'NALGO members have been at the forefront of campaigns up and down the country to fight opt outs at their local hospitals.'[81]

The 1990 conference adopted its own vision for the future of the NHS in the paper *Patients before Profits*, but, as the NHS and Community Care Act became operative on 29 June 1990, NALGO was not hopeful:

Things are likely to get worse, with opted-out trusts haggling in the market place over local health care, and profits being put before patients. For the 64,000 NALGO members who work in the NHS, the prospects are bleak. *Trusts will be run by boards of directors who will not be accountable to the local community. Employees working for them will have no protection of jobs, pay or conditions. There's no guarantee that NALGO or any other union will be recognised by a trust. And trusts will also have power to flog off NHS land or buildings as they see fit.*[82]

---

[76] Ibid. 46.
[77] LRD, *Privatisation and Cuts: The Government Record* (London: LRD, 1990), 3–4.
[78] *News Now* (Sept. 1990), 1.   [79] *PS* (Nov. 1990), 8.   [80] Ibid. (May 1990), 7.
[81] Ibid. (Aug. 1990), 13.   [82] Ibid. 1.

The second wave of opt-outs began in 1991, and the union gave ten reasons to oppose it—it is undemocratic, divisive, destroys planning, boosts private practice, leads to asset stripping, produces no extra cash, could mean bankruptcy, it is secretive, it threatens pay and conditions, and it is unpopular. The new system brought about a particularly acute crisis in London, with severe job losses as Trusts vied with each other to be the government's flagship. As the year ended the government proposed further reforms in another Green Paper, *The Health of the Nation*, which the union opposed:

The effects of its policies will be to cripple the NHS as a free service at the point of need and force those who can barely afford it into private health care. And increasingly what passes for a national health service will put commercial needs before the needs of patients . . . Only private health insurance, private health care and cowboy contractors stand to benefit—and, of course, the unelected and unaccountable trust boards in charge of the shambles . . . The government has cleared the way for staff to be squeezed by virulent trust boards determined to act as a health industry rather than a health service.[83]

Markets in education

LMS schemes, being prepared by all LEAs under the Education Reform Act, had implications for both school administration and LEA authority. The National Local Government Committee drew up recommendations for action: 'The main thrust of branch activity now should be on the *development of agreements at LEA level to accompany the scheme*, setting out specific provisions which apply to APT&C staff in schools. The second main area should be in *approaches to governing bodies*, both directly and through the LEA.'[84] The union produced a training pack, *LMS for Administrative Staff*. 'The pack seeks to explain to school secretaries and administrators how to perform the different areas of their work, and provides advice and guidance, in particular of the "good practice" variety, to help them carry out their duties.'[85] This was linked to pay issues: 'Most authorities have been gradually piling responsibilities on to beleaguered secretaries for over a year in the run up to the full implementation of LMS, and now secretaries all over the country are demanding regradings in line with additional work.'[86]

NALGO opposed the government's White Paper *Higher Education: A New Framework*, not because it proposed the ending of the specious 'binary' division between universities and polytechnics but because it would not be funded and would add to competition in the sector. Before 1991 was out the union identified how college cuts threatened jobs and infrastructure:

[83] *PS* (local government) (Nov. 1991), 6.   [84] *NN*, 19 Jan. 1990, 4–5.
[85] Ibid., 23 Feb. 1990, 4–5.   [86] Ibid. 8.

'Cracks, leaks, unmet bills, unpaid rises—an everyday picture of London's colleges.'[87]

Markets for local-government services

Local authorities took the largest funding cuts in 1990: 'Poll tax capped councils decided on £230 million worth of cuts . . . and there is worse to come as jobs and services go.'[88] Cuts in 1991 were even deeper, following Michael Heseltine's announcement of yet more reforms in a statement to the House of Commons:

The government believes that this structure of two tiers needs to be re-examined for the following reasons. First, unitary authorities are more clearly responsible for the delivery of services . . . second, two tiers may lead to excessive bureaucracy . . . third, the government is committed to the concept of enabling authorities . . . fourth, the government intends to increase the momentum of their existing policies . . . fifth, the present structures of local government do not universally win favour with local people.[89]

NALGO responded in detail to the two consultation documents, *The Structure of Local Government in England* and *A New Tax for Local Government*:

This Association is deeply committed to strong, effective and independent local government, and to the principles of local democratic control of many public services . . . We have a deep suspicion that this review exercise is not genuinely aimed at identifying the real problems and devising solutions which strengthen local democracy . . . There are hints within the document . . . that there is a set of preconceived ideas . . . to undermine and marginalise local government.[90]

Such worries were shown to be well founded when further cuts were announced, confirming NALGO's view: 'The present government has a secret agenda for local government. This agenda involves an attempt to undermine local democracy and to dismantle the network of services which local authorities provide for and on behalf of the community.'[91] More evidence of the government's intentions came with new CCT proposals: 'CCT, which forces local authority services into an ideological straightjacket, is due to be extended. Both the current law and planned legislation are minefields, dependent on the "guidance" of the Secretary of State.'[92] The consultation paper, *Competing for Quality*, proposed extending CCT into 'professional' areas.

As funding caps caused more job losses, branches responded with action. There was a particularly bitter strike in Liverpool:

[87] *PS* (education) (Nov. 1991), 1. [88] *PS* (Sept. 1990), 1.
[89] *NN*, 3 May 1991, 6. [90] Ibid., 28 June 1991, 3.
[91] Ibid., 11 Oct. 1991, 4. [92] Ibid., 15 Nov. 1991, 4–5.

NALGO council workers in Liverpool have voted to take strike action in protest at plans to axe over 1,000 jobs. In a ballot last week, members gave their overwhelming support for three days of strike . . . Union negotiators arrived at talks over a planned 386 redundancies last week to hear news that the council wishes to shed a further 684 jobs . . . NALGO, which stands to lose 40 jobs if the cuts package goes ahead, was among unions which put forward alternative plans to compulsory redundancies to avoid poll tax capping.[93]

The strike went ahead:

Liverpool city council was brought virtually to a standstill as workers halted services during a three day strike . . . The strike was solid as reports came in of leisure centres, libraries, social services offices and housing offices closed down . . . Keith Dovaston, NALGO steward and secretary of the Joint Trade Union Committee, said: 'At least 20,000 are out, council services are pretty well at a standstill.'[94]

When a small group of Liverpool councillors took control of the employers' side and tried to push through an additional 590 compulsory redundancies, the dispute turned nasty: the council revoked time-off agreements; fourteen people were arrested on picket duty after intervention by the Special Branch; and there were reports of black members on picket lines being racially abused. Judy Cotter, branch vice-chair, said that the council was becoming increasingly hostile towards the unions. The *Liverpool Echo* captured the atmosphere: 'Defiant union leaders today announced a programme of industrial action aimed at crippling Liverpool City Council services.'[95] Later: 'Jobs-cutting Liverpool City Council has sent out its first compulsory redundancy notices—escalating the bitter confrontation with its workforce.'[96] The dispute cost the union £3,750,000 in strike pay.

The precarious state of local-authority funds was further revealed by the collapse of the bank BCCI. This illustrated how the government's failure to regulate the private sector, and its advice to local authorities on their savings and investments, made funds more vulnerable. Many local authorities lost money as a result: 'Billions Frozen as Bank Closes in Fraud Enquiry' ran *The Times's* headline, with allegations of laundering drug money.[97]

Managers in the markets

This mixture of financial uncertainty, constraints, and political attacks on public services started to affect management practice, throwing up odd examples of what were to become widespread practices later on. Management attitudes and behaviour towards both collective bargaining and trade

[93] *NN*, 5 Apr. 1991, 1.   [94] Ibid., 19 Apr. 1991, 1.
[95] *Liverpool Echo*, 3 Apr. 1991, 1.   [96] Ibid., 9 Apr. 1991, 1.
[97] *The Times*, 6 July 1991, 1, 25.

unionism were changing significantly. Some managers welcomed the 'empowerment' associated with the 'freedom' to manage local budgets. Some just went along with it, responding to increased pressure to toe the line themselves by intensifying the pressures on their staff. Others opposed both the changes and the new direction of management, and either took early retirement or watched ruefully as an important tradition of public-sector management, indeed the wellspring of the original NALGO, was swept aside in a tide of managerialist zeal. Traditional forms of management practice, rooted in a public-service-sector ethos, embracing both service users and service staff, were simply no longer appropriate in the new world of self-declared modernity and market mechanisms.

In 1990 much of this was yet to become apparent in the services remaining in the public sector—it was only after the 1992 Conservative election victory that the floodgates really opened for the new management experts to take their place at the forefront of the public services. Nevertheless, examples of practices long established in the private profit-making sector were already emerging. There were local employer-based pay schemes for white-collar staff at Macclesfield Borough Council with merit and loyalty pay. Kent County Council opted out of national pay bargaining altogether, and went over the head of the NALGO branch to implement this with staff. In Coventry the first Labour council introduced performance-related pay, designed by management consultants Hay MSL. Similar schemes were being considered by Braintree and Buckinghamshire councils.[98]

This unilateral imposition of new pay systems was symptomatic of a wider assertion of managerial prerogative, to worsen conditions of service and to alter working practices. Thirty-six NALGO members were locked out by British Gas in Norwich for opposing new working practices. In the electricity supply industry *NALGO News* pointed to 'problems continually arising from the new "macho" management approach' as part of the rush to privatization.[99]

There were a few victories to change employers' minds, as when Croydon council dropped their plans to transfer fifteen homes for the elderly into the private sector. *Public Service* reported: 'Local union leaders warned the social services department that costs would rocket and staff threatened industrial action when they learnt there was no guarantee that trade unions would be recognised or national agreements maintained.'[100] There was a fifteen-week strike by 130 Islington childcare staff over workload, which ended when the staff returned to work accepting an increase in the staff/child ratio of 11 per cent instead of 27 per cent as originally intended by the council. At the

[98] Association of District Councils Human Resources Commitee, *Reports on National Pay Bargaining* (London: Association of District Councils, 1990).

[99] *NN*, 2 Feb. 1990, 6.   [100] *PS* (May 1991), 3.

national level, 'NALGO has won a victory in the fight to stop piecemeal privatisation of Britain's canal sides.'[101] But such victories could not disguise the main flow of events, as even wealthy institutions such as Imperial College in London planned to privatize their security and messenger services and Berkshire NHS support services were being put out to private tender.

However, the scandal over the collapse of privatized computer firm Qa Business Services, created in 1989 through a management buyout of the West Midlands Regional Health Authority's computer bureau, was a significant setback for the government. *NALGO News* reported: 'Devastated staff working for the troubled Qa Business Services health company in the West Midlands have been told they will not be paid . . . It is believed the bank has frozen the company's account . . . The company, which pioneered the Department of Health's waiting list initiative, was one of the first major sell offs of the NHS administration in Britain.'[102] Things then became much worse: 'Distraught health workers have been thrown out of work without any money following the collapse of Qa Business Services, the government's flagship privatisation firm.'[103]

NALGO, NUPE, and COHSE commissioned the West Midlands Health Monitoring Unit to compile a report on the fiasco, which identified a pattern that became all too familiar: decreasing public accountability; increased secrecy under the smokescreen of commercial confidentiality; purchase of public assets at knockdown prices; loss of employment rights; and exclusion of trade unions. In this case the staff received short shrift: 'There is no happy ending to this story of the attempt to transform a supposedly ugly duckling from the public sector into a private sector swan. No one arrived on a white horse to save Qa at the last moment. The innocent suffered, while those perhaps not so innocent escaped punishment.'[104] This particular battle was still going on in 1999, when UNISON finally won £4 million compensation for forty-nine Qa staff who lost their pensions.[105]

Reports of the Death of Collective Bargaining— Greatly Exaggerated

Changes in workplace industrial relations during the 1980s were tracked by the Workplace Industrial Relations Surveys. The 1990 survey[106] revealed a

---

[101] *PS* (May 1991) 16.   [102] *NN*, 27 Sept. 1991, 1.   [103] Ibid., 4 Oct. 1991, 1.

[104] COHSE, NALGO, and NUPE, *Qa Business Services: The NHS Privatisation that Failed* (London: NALGO, 1992), 25.

[105] *Morning Star*, 22 Nov. 1999, 4.

[106] N. Millward, M. Stevens, D. Smart, and W. Hawes, *Workplace Industrial Relations in Transition* (Aldershot: Dartmouth, 1992).

decline in traditional post-Donovan industrial relations, with a marked shift away from national bargaining in private-sector manufacturing and services. However, there was only a relatively small dip in the dominance of the old Whitley system in the public sector. The survey reported that levels of public-sector union density remained high at 72 per cent among both manual and non-manual employees.[107] Collective bargaining still dominated industrial relations in the public sector with 84 per cent of employees covered by collective agreements, involving over four million workers.[108] Nearly every establishment in the public sector had grievance (96 per cent) and disciplinary (98 per cent) procedures.[109]

This was before the main reforms of health, education, local government, and the Civil Service were fully in place. Further data from the 1998 survey[110] suggest that Whitleyism was weakened during the 1990s. Ninety-five per cent of public-sector workplaces had a recognized union,[111] with union density at 57 per cent.[112] The existence of formal disciplinary and grievance procedures remained unchanged, but collective-bargaining coverage had fallen to 63 per cent.[113] However, this did not count over a million employees covered by pay review bodies. Collective bargaining remained an important part of industrial relations throughout the public services. National pay claims were settled without industrial action, but local initiatives to combat low pay through regradings led to a spate of local disputes, which turned nasty where managers sought to seize unilateral control over job regulation by undermining the union.

The National Health Service

The ambulance dispute continued into 1990 with great popular support against entrenched government ministers and angry managers, reported by Astrid Stubbs in *NALGO News*: 'Four months of industrial action has failed to break the resolve of ambulance workers fighting for a decent wage . . . meanwhile the union's assistant national officer for health Owen Davies, praised the action of control staff in London who were suspended after refusing to transfer to Waterloo to take over jobs of staff who have already declared themselves suspended'.[114] The cost of the dispute to the government escalated: 'South Yorkshire police will be passing on to the NHS bills for £26,000 a day for providing emergency cover . . . Health secretary Kenneth Clarke faced criticism from all sides this week—even from within his own party—

---

[107] Ibid. 59.   [108] Ibid. 91.   [109] Ibid. 187.

[110] M. Cully, S. Woodland, A. O'Reilly, and G. Dix, *Britain at Work* (London: Routledge, 1999).

[111] Ibid. 92.   [112] Ibid. 88.   [113] Ibid. 242.   [114] *NN*, 5 Jan. 1990, 1.

over his handling of the ambulance dispute.'[115] The mass rally in London on 13 January attracted over 35,000 supporters, and leader of the Labour Party Neil Kinnock handed in a petition with 4,446,208 signatures supporting the unions' demands for arbitration to end the dispute. One million people stopped work for fifteen minutes, as hundreds and thousands joined marches and rallies throughout the country.

In the end the dispute was resolved through an increased pay offer. NALGO advised members to accept 'the deal worth 9.2 per cent in cash terms in the first year, and over two years ambulance staff salaries will rise by at least 17.6 per cent. If two per cent local supplements are also agreed, unions are confident the deal could be worth 19.6 per cent for all—compared to the original 6.5 per cent the Government was offering.'[116] This was NALGO's best gloss on the agreement. In reality, after such a long and bitter struggle, the improvement was marginal.

The 1990 claim for the 150,000 staff on A&C grades, for a 12 per cent or £18 increase, had two main aims:

The first is to build on the progress which was made last year in addressing the problems of absolute low pay in the structure particularly for women. The second is to improve the position of the group as a whole in relation to average earnings and to earnings in comparable areas so that the NHS is in a position to offer a rate of pay for the demanding work undertaken by its A&C staff.[117]

Negotiations stalled as the union side rejected a management offer and took the issue to the branches:

NALGO has delivered a hard hitting message to its NHS administrative and clerical workers to vote in favour of industrial action for better pay. At a national delegate advisory meeting last Friday, members voted by nearly three to one to reject the 7.7 per cent offer and to go to a ballot on a programme of summer strikes and overtime bans. Figures on a card vote were 36,685 in favour of a ballot with 13,662 against. The ballot, to be held in coming weeks with the result announced on 14 June, will be accompanied by a mass media advertising campaign making a no-nonsense call to members to throw out the offer and take action for a living wage.[118]

However, the majority of the members, perhaps with an eye on the ambulance dispute, did not have the stomach for a fight—the ballot showed a clear majority in favour of the overtime ban but not in favour of strike action, and the reconvened group meeting voted to accept the offer.

In 1991 the A&C claim called for a thirty-five-hour week, improved long service leave, a 5 per cent plus £25 pay increase, and deletion of the most junior grades: 'The A&C structure is still marked by low pay in absolute and

---

[115] *NN*, 12 Jan. 1990, 1. [116] Ibid., 2 Mar. 1990, 3. [117] Ibid., 2 Feb. 1990, 4–5.
[118] Ibid., 25 May 1990, 1.

relative terms and by wide and unacceptable discrepancies between the earnings of men and women within it.'[119] Low-paid women on A&C grades were urged to write to the Secretary of State for Health, Virginia Bottomley. The union briefed NHS stewards on the possibility of industrial action, based on the successful 1989 local-government strike: 'NALGO's strategy is for a limited programme of national action involving all members, backed up by indefinite strike action to be undertaken by key groups of members. Limited national action would allow for periods of one, two and three day strikes.'[120] By April the employers responded with an offer of 7.4 per cent, and their final offer was accepted in the summer: '56,000 staff on A&C grades one and two and 13,500 PT'B' staff on scale point 10 and below will be £600 better off while those above that point will receive a 7.9 per cent rise' (see Tables 2.7 and 2.8).[121] An identical claim was submitted for ambulance officers and controllers, supported by arguments about inflation, comparability, labour shortages, and increased responsibilities in the age of information technology. A 15 per cent claim went in for the 45,000 PT'B' staff in committees 'A' (pathology laboratory staff), 'T' (medical technical staff and dental auxiliaries), and 'W' (works/estates staff).

NHS restructuring began feeding into the bargaining arena, as managers of some of the first Trusts called for local pay determination. NUPE Assistant General Secretary Roger Poole, speaking at a conference organized by management consultants KPMG, typified the union position: 'There will not be local pay bargaining in the NHS. We can now say it very confidently indeed. The Whitley Councils are going to stay, review bodies are going to stay . . . local pay bargaining is not going to see the light of day.'[122] NALGO argued that Trust status 'radically undermines the national, comprehensive and universal character of the service',[123] and that it opened the door for changes in labour management practices aimed at cheapening staff costs and reducing the influence of staff groups. Talks about gradings for PAMs hit difficulties when the management side engineered a collapse of the negotiations, under government guidance, symptomatic of the growing trend towards managerialism. Lincolnshire Ambulance Trust tried to undercut Whitley by offering staff less than the national agreement. They backed down under union pressure, but then turned against crews with temporary contracts, terminating them and re-employing them on worse 'trust contracts'.

In their joint submission to the pay review body NALGO and the other NHS unions urged employers to 'outlaw low pay among undervalued nurses, midwives and health visitors'.[124] However, the government announced that

[119] Ibid., 1 Feb. 1991, 8.   [120] Ibid., 15 Feb. 1991, 4–5.
[121] *PS* (health) (June 1991), 1.   [122] *NN*, 22 Mar. 1991, 3.
[123] Ibid., 28 Mar. 1991, 5.   [124] *PS* (health) (Nov. 1991), 3.

awards for both nurses and PAMs were to be staged, with 7.5 per cent in April and the rest (2.2 per cent for nurses and 3.3 per cent for PAMs) in December.

National committee chair John Pestle assessed the union's campaign and the negotiating climate in 1991:

NALGO's NHS workers had fought on all fronts in the past year—for improved gradings, service conditions, opposing creation of trusts and for negotiating rights in opted out units. There was nothing wrong, he said, in the union staying its hand over action at this stage. Acceptance of the offer was merely the close of one small episode in a long battle against a government that, despite its rhetoric, cared nothing for the NHS, he said. 'We have taken some hard knocks in the last year but the lessons we have learned have strengthened our resolve to take on the awesome tasks that still confront us,' said Mr Pestle.[125]

Local government

The 1990 APT&C claim for a flat-rate increase of £1,500 was seen as part of the solution to low pay among the 500,000 members. Improvements claimed in service conditions included a thirty-five-hour week and twenty-five days' basic leave. Responding to the employers' offer, NLGC chair Jim White angrily stated: 'The real world dictates that 8 per cent is totally unrealistic and unacceptable. We reject it. It does nothing to protect our members from the ravages of soaring interest rates nor the effects of the poll tax . . . it is less than the rate of inflation and less than pay settlements in other sectors.'[126] After further negotiations the union side accepted 9.39 per cent, and he argued that 'this is not a victory for the low paid or for the general membership, it's a settlement which meets by and large the aspirations of the membership and we had no option but to recommend acceptance'.[127]

During the summer of 1990 NALGO representatives from the twenty-one poll-tax-capped authorities met in London to discuss a common strategy. The main motion of the day

set out minimum standards for co-operation with local authorities, including no compulsory redundancies, protection of conditions of service, full consultation and maintenance of local and national agreements. It also calls on branches in poll-capped authorities to monitor cuts and unfilled vacancies, to refuse to do planned overtime resulting from capping and to educate and inform stewards and service users.[128]

Examples of this kind of action could be seen in many councils. Haringey threatened up to 800 forced redundancies to make up a budget shortfall of £14 million. The unions presented a counter-strategy, whereby cuts would be achieved through negotiation as an alternative to significant levels of

---

[125] *PS* (health) (June 1991), 1.   [126] *NN*, 18 May 1990, 1.

[127] *PS* (July 1990), 12.   [128] *NN*, 6 July 1990, 1.

industrial action. In Avon the NALGO branch made 'it very clear to members that work due to unfilled posts, caused by poll tax capping, should be left undone so that people can see the effects of the government's policy'. In North Tyneside, facing cuts of 1,100 jobs, the branch secretary spoke of 'unimaginable levels of chaos . . . we are talking about the effective collapse of an authority as a provider of services . . . no section of the workforce will be immune from these cuts.' In Derbyshire 'huge cuts will almost certainly result in job losses'; in Brent with a hung council cuts were being made despite a balanced budget; in Doncaster the council 'defied the government this week by setting a poll tax level above that determined by environment secretary Chris Patten'; and in capped Lambeth the council decided that 'co-operation and compromise with staff unions were the watchwords'.[129]

Activists aimed to protect collective bargaining by developing a strong national strategy that would support local action against cuts. More and more councils that were making cuts were Labour councils. Nevertheless, the local union responses were inevitably patchy, as members in some areas were ready to fight but others were less enthusiastic. In Southwark, for example, a branch meeting to discuss job losses was inquorate.

The 1991 APT&C claim was supported by a Low Pay Unit report showing that discrimination was at the heart of low pay. New NLGC chair Jean Geldart told a fringe meeting at NALGO's women's conference that 'low pay is a women's issue'.[130] Dennis Reed, the national officer for local government, highlighted the difficult negotiating climate as the claim was being drawn up:

Local authority employers have already made great play of the fact that this has been a difficult year for local authorities with poll tax capping and so on. They issued a barrage of press releases about how difficult it is going to be to meet our pay claim before we'd even lodged it. It is a difficult year for negotiations, but we are not prepared to accept the continuing erosion of APT and C terms compared to other sectors and within council employment. We are also not prepared to allow the employers to rubbish our claims on behalf of low paid members in local government.[131]

The main elements of the claim were for 12 per cent, deletion of the first four spinal points and reduction in hours. The employers countered with the assertion that, as teachers had received 6 per cent, so others in local government could not realistically expect more than that. They also rejected the low-pay case, referring to rising unemployment as a reason for not worrying about recruitment and retention. In May *NALGO News* reported on the employers' delaying tactics: 'A summer of local government industrial action

[129] Ibid., 10 Aug. 1990, 1.   [130] Ibid., 1 Nov. 1991, 3.
[131] Ibid., 8 Feb. 1991, 1.

came one step nearer this week as the national employers failed once again to make an offer in response to NALGO's pay claim.' Dennis Reed said: 'Our members are going to be very angry if an offer has not been made by the time of the group meeting.' National committee chair Jim White echoed the sentiment: 'NALGO members hate being betrayed and that is what the employers seem to be doing.'[132] Their frustration was encapsulated in a *Public Service* headline in June 1991: 'Anger as Bosses Drag Feet over Pay Offer'.

When the employers did finally respond, the situation only worsened: 'Furious NALGO negotiators this week dismissed the local government employers [*sic*] pay offer of 6.1 per cent as "ridiculous and insulting"'[133] (see Tables 2.5–2.8). The NLGC called on the group meeting delegates for: 'Support for the staff side's rejection of the offer of 6.1%; continued negotiations; preparation of plans for a ballot on industrial action; and a national lobby of the NJC.'[134] Journalist Kay Holmes reported on the NJC meeting in *NALGO News*:

The local government employers have raised their pay offer by a mere 0.3 per cent, bringing the offer to 6.4 per cent, with nothing to address the problem of low pay or working time. The staff side of five unions unanimously rejected the offer and NALGO negotiators are recommending a ballot for 10 days all out strike action over a period of eight weeks plus selective strike by key workers.[135]

This call was supported by the local-government group meeting and the union campaigned for a yes vote, issuing an emergency edition of *Public Service*. Dennis Reed's anger with the employers was clear: 'We could have reached a settlement, but the employers cynically and contemptuously engineered a breakdown in the talks because of the opposition to giving more money to the lower paid. We are also concerned that their aim is to break down the national negotiating machinery.'[136] However, the members voted heavily against action (95,758 in favour, 202,340 against) and the 6.4 per cent offer was accepted.

Higher and further education

The 1990 claim for university clerical staff was for 15 per cent or £1500. The employers offered 8.2 per cent plus £100 and this was accepted. Staff in colleges and polytechnics rejected a similar offer of 8.2 per cent, but national negotiations were dogged by employer moves towards employer-level local bargaining.

---

[132] *NN*, 17 May 1991, 1.   [133] Ibid., 31 May 1991, 1.
[134] Ibid., 7 June 1991, 6.   [135] Ibid., 12 July 1991, 1.
[136] *PS* (local government) (Aug. 1991), 1.

In 1991 the universities group claimed 15 per cent or £1500 to protect members from inflation and from low pay, and to catch up for recent relative decline. As Elaine Harrison, national officer, commented: 'We hope this meets the aims and aspirations of all our members and they will rally round in support.'[137] Janet Richardson, chair of the national committee, added: 'We have got a long way to go to make up the ground we lost in the past ten years. It's appalling that 58 per cent of staff are still low paid. This claim is aimed at ensuring that staff get proper recognition for the work they do.'[138]

NALGO rejected the employers' opening offer of 5 per cent with the possibility of a pay review body in the future, and campaigned for a better deal while the Committee of Vice-Chancellors and Principals (CVCP) negotiated with the government for more funds. The union supported this push from the employers for some respite from cuts in the sector, and branches campaigned to draw attention to the plight of universities. A revised offer of 7 per cent was seen as inadequate, but the union negotiators conceded that the employers had offered what they could afford given the continued squeeze on finances. Janet Richardson was pleased that the employers had accepted the union's case: 'I would like to pay tribute to activists around the country who have worked hard and it has paid off. You changed the employers [*sic*] mind. You have influenced their strategy. The employers have at least accepted our arguments that our salaries have fallen behind our comparators in real terms.'[139]

In the newly reformed higher and further education sectors the union had an even harder task with worse results. Restructuring under the Education Reform Act 1988, allied with a continuing squeeze on the unit of resource, created a situation similar in some ways to that in the health sector. The employers were aiming to introduce new contracts with a weaker national agreement, and to undermine the union's position at local level by threatening to reduce time off for trade-union duties and activities. The campaign for APT&C staffs in the polytechnics and colleges in the Polytechnic Central Funding Council (PCFC) sector included a claim for 15 per cent or £1500, better leave, shorter hours, and the deletion of the bottom grades. Branches were advised that 'membership participation and support is the very basis of the campaign' and that they could 'hold workplace or constituency meetings; issue local publicity highlighting local issues . . . get stewards to distribute leaflets . . . and put posters and stickers in prominent positions'.[140]

Negotiations were hampered by the general lack of funds in the system and by divisions among the employers, and the first offer drew an angry response:

---

[137] *PS* (Jan. 1991), 1.   [138] Ibid. (Mar. 1991), 13.
[139] *PS* (education) (Sept. 1991), 2.   [140] *NN*, 10 May 1991, 4–5.

College and polytechnic staff have been warned to brace themselves for industrial action over the latest 6 per cent national pay offer. Mike Clarke of the national polytechnics and colleges committee warned delegates at the annual group meeting 'I personally believe we will have to go to industrial action. We will be very lucky to get an extra 0.3 per cent improvement in the offer. To me, that is nowhere near enough.' Members unanimously backed the emergency motion that the 'wholly inadequate' pay offer be thrown out. They recognised that industrial action may be needed to support their claim, and they agreed that the membership should be fully consulted on the best form of protest.[141]

A slightly improved offer was also rejected: 'A campaign for support of industrial action has been given the go-ahead by the national polytechnics and colleges committee following the employers' offer of 6.2 per cent or £600.'[142] Finally the issue came to a head in the autumn:

Delegates to a group meeting last week overturned a recommendation by the national polytechnics and colleges committee to reluctantly accept a 6.3 per cent or £600 increase. Instead a card vote revealed 2,903 to 1,959 in favour of an amendment rejecting the offer and calling for a ballot on a ban on all non-contractual overtime, a one-day national strike and selective action.[143]

The union campaigned for a yes vote, but the ballot went against:

NALGO's polytechnics and colleges APT&C staff have voted narrowly against strike action in protest at this year's pay offer. The result of a ballot on industrial action this week revealed 3,599 (47.58 per cent) in favour of a one day strike to improve the 6.3 per cent or £600 offer with 3,915 (51.76 per cent) against. Even so, in a high 68.21 per cent turnout, staff voted decisively in favour of an overtime ban. There were 4,424 votes (58.49 per cent) in favour of the ban with 2,950 (39 per cent) against.[144]

In the private sector—utilities and buses

Bargaining in the recently privatized sector took a somewhat different form, as negotiators came to terms with both the new bargaining machinery and the new commercial realities of their private employers. British Gas staff argued for a substantial pay rise in 1990, based on 'profitability and productivity' and giving detailed facts and figures in support of their case (see Tables 2.11 and 2.12). After a split in the national committee, with a minority wanting to ballot members, an offer of 9.75 per cent was accepted. The 1991 claim for 'a substantial increase' was based on British Gas profits. The employer offered £750 to all staff from 1 September and a further 4 per cent on all scales from March 1992, in exchange for some changes in working practices.[145] Roy

---

[141] *PS* (education) (July 1991), 2. [142] *NN*, 9 Aug. 1991, 1.
[143] Ibid., 4 Oct. 1991, 3. [144] Ibid., 22 Nov. 1991, 1.
[145] NALGO, *Under Review: Your NALGO Guide to the GSSO Review* (London: NALGO, 1991).

Jones, chair of the national committee, said: 'It has been a long hard set of negotiations but we have finally brought them to a conclusion which I believe will be acceptable to the majority of our members.'[146] However, the group meeting disagreed, as *Public Service* journalist Jeff Spooner reported:

Delegates threw out the committee's motion which called for a recommendation of acceptance when the GSSO [Gas Staffs and Senior Officers] members vote in a secret ballot on the review terms which have taken more than three years to negotiate. The committee was defeated on a card vote of 11,815 for to 14,905 against. And the meeting went on to decide to make no recommendation to members.[147]

In the end the members sided with the national committee, voting to accept the offer by 18,868 (77.3 per cent) in favour and 5,552 (22.7 per cent) against.

Electricity national officer Mike Jeram put in the 1991 claim using the same formulation as gas colleagues for a 'substantial increase'. Receiving an offer of 8.9 per cent on pay but nothing on hours and equal pay issues, NALGO's first response was to get the annual group meeting to instruct the National Electricity Committee to prepare for industrial action if necessary, but the clear feeling of the members was to accept what was on the table (see Tables 2.11 and 2.12).

Water industry settlements varied a little in 1990, under company-level bargaining (see Table 2.13). For example, staff in Welsh Water accepted a 9.6 per cent deal over nine months, and at the Portsmouth Water Company a settlement of 12.25 per cent over fifteen months was reached. In North West Water members rejected the 9.4 per cent offer and went to ballot on industrial action, and Anglian Water settled at 9.5 per cent.

In 1991 the new bargaining arrangements began to throw up variations in the ways employers and NALGO branches settled pay. For example, at Wessex Water the union linked pay with company profits and settled for 9 per cent. Managers at Thames Water and Yorkshire Water wanted to tie pay this year to the move to single-table bargaining. In the end Thames settled for 7.5 per cent and Yorkshire Water received 9.5 per cent. Among other companies ballots on offers resulted in acceptance as follows: North West 7.25 per cent, Northumbria 6.9 per cent, Severn Trent 9.5 per cent, Anglia 8 per cent, Southern 8.3 per cent, Easy Surrey 8.7 per cent, York 6.5 per cent, Sutton 7.5 per cent. A major exception was at North West Water, where NALGO members held the first ever strike in the privatized industry when their claim for 9 per cent and £300 was followed by an offer of 7.25 per cent. The one-day strike included picketing of local offices and support from the GMB. The dispute was resolved after an improved offer from the company, which included an extra 1 per cent.

---

[146] *PS* (gas) (June 1991,) 1.   [147] Ibid. (July 1991), 1.

British Waterways Board staff claimed 15 per cent in 1990 and settled at 9.5 per cent. In 1991 they claimed 10 per cent and improved conditions on hours and equal opportunities. After an unsatisfactory set of negotiations the employers' offer of 6.5 per cent went to a ballot and was accepted.

In passenger transport the PTE employers responded to NALGO's 1990 claim for 12 per cent with an initial offer of 6 per cent, which was rejected. An increased 7 per cent offer with strings was again rejected, but later accepted, as national officer Alex Thompson explained: 'No one is happy with the offer but the negotiators felt that there was no alternative to making the recommendation to accept the offer other than industrial action—branches will now decide.'[148] Bus company settlements included GM buses at 8.5 per cent, Busways at 10 per cent, Lincoln City at 5 per cent, and Eastern National at 8.3 per cent.

Low pay and regradings

Low pay was explicitly raised in every national claim—as John Daly noted, 'even in Dickens' time the low paid were better off, relative to average earnings, than they are today'.[149] Jim White told us: 'Low pay was becoming a major issue within local government . . . the straight percentage settlement year in year out was only increasing the cash differential.' Rita Donaghy agreed: 'the low pay issue and bargaining became the old flat rate versus percentage debate.' The arguments extended into important broader issues of incomes differentials and skills valuation, taken up by John Pestle, chair of the Health Service Committee, when he said that members wanted 'a fair reward for their contributions'.[150] In the context of merger discussions NALGO needed to bring its claims and concerns into line with NUPE's strong fight for the introduction of a national minimum wage, and to highlight the identity of interest of low-paid manual and non-manual employees.

Public Service and *NALGO News* carried regular features on the plight of low-paid NALGO members, as in this report by Kay Holmes:

Wearing a white collar to work is not a passport to a life of comfort and luxury. Despite the 'cushy' image of local government jobs, more than a quarter of a million white collar workers are trapped in a low pay ghetto. Insecurity, poor prospects and pitiful pay were the experiences of local government workers interviewed for a Low Pay Unit survey published last week. The survey, commissioned by NALGO, reveals that low pay is a major problem among non-manual local government staff, with four in 10 APT and C workers earning less than the Council of Europe's decency threshold.[151]

---

[148] *PS* (transport) (July 1991), 2.   [149] *PS* (Apr. 1990), 6.
[150] Ibid. (Jan. 1991), 1.   [151] *NN*, 13 Apr. 1990, 1.

The low-pay theme continued in 1991, with claims supported by the union's *Low Pay Charter*. In local government:

NALGO has drawn up a 10-point charter on low pay to help branches to address the issue in negotiations. The union's document points out that nearly 40 per cent of local authority staff earn below the Council of Europe's 'decency threshold' . . . NALGO's 1991 pay claim includes a demand for a flat-rate element bringing all adult workers up to the decency threshold.[152]

Some feared that this emphasis on low pay would appear to neglect the interests of members in higher levels of management, resulting in a loss of membership. Mike Blick hinted at some division at national level when he told us: 'We didn't just represent lower paid people . . . the national committee didn't want the union to become a low paid union.' However, in practice most settlements were predominantly percentages. So, with downward pressure on everyone's pay, the relative position of the lower paid remained mainly unchanged.

As pay rates were squeezed nationally, with settlements frequently no higher than inflation, attention focused on the local employer. Unable to deal with relatively low pay through national action, local grading claims took an increasingly important role in securing promotion and recognition. There were some successes in the utilities. Members in the South Eastern electricity branch won regrading through an equal-pay claim:

Sue Houlton and Stella Sanderson had worked in Seeboard's salary section for nine years and had been demanding a regrading since 1982. They were joined by Marika Hoare who started in 1984 and the three, defended by NALGO, pursued their claim to an Industrial Tribunal. District Officer John Smith said 'we realised there was a fourth person involved, working in the same section, doing the same work, only this person was a man and he was on a higher scale.'[153]

The employer settled out of court adding £1,500 to their salaries. In another example, a strike started in the North West Region when 250 members walked out in support of three colleagues who were suspended for refusing to accept training on new computers during a dispute over regrading. Indicating the strike's significance for the union, 'NALGO's new president, David Stockford, made the gas staff's picket lines his first engagement in his year of office'.[154] The 'Preston Three' were eventually reinstated and good faith negotiations on regrading took place.

But the main action in 1990 was in the NHS and in local government. Medical secretaries throughout the country took action against their employers, frequently successfully. For example, in Gwynedd Health Authority

[152] *PS* (local government) (June 1991), 2.   [153] *NN*, 16 Feb. 1990, 1.
[154] Ibid., 22 June 1990, 1.

sixty-eight members took strike action at the end of April, receiving £50 per week strike pay from the national union, with members in other branches being asked to donate funds for the dispute. There was a one-day strike over regrading by secretarial and clerical staff at Bromsgrove and Redditch Health Authority, and a half-day strike by 120 nursery workers in Leeds. Hospital receptionists in Southampton escalated their dispute: 'Low paid NALGO workers at Princess Anne hospital in Southampton started indefinite strike action on Monday in their fight for regrading.'[155] This dispute escalated: 'Bread-line NALGO members have been sacked from a Southampton hospital after going on strike. The 16 long-serving clerks and receptionists . . . have been out in dispute for more than a month in a demand for regrading. Last week, management took the brutal step of dismissing them. Their jobs are to be readvertised.'[156] They were reinstated after the threat of indefinite action by the rest of the Southampton health branch. The union's decision to pay full take-home pay to the strikers after their dismissal contributed to the victory. But the most bitter and difficult regrading dispute was the strike of medical records staff at Oldham Royal Infirmary (see Box 15).

In local government, many claims reflected changes in the workplaces. As services were reorganized and working practices altered, so the job tasks changed, providing a basis for arguments in support of regrading claims. Two extracts from NALGO journals illustrate this: 'Low paid Manchester library staff were on strike this week in support of a six year old regrading claim. More than 140 staff took strike action and picketed all the city's libraries. Most of the workers are on scales one or two, and the branch is seeking an overall regrading for all library staff.'[157] And: 'Liverpool fire brigade technicians have blazed to victory after 48 days of strike action. The seven staff who maintain the central communications unit of the Merseyside Fire and Civil Defence Authority had been on the same grade since 1974.'[158] Occupational therapists in local government put in for new gradings based on those of social workers, and in Haringey school secretaries took action over their pay rates. In Sheffield, the anti-discrimination legislation was used to help women school meals catering officers win regrading through an equal-value case after five years.

Box 15. NALGO and the Regrading Claims of Medical Secretaries

Medical secretaries work for hospital consultants and their team of doctors. They deal with correspondence, with patients and relatives, and with general practitioners.

[155] *NN*, 9 Feb. 1990, 1.   [156] Ibid., 9 Mar. 1990, 1.
[157] Ibid., 3 May 1991, 1.   [158] *PS* (local government) (Oct. 1991), 1.

They organize case conferences, prepare the agendas and minutes of meetings, and some maintain waiting lists and arrange admissions to hospital. On 9 March 1986 thirty-four of the thirty-eight secretaries at Luton and Dunstable Hospital started a strike after thirteen years of trying to persuade their managers to discuss their case for a higher grade.

They were on the 'Personal Secretary' grade, the lowest grade for NHS administrative and clerical (A&C) workers, which covers general clerical duties involving 'particular matters of minor importance'. They believed that they should be on the 'Higher Clerical Officer' (HCO) grade, and went through the regrading procedure: the first stage was an application to local management; secondly, an appeal against management's decision to a joint panel at the level of the Regional Health Authority; and, finally, an appeal to a joint panel of the national Whitley Council. As happened with most cases, management turned down their applications, and the appeals panels failed to agree, with the union representatives supporting and the employer representatives opposing. Their last remaining option was industrial action, and they decided to strike.

There was widespread support for their case. Ada Maddocks, national officer for health, said: 'We support the secretaries' action because it is a challenge by low-paid women workers to management down-grading of their skills, talents and responsibilities.' Consultants at their hospital donated £2,000 to their hardship fund and then voted to stop doing routine work and to cover emergencies only. Messages of support came from branches all over the country and from patients, district full-time officers attended picket lines and gave practical organizing support, and national publicity officers helped to publicize their case.

After less than four weeks management agreed to a minimum of twenty upgrades as the basis for talks, and the strike was suspended. Their spokeswoman Jean Taylor said, 'We are very pleased that it has been so effective in making management listen to our demands and are confident that we now have a sound basis for negotiation.'

This victory spurred medical secretaries throughout the country to press forward with their own demands. Thirty-nine secretaries at Birmingham's Selly Oak Hospital, who had lodged a claim in February 1986, started a work to rule in December. Seven weeks later management threatened them with a pay cut of one-third unless they returned to normal working. Their response was to strike, and to organize a picket, a lobby of the health authority, and a petition. Six days later they were back at work with a deal that gave them up to £14 a week extra pay backdated to February, and automatic progression to the HCO grade after one or two years' service.

Threatened strikes in hospitals and health authorities all over the country resulted in similar deals—in Bradford, Hartlepool, Blackpool, Wyre and Fylde, and Mid-Glamorgan. In Coventry seventy-seven medical secretaries, half in NALGO and half in NUPE, marched back to work victorious after a six-week strike for the HCO grade. One of them, Rashbinder Chahal, accused management of harassing pickets and of using 'emotional blackmail' to deter the women from striking. She pointed out the loyalty between medical secretaries, their consultants, and their patients, and that they had been 'fobbed off' by management for six months. A nine-week strike of thirty-five secretaries in North West Durham won regrading for full-timers, also to be applied to the six part-timers. Agreements followed in Tameside, and in University Hospital Cardiff, where sixty-five members of NALGO and COHSE were locked out by management for taking limited industrial action. During 1988 there were more successful deals, in Inverness after a two-week strike, in Southampton, Aylesbury, West Glamorgan, and Northampton after a five-week strike. In this wave of action it seemed that any group of low-paid workers with a strong case and the right amount of determination and organization could take on the management and secure some degree of justice at work. Then came the dispute at Oldham.[159]

On 27 February 1991 sixty-three NALGO members in the Royal Oldham Hospital's Health Records Department went on strike. A year later NALGO's Emergency Committee terminated the dispute without having reached a settlement, and in March 1993 the union was still making hardship payments to nine members who remained unemployed as it prepared to enter UNISON.

At the 1990 annual conference the Health Group resolved to support any members taking industrial action to support a regrading claim, as part of the union's push to use bargaining opportunities within the newly introduced grading structure. The Oldham stewards lodged their claim in July for regrading from grade two (£122–£143 per week) to grade three (£143–£167 per week), covering medical secretaries, medical records staff, and ward clerks (Whitley Council grading definitions). Six months later management offered eight posts at grade three, with greater levels of responsibility, open to competition among existing staff. The stewards stood by the original claim and rejected the offer. Soon afterwards the members found that non-NALGO staff in another section of the department had been regraded in a secret deal.

Management met the stewards on 20 February, but would not shift their position. The incensed members started their strike after voting in a ballot, setting up a strike office in the Clayton Arms for daily strikers' meetings. The branch produced a regular *Strike Bulletin* to present the strikers' case and to counter management propaganda issued in their *Hospital Bulletin*.

Immediately the strike started Hospital Manager Terry Windle wrote to each striker to tell them they could be dismissed if they failed to resume normal working. Two days later management increased its offer slightly to include the addition of two increments to the top of grade two, but it refused to negotiate until the strikers returned to work and it made further dismissal threats. A strikers' meeting rejected the offer, and management issued a letter to each striker requiring them to return to work no later than 7 March. The deadline passed, with a large demonstration of hospital staff supporting them outside the hospital gates.

Senior management's hard line, a changed approach to industrial relations and to negotiations from the traditional NHS model, forced the stewards to revise their position, dropping their demand for grade three and proposing the addition of two increments to the top of grade two and the deletion of two increments from the bot-

[159] A. Gilmore, 'Analysis of the Attitudes of Oldham Health Authority Management to Recent Strike Action from the Strikers' Perspective', MA thesis (Keele, 1992).

tom. Management rejected this, issued a final ultimatum of dismissal without notice on 11 March, and withdrew all its previous offers. A strikers' meeting voted to continue the strike. Twenty-nine members returned to work on 11 March, with much distress on the picket line; thirty-four strikers with a combined length of service of 250 years were sacked.

Weekly demonstrations followed, with the sacked strikers receiving support from within the hospital. As Avis Gilmore, steward for the Chartered Society of Physiotherapy members at the hospital, put it: 'Every Wednesday lunchtime for the next seven months found hundreds of us eating our sandwiches with the sacked strikers whatever the weather.' They won support from trade unionists in the Oldham area, speaking at meetings of union branches, trades councils, and Labour and Liberal Democrat parties. NALGO's Health Group called for the dispute to be put at the forefront of union campaigning and for the sacked strikers' case to be publicized among the entire membership and the general public. Shop steward Annemarie Sykes, who had given eighteen years service to the health authority before they sacked her, received a standing ovation when she addressed the annual conference in Glasgow, which pledged its 'full support'. Management recruited replacement employees.

Throughout the summer of 1991 national and district officers attempted to secure discussions with management about reinstatement. As it became clear that management was not going to back down, they shifted to seeking re-employment in different jobs. By the end of August the strikers discovered that seventeen posts in their department had been regraded to grade three, management refused to re-employ all strikers, and five strikers had obtained new jobs with the health authority. The remaining few kept up picketing throughout September and October, sustained by strike pay, donations, demonstrations, and social functions, but their number dwindled to eighteen as some of them took jobs with other employers. The dispute gradually petered out as morale collapsed and picketing became a terrible chore, until in February 1992 only eleven remained out of work. NALGO was committed to continuing strike pay and providing other forms of support until they found satisfactory employment, and the remaining strikers agreed that the dispute should be officially ended without any fuss.

Management's new hostility was rooted in the changes taking place in the NHS at the time, linked to their application for self-governing trust status. As the new national officer for health Paul Marks said when commenting on both the Oldham situation and similar management threats against 100 NALGO medical records staff on strike in Dudley in May 1991: 'It's difficult to divorce that from what's happening to the NHS as a whole. It can hardly be coincidence that this change in attitude comes at a time when the service is primed for virtual dismemberment with opting out.'

Many disputes escalated into deeper struggles over the frontier of managerial control when local managers tried to weaken the union by victimizing activists or reneging on agreements in order to gain unilateral control over the labour process. A dispute between 200 senior social workers and Strath-clyde Regional Council over a regrading claim escalated into strike action when the council disciplined a member for operating the union's work to rule. After nine weeks on strike 1,400 other staff, including social work assistants and managers, voted in a ballot to take supporting action, leading to a settlement.[160]

In November 1989 the Tameside Branch AGM resolved, *nem. con.*:

In view of the apparent unwillingness of our employer to seriously consider the legitimate claim of Libraries and Arts staff for improved grades and the inability of our trade union representatives to negotiate these during the last few weeks owing to the removal of the Facilities Agreement this AGM meeting requests the Branch Executive to arrange for a ballot of members in Libraries and Arts Department on a proposal that all members cease work on the introduction of LIBS100 system at any more locations.[161]

In some cases local industrial relations broke down completely, as in Greenwich in 1990. Under the headline 'Nalgo Strikers to be Punished', the local paper reported that 'Council services could be crippled tomorrow when 2000 housing workers walk out in support of striking colleagues accused of boozing, bingeing and bullying on the picket line . . . Council chiefs said some strikers must be punished . . . They are considering disciplinary action against 15 strikers.'[162] *NALGO News* took up the story:

The increasingly bitter housing dispute at Greenwich council looked set to worsen this week as action involving 147 strikers went into its fifth month. At an emergency branch meeting last Thursday, NALGO members endorsed a motion deploring a decision by the Labour-controlled council to victimise strikers and to employ temporary strike breakers to cover their jobs. The branch went on to call on the NEC to ballot key groups of workers on all out indefinite action until the victimisation had been lifted.[163]

Gas showroom staff in the East Midlands threatened to take industrial action after management imposed new working practices and refused to disclose information for bargaining purposes. Careers officers in Gateshead took indefinite strike action with full pay 'in protest at the suspension of a member for taking limited industrial action'.[164] That dispute escalated when the council agreed to resume talks on the future of the careers service and then abandoned them. It then sacked some of the strikers, and later the council withdrew all union facilities prompting yet further industrial action.

---

[160] *NALGO Emergency Committee Meeting Minutes*, 19 (London: NALGO, 1990), 29.
[161] Ibid. 68.   [162] *Greenwich and Eltham Mercury*, 16 Aug. 1990, 5.
[163] *NN*, 31 Aug. 1990, 1.
[164] *NALGO Emergency Committee Meeting Minutes*, 20 (London: NALGO, 1991), 18.

The London Borough of Camden also decided to take on the NALGO branch when it supported a member threatened with dismissal. There was a one-day strike 'on 29 January 1991 to match the changed date of the dismissed member's appeal hearing'.[165] Such was media and government interest that even *The Times* reported that 'council staff have called a one day strike . . . in support of Michael Henegan, a housing officer, as the council considers an internal appeal by him against his dismissal'.[166]

Six months later Camden social workers were in dispute after the council refused to implement a national agreement. A report to the Emergency Committee summarizes the issues:

The Camden NALGO branch has been attempting to negotiate the implementation of the National Regrading Agreement for Social Workers and Social Work Assistants since February 1990. The National Agreement applies to all Authorities which were operating either the previous national grading scheme or a scheme based on it. Camden falls into the latter category and the agreement should therefore be applied. Despite continued correspondence the management have refused to implement the agreement and have suggested that the matter be referred to the Greater London Whitley Council Disputes Procedure. It is the view of the branch supported by the secretary of the National Staff Side, copy of letter attached, that as this is a clear interpretation of a National Agreement it does not require further discussion outside Camden and the appropriate way to resolve the dispute is through local negotiation.[167]

The social workers started an indefinite strike in June, after a vote of 121 for and 38 against in a ballot of 203 members. By September, despite the use of ACAS and the disputes procedure, the strike remained unresolved. In November District Organization Officer Andrew Jack reported that a management offer had been rejected, and that the branch should give more support to the social workers on strike, especially in view of the implementation of the Children's Act.[168] As the year ended the dispute was still running and the union, although digging in on the principle of the local implementation of national agreements, had failed to win any more local backing for the social workers. By this time the dispute had cost NALGO £805,172 in strike pay and associated costs.

Another vivid example of the toughening management approach was in the crackdown on sickness absence:

All 2,600 members at Tower Hamlets London Borough are to be pulled out on a day's strike next Tuesday in support of a sacked colleague suffering post natal depression.

---

[165] Ibid. 20.   [166] *The Times*, 29 Jan. 1991.

[167] *NALGO Emergency Committee Meeting Minutes*, 20 (1991), 127.

[168] Ibid. 327.

Some 250 NALGO members at the Labour controlled Isle of Dogs neighbourhood have already been on strike for more than four weeks after the council refused to re-employ Gail Ogbuhei, the Isle of Dogs chief race adviser.[169]

This pattern of limited local action up and down the country had considerable success in terms both of winning regrading disputes and of cementing members' support for the national union through local recognition of deeds well done. It raised morale and it gave the union a high profile as one that defends all its members. NALGO had proven capacity both to mobilize national strikes and to support local struggles.

Employers in both the private and public sectors were on the offensive, aiming to sweep Whitleyism aside. Branches were confronted by increasingly unitarist managers aiming to cut costs for their employers, cash-strapped in the public sector and profit-seeking in the private, bringing a range of new issues to the fore. Jeff Spooner outlined the process in *Public Service*:

Growth of big business methods in the public services is one of the thorniest problems for the trade union movement. A host of management consultants and private financial advisers have been engaged, at a price, to help foster commercial practices. The idea is to get more work from the same staff, to offset the government squeeze on public spending. Performance-related pay and performance management is perhaps the biggest threat to organised labour. It puts a locally fixed price on the individual according to work targets achieved, rather than following a nationally negotiated rate for the job . . . Many public service staff, initially lured by the prospect of additional money, have found in the end that the rewards are not so great. In the process, hard fought for rights have disappeared.[170]

Worries about the cost of introducing or maintaining performance-related pay (PRP) did cause some employers to hesitate, but Jeff Spooner identified other concerns: 'the nightmare for many NALGO members signed up in PRP schemes may yet be realised—schemes could now be used by cost cutting councils to hold pay down'. As assistant organizer John Findlay argued, 'performance-related pay rises are not negotiated, they are at the discretion of the employer'.[171] The activists' view of the management consultants who promoted PRP and other HRM initiatives was expressed by one branch secretary: 'It's obvious now that they are "tools of the bosses" and a shop stewards' committee caught cold can find themselves agreeing with job losses without realising it.'[172]

Public-sector management traditions were eroded as managers turned to HRM techniques under the pressure of their budget shortfalls. Examples cropped up in all services. In the NHS there was local pay. In schools, assis-

---

[169] *NN*, 11 Jan. 1991, 1.   [170] *PS* (Jan. 1991), 8.   [171] Ibid. (Apr. 1991), 6.
[172] LRD, *Management Consultants and New Management Techniques* (London: LRD, 1992), 3.

tant national officer for local government Jon Skewes identified the workload pressures arising from LMS: 'The major increase in the administrative and clerical role for individual schools has put a greater burden of work on office staff.'[173] Job evaluation was more widespread, including the Hay scheme for National Rivers Authority (NRA) and British Gas staff. The threat to the national grading system covering staff in colleges and polytechnics was partially averted with the agreement of a framework arrangement within which a national system could be locally varied. British Gas management in North Thames threatened to sack staff away on sick leave.

More aggressive attitudes towards labour management were accompanied by attacks on the trade unions, typified by Wandsworth Council, which, anticipating government legislation, threatened to end the check-off. Northumbrian Water Group attempted to derecognize unions and replace negotiations with a company council—the unions managed to retain recognition in Northumbrian Water Ltd., but not in many subsidiaries of the main group. British Gas avoided negotiations while pressing ahead with its regional organization review. Electricity companies moved to introduce single table bargaining at company level.

Part and parcel of the help for local activists in dealing with these developments centred around education courses and materials on the introduction of private-sector business methods into public services. As the TUC's Public Service Committee noted, 'there was a particular need to seize the initiative in this area in the face of developing human resource management strategies, some of which could undermine collective representation'.[174] NALGO celebrated the seventieth anniversary of its education department with an appreciation by Asa Briggs.[175]

Concluding Remarks

The fortunes of both the Conservative government and the labour movement shifted during the early years of the new decade. On the one hand, Thatcherism was running out of time: reforms in health, education, and local government were neither popular nor coherent; privatization of water was deeply resented throughout the political spectrum; and the electricity sell-off was a messy business. The economic miracle of Nigel Lawson turned sour once again, and the campaign against the poll tax united many citizens in mass action. Shaken to its core, the government ditched the helmswoman in favour of John Major.

---

[173] *PS* (May 1991), 4.   [174] *TUC Annual Report 1991*.   [175] *NN*, 7 Dec. 1990, 3–6.

There were genuine grounds for optimism at home, fed by the triumphant release of Nelson Mandela. However the Labour Party and much of the trade union national leadership had shifted to the right. The 'official' labour movement avoided hard policy issues, disavowed the mass movement around the poll tax, and began the long retreat from nationalization, from well-funded public services, and from welfare as a right not as a gift. As the next chapter shows, the defeat of Labour in the 1992 election was a terrible blow for the labour movement, which might have stood firm with NALGO and other sections of the movement but instead withdrew into even more cautious policies. It also provided the final argument for NALGO to join with COHSE and NUPE in UNISON.

Appendix

TABLE 8.1. *NALGO membership, 30 September 1990*

District	Number of branches (1)	Voting members (2)	Members in arrears (3)	Membership of branches excluded from voting (4)	Total ordinary membership (cols. 2-4) (5)	Retired (6)	Student (7)	Unemployed (8)	Honorary (9)	Total membership (cols. 5-9) (10)	Total membership 30 Sept. 1989 (11)	Increase/ decrease (12)	Increase/ decrease (%) (13)
Eastern	117	41,535	4	342	41,881	7,009	13	38	—	48,941	47,733	+1,208	+2.53
East Midland	100	43,651	29	408	44,088	5,438	36	24	—	49,586	49,940	−354	−0.71
Metropolitan	133	87,203	699	485	88,387	13,830	51	82	—	102,350	104,854	−2,504	−2.39
North Eastern	75	41,858	38	136	42,032	3,046	4	14	—	45,096	44,762	+334	+0.75
North Western and North Wales	139	107,015	12	0	107,027	10,549	25	110	—	117,711	119,134	−1,423	−1.19
Scottish	107	78,454	50	66	78,570	3,096	19	19	—	81,704	82,428	−724	−0.88
South Eastern	92	31,805	52	399	32,256	5,762	13	31	—	38,062	40,456	−2,394	−5.92
Southern	79	30,632	17	390	31,039	4,966	18	26	—	36,049	37,001	−952	−2.57
South Wales	81	32,220	34	323	32,577	2,650	17	8	—	35,252	35,216	+36	+0.10
South Western	95	43,378	6	0	43,384	4,992	22	29	—	48,427	47,702	+725	+1.52
West Midland	89	66,330	1	484	66,815	7,948	17	19	—	74,799	75,000	−201	−0.27
Yorkshire and Humberside	74	61,637	20	0	61,657	4,747	12	21	—	66,437	66,236	+201	+0.30
Honorary members	—	—	—	—	—	—	—	—	39	39	40	−1	−2.50
TOTAL	1,181	665,718	962	3,033	669,713	74,033	247	421	39	744,453	750,502	−6,049	−0.81

343

TABLE 8.2. Allocation of NALGO membership, 30 September 1990

District	Local government	Gas	Electricity	Health	Transport	Water	New Towns	Port authorities	Universities	Police authorities	Polytechnic colleges	Retired	Student, unemployed	Total membership
Eastern	29,936	2,174	2,453	2,955	247	2,096	192	1.1	434	956	427	7,009	51	48,941
East Midland	31,097	3,046	2,235	4,936	219	0	0	0	435	1,240	880	5,438	60	49,586
Metropolitan	67,268	4,193	3,594	6,566	203	3,115	325	0	1,280	0	1,843	13,830	133	102,350
North Eastern	30,047	1,999	1,625	4,327	703	903	37	73	261	939	1,118	3,046	18	45,096
North Western and North Wales	76,275	4,250	5,096	10,903	1,497	3,448	196	29	1,232	2,134	1,967	10,549	135	117,711
Scottish	61,378	2,266	3,607	7,991	339	20	1,140	31	1,525	273	0	3,096	38	81,704
South Eastern	20,616	2,288	1,813	4,037	45	1,801	0	11	720	505	420	5,762	44	38,062
Southern	19,950	1,923	1,935	4,587	0	0	294	0	889	621	840	4,966	44	36,049
South Wales	22,596	1,602	1,084	3,493	149	1,879	84	0	762	928	0	2,650	25	35,252
South Western	31,586	1,538	2,220	3,345	54	1,907	0	2	603	1,387	742	4,992	51	48,427
West Midland	45,207	4,259	2,853	7,061	989	3,351	0	0	818	1,070	1,207	7,948	36	74,799
Yorkshire and Humberside	47,806	1,286	2,673	3,846	778	2,105	0	0	1,190	676	1,297	4,747	33	66,437
1990 totals	483,762	30,824	31,188	64,047	5,223	20,625	2,268	157	10,149	10,729	10,741	74,033	668	744,414
Percentages	64.99	4.14	4.19	8.60	0.70	2.77	0.31	0.02	1.36	1.44	1.44	9.95	0.09	100.00
1989 totals	487,189	32,361	31,417	64,642	5,694	20,878	2,387	166	9,582	10,732	10,412	74,156	846	750,462
Percentages	64.92	4.31	4.19	8.61	0.76	2.78	0.32	0.02	1.28	1.43	1.39	9.88	0.11	100.00

TABLE 8.3. *NALGO membership, 30 September 1991*

District	Number of branches	Voting members	Members in arrears	Membership of branches excluded from voting	Total ordinary membership (cols. 2–4)	Retired	Student	Unemployed	Honorary	Total membership (cols. 5–9)	Total membership 30 Sept. 1990	Increase/decrease	Increase/decrease (%)
	(1)	(2)	(3)	(4)	(5)	(6)	(7)	(8)	(9)	(10)	(11)	(12)	(13)
Eastern	110	41,900	2	186	42,088	7,283	11	53	—	49,435	48,941	+494	+1.01
East Midland	94	42,891	210	1,557	44,658	5,741	41	30	—	50,470	49,586	+884	+1.78
Metropolitan	130	83,511	186	2,318	86,015	14,896	55	152	—	101,118	102,350	−1,232	−1.20
North Eastern	60	42,509	38	282	42,829	2,972	6	27	—	45,834	45,096	+738	+1.64
North Western and North Wales	138	104,925	11	2,914	107,850	11,965	45	105	—	119,965	117,711	+2,254	+1.91
Scottish	105	79,417	10	253	79,680	3,421	19	27	—	83,147	81,704	+1,443	+1.77
South Eastern	91	30,948	5	1,357	32,310	7,422	16	41	—	39,789	38,062	+1,727	+4.54
Southern	80	31,251	1	871	32,123	5,017	17	31	—	37,188	36,049	+1,139	+3.16
South Wales	79	31,860	174	1,686	33,720	2,844	5	15	—	36,584	35,252	+1,332	+3.78
South Western	97	44,121	1	1,535	45,657	5,244	10	27	—	50,938	48,427	+2,511	+5.19
West Midland	87	66,210	43	1,752	68,005	8,603	13	39	—	76,660	74,799	+1,861	+2.49
Yorkshire and Humberside	70	62,806	14	0	62,820	5,688	29	33	—	68,570	66,437	+2,133	+3.21
Honorary members	—	—	—	—	—	—	—	—	37	37	39	−2	−5.13
TOTAL	1,141	662,349	695	14,711	677,755	81,096	267	580	37	759,735	744,453	+15,282	+2.05

345

TABLE 8.4. Allocation of NALGO membership, by service, 30 September 1991

District	Local government	Gas	Electricity	Health	Transport	Water	New Towns	Port authorities	Universities	Police authorities	Polytechnic colleges	Retired	Student, unemployed	Total membership
Eastern	30,220	2,251	2,290	2,915	218	2,111	188	12	442	977	464	7,283	64	49,435
East Midland	31,851	3,047	2,067	4,896	200	0	0	1	448	1,277	871	5,741	71	50,470
Metropolitan	66,005	4,317	2,514	6,511	192	2,974	309	0	1,250	0	1,943	14,896	207	101,118
North Eastern	30,526	2,121	1,574	4,581	643	882	28	69	250	981	1,174	2,972	33	45,834
North Western and North Wales	77,569	4,427	4,673	10,929	1,398	3,139	175	29	1,265	2,232	2,014	11,965	150	119,965
Scottish	62,719	2,365	3,612	7,794	291	20	1,030	3.1	1,542	276	0	3,421	46	83,147
South Eastern	20,774	2,330	1,565	4,058	33	1,852	0	8	469	847	374	7,422	57	39,789
Southern	20,976	2,016	2,133	4,409	0	0	285	0	889	628	787	5,017	48	37,188
South Wales	23,372	1,644	1,273	3,536	126	1,990	98	0	769	912	0	2,844	20	36,584
South Western	33,505	1,556	2,546	3,264	70	1,989	0	1	576	1,494	656	5,244	37	50,938
West Midland	47,032	4,462	2,212	6,835	974	3,391	0	0	818	1,116	1,165	8,603	52	76,660
Yorkshire and Humberside	48,514	1,221	3,269	3,829	783	2,075	0	0	1,162	731	1,236	5,688	62	68,570
1991 totals	493,063	31,757	29,728	63,557	4,928	20,423	2,113	151	9,880	11,471	10,684	81,096	847	759,698
Percentages	64.90	4.18	3.91	8.37	0.65	2.69	0.28	0.02	1.30	1.51	1.41	10.67	0.11	100.00
1990 totals	483,762	30,824	31,188	64,047	5,223	20,625	2,268	157	10,149	10,729	10,741	74,033	668	744,414
Percentages	64.99	4.14	4.19	8.60	0.70	2.77	0.31	0.02	1.36	1.44	1.44	9.95	0.09	100.00

346

9

NALGO's Last Year

Tis last of NALGO's eighty-eight years saw the union more deeply involved in action against the government than ever. It campaigned strongly in the 1992 general election, reaffirming its commitment to public ownership, to fully funded public services, and to trade-union rights. Meanwhile, the Labour Party, the TUC, and many trade-union leaders embraced yet more of the big business agenda, supporting the logic of the market and its associated HRM techniques. Gaining 43 per cent of the vote, against Labour's 35 per cent, the Tories snatched victory from the jaws of defeat.

Even the Tories were surprised that they were still in government, and they set about consolidating their reforms in education, health, and local government. In the election aftermath the union pursued merger with renewed urgency. After the election NALGO's main policy concern was to consolidate the merger. It clarified its policies against pay limits, the anti-union laws, the single European market, and further cuts in public services. It fought to maintain national collective bargaining and to protect conditions of service, but was forced to settle at the 1.5 per cent pay limit in 1993. Its last months saw some of the most bitter strikes against job losses, especially in Labour-controlled councils.

The Tories—Five More Years!

There was a general climate of optimism in the labour and trade-union movement at the start of 1992. With the Conservative Party bitterly divided over Europe, torn by personal and political rivalries, and deeply unpopular with significant sections of the population, its removal from government seemed

347

certain. There was growing concern within the electorate about the need to restore the public services and about issues such as equality and social justice. Yet the Labour Party, although much restored in opposition from the depths of the mid-1980s, somehow failed to capitalize on these opportunities.

The NEC was well satisfied with the union's £2 million national election campaign:

Once again, NALGO showed that, through its Political Fund, it has established itself as the leading pressure group in terms of advertising to influence public opinion at election times. The impact of its national newspaper advertising campaign before the 1992 General Election was assessed by opinion research afterwards, and very high levels of public response were measured. The hard-hitting advertisements, which combined striking visual images with sharp humour, emphasised the need for a change in Government policy towards the cash starved public services.[1]

Advertisements depicting the consequences of government policy on the public services became election issues in their own right, attracting national publicity: 'NALGO has hit the headlines with its latest advertising campaign in defence of public services. The first advert in the eight-part project appeared in national papers last week. It points out that education is suffering under government policies. The advert provoked an attack from Education Secretary Kenneth Clarke, who accused the union of "doing Labour's dirty work for them".'[2] Deputy General Secretary Dave Prentis responded to an attack by the local-government minister: 'Mr Portillo and his government are in a state of panic at the success of our adverts in highlighting the true extent of their rotten record on the public services.'[3] NALGO kept up the pressure: 'Signs that ministers are getting increasingly rattled by NALGO's national newspaper advertising campaign against government neglect and cuts in services surfaced this week. The Advertising Standards Authority, the industry's self-regulatory body, confirmed that it had received a complaint from Employment Secretary, Michael Howard.'[4]

Despite such a positive campaign, the election was lost. It was a massive setback for the Labour leadership under Neil Kinnock (soon to be replaced by John Smith), and for unions such as NALGO that had pinned so much hope and spent large amounts of time and money on the election campaign. As Alan Jinkinson said: 'We are going to have a fight on our hands, starting right now. The Tories hate trade unions, they hate public service trade unions in particular, and they seem to have developed a special kind of hatred for NALGO.' The task ahead for NALGO 'will be to survive the next four years

[1] *NALGO Annual Report 1992* (London: NALGO, 1993), 77.
[2] *NALGO News (NN)*, 14 Feb. 1992, 1.   [3] Ibid., 21 Feb. 1992, 1.
[4] Ibid., 28 Feb. 1992, 1.

and emerge from them strengthened and still able to defend our members and the services on which the public depends'.[5] In his speech to conference President Mike Blick said: 'The three Conservative governments of the '80s have used their power . . . to apply their prejudices to fundamental changes in the democratic structure and organisation of our society. Nowhere is this more blatant that in the systematic downgrading of the role of local government, coupled with a remorseless shift of power to central government and its agencies.'[6]

John Major himself was somewhat bemused: 'The uncelebrated success of the 1992 Conservative election campaign was winning in a recession, against the shadow of the poll tax, and with barely a mention of Europe.'[7] On the world stage, with the counter-revolutions in Central and Eastern Europe foreshadowing a general retreat from social democracy throughout Northern and Western Europe, the election result set the scene for the Major government to pursue a yet more virulent version of the Thatcher agenda. With most of the formerly nationalized industries and utilities under private ownership, the force of reform fell most heavily on health, education, and local government. Restructuring into business units, along with wider and deeper changes in the ways that services and service workers were managed, heralded a period of unprecedented crisis and decline in these sectors.

In the general economy things went from bad to worse, culminating in the catastrophic collapse of the pound on Black Wednesday, 16 September. The Prime Minister acknowledged that it was 'a political and economic calamity. It unleashed havoc in the Conservative Party and it changed the political landscape of Britain.'[8] The Chancellor, Norman Lamont, was ruined and he typically blamed his colleagues: 'It was the politicians who had interfered with the technicians and only succeeded in making things even worse with their amateur and bungling intervention.'[9] The crash of the pound and the exit from the ERM split the government on Europe, damaged its reputation for economic management, and allowed the Labour Party under John Smith to take a dominant lead in the opinion polls, which remained pretty well unchanged when Tony Blair became leader and won the 1997 election. The NEC's annual report looked back on the year with some dismay:

1992 proved to be an extraordinary year and a significant turning point in Britain's economic history. The final collapse of the last of a series of disastrous economic policies stretching back to the late seventies occurred in September, but not before many more months of deepening recession. Falling output, plummeting investment, tens

---

[5] Ibid., 8 May 1992, 3.   [6] *Public Service* (PS), July 1992, 13.

[7] J. Major, *The Autobiography* (London: Harper Collins, 1999), 291.   [8] Ibid. 312.

[9] N. Lamont, *In Office* (London: Little, Brown & Co., 1999), 251.

of thousands of bankruptcies and housing repossessions, and unemployment surging to levels unimagined a generation ago mean that 1992 was indeed a terrible year for millions of ordinary people. The recession was proving to be the worst for 60 years, induced and reinforced by the same destructive economic policies which had produced the inter-war slump and led in turn to fascism and the second world war.

Your Council continued to press for radical changes in economic policy, arguing as they had done throughout 1991 that the pound was substantially overvalued in the European Exchange Rate Mechanism and that high interest rates were devastating the economy and would continue to do so. Even within the trade union movement, NALGO's voice was almost alone in calling for devaluation and a cut in interest rates, claiming not only that such policies were vital for any possibility of economic recovery, but sooner or later the pound would crash and new policies would be forced on the Government. Your Council's prediction came true on 16 September, when the pound fell out of the ERM and a stubborn, dogmatic and incompetent Government was humiliated.[10]

NALGO, along with most other unions and the TUC, started 1992 in hope and ended it in the realization that another five years of hard conservatism were upon them. This combination of political defeat, economic neglect, and employment restructuring sealed the argument for merger, as a defensive measure against further attacks on the members, their jobs, and their unions. It was also an offensive measure, part of trade-union restructuring aimed at mounting more effective campaigns and industrial action. And it was a political measure to seek to secure pro-public-sector, pro-equality, and left-of-centre policies within British and, increasingly, European trade unionism.

Campaigning, Merging, and Holding the Line

The government carries on regardless

The government's reaction to the pound's collapse was predictable: 'The Chancellor singled out public sector employees for attack in his Autumn Statement, imposing a 1.5% ceiling on pay rises for all public sector workers and reinforcing constraints on local authority spending in particular, which was certain to bring massive job losses and serious cuts in services.'[11] NALGO's Anne Middleton made the point at the STUC women's conference in November 1992 at Perth: 'The restriction on public sector pay means that our members have to bear the brunt of the government's economic mistakes.'[12] Alan Jinkinson commented:

---

[10] *NALGO Annual Report 1992*, 10.   [11] Ibid. 12.   [12] *NN*, 27 Nov. 1992, 9.

Coming just days after the government announced it will abolish the wages councils, which fix minimum wage levels in a range of industries, its new public sector incomes policy confirms that the government wants ordinary people to pay for its problems by driving wages down. Its strategy is to create a low wage and low skill economy. Government mismanagement of the economy is to be paid for by the likes of low paid APT&C staff and nurses.[13]

In Chapter 1 we set out our general position on the cheapening of the public services through the downgrading of public-service labour. The situation in health, education, and local government was broadly similar. Service managers were put into competition with each other, and they competed mainly on cost—successful business units were the ones that operated within government guidelines at least cost. Action to reduce unit labour costs aimed to maximize the work done for the minimum total wage bill through a range of initiatives, including: reduced staffing levels; flexible working patterns, including shift and weekend working at plain time; increased intensity of work; changed skill mix through substitution of less-skilled workers for more-skilled workers; changed grading structures, through management techniques such as job evaluation; links between pay and effort through merit pay and performance-related pay; and, finally, tighter controls over performance through appraisal, TQM, and other similar quality initiatives, and debatable measures of effectiveness such as performance indicators. To this list of HRM techniques could be added the managerial notions of partnership, empowerment, and employee involvement.

The government's consultation paper, *Competing for Quality*, set out its aim of securing 'value for money' through the introduction of market competition in the public services, supported by 'charters' of rights for service users. In a joint response, NALGO, NUPE, GMB, and TGWU rebutted the government's argument: 'It is made up of little more than a recital of complaints by a number of unnamed private contractors. The consultation paper states that the government wants to promote fair competition in local government. Yet its proposals simply discriminate in favour of private contractors and against DSOs.'[14] Linking quality issues to labour management issues, Alan Jinkinson argued: 'You cannot expect to get high quality services when staff are demotivated, demoralised, underpaid, undertrained and fearful for their jobs. When the service user is turned against the service provider, nobody benefits.'[15]

[13] *PS* (Dec. 1992), 8.
[14] NUPE, NALGO, GMB, and TGWU, *A Response to the Department of the Environment's Consultation Paper 'Competing for Quality'* (London: NALGO, 1992), 1.
[15] *TUC Annual Report 1992* (London: TUC, 1993), 363.

In a grim reminder of the government's lack of concern for the consequences of their policies, the axe hanging over the coalfield communities
started its final swing as 1992 drew to a close and Michael Heseltine started a
review of the industry. A wave of protest against the anticipated closures and
in solidarity with the miners swept the country. On 25 October 200,000
marched through London in the pouring rain to call for the pits to be kept
open. The TUC met outside London for the first time in its history: 'The
TUC general council took the radical step of meeting in Doncaster last week
showing solidarity with miners facing alleged harassment to take redundancy.'[16] All to no avail, as the next year saw the virtual closure of the state
coal-mining industry.

Margaret Thatcher was still certain that closures were inevitable: 'How
many of the pits had a long-term commercial future was unclear. We were
still mining too much high-cost, deep-mined coal—a situation which had
come about because of the protected and monopolistic market the nationalized coal industry had enjoyed. So there would have to be closures.'[17] But
Prime Minister Major realized too late this was another error of judgement
that would help them lose votes later: 'We then found ourselves in combat
with the miners after a mistake that was to inflame public opinion more spon-
taneously than any other event in my years at Downing Street.'[18] To add
insult to injury the Chancellor admitted that 'one of the problems was that the
DTI [Department of Trade and Industry] was none too sure of its own
costings for the viability of individual pits',[19] but he put the blame for the
debacle fully onto Michael Heseltine.

NALGO donated £100,000 to the TUC's jobs and recovery campaign and
joined the campaign to defend miners and their communities, supporting the
NUM's final bid to stave off the industry's closure. NALGO was specially
prominent in supporting 'Women Against Pit Closures' campaigns, which
included setting up camps outside seven threatened collieries. On 29 March
there were further lobbies and marches organized by the TUC to save pits,
and on 2 April there was a series of rallies in several towns and cities as part of
a TUC day of action in protest against government policies on pits, transport,
public services, and unemployment.

NALGO News published union researcher Kelvin Hopkins's analysis of
the state of Britain's economy, continuing to press not only NALGO's
justified case against the government's policies but also the failure of the
Labour opposition to present a credible alternative:

---

[16] *NN*, 4 Dec. 1992, 4–5.
[17] M. Thatcher, *The Downing Street Years* (London: Harper Collins, 1993), 686.
[18] Major, *The Autobiography*, 668.   [19] Lamont, *In Office*, 294.

The country is staring long-term economic disaster in the face. Hundreds of thousands march to save the mining industry, bankruptcies and redundancies bring misery to thousands more every week while the Parliamentary front benches shadow box in a charade of fierce antipathy, tacitly conspiring to keep Maastricht alive and get back on track for ERM, European monetary union and European deflation.[20]

The article set out NALGO's opposition to the EU's Maastricht Treaty, believing it would lead to more unemployment and to less democracy.

The discredited Chancellor's next budget confirmed the union's worst fears, leading the way to recession, higher unemployment, and lower investment, while pushing the costs onto the most vulnerable citizens through the imposition of VAT on fuel and, of course, with further planned reductions in public expenditure. Alan Jinkinson responded:

Mr Lamont should realise that the whole country is frightened about the future, frightened about losing jobs, frightened about not finding work again, frightened about their homes being repossessed, frightened about their firms going bankrupt and frightened for their children's futures. The budget will do nothing to reduce this fear, or to encourage people to go and spend in the shops to revive the economy.[21]

Lamont remains unrepentant: 'Looking back at the 1993 budget now, it did go a long way to achieving its objective of a massive switch of resources back towards reducing the deficit. It was the largest increase in taxation for years. Obviously I wasn't pleased about that, but it had to be done.'[22] Against the background of continuing recession this became an albatross around the government's neck, and Lamont was soon replaced by Ken Clarke.

But the harshest of all harsh realities was the growing number of unemployed. Here was the symbol of Toryism: policies designed to cheapen labour as a commodity went side by side with those aimed at helping wealthy individuals and corporations to accumulate ever more wealth, and the consequence was widespread unemployment. One feature of the supply-side argument was that the tax and benefit system might result in a range of potential workers preferring to remain unemployed, thereby creating a culture of dependence on the state. This was a mishmash of two reactionary traditions in British politics: the old fashioned high Tory distinction between the deserving and the undeserving poor; and the classic liberal position of tough love. Social welfare should not be wasted on those who do not need it—the undeserving—it can be better targeted on the deserving. The Labour Party leadership and some sections of the labour movement embraced the Thatcherite view that a dependency culture existed, and that some organizations wrongly defended it—trade unions, left-wing councils, some religious

---

[20] *NN*, 15 Jan. 1993, 4.   [21] *PS* (Apr. 1993), 6.   [22] Lamont, *In Office*, 357–8.

and voluntary bodies, sections of the professions, and those in favour of some notion of state planning.

Alan Jinkinson took a strong line on such cant: 'Workfare, or any scheme to force unemployed people into workhouse schemes, is about undercutting public service jobs and cutting public spending on vital work. And it is about diverting the blame for government policies onto unemployed people—implying that they're shirkers living a cushy life on the tax payer. It should be resisted at all costs. It is an obscenity.'[23] He continued this theme in a fierce attack on the government at the STUC Annual Congress in Glasgow. 'We have mass unemployment, collapsing industries, crumbling infrastructure, increasing poverty, social breakdown, young people with no hope drifting into street crime and drug addiction, and over-stretched and under-resourced public services. And all of this derives from monumental economic policy failures by successive governments.'[24]

The logic of supply-side economics provided justification for the government to further deregulate labour markets, weaken collective-bargaining machinery, tighten the laws on industrial action, and abolish Wages Councils. The TUC stood against the full extent of the free-market tide, calling for increased investment to stimulate demand for jobs in its *Strategy for Full Employment* paper. When the government published the Trade Union Reform and Employment Rights Bill, with its further restrictions on strike ballots, fussy rights on scrutiny of union finances, and even a Commissioner for Protection against Unlawful Industrial Action, NALGO and the TUC responded. NALGO's final conference agenda was replete with motions against anti-union laws, and the TUC's counter-attack included a twelve-point plan, *Employment Charter for a World Class Britain*, which would give all people at work certain entitlements: a safe and healthy working environment; equal treatment at work regardless of sex, race, disability, sexuality, or age; education and training rights; a contract of employment in written form; more help for parents and carers; equivalent treatment whatever type of contract; fair pay and conditions of service; fairness in disciplinary action; information and consultation; fair treatment in redundancy; proper protection in transfer; and the right to join and be represented by an independent trade union.

However, while the TUC stood firm on some specific employment issues, on broader economic policy it lined up with the Labour Party's support for resource allocation through market efficiency, flexible labour markets, and HRM practices. Lord McCarthy's analysis for the TUC identified the changes confronting the trade-union movement: increased competition in

---

[23] *PS* (Mar. 1993), 8.   [24] *NN*, 23 Apr. 1993, 1.

the private and public sectors; use of management techniques to reduce unit costs; shift in the composition of the labour force from traditional manufacturing to private service employment, and from full-time and permanent to part-time and temporary; and a reduced commitment to full employment, equality, community, and collectivism. The General Council used this as the basis for its report, *TUC towards 2000*, but its programme for the movement embraced the business logic of market individualism and went with the flow, setting out four broad objectives:

to establish trade unions as strong sound partners in a successful economy measured against the highest international and European standards; to strengthen our own organisation and competence at every level in a rapidly changing labour market; to develop the TUC role as a campaigning organisation with a high public profile; to develop the TUC as a well-managed source of information and centre of excellence.[25]

NUPE and COHSE had few problems in following, but NALGO was far less happy to abandon either its historic support for the now widely forgotten AES or its opposition to anti-union legislation. This fed the battles over future UNISON policy, between NALGO's progressive left and NUPE's and COHSE's support for the nascent new Labour.

At the 1993 TUC Annual Congress in Blackpool there was the unusual sight of the Director General of the CBI, Howard Davies, on the platform— a powerful symbol of the social partnership tradition. 'His appearance was controversial. NALGO had opposed the invitation but having registered its strong objection did not feel there was anything to be gained by joining a walk out of delegates.'[26] Alan Jinkinson responded robustly to the CBI's assertions that there should be no increase in the public-sector pay bill, which implied that either no one should get a pay increase, or some could take a pay increase while others either take a pay cut or lose their jobs: 'Better quality public services is what we are about. And I say to Howard Davies that improving quality and driving down pay is an equation which won't work.'[27]

Preparing for merger

NALGO faced two challenges in its final year of existence: first to deal with the old enemy of a government set to reduce further employees' rights, trade-union rights, bargaining rights, and public expenditure, and to deregulate labour markets and employment practices; but, secondly, to protect the union's ways of working, supporting members, and developing policy, minimizing compromises to these positions while also respecting the traditions of

[25] *TUC Annual Report 1992*, 5.   [26] *NALGO Annual Report 1992*, 82.
[27] *PS* (Oct. 1992), 16.

NUPE and COHSE. While the union maintained its efforts to defend the pay and conditions of service for all members in all sections, it also had to resolve the central problems of implementing and cementing the merger into the new union UNISON. Most of the national and local leaders, officials and activists, had fought for the principle of the new union, but some key questions now needed to be answered. How was it to be organized? What policies and traditions should be fought for within the new political and organizational setting? These positions were contested through NALGO's traditional arenas of branch and district meetings, conferences and group meetings, and through the pages of its journals and publicity department pamphlets.

A lengthy report in *The Times* quoted the president of the Society of Chief Personnel Officers in local government, Alwyn Rea, on the prospects for merger: 'It might ease the relationship, because the unions will be speaking with one voice, rather than three. It might facilitate agreements.' The article also referred to a leaked NHS document that stated 'it would be very difficult for a SGT to resist recognition of such a large organization'. It also reported on opposition to the merger from within NALGO on the grounds that it would be unworkable, it would be 'spanning bosses and workers', and it would be an 'unwieldy political juggernaut', with too much representation for women and part-timers.[28]

This was followed the next day by an editorial in *The Times*, which attacked both the idea of merger and trade unionism more generally:

[NALGO, NUPE and COHSE] members have in common only one thing: that they rely for their hire and reward on the taxpayer. From now on these unions will cry with a single voice for ever-increasing public expenditure to maintain their members' incomes. Whether they will be able to put the muscle of collective action behind that cry is more doubtful. . . . Labour organisation in the competitive 1990s is unquestionably in the decline. The age of the sub-contractor, the freelancer, the 'lump' and the individual contract will see ever less scope for the great combinations of labour. Merger mania will solve nothing. The fate of the unions, as national institutions, will be one every marxist is familiar with. They will simply wither away.[29]

As NALGO's penultimate conference prepared to vote on the merger, Alan Jinkinson was in no doubt about the significance of the impending decision: 'It will determine the future of British public service trade unionism well into the next century'.[30] He made it clear why the merger was so important:

Never before has it been so necessary for public service workers to speak with one voice and to demonstrate the fundamental trade union value of unity, which the

[28] *The Times*, 4 Mar. 1992, 21.   [29] Ibid., 5 Mar. 1992, 15.
[30] *NN*, 12 June 1992, 4.

name UNISON implies. We must not allow employers to drive a wedge between the manual and white-collar workers. Nor can we allow a hostile government, intent on running down and privatising the NHS, to benefit from wasteful multi-unionism.[31]

The delegates voted in favour by 424,888 to 174,388 on a card vote, to be ratified by a ballot of all members in November.

The 1992 conference also confirmed NALGO's policies on a range of crucial issues. For example, 'Rita Donaghy pledged that the union's leadership had no intention of backing down from the commitments contained in NALGO policy and no intention of joining the TUC or Labour Party in diluting the trade union movement's opposition to Tory anti-trade union law'.[32] That issue had such a high priority that the delegates gave it top billing for the union's motion to the TUC.

The self-organized groups also prepared for life in UNISON, reviewing their progress in NALGO and identifying the work still to be done. The national conference for black members in London in November 1992 applauded the achievements of ten years of self-organization and pledged to fight on in the new union. The strong position of black members in NALGO contrasted vividly with the situation in the trade unions more generally, as reported in *NALGO News*: 'Astrid Stubbs reports on TUC research that shows lack of trust in the services which unions provide for black members, poor representation on decision-making bodies and outmoded employment policies.'[33] The TUC black workers' conference called for self-organization within unions, support for the Anti-Racist Alliance (ARA) and more union help for black workers. NALGO member Jackie Burnett told the conference about the murder of her 18-year-old cousin, Stephen Lawrence, by racist youths in south London three weeks earlier.[34] NALGO (and then UNISON) and the TUC gave long-term support to the Lawrence family in their quest to bring the killers to justice. The ARA stepped up its campaign to close down the British National Party's bookshop and office in Welling, with NALGO and TUC support.

Similar themes of equality and justice were on the table at the national disability conference in Port Talbot, which also discussed the importance of educating stewards on the issues and presenting positive images of disabled people. Delegates at the 1992 lesbian and gay members' conference were pleased with recent progress in NALGO, but noted with some caution that COHSE was about ten years behind them in terms of union policies and awareness. Throughout its last year the union continued its high profile work

---

[31] *PS* (July 1992),1. [32] Ibid. 5. [33] *NN*, 31 Jan. 1992, 7.
[34] *NALGO Black Action* (London: NALGO, 1993).

on equality and against discrimination. There was special attention to how the union can support women's struggles for wider and deeper equality: 'Every day NALGO women are fighting to get a better deal—at work, at home, in terms of their health and in their union—whether they are white, heterosexuals, black, lesbian or disabled.'[35]

Against this background the impetus for merger gained strength, culminating in the historic ballot right at the end of 1992. 'The main event of the year was the ballot of COHSE, NALGO and NUPE members who voted by a 4 to 1 majority to form Britain's biggest union—UNISON—with 1.4 million members. In total 451,225 (82.12%) voted in favour and 98,243 (17.88%) voted against on a 35% poll. In NALGO there was a higher poll (38.45%) but a lower percentage vote in favour (73.17%). UNISON will come into being officially on 1 July 1993.'[36] Alan Jinkinson declared: 'Members will benefit greatly from its democracy, from its fair representation policies and from its strength and resources. Employers will no longer be able to divide us.' NUPE's Rodney Bickerstaffe added that the new union was 'good news for public employees, the public they serve and the services they provide'; and, for COHSE's Hector MacKenzie, 'A strong, effective people-centred union, UNISON will take us forward to meet the challenges ahead.'[37]

NALGO's last President, Ralph Gayton, struck a similar note of optimism in his New Year message, referring to the mass opposition to pit closures: 'The trade union movement must keep the momentum going. In particular the trade union movement as a whole must redouble its attack on the evils of continuing rising unemployment as well as opposing the assaults on our living standards and the destruction of our public services.'[38] 'Seize the time' is not always a popular slogan among British labour-movement leaders, but Ralph Gayton's analysis accurately portrays the concept of a movement in motion, and the dynamic nature of political events. It suggests a deep concern that at times some trade-union leaders, alongside others from the Labour Party, have been hesitant in harnessing mass discontent into more effective opposition to government policies.

NALGO's final conference in June 1993 reaffirmed most of the union's main principles and policies for its 764,000 members (see Tables 9.1 and 9.2), including a renewed commitment to public ownership and to equality. The last edition of *Public Service* gave reminders of how members had fought for those principles through thick and thin, in one form or another, since its foundation eighty-eight years ago. Sadly the final months of NALGO also saw the death of Geoffrey Drain, General Secretary from 1973 to 1983, on 2 April

[35] *PS* (Aug. 1992), 6.   [36] *NALGO Annual Report 1992*, 10.
[37] *PS* (Jan. 1993), 1.   [38] Ibid.

1993. In an obituary in the *Guardian* Keith Harper described him as 'a Pick-wickian figure . . . who looked for all the world like a bank manager . . . and applied an incisive mind to debates'.[39] *The Times* reported: 'He initiated a number of new developments, including a series of studies of public policy and efforts at bridge-building with other unions.'[40]

Recession, Redundancies, and Falling Relative Pay

Public-sector pay continued its relative decline in the 1990s, and successive reorganizations increased the proportion of lower-paid white-collar jobs. NALGO continued to shift its pay-bargaining policy towards combating low pay, which sat well with NUPE's historic fight for a national minimum wage and with COHSE's concern for poor wages in the health service.[41] In 1990 a *National Low Pay Strategy* committed the NLGC to 'prepare proposals for a long term negotiating strategy, with detailed negotiating objectives, includ-ing a national minimum wage for APT&C staff'.[42] In 1992 this was incorpo-rated into proposals for a 'long term strategy' that included the objective of 'harmonisation of terms and conditions of employment of all workers in local government'.[43] The *Long Term Pay Strategy* was published in 1993, with the first objective being 'To protect national bargaining from attacks by central government'. Other service groups adopted similar objectives. However, single-employer bargaining was already established in many of the privatized utility companies. The union had to resource more negotiations in more bar-gaining units.

The remainder of this chapter identifies how the union responded to pres-sures on bargaining during this last year before merger. In the private sector the union faced pressures of intensifying competition, profit-taking, and changes to national collective bargaining. In the public-service sector it faced market pressures, declining budgets, and in 1993 a 1.5 per cent pay norm set by the government. In both sectors it meant yet more attacks on pay, on jobs, on conditions of service, and on trade-union organization.

Transport

Further deregulation and cartelization meant a harsh collective-bargaining climate on the buses, with job losses and modest pay awards. The union's

[39] *Guardian*, 7 Apr. 1993, 10.   [40] *The Times*, 5 Apr. 1993, 17.
[41] M. Carpenter, *Working for Health: The History of COHSE* (London: Lawrence & Wishart, 1988); R. Fryer and S. Williams, *A Century of Service: An Illustrated History of the National Union of Public Employees, 1889–1993* (London: Lawrence & Wishart, 1993).
[42] *NN*, 8 May 1992, 4.   [43] Ibid., 15 May 1992, 4–5.

national transport committee summarized the impact of the 1985 Transport Act in *Moving Forward: A NALGO Policy Statement on Public Transport for the 1990s*: 'By 1990 Britain was saddled with a bus industry which was costing passengers more, providing a poorer service to those who needed it most, where the vehicles were generally older, inconvenient and uncomfortable, where the staff were disgruntled and worse off and with British bus building virtually at a standstill.'[44] Shadow Transport Secretary John Prescott pledged to repeal it. After the election the union continued to oppose further deregulation and the enforced privatization of the municipal bus companies. It funded a research post at the Public Transport Information Unit, supported a Women's Transport Charter launched by a number of women's organizations, and participated in activities of Transport 2000 and the Public Transport Campaign Group.

Deregulation brought about more management buyouts, higher fares, worse services, and poorer employment conditions for staff. It added significantly to the general crisis of transport, with congested motorways, investment-starved rail, and deteriorating buses. This problem of service provision was compounded by the domination of bus companies by a handful of large firms often with other transport interests. One important new development was employee buyouts through Employee Share Ownership Plans (ESOPs). NALGO issued guidance on this,[45] anticipating DTI approval for a staff buyout of Merseybus.

In the Public Transport Information Unit's report *Privatisation of the Scottish Bus Group*, Henry McLeish MP argued that 'nothing that has happened since the sell off was announced bears any resemblance to [the government's] ridiculous claims. . . . There is now a chasm between the empty rhetoric of the government ministers and the realities facing bus users.'[46] Other reports stressed the consequences: 'Six years of deregulation have jammed the roads with buses, and passengers are still waiting for a better service.'[47] Official reports provided further evidence: 'Instability in the local bus market is driving people off the buses, according to the latest annual reports of the traffic commissioners, the civil servants who issue licences and register bus services throughout the country.'[48]

As the bus services deteriorated under the impact of deregulation, so did wages and service conditions, intensified by the withdrawal of government

---

[44] NALGO, *Moving Forward: A NALGO Policy Statement on Public Transport for the 1990s* (London: NALGO, n.d., c.1992), 6.

[45] NALGO, *For Sale: A Report on the Sale of Local Authority Owned Bus Companies* (London: NALGO, 1992).

[46] *PS* (transport) (Aug. 1992), 2.   [47] Ibid. (Sept. 1992), 1.

[48] Ibid. (Nov. 1992), 12.

The Poll Tax is being scrapped, but billions of pounds have been wasted
trying to make it work. Now the Government plans to replace it with the Council Tax. Another tax
designed to put the squeeze on councils and prevent them from providing
better local services. It isn't just the Poll Tax which has to go. It's the attitudes behind it.

You can choose a better future. Make sure you do.

Strange, isn't it? Thirteen years of NHS underfunding.
And now, all of a sudden, a frantic, money-no-object scramble to shorten the waiting list.
And what date have Health Service Managers been given to achieve
this reduction? April 1st. Just 8 days before the election. Now there's a coincidence.

You can choose a better future. Make sure you do.

Once again, under this Government, there are almost 3 million people on the dole. Yet British industry is desperate for skilled workers. With proper training schemes, industry could have the skilled workers it needs. But not with the sort of half baked training schemes this Government has created – leaving people unqualified, jobless or doing unsuitable work. If individuals can't fulfil their potential, how can we as a nation fulfil ours?

You can choose a better future. Make sure you do. NALGO

The State education system is crumbling through lack of Government investment.
Overcrowded classes. Dilapidated buildings. Demoralised teachers. No wonder our children are less well educated than those in other European countries. The problem is underfunding.
A national curriculum and opting out won't solve it. That's a lesson this Government still needs to learn.

You can choose a better future. Make sure you do.

Thirteen years of neglect and cuts will never be put right by a few hundred pages
of empty promises. The Government's Charters profess to guarantee quality in public services. Of course
we all want quality, but quality can only be guaranteed by investment. The same people
who have run down public services since 1979 now want us to believe that they care. Who are they kidding?

You can choose a better future. Make sure you do.

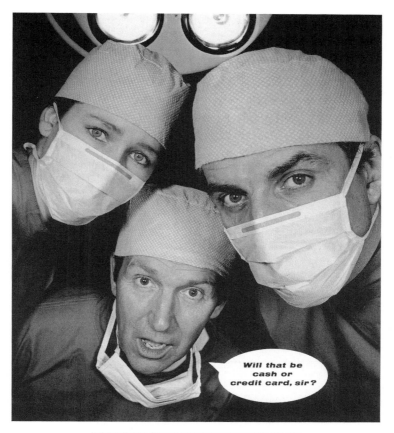

Will that be cash or credit card, sir?

In the last 12 years, the NHS has lost nearly a quarter of its beds through underfunding. Wards have closed and re-opened as private wards. Health authorities are refusing to carry out routine operations on the NHS. As a result, those who can, pay. Those who can't, pay too. By joining a waiting list still so long that people die waiting.

You can choose a better future. Make sure you do.

This Government invests less money in public transport, as a proportion
of national income, than any other in Europe. The result is unreliable services, queues,
overcrowding and high fares. So more people travel by car – often in traffic
jams which cost the economy £15 billion a year. It's a transport policy that's going nowhere.

You can choose a better future. Make sure you do.

subsidies, enforced sales of local-authority services, and falling profits for many of the new private operators. The Transport Committee agreed a 1992 claim for non-manual staff in the six English PTEs, for an '8 per cent pay rise with a minimum £750 increase, progress towards a 35 hour week and at least 24 days' annual leave'.[49] This was intended to stop the relative decline in pay, but the settlement reached at the end of March was for 4.9 per cent. This was in line with settlements of between 4 and 5 per cent in the private bus companies, with some exceptions, such as the 7 per cent increase at Strathclyde buses.

Water

NALGO now had to support pay negotiations in all the private water companies as well as in the NRA and BWB. A going rate of 4–5 per cent for most private companies was matched in the NRA and BWB in 1992. Negotiations were hard going in the aftermath of privatization. In an effort to reduce the difficulties for negotiators in so many companies, NALGO and NUPE joined forces to produce *The New Water Companies*, which gave details of company finances and other bargaining information. NUPE's national officer for water Virginia Branney argued: 'Increasingly, manual, craft and staff are having to work together to compile pay claims and prepare for negotiations as water companies move towards single table bargaining and harmonisation.'[50] Pay itself became increasingly hard to assess, with basic awards being supplemented by performance-related pay deals, profit-related pay, market options, and share option schemes, further complicated by the introduction of new grading structures.

There were further revelations that the government had botched the privatization of the industry with an estimated extra loss of £2.36 million. *Public Service* summed this up: 'When the Conservative government took power, access to clean, fresh water was an undeniable right for everybody. Today it is a commodity privately owned for profit.'[51] The union was in no doubt that pre-tax profits showed that the companies could afford to pay more. Staff in Yorkshire water rejected a 4.3 per cent offer and later accepted 5 per cent, and North East Water accepted a 5.1 per cent offer after a ballot. Other deals included 4.3–4.8 per cent at Severn Trent, 5 per cent at South Staffordshire, and 4.5 per cent at both Southern Water and North West Water. Thames Water faced its first strike since privatization when 250 staff went out for the day at Swindon over back pay and over assimilation of staff onto the company's new pay grades. North West Water announced 700 redundancies and

[49] Ibid. (Mar. 1992), 2.   [50] *PS* (water) (Feb. 1992), 16.
[51] Ibid. (Mar. 1992), 1.

its withdrawal from collective bargaining. More threats to union organization and recognition rights came from Yorkshire Water and Wessex Water.

NRA negotiators agreed a 4.3 per cent rise after a 7 per cent claim and an initial offer of 3.6 per cent, but the main bargaining issue remained the new job evaluation scheme based on the Hay method for over 5,000 jobs—the union view was that it was about introducing performance-related pay. The NRA demanded a reduction in conditions of service but NALGO just refused. On a brighter note, the NRA agreed to tackle equal opportunities with NALGO as an increasing priority.

Rising public concern about water conservation, purity, and purification was fuelled by incidents such as the pollution of the Carnon River in Cornwall. NALGO was involved, along with other unions and the environmental lobby, in a successful campaign to keep the NRA as a single entity. However, later in 1992 Michael Howard, Secretary of State for the Environment, announced that the NRA was to be market tested. NALGO recognized the implications: 'Market testing, where government departments and quangos are subjected to scrutiny on the basis of efficiency and value for money, is seen as the first stage to competitive tendering and privatisation.'[52] Deputy national officer for water, Steve Bloomfield, responded: 'Our assessment is that it is essentially about reducing the number of jobs.' As all NRA regions faced market testing, so the fears of job losses mounted: 'Market testing is an expensive experiment in ideological dogma that deserves to fail. Both NALGO and NUPE will be working closely together now and in UNISON (from July 1993) to protect jobs and services and to promote the values of public service.'[53]

British Waterways staff claimed a 7 per cent pay increase in 1992, and settled for 4.3 per cent in June. BWB announced the closure of its south-west regional office with job losses and transfers. Steve Bloomfield said: 'For an organisation which proclaims its commitment to its staff, British Waterways has behaved with a reckless high handedness strongly condemned by NALGO.'[54]

In the summer of 1992 Scottish Secretary Ian Lang announced that Scottish water was to be privatized, in the face of opposition from the majority in Scotland. *Public Service* reported: 'Scotland is gearing up for the biggest anti-privatisation campaign mounted in Britain',[55] and opposition increased in 1993. Matt Smith, Scottish District Officer, said: 'It's quite obvious that the idea of franchising or privatisation are the preferred government options.'[56]

---

[52] *PS* (water) (Oct. 1992), 2.
[53] NALGO and NUPE, *A Negotiator's Guide to Market Testing in the NRA* (London: NALGO and NUPE, 1992).
[54] *NN*, 3 Apr. 1992, 1.   [55] *PS* (water) (Dec. 1992), 1.   [56] Ibid. (Jan. 1993), 2.

A mass movement developed, as the STUC campaigned with a range of organizations joined together to protest against the government's plans and to coordinate opposition. As *Mac* reported:

The secretary of state has at last published his 'consultation paper' on the future of Water and Sewerage in Scotland. Scottish NALGO and branches throughout the country have put in responses to the paper and a joint UNISON union demonstration was being arranged for 30 January to underline the point. 'Turn the Tide' is the slogan for the campaign designed to save Scotland's water and sewerage public services.[57]

The march and rally in Glasgow was attended by people from all over the country.

Gas

Post-privatization restructuring of British Gas gained momentum: 'Staff are set for further uncertainty and disruption in the wake of the three-way agreement between the company, the Office of Fair Trading and industry regulator Ofgas.'[58] More showrooms were closed, bringing to over fifty the total shut during the year, as the unions and other groups prepared to submit reports to the MMC investigations. The actual nature of the future shape of the industry was still undecided in 1993, as less than open negotiations continued between the MMC, Ofgas, the DTI, and the company, with the unions sniping from the sidelines. British Gas was prepared to shed up to 3,000 jobs in the regions.

National officer Dave Stirzaker summarized the impact of this on industrial relations: 'The problem for NALGO members is the way in which the personnel philosophy has switched from traditional industrial relations to the new style Human Resource Management approach.' This included a shift away from encouraging union membership, a reduction in the scope of the bargaining agenda, and large-scale job losses.[59] Managers tried to ignore the union and to avoid negotiations in the Information Services sector of British Gas. Dave Johnson, deputy national officer, said: 'We said British Gas must wake up to the level of discontent and treat staffing issues with the seriousness they deserve.'[60]

The company's overall performance improved so negotiators argued that this depended on staff performance and asked for 'a substantial above inflation pay increase' as well as a thirty-five-hour week and improvements in paternity leave and career breaks in the 1992 claim. The union rejected the company's opening offer in May of 3.9 per cent as 'derisory and insulting'.

[57] *Mac* (Feb. 1993), 1.   [58] *PS* (gas) (Feb. 1992), 1.
[59] Ibid. (May 1992), 2.   [60] Ibid. (Jan. 1992), 1.

Delegates at the gas group annual meeting confirmed rejection of the offer, and also opposed further showroom closures. An increased offer of 4.3 per cent was also rejected by the negotiating team. Dave Stirzaker drummed up support for industrial action: 'We know how angry our members are. They will vote for action.'[61] But the ballot vote went against action, reflecting the uncertainty among the union's 32,000 members as the company, the MMC, and Ofgas talked about splitting up the company, and the union finally accepted 4.3 per cent.

The 1993 claim for 5 per cent or £600 minimum was based on the same arguments, as chair of the national gas committee, Roy Jones, explained: 'The company's performance and profitability mean they are able to fund the claim in full.'[62] By the end of March the company managed to offer 2.1 per cent, despite awarding dividends to shareholders of 6 per cent, and negotiations were still continuing as NALGO went into UNISON.

Electricity

In the final year of national collective bargaining the negotiators won settlements slightly above the general going rate. There were clear dangers in the new bargaining regimes being established in the branches of the industry. National Power targeted 200 senior professional and technical staff for personal contracts. Norweb unilaterally imposed new pay scales on new starters, but was forced to abandon performance-related pay based on gold–silver–bronze assessments after the 700 NALGO members threatened industrial action. Staff at SWEB were asked to accept pay cuts or lose jobs. There was a storm of protest at PowerGen after a leaked secret document revealed the company's intention to sack up to one-third of the workforce, about 2,000 jobs.

Mike Jeram, national officer, compared these attacks on the workforce with the pay-offs for shareholders and top managers: 'These huge profits as a reward for disposing of jobs make bounty hunters appear like charity workers. It underlines that privatisation of the industry was carried out only to create mega profits for the City and similar pay rises for senior management.'[63] The electricity industry regulator, Stephen Littlechild, was attacked for his failure to enforce regulations concerning economic purchasing licences. His office, Offer, was accused by a joint union and consumer pressure group, Coffer, of failures that would lead to job losses throughout the industry.

At a seminar at Ruskin College, Oxford, Dennis Gregory spoke about the changes in management techniques in the industry: 'It goes under a number of titles: human resource management, total quality management, teamwork

[61] *NN*, 17 July 1992, 1.   [62] *PS* (gas) (Feb. 1993), 1.   [63] *NN*, 17 July 1992, 1.

for performance, team talk. Whatever the name, it's eroding workers' rights and conditions of service and undermining NALGO.'[64]

As 1992 was the last year of national negotiations in the electricity supply companies, activists urged the union officers to move closer to the members in order to sustain trade-union organization and bargaining capability. Unions representing the 130,000 staff launched a joint pay campaign. Given reports of strong profits among the electricity supply companies, they aimed their claim at a figure above inflation. They recommended acceptance of a 5.5 per cent offer, agreed by the members in a ballot, and they approved the new single-table arrangements. NALGO was eager for its 60 per cent women membership to participate more fully in union affairs in readiness for company-level negotiations in 1993. Assistant national officer Judith Secker launched a bargaining pack, *Improving Working Life*, which included a fully integrated equal opportunities agenda.

National Power was shedding jobs in readiness to embark on international competition. Another 2,500 jobs were to go, in addition to the 6,500 already lost. New company bargaining arrangements were put forward at the end of 1992, including eleven new salary grades in a single structure, a 3.95 per cent pay rise from March, a one-off lump-sum payment, better annual leave, and some aspects of performance-related pay to be negotiated with NALGO. This package was widely accepted in a vote of the members.

Meanwhile PowerGen was also involved in wide-ranging talks in which agreement on single-table bargaining would be met by beneficial changes to the salary structure and favourable negotiations on related issues such as maternity leave, hours of work, and flexibility. This included an important condition of equal pay for work of equal value, and a 'bumper' deal on pay of 5.5 per cent basic plus £400 plus 2 per cent for accepting company bargaining as well as improvement associated with assimilation onto new grades.

In 1993 pay claims were framed with the large profits from privatization in the minds of the negotiators. Increases in profitability ranged from 15 per cent at Scottish Power to 127 per cent at Norweb from 1991–2. Hydroelectric staff called for industrial action after the company threatened pay cuts, but the company climbed down after a ballot on action. At Southern Electric there was a 2.9 per cent offer with a 4.5 per cent one-off payment as part of the new single-table bargaining arrangements. This was in line with other companies such as a 4.7 per cent equivalent at Yorkshire Electric, but more than the 2.4 per cent and £100 lump sum at East Midlands. At National Grid the staff agreed with NALGO's recommendation to accept an offer of 3.95 per cent plus a lump sum linked with new bargaining arrangements. PowerGen staff

---

[64] *PS* (electricity) (Dec. 1992), 20.

accepted an offer of 2.5 per cent and £250–£550 (an average of 4.5 per cent), also following the union's recommendation.

NALGO's hostility to the entire electricity privatization programme had been maintained for nearly a decade. While the union now had to come to terms with new bargaining arrangements in order to secure the best possible conditions for the members in the new private companies, this principled hostility continued. As Mike Jeram commented: 'NALGO wants electricity run in the public interest. Its strategic importance must be recognised for the economy and the environment. NALGO would support bringing National Grid back into public ownership. There should be a planned energy policy.'[65]

Education

In schools the locus of local bargaining for non-teaching staff moved to the school head and governors, as the LMS system weakened the LEAs' role. NALGO's first priority was to keep staff on national local-government APT&C conditions. It argued for framework agreements with LEAs as a basis for protecting conditions of service, and for a network of school-based NALGO representatives with regular access to the head and relevant governors.[66] Harrow moved early, ditching national pay and conditions for non-teaching staff in its schools. A new Education Bill contained several measures designed further to reduce the authority of the LEAs and transfer their powers to central government agencies, thus increasing the loss of local democratic accountability and marginalizing staff and their unions, as well as users, from decision-making.

Articles in *Public Service* identified the main problems in further and higher education in 1992: 'Under funding has been the hallmark of the British education system in the last 13 years,' and: 'Job losses caused by closure of departments or privatisation to keep costs down have become increasingly fashionable in the sector.'[67] A strike by staff at Imperial College London over sackings, a similar show of solidarity at King's College London over threatened cuts and job losses, and disputes and days of action at the Universities Central Council on Admissions (UCCA) headquarters in Cheltenham over job-evaluation schemes, were symptomatic of the situation. This was worsened by the hastily enacted Further and Higher Education Act, aimed at restructuring funding councils and allowing polytechnics and larger colleges to become universities.

University administrative and clerical staff put in a pay claim for 1992 of 12 per cent or £1,200 per year whichever was the greater. As negotiations got

---

[65] *PS* (electricity) (Mar. 1992), 24. [66] *NN*, 24 Jan. 1992, 6.
[67] *PS* (colleges, polytechnics, and universities) (Mar. 1992), 1, 24.

under way, Janet Richardson, chair of the National Universities Committee, said: 'Employers will always argue that they can't afford to pay us what they would like to. We are saying that they could pay us more if they altered their priorities.'[68] They settled for 5.5 per cent and some grading changes at the end of April.

Things went less smoothly in colleges and polytechnics. The 1992 claim for 10 per cent or £1,000 was followed by an employers' offer of 4 per cent, increased to 4.3 per cent at the June negotiating meeting. These were rejected, and the union leadership campaigned vigorously for a yes vote in a strike ballot. Elaine Harrison, national officer, described the offer as 'a kick in the teeth for all the hard work of the last three years in helping maintain an increase in student numbers'.[69] The union gave ten good reasons for the action, including pay, which had fallen far behind equivalent comparators; hours of work were the same as in 1972; student numbers had increased; the university sector had won 5.5 per cent; and the employers could afford it. With a 54.7 per cent vote for action, the one-day protest strike went ahead on 20 August. As Alison Shepherd, chair of the Polytechnic and Colleges Committee, pointed out, it was NALGO's 'first ever national strike action to tale place in the polytechnic and colleges sector'.[70] There was a two-day strike at the end of September because, as Elaine Harrison said, members 'felt cheated'. At the end of October members were taking selective action throughout the country, but by November the union had no alternative but to call off the action and accept the 4.3 per cent.

At one point during that dispute the employers tried to block the strikes by using the anti-union laws. They claimed that the union should have balloted members separately in each institution, which would have made the balloting process even more onerous and open to nit-picking challenges from individual employers.[71] The union defeated this legal challenge to effective union organization, winning a crucial decision in the High Court. Val Cook, deputy legal officer, said: 'It's given us very good authority to call a ballot nationally on national services where there are multi employers.'[72]

Education-sector staff were furious at the start of the 1993 pay round, not only about the 1.5 per cent general pay freeze but also about comments by Secretary of State John Patten that future pay would also be kept down. This was made worse by both a serious lack of funding and a lack of coherent policy direction, according to the heads of the new universities. As part of the new managerialism entering the university system at a time of intense

---

[68] Ibid. (May 1992), 2.   [69] Ibid. (Aug. 1992), 1.   [70] Ibid. (Sept. 1992), 16.
[71] J. McMullen and P. Kaufman, *Labour Law Review 1993* (London: Institute of Employment Rights, 1993), 4.
[72] *NN*, 21 Aug. 1992, 1.

stringency the vice-chancellors started to consider local bargaining with a single salary spine. The unions rejected their 1.5 per cent offer and campaigned for a substantial real rise in pay, but, as with the other services, members received only the 1.5 per cent allowed for by government. This left the 30,000 clerical and administrative grades in the 'old' universities on salaries ranging from £19,220 at the top of grade 6, down to £6,834 for those at the bottom of grade 1.[73] The prospects were not good.

The National Health Service

NALGO News described the serious situation facing the NHS in 1992, after thirteen years of Tory government: 'Gross under funding, internal market, opt-out hospitals, privatization, attacks on health workers and their unions— they're all chronic news for patients and health service workers. What's worse, they attack the very idea of a National Health Service offering comprehensive treatment, which is free and equal for all.'[74] In the run-up to the election, *NALGO News* reported on the Labour Party's commitments:

A future Labour Government will abolish the internal market, opt outs and GP fund holding, pledged Neil Kinnock last week. Launching the party's white paper, *Your Good Health*, Mr Kinnock said the government was 'promoting the privatisation of the NHS in Britain'. In contrast the Labour Party says it will bring an end to fragmentation and commercialisation of the NHS.[75]

NALGO continued its opposition to the setting up of Trusts and the creation of an internal market, and in 1992 issued joint advice with COHSE, GMB, and TGWU in the booklet *Competition for Patient Transport Services: A Guide for the Ambulance Services*.

London's health service was descending into chaos. Over thirty hospitals and a quarter of acute beds had been closed since 1979. Cuts in jobs were announced at the Royal London, Riverside, Middlesex, and Barts hospitals as financial problems mounted. In early August there were protest strikes by staff from Charing Cross and Westminster hospitals. Unions argued for a full strategy for London health care before any hospital mergers, but in October the Tomlinson Report recommended the closure of ten hospitals: 'Health union fears over the future of health services in London increased this week following the government's announcement on the Tomlinson report. NALGO accused health secretary Virginia Bottomley of fudging . . . The union warned that without intervention the internal market will take its toll regardless.'[76]

---

[73] IDS, *Pay in the Public Services: Review of 1993, Prospects for 1994* (London: IDS, 1994), 101.
[74] *PS* (health) (Mar. 1992), 1. [75] *NN*, 28 Feb. 1992, 6.
[76] Ibid. 19 Feb. 1993, 8.

The emergency reached new depths at the start of 1993 when all London hospitals were put on 'yellow' alert over bed shortages.

In Birmingham the 'Save our Services' campaign, mounted by health and patient groups and supported by the unions, presented Virginia Bottomley with a 35,000-signature petition expressing concern about the future of the city's NHS services. The three merger partner unions coordinated plans to hold days of action and lobbies of Parliament, and they produced a report, *In the Firing Line: The Impact on Staff*, covering the impact of the internal market on health care.

NALGO's 1992 pay claim was for £16 per week or 10 per cent, whichever was the greater, as the unions launched a campaign against low pay. A&C members accepted an offer of 4.75 per cent or £400 per year, as did PTB staff and ambulance officers and control assistants. Staff covered by pay review did better, as nurses received between 5.7 per cent and 5.8 per cent and PAMs got 6.3 per cent. As the claims were settled, some early signs of Trust management thinking about staff management began to emerge, with performance-related pay for senior managers being viewed with deep unease.[77] A NALGO survey found that one in five NHS managers were not receiving the appropriate level of pay under their performance-related pay schemes.

Later, and more positively, there was a national agreement to safeguard the abuse of extra 'stat' days, and NALGO won its first clinical nurse grading appeals at national level. However, these successful appeals revealed how management had underpaid experienced but unqualified nurses, exploiting their work knowledge through an unfair interpretation of the rigid guidelines on qualifications. This was part of a more general move to cut unit labour costs by changing the skill mix, a tactic made easier by the government's introduction of health-care assistants who were not covered by the national arrangements for determining pay and conditions.[78]

Some local bargaining emerged, but only on a piecemeal basis, as local managers began to test out the limits of their new-found freedom to determine employment issues. For example, Alan Davison, chief executive of Essex Rivers Healthcare Trust, threatened to tear up national Whitley agreements: 'The boss of an opted-out Essex trust has spelt out his commitment to cut staff pay and if possible sell off entire support services in a management document leaked to London Health Emergency.'[79]

[77] NALGO, *Performance Pay in the Health Service: A Negotiating Guide* (London: NALGO, 1993).
[78] C. Thornley, 'Contesting Local Pay: The Decentralization of Collective Bargaining in the NHS', *British Journal of Industrial Relations*, 36/3 (1998), 413–34.
[79] *NN*, 13 Mar. 1992, 1.

The signs for collective bargaining in 1993 were not good: 'Chancellor Lamont's 1.5 per cent pay ceiling will have a particularly severe affect on already low paid NHS workers.'[80] The claim for nurses and midwives went in at 8.7 per cent, and all the unions representing white-collar staff rejected the 1.5 per cent pay limit in the run-up to the 1993 negotiations. NALGO national officer, Paul Marks, said: 'The management side should be aware that our claim has been presented in the context of bitterness and resentment on the part of the staff whom we represent at the way in which they are being undervalued. We shall be totally ignoring the 1.5 per cent figure.'[81] Unions representing PTB staff rejected an offer of 1.5 per cent. The government response was to make sure the pay review bodies offered only 1.5 per cent and that Trust managements also stuck by the freeze. The unions consulted their members on industrial action, and organized a pre-budget lobby of Parliament in March. In June, delegates at the union's last health group meeting accepted the 1.5 per cent offer.

The sadly mis-named 'Care in the Community' arrangements came into effect on 1 April 1993. The general view was that 'it is union members who will be expected to bear the brunt of service failures as a result of gross under funding'.[82] NALGO commissioned the Institute for Public Policy Research to investigate the experiences of service users, carers, and service providers, reported in *Community Care: Users' Experiences*. In 1993 the union issued *Community Care: Handbook for Local Government Branches*, which highlighted the issues involved in splitting the purchasing and providing functions of local-authority social service departments into separate arms of service organization.

By the time NALGO became part of UNISON there was some 'devolution of decision-making on pay and conditions to local managers . . . [but] the overwhelming majority of NHS staff are currently still employed on nationally determined pay and conditions'.[83] All groups settled at the 1.5 per cent government limit, which undermined the independence of the review bodies as much as it made a mockery of the collective bargaining system for other groups. Most staff on A&C grades remained on the national pay structures, somewhere between a minimum of £6,561 at the bottom of grade 1 and £33,679 at the top of grade 10.[84] As yet there was virtually no move to local pay bargaining, despite trust managers apparently having the freedom to break away from the national systems.

---

[80] *PS* (health) (Dec. 1992), 1.   [81] *NN*, 15 Jan. 1993, 1.
[82] *PS* (health) (May 1993), 8.   [83] IDS, *Pay in the Public Services*, 63.
[84] Ibid. 78.

Local government

Local government was now taking the brunt of the government attack. Secretary of State Michael Heseltine announced the financial settlement for 1992, he put the Local Government Bill before Parliament, with its proposals to extend CCT, and he established a Local Government Commission, which later led to the biggest reorganization since 1974. Alan Jinkinson slammed Heseltine's proposals in an open letter published in *Public Service*:

You are on the verge of eliminating the last vestiges of the financial independence of local government. Effective and vigorous local democracy cannot survive within a system which provides that 85 per cent of a council's funds is directly allocated to them by you and that the other 15 per cent is effectively controlled by you as well. The gradual process by which you have acquired effective control over local government finance is a threat not just to the continuing provision of high quality public services but also to the constitutional fabric of our democracy.[85]

The union's lead negotiator also took up the issues, in a *Public Service* interview:

Thirteen years of alternating attack and neglect have left local government bloody and battered. The strain of trying to force a square peg into a round hole—to force local government to act like a commercial enterprise—has told on both local authorities and NALGO members. 'When you look back and go through all the different attacks there have been in the last twelve years or so, the more it becomes miraculous that local government has survived at all during this period,' says NALGO national officer Dennis Reed.[86]

One of the union's main concerns at this time was the extension of CCT, taken up in another report:

A leaked secret report has revealed that the government ignored professional advice on its plans to extend compulsory competitive tendering in local government. The government employed the PA consulting group to advise it on the changes included in the Local Government Bill which is currently before Parliament. But it kept the PA report secret—with good reason, as the document contradicts many of the government's plans. The report clearly states that there is currently no viable market for many local government services. And it gives advice that certain services are not candidates, or not good candidates, for compulsory competitive tendering.[87]

The General Secretary continued the theme: 'Privatisation is about providing shoddy goods on the cheap, and now the government want to extend CCT to white-collar services, despite widespread hostility.'[88] NALGO

---

[85] *PS* (Jan. 1992), 6. [86] *PS* (local government) (Mar. 1992), 1.
[87] Ibid. (Feb. 1992), 1. [88] Ibid. (July 1992), 4.

identified some specific arguments against white-collar CCT: 'In many cases there is no identifiable private market. Even where a private market does exist it is often far more expensive than local authority provision. There is a need for certain services either because of their statutory or specialist nature to be done in-house.'[89] However, in early November Environment Minister Michael Howard announced that CCT would indeed apply to white-collar services.

As part of its practical fight back the union issued guidelines on *Ways to Tackle the Tender Trap*. It aimed 'to limit non-enforced tendering and privatisation and to protect the jobs and conditions of service of our members'. The NHS Privatization Unit became the Public Services Privatization Research Unit (PSPRU), funded by NALGO, NUPE, COHSE, Northern Ireland Public Services Alliance (NIPSA), National Union of Civil and Public Servants (NUCPS), and TGWU, with its role expanded to cover local government and the Civil Service. PSPRU's 1992 report, *Privatisation: Disaster for Quality*, started baldly: 'This booklet examines how privatisation in the public sector has cheated us all out of quality services.' In the same year NALGO's Metropolitan District and three branches, Westminster, Wandsworth, and Kensington and Chelsea, commissioned the Centre for Public Services to write up their experiences in *Competition Cuts and Contractors: Lessons for Trade Unionists from Three Flagship London Boroughs*.

In February 1993 the Local Government Group Meeting agreed a Compulsory Competitive Tendering Strategy, which set out a programme of action for the national committee, district committees, and branches. Central to the strategy was the establishment of negotiations and consultations with local authorities over the implementation of the CCT regime. This was supplemented by a joint NALGO, NUPE, GMB, and TGWU booklet *Competitive Tendering Strategy Handbook*, prepared by the Centre for Public Services (formerly SCAT), which argued 'Experience shows that in those local authorities where a comprehensive strategy has been adopted by both trade unions and management there has been a greater success in retaining services in-house'. The unions' battle was not helped when the Shadow Secretary of State for the Environment, Jack Straw, told the Labour Party local-government conference in Bournemouth that he approved of CCT, the council tax, and the internal market based on the purchaser–provider split.

In the national bargaining arena, 1992 started with a breakthrough for residential social workers with substantial gains in two areas of traditional contention: extra payments in recognition of special working hours and conditions, and the deletion of some unpopular grades that created unfair dif-

---

[89] *NN*, 12 Mar. 1992, 4–5.

ferentials with field social workers. The Howe inquiry into pay and conditions made recommendations that fell far short of the members' aspirations, but Alison Mitchell, deputy national officer, saw further potential in the agreement: 'Acceptance of the offer means that the Howe inquiry will continue and there are other things coming out of that inquiry in respect of career grades and training.'[90]

Meanwhile the 1992 national local-government pay claim was formulated in January and called for a £1,000 annual pay rise. Jean Geldart, chair of the national committee, announced the claim after consultation with districts and branches: 'This claim is the one that meets the needs and aspirations of every single NALGO member.'[91] The claim stated: 'The staff side strongly believes that the 1992 pay settlement should reflect the value of services provided by local government staff and the commitment of these staff in very difficult times. The staff side believes that particular recognition should be given to low paid staff, many of whom are in the front line of providing services to the public.'[92] The claim also defended national bargaining, firmly rejecting the employers' proposals to weaken it through much publicized ideas such as kitty bargaining.

As the employers failed to respond, Dennis Reed, NALGO's staff side secretary of the APT&C negotiating committee, wrote an open letter to the employers' side secretary, Charles Nolda, passing on the union's data on the extent of discrimination against women staff: 'What it uncovers is a shocking indictment on the level of institutionalised discrimination in local government.'[93] The union's survey showed that 92 per cent of full-time staff on Scale 1 were women and that 89 per cent of full-time workers paid below the Council of Europe decency threshold were women. During May the employers rejected the flat-rate element and then offered 3.6 per cent which was slammed by Dennis Reed: 'It is a miserable offer—a real wage cut for all of our members.'[94] This, and a subsequent slightly improved offer of 3.8 per cent, was rejected by the union negotiators. In a report to the June annual group meeting the national committee agonized over its dilemma: on the one hand, it was bound by a 1991 decision for a substantial flat-rate increase supported by industrial action if necessary, but, on the other hand, it was confronted by employers unwilling to offer either a flat-rate or a substantial increase, and it feared the debilitating impact of another failure to win membership support in a ballot for industrial action. Soundings amongst members and activists indicated no mood for action in the aftermath of the general-election results. As a result, the way forward seemed to be to continue to

[90] Ibid., 7 Feb. 1992, 6.   [91] Ibid., 24 Jan. 1992, 1.   [92] Ibid., 31 Jan. 1992, 6.
[93] Ibid., 20 Mar. 1992, 2.   [94] Ibid., 15 May 1992, 1.

negotiate with the threat of some form of action, and the group meeting agreed.

The employers increased their offer to 4.1 per cent of the pay bill; the negotiators were unhappy with this but decided to consult widely in advance of the reconvened group meeting. Dennis Reed summed up the negotiators' feelings: 'The offer is very disappointing from all points of view. Our members at all levels have kept local government from going under in very difficult circumstances. Low pay has subsidised councils facing severe cuts.'[95] As the group meeting reluctantly voted to accept the offer, Jean Geldart, chair of the national committee, put the decision in perspective: 'To achieve a substantially better settlement, we would have to take major industrial action. There are times when you make a tactical retreat in order to fight better on other issues.'[96] And there was no shortage of 'other issues' to fight on.

Cuts in local-government spending, enforced by the government, provoked local authorities into two particular responses that caused industrial-relations problems at local level. Job losses continued, with increasing numbers of compulsory redundancies, and employers considered breaking away from the constraints of the national agreement, especially on pay. For some, this became necessary because of labour shortages among certain categories of employee. Some employers wanted new payment systems and structures outside the traditional national Whitley agreements, and by the end of 1992 about thirty local authorities had introduced local pay schemes for APT&C staff.[97] Kent County Council led the field with their 'pay plus scheme' in 1991, subsequently imposing a 4.5 per cent pay award on 10,000 staff who had opted out of the national pay scales. *NALGO News* reported on union concerns about other breakaway councils: 'Fears are growing that thousands of senior council staff in southern Britain who signed up for local, market-related, pay schemes may be asked to accept salary standstills and even cuts this year.'[98]

But the biggest conflicts were over redundancies, and 1992 was dominated by some bitter trials of strength. *NALGO News* reported on one such dispute in Scotland: 'Strathclyde NALGO wants to escalate a strike in support of community education workers suspended for refusing work from recently redundant posts.'[99] There were already 228 community education staff on strike, and, as they sought further support from the branch, it was decided to ballot over 600 members in strategic parts of the council.[100] This was followed by an acrimonious debate within the union as to whether all members should

[95] *NN*, 3 July 1992, 1.   [96] *PS* (local government) (Aug. 1992), 1.
[97] IDS, *Local Pay in the Public Sector*, study 510 (London: IDS, 1992).
[98] *NN*, 13 Mar. 1992, 1.   [99] Ibid., 17 Jan. 1992, 2.
[100] *NALGO Emergency Committee Meeting Minutes*, 21 (London: NALGO, 1992–3), 4.

be covered in one single ballot or in separate ballots for members in each of the six relevant sections. In the end there were 265 in favour of a strike and 249 against, with 103 not voting. The strike went ahead, growing to some 1,000 members, including 203 community education staff, 610 finance staff, and 180 other finance staff. It ended with an agreement acclaimed by branch secretary, Chrissie Carmouche, who said: 'The agreement recognises our view that members should not be required to do redundant work, and our members have been prepared to accept it on this basis.'[101]

Later in 1992 an even larger and longer dispute saw over 2,000 Newham council members on strike, after a 63 per cent yes vote in a ballot, to protest at the threat of compulsory redundancies. Branch chair Phil Thompson said: 'We regret the major disruption this strike will cause the people of Newham but the blame for it has to be laid firmly at the door of the council. Firstly it refuses to talk to the union and then it attacks our members on official strike action.'[102] The annual group meeting discussed the council's attacks on the strikers, the use of the anti-union laws to try to frustrate the strike, and the threat to withdraw check-off facilities. Reflecting the delegates' concern that other employers might follow Newham's example, the meeting pledged its full support for the strikers and their branch, declaring the strike 'a test case dispute'. Later that week the union's Emergency Committee recorded its support.[103]

Newham council took the union to court to stop it campaigning for a yes vote for strike action, adding a fresh twist to the anti-union legislation—if successful it would mean that unions could ballot their members on industrial action but would not be allowed to encourage them to vote in favour. In the High Court Mrs Justice Ebsworth sided with the employer, arguing that the union was in breach of the Employment Act 1990, but the next week the Court of Appeal reversed that decision on the grounds that there was a legitimate dispute, that ballots had been properly held, and that the union had rightly campaigned for a yes vote. The dispute ended in late September after eight weeks with the re-employment of sacked members, but with the return to work came a fresh dispute that required another ballot this time over redeployment and restructuring. Another strike of 1,600 staff after a 57 per cent yes vote continued when the council refused to negotiate back-to-work procedures. In December, with 900 still out, the council finally agreed to talks through ACAS. The strike ended in February 1993 without an agreement, as the emergency committee decided that, with two-thirds of the branch membership not on strike and with no sign of the Labour council backing down,

---

[101] *NN*, 7 Feb. 1992, 8.   [102] Ibid., 7 Aug. 1992, 1.
[103] *NALGO Emergency Committee Meeting Minutes*, 21 (1992–3), for 18 June, n.p.

the strike could not be won. An emergency debate at the group meeting on pay saw a narrow vote to reinstate the dispute as a test case, but the NEC agreed with the Emergency Committee's analysis and confirmed that the strike was to be wound up. This view was not shared by local branch officers, but they nonetheless accepted the position.

In another attack on a NALGO branch, Bury Metropolitan Borough Council sacked branch secretary Rob McLaughlin, after he distributed union leaflets against the council's £40 million cuts proposals. A special general meeting of the Bury Metropolitan Branch carried a motion calling for action: 'This branch resolves to request the district organisation officer to conduct a ballot for a campaign of action against the continuing attack on this branch and this union by the employers. This will involve a programme of all-out action and selective action by key groups in key areas.'[104] An IT ordered the council to put him back on the payroll until a full hearing of his claim, but council leader Colin Jones responded by threatening to withdraw union facilities and the strike ballot went ahead—there was a clear majority for action.

Redundancies in the London Borough of Greenwich provoked another important dispute. Nine NALGO members were made redundant from the Elmley Street family centre in March. When the council opened a new centre in the borough a few months later it prompted further union action, and over 175 staff started a programme of walkouts, strikes, and picketing of benefit offices. During July over 500 staff in eleven different shops took action 'so as to cause maximum disruption'.[105] Further escalation took place with a request for official support for strike action by 230 members. A ballot of more key workers resulted in a clear majority among 121 estate management staff, but a very small majority of staff in advice and benefits. The branch leadership wanted a ballot of the entire branch while the emergency committee at national level recommended only a vote of strategic work groups.[106]

There was a similarly difficult dispute at Skellow Hall, an assessment centre for children in Doncaster, which the council planned to close in favour of smaller units. The centre had a history of problems with staff unable to cope with aspects of care and control owing to lack of management support. Despite the union's efforts to negotiate a settlement and the conditions of the Children's Act the Council announced immediate closure in May 1992. A strike resulted in an agreement on the future of the centre in June.[107]

Camden's long and bitter strike by social workers continued into 1992, culminating with the sacking of the strikers despite negotiations including meetings between the joint secretaries of the Greater London Whitley Council.

---

[104] *NALGO Emergency Committee Meeting Minutes*, 21 (1992–3), for 25 Nov., n.p.
[105] Ibid., for 22 July, n.p.   [106] Ibid., for 28 Sept., n.p.
[107] Ibid., for 22 July, n.p.

NALGO News reported: 'Camden council has sacked 133 social workers who have been on strike for more than nine months. Strikers had been issued with new job descriptions after a council restructuring and were told to either reapply for new "care manager" posts or lose their old jobs. NALGO branch secretary David Eggmore said that the branch would be campaigning for reinstatement of the workers.'[108] The council decided to impose changes on the strikers, making it a national issue of employment rights. The Emergency Committee supported both the decision of the strikers to refuse the new jobs and the support for them by other staff.[109] The dispute finally ended, after one year of action, with a return to work, but subsequently over twenty staff were sacked. The Emergency Committee agreed that 'financial assistance be given to the 22 social workers who obeyed the instruction to return to work on 26 May 1992 and have had their services terminated'.[110]

More and more councils were badly hit by cuts and redundancies: 'Job losses in local government are growing fast from a trickle into an avalanche.'[111] Several NALGO branches were involved in a type of industrial action that was relatively unknown to the union—the long-drawn-out trial of strength, rather than the short demonstration of anger and frustration. It was, perhaps, an inevitable outcome of NALGO's continued strong line of fighting job losses by refusing to cover for unfilled posts. The union's position was clear:

Every cut has its effects and the end result is job losses and impaired services. The effects of the government's policies are savage, insidious and long-term. Action to oppose them must be resolute because it is not only members' jobs NALGO is defending, but services to the public too. . . . If you take on extra work because of an unfilled vacancy you are accepting a worsening of your conditions of service and more stress and pressure. Your service to the community and your performance will suffer. You are showing to your employers that you will accept the consequences of the cuts without opposition. Once you have accepted the extra duties, they are unlikely to be removed.[112]

As councils searched for ways of operating within the government's new framework they shifted their management structures in line with new models of service delivery. Birmingham, like many other councils, was decentralizing services geographically, as well as altering staffing structures to substitute cheaper labour for qualified staff: 'Plans to replace "front line" social workers with super receptionists at Birmingham social service offices have been slammed by the NALGO and NUPE branches as a cost cutting

---

[108] *NN*, 21 Feb. 1992, 1.
[109] *NALGO Emergency Committee Meeting Minutes*, 21 (1992–3), for 12 Feb., n.p.
[110] Ibid., for 3 June, n.p.   [111] *NN*, 22 Jan. 1993, 1.   [112] Ibid., 5 Mar. 1993, 6.

exercise which would lead to a poorer service.'[113] And later there was a strike by 450 neighbourhood office staff over inadequate staffing levels. Meanwhile other councils were reorganizing with the market model in mind, as Berkshire County Council became the first local authority to set up business units within the council structure. Members at Westminster held a one-day strike against that council's plans to bring in business units with their own pay and conditions packages.

At national level, all the council unions declared their opposition to the Chancellor's continuing 1.5 per cent pay freeze, a position supported by the local-government group meeting, which urged the union to organize massive demonstrations. Jean Geldart said: 'Imposition of the government's pay control policy is something that members feel extremely angry about, and they feel equally angry that their employers have now accepted pay control.'[114] The main UNISON unions' joint claim in 1993 was for £700 flat rate, merger of scales 1 and 2, and payment of minimum adult rate at age 18, not 21. But the employers refused to shift from their opening offer of 1.5 per cent and as a result the staff side started its consultations on industrial action. At the final NALGO conference the NLGC recommended acceptance of the 1.5 per cent, but group meeting delegates voted instead for a ballot of members on the issue.

By the time NALGO went into UNISON, negotiators still faced the intransigence of a government pay limit: 'All local authority national bargaining groups agreed pay increases within the Government's 1.5 per cent public sector pay limit for 1993.'[115] Over 50,000 jobs had been lost through a combination of redundancies, early retirements, and the non-replacement of those on short-term contracts and others leaving. In specific cases the central government's tight settlement created difficult situations—for example, in Sheffield there was a deal to cut pay by 3.25 per cent in return for a shorter working week and no redundancies. Opted-out councils were also urged by government ministers such as John Redwood to show pay restraint. In the event most settled for 1.5 per cent—so much for local management empowerment. Other related issues such as the use of merit pay and the move to harmonization of service conditions remained very much a minority pursuit. For the 740,000 white-collar staff on APT&C grades, with pay rates ranging from £5,307 at the bottom of scale 1 to £26,961 at the top of the principal officer range,[116] their situation had not changed much in these early years of the 1990s.

---

[113] *NN*, 3 Apr. 1992, 4.
[115] IDS, *Pay in the Public Services*, 33.
[114] Ibid., 9 Apr. 1993, 1.
[116] Ibid. 44.

Concluding Remarks

The union's campaigning activity was pulled and pushed by several significant forces in its last year: the first imperative was to generate an anti-Conservative or pro-Labour vote in the general election; the second was to defend policies on publicly owned public services in the TUC and the Labour Party; the third was to win the merger vote; and the fourth was to reach policy agreements and accommodations with NUPE and COHSE in order to lock up the merger itself. Thus NALGO's role in the wider labour movement throughout 1992 was increasingly driven by the general election and the merger, as the union sought to protect its policies while aiming for a Labour victory and for a set of viable agreements with the COHSE and NUPE leaderships.

John Major's government went into the general election in a totally shambolic state and in the midst of a deep economic recession of its own making. The labour-movement tactic of winning votes by moving right simply failed to capitalize on the Tories' disarray, and the election result was a huge setback. For NALGO members, activists, and leaders it was all too much. The tide was out and any chance of catching it seemed to rest with size: getting bigger was the only strategy left for getting better. The union had grappled with its bargaining weaknesses, with the limitations of campaigning, and with the ease with which legislative gains could be reversed. Recognizing the need to move forwards, sadly the union became extinct—the time had come for a new and modified union to represent the members' interests.

This account of NALGO's last fifteen years of existence ends as it began in 1979, focused on collective bargaining, the core of all trade-union methods. This basic union function of supporting workers in struggle is often unrecorded, frequently unrewarded, and deliberately understated, so as to reduce its importance, to ignore the enduring conflict inherent in the employment relationship, and to avoid the hard questions asked about deeper inequality in the wider society. This book has purposefully elaborated pay claims and disputes, struggles over jobs and conditions of service, and campaigns to save services at home and to support comrades abroad. It has endeavoured to include national as well as local action, activities in large cities and small towns, demonstrations of anger in Scotland, Wales, and most regions of England. It has attempted to go beyond NALGO's majority membership of APT&C grades in local government to include members in various occupations in other industries such as health, the utilities, buses, and education. It has recounted the separate and united efforts of women members, black members, disabled members, and gay and lesbian members in their fights within NALGO and at work. But it has mainly been concerned to display the character and integrity of the whole union, within the mainstream of the TUC, and within the wider labour movement. It is not our concern here to follow NALGO into UNISON, but the final chapter does make an assessment of the main impulses underlying the merger.

Appendix

TABLE 9.1. NALGO membership, 30 September 1992

District	Number of branches (1)	Voting members (2)	Members in arrears (3)	Membership of branches excluded from voting (4)	Total ordinary membership (cols. 2-4) (5)	Retired (6)	Student (7)	Unemployed (8)	Honorary (9)	Total membership (cols. 5-9) (10)	Total membership 30 Sept. 1991 (11)	Increase/decrease (12)	Increase/decrease (%) (13)
Eastern	113	42,680	15	0	42,695	7,850	22	67	—	50,634	49,435	+1,199	+2.43
East Midland	93	43,640	11	1,496	45,147	6,164	38	41	—	51,390	50,470	+920	+1.82
Metropolitan	131	81,846	208	3,220	85,274	15,274	45	206	—	100,799	101,118	−319	−0.32
North Eastern	59	40,241	37	2,670	42,948	3,547	5	41	—	46,541	45,834	+707	+1.54
North Western and North Wales	137	105,382	9	2,174	107,565	11,621	51	134	—	119,371	119,965	−594	−0.50
Scottish	105	78,749	19	1,263	80,031	3,502	47	41	—	83,621	83,147	+474	+0.57
South Eastern	84	31,014	13	1,058	32,085	7,692	14	56	—	39,847	39,789	+58	+0.15
Southern	77	30,292	6	1,470	31,768	5,204	18	48	—	37,038	37,188	−150	−0.40
South Wales	76	32,945	13	807	33,765	2,991	5	16	—	36,777	36,584	+193	+0.53
South Western	96	42,929	31	2,086	45,046	5,944	23	74	—	51,087	50,938	+149	+0.29
West Midland	79	67,492	15	370	67,877	8,935	32	56	—	76,800	76,660	+140	+0.18
Yorkshire and Humberside	71	63,404	0	0	63,404	6,641	23	52	—	70,120	68,570	+1,550	+2.26
Honorary members	—	—	—	—	—	—	—	—	37	37	37	0	0.00
TOTAL	1,121	660,614	377	16,614	677,605	85,265	323	832	37	764,062	759,735	+4,327	+0.57

TABLE 9.2. *Allocation of NALGO membership, by service, 30 September 1992*

District	Local government	Gas	Electricity	Health	Transport	Water	New Towns	Port authorities	Universities	Police authorities	Polytechnic colleges	Retired	Student, unemployed	Total membership
Eastern	30,646	2,117	2,388	3,103	183	2,025	191	11	434	1,075	522	7,850	89	50,634
East Midland	32,410	2,786	2,048	5,140	158	0	0	1	442	1,252	910	6,164	79	51,390
Metropolitan	65,074	4,178	2,999	6,351	168	2,915	321	0	1,283	0	1,985	15,274	251	100,799
North Eastern	30,290	2,165	1,541	4,868	616	876	26	61	249	988	1,268	3,547	46	46,541
North Western and North Wales	77,589	4,223	4,637	11,067	1,253	2,842	160	34	1,228	2,378	2,154	11,621	185	119,371
Scottish	63,562	2,251	3,246	7,950	222	20	986	19	1,440	283	52	3,502	88	83,621
South Eastern	20,411	2,215	1,565	4,281	28	1,798	0	3	463	823	498	7,692	70	39,847
Southern	20,657	2,006	2,229	4,375	10	0	0	0	913	640	938	5,204	66	37,038
South Wales	23,613	1,563	887	3,771	105	2,033	93	0	777	903	0	2,991	21	136,777
South Western	33,042	1,564	2,288	3,225	66	1,949	0	1	527	1,483	901	5,944	97	51,087
West Midland	47,263	4,488	1,882	6,693	859	3,440	0	0	794	1,202	1,256	8,835	88	76,800
Yorkshire and Humberside	49,321	1,236	2,620	4,107	749	2,118	0	0	1,206	709	1,338	6,641	75	70,120
1992 totals	493,898	30,792	28,330	64,931	4,417	20,016	1,777	130	9,756	11,736	11,822	85,265	1,155	764,025
Percentages	64.64	4.03	3.71	8.50	0.58	2.62	0.23	0.02	1.28	1.53	1.55	11.16	0.15	100.00
1991 totals	493,063	31,757	29,728	63,557	4,928	20,423	2,113	151	9,880	11,471	10,684	81,096	947	759,699
Percentages	64.90	4.18	3.91	8.37	0.65	2.69	0.28	0.02	1.30	1.51	1.41	10.67	0.11	100.00

10

In UNISON

IN this history we have traced the actions and concerns of NALGO members, activists, and leaders, concluding with the merger into UNISON. This chapter locates the merger in wider debates. In the first section we argue that most academic explanations of mergers generally neglect two important factors: the underlying dynamics of change among the merging unions' memberships; and the political role of leaders and activists in shaping decisions about whether or not to merge. In the second section it is argued that, in the case of NALGO members, the move to merge was rooted in their experiences as employees during the 1980s. First was the deepening exploitation and alienation, as employment in the public sector became more like employment in the private sector, and management practices became increasingly concerned with cheapening labour. Second was the experience of fighting back, and a growing awareness of how important it was to make common cause with other groups of members, with other unions, with other campaigners, and with the public at large. If UNISON was born out of this combination of action and understanding, then its future may depend on it too.

The Cold Logic for Merger

In the run-up to the merger, all three union executives contained large majorities in favour. The dominant view was that the objective circumstances of the time, which Jim White called the 'cold logic', meant that the constituent unions could only meet their aims together, through UNISON. The arguments in favour were broadcast loud and long, not only internally but also in the friendly press—the *Morning Star* proclaimed the virtues of the new union, which would wage 'a nationwide campaign' to save the NHS, act as

383

an advocate for staff and service users, secure public accountability in the utilities, and continue 'the struggle to retain local government services'.[1]

Thus the merger was seen as strengthening the three main aspects of trade unionism—independence, collective bargaining, and related action. A higher profile, more and better services to members, and the momentum derived from the merger process itself, would increase both recruitment and retention. Along with efficiency gains and assumed economies of size, this would strengthen the union's financial position. The resulting robust membership list, rationalized services, and tighter organization would protect the union's independence from employers and from government. UNISON's internal government would be strengthened through 'a more democratic structure than any of its predecessors'.[2]

In collective bargaining—making collective agreements, implementing them at the place of work, and representing individual members in grievance and disciplinary cases—the new union would have to maintain informal and formal activity, at all levels, in a multiplicity of units. It would also have to protect the scope of the bargaining agenda against union exclusion strategies.[3] The merged union would deliver better agreements through bigger (single status) bargaining units, especially in local government,[4] through simplified (single table) bargaining structures, and through a well-supported lay representatives' network. Bargaining priorities would be set to produce both better outcomes for the majority and protection for minorities. The combination of national framework agreements alongside monitored local deals would, it was hoped, stem the adverse tide of weaker national bargaining and worsened local conditions of service driven through by local employers seeking further fundamental changes in working practices.

Finally, the new union would be better able to take the action required to enforce its bargaining methods. Industrial action would be strengthened through the higher level of resources available to all sections within the larger organization. The campaigns necessary to apply political pressure on public-sector policy-makers, in government and in senior management positions, would be more effective because they would include a wider range of employees, and because of the union's extra clout in both the TUC and the

---

[1] *Morning Star*, 1 Mar. 1993, 4–5.

[2] M. Terry, 'Negotiating the Government of UNISON: Union Democracy in Theory and Practice', *British Journal of Industrial Relations*, 34/1 (1996), 87–110.

[3] P. Smith and G. Morton, 'Union Exclusion and the Decollectivization of Industrial Relations in Contemporary Britain', *British Journal of Industrial Relations*, 31/1 (1993), 97–114; P. Smith and G. Morton, 'Union Exclusion in Britain—Next Steps', *Industrial Relations Journal*, 25/1 (1994), 3–14.

[4] IRS, 'Survey of Employee Relations in Local Government', *Employment Trends*, 594 (1995), 6–13.

Labour Party. NALGO activists, keen to defend broad left policies and an open leadership style, hoped that the new union's political culture would be based on NALGO's democratic internal decision-making mechanisms for allocating resources to local, national, and sectional campaigns.

Those objectives for the merger can be located within academic explanations of the wider pattern of union mergers in general. Academic interest grew with the large-scale mergers of the 1980s and 1990s. In the five years preceding the creation of UNISON, ASTMS and TASS merged to form MSF, SCPS and the Civil Service Union (CSU) to form NUCPS, the NGA and SOGAT to form the GPMU, the NUR and the National Union of Seamen (NUS) to form the National Union of Rail, Maritime, and Transport Workers (RMT), and APEX went into the GMB. In the following three years the AEU merged with the EETPU to form the AEEU, the UCW with the National Communication Union (NCU) to form the CWU, and the Inland Revenue Staff Federation (IRSF) with NUCPS to form the Public Services, Tax, and Commerce Union (PTC). Between 1996 and 1999 there were two more notable mergers, of the PTC with the Civil and Public Service Association (CPSA) to form the Public and Commercial Services Union (PCS), and the banking unions the Banking, Insurance, and Finance Union (BIFU), UNiFi, and the National Westminster Staff Association (NWSA) to form a new UNIFI.

All of those mergers could be seen as defensive/consolidatory rather than expansionist, and as reflecting the relative bargaining weakness of the unions, the changing composition and nature of the employers, the more hostile legal and political environment, and changes in labour markets.[5] This explanation emphasizes long-term factors, outside the control of unions, which push them to reconsider the efficacy of their existing structures.[6] Others concentrate on the peculiarity of any given merger in order to provide a political and personal assessment of change.[7] Jeremy Waddington[8] tries to synthesize both positions and to develop a new explanatory framework through regression analysis of mergers between 1893 and 1979. However, this mechanistic

---

[5] J. Waddington and C. Whitston, 'The Politics of Restructuring: Trade Unions on the Defensive in Britain since 1979', *Relations Industrielles*, 49/4 (1994), 794–819.

[6] R. Buchanan, 'Mergers in British Trade Unions', *Industrial Relations Journal*, 12/3 (1981), 40–9; R. Buchanan, 'Measuring Mergers and Concentration in UK Unions 1910–1988', *Industrial Relations Journal*, 23/4 (1992), 304–14.

[7] R. Undy, 'Negotiating Amalgamations: Territorial and Political Consolidation and Administrative Reform in Public Sector Service Unions in the UK', *British Journal of Industrial Relations*, 37/3 (1999), 445–63; R. Undy, V. Ellis, W. McCarthy, and A. Halmos, *Change in Trade Unions: The Development of UK Unions since the 1960s* (London: Hutchinson, 1981).

[8] J. Waddington, 'Trade Union Mergers: A Study of Trade Union Structural Dynamics', *British Journal of Industrial Relations*, 26/3 (1988), 409–30.

approach to the common features of merged organizations neglects both policy debates and merger outcomes.

Another group of writers rationalizes mergers as responses to perceived resourcing problems: membership losses or potential losses and the associated financial problems; and wasteful competition and aggravation between rival unions.[9] However, these clearly are neither necessary nor sufficient conditions for mergers. Financial troubles have not necessarily been reduced through merger, nor indeed has membership loss been unequivocally halted.[10] According to one survey, union finances generally improved throughout the 1980s.[11] While some expensive competitive pressures may be relieved, others may remain, appear, or reappear—UNISON competes with the GMB in local government and the RCN in the NHS, but there have been no merger discussions. Teacher unions, especially the NUT and National Association of Schoolmasters and Union of Women Teachers (NASUWT), are fierce rivals and on their own admission spend too much time and effort fighting each other, but as yet that has not created the conditions for merger. The true relationship between membership growth and sound finances was, as Oscar Wilde might have said, neither pure nor simple.

The creation of so-called super unions is rationalized by some writers through the notion of market share of membership: 'administratively effective unions focus on an organizable job territory, control costs and avoid competition. Representative effectiveness is defined by the degree of employer dependence, the balance of services and the degree of centralization. We argue that the prevailing tendency for concentration through merger often damages representative effectiveness while yielding few administrative benefits.'[12] This echoes the case made by Ben Roberts in the 1950s in favour of less democratic and more businesslike trade unionism. It ignores the political dimension, not only of mergers themselves, but also of the academic studies of mergers. Many analyses fail to disentangle what *is* happening from what *ought* to be happening and from what *might* have happened. Finally, there is a distinct lack of post-merger studies to assist analysis. Most academic explanations do not reveal why some unions merge and others do not, even though they face similar circumstances.

[9] P. Willman, 'Merger Propensity and Merger Outcomes among British Unions, 1986–1995', *Industrial Relations Journal*, 27/4 (1996), 331–8.

[10] Waddington and Whitston, 'The Politics of Restructuring', 803.

[11] P. Willman, 'The Financial Status and Performance of British Trade Unions, 1950–1988', *British Journal of Industrial Relations*, 28/3 (1990), 313–28.

[12] P. Willman and A. Cave, 'The Union of the Future: Super-Unions or Joint Ventures?', *British Journal of Industrial Relations*, 32/3 (1994), 395.

Our approach recognizes that merger is one option among many. While the cold logic of capital creates the conditions for all union action, including merger, any particular actual course of action is the outcome of internal struggle, debate, and policy development. This approach is consistent with the responses of NALGO officers and activists, white–collar public-service trade unionists, to the conditions they faced in the 1980s and 1990s. The UNISON merger was not a self-evident technical solution to a set of obvious problems. Nor was it mechanically determined by circumstances that left no viable alternative but to merge. It was driven through by leaders and activists on the basis of their political assessment of the best way forward.

There had been some clear areas of convergence among public-service unions for most of the 1970s and 1980s. These included membership growth, the development of links with the wider labour movement especially through the TUC, expansion of workplace representative networks, internal reforms, more employer-based bargaining, the growth of industrial action and political campaigns, and the increasingly important role played by women and other groups hitherto noticeable by their absence in union decision-making.[13] By the mid-1980s public-service trade unions accounted for about half of all trade unionists, over two-fifths of TUC affiliates, and averaged over 70 per cent density.

Bob Fryer notes the emergence and importance of steward systems for all three unions during the 1970s. He makes seven points: the rapid growth of steward numbers; the extension of local bargaining machinery; the sponsorship of most steward systems by the national union and/or full-time officers; the recognition of stewards in collective agreements; the official incorporation of stewards into union structures; the huge increase in formal procedures along with the expanded personnel function; and the development nationally of local rights such as with health and safety and sick pay schemes. Unions such as NALGO, NUPE, and COHSE tended to have more regular branch meetings than most others, all three had to deal with a diverse membership in terms of services, units, occupations, and competitor unions. By the late 1980s the three unions had initiated 'positive action programmes' on issues of minority representation and under-representation.[14]

Another important feature that began to bring the unions together in the 1970s was in the use of industrial action. Incomes policies were crucial in persuading unions such as NALGO to affiliate to the TUC, and to become involved in protest and action against relative falling wages. For most

[13] R. Fryer, 'Public Service Trade Unionism in the Twentieth Century', in R. Mailly, S. Dimmock, and A. Sethi (eds.), *Industrial Relations in the Public Services* (London: Routledge, 1989), 17–67.
[14] Ibid. 35–7.

members it was their first experience of militancy. Most disputes were official and national, they involved large numbers of women, and they were often intensely bitter.[15] Other distinctive features of the public-service strike wave included the innovative nature of action taken, the fact that it was service users who suffered far more than the employers, and that most disputes were about pay, especially issues of comparability versus those of performance. Fryer argues that 'the upsurge in public service union militancy in the 1970s not only changed the internal character of several unions, it also sharply revised their public profile'.[16]

The mobilization required to take action is quite a different type of activity from peaceful national bargaining, with or without arbitration.[17] In the 1980s there were more local disputes, mainly over issues such as redundancies and work reorganization associated with privatization and/or employer restructuring. Fryer concludes that the success of public-service unionism after the 1987 election would depend on winning public support through campaigns to save services and jobs. Our account shows that, while such a road was exceedingly hard, it was the best one to take. In that context, the merger can be seen not only as defensive but as partly born out of sheer exhaustion.

One academic summary of industrial relations in the public sector, written just before the merger, made the obvious point that

in the immediate future under the present Conservative government the basic environment in which public sector collective bargaining operates is likely to be one characterized by restrictions on public expenditure growth, further employment reductions, increased privatization and competitive tendering initiatives, public sector wage constraints and pressures to decentralize wage bargaining arrangements.[18]

This list formed part of the merger case for securing larger and more uniform bargaining units, but it does not capture either the important role of politically minded activists or the grave feelings of uncertainty amongst members that turned the cold logic into an actual move to merge.

The Dialectics of Exploitation—Losing Control and Controlling Loss

In her autobiography, Margaret Thatcher entitles a chapter 'The World Turned Right Side Up'. She welcomes the *pax Americana* with open arms, cel-

[15] D. Winchester, 'Industrial Relations in the Public Sector', in G. Bain (ed.), *Industrial Relations in Britain* (Oxford: Blackwell, 1983), 155–78.

[16] Fryer, 'Public Service Trade Unionism in the Twentieth Century', 51.

[17] J. Kelly, *Rethinking Industrial Relations* (London: Routledge, 1998).

[18] P. Beaumont, *Public Sector Industrial Relations* (London: Routledge, 1992), 173.

ebrating freedom in a better world after the defeat of leftist forces around the globe. Conservative hegemony appeared complete: 'The New Right has enlisted not just the British state structures but the deep-seated conservatism embodied in Britain's economic and political institutions and wider value system to support its cause.'[19] As the 1990s started, the economic situation facing most NALGO members was far from terrible in some important respects: few would experience unemployment, and most would enjoy real increases in wages, although at a lower rate than the average. However, under the dominance of capitalist managerial and market relations that were increasingly unhindered by either social/cultural opposition or alternative models of operation, their conditions of service, their workload, and their jobs, all deteriorated. The real dangers they faced stemmed from their increasing loss of control within their services and their employment situation.

This applies to members in all sectors: to those in water, gas, electricity supply, and buses switched from public-sector to private-sector employment through direct privatization; to those who stayed within the restructured public sector, in NHS Trusts, incorporated FE colleges, and LMS schools; and to those in local government and higher education who experienced new internal management structures. All came under severe cost limits and associated audit. Most were forced into some form of beggar-my-neighbour competition, either with each other within an industry such as hospital-providers, schools, and local authorities, or with other national and international competitors through CCT in health and local government, bus deregulation, and privatized utilities. The result, at a time of high unemployment, hostility to union organization and action, and aggressive restatement of management's right to manage, was greater management control of labour itself.

Private-sector managers and/or owners facing declining budgets or profits could shut down part or all of the business, or alter core business activities, options not available to managers in public services. In private-sector labour intensive industries, managers could slash wage rates and other conditions, but a combination of TUPE regulations, national agreements, and government regulators prevented that as well in most cases. Born-again public-service managers had only one viable option—to reduce their unit labour costs through a series of pay and performance measures, based on a flexible labour force, and implemented through HRM and TQM initiatives. In particular there were job losses. Reductions in staffing levels had two consequences for those remaining: a general fear of job loss, which resulted in an atmosphere of individual weakness and union inaction; and an increase in workload as jobs were shed faster than work was reduced.

---

[19] W. Hutton, *The State We're In* (London: Vintage, 1996), 32.

As well as cheapening labour costs, management also needed to ensure services matched up to the government's performance indicators, so they applied performance management techniques: job measurement and controls through job evaluation, appraisal, and work reorganization; skills substitutions with lower-skilled workers replacing higher-skilled ones, younger replacing older, and cheaper replacing more expensive; and the undermining of national wage setting with the use of bonus schemes, such as performance-related pay, attached to managerialist conceptions of performance. As these worked their way through departments, teams, and units, so there were more disciplinary cases, more victimization of union activists, more discrimination against women and other groups, and more grievances and tribunal claims as unions sought to gain what little redress was available. The result was the endless stream of local disputes visible in this history. Each one tells a story of lessons learnt from the experience of fighting back.

Intense pressure to cut costs and improve performance resulted in yet more workplace change: new technology, new management structures, and new forms of work organization. More control meant more managers managing fewer direct service workers. New technologies were used to automate more and more tasks, to redistribute tasks between workers, and to strengthen the hierarchy of supervision. This enhanced managerial control over work processes and work speed, resulting in a general lowering of skill levels within the workforce, even if some sections perceived themselves to be 'upskilled'. No one was immune, no job escaped scrutiny, all came under the watchful gaze of the latter-day scientific managers—the management consultants and business-school graduates. The experience of work became ever more grim: longer hours, harder hours, less secure hours, worse pay per hour, and more closely supervised hours. More and more labour time came under the control of the time-and-motion study technicians, with their new tools of the computerized stop watch, the video camera, and the self-supervising quality circle. Public-service notions of collective good, community action, universal service, and democratic control disappeared into the realm of managerially manufactured service standards. Those significant shifts in the management of the labour process, in the form and content of exploitation, and in the alienation of public-service workers from their services, narrowed the real and assumed gap between manual and non-manual. Their sharing of common threats and experiences was the key factor behind the merger.

This history shows how the impact of government policies began to influence first one group and then another, as they (re)defined their interests inside the employment relationship and equally within the broader service, community, and class. When one group of members went on strike over conditions of service issues, they became aware of the link with others fighting similar battles. When local-government APT&C grades fought for a comparability pay deal in 1980, there was common cause with all public-sector workers opposed to government pay limits. When individual trade-union activists were victimized, or threatened with deportation, it revealed the hands of employers and government arbitrarily determining people's livelihoods. Privatization threatened white-collar and manual jobs alike in the utilities, and their fears were shared with the service users if not with the new share owners. Joint committees were among the main campaigning forces against privatization. When old people's homes were shut, when hospitals were rationalized, when educational establishments were starved of funds, then the coming-together of providers and users to defend services provided a local focus for struggles against increasingly undemocratic state functions.

Wider common cause was forged in battles to rebuff anti-union laws, to reinstate trade-union rights at GCHQ, to defend miners and print workers against over mighty state force, and to release Nelson Mandela and help topple the apartheid regime. The sheer spread of activities involved thousands of activists, each arguing their case with work colleagues just like Owen with his ragged-trousered philanthropists. They developed the habits of organization and the skills of campaigning, and they built solidarity with others such as the women at Greenham, environmentalists, and the mothers of victims of Pinochet's terror squads, creating bonds, random and haphazard, but secure and remembered. Common cause campaigns were taken to the TUC, fighting unemployment, public-service cuts, and the unpalatable monetarist medicine prescribed to cure inflation. This found expression through the AES, a mixture of Keynesianism and socialism that provided a platform for the broad left in many unions. The more specific NALGO campaigns, 'Put People First' and 'Make People Matter', also brought into the fray new activists, including younger members and others not traditionally involved in union activity.

Such struggles were deepened by mobilizations against discrimination, confronting a range of reactionary social forces in our society: racism, sexism, homophobia, and prejudice against disabled people. Each of these pointed to wider inequality, and to the lack of real democracy in 'liberal' democracies. Campaigns at work fed into and from both the unions and the wider social and cultural movements of the day. Self-organized groups, supported by union funding and expertise, encouraged and enlivened the wider interest formation. Sometimes infighting and muddle made the movement arid and directionless, but the union's outward-looking and broadly based policies steered it towards survival, struggle, and social justice.

Conclusion

Over-rational and deterministic merger models fail to represent the sense of unease, the fears, and the worries of NALGO members up and down the country in a myriad of workplaces dispensing a variety of services to a shifting mass of service users and citizens. The degradation of public services and of public-service work, combined with the experiences of fighting back and of establishing common cause with others opposing the dominance of state monopoly capital both in the workplaces and in the wider political sphere, together led the majority to conclude that their historic organizational identity, NALGO, should be transformed. Leaders and activists successfully articulated their analysis of increasing union weakness in the face of neoliberal economic policies. They linked the members' experiences and fears to a wider critique of capitalism and its British, European, and global institutions, and they argued for a credible set of alternatives.

NALGO's policies taken into UNISON, summarized in the union's policy guide, included: a principled opposition to monetarism; a continuing belief in the value of public ownership, the concept of public service, and the direct provision of services by public authorities; a belief in universality as a unifying principle for the allocation of resources, rather than 'targeted' benefits; a commitment to greater equality; acting as an independent voice within the TUC, producing detailed responses to government or opposition proposals; and being an outgoing union with a wide range of links and affiliations at home and abroad, at branch and national levels.[20] When NALGO members voted so heavily in favour of merger, they voted for a UNISON that would be bigger, more inclusive, and more representative than any other British union, and would protect and further the progressive ideals that underpinned NALGO's distinctive brand of trade unionism.

[20] NALGO, *NALGO into UNISON: A Short Policy Guide* (London: NALGO, 1993).

Bibliography

Primary Sources

Journals

NALGO

Public Service (*PS*) (NALGO national journal for members)
Edlines (NALGO journal for Eastern District members)
Empress (NALGO journal for East Midland District members)
Mac (NALGO journal for Scottish District members)
Met District News (NALGO journal for Metropolitan District members)
NALGO News (*NN*) (NALGO national journal for activists)
News NoW (NALGO journal for North Western and North Wales District members)

General

Birmingham Evening Mail
Bolton Evening News
Cambridge Evening News
Cornishman
Daily Telegraph
Dundee Courier and Advertiser
Ealing Gazette
The Economist
Evening Chronicle
Evening Mail
Evening Chronicle
Gazette
Greenwich and Eltham Mercury
Guardian
Hartlepool Mail
Independent
Islington Gazette
Journal
Kentish Gazette

Leicester Mercury
Luton News
Liverpool Echo
Manchester Evening News
Morden News
Morning Star
New Society
New Statesman
North East News
Scotsman
Star
The Times
Western Morning News

Leaflets and pamphlets

NALGO

51 per cent (London: NALGO, 1986).
The Alternative Economic Strategy (London: NALGO, 1983).
Be Fair to Those Who Care (London: NALGO, 1981).
Behind Closed Doors (London: NALGO, 1979).
The Bradford Experiment: Counting the Cost, Bradford Branch (Bradford: NALGO, 1990).
Building Friendship—Working for Freedom: Report of a NALGO Delegation to South Africa (London: NALGO, 1987).
Central America: The Right to Live in Peace (London: NALGO, 1989).
Community Care: Users' Experiences (London: NALGO, 1992).
Community Care: Handbook for Local Government Branches (London: NALGO, 1993).
Council Non-Manual Workers and Low Pay (London: NALGO, 1986).
Crisis in Construction (London: NALGO, 1981).
Disability is No Handicap: Negotiating on Behalf of the Disabled Worker: A NALGO Guide (London: NALGO, n.d., *c.*1986).
The Economy: A NALGO Review (Part 1) (London: NALGO, 1991).
Energy for the Future (London: NALGO, 1982).
Equal Rights Survey: Preliminary Results of the NALGO 1979 Branch Survey Prepared for the 1980 Annual Conference (London: NALGO, 1980).
Equality? Report of a Survey of NALGO Members (London: NALGO, 1981).
The European Community and 1992: The Report of the National Executive Council's Single European Act Working Party (London: NALGO, 1990).
Fighting Privatisation in Local Government: Campaign Handbook (London: NALGO, n.d., *c.*1987).
Fighting Privatisation: A NALGO Campaign Guide for Districts and Branches (London: NALGO, 1982).
Fighting against Prejudice (London: NALGO, n.d., *c.*1986).
For Sale: A Report on the Sale of Local Authority Owned Bus Companies (London: NALGO, 1992).

Gas Action News (London: NALGO, 1981).

Gay Rights: NALGO Fighting against Prejudice (London: NALGO, n.d., c.1983).

Give Britain a Boost: NALGO's Case for an Alternative Economic Strategy (London: NALGO, 1981).

How Equal are your Opportunities? (London: NALGO, 1986).

I Can't Afford to Work Here Any More: The Recruitment and Retention of Administrative and Clerical Staff in the NHS (London: NALGO, 1989).

Improving Working Life: Advice for Negotiators in Electricity (London: NALGO, 1992).

In Defence of New Towns (London: NALGO, 1981).

Ireland: A Trade Union Concern (London: NALGO, n.d., c.1988).

Long Term Pay Strategy (London: NALGO, 1992).

Low Pay Charter (London: NALGO, 1991).

Maastricht: Implications for Public Services, North Western and North Wales District Council (Manchester: NALGO, 1993).

More than Ramps (London: NALGO, 1986).

Moving Forward: A NALGO Policy Statement on Public Transport for the 1990s (London: NALGO, n.d., c.1992).

Muhammad Idrish: The Case against Deportation (London: NALGO, 1984).

NALGO Black Action (London: NALGO, 1993).

NALGO into UNISON: A Short Policy Guide (London: NALGO, 1993).

NALGO Negotiating Guidelines: Job Sharing (London: NALGO, 1986).

NALGO Negotiating Guidelines: Part-Time Work (London: NALGO, 1986).

NALGO Visit to Israel and the Occupied Territories 1987 (London: NALGO, 1988).

Namibia: The Forgotten Colony (London: NALGO, 1988).

National Low Pay Strategy (London: NALGO, 1990).

Our Buses our Fight (London: NALGO, 1984).

Patients before Profits: A Positive Agenda for the NHS (London: NALGO, 1990).

Performance Pay in the Health Service: A Negotiating Guide (London: NALGO, 1993).

Poll-Taxed or Pole-Axed? (London: NALGO, 1988).

Post-School Education (London: NALGO, 1981).

Public Transport Now (London: NALGO, 1982).

Public Expenditure: Into the Eighties (London: NALGO, 1979).

Race and Racism, Lambeth NALGO (London: NALGO, n.d., c.1981).

Report of a Delegation to Ireland, 21–25 October 1990, Metropolitan, North Western and North Wales, and Scottish District Councils (London: NALGO, n.d., c.1990).

Rights of Working Parents (London: NALGO, n.d., c.1982).

Sanity in Our Time: Why NALGO is Affiliated to the CND (London: NALGO, 1985).

Sexual Harassment is a Trade Union Issue (London: NALGO, 1980).

Steward's Guide to Recruitment (London: NALGO, 1986).

Stop the Cuts Action Bulletin, nos. 1–39 (London: NALGO, October 1979 to February 1982).

Stop your Council Contracting, bulletin (London: NALGO, 1988).

They Sell We Pay (London: NALGO, 1984).

Under Review: Your NALGO Guide to the GSSO Review (London: NALGO, 1991).

Underpaid and Undervalued: Secretarial and Clerical Workers in the NHS (London: NALGO, 1986).
Unemployment or Prosperity: The Battle for Lothian (London: NALGO, 1981).
Water down the Drain? The Case against Privatising the Water Industry (London: NALGO, 1988).
Ways to Tackle the Tender Trap (London: NALGO, 1992).
Why NALGO Opposes the Abolition of the Metropolitan Counties and the GLC (London: NALGO, 1984).
Workplace Nurseries: A Negotiating Kit (London: NALGO, n.d., c.1980).

NALGO and NUPE

Local Government under Attack (London: NALGO and NUPE, 1981).
A Negotiator's Guide to Market Testing in the NRA (London: NALGO and NUPE, 1993).
The New Water Companies: Information and Data for NALGO and NUPE Local Negotiators (London: NALGO and NUPE, 1991).
Scottish Local Government under Attack (London: NALGO and NUPE, 1981).

NALGO, NUPE, and COHSE

The Challenge of the New Union: Report of the COHSE, NALGO and NUPE National Executives to the 1990 Annual Conferences (London: COHSE, NALGO, and NUPE, 1990).
A Framework for a New Union: Report of the COHSE, NALGO and NUPE National Executives to the 1991 Annual Conferences (London: COHSE, NALGO, and NUPE, 1991).
In the Firing Line: The Impact on Staff (London: COHSE, NALGO, and NUPE, 1993).
Qa Business Services: The NHS Privatisation that Failed (London: NALGO, 1992).

Other pamphlets and leaflets

Bury Joint Trade Union Committee, *Hands off Bury's Bins: How We Stopped Privatisation* (Bury: Bury Joint Trade Union Committee, 1984).
Centre for Public Services, *Competition Cuts and Contractors: Lessons for Trade Unionists from Three Flagship London Boroughs* (Sheffield: Centre for Public Services, 1992).
COHSE, GMB, NALGO, NUPE, and TGWU, *Competition for Patient Transport Services: A Guide for the Ambulance Services* (London: COHSE, GMB, NALGO, NUPE, and TGWU, 1992).
GMB, NALGO, NUPE, and TGWU, *Competitive Tendering Strategy Handbook* (London: NALGO, 1993).
———————— *Who Cares Wins: A Trade Union Guide to Compulsory Competitive Tendering for Local Services* (London: GMB, NALGO, NUPE, and TGWU, n.d., c.1989).
———————— *Tender Care: Ground Maintenance: Joint Guidelines to Compulsory Tendering for Local Services* (London: GMB, NALGO, NUPE, and TGWU, n.d., c.1989).

——————————*Tender Care: Building Cleaning: Joint Guidelines to Compulsory Tendering for Local Services* (London: GMB, NALGO, NUPE, and TGWU, n.d., *c*.1989).

——————————*Tender Care: Refuse and Street Cleaning: Joint Guidelines to Compulsory Tendering for Local Services* (London: GMB, NALGO, NUPE, and TGWU, n.d., *c*.1989).

——————————*Tender Care: Catering: Joint Guidelines to Compulsory Tendering for Local Services* (London: GMB, NALGO, NUPE, and TGWU, n.d., *c*.1989).

GUARD, *Before you Decide, Read the Facts* (London: GUARD, 1986).

Joint NHS Privatisation Unit, *The NHS Privatisation Experience* (London: Joint NHS Privatisation Unit, 1990).

NALGO, GMBATU, NUPE, TGWU, TWSA and UCATT, *Hands Off!* (London: NALGO, GMBATU, NUPE, TGWU, TWSA and UCATT, 1985).

NUPE, NALGO, GMB, and TGWU, *A response to the Department of the Environment's Consultation Paper 'Competing for Quality'* (London: NALGO, 1992).

Public Services Privatisation Research Unit, *Privatisation: Disaster for Quality* (London: Public Services Privatisation Research Unit, 1992).

TUC/Labour Party Liaison Committee, *A New Partnership—A New Britain* (London: TUC/Labour Party Liaison Committee, 1985).

——*People at Work: New Rights New Responsibilities* (London: TUC/Labour Party Liaison Committee, 1986).

——*Low Pay: Policies and Priorities* (London: TUC/Labour Party Liaison Committee, 1986).

Wandsworth Trade Union Publications, *Public Jobs for Private Profit: Fighting Contractors in Wandsworth* (London: Wandsworth Trade Union Publications, 1983).

Water Joint Trade Union Committee, *Public Ownership: A Water Tight Case* (London: Water Joint Trade Union Committee, n.d., *c*.1989).

Reports

NALGO Annual Conference Minutes (London: NALGO, 1979–93).

NALGO Annual Reports (London: NALGO, 1978–93).

NALGO Emergency Committee Meeting Minutes (London: NALGO, 1978–93).

NALGO Scottish District Council Annual Reports (Glasgow: NALGO, 1978–93).

NALGO in the Eighties, First Report (London: NALGO, 1981).

National Joint Council for Local Authorities' Administrative, Professional, Technical, and Clerical Services, *Schemes of Conditions of Service*, known as the Purple Book (London: NJC for Local Authorities' APT&C Services, 1978–93, updated annually).

TUC Annual Reports (London: TUC, 1978–93).

UNISON rule book 1993 (London: UNISON, 1993).

SECONDARY SOURCES

AARONOVITCH, S., *The Road from Thatcherism: The Alternative Economic Strategy* (London: Lawrence & Wishart, 1981).

397

ACAS (Advisory, Conciliation, and Arbitration Service), *Industrial Relations Handbook* (London: HMSO, 1980).

ALLEN, V., *Power in Trade Unions* (London: Longman, 1954).

——*Militant Trade Unionism* (London: Merlin Press, 1966).

——'The Differentiation of the Working Class', in A. Hunt (ed.), *Class and Class Structure* (London: Lawrence & Wishart, 1977), 61–9..

ANDREWS, K., and JACOBS, J., *Punishing the Poor: Poverty under Thatcher* (London: Macmillan, 1990).

ARTHURS, A., 'Management and Managerial Unionism', in K. Thurley and S. Wood (eds.), *Industrial Relations and Management Strategy* (Cambridge: Cambridge University Press, 1983), 13–18.

ASSOCIATION OF DISTRICT COUNCILS Human Resources Committee, *Reports on National Pay Bargaining* (London: Association of District Councils, 1990).

BACON, R., and ELTIS, W., *Britain's Economic Problem: Too Few Producers* (London: Macmillan, 1976).

BAIN, G., *The Growth of White-Collar Unionism* (Oxford: Oxford University Press, 1970).

——(ed.), *Industrial Relations in Britain* (Oxford: Blackwell, 1983).

BARAN, P., and SWEEZY, P., *Monopoly Capital* (Harmondsworth: Pelican Books, 1966).

BAROU, N., *British Trade Unions* (London: Victor Gollancz, 1947).

BEAUMONT, P., *Public Sector Industrial Relations* (London: Routledge, 1992).

BEESLEY, M., and LITTLECHILD, S., 'Privatization: Principles, Problems and Priorities', *Lloyds Bank Annual Review*, 149 (July 1983), 1–20.

————'The Regulation of Privatized Monopolies in the United Kingdom', *RAND Journal of Economics*, 20/3 (1989), 454–72.

BELL, K., 'A History of NALGO in Scotland', Ph.D. thesis (Strathclyde, 1989).

BLACK, SIR DOUGLAS, *Inequalities in Health—the Black Report* (Harmondsworth: Penguin, 1982).

BLACKBURN, R., *Union Character and Social Class* (London: Batsford, 1967).

——and PRANDY, K., 'White Collar Unionization: A Conceptual Framework', *British Journal of Sociology*, 16 (1965), 111–22.

BLACKWELL, R., and LLOYD, P., 'New Managerialism in the Civil Service: Industrial Relations under the Thatcher Administration 1979–1986', in R. Mailly, S. Dimmock, and A. Sethi (eds.), *Industrial Relations in the Public Services* (London: Routledge, 1989), 68–113.

BLAIR, A., 'Consensual Feelings', *Unions Today* (Jan. 2000), 8–10.

BLAKE, R., *The Conservative Party from Peel to Thatcher* (London: Methuen, 1985).

BLYTON, P., and URSELL, G., 'Vertical Recruitment in White-Collar Trade Unions: Some Causes and Consequences', *British Journal of Industrial Relations*, 20/2 (1982), 186–94.

BRAVERMAN, H., *Labor and Monopoly Capital: The Degradation of Work in the Twentieth Century* (New York: Monthly Review Press, 1974).

BROWN, W., *The Changing Contours of British Industrial Relations* (Oxford: Blackwell, 1981).

——and LAWSON, M., 'The Training of Trade Union Officers', *British Journal of Industrial Relations*, 11/3 (1973), 431–48.

——and ROWTHORN, R., *A Public Services Pay Policy*, Fabian Society Tract no. 542, (London: Fabian Society, 1990).

BUCHANAN, R., 'Mergers in British Trade Unions', *Industrial Relations Journal*, 12/3 (1981), 40–9.

——'Measuring Mergers and Concentration in UK Unions 1910–1988', *Industrial Relations Journal*, 23/4 (1992), 304–14.

BURNS, E., *Rightwing Labour* (London: Lawrence & Wishart, 1961).

BYATT, I., *The British Electricity Industry 1875–1944* (Oxford: Clarendon Press, 1979).

CALLAGHAN, J., *Time and Chance* (London: Collins, 1987).

CARPENTER, M., *Working for Health: The History of COHSE* (London: Lawrence & Wishart, 1988).

CARTER, R., *Capitalism, Class Conflict and the New Middle Class* (London: Routledge & Kegan Paul, 1985).

CHOMSKY, N., *Profit over People: Neoliberalism and the Global Order* (New York: Seven Stories Press, 1999).

CLAY, H., *The Problem of Industrial Relations* (London: Macmillan, 1929).

CLEGG, H., *How to Run an Incomes Policy, and Why We Made a Mess of the Last One* (London: Heinemann, 1971).

——*The System of Industrial Relations in Great Britain* (Oxford: Blackwell, 1972).

——*The Changing System of Industrial Relations in Great Britain* (Oxford: Blackwell, 1979).

——KILLICK, A., and ADAMS, R., *Trade Union Officers: A Study of Full-Time Officers, Branch Secretaries and Shop Stewards in British Trade Unions* (Oxford: Blackwell, 1961).

COATES, K., and TOPHAM, T. (eds.), *Workers' Control* (London: Panther Books, 1970).

——*Trade Unions in Britain* (London: Fontana Press, 1988).

COHEN, G., *Karl Marx's Theory of History: A Defence* (Oxford: Clarendon Press, 1978).

COLE, G. D. H., *British Trade Unionism Today* (London: Gollancz, 1939).

COLLING, T., 'Privatization and the Management of Industrial Relations in Electricity Distribution', *Industrial Relations Journal*, 22/2 (1991), 117–29.

COMMONS, J., and ASSOCIATES, *History of Labor in the United States* (New York: Macmillan, 1918).

CONNOLLY, J., 'Old Wine in New Bottles', in P. Ellis (ed.), *James Connolly: Selected Writings* (Harmondsworth: Penguin, 1973), 175–80. Originally published 1914.

CULLY, M., WOODLAND, S., O'REILLY, A., and DIX, G., *Britain at Work* (London: Routledge, 1999).

CURRIE, D., 'World Capitalism in Recession', in S. Hall and M. Jacques (eds.), *The Politics of Thatcherism* (London: Lawrence & Wishart, 1983), 79–105.

DAVIDSON, J., *Privatization and Employment Relations: The Case of the Water Industry* (London: Mansell, 1993).

DAVIS, J., *Blue Gold: The Political Economy of Natural Gas* (London: George Allen & Unwin, 1984).

DEPARTMENT OF EMPLOYMENT, *Democracy in Trade Unions*, Cmnd 8778 (London: HMSO, 1983).

DEPARTMENT OF ENERGY, *Privatizing Electricity: The Government's Proposals for the Privatization of the Electricity Supply Industry in England and Wales*, Cm 322 (London: HMSO, 1988).

—— *Privatizing Electricity: The Government's Proposals for the Privatization of the Electricity Supply Industry in Scotland*, Cm 327 (London: HMSO, 1988).

DEPARTMENT OF THE ENVIRONMENT, *Streamlining the Cities*, Cmnd 9063 (London: HMSO, 1983).

—— *Competition in the Provision of Local Authority Services* (London: HMSO, 1985).

—— *Paying for Local Government* (London: Department of the Environment, 1986).

DEPARTMENT OF HEALTH, *Caring for People: Community Care in the Next Decade* (London: HMSO, 1989).

DEPARTMENT OF TRANSPORT, *Buses*, Cmnd 9300 (London: HMSO, 1984).

DHSS (Department of Health and Social Security), *Patients First: Consultation Paper on the Structure and Management of the NHS in England and Wales* (London: DHSS, 1979).

DICKINSON, M., *To Break a Union: The Messenger, the State and the NGA* (Manchester: Booklist Ltd., 1984).

DONOVAN, LORD, *Royal Commission on Trade Unions and Employers' Associations*, Cmnd 3623 (London: HMSO, 1968).

DUNLEAVY, P., *Democracy, Bureaucracy and Public Choice: Economic Explanations in Political Science* (New York: Harvester Wheatsheaf, 1991).

DUNN, M., and SMITH, S., 'Economic Policy and Privatisation', in S. Savage and L. Robins (eds.), *Public Policy under Thatcher* (London: Macmillan, 1990), 23–44.

DUNN, S., and GREGORY, M., 'Chronicle: Industrial Relations in the United Kingdom, April–July 1980', *British Journal of Industrial Relations*, 18/3 (1980), 377–92.

—— —— 'Chronicle: Industrial Relations in the United Kingdom, August–November 1981', *British Journal of Industrial Relations*, 19/1 (1981), 94–105.

DURKHEIM, E., *The Division of Labour in Society* (Toronto: Macmillan, 1964). Originally published 1933.

EDELSTEIN, J. D., and WARNER, M., *Comparative Union Democracy* (London: Allen & Unwin, 1975).

EDWARDS, P., *Conflict at Work* (Oxford: Blackwell, 1986).

—— 'Industrial Conflict', *British Journal of Industrial Relations*, 30/3 (1992), 361–404.

—— (ed.), *Industrial Relations* (Oxford: Blackwell, 1995).

—— and SISSON, K., *Industrial Relations in the UK: Changes in the 1980s* (ESRC Research Briefing, London: ESRC, 1990).

EVANS, E., *Thatcher and Thatcherism* (London: Routledge, 1997).

EWING, K., *The Employment Act 1990: A European Perspective* (London: Institute of Employment Rights, 1991).

FARNHAM, D., 'Sixty Years of Whitleyism', *Personnel Management* (June 1978), 29–32.

FERNER, A., and COLLING, T., 'Privatization, Regulation and Industrial Relations', *British Journal of Industrial Relations*, 29/3 (1991), 391–410.

——— 'Electricity Supply', in A. Pendleton and J. Winterton (eds.), *Public Enterprise in Transition: Industrial Relations in State and Privatized Corporations* (London: Routledge, 1993), 100–33.

FLANDERS, A., 'Collective Bargaining', in A. Flanders and H. Clegg (eds.), *The System of Industrial Relations in Great Britain* (Oxford: Blackwell, 1954), 252–322.

—— *Management and Unions* (London: Faber & Faber, 1968).

—— *Trade Unions* (London: Hutchinson University Library, 1968).

—— and CLEGG, H. (eds.), *The System of Industrial Relations in Great Britain* (Oxford: Blackwell, 1954).

FONER, P., *History of the Labor Movement in the USA* (New York: International Publishers, 1947).

FORRESTER, K., 'Buses', in A. Pendleton and J. Winterton (eds.), *Public Enterprise in Transition: Industrial Relations in State and Privatized Corporations* (London: Routledge, 1993), 211–31.

FOSH, P., and HEERY, E. (eds.), *Trade Unions and their Members: Studies in Union Democracy and Organization* (Basingstoke: Macmillan, 1990).

FOSTER, D., 'Privatization Policy in Local Government: The Response of Public Sector Trade Unions', Ph.D. thesis (Bath, 1991).

FOWLER, N., *Ministers Decide* (London: Chapmans, 1991).

FOX, A., *Industrial Sociology and Industrial Relations* (Research Paper 3, Donovan Commission, London: HMSO, 1966).

FREDMAN, S., and MORRIS, G., 'The State as Employer: Setting a New Example', *Personnel Management* (Aug. 1989), 25–9.

FRIEDMAN, M., *Free to Choose* (Harmondsworth: Penguin, 1980).

FRYER, R., 'Public Service Trade Unionism in the Twentieth Century', in R. Mailly, S. Dimmock, and A. Sethi (eds.), *Industrial Relations in the Public Services* (London: Routledge, 1989), 17–67.

—— and WILLIAMS, S., *A Century of Service: An Illustrated History of the National Union of Public Employees, 1889–1993* (London: Lawrence & Wishart, 1993).

—— FAIRCLOUGH, A., and MASON, T., *Organisation and Change in the National Union of Public Employees* (London: NUPE, 1974).

GAMBLE, A., 'Thatcherism and Conservative Politics', in S. Hall and M. Jacques (eds.), *The Politics of Thatcherism* (London: Lawrence & Wishart, 1983), 109–31.

GEARY, R., *Policing Industrial Disputes: 1893 to 1985* (Cambridge: Cambridge University Press, 1985).

GENNARD, J., GREGORY, M., and DUNN, S., 'Throwing the Book', *Employment Gazette*, 88/6 (1980), 591–600.

GILL, W., IRONSIDE, M., and SEIFERT, R., 'The Reform of English Local Government Finance and Structure, and the Consequences for the Management of Labour', paper for the Critical Perspectives on Accounting Conference, New York (1999).

GILMORE, A., 'Analysis of the Attitudes of Oldham Health Authority Management to Recent Strike Action from the Strikers' Perspective', MA thesis (Keele, 1992).

GILMOUR, I., *Dancing with Dogma: Britain under Thatcherism* (London: Pocket Books, 1992).

GOLDSTEIN, J., *The Government of British Trade Unions* (London: Allen & Unwin, 1952).

GOODRICH, C., *The Frontier of Control* (London: G. Bell & Sons, 1920).

GRAMSCI, A., *Selections from the Prison Notebooks* (London: Lawrence & Wishart, 1971). Originally published 1930.

GRIFFITHS, R., *NHS Management Inquiry* (Letter to Secretary of State, London: DHSS, 1983).

HALCROW, M., *Keith Joseph: A Single Mind* (London: Macmillan, 1989).

HALL, S., 'The Great Moving Right Show', in S. Hall and M. Jacques (eds.), *The Politics of Thatcherism* (London: Lawrence & Wishart, 1983), 19–39.

HAYEK, F. VON, *The Road to Serfdom* (London: Routledge, 1944).

——*1980s Unemployment and the Unions* (London: IEA, 1984).

HEALD, D., 'Tory Policies towards the Public Sector', *Scottish Trade Union Review*, 7 (1979), 4–10.

HEERY, E., 'Chronicle: Industrial Relations in the United Kingdom April–July 1987', *British Journal of Industrial Relations*, 25/3 (1987), 437–50.

HEMMINGWAY, J., *Conflict and Democracy* (Oxford: Oxford University Press, 1978).

HESELTINE, M., *Where There's a Will* (London: Hutchinson, 1987).

HIBBS, J., 'Privatization and Competition in Road Passenger Transport', in C. Veljanovski (ed.), *Privatization and Competition* (London: IEA, 1989), 161–77.

HILL, L., 'The Municipal Service', in H. Laski, W. Jennings, and W. Robson (eds.), *A Century of Municipal Service: The Last Hundred Years* (London: George Allen & Unwin, 1935), 109–52.

HOBSBAWM, E., *Age of Extremes: The Short Twentieth Century 1914–1991* (London: Michael Joseph, 1994).

HOLMES, M., *The First Thatcher Government 1979–1983* (Boulder, Colo.: Westview Press, 1985).

HORTON, S., 'Local Government, 1979–1989', in S. Savage and L. Robins (eds.), *Public Policy under Thatcher* (London: Macmillan, 1990), 172–86.

HOWE, G., *Conflict of Loyalty* (London: Macmillan, 1994).

HOXIE, R., 'Trade Unionism in the United States' (pp. 44–52), in E. Bakke and C. Kerr (eds.), *Unions, Management and the Public* (New York: Harcourt, Brace, & Co., 1948), 152–5. Originally published 1920.

HUGHES, J., *Trade Union Structure and Government* (Research Paper 5, Donovan Commission, London: HMSO, 1966).

HUTT, A., *British Trade Unionism: A Short History* (London: Lawrence & Wishart, 1975).

HUTTON, W., *The State We're In* (London: Vintage, 1996).

HYMAN, R., *Industrial Relations: A Marxist Introduction* (London: Macmillan, 1975).

——'Trade Unions: Structure, Policies and Politics', in G. Bain (ed.), *Industrial Relations in Britain* (Oxford: Blackwell, 1983), 35–65.

——*Strikes* (London: Macmillan, 1989).

——PRICE, R., and TERRY, M., *Reshaping the NUR* (London: NUR, 1988).

IDS (Incomes Data Services), *Pay in the Public Sector*, study 263 (London: IDS, 1982).

—— *Local Pay in the Public Sector*, study 510 (London: IDS, 1992).

—— *Pay in the Public Services: Review of 1993, Prospects for 1994* (London: IDS, 1994).

INDUSTRIAL WORKERS OF THE WORLD, 'Preamble', in S. Larson and B. Nissen (eds.), *Theories of the Labor Movement* (Detroit: Wayne State University Press, 1987), 66. Originally published 1908.

INGHAM, M., 'Industrial Relations in British Local Government', *Industrial Relations Journal*, 16/1 (1985), 6–15.

IRONSIDE, M., and SEIFERT, R., *Industrial Relations in Schools* (London: Routledge, 1995).

IRS (Industrial Relations Services), 'Pay Comparability: The Standing Commission Reports', *Industrial Relations Review and Report*, 206 (1979), 2–5.

—— 'Training Union Representatives: NALGO's Policy', *Industrial Relations Review and Report*, 225 (1980), 9–10.

—— 'Doomed Comparability Commission Forecasts its Rebirth', *Industrial Relations Review and Report*, 231 (1980), 10–11.

—— 'Local Government Staff Win 15% Arbitration Award', *Industrial Relations Review and Report*, 239 (1981), 10.

—— 'Arbitration as a Means of Settling Disputes: 1. The Public Sector', *Industrial Relations Review and Report*, 259 (1981), 2–7.

—— 'Union Procedures on the Admission and Expulsion of Members', *Industrial Relations Review and Report*, 272 (1982), 2–7.

—— 'Survey of Union Strike Rules. Part 1: Authorisation and Procedure for Calling Industrial Action', *Industrial Relations Review and Report*, 276 (1982), 2–12.

—— 'Union Strike Rules. Part 2: Strike Pay, Strike Committees and Disciplinary Rules', *Industrial Relations Review and Report*, 279 (1982), 2–9.

—— 'Union Rules: Election Procedures for Officials and Governing Bodies', *Industrial Relations Review and Report*, 282 (1982), 2–11.

—— 'Survey of Employee Relations in Local Government', *Employment Trends*, 594 (1995), 6–13.

JACKSON, P. (ed.), *Implementing Government Policy Initiatives: the Thatcher Administration 1979–1983* (London: Royal Institute of Public Administration, 1985).

JENKINS, C., and SHERMAN, B., *White Collar Unionism: The Rebellious Salariat* (London: Routledge & Kegan Paul, 1979).

JENKINS, P., *Mrs Thatcher's Revolution* (London: Jonathan Cape, 1987).

JOHNSON, C. (ed.), *Privatized Ownership* (London: Pinter, 1988).

KAHN-FREUND, O., *Labour and the Law* (London: Stevens, 1977).

KAVANAGH, D., *Thatcherism and British Politics* (Oxford: Oxford University Press, 1987).

KELLY, J., *Trade Unions and Socialist Politics* (London: Verso, 1988).

—— *Rethinking Industrial Relations* (London: Routledge, 1998).

—— and RICHARDSON, R., 'Annual Review Article 1988', *British Journal of Industrial Relations,* 27/1 (1989), 133–54.

—— and HEERY, E., *Working for the Union* (Cambridge: Cambridge University Press, 1994).

KENDALL, I., and MOON, G., 'Health Policy', in S. Savage and L. Robins (eds.), *Public Policy under Thatcher* (London: Macmillan, 1990), 103–16.

KERR, A., and SACHDEV, S., 'Third among Equals: An Analysis of the 1989 Ambulance Dispute', *British Journal of Industrial Relations*, 30/1 (1992), 127–43.

KESSLER, I., 'Shop Stewards in Local Government Revisited', *British Journal of Industrial Relations*, 24/3 (1986), 419–41.

—— 'Bargaining Strategies in Local Government', in R. Mailly, S. Dimmock, and A. Sethi (eds.), *Industrial Relations in the Public Services* (London: Routledge, 1989), 159–98.

—— and WINCHESTER, D., 'Pay Negotiations in Local Government—the 1981–82 Wage Round', *Local Government Studies* (Nov.–Dec. 1982), 19–31.

KESSLER, S., and BAYLISS, F., *Contemporary British Industrial Relations* (London: Macmillan, 1998).

KINNERSLEY, D., *Troubled Water: Rivers, Politics and Pollution* (London: Shipman, 1988).

KINNOCK, N., *The Future of Socialism*, Fabian Society Tract no. 509 (London: Fabian Society, 1986).

KLINGENDER, F., *The Condition of Clerical Labour in Britain* (London: Martin Lawrence, 1935).

KNOWLES, K., *Strikes—a Study in Industrial Conflict* (Oxford: Blackwell, 1952).

KOCHAN, T., KATZ, H., and McKERSIE, R., *The Transformation of American Industrial Relations* (New York: Basic Books, 1986).

LABOUR PARTY, *The New Hope for Britain—Labour's Manifesto 1983* (London: Labour Party, 1983).

—— *Social Justice and Economic Efficiency* (London: Labour Party, 1988).

LAMONT, N., *In Office* (London: Little, Brown & Co., 1999).

LANE, T., *The Union Makes Us Strong* (London: Arrow Books, 1974).

—— 'The Tories and the Trade Unions: Rhetoric and Reality', in S. Hall and M. Jacques (eds.), *The Politics of Thatcherism* (London: Lawrence & Wishart, 1983), 169–87.

LAWSON, N., *The View from No. 11* (London: Corgi Books, 1992).

LENIN, V., *What Is To Be Done?* (Oxford: Oxford University Press, 1963). Originally published 1902.

LERNER, S., *Breakaway Unions and the Small Trade Union* (London: Allen & Unwin, 1961).

LIPSET, S., TROW, M., and COLEMAN, J., *Union Democracy: The Internal Politics of the International Typographical Union* (Glencoe, Ill.: Free Press, 1956).

LOCKWOOD, D., *The Black Coated Worker* (London: Allen & Unwin, 1958).

LRD (Labour Research Department), 'Goodbye, Mr Clegg', *Labour Research*, 69/9 (1980), 196–8.

—— 'Attacks on Local Councils', *Labour Research*, 71/10 (1982), 218–20.

—— *Rate Capping and Abolition* (London: LRD, 1984).

—— *Defending the NHS* (London: LRD, 1984).

—— *The Poll Tax* (London: LRD, 1990).

——*Privatisation and Cuts: The Government Record* (London: LRD, 1990).

——*Women in Trade Unions* (London: LRD, 1991).

——*Management Consultants and New Management Techniques* (London: LRD, 1992).

——SCAT, and Birmingham TURC, *Putting the Rates to Work* (London: LRD, 1985).

LUMLEY, R., *White Collar Unionism in Britain* (London: Methuen & Co., 1973).

McBRIDE, A., 'Reshaping Trade Union Democracy: Developing Effective Representation for Women', Ph.D. thesis (Warwick, 1997).

McCARTHY, W., *Making Whitley Work: A Review of the Operation of the NHS Whitley Council System* (London: HMSO, 1976).

McCHESNEY, R., 'Introduction', in N. Chomsky, *Profit over People: Neoliberalism and the Global Order* (New York: Seven Stories Press, 1999), 7–16.

McMULLEN, J., and KAUFMAN, P., *Labour Law Review 1993* (London: Institute of Employment Rights, 1993).

McVICAR, M., 'Education Policy', in S. Savage and L. Robins (eds.), *Public Policy under Thatcher* (London: Macmillan, 1990), 131–44.

MAILLY, R., DIMMOCK, S., and SETHI, A. (eds.), *Industrial Relations in the Public Services* (London: Routledge, 1989).

MAJOR, J., *The Autobiography* (London: Harper Collins, 1999).

MANN, T., *Memoirs* (London: Labour Publishing Company, 1923).

MANZER, R., *Teachers and Politics* (Manchester: Manchester University Press, 1970).

MARSDEN, D., 'Chronicle: Industrial Relations in the United Kingdom August–November 1982', *British Journal of Industrial Relations*, 21/1 (1983), 115–26.

—— 'Chronicle: Industrial Relations in the United Kingdom, August– November 1985', *British Journal of Industrial Relations*, 24/1 (1985), 121–33.

MARTIN, R., 'Union Democracy: an Explanatory Framework', in W. McCarthy (ed.), *Trade Unions* (Harmondsworth: Penguin, 1985), 224–42. Originally published 1968.

MARTIN, R. M., *The TUC: the Growth of a Pressure Group, 1868–1976* (Oxford: Clarendon Press, 1980).

—— *Trade Unionism: Purposes and Forms* (Oxford: Clarendon Press, 1989).

MARX, K., 'Preface to a Contribution to the Critique of Political Economy', in K. Marx and F. Engels, *Selected Works Volume One* (Moscow: Progress Publishers, 1969), 502–6. Originally published 1859.

——'The Eighteenth Brumaire of Louis Bonaparte', in K. Marx and F. Engels, *Selected Works Volume One* (Moscow: Progress Publishers, 1969), 394–487. Originally published 1869.

——and ENGELS, F., 'Manifesto of the Communist Party', in K. Marx and F. Engels, *Selected Works Volume One* (Moscow: Progress Publishers, 1969), 98–137. Originally published 1848.

MAYNARD, A., 'Privatizing the National Health Service', in C. Johnson (ed.), *Privatization and Ownership* (London: Pinter, 1988), 47–59.

MEGAW, J., *Report of an Inquiry into Civil Service Pay*, Cmnd 8590 (London: HMSO, 1982).

MERRISON, A., *Royal Commission into the NHS*, Cmnd 7615 (London: HMSO, 1979).

MICHELS, R., *Political Parties* (New York: Hearsts, 1915).

MILIBAND, R., *The State in Capitalist Society* (London: Quartet Books, 1973).

——'Freedom, Democracy and the American Alliance', in *Socialist Register 1987* (London: Merlin Press, 1987), 480–501.

MILLWARD, N., STEVENS, M., SMART, D., and HAWES, W., *Workplace Industrial Relations in Transition* (Aldershot: Dartmouth, 1992).

MMC (Monopolies and Mergers Commission), *North of Scotland Hydro-Electric Board*, Cmnd 9628 (London: HMSO, 1985).

——*The Revenue Collection Systems of Four Area Electricity Boards*, Cmnd 9427 (London: HMSO, 1985).

MORGAN, K., *The People's Peace: British History 1945–1989* (Oxford: Oxford University Press, 1990).

——*Callaghan: A Life* (Oxford: Oxford University Press, 1997).

NALGO ACTION GROUP, *Fighting the Cuts* (London: NAG, 1980).

NEAL, L., BLOCH, L., and GRUNFELD, C., *Essential Services—Whose Rights?* (London: Centre for Policy Studies, 1984).

NEILL, C., 'Nalgo and the Development of Occupational Associations in Local Government', *Industrial Relations Journal*, 10/2 (1979), 31–40.

NEWMAN, G., *Path to Maturity: NALGO 1965–1980* (London: NALGO, 1982).

NICHOLSON, N., and URSELL, G., 'The NALGO Activists', *New Society*, 15 Dec. 1977, 581–2.

————and BLYTON, P., *The Dynamics of White-Collar Unionism* (London: Academic Press, 1981).

——————'Social Background Attitudes and Behaviour of White-Collar Shop Stewards', *British Journal of Industrial Relations*, 18/2 (1980), 231–9.

NISKANEN, W., *Bureaucracy and Representative Government* (Chicago: Aldine Atherton, 1971).

——'Bureaucrats and Politicians', *Journal of Law and Economics*, 18/3 (1975), 617–43.

O'DONNELL, K., and SAWYER, M., *A Future for Public Ownership* (London: Lawrence & Wishart, 1999).

OGDEN, S., 'The Trade Union Campaign against Water Privatization', *Industrial Relations Journal*, 22/1 (1991), 20–35.

——'Decline and Fall: National Bargaining in British Water', *Industrial Relations Journal*, 24/1 (1993), 44–58.

——'Water', in A. Pendleton and J. Winterton (eds.), *Public Enterprise in Transition: Industrial Relations in State and Privatized Corporations* (London: Routledge, 1993), 134–65.

——'The Reconstruction of Industrial Relations in the Privatized Water Industry', *British Journal of Industrial Relations*, 32/1 (1994), 67–84.

PARKINSON, C., *Right at the Centre* (London: Weidenfeld & Nicolson, 1992).

PEET, J., *Healthy Competition: How to Improve the NHS* (London: Centre for Policy Studies, 1987).

PELLING, H., *A History of British Trade Unionism* (Harmondsworth: Penguin, 1976).

PENDLETON, A., and WINTERTON, J. (eds.), *Public Enterprise in Transition: Industrial Relations in State and Privatized Corporations* (London: Routledge, 1993).

PERLMAN, S., *A Theory of the Labor Movement* (New York: Macmillan, 1928).

PHELPS BROWN, H., *The Inequality of Pay* (Oxford: Oxford University Press, 1977).

PIERSON, P., *Dismantling the Welfare State? Reagan, Thatcher and the Politics of Retrenchment* (Cambridge: Cambridge University Press, 1994).

PINKERTON, A., *Strikers, Communists, Tramps and Detectives* (New York: G. W. Carleton & Co., 1878).

POLLITT, C., *Managerialism and the Public Services: Cuts or Cultural Change in the 1990s?* (Oxford: Blackwell, 1993).

PRANDY, K., STEWART, A., and BLACKBURN, R., *White-Collar Unionism* (London: Macmillan, 1983).

PRIMEAUX, W., 'Electricity Supply: An End to Natural Monopoly', in C. Veljanovski (ed.), *Privatization and Competition* (London: IEA, 1989), 129–34.

PYM, F., *The Politics of Consent* (London: Hamish Hamilton, 1984).

REINER, R., *The Blue-Coated Worker: A Sociological Study of Police Unionism* (Cambridge: Cambridge University Press, 1978).

RIDDELL, P., *The Thatcher Government* (Oxford: Blackwell, 1985).

RIDLEY, N., *My Style of Government* (London: Hutchinson, 1991).

ROBERTS, B., *Trade Union Government and Administration in Great Britain* (London: G. Bell & Sons, 1956).

—— *Industrial Relations: Contemporary Problems and Perspectives* (London: Methuen & Co., 1968).

ROBERTS, J., ELLIOTT, D., and HOUGHTON, T., *Privatising Electricity: The Politics of Power* (London: Belhaven Press, 1991).

ROLPH, C., *All those in Favour: The ETU Trial* (London: André Deutsch, 1962).

ROSE, M., *Industrial Behaviour: Theoretical Development since Taylor* (Harmondsworth: Penguin Books, 1988).

ROSLENDER, R., 'The Engineers' and Managers' Association', *Industrial Relations Journal*, 14/2 (1983), 41–51.

ROTHWELL, T., 'Violence to Staff—the National and Local Responses', *Local Government Employment*, 31/5 (1987), 9.

ROUTH, G., *Occupation and Pay in Great Britain 1906–1979* (London: Macmillan, 1980).

SAMUEL, R., BLOOMFIELD, B., and BOANAS, G. (eds.), *The Enemey Within: Pit Villages and the Miners' Strike of 1984–5* (Routledge & Kegan Paul, 1986).

SASSOON, D., *One Hundred Years of Socialism* (London: Fontana Press, 1996).

SAVAGE, I., *Deregulation of Bus Services* (London: Gower and Institute for Transport Studies, 1985).

SAVAGE, S., and ROBINS, L. (eds.), *Public Policy under Thatcher* (London: Macmillan, 1990).

SCHUMPETER, J., *History of Economic Analysis* (London: George Allen & Unwin, 1963).

SCHWARZ, B., 'The Thatcher Years', in *Socialist Register 1987* (London: Merlin Press, 1987), 116–55.

SEIFERT, R., 'Some Aspects of Factional Opposition: Rank and File and the National

Union of Teachers 1967–1982', *British Journal of Industrial Relations*, 22/3 (1984), 372–90.

SEIFERT, R., *Teacher Militancy: A History of Teacher Strikes 1896–1987* (Sussex: Falmer Press, 1987).

——*Industrial Relations in the NHS* (London: Chapman & Hall, 1992).

SECRETARY OF STATE FOR EMPLOYMENT, *Employment: The Challenge for the Nation*, Cmnd 9474 (London: HMSO, 1985).

SECRETARIES OF STATE FOR HEALTH, WALES, NORTHERN IRELAND AND SCOTLAND, *Working for Patients*, Cm 555 (London: HMSO, 1989).

SECRETARY OF STATE FOR HEALTH, *The Health of the Nation*, Cm 1986 (London: HMSO, 1992)

SIMPSON, D., 'Managers in Workers' Trade Unions: The Case of the NUJ', in K. Thurley and S. Wood (eds.), *Industrial Relations and Management Strategy* (Cambridge: Cambridge University Press, 1983), 19–26.

SISSON, K., *The Management of Collective Bargaining* (Oxford: Blackwell, 1987).

SLOANE, A., *Hoffa* (London: MIT Press, 1991).

SMITH, C., *Technical Workers: Class, Labour and Trade Unionism* (London: Macmillan, 1987).

SMITH, K., *Water in Britain* (London: Macmillan, 1972).

SMITH, P., and MORTON, G., 'Union Exclusion and the Decollectivization of Industrial Relations in Contemporary Britain', *British Journal of Industrial Relations*, 31/1 (1993), 97–114.

————'Union Exclusion in Britain—Next Steps', *Industrial Relations Journal*, 25/1 (1994), 3–14.

SNAPE, E., and BAMBER, G., 'Managerial and Professional Employees: Conceptualising Union Strategies and Structure', *British Journal of Industrial Relations*, 27/1 (1989), 93–110.

SPOOR, A., *White Collar Union: Sixty Years of NALGO* (London: Heinemann, 1967).

STEEL, D., and HEALD, D., 'The Privatization of Public Enterprises 1979–1983', in P. Jackson (ed.), *Implementing Government Policy Initiatives: The Thatcher Administration 1979–1983* (London: RIPA, 1985), 69–91.

SWABE, A., COLLINS, P., and WALDEN, R., 'The Resolution of Disputes in the NHS', *Health Services Manpower Review*, 12/1 (1986), 3–5.

TAYLOR, F., *Scientific Management* (New York: Harper & Bros., 1911).

TAYLOR, R., *The Fifth Estate* (London: Routledge & Kegan Paul, 1978).

TEBBIT, N., *Upwardly Mobile* (London: Weidenfeld & Nicolson, 1988).

TERRY, M., 'Organising a Fragmented Workforce: Shop Stewards in Local Government', *British Journal of Industrial Relations*, 20/1 (1982), 1–19.

——'Negotiating the Government of Unison: Union Democracy in Theory and Practice', *British Journal of Industrial Relations*, 34/1 (1996), 87–110.

THATCHER, M., *The Downing Street Years* (London: Harper Collins, 1993).

THOMASON, G., 'The Pay Review Bodies', *Health Services Manpower Review*, 11/3 (1985), 3–6.

THORNLEY, C., 'Contesting Local Pay: The Decentralization of Collective Bargaining in the NHS', *British Journal of Industrial Relations*, 36/3 (1998), 413–34.

THURLEY, K., and WOOD, S. (eds.), *Industrial Relations and Management Strategy* (Cambridge: Cambridge University Press, 1983).

THE TREASURY, *The Next Ten Years: Public Expenditure and Taxation into the 1990s*, Cmnd 9189 (London: HMSO, 1984).

TRESSELL, R., *The Ragged Trousered Philanthropists* (London: Panther Books, 1965). Originally published 1912.

TROPP, A., *The School Teachers* (London: Heinemann, 1957).

TUC (Trades Union Congress), *Improving Industrial Relations in the NHS* (London: TUC, 1981).

——*Plan for Growth* (London: TUC, 1981).

——*Unemployment: The Fight for TUC Alternatives* (London: TUC, 1981).

——*Keep Public Services Public—the TUC Case against Contracting out* (London: TUC, 1982).

——*The Battle for Jobs: TUC Economic Review 1983* (London: TUC, 1983).

——*Stripping our Assets—the City's Privatisation Killing* (London: TUC, 1985).

——*Privatisation by Order—the Government Plan for Local Services* (London: TUC, 1985).

——*The £16 Billion Gas Bill* (London: TUC, 1986).

——*Privatisation and Top Pay* (London: TUC, 1986).

——*TUC Budget Submission* (London: TUC, 1991).

——*Towards 2000* (London: TUC, 1992).

——*Strategy for Full Employment* (London: TUC, 1993).

——*Employment Charter for a World Class Britain* (London: TUC, 1993).

TURNER, H., *Trade Union Growth, Structure and Policy* (London: Allen & Unwin, 1962).

UK GOVERNMENT, *Winning the Battle against Inflation*, Cmnd 7293 (London: HMSO, 1978).

——*Alternative to Domestic Rates*, Cmnd 8449 (London: HMSO, 1981).

——*Privatisation of the Water Authorities in England and Wales*, Cmnd 9734 (London: HMSO, 1986).

——*Higher Education: a New Framework*, Cm 1541 (London: HMSO, 1991).

——*Industrial Relations in the 1990s—Proposals for Further Reform of Industrial Relations and Trade Union Law*, Cm 1602 (London: HMSO, 1991).

UNDY, R., 'Negotiating Amalgamations: Territorial and Political Consolidation and Administrative Reform in Public-Sector Service Unions in the UK', *British Journal of Industrial Relations*, 37/3 (1999), 445–63.

——ELLIS, V., MCCARTHY, W., and HALMOS, A., *Change in Trade Unions: The Development of UK Unions since the 1960s* (London: Hutchinson, 1981).

UNISON, *Getting the Balance Right: Guidelines on Proportionality* (London: UNISON, 1994).

VELJANOVSKI, C. (ed.), *Privatization and Competition* (London: IEA, 1989).

——'Privatization: Monopoly Money or Competition?', in C. Veljanovski (ed.), *Privatization and Competition* (London: IEA, 1989), 26–51.

VOLKER, D., 'NALGO's Affiliation to the TUC', *British Journal of Industrial Relations*, 4/1 (1966), 59–66.

WADDINGTON, J., 'Trade Union Mergers: A Study of Trade Union Structural Dynamics', *British Journal of Industrial Relations*, 26/3 (1988), 409–30.

——and WHITSTON, C., 'The Politics of Restructuring: Trade Unions on the Defensive in Britain since 1979', *Relations Industrielles*, 49/4 (1994), 794–819.

WALKER, P., *Staying Power* (London: Bloomsbury, 1991).

WALSH, K., 'Centralisation and Decentralisation in Local Government Bargaining', *Industrial Relations Journal*, 12/5 (1981), 43–54.

WALTON, R., and MCKERSIE, R., *A Behavioral Theory of Labor Negotiations* (New York: McGraw Hill, 1967).

WATSON, D., *Managers of Discontent* (London: Routledge, 1988).

WEBER, M., *The Protestant Ethic and the Spirit of Capitalism* (London: Unwin University Books, 1970). Originally published 1904.

WEBB, S., and WEBB, B., *The History of Trade Unionism* (London: Longman, 1894).

——— *Industrial Democracy* (London: Longman, 1897).

——— 'Special Supplement on Professional Associations, Part Two', *New Statesman*, 9/212 (1917), 25–48.

——— *The History of Trade Unionism* (London: Longman, 1920).

WEDDERBURN, LORD, *The Worker and the Law* (Harmondsworth: Penguin, 1986).

WIDDICOMBE, D., *The Conduct of Local Authority Business: Report of the Committee of Inquiry into the Conduct of Local Authority Business*, Cmnd 9797 (London: HMSO, 1986).

WILLIAMS, T., *A History of the British Gas Industry* (Oxford: Oxford University Press, 1981).

WILLMAN, P., 'The Financial Status and Performance of British Trade Unions, 1950–1988', *British Journal of Industrial Relations*, 28/3 (1990), 313–28.

——'Merger Propensity and Merger Outcomes among British Unions, 1986–1995', *Industrial Relations Journal*, 27/4 (1996), 331–8.

——and CAVE, A., 'The Union of the Future: Super-Unions or Joint Ventures?', *British Journal of Industrial Relations*, 32/3 (1994), 395–412.

WINCHESTER, D., 'Industrial Relations in the Public Sector', in G. Bain (ed.), *Industrial Relations in Britain* (Oxford: Blackwell, 1983), 155–78.

WOOTTON, B., *The Social Foundations of Wage Policy* (London: Unwin University Books, 1962).

WRIGHT MILLS, C., *The New Men of Power* (New York: Harcourt Brace, 1948).

YOUNG, H., *One of Us: A Biography of Margaret Thatcher* (London: Macmillan, 1991).

Index